E. F. Haskell

The Housekeeper's Encyclopedia of Useful Information for the

Housekeeper

In all branches of cooking and domestic economy

E. F. Haskell

The Housekeeper's Encyclopedia of Useful Information for the Housekeeper
In all branches of cooking and domestic economy

ISBN/EAN: 9783744785150

Printed in Europe, USA, Canada, Australia, Japan

Cover: Foto ©Lupo / pixelio.de

More available books at **www.hansebooks.com**

HOUSEKEEPER'S ENCYCLOPEDIA

OF

Useful Information for the Housekeeper

IN ALL BRANCHES OF

COOKING AND DOMESTIC ECONOMY:

CONTAINING

THE FIRST SCIENTIFIC AND RELIABLE RULES FOR PUTTING UP ALL KINDS OF HERMETICALLY-SEALED FRUITS, WITH OR WITHOUT SUGAR, IN TIN CANS OR COMMON BOTTLES;

ALSO

RULES FOR PRESERVING FRUITS IN AMERICAN AND FRENCH STYLES;

WITH

TRIED RECEIPTS FOR MAKING DOMESTIC WINES, CATSUPS, SYRUPS, CORDIALS, ETC.;

AND PRACTICAL DIRECTIONS FOR THE CULTIVATION OF VEGETABLES, FRUITS, AND FLOWERS, DESTRUCTION OF INSECTS, ETC., ETC.

BY

MRS. E. F. HASKELL.

NEW YORK:
D. APPLETON & CO., 443 & 445 BROADWAY.
1861.

ENTERED, according to Act of Congress, in the year 1860, by
D. APPLETON & CO.,
In the Clerk's Office of the District Court of the United States for the Southern
District of New York.

PREFACE.

In our grandmothers' time, no greater praise could be spoken of a lady, than to say she was a perfect housekeeper; while in the present generation, woman is taught too much to look on the happiness, health, and comfort of her family as in no way ... with the every-day management of her house, table, ...der many intelligent men look with abhorrence ... d ladies, shunning them for life companions, and choosing women below themselves in education and intellect, far less congenial in every respect, and wholly unable to fill with credit the station they are called to occupy in public, or to sympathize in private with the refined tastes of their husbands. The more intelligent the woman, the more perfectly should she perform the several duties of her station. An educated man does not consider his intellect degraded by bringing to his assistance in the every-day business of life, the whole power of his mind, natural or acquired, and the more intelligent the man, the better success, all things being equal, attends his efforts. We educate our sons that they may fill with honor to themselves, and the good of the community generally, the various stations they may be called upon to occupy; should we not use the same good sense, in the education of our daughters? preparing them for useful and happy wives, mothers, and mistresses, as well as polished, graceful ladies; capable of giving pleasure to all who come within their influence, as well in the home circle as in public. Ladies with cultivated minds should be not only more congenial companions and judicious mothers, but better housekeepers, than those who have been less favored. That this is not generally the case, too many sadly neglected households of ladies, who shine in literary circles, bear witness. Surely, she who neglects present duties, while crowding the mind, must lack some of the essentials necessary to the character of a true woman. Housekeeping, in its several branches, is itself a study not to be despised. To excel, as in any other branch of education, it must be pursued with interest, patience, system, and perseverance. No woman exists, deserving the name of wife and mother, who would not feel complimented, to establish the reputation of making her home happy for her family, as well as pleasant for her guests. To become an intelligent housekeeper, a lady must acquaint herself with the laws of the human constitution the qualities of provisions, and the mode of preparing healthy, and, at the same time, palatable dishes. The great efforts of housekeepers should not be confined to the present enjoyment of elegant dishes, formed to please the taste without regard to utility. The daily food for a family should consist of the elements most needed by its members, to develop their systems, mentally and physically; taking into account their ages, health, employment, and tastes. Many seem to imagine the coarsest food most conducive to health, and conscientiously avoid the little made dishes, shunning them as so much poison. They say, "Our grandmothers always supplied such food to their families, and if we succeed in bringing up our children with as firm constitutions as our parents, we shall be satisfied; we think there are more important duties to be performed in the world, than beating eggs and making pastry." These housekeepers do not stop to think of the difference in the times.

Our grandparents enjoyed their pork and beans as well, no doubt, as we now do the more elaborate cooking of the present day, but then they chopped their own wood, ploughed, threshed, mowed, raked, etc., with their own right arm, with no aid from machinery. The girls in those days walked three miles to school in winter, and spun and wove in summer; rode the wildest colts without saddle, etc. The boys, meantime, studying in winter, and farming during the summer. Ladies rode hundreds of miles on horseback, or if in wagons, jolted without springs over byways, etc., consuming more oxygen in one day than their descendants do in three; pork was needed to sustain them; but let us live in the same manner, with no more exercise than we at present take, and we should soon see the effect in feeble constitutions, and scrofulous diseases. According to the necessities of the times, our grandmothers were, as a general thing, ahead of us in housekeeping; their mode of cooking was what their families needed, as the well-developed frames, and strong constitutions of our parents attest. Some again err the other way; thinking nothing fit to eat, unless as rich with butter, spices, etc., as possible. These err as much in their ideas as the first; they forget that rich, oily food is nearly the same to the stomach, in whatever form it is produced. The French mode of preparing food is, perhaps, as palatable and healthy as any (except always the spices), which forms the objection to their mode of cooking. This defect can be avoided; it is unnecessary to spice fish and meats; and to American tastes is not as agreeable. The more perfectly the flavor of the meats are preserved, the more healthy, and, usually, the more palatable the dish. The same may be said of fruits; the art of preserving these naturally, was first discovered by the French. In this work, full and explicit directions are given for preserving all American fruits, and a few which are imported. Fruits prepared in this manner, are much more conducive to health when used as dinner desserts, than so much rich pastry. We have endeavored to make this work a complete encyclopedia for the housekeeper; going minutely into many things, which, to an experienced person may seem superfluous, but which would, had she possessed them, been of benefit to the writer, in her first housekeeping. Many of the receipts are original, and we think all good. Those appertaining to fruits, except a few French rules, originated with the author. Many persons put up fruits, who have never published their rules. She thinks the directions for preserving hermetically sealed fruits in this book are the first reliable rules published.

E. F. H<small>ASKELL</small>

TABLES OF WEIGHTS, MEASURES, ETC.

Ale or Beer Measure, used for Measuring Milk, etc.

			MARKED.				MARKED.
2 pints	make	1 quart	qt.	36 gallons	make	1 barrel	bar.
4 quarts	"	1 gallon	gal.	54 gallons	"	1 hogshead	hhd.

Dry Measure, used for Measuring Coarse Vegetables, and, in some Markets, Berries.

2 pints	make	1 quart	qt.	4 pecks	make	1 bushel	bu.
8 quarts	"	1 peck	pk.	36 bushels	"	1 chaldron	ch.

Avoirdupois Weight, used in Weighing Tea, Sugar, Butter, etc.

16 drachms	make	1 ounce	oz.	4 quarters make	1 hundredweight	cwt.
16 ounces	"	1 pound	lb.	20 hundredweights make	1 ton	T.
25 pounds	"	1 quarter	qr.			

Troy Weight, used in Weighing Gold, Silver, etc.

24 grains	make	1 pennyweight	pwt.	12 ounces	make	1 pound	lb.
20 pennyweights	make	1 ounce	oz.				

Apothecaries Weight, used in Preparing Drugs, etc.

20 grains	make	1 scruple	℈	8 drachms	make	1 ounce	℥
2 scruples	"	1 drachm	ʒ	12 ounces	"	1 pound	℔

Miscellaneous.

12 units	make	1 dozen.	A sheet folded in 24 leaves	24mo.
12 dozen	"	1 gross.	" " 32 "	32mo.
12 gross	"	1 great gross.	24 sheets of paper make	1 quire.
20 things	"	1 score.	20 quires " " "	1 ream.
100 pounds	"	1 quintal of fish.	2 reams " "	1 bundle.
196 pounds	"	1 barrel of flour.	5 bundles " "	1 bale.
200 pounds	"	1 barrel of pork.	1 quart of flour weighs	1 lb.
18 inches	"	1 cubit.	1 quart of powdered loaf-sugar	
22 inches	"	1 sacred cubit.	weighs	1 lb. 1 oz.
14 pounds of iron or lead	make	1 stone.	1 quart of Indian meal weighs	1 lb. 2 oz.
21¼ stones	"	" 1 pig.	1 common sized teacup of hard	
8 pigs	"	" 1 fother.	butter weighs	¼ lb.
A sheet folded in 2 leaves is a folio.			8 large table-spoonfuls measure	1 gill.
" " 4 "	quarto, or 4to.	25 drops fill a common teaspoon.
" " 8 "	octavo, or 8vo.	4 common table-spoons fill a wine-glass.
" " 12 "	12mo.	A common wine-glass holds half a gill.
" " 16 "	16mo.	A common tumbler holds half a pint.

Cloth Measure, used in Measuring all Goods.

			MARKED.				MARKED.
2¼ inches, (in.)	make	1 nail	na.	4 quarters	make	1 yard	yd.
4 nails	"	1 qr. of a yard	qr.	5 quarters	"	1 ell English	E. E.
3 quarters	"	1 ell Flemish	E. F.				

Linear Measure, used in Measuring all distances.

12 inches	make	1 foot	ft.	8 furlongs	make	1 mile	mi.
3 feet	"	1 yard	yd.	64¼ statute, or 60 geographical miles,		make 1 degree of the equator	deg. or °
5½ yards	"	1 rod, perch, or pole	rd.	360 degrees, a circumference of the earth.			
40 yards	"	1 furlong	fur.				

Square Measure, used in Measuring Land, Rooms, etc.

144 square inches (sq. in.) make 1 square foot (sq. ft.).

9 square feet make 1 square yard (sq. yd.).

30¼ square yards make 1 square rod, or perch (P.).

40 square rods, or perches make 1 square rood (R.).

4 square roods make 1 square acre (A.).

640 square acres make 1 square mile (M.)

Cubic Measure, used in Measuring Wood, etc.

1728 cubic inches (cu. in.) make 1 cubic foot (cu. ft.).

27 cubic feet make 1 cubic yard (cu. yd.).

40 feet round, or 50 feet of hewn timber, make 1 ton (T.).

42 cubic feet make 1 ton of shipping (T.).

16 cubic feet make 1 cord foot of shipping (cd. ft.).

8 cord feet, or 128 cubic feet, make 1 cord of shipping (c.)

English Money, used in England and Canada.

4 farthings (far.) make 1 penny (d.).

12 pence make 1 shilling (s.).

20 shillings make 1 pound or sovereign (£).

21 shillings make 1 guinea.

United States Money, used in the United States.

10 mills	make	1 cent	ct.	1/4 of a dollar	is	25 cents	2/-
10 cents	"	1 dime	d.	1/5 of a dollar	"	20 cents.	
10 dimes	"	1 dollar	$	1/8 of a dollar	"	12½ cents	1/-
10 dollars	"	1 eagle	E.	1/10 of a dollar	"	10 cents.	
1 dollar	is	100 cents	$	1/16 of a dollar	"	6¼ cents.	
1/2 of a dollar	"	50 cents	4/-	1/20 of a dollar	"	5 cents.	
1/3 of a dollar	"	33⅓ cents.		1/2 of a cent	"	5 mills.	

The table used for weighing the proportions of cakes used in this book is avoirdupois—16 ounces to the pound.

For measuring ale or beer, measure four quarts to the gallon.

CONTENTS.

PART I.
ADVICE TO YOUNG HOUSEKEEPERS AND THEIR HOUSEHOLD.

CHAPTER	PAGE
I. Selecting House and Furniture,	1
II. System and Management of Servants,	4
III. Economy in Cooking well, Cheerfulness, etc.,	7
IV. Washing, Ironing, Starching, etc.,	12
V. Directions for entertaining Visitors, etc.,	24
VI. To Husbands—Excuses for the Mistakes of Housekeepers,	27
VII. Advice to Servants,	31
VIII. Carving,	37

PART II.
NUTRITION, ELEMENTS OF FOOD, ETC.

I. Nutrition,	43
II. Elements of Food,	47
III. Marketing,	51

PART III.
GENERAL COOKERY.

I. Soups, Gravies, and Sauces,	58
II. Fish,	74
III. Beef,	84

CHAP		PAGE
IV.	Pork,	91
V.	Venison, Veal, Lamb, and Mutton,	100
VI.	Poultry and Game,	106
VII.	Vegetables,	116
VIII.	Puddings and Dinner Desserts,	133
IX.	Pastry and Pies,	153
X.	Yeast, Bread, and Biscuits,	159
XI.	Cakes,	169
XII.	Confectioneries, Creams, etc.,	190
XIII.	Tea,	204
XIV.	Coffee and Chocolate,	207

PART IV.

BREAKFAST DISHES, COLD DINNERS, ETC.

I.	Breakfast Dishes,	212
II.	Hashes,	217
III.	To Select Eggs, Preserve, Cook, etc.,	219
IV.	Economy Dishes,	223
V.	Cold Dinners,	226

PART V.

FRUIT HERMETICALLY SEALED, PRESERVED, DRIED, COOKED, ETC.

I.	Apples,	229
II.	Peaches,	236
III.	Pears and Quinces,	244
IV.	Plums,	248
V.	Cherries,	257
VI.	Small Fruits,	263

PART VI.

WINES, BRANDIES, VINEGARS, CORDIALS, ETC.

I.	Wines and Table Beer,	272
II.	Fruit Brandies,	278

CHAPTER	PAGE
III. Fruit Vinegars,	281
IV. Cordials and Extracts,	283

PART VII.
FLAVORED VINEGARS, PICKLES, MANGOES.

I. Catsups,	286
II. Salads,	289
III. Flavored Vinegars,	292
IV. Pickles and Mangoes,	296

PART VIII.
GARDENING AND INSECTS.

I. Kitchen Garden,	306
II. Fruit Garden,	319
III. Flowers,	329
IV. Hot-beds,	343
V. Insects injurious to the Garden, and troublesome to Housekeepers,	349

PART IX.
CURING MEATS, AND DAIRY WORK.

I. Curing Meats,	360
II. Milk, Butter, and Cheese,	362

PART X.

I. Spring Work for the Housekeeper,	367

PART XI.
SICK-ROOM, REMEDIES, INFANTS, COOKING FOR INVALIDS.

I. Sick-room, What it should be, etc.,	371
II. Simple Remedies,	374

CHAPTER	PAGE
III. CARE OF INFANTS FROM BIRTH TO WEANING, ...	383
IV. COOKING FOR THE INVALID AND CONVALESCENT, . . .	391

PART XII.

MISCELLANEOUS, ... 398

INDEX, ... 421

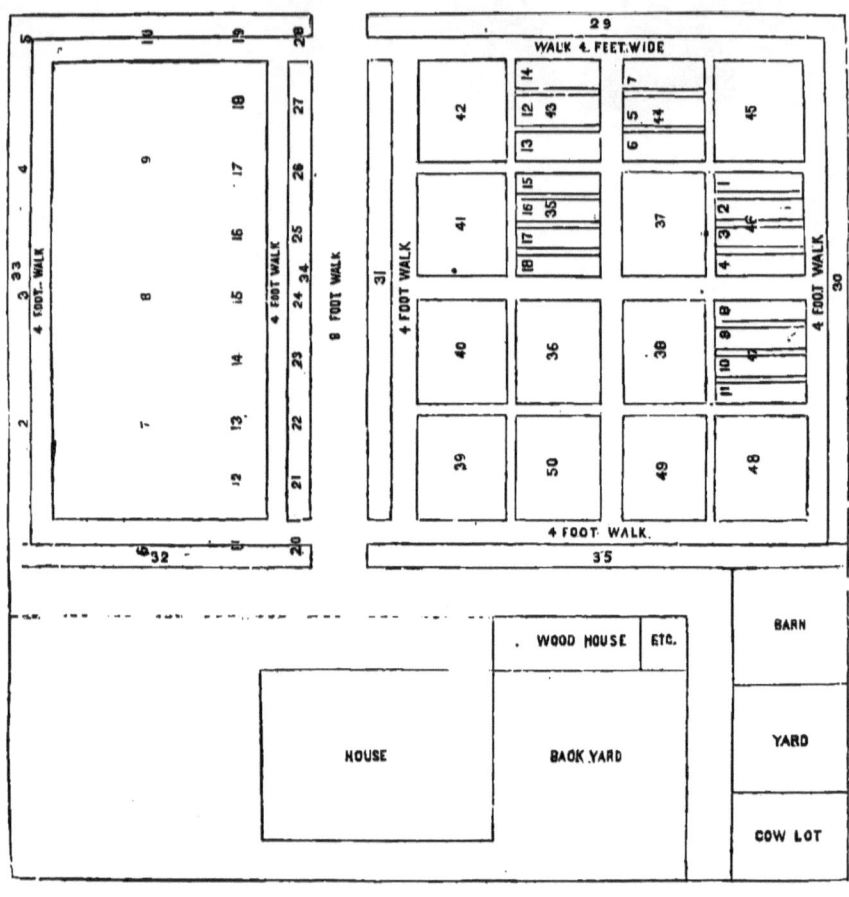

HOUSEKEEPER'S ENCYCLOPEDIA.

PART I.

ADVICE TO YOUNG HOUSEKEEPERS, ETC.

CHAPTER I.

HINTS TO YOUNG HOUSEKEEPERS, IN SELECTING HOUSE AND FURNITURE.

In selecting a house choose one not only within your means, but with reference to the number of persons in your family.

A large, empty house is only a burden, especially when good servants are scarce, and means limited. If possible, obtain one with a good hall, the principal rooms opening from it: rooms interfering with others are a great annoyance to housekeepers, as it is impossible to keep a room tidy when used as a thoroughfare by members of the family without frequent use of broom and duster, which is a constant wear on carpet and patience. The dining-room ought either to open out of the kitchen, or be separated by a hall; each should have a closet opening from them; and the kitchen have a passage to the cellar, and an outside door. The parlor is the most pleasant facing north, and should be independent of the other part of the house. The nursery is most convenient on the principal floor. Small bed-rooms are preferable with closets to large ones without. Spring and rain water should be near the kitchen. Furniture appears well in small, that would hardly be called respectable in large, rooms.

Furnish your house with uniformity; nothing looks more vulgar than a splendidly furnished parlor, while the remainder of the house is hardly decent.

Decide how much you can afford to spend on furniture; commence in the kitchen, and go through the house, making a list of all necessary articles, with their prices. If, after this is done, you find the sum appropriated not expended, select the superfluities, being careful not to crowd the parlors.

NECESSARY KITCHEN FURNITURE.—Range, or stove, for cooking; pot and kettle with covers; two small kettles with oval bottoms; tin boiler with steamer; tea kettle and steeper; coffee pot and mill; dripping pan and spider; gridiron and meat fork; preserving kettle and saucepan; griddle and pancake turner; iron ladle and spoons; knives, with forks strong and large; butcher and bread knife; dippers, quart and pint, colander and large skimmer; waffle irons with rings; butter ladle and potato pounder; bread board and rolling pins; sieve, cake pans, and grater; mixing and baking pans, for bread; milk pans and strainer; milk pail and small skimmer; pie plates and pudding bakers; pepper shaker and wooden salt dish; flour dredge and cooky or biscuit cutter; bowls of common ware and dishes; jars for soda, cream of tartar, and spices; canisters, or bottles, for tea and coffee; tin box for bread, and one for cake; jugs for molasses and vinegar; spring and rain water, cleaning, and swill pail; iron ash pail and firebox; shovel, tongs, and match safe; kitchen table and chairs; candlesticks and snuffers; broom, dust pan, and scrubbing brush; bottle cleaner and stove brush; boxes with handles for sugar, etc.; wash-boiler, and wash-tubs; clothes line, washboard, and clothes pins; flat irons, ironing blanket and sheet; skirt and bosom board; clothes basket; knife and spoon basket; market and chip basket; dish pans and towels.

With these necessary articles, the writer closes the list, although there are many conveniences not enumerated, which are pleasant to use.

DINING-ROOM.—Table and chairs according to family; tea and dining set, full or not, as desired; knives and forks for dinner and tea; tea and table spoons; mats and waiter; carpet or oil-cloth on the floor; two high lamps, or candlesticks; small side table; tablecloths and napkins; tea and coffee pot with stands; covers for meats, of wire; castor, butter knife, and carver; fly broom, pitchers, and goblets.

HALL.—Oil-cloth, lamp, and hat-stand.

Almost all prices being fixed to these articles according to their beauty and value, the purchasers must be governed by their means and taste.

FAMILY BED-ROOM.—Bedstead, with furniture and crockery; bureau, washstand, washbowl, and pitcher; slop jar, soap dish, foot bath, and two pint mugs; rocker, and other chairs; footstool, stove, and window shades; looking-glass, and small table; carpet, broom, and dust brush.

PARLOR.—Carpet, table, chairs, sofa, lamp, footstools, shades.

LIBRARY.—Book-case, with all conveniences for writing; table, chairs, and oil-cloth or carpet.

SPARE CHAMBER.—Bedstead and furniture; washstand and furniture; Foot bath, slop jar, teeth mugs, and towel rack; dressing bureau, or table with glass; small stand, stove, chairs, window-shades, and carpet.

BED-ROOMS.—Carpet, bedstead and furniture; washstand, bowl, and pitcher; looking-glass, small table, and chairs; window-shades.

SERVANTS' ROOMS.—Bedsteads, chairs, small stand, looking-glass.

This catalogue will enable inexperienced persons to make the list before advised, in order to furnish the house with uniformity, and yet keep within the sum specified.

CHAPTER II.

SYSTEM AND MANAGEMENT OF SERVANTS.

AIM to be as systematic as possible in arranging your regular work; make rules most convenient for your family, and have the servants understand they are to be obeyed. Never allow yourself to speak in a fretful manner to your help, as by so doing you lose your self-respect, and their esteem. When any fault needs correcting, do it in kindness, speaking in a lady-like manner. Take interest in the moral welfare of your help, and show yourself their friend, and a servant worth keeping will fully repay your kindness by faithful service. We should hear less complaints of servants if mistresses would oftener do their duty to those under them. Servants that will not be influenced by kindness can never be trusted; make it a rule to dismiss help that will not work without scolding as soon as possible. Not only is it necessary to point out delinquencies kindly, but every improvement should be as constantly noticed "Sally, your floor looks nicely," goes a long way towards another scrubbing. When any article is broken, unless it happened through disobedience to some order, pass it lightly, with "I am sorry it is broken, try to be more careful for the future;" and generally it will have the desired effect. Never dismiss help in anger, they will surely give you a bad name. Sometimes servants are very quick tempered and will themselves speak improperly; leave them immediately, without noticing what they say, and they will soon cool down, and often ask forgiveness. If they do not, leave it, for the present, as though forgotten, and at some future time, when all things have gone well, and the kitchen unusually pleasant, bring it up, and try to convince her of her fault, and say decidedly, "If we cannot get along pleasantly we must part." This plan, if always followed, will be found to work well.

Rémember that to govern a family well, you must first govern yourself; live up to this rule and but little trouble will be found in managing other members of the household.

Order and system is of more importance to a family than is generally supposed; many a man is driven from his home for the want of this alone, and in no place is the comfort of a family more affected by the want of it than at the table. Aim to prepare the meals at regular hours, and what you have well cooked; let the tablecloth be always white, clean, and well ironed; the napkins in their rings in proper order; place the platter, or dish with meat, directly before the person who carves, with the potatoes always on the right of the meat; if two other vegetables, put one on the left, and two on the right; the gravy tureen on the left, near the carver, with the spoon towards him. When tea or coffee is served at the table, place the tray opposite the carver. The tray should contain cups, saucers, sugar, cream, spoons in a holder, slop bowl, one plate, knife, fork, and napkin. Near the middle of the table place the castor, the butter one side of it, and the pickles or some other relish to balance the table on the other. The bread should be on a corner, generally on the right hand from the carver, and crackers on the left; carving knife and fork should be just before the carver, the steel lying with the handle towards him, on his left. Table-spoons should be laid within his reach. The plates, during fly season, should be turned bottom side up, the knife above the plate, the handle towards the host, if at his left, and hostess, if at her right, the fork on the left, with the handle towards the edge of the table, the napkin in the same position on the right as the fork occupies on the left. Spoons at the right. Small or individual salts towards the centre of the table, near the plate, but far enough from it to avoid being displaced by moving the knife. Goblets on the right, a little mid-way from the next plate, that the water may be poured with ease by the waiter; some prefer filling the glasses on a side table, but the more glass on the table the better it looks. If extra relishes are to be served, the lady of the house, if not before the tray, if so, a servant, or any person at the table, if no servant waits, should dish them—the carver never; he has sufficient business before him.

If not absolutely necessary, no person should leave the table to supply deficiencies, or replenish dishes; a bell should be used, instead of calling a servant by name, when she is needed to wait upon the table. When there is no servant in the family, arrange all articles for the dessert on the side table near by, that the table can be cleared and the dessert brought on without confusion. When a servant waits on the table properly, she first removes the meats and vegetables, then the plates, knives, forks, and extra dishes; after this the butter, castor, pickles, salt, and bread, unless wanted. She then removes the crumbs, taking a plate in her left hand, and brush in her right. After this the plates on which the dessert is to be served is set on the left of the lady of the house, unless she is seated before the waiter, in that case, before the carver or eldest daughter, in the same position; the knives and forks, or spoons, are to be placed on the right, and the dessert in the place occupied by the dining plate, though not quite as near the edge of the table. The lady of the house should be the last one waited on. For serving tea and coffee, see TEA AND COFFEE.

This manner of setting the table, with slight variation, is proper for breakfast and dinner.

For tea, the knife and fork should both be placed on the right hand, with the handle towards the edge of the table. The waiter should occupy the same place as at dinner or breakfast. The cake the place of the castor, about four inches from the waiter, butter on the left, cheese or other relish on the right. The sweetmeats where the meat is placed at dinner, sauce dishes on the left, spoons on the right. Table-spoons near. The bread or biscuit on the right, mid-way between the cheese and sauce plates, crackers to match on the left. Bread should first be passed, then butter, after which the sauce. When two kinds of cake are on the table, on separate plates, pass the plainest first; the same rule applies to sweetmeats.

Make as much variety as possible with your means; plain food can be cooked in many different ways; take potatoes for instance, they can be baked, boiled, fried, mashed, browned in balls, broiled, heated in cream, etc.

DIRECTIONS IN REGARD TO CHAMBERS.—Have the beds well aired, the furniture well washed, never turn down, or leave covers on chamber ware. If possible, this part of the work should be done early in the morning, the chamber pail should be always rinsed, and left in the air. Pails japanned never smell or rust.

GENERAL DIRECTIONS.—If you wash Monday, bake Tuesday, iron Wednesday, clean Thursday, mend Friday, and bake Saturday. Of course you will be somewhat governed by the peculiar situation of the family; but it will be found to be a good plan to have a regular routine for each day. If you keep but one servant, it will be found more convenient to wash Tuesday, putting the clothes in soak Monday. There can then be a nice cold dinner prepared for washing day, and the same can be arranged for ironing day. Special directions for cold dinners are given in another part of the book.

DIRECTIONS FOR WASHING DISHES AND CLEANING SILVER, ETC.—Always have two pans of clean, soft water, one with a little soap dissolved in it, and a nice dish cloth; wash all the glass first, and wipe them from the clear water while hot, lay tumblers on the side, partly filled, and hot water will not crack them. The silver should be next washed, and rinsed as the glass, rubbing it when dry with wash leather; if any articles are spotted, rub with whiting, never put away discolored silver. The cups, and all dishes free from grease, should now be washed, rinsed, and turned down to drain; after this wash the platters, etc. Wipe the first put to drain while the last are draining. Wash all tins next that are free from milk, rinse well, wipe, and stand them near the fire until perfectly dry. Wash the dish cloth, rinse, and hang it to dry. Get the pot cloth, wash all the kettles, inside and out, rinse and dry them perfectly. Wash the pot cloth, and put it to dry. Get the stove cloth, wash the stove in the suds, cleanse the cloth and hang it to dry. If you keep a cow, always fill the milk pail with cold water, as soon as the milk is strained, leaving in the strainer; a separate cloth should be used for washing the milk pail and pans; after they are perfectly free from milk, wash them in suds, scald in boiling water; and dry perfectly by the fire, or in the hot sun. Scald the milk cloth, and hang it to dry.

Knives should be scoured every time they are used, and thoroughly dried; the handles must never be dipped in hot water, a fine sandpaper will remove spots from ivory or bone handles. If knives are wrapped in chamois leather they will never rust, unless put away damp.

Every member of the family should have a bag for soiled clothes; where there are closets in the bed-rooms it is well to fasten them on the inside of the closet doors; take one yard and a quarter of dark drilling, fold it so as to make a bag a half-yard deep, with the quarter projecting beyond, bind it all around with strong colored tape, make loops in the corners to hang up by, and put them on the door with carpet tacks. Bags are more convenient for patches, etc., than boxes, they take up less room, and will last, when made of good material, a lifetime. A good method is to have a bag for each variety of patch, cotton, woollen, silk, etc., and sew a square patch on each bag, to show what they contain; for instance, on the calico patch bag sew a square of print, on the silk, a silk patch, etc.; we find this the most convenient method of designating them, as we often have help who cannot read sufficient English to bring a bag with the contents written or printed on it.

A bag made in the form of the old-fashioned needle-books, with pockets just deep enough to hold shoes, and one in the same form for combs and brushes, will be found convenient. A paper bag should hang in the kitchen, containing refuse paper for covering cake, etc., when baking. One with bits of woollen and cotton for holders and iron wipers; and one to contain the bits of twine which come around bundles.

We ourselves would not know how to keep house without these bags. Every spring they are assorted, and all superfluous patches put with carpet or paper rags, which keeps them in good order the year round, and saves much needless trouble in hunting patches, buttons, etc., from among quantities of rubbish.

CHAPTER III.

ECONOMY IN COOKING WELL, ETC.

ECONOMY in cooking does not consist in the use of very little of what are called the necessaries, but rather in always getting up, even the most common dishes, in such a manner, as not only to relish, but also to present, at table, a good appearance. Some housekeepers who have come within the range of the writer's observation, appear, in a remarkable degree, to possess this faculty. A poor meal is never seen on their table, or ever a time known when friends happening in at meal time put them out of sorts. The plainly furnished table is always neat, the cloth white, and carefully spread, the knives and forks bright as brick-dust can make them, and the silver looking its very best; while the clean floor, well-dusted furniture, cheerful fire in winter, or pleasant breeze and vases of flowers in summer, wonderfully assist the appetite, and add greatly to the enjoyment of the *plain* but *excellent* fare. Cheerful faces, too, add to table enjoyment more than is generally supposed. What husband and father, coming from the drudgery of business, would not rather find at the head of his table a cheerful, happy-looking wife, neatly dressed, and pleasant children, with a plain, well cooked, but simple dinner, than be seated at a sumptuous feast spread on an untidy table; the room in confusion, and every thing betokening ill-humor; the wife heated, full of complaints of the fatigue of cooking; the children's faces and hair in any thing but tidy order, reflecting, as children generally will, the unhappy state of their mother. It will indeed be a wonder if one or two are not sent from the table, or punished in some other manner, before the meal is over.

No matter with how much care the meal has been prepared, every article on the table may be perfect in itself, and perfectly cooked, and the only motive in getting it up may have been to give pleasure to the family, still, after all, we find the principal relish wanting; the only seasoning which gives enjoyment to viands, however costly, absent; the outlay worse than wasted, and the fatigue endured for naught. Many housekeepers fail here in making their table attractive, but do not realize the cause. No doubt often there are little trials, known only to themselves, which cloud the brow, but they should always make it the rule never to let such troubles be the cause of ill-humor in the family, especially at meal time. When the dress is changed for dinner, let it be the rule to clear the brow from all its clouds. If necessary, put on a cheerful air, and soon the spirit itself will pervade the soul, repaying fully the effort to subdue the evil by filling the bosom with joy and peace, and the next effort will be found much more easy. Perhaps this may be called digression, but the writer thinks not; her object is to benefit the young, whose habits as housekeepers are not fixed, but who have an idea of making home pleasant, they hardly know how, unless by cooking fine meals, etc.

She wishes housekeepers with limited means to understand the economy of cheerfulness, it will cover the many defects of cooking, or mistakes of judgment, to which the young housekeeper is daily exposed; and we think, too, a cheerful-tempered lady will, in the end, make a more finished housekeeper than one who habitually gives way to gloom. Hope is every thing in the family, and no member needs it more than the wife and mother. Be particularly mindful to cultivate this habit of mind if you find your husband inclining to despondency. Wives, even by silent influence, often uphold a sinking husband; many times all a man wants is courage, and a hopeful wife can impart all that he needs. Our sphere is large, no one can say how large; let us fill it in view of the future, with pure motives, not, like too many of our sex, think only of our ease, without regard to consequences. Be careful that every bit left is put to the best advantage; many times have we seen sufficient bread in the swill-pail to give a small family a meal. "Wilful waste makes woful want." Not that, under any circumstances, we would advise the use of unhealthy food, such as sour bread or biscuit. When this accident occurs, which ought not to be oftener than once to any housekeeper, and for which there is no excuse, throw it away; better by far bake again than allow a family to eat sour bread. One of the rules given to servants should be, that if the bread is sour another baking must take its place immediately. We have found this to work well. Servants don't like to do work twice when a little care will save them the trouble. Dry and heavy bread can be used. (*See* DIRECTIONS FOR USING DRY BREAD.) Much waste is also experienced in the boiling, etc., of meats. Unless watched, the cook will throw out the water without letting it cool to take off the fat, or scrape the dripping pan into the swill-pail. This grease is useful in many ways. It can be burned in lamps mixed with lard; or, when no pork has been boiled with it, made into candles. When pork is boiled alone it will do to fry cakes, if cleansed. (*See* CLEANSING GREASE.) Again, bits of meat are thrown out which would make good hashed meat, or hash. (*See* HASHES.) The flour is sifted in a wasteful manner, or the bread pan left with dough sticking to it. Pie crust is left and laid by to sour, instead of making a few tarts for tea, etc. Cake batter is thrown out because but little is left. Cold puddings are considered good for nothing, when often they can be steamed for the next day, or, as in case of rice, made over in other forms. Vegetables are thrown away that would warm for breakfast nicely. Dish towels are thrown down where mice can destroy them. Soap is left in water to dissolve, or more used than is necessary. If Bath brick is used, whiting, rotten stone, etc., much is wasted uselessly. The scrub brush is left in water, pails scorched by the stove, tubs and barrels left in the sun to dry and fall apart, chamber pails allowed to rust, tins not dried, and iron-ware rusted; nice knives used for cooking in the kitchen, silver spoons are used to scrape kettles, or forks to toast bread. Rinsings from sweetmeats, and skimmings of syrup, which make good vinegar, are thrown out; cream is allowed to mould, and spoil; mustard to dry in the pot, and vinegar to corrode the castor; tea, roasted coffee, pepper, and spices, to stand open and lose their strength. The molasses jug loses the cork, and the flies take possession. Sweetmeats are opened and forgotten. Vinegar is drawn in a basin, and allowed to stand, until both basin and vinegar are spoiled. Sugar is spilled from the barrel, coffee from the sack, and tea from the chest. Different sauces are made too sweet, and both sauce and sugar wasted. Dried fruit has not been taken care of in season, and becomes wormy. The vinegar on pickles loses strength, or leaks out, and the pickles become soft. Potatoes in the cellar grow, and the sprouts are not removed until they become worthless. Apples decay for want of looking over. Pork spoils for want of salt, and beef because the brine wants scalding. Hams become tainted, or filled with vermin, for want of the right protection. (*See* HAMS.) Dried beef becomes so hard it can't be cut. Cheese moulds, and is eaten by mice or vermin. Lard is not well tried in the fall, and becomes tainted. Butter spoils for want of being well made at first. Bones are burned that will make soup. Ashes are thrown out carelessly, endangering the premises, and wasting them. Servants leave a light, and fire burning in the kitchen, when they are out all the evening. Clothes are whipped to pieces in the wind; fine cambrics rubbed on the board, and laces torn in starching. Brooms are never hung up, and soon are spoiled. Carpets are swept with stubs, hardly fit to scrub the kitchen, and good new brooms used for scrubbing. Towels are used in place of holders, and good sheets to iron on, taking a fresh one every week, thus scorching at last nearly all in the house. Fluid if used is left uncorked, endangering the house, and wasting the alcohol. Caps are left from the lamps, rendering the fluid worthless by evaporation. Table linen is thrown carelessly down, and is eaten by mice, or put away damp and is mildewed; or the fruit stains are forgotten, and the stains washed in. (*See* REMOVING FRUIT STAINS.) Tablecloths and napkins, used as dish wipers; mats forgotten to be put under hot dishes; teapots melted by the stove;

water forgotten in pitchers, and allowed to freeze in winter; slops for cow and pigs never saved; china used to feed cats and dogs on; and in many other ways, a careless or inexperienced housekeeper will waste, without heeding, the hard-earned wages of her husband; when she really thinks, because she buys no fine clothes, makes the old ones last, and cooks plainly, she is a most superior housekeeper. The old saying of our grandmothers is only too true, which says, "A woman can throw out with a spoon, faster than a man can throw in with a shovel."

I am thus particular, in noting the little things, in which housekeepers fail, because I know, from my own early experience, how necessary it is to know and feel the importance of economy in small matters. It is seldom that a lady can assist in any other manner, in lightening the load of her husband, and, indeed, this should not be neglected, let her talents be what they may. The first duty of a wife is to make the home pleasant; if this can be done, and other labor accomplished, all is well; but that is an absolute necessity, never to be thought lightly of, or classed among the secondary duties of woman: "a word to the wise is sufficient." The duties of woman are everyday duties; we cannot let go awhile and pick up where we left off; it is like a stich, dropped in intricate knitting, it goes down and down, until the whole work is spoiled. Sometimes ladies go into the kitchen ill prepared, in dress, for the work to be done; it certainly is better economy, to buy common dresses for such purposes, than to spoil one that would buy a dozen such. Large aprons, with sleeves, will be found convenient to put on for a few moments, when company is in the parlor, to assist in taking up tea. A novice in kitchen work will soil her clothes more in a half-hour, than an adept in a week. Rings with stones must always be removed before putting hands in dough. This may seem superfluous advice, but the writer well remembers seeing, many years since, dough in the ring of a young housekeeper. When a lady first becomes a housekeeper, she is very anxious to do her best. She asks of this and that friend the advice she needs. Some are good advisers, and some not; and thus often mistakes occur. It is well to keep a record of all the mistakes you make, they will be less apt to happen again. When you make a good batch of bread, etc., write immediately in your journal the whole process; it will enable you to do the same again. Memory is not a safe guide for housekeepers, more than others; it often fails, and this is one reason why there is such a difference in the every-day cooking in a family. If you possess a cook book, mark every receipt you try; those you like with one, and those which do not suit with another mark. Always, in trying receipts, be attentive to copy the rule not only, but the directions. There is as much in putting cakes together as in getting the proportions. Many do not consider, that the cake must be baked as directed, to insure success; but that this is highly important experienced housekeepers are well aware, and a stove with a poor oven is pronounced a worthless appendage to the kitchen.

CHAPTER IV.

WASHING, STARCHING, IRONING, AND FOLDING LINEN.

If you wash Monday, put the clothes to soak in strong suds Saturday evening, the fine and coarse in separate tubs. If the washing is done Tuesday, soak them from Monday night, as in warm weather the suds would sour, standing from Saturday until Tuesday. The table and bed linen should be by themselves; change the beds Saturday morning, so as to have the sheets soak. On Monday, prepare a boiler of rain water in the following manner: to every pail of water, take a small table-spoonful of sal soda pounded fine, enough hard soap to make a suds, and to five pails of water a table-spoonful of spirits of turpentine; wring out all the table and bed linen, and boil them without rubbing, a good half-hour hard, frequently pushing them down with the clothes stick. Then take them out, and rinse in three tubs of rain water, blue in the last. If in time of fruit, the table linen should be examined before wetting, and boiling water poured through each stain, after which they can be put in the suds; this generally removes fruit stains. While the first boiler is on the fire, the fine clothes should be looked over, the wristbands, bosoms of shirts, and all articles that are soiled by contact with the skin or ground, be rubbed through one suds, when the first clothes are taken from the boiler; cool the water, adding a little soda, and boil the fine clothes, and afterwards, in the same manner, the coarse, and lastly, the brown towels. Fine linen embroideries, or cambrics, should never be rubbed on the washboard, and be always boiled in bags. Do not let clothes remain on the line after they are dry: the wind whips the hems, and wears more in an hour, than good use would in a month's time. This has been the manner of washing for the most part for ten years in the writer's family, and we are satisfied, from experience, that it saves clothes, labor, time, and soap. One half the soap can be saved, if well managed, that is ordinarily used in washing. Notice that clothes should never be washed in hot water; blood heat is sufficient to remove all soil.

STARCHING SHIRTS AND COLLARS.—Allow one teaspoonful of good starch to each shirt and collar, take just enough cold water to wet the starch, mash it free from lumps, add a little more, and stir it well; add, for each shirt, a piece of sperm or white wax, as large as a dry pea, and a quarter of a spoonful of clean salt to three of starch, pour on boiling water, slowly stirring all the time, let it boil hard fifteen minutes without scorching, skim and strain it while hot; this can be done only by dipping the strainer in cold water, while the starch is in the bag, and squeezing it immediately before it becomes hot. It is impossible to give a rule for the quantity of water to the spoonful of starch, as there is such a diversity of taste, in regard to the stiffness of bosoms and collars. Wet the bosoms and collars in hot water, wring them very dry, and starch while wet; rub them well, that the starch may penetrate, and wring them in a dry towel, to remove all the starch left on the outside; spread them out evenly, rub them down with a dry cloth and roll them tightly, let them lay two or three hours, and then iron them.

FOLDING AND IRONING.—Fold all clothing, so that when ironed, they will open on the right side. Pillow-cases, napkins, and towels, should be folded width-wise, first in the middle, then back and forth, to make three distinct folds, and in the same manner length-wise. The ironing should be finished as soon as possible after the clothes have lain three hours folded, as they soon become sour. In winter they can lie longer, even over-night, but in hot weather it is not safe to trust them, though it is often done. Examine the clothes-basket to be sure that every article is finished up, and not left damp to mildew, even to old cotton; if worth washing it is worth ironing. Fold the linen handsomely, hang it evenly on the bars, and let it remain until bone-dry. In folding the clothes, select such as need repairing, and lay them in the basket, or drawer appropriated to such articles, until mending day, when it should all be finished, and put in place; pile the sheets by themselves, also pillow-cases, towels, napkins, etc., so that, in getting one article, the whole drawer may not be disturbed. Fold shirts, so that the bosoms will be folded in, without bending; collars should be kept in round boxes. Ladies' under-clothing should be folded with the sleeves and necks on the outside. Skirts should be ironed on a board, without folding; these should be about as stiff as new cotton; iron stockings flat, with no fold on the instep. Embroideries must be laid on thick flannel and pressed on the wrong side; also dotted muslins, laces, curtains, bedspreads, and very fine cambric handkerchiefs. A cassimere vest is about as difficult an article to iron as there is of gentlemen's wear. The padding should be removed before it is wet; it must be starched, and dried thoroughly, the right side hanging inside; a speck of dust would make it necessary to wash it over. When quite dry, sprinkle it, and pull it in shape as much as possible, and roll it up true. It can be ironed best on a bosom-board such as described below. The irons should be hot, but not scorching; iron first the back lining and pockets, lay on the outside a damp cloth, unless the vest is sufficiently damp; if so, a dry one, and press it with a heavy iron; the pockets should not be turned in, until the vest is finished; be careful not to misshape the collar, and do not bend it in the least; gentlemen prefer shaping their own vests.

To IRON SHIRTS well, a bosom-board is essential. It should be made in the following manner: The board ought to be well-seasoned pine free from gum; it should be one and a half inches thick, one foot nine inches long, and eighteen inches wide; very smooth, and straight, rounded on one end, and cut smooth leaving no edge; the square end should be smooth, with a hole in the middle near the edge, large enough to let through a strong spike, or nail, to hang it by; cover the board on one side with flannel, until it is as thick as a common cotton comfortable, tacking each layer to the edge so as to draw it tightly over the board; the last two layers should be Canton flannel. The other side cover with thick flour paste, and cover it with Canton flannel; after it is perfectly dry, paste on another layer, and so on until four layers are pasted smoothly to the board. Make cotton cases, to slip the board in, and change them every week. The soft side is for embroidery ironing, Marseilles vests, and other figured articles; and the hard side is to be used in giving a polish to shirts and collars. A clean ironing sheet should be spread on the table before ironing the starched articles; iron first the neck binding, after that the back folded in the middle, then the sleeves, and remainder of the body, the collar, if on the shirt, and lastly, the bosom. If desired to have the collar and bosoms polished, turn the board, which should have been placed the soft side up, under the bosom on the hard side, pass the bosom over lightly with a damp cloth, and iron it hard and quickly with a polishing iron, which differs from others by being rounded instead of flat, without an edge, and being smooth as glass, leaves no mark of the iron, as common flat-irons do. This iron is useful in ironing vests, caps, and many other articles. Collars, although a small article, are seldom ironed well, being easily drawn out of shape; pass the iron quickly over the wrong side of the collar, then iron the band, and lastly the front side of the collar, until it is nicely polished. Gentlemen's pants are always starched; to iron them well, a pant-board should be made, as directed for the soft side of the bosom-board, on both sides to reach as near the full length as possible. The pockets should be turned out, before ironing, and no folds should be made in the pants, if possible to avoid it; hang them to air by the straps on the waistbands. A skirt-board should be in every house, to iron dresses and skirts; it should be six feet long, eighteen inches wide, one and a half inches thick, and rounded at one end; cover one side, as directed for the soft side of the bosom-board, and make cases to slip on and off, of strong cotton cloth. To use it, slip the skirt-board through the skirt, by the round end, letting the part not on the board fall on a clean cloth under the board while it is being ironed; when finished draw it carefully off the board, and hang it, if in fly-time, immediately away. Fringed doilies or cake napkins should be whipped on the skirt-board, to straighten the fringe. Damask must, to look well, be pressed rather damp, on the right side, with heavy irons until quite dry; the ironing table should be neither too hard nor too soft; a thick blanket doubled, makes the thickness about right, when covered with a sheet. Iron-holders should have cases that can be taken off to wash, or they should be made of quilted cotton, and one washed each week. The irons must be kept free from dampness, always standing on the end, it ruins flats to set them on their faces; should they become rusted send them to the emery mill, and have them ground off, or scour them with fine emery until quite smooth on a board. To cleanse them from burned starch, or other impurities, rub on a cloth or smooth board a bit of hard soap, and scour the iron on it while hot, and afterwards rub it on a damp cloth, until the soap is entirely removed. Muslin dresses should be as stiff as new muslin; the starch should be mixed through the rinsing water. White gum-arabic added to the starch, gives a new appearance to muslins, and they retain the stiffness longer than when starch alone is used. Dark muslins should be starched with the gum alone, or in rice water.

To WASH PRINTED INDIA MUSLINS WITH FAST COLORS.—Make

a suds of good hard soap, and squeeze them through it carefully, without rubbing; repeat the process three times, each suds being no warmer than blood heat. If the groundwork is white, put it in clear cold suds, and heat it boiling hot; after it has boiled three minutes, rinse it in soft water until the rinsing water is perfectly clear; then take three gallons of clear spring water, mix with it eighty drops of the elixir of vitriol, and one gallon of rice-water, made by boiling a pound of rice in four quarts of water until perfectly soft, adding boiling water to the rice, as fast as it evaporates, so that it is boiling in the first quantity constantly; it should be frequently stirred, and broken as much as possible while cooking. When the rice is dissolved as much as it will, pour the whole into the water and vitriol, strain it all through a thick cloth, and rinse the muslin in it; wring the dress as dry as possible, shake it out well, and hang it in the shade, until sufficiently dry to iron. Press it on a skirt-board, on the wrong side. If the waist is so made that this cannot be done, lay a thin cloth between the muslin and the iron, and press until quite dry.

To Wash Muslins of Doubtful Colors.—Take rice-water, and wash them quickly, without soap, until perfectly clean. If there is grease to be removed, or soil from the skin, rub the spots with the yolk of eggs, and wash it as though the egg was soap; rinse in hard water, and to the second rinsing add, to each gallon of water, forty drops of elixir of vitriol; strain the water, after adding the vitriol, that it may be thoroughly mixed through; wring dry; hang it in the shade, wrong side out, where it will get the air and dry quickly; fold as soon as sufficiently dry, and iron in two hours, on the wrong side.

Prints with Fast Colors.—These should be washed in warm suds, and scalded, if the ground is white, by pouring boiling water over them, but if dark, the scalding should be omitted. Rinse thoroughly, and add a little starch to the last water, merely sufficient to give them a fresh look, without stiffening them. Iron as soon as possible, after being starched. Prints soon sour.

To Wash Doubtful Colored Prints.—Prepare, before commencing, two tubs of suds, made of hard soap; throw in each a handful of salt; strain the suds, or bits of soap may come in contact with, and spot the print. Have three rinsing waters ready, in the last put forty drops to the gallon of elixir of vitriol, and a teaspoonful of dissolved gum-arabic to each gallon of hard water; strain the prepared water through a thick cloth. Look over the dress, and rub yolk of eggs instead of soap, on all grease spots, and wash them, in clear warm water, until they are removed; after which, pass it through two suds, rinse in two waters, and lastly, in the water with the vitriol and gum; wring dry, hang in the shade, where it will quickly dry from wind, and press it on the wrong side.

Swiss Muslin, India, and other thin muslins, should be gently squeezed but never rubbed. These and all handkerchiefs, collars, and small articles, should be boiled in bags for the purpose, made sufficiently large to allow them to be rinsed, ready to put on the clothes-line, without removing them from the bag. In hanging such articles to dry, care is needed to prevent their being torn or soiled; they should be pinned to sheets, or other large articles, instead of the line, and be taken in, as soon as dry. Rice-water is very nice for all thin muslins; requiring but little starch; the iron does not stick as badly with rice as other starch. Iron all muslins, if possible, on the wrong side.

To Wash Mourning Prints.—The suds should be very weak, and prepared as directed for prints with doubtful colors, omitting the vitriol; ox-gall is excellent for setting the color of black prints, but the odor is disagreeable to most persons.

Flannels should be washed in tepid water; no soap should be rubbed on them, if possible to cleanse them without. Suds should be prepared for the whole process before wetting the flannels; generally two suds are necessary, and two rinsings for fine flannels; the water should be barely softened for the last rinsing with toilette soap, or liquid ammonia; a teaspoonful of the ammonia to a gallon of water is sufficient. Each suds and rinsing water should be the same heat. Hot or cold water shrinks woollens, more than tepid water. New white flannels should soak in good suds all night, to remove the gluten, that is always in them, or when washed they will look spotted. If flannels are washed with the hand, the shrinkage will be less than if rubbed on the board. Blue white flannels a trifle in the last rinse; wring dry, and snap them out until there are no wrinkles left from the wringing; hang them in the shade to dry, and press them slowly with heavy irons until perfectly dry; if embroidered, iron the embroidery on the wrong side, on the soft side of the skirt-board. If skirts, use the dress-board to press them on. If bound with linen or cotton, rinse the bindings in boiling soft water, after the article is rinsed, without wetting the flannel; wring the binding in a towel as dry as possible, hang it to dry by the binding, and iron the binding before the other part of the garment.

Nice fine white woollen hose, if washed, and dried on frames, the shape of the stocking will never shrink; black or colored woollen stockings, to be washed well, will need two suds; the first suds the stocking should be rubbed well, and turned, and afterwards, if much soiled, rubbed through another, rinsed quickly, wrung dry, pulled in shape, and dried in the shade. White woollen stockings ought to be washed with as much care as fine flannels, and in the same manner.

PRINTED DELAINES need careful washing. The skirts ought to be ripped from the waist, and if desired to look like new, the whole dress must be ripped up. Wash quickly in from one to two suds prepared as for mourning prints, adding ox-gall, if possible, to the water; rinse as directed in doubtful prints, or substitute strong vinegar or alum for the vitriol, and twice as much gum-arabic; iron it on the wrong side; as soon as the iron will pass over it without sissing, until perfectly dry. If the linings are left in, dry the dress, and iron in the same manner as a print.

TO WASH COLORED MERINOES AND PLAIN DELAINES.—After the dress is ripped, look it over carefully, and rub on each grease or badly soiled spot the yolk of eggs; let it remain on the dress until the next day, or longer, if convenient. Prepare weak suds, sufficient to wash each piece by itself; it will not do to put such goods in the water, to remain while the whole is being washed, neither will the same tub of suds do for each piece separate, as the dye, in the fabric, will partially destroy the alkali, so that each successive breadth will have less strength of the suds, which will give a different shade to each piece, if the color is affected by the lye in the soap. Therefore the only sure method of giving the goods the same shade and stiffness is to wash and rinse each breadth and piece by itself. Wash each part first in clear soft water about blood heat, rubbing off all the egg; then in the suds the same heat, after which give two rinsings in warm rain-water, and stiffen with gum-arabic, using for each gallon of water a table-spoonful. To prepare it for a dress, take two table-spoonfuls of the gum, and a gallon of boiling rain-water; after it is dissolved, add another gallon of cold rain-water, and strain it through a thick cloth. Take a small part for each bit of the goods, dip in the merino, wring hard, and hang it by the edge to drain, where the sun will not strike it; after it drains, take it down, and shake it until the marks of the wringing is gone, and the water snapped out of it; roll it in a sheet for an hour, and press it slowly on the side that is to be turned in when made up. If double-width goods, fold the breadths evenly after it is ironed, lay a damp strip of cotton on the fold, and press the edge with a warm heavy iron, moving it constantly, so as not to leave the impression of the flat on the goods. The fold should be on the side it is intended to be made up.

PLAIN DELICATE COLORED MERINOES AND DELAINES.—Boil a peck of bran in a washboiler of soft water three hours; let it settle, and become cold; when clear, strain it through a thick cloth, and wash the goods in the water, passing each piece through a part of the bran-water by itself; rub it through three waters; rinse, stiffen, dry, and iron, as directed for colored goods of the same fabrics.

To WASH PRINTED MERINOES, DELAINES, OR OTHER PRINTED WOOLLEN GOODS.—Prepare a bran-water, and wash quickly as possible, each piece by itself, as directed for delicate colored goods of the same fabrics. Rinse, stiffen, dry, and iron the same, except the addition of twenty drops to the gallon of elixir of vitriol in the stiffening water, remembering always to strain the water after putting in the vitriol. Wash articles, that are almost certain to fade, in bran-water, adding to each gallon of water twenty drops of elixir of vitriol, and dry quickly in the shade; select a windy day to wash them, and wring the article, if there are gathers or linings, in cloth, until all the moisture possible is absorbed by the cloth. Such goods ought to be washed before badly soiled, if possible.

To WASH CHINTZ SPREADS WITH GREEN OR BLUE GROUND.—Rub them through three bran-waters; to the last, add to each gallon twenty drops of elixir of vitriol to brighten the green. Hang them up single, without wringing, to drain, where the sun cannot fade them. If double on the line, it will be too long drying, and the colors become mixed. If tapes are sewed on at regular intervals before they are wet, to hang them by, they can be fastened securely, without doubling the edge. If there is cotton quilted in the spread, rinse in clear well-water three times, without stiffening, each rinsing water containing the proper proportion of vitriol carefully strained, and wring them as dry as possible. When either the single or quilted spread drains so as to fill the lower part with water, while the top is nearly dry, wring the lower part; this will need to be repeated several times while drying. When nearly dry, fold the single spreads evenly, and roll them up for two or three hours, after which press them slowly on the skirt-board, without doubling. The quilts, after they are nearly dry, may be stretched on frames, or the carpet, until sufficiently aired, to spread on the beds.

To WASH CHINTZ WITH RED GROUND, TURKEY RED, OR OTHER RED PRINTS.—Prepare the bran-water as directed; add to each water an ounce of cream of tartar; should this not keep the color from discharging, add ten drops of the muriate of tin to each gallon of the second water; hang the chintz in the shade, after passing through three waters.

To WASH BROWN AND OTHER COLORED CHINTZES.—Mix in the bran-water ox-gall, and rub each article through three bran-waters, and rinse in well-water. The water for all colored articles should never be hot. Dry in the shade.

To WASH SCARLET MERINOES, DELAINES, ETC.—Prepare bran-water; to each pailful add a table-spoonful of good cream of tartar. If the color is discharged in the water, add to each gallon of water twenty drops of the muriate of tin. In the last rinse, omit bran or tin, unless the last water was colored; if so, add the tin. Press evenly, when in the proper state to iron, with as cool a flat as can be used without soiling the goods, until perfectly smooth. If the irons are very hot the goods may be discolored by the heat. In putting in the folds, be careful not to have the cloth much damp, so as to require a very hot iron, and pass it over lightly until the fold is well pressed in.

To WASH BLUE, BROWN, AND BLACK MERINOES, ETC.—If there are any grease or other badly soiled spots from contact with the skin, make a paste of fuller's earth and boiling water, rub the spots with the paste, and dry it by the fire. While drying, mix in two tubs, containing two pails of soft warm water each, a half-pint of ox-gall, and four quarts of old urine in each tub, and strain the water before putting in the goods. Wash the article quickly, each breadth in a small part of the water, and afterwards rinse twice, adding gum-arabic to the last rinsing. Dry, and iron, as directed for colored merinoes. If the articles washed, are broadcloths, etc., treat the goods as follows: rinse, without stiffening, in water rather more than blood-heat, and dry them, without wringing, on the wrong side; when nearly dry pull them in shape, press them with a hot iron on the wrong side, to remove all wrinkles, and hang them up again until dry, after which turn and brush them the wrong way of the nap, until a little rough, and then the right way until smooth. Have ready whiskey and water, half and half, with which wet a linen cloth, and wring it dry; the irons should be hot, but not scorching, and heavy; lay the wet linen over the article on the right side, and press slowly, moving the iron constantly the way of the nap. If the iron stands, it will mark the goods with its shape. Broadcloths, managed in this manner, look like new.

GINGHAMS.—Ginghams should be washed carefully; never allow them to lie wet or in the suds. Dark ginghams and prints should never be washed with the light; salt in the water helps to keep the colors bright. If washed in bran or rice-water, they will not fade nor be injured; dry in the shade, and iron on the wrong side.

To WASH EMBROIDERIES.—Prepare a strong suds with good hard soap. Look over and mend all broken places in the work, and soak the articles until the next day. Squeeze them carefully out of the suds, passing each article through the hand several times; prepare other suds, and wash them in the same manner until the suds is left perfectly clean. If you scald them, put the collars, etc., in a bag, pour over them cold suds, heat gradually, and boil five minutes. If very yellow by lying, put them in a white earthen wash-bowl, make a nice suds, lay them in the bowl, and set it in the sun for two or three days, changing the water daily. The articles must be frequently pressed under the water, and stirred up, so as to bring each to the influence of the sun. Rinse, without wringing much, until the water is quite clear, then add a little blue to the rinsing water; strain it through a thick white cloth; dip each article in, one by one, and wring, by pressing them in a towel. If desired very stiff, dry before starching; if not, have the starch ready, dip them in while it is boiling hot, and press out all that is possible in a towel. As fast as a piece is starched, spread it on plain cotton; stretch the work properly, and roll it tightly. This has the same effect as clear starching, which not only wears the embroidery, but is very fatiguing. Iron when in a proper state, on the wrong side, using the soft side of the bosom-board. The ironing should be done slowly, with moderate irons, and it is well to lay a thin cloth over the collars on the wrong side while passing the iron over the first time. If rubbed instead of pressed, the work, if heavy, will be apt to break. The starch made from rice does not stick to the iron as badly as wheat or flour starch.

To Prepare Starch for Embroideries.—Take as much as is needed of good clean starch, that has no sour taste. A teaspoonful will starch a collar, if but one is to be done up; a table-spoonful will starch six if all the starch is squeezed back into the basin as each article is dipped. Look carefully at the starch, see that no specks of fine dust are mixed with it, mix it smoothly with cold water. Have ready clear soft water, boiling hot, in the starch basin; add a little to the starch, stir it up, and add it gradually to the boiling water; stir it until boiled perfectly clear, then boil slowly fifteen minutes, without stirring; remove the skin that forms over the top, add to each table-spoonful of starch, a bit of sperm as large as a hazel-nut. Have ready one quarter of a teaspoonful of pure loaf-sugar boiled in a table-spoonful of water, until quite clear, without scorching; remove the scum from the sugar, and mix it thoroughly in the starch; after which strain the starch hot. This can be done by using a starch bag, pressing the starch through with a spoon. Articles done up in this starch look beautifully. If it is used for plain linen collars, add a little white wax to give a polish.

Starch for Heavy Skirts can be made with wheat flour, mixed as directed for starch, adding salt instead of sperm or wax; boil until clear, and strain it through a bag while hot. Some say if the starch is salted freezing will not destroy the stiffness, but this is not so; if frozen, the articles will hardly show the starch.

To Wash Thread Edging.—Get quart bottles that have never been used, sew around them a fold of cotton cloth, and wrap the lace carefully on them, so that the edge of the whole piece can be seen; soak it in several suds until the whole is clean. If the lace is desired white, lay the bottle in cold suds, heat it to a scald, and rinse in clear water until the water is free from soap; press it in a towel, and hang up the bottle by the neck until the lace is dry. If desired the color of new lace, rinse until clear from the soap, and then put it in a weak suds made from white toilet soap, and dry on the bottle as before directed. The suds will stiffen the lace sufficiently. When nearly dry take the lace from the bottle, pick out the edge, lay over it a cloth and press lightly, without perfectly drying the fabric, with the heat of the iron, after which roll it on a block or card until wanted.

To Wash Silks.—First know what mordants were employed by the dyers, and use those of the same nature, if possible, in the bran-water while washing. If reds, the muriate of tin; for greens, blues, crimson, maroon, and bright yellow, use oil of vitriol. When badly soiled, the bran-water must be used alone, and the goods be rinsed in water containing the mordant. Proceed as follows: First rip the dress, and look it over; if greased, rub the spots in the yolk of egg, and let them dry; then spread the silk on a clean whitewood board, and wash each breadth with a sponge or woollen cloth, first one side, and then the other, as quickly as possible; rinse in the prepared water without wringing. If very much soiled, it may need going over twice; if so, finish the washing before drying the egg, using it after first rinsing in the water prepared. Dry in the shade, stiffen with a very small bit of gum-arabic in the last rinse, unless the silk is heavy; if so, it will look better without. The best manner in which laundry maids can iron a silk dress is, to have a nice new piece of stove pipe, which is perfectly clean, heated and placed through a stick, so that it cannot roll, the stick being longer than the pipe, and laying across the back of chairs, or on tables; let two persons take hold of the silk and draw it over the pipe until well pressed; this is much better than ironing in the usual manner. Light fawn and brown silks usually wash well, and need no mordants. Ribbons can be washed in the same manner, and ironed when dry by drawing them across the flat iron. Soft India silks can be squeezed in the water, and ironed on the wrong side with a cool iron. Black silks should be sponged in a water prepared with gall and bran-water.

To Wash Bombazines.—Make a good suds, add gall, and squeeze through the hand without rubbing. Rinse thoroughly, and stiffen a very little with gum-arabic. Do not wring the goods; when nearly dry, roll it in black cambric; press slowly over black with a heavy iron on the wrong side, leaving no marks of the iron, and put into it a fold as described in the directions to wash colored merinoes.

To Wash Lace and Embroidered Curtains.—Pursue the same plan of washing as advised for embroideries. Prepare the starch in the same manner, using as much more water as is needed. Starch them in the same way, and roll them up until nearly dry enough to press. Pin sheets on the carpet, spread out the curtains, carefully shaping every scollop on the sheets, be careful to lay them perfectly straight, pin them in place, and leave them until quite dry. Barred muslins and harness pattern drapery better be ironed on the wrong side, as the trouble of spreading is much more than ironing, and they look very well ironed.

To Iron Cotton Sheets.—Cotton sheets, if folded evenly, and laid under the ironing sheet, will be well pressed by ironing the other linen. Linen sheets need hard pressing over the whole surface and both sides of the hems.

To Wash a White Counterpane.—Soak it in a strong solution of soap and soda for forty-eight hours. If there are spots, rub them; if not, boil it one hour in a boiler of suds, with three table-spoonfuls of soda, and two of turpentine. Rinse in three waters without wringing; in the fourth rinsing put a little blue, and wring the way the warp runs. When it drains, squeeze out the water from the edges, and when partly dry spread it out carefully, that no creases from the wringing or line may be left. When dry, stretch and fold it evenly, and press it by laying a weight upon it.

To Wash Blankets.—Wash them in good suds until quite clean; if much soiled, they will require two or three waters. Rinse them in tepid water until clear, adding to the last rinsing water a very little fine soap. Hard or hot water should never be used in washing or rinsing any woollen goods. They should be wrung very dry, snapped well to remove the wrinkles, and dried as soon as possible; when dry, press with a moderate iron until smooth.

Directions for scouring carpets, etc., and receipts for bleaching, labor-saving soap, etc., will be found in another part of this work.

CHAPTER V.

DIRECTIONS FOR THE ENTERTAINMENT OF VISITORS.

When inviting company never undertake more than you can perform with credit to yourself; understand your resources, and what ought to be expected of you in your circumstances. Do not aim to an equality in entertainments with more wealthy people.

To serve a Good Dinner for a Party of Gentlemen who do not use Wine.—Unless the table is very handsome it should first be covered with a colored table-cloth, after which a white cloth must be spread evenly over the table. If twelve guests are invited, set fourteen plates, as before directed, with knife, fork, table-spoon, napkin, goblet, and salt; place the knife with the handle towards the right; the fork on the left, with the handle towards the edge of the table; napkin and goblet on the right; spoon between goblet and plate; and salt on the left. A side table should be spread, containing water, a plate of bread, extra napkins, fourteen large and twenty-eight small plates, also fruit, nuts, and fruit napkins; as many large and small knives and forks as there are small plates.

The bread should be cut in squares, and a piece laid on each napkin. The castor should be placed in the centre of the table, jellies and relishes at the corners, spoons put on tastily in places convenient for the dishes. When dinner is ready the lady of the house may inform her husband. The soup should be placed before the lady of the house, the soup plates having been placed beside her plate when the table was laid; a waiter should fill the goblets while the soup is passing, which should be offered to every guest, commencing at her right hand, without remark. The host in the mean time should notice if any guest refuses soup; if so, he will serve them with fish which stands before him. The waiter must notice when the guests are through with soup, take the plate immediately, and bring him fish if desired. The hostess must help the host last, and the host the hostess in like manner. When the fish has been served, remove soup, fish plates, knives, and forks. A boiled turkey is placed before the host, oyster sauce on his left, with the handle of the ladle towards the edge of the table; potatoes on the right, which should be mashed; and turnips on the left. It is not fashionable now for a lady to carve. Another platter containing beef may be placed before a guest, who is requested to carve; and another to balance on the other side, with duck, or some other fowl, may be set before some other guest, who should also be requested to carve. If ham or beef is on the table with the turkey, it will be all sufficient, but two distinct varieties of meat are absolutely necessary for a genteel dinner. When the guests have finished with this course, the table must be entirely cleared, and the first cloth removed; the pudding should then be placed before the hostess, and the relishes before the host. She commences at the right as before, and passes a piece to each guest, the host passing the relishes. When this is finished the waiter brings on the fruit, nuts, etc.; the plates, napkins, knives, etc., are placed before each guest with as little parade as possible. When the dessert is finished, the lady gives a signal to the host, and rises from the table, taking the arm of her escort, who should have been seated at her right, and leads the way to the parlor, where coffee should be immediately served, unless served at the table as a last course.

DIRECTIONS FOR EVENING PARTIES.—It is fashionable now to spread a table in the dining-room, to which the guests are invited for refreshment. Much taste can be employed in decorating the table; where flowers are plenty, nothing is more beautiful than well-arranged bouquets. A few articles are deemed essential for parties; chicken salad, ice cream, whips or flummeries, jellies, fruits, nuts, coffee and tea, sandwiches, cakes, and fancy confectioneries.

The large dishes should stand at the head and foot of the table, fancy dishes in the centre, to balance each other, and smaller in groups. Any person of taste can arrange to suit themselves much better than they can be directed. If you wish good coffee, don't allow it to be put on the fire until just before time to serve the refreshments; it is quite common to smell coffee two or three hours before it is served. For directions in preparing dishes, see different recipes in this work.

If possible, have all your arrangements concluded early, that you may not look jaded or care-worn. Do not appear anxious if any accident occurs, take no notice of it, or pass it lightly; don't ask if this or that relishes, or if the evening has passed pleasantly; take it for granted your guests are happy; nothing embarrasses visitors more than a fussy anxiety, fearing they are dull, etc. Be easy yourself, and your guests will feel the same. In your dress be simple, not pretending to make a show, that no person may feel that you are better dressed than themselves. Spend but little time with each guest, that all may receive your attentions, let your manners be quiet and dignified. If any guest brings a stranger uninvited, be particularly polite to them; if a gentleman, introduce him first to your husband, and then to others near; if a lady, introduce to the host, who will introduce her to others. In short, act the lady, and you will succeed in making your entertainments pleasant for your guests.

HOW TO TREAT ACCIDENTAL COMPANY.—In the first place, make your friends welcome; but do not make a fussy parade or show in doing it. If you can possibly do so, avoid cooking on their account; it makes a person feel uncomfortable to find themselves the occasion of extra trouble. Better by far give them without comment the best the house affords ready prepared, and spend the time of the visit in their society. It is generally supposed our friends are not obliged to make visits to supply the deficiencies at home; and we are to take the visit as a desire for our society rather than the costly viands with which we might load our table. When friends come from a distance, be particularly careful not to have them imagine their visit ill-timed; do not complain of poor help, or want of room to make them as comfortable as you would wish. If you have a good room, give it them; if, on the other hand, your accommodations are not such as you would desire on their account and your own, make no apology, do not let them see your mortification, but act as though you felt satisfied with yourself and the world. If you have all you need, and your friends have hardly as much of this world as would be for their comfort, be careful not to wound their feelings by an ostentatious show of the comforts you happen to be blessed with, but appear as though your friends were accustomed to every luxury, and these trifles were only a matter of course. When a friend arrives, it is expected they need the refreshment both of toilet and table; as soon as congratulations are over, and their luggage arrived, show them to their rooms. Be sure that every article needed is there before you go up. Do not be obliged to call for water, towels, etc., but let them think the room was in order for company before their arrival. A bit of meat relishes well after a journey, if it can be obtained without too much trouble. Do not hurry your guests at their toilet, but be ready as soon as they have finished their toilet, to serve refreshments.

Allow them to propose retiring at night, instead of saying yourself, " Our friends must be fatigued after their journey, and we will retire early on their account." If convenient, their room should be put in order while breakfast is serving; if not, as soon as possible after. Do not allow a guest ever to feel that you are putting yourself to trouble on their account. If you make changes, do it quietly, that it may not be noticed. It is much more agreeable to a guest to be treated to plain fare than to feel that they are making needless trouble.

CHAPTER VI.

CHAPTER TO HUSBANDS—EXCUSE FOR HOUSEKEEPERS.

FIRST of all you will say, Why was this chapter written? What have husbands to do with housekeeping? If they furnish the funds to supply the family, is not that sufficient? What more can be expected of us? We love our families, and work hard to maintain them. Surely we cannot be expected to be housekeepers too. When we married, we expected to find a housekeeper as well as companion in our wife—we never agreed to carry all the burdens of the family. True, and no true wife wishes it. We know you love your families, and often overtask yourself, in your unwearied efforts to maintain them. Yet most of you, perhaps not all, in trifles that to you appear as light as air, add, unconsciously to yourself, many a care to your overburdened wife. It is with the hope, perhaps a vain one, of opening the eyes of young husbands, before their habits are fixed, to the importance of thoughtfulness in minor matters, to ensure the comfort and happiness of the family circle, that this chapter is written. Want of punctuality, particularly at the mid-day meal, is perhaps one of the greatest of your failings. If you are able to furnish plenty of servants, it is a less trial than where none or only one can be employed. The first object in all private families, as far as cooking is concerned, is, or should be, to suit the gentlemen of the family, especially the head of the house. The dishes that please him most, are the oftenest served; many times the wife exerts herself beyond her strength in the hope of pleasing her husband, by placing before him choice viands elaborately prepared, when by the delay of fifteen minutes, the whole dinner, which was perhaps a forenoon's work, is ruined. Sometimes delay is unavoidable, but usually business arrangements can be made, with sufficient accuracy, to ensure punctuality, provided its importance is appreciated. It is too often true, that something besides the regular business detains you—politics, arguments, long stories; etc., etc. These matters surely can be deferred to a more convenient time. We have known a few gentlemen who always closed business at a given hour, let who would be waiting, and they succeeded in the world too. If this is the habit of a man, his friends and customers soon find it out. It would take but a few decided efforts to accomplish this. "Gentlemen, this is my hour for dining," is sufficient excuse to all lovers of good cheer, and there are but few of the "lords of creation," who do not fully sustain this character. Do you not remember, if you have been married a few years, many times to have found your dinner spoiled, wife out of tune, and yourself seriously annoyed, when you could, without injury to business, or even trespassing on the laws of courtesy, have been punctual to the moment? And again, when for important reasons you desire the dinner prompt, you have found it far from ready, have you not found fault, and been reproached with such want of regularity yourself, as to make it impossible to keep up a proper system in the family? If not, you are a pattern husband, whose example it would be well for many to copy. If your wife has no servants, or not a sufficient number to do the work of the family, her time is as precious as yours, and the moments wasted waiting for you, must be made up by extra exertion through the day, or taken from the hours necessary for repose at night. You think little of this, or your practice would be different.

FAULT-FINDING.—This too is a serious trouble, especially with the inexperienced houskeeper. Don't find fault, if you can avoid it, especially when the matter which annoys is before you. If the dinner is poor, it will not be improved by ill-nature. You may have, in selecting a companion, chosen one highly accomplished, without a particle of household knowledge; you ought to have seen this defect removed before marriage. Few sensible young ladies, but would gladly educate themselves for accomplished housekeepers, could they have the time to do so, after they have been selected to fill the station of wife, but usually the young lady returns from school ignorant of all household matters, and marries almost immediately after; you should take a part of the blame of the housekeeping mistakes on yourself, and charge her mother with the remainder. Encouragement will go further with the young wife, than blame. Never wish for the dishes your mother prepared for you when a boy. There is nothing of which a wife is more jealous than a mother-in-law's cookery; besides, there is scarcely a doubt, that the very dishes so much longed for, would fail to please you now. When a boy, every thing relished with boyish zest; but now, even your mother, noted for her cookery of the old-fashion dishes, if you have become accustomed to the more modern styles, would be found faulty. But suppose she was, and is now, a perfect housekeeper in all respects, is it kind or gentlemanly to put your mother, with her years of experience, in competition with your young and inexperienced wife? You must bear and forbear, as very likely your father did before you, or you will never have a housekeeper in your wife. Avoid ridicule and bringing up mistakes, however absurd, before a third person, and never, under any circumstances, make apologies for your wife's failings before company at the table; mistakes will be noticed less, if passed without remark, and your wife's feelings are of more account than the whole dinner, and your own mortification besides. The want of order in husbands, is also a trial of no small moment to wives; it is as easy for a gentleman to hang up his coat, put away his overshoes, papers, books, etc., as for his wife to follow him as she would a child, rearranging all that he lays his hand on. The want of cleanliness, often tries patience sadly: what could have been prevented by a little forethought in a few moments' time, takes hours, perhaps, to remedy. Boots are not wiped on the rug, and soil the carpet; umbrellas left in the hall to drain, stain the carpet; marble hearths are stained with tobacco juice, when spitoons are at hand, (we regret the necessity of alluding to this miserable habit;) and in many other ways an untidy man will increase the labor of the family. Sympathize with your wife in her trials; these are not few, although you may wonder what she can have to trouble her. You expect her to be ready to listen to all that troubles you in business matters, while you are too apt to think she has no right to be tired by her cares. If you find her fatigued, you are sure she has been doing unnecessary work. You cannot see how a little sweeping, dusting, cooking, washing, ironing, mending, etc., with only two to provide food and clothing for, need to fatigue so much; think she must be a poor manager; your mother did all her work, and never complained of being tired; and with a good girl, the work in such a small family ought to go on as smooth as oil. You forget that the duties she owes to society take more time than in your mother's day; that servants do better with an eye on them, and are often almost worse than no help. You forget how often her head aches, for want of the walk or ride, to which she was accustomed at her father's, and how cheerfully she submits to your circumstances, when perhaps she never made her own bed before she became your wife. If she has children, she often gets no rest night or day; she never knows freedom from anxiety and care. Would you exchange cares with her? You know she suffers when your brow is clouded, perhaps more acutely than yourself, and also bears her own burdens. Do you not feel that your wife is under a species of obligation to you, for furnishing her with the comforts of life; and do you not think you ought to be paid for it, by a relief, not only from hearing of the petty home troubles, but in being waited on, while at home, with anxious care; the slippers and gown ready by the chair, and every thing to match, that selfish love would prompt? Do you think it necessary, when only wife is there, to be entertaining, or is the newspaper of more interest than her conversation? Do you know that these trifles make up a woman's life, and that you are adding drop by drop to the cup of care, which is fast robbing her cheek of bloom, and hastening her departure to the land where the "weary soul finds rest"?

This chapter is intended for the affectionate husband, one that the world calls perfect, in this relation; not for brutes, who care only for themselves without regard to others. Woman's nature is delicate, and easily chilled; many a husband will be called upon to answer for a broken heart, and untimely death, who never dreamed of unkindness or neglect. Treat your wife with the same politeness you would were you not married to her. Too many, in public and private, are polite to every one but their wife; this is wrong, and a sensitive lady feels it sadly. You should not deceive your wife in regard to your income; if sufficient to allow her luxuries, help, etc., she should know it; if economy is necessary, she should practise it: if once deceived, and trouble comes, she will be constantly on the look out for it. In short, be her companion in all things, and let the union betwen you be perfect in every sense. As you desire her to please you, so should you cultivate that which is pleasing to her; never expecting the perfection in a wife, which you know she will not find in you. There are too often good excuses for failures in cooking, unknown to you. The cook-stove may be new, and as yet untested, or it may prove a poor baker, either drying or burning every thing that goes into the oven. Company may unavoidably detain the housekeeper so long, that the intended dessert cannot be prepared. A new dish may fail through a defect in the recipe, and in many other ways the best efforts of the housekeeper, especially the young, may fail. Learn to bear those petty trials, not like a martyr, but receive with grace and good nature all reasonable excuses, or your young wife will become discouraged, and fail to become what you so much desire—a finished housekeeper.

CHAPTER VII.

ADVICE TO SERVANTS.

A HOUSEKEEPER should possess decision of character, good temper, energy, system, neatness; with a thorough knowledge of the different branches of housekeeping generally; sufficient education to enable her to keep accounts accurately, and should understand enough of the usages of society, to know how to order, without confusion, the daily routine of a genteel family. She is expected to look after all the female servants in the house, to know that they understand their duties, and discharge them faithfully; that nothing is wasted, or destroyed by carelessness or neglect. She takes charge of the store-room; gives out the supplies to the cook, sees that she wastes nothing; looks over the linen, and removes the stains before giving the soiled clothing to the laundry-maid; examines and lays away the linen after ironing, mending all that requires it; looks after the furniture; counts and takes the charge of the silver; if there is no butler, does the marketing; keeps the family accounts; etc. It is usually her duty to attend to the curing of the meats; the preserving of fruits for winter use; the preparation of the sweetmeats, pickles, catsups, confectionaries, etc.; to see that the table is well laid, and the dessert arranged to send in at the proper time. She should show herself willing to be directed, and anxious to please the family. In giving orders, she should be mild, but firm, never passing over wilful neglect, or any misbehavior; she should show no partiality in the kitchen, treating all with kindness, yet requiring a strict fulfilment on the part of each servant of her respective duties. She should feel the same interest for her employers, that she would for herself, and consider that she is responsible for all under her.

DUTIES OF THE COOK.—A first-rate cook should understand the art of dressing meat in every manner, the cooking of vegetables, preparations of desserts, etc.; should be energetic, prompt, orderly, and, above all, neat with her cooking, as well as in her person and kitchen. If she has no assistant, which is often the case, in moderate families, she should so plan her work that the vegetables are ready in time to be dished with the meat, that the one may not be spoiled, waiting for the other. She should keep the kitchen clock full up to the town time, and never keep the gentlemen waiting for dinner one moment. In the morning, she should be the first person astir in the house, and unless she has a scullion or chore-boy to do it for her, clean her grate or stove thoroughly, make the fire, sweep and dust her kitchen, and wipe off the stove; while the fire is kindling, should go to her room, wash, arrange her hair, and dress neatly, and then proceed with her breakfeast. No cook should allow herself ever to dress her hair in the dress she is to wear about her cooking, as there is always danger of loose hair hanging to the dress. While the family are at breakfeast, she should wash all the dishes and kettles soiled in the preparations for breakfast. If fowls are to be dressed for dinner, they should be killed, or any other preparations for dinner may be commenced. If any thing is needed for the kitchen, and there is no housekeeper, make a list of the articles and send them to the lady of the house, before the master goes out, that he may order them sent home. Examine the meats on hand; if there is danger of loss from longer keeping, either lay it in brine, or contrive some method to cook it. See that flies do not get to the fresh meat; if it is already blown, cut the part off without delay. In dishing dinner, serve first such things as will injure the least by standing in the oven to keep hot, and last that which should be eaten as soon as served; if many dishes are in progress, she cannot dish the whole dinner herself, without the danger of spoiling some; therefore some person should assist her in this. The most important dishes, making of gravies, etc., she should take wholly upon herself, and not allow a dish sent to the table without inspection. The platters and covered dishes should be heated, ready, so that there will be no confusion attending the serving of the viands. Each dish should be wiped, with a clean towel, before sending it to the table, or spatters of gravy, butter, etc., will give the whole an untidy look.

A cook is often nervous, especially when dishing dinner; this is a serious failing, and can be overcome with watchfulness and system combined; the trouble generally is, she either does not understand her duties, lacks system, or undertakes more than with the conveniences furnished her she can well perform. It requires patience to overcome difficulties in every station in life, and perhaps the cook, living as she does over a heated stove, constantly anxious for the success of her dishes, feeling tried with failures which must sometimes occur, requires a double amount to enable her to perform her duties cheerfully, with comfort to herself and others. There is certainly nothing more uncomfortable in a family, than an ill-natured disobliging cook, ready to snap at every person coming into her domain, like a cross dog gnawing a bone. The cook, too, can destroy and waste more than any other servant in the family, unless she feels the importance of being faithful in small things, without realizing that she is failing in any part of her duty to the family who employ her, and would be highly offended at even a hint of the fact, when at the same time, did she realize the truth, she would herself be the first to correct it. It is not that servants have no wish to be faithful, that they so often fail, but because their consciences are uneducated in these respects; a careful and consistent mistress, who shows she is willing to do her duty to her servants, can, by proper instruction, enlighten them, and so impress their minds with the importance to themselves, as well as others, of fulfilling their duties conscientiously in every matter that comes within their province.

CHAMBERMAID.—The chambermaid is generally also the housemaid; she is expected to make up the beds, do all the other part of the chamber-work, sweep and dust the parlors; wipe the paint, etc. In most small families, where few servants are employed, she sets the tables, waits at dinner, cleans the silver, and assists in the ironing. When her duties are various, she will find it very important to be up in good season, that the parlors may be arranged, before the family leave their rooms. If the cook or laundrymaid waits at breakfast, she should, while this meal is being served, air the chambers, shake up the beds, carry down the slops, and wash the chamber-crockery. If she has the charge of the dining-room, putting it in order is her first work after breakfast; when this is finished make up the beds, sweep and dust the chambers. The next thing in order is the sweeping and dusting of hall and stairs; and lastly, the porch or portico. After this, a pail of clean suds should be prepared, and every spot of soil on the paint be removed, wiping each place wet with the suds, with a soft dry cloth. If any spots are to be seen on the carpets, let them be rubbed out; and if the windows are dusty, or fly-specked, cleanse them. (*See* HOUSE-CLEANING.) If it is her duty to wait at dinner, she should change her dress, after arranging her hair, etc.; putting on a neat print, with a white apron: nothing looks more silly than a table-waiter decked in finery. A chambermaid should particularly guard against curiosity; never meddling with any thing belonging to ladies occupying the chambers, or using their combs, etc. The dress of a chambermaid should never look soiled; as her work is neat, there is no excuse for a slovenly appearance. Particular directions on the care of chambers will be found in another part of this work.

LAUNDRYMAID.—Directions for washing are contained in another chapter of this work; but a few hints farther on this subject, may not be deemed superfluous. The laundrymaid will do well to bring in, the evening before washing, as much water as her extra tubs, etc., will conveniently contain. She should know that all her washing apparatus is in order; that she has in the house, soap, starch, indigo, or whatever she may need on the morrow. She should rise very early to enable her, in winter, to dry the linen the same day it is washed; and, in summer, to secure the cool of the morning for the most fatiguing part of the work. The clothes should be hung up systematically on the line, the shirts and articles to starch by themselves so that, when taken down, the folding can be done without handling them twice. If any part of the linen is necessarily hung in an exposed part of the yard, let the table and bed linen be selected to occupy that part of the line. As fast as the clothes dry, bring them in, and lay them on a clean table. If possible, fold as many of the plain clothes, the evening after washing, as can be ironed the next day. In ironing, be careful not to break buttons or bend hooks. (*See* DIRECTIONS FOR WASHING, STARCHING, IRONING, ETC.)

NURSEMAID.—A very young person should never be trusted with the entire care of children, especially infants. It requires more judgment and experience than they usually possess, to fill a place of such importance in the family. Many children have been ruined for life, by employing young girls to take the charge of them. A woman employed to take the care of children, should be possessed of good common sense, a kind heart, decision of character, without being stern; an agreeable countenance, without deformity of eye or impediment of speech. She should be a person of known integrity, and particularly truthful. Her health should be robust, particularly if the children occupy the same room; expert with the needle, and in person scrupulously neat and orderly. It is the duty of the nursemaid to wash, dress, and feed the children; to join them in their sports; amuse them by pleasant stories; walk and ride with them at stated times; and attend to all their habits. A judicious nurse will not be governed by the children, neither will she find it necessary to resort to corporeal punishment. She should carefully avoid irritating, or bringing into notice forbidden objects; but for the child's sake, should never give up to its caprices. If the same nurse has the charge of a child the three first years of its life, she can form its character at will; that is, always provided her influence is not interfered with. If the nurse is passionate, untruthful, deceptive, or superstitious, the child will be tainted. Many a person suffers through life from the superstitions received from the nurse in babyhood. She must carefully watch the child's diet, allowing what appears to agree with it only. If teething, the state of the bowels must be particularly noted. If it has taken cold, its breathing must be watched with care. If infectious diseases are prevalent, the symptoms must be looked for; and in many other ways, a good nurse will, with watchful, zealous care, look out for the wellbeing of the little ones under her care. (*See* INFANTS.)

MAID OF ALL WORK.—Most people employ but one female assistant in the kitchen, and but few employ three; unless there are a number of small children who need the constant attention of a nurse. The maid of all work is expected to cook plain food well, the mistress usually preparing desserts, making cakes, sweetmeats, pickles, etc.; she also expects to assist, if the family is large, on washing day, takes care of the parlors, etc. Unless the help is efficient, she expects to teach her, and if the help is naturally intelligent, she soon becomes expert in all the branches of housework. Each servant in the family adds to as well as performs her part of the labor of the family; and in families where so much is to be done that each department requires its especial servant, it is usually the case that the work for each is perhaps harder than that performed by the one assistant in a small family, besides being much more healthy from its variety. It is much more fatiguing to be employed in one steady routine than to work more hours with constant change; no females show better health than our country girls, hastening from one thing to another, from morning till night—washing, baking, ironing, etc., as each day's duties come around. Every effort should be made to lighten the kitchen burdens: the wood and water should be near; the kitchen and dining-room, if possible, should be on the same floor with the cellar. Punctuality in meals is highly important, and where three meals are prepared, an early breakfast is a great lift to a day's work. The maid should learn to save steps. When clearing and setting table, use a small waiter to carry the articles needed, instead of taking one thing at a time. Sheets can be nicely pressed by laying them under the ironing sheet while doing the other part of the ironing; and in many ways steps can be saved and fatigue avoided while performing the labor fully as well. The situation of maid of all work is more pleasant, in one respect, in the family than that of cook, chambermaid, etc., in large families; she is by herself, and not troubled by the petty quarrels which are almost always occurring between servants of the same household. When her day's work is over she has nothing to trouble her; she can sew, read, or in some other pleasant manner spend her evenings; while usually where a number fill the kitchen, the time, if not wickedly spent, is foolishly wasted.

DRESS OF SERVANTS GENERALLY.—Never ape those who you. You are much more respectable in a plain dress tha⁻ in silks. A plain but neat dress would become you m⁺ showy finery; but, however you may choose to dreṣ ͺoing out, never appear about your work in any thing the leaṣ ͺproaching to finery; let your hair be always smooth, and your dress neatly fitted and well made, of a material that will wash without injury. When waiting at table, ironing, or baking, a white apron looks both neat and becoming. Always have a neat sun-bonnet to wear when doing the errands of the house; keep your feet neat, wear light shoes in the dry season, but guard against wetting your feet washing days. Bathe your person often, particularly the feet; being over the stove heat so much as is necessary for you in your several duties, occasions your feet to perspire so much as often to make you disagreeable. India-rubbers, too, have the same effect if constantly worn, and are very unhealthy.

CHAPTER VIII.

CARVING.

BUTCHERS divide a bullock into eighteen different parts. Sirloin, which is the best part of the animal, extending from the rump to the fore ribs; rump, which lies back of the sirloin; fore ribs, between the sirloin and middle ribs; middle ribs, between the fore ribs and chuck ribs; chuck ribs, between the middle ribs and sticking place; sticking place, between the chuck ribs and cheek; thin flanks, the belly under the sirloin; brisket, under belly, below the ribs; edge bone, under the rump; buttock, under the edge bone; mouse buttock, under the buttock, being part front of edge bone and buttock, and back of the thin flanks; leg of mutton piece, on the fore shoulder, between the chuck ribs and shin; shin, the lower part of the foreleg; leg, the lower part of the hind-leg; cheek clod, on the breast below the sticking place; thick flank, the front and upper part of the hind-leg. Besides these parts, there is the heart, the liver, tongue, palate, sweetbreads, kidneys, skirts, and tripe. The tripe is the prepared stomach. The sweeetbreads are situated between the bottom of the stomach and vertebræ of the loins, extending from the liver to
n. The skirt is the respiratory muscle which divides the to two cavities: the thorax and the abdomen.
est roasts and steaks come from the sirloin. The best slices ear the ribs, extending from five to eight inches on the side ef. These steaks are called "Porter-house steaks." Next r-house comes sirloin. The whole ham is used for dried e best boiling pieces of corned beef come from the brisket. Good steaks are also cut from the fore shoulder. The best soup bone

is the shank of the hind leg, called the leg by butchers. The part called the sticking piece, is usually boiled for mince pies.

The terms butchers use in dividing a calf are, loin, (kidney end,) loin, (chump end,) fillet, hind knuckle, fore knuckle, neck, (best end,) scrag, blade bone, breast, brisket, head, pluck, liver, light, or lungs, heart, sweetbreads; the largest of which is called the throat sweetbreads, and the smallest the wind-pipe sweetbreads; the rennet or stomach, and the feet. The loin chump end lies from the end of the backbone to the kidney loin; next to this from the backbone to the breast, and between the chump loin and the best neck end. The scrag lies between the head and the best neck piece. The brisket is below the scrag on the front. The breast is the belly; the fore-knuckle is the fore leg; the hind knuckle is the hind leg. The fillet lies between the hind knuckle and the chump loin, and extends to the breast. The feet embrace the leg to the knee. The head embraces the brain and tongue. The fillet is usually stuffed and roasted. The loin, breast and shoulders are roasted plain. Pies are made from the breast or neck. Cutlets are cut from the fillet. Pot-pies are made from the neck; stews from the knuckle; soups from the feet.

The parts of a lamb are fore and hind quarters. The fore quarter includes one shoulder, with half the neck and breast, and the hind quarter consists of one leg, and half the loin. A leg of lamb is usually boiled, also the shoulder. Whole quarters are roasted.

Mutton is cut up by the butchers into the leg, loin, (best end,) chump end of loin, neck, (best end,) scrag, shoulder, breast. The leg is boiled; also the neck. The shoulder is stewed. The two loins are roasted together, and are called a saddle of mutton.

The butchers divide the hog into the spare rib. It lies between the head and fore-loin, and is usually roasted. The hands are the fore shoulders; the spring is the belly, the legs or hams, the fore and hind loin, between the leg and spare rib. The leg is boiled or roasted; when salted is called a ham. A hand is usually fried, and when salted is called a shoulder. The belly pieces and loins are fried or baked; when salted, the bones should be removed. The head and feet are best boiled for souse or head-cheese. The tenderloin makes the best steak.

DIRECTIONS TO CARVE A ROAST OF BEEF.—The knife should be of good steel, and sharp, and not too heavy. A large heavy-handled carving-knife is very awkward to manage. The platter containing the beef should be near the carver, that he may not be obliged to reach over the table. His seat should be high, or if not, he may be allowed to stand while carving. In a sirloin of beef, cut the outside pieces thin, lengthwise of the bone, drawing the knife through with a quick movement, and laying them in order on the platter, until there are as many slices cut as there are persons to be helped. Now cut the inside meat in the opposite direction, cutting across the bone, laying the slices, which should be very thin, in order by themselves. When filling the plates, give each person an outside and inside piece, that the beef may be equally enjoyed by all, but do not overload the plates, nothing destroys a delicate appetite sooner than an overloaded plate. If the slices are large, divide them.

To CARVE A LEG OF MUTTON.—Lay the joint back down; cut the first slice across the lower part, about one-fourth of the distance between the knuckle and cramp bone. Cut the slices towards the thickest part, until it is sliced to the bone. Then cut the thin part near the thickest part until it is sliced to the bone. Then cut the part near the knuckle lengthwise. The best pieces are in the thickest part of the leg, but those near the knuckle are miserable cold. If any is left, let it be the thickest and best part.

To CARVE A HAUNCH OF VENISON.—Place the joint lengthwise on the platter, bringing the thickest part nearest the carver. Make the first cut to the bone across the haunch, about one-fourth of the distance between the knuckle-bone, and the extreme end of the haunch; then cut slices lengthwise from the first cut to the bone at the opposite end. A haunch of mutton is carved in the same manner.

To CARVE A SADDLE OF MUTTON.—Cut the slices lengthwise from end to end on each of the back-bones. If too large, divide them, and give each person a bit of fat from the sides.

To CARVE A LOIN OF VEAL.—Carve exactly as you would a sirloin of beef, except this: the carver turns over the loin, and removes both kidney and fat, before cutting any slices. These are helped with the veal.

To CARVE A SHOULDER OF MUTTON.—Lay the joint on the platter, with the back uppermost. Cut the leanest parts to the bone across the joint. The most delicate slices are cut each side of the blade-bone. The most tender of the meat is under the blade-bone, and the best fat lies at the under part of the thick end. A shoulder of veal is managed much as a shoulder of mutton.

To Carve a Fillet of Veal.—Give to each person a thin slice cut through, with the dressing and some of the outside.

To Carve a Breast of Veal.—The ribs should be separated from the brisket. Cut the small bones and serve them, divide the long ribs, and help to suit the different individuals at the table.

To Carve a Leg of Lamb.—Carve as a leg of mutton. Lay it in the platter back down.

To Carve a Fore Quarter of Lamb.—The cook should cut round the shoulder, and lift the meat without marring the joint; and crowd in between the ribs butter, pepper, salt, and, if relished, lemon juice; then replace the shoulder; put a ruffle of paper on the joint, lay it on a clean dish, and send it to the table. It is first cut similar to a shoulder of mutton; then the neck is separated from the ribs, and served according to choice.

To Carve a Ham.—Lay the back up; cut slices as thin as possible near the middle of the ham to the bone; and also near the thin end of the ham. Help a bit of lean and fat together.

To Carve a Boiled Calf's Head.—Calf's head consists of a number of choice parts; which should be divided so that each person may have a share. The sweetbread lies at the fleshy part of the neck-end. Cut slices across the cheeks to the bone lengthwise. Remove the eye with the point of the knife from the socket; divide it and help those with it who prefer it. Remove the jaw-bone and carve the lean meat under it. The palate lies under the head, and by some is much esteemed. Divide the parts, giving every person some of each.

To Carve a Tongue.—The best slices are midway between the root and the tip of the tongue. Cut the tongue through, dividing it, and slice quite thin; help those who desire them, to the fat and kernels.

To Carve a Roast Pig.—If the pig is served whole at the table, the carver first removes the head, striking the neck joint; this is laid on a plate, and divided for those who prefer that part of the pig. It is then laid open at the back-bone from neck to tail, and laid crackling side down. After this is done, divide the ribs, and serve a part of the crackling and dressing to each person. If the pig is partly carved by the cook, the carver may finish as already directed.

To Carve a Fowl.—Place the fork firmly into the thick part of the breast; take slices from each side of the breast-bone, extending the whole length of the fowl; joint and remove the wings, and divide them at the first joint. Divide the ligaments of the legs, and twist them out of their sockets, and separate them at the first joint. Now enter the point of the knife at the breast in the direction of the merry-thought or wish-bone, which is displaced by lifting the bone, and pressing backward. The collar-bones, which lie on each side of the merry-thought, must now be lifted up by the knife, at the broad end, and forced towards the breast-bone, until the part to which they are fastened, breaks off; cut through the ribs on each side, and remove the breast. Now turn up the back-bone, and press the knife firmly across it near the middle, lifting the lower end at the same time with the fork, until the bone gives way; then turn the lower end of the back from the carver, and remove the bones from each side; this is easily done by placing the point of the knife on the place where the side bones are joined to the vertebræ. There is much choice in the parts of a fowl: the white meat being esteemed the most delicate; some, however, prefer the dark meat. The drum-stick is the coarsest part of the fowl. Duck is carved in the same manner, as also prairie-hens.

To Carve a Turkey or Goose.—The art of carving these consists in cutting as many slices as possible from them without cutting up the carcass. The wings and legs are removed in the same manner as fowls. When the carcass is divided, proceed as directed in carving fowls. Pheasants are carved like a turkey; cut as many slices from the breast as possible.

Partridges are carved like a common fowl; though the merry-thought is never removed unless the bird is unusually large.

To Carve Pigeons and Quails.—All birds of this size are divided in the middle of the back. Blackbirds are served whole.

To Carve a Hare or Rabbit.—In this country the hare is seldom served; it is carved the same as a rabbit. Enter the knife at the shoulder on each side of the back-bone, and cut lengthwise the whole length of the animal, dividing it in three different parts; then divide the back-bone of a rabbit into two and that of a hare into four parts. The back and legs of a hare are the best parts, although the shoulders are much prized by some. The best parts of a rabbit are the back and legs. Some prefer removing the head of a rabbit before sending it to the table.

To CARVE FISH.—To carve fish well a fish-trowel is very necessary, as with this instrument they may be carved without breaking the flakes.

To CARVE A COD'S HEAD.—Cut slices from the fish through the back, reaching half down the sides. Commence to cut the slices some few inches from the head, and serve with them a part of the sound, which lies under the back-bone, and lines it. The most of the head is considered very fine. The palate and soft part about the jaw-bone are much esteemed.

To CARVE SALMON.—Cut salmon lengthwise, as also all other short-grained fish. In serving this fish, do not help one person to the thick and another to the thin part, but divide the two parts equally.

To CARVE HADDOCK.—This is a long-grained fish, and the slices should be cut round the body.

To SERVE MACKEREL.—Cut slices of this lengthwise, from the head to the tail.

To SERVE A BAKED FISH.—If the grain is coarse, pass the fish-trowel through, taking round slices with the dressing. If fine-grained fish, cut them the other way, and serve some of the dressing with it.

TURBOT.—Enter the fish-trowel at the head, and press it along the back-bone the whole length of the fish. Slices may then be served from the back-bone to the fins on both sides, those nearest the centre being most prized. When the upper side is served, lift the back-bone with the fork, and divide the lower part in the same manner. The fins are considered the most delicate, a portion of which should be served with the other part of the fish.

To SERVE EELS.—These are cut into pieces through the bone; the middle slices are the choice bits.

PAN FISH.—If very small, they are served whole; if large, they are cut in pieces by the cook before frying.

To SERVE SOUP.—If soup is served for a first course by the carver, he should pour but one ladlefull into a plate. Persons are often overtaxed to get rid of the contents of their soup-plate.

PART II.

NUTRITION.—ELEMENTS OF FOOD.—MARKETING.

CHAPTER I.

NUTRITION.

NUTRITION consists in the process by which food, taken into the stomach, is changed and prepared to repair the natural loss of the system. The first change is produced by a substance or juice, unlike any other, placed in the stomach of each animal by the All-Wise. It is called Gastric Juice, and is said to consist of hydrochloric acid, gastric mucus, and water. It is very powerful, reducing all substances capable of digestion to a uniform paste of a grayish color, called Chyme, which, passing into other organs, meets Bile, Pancreatic Juice, and other acids, and changes to a milky substance called Chyle, which, in its turn, being taken up by minute vessels called Lacteals, goes through another transformation, until it finally reaches and is united with the blood, and by it is carried to every part of the body, thoroughly renovating the system in its course. It is a well-known fact, that the animal system experiences a daily waste; but few are aware to how great an extent it may be said we decay to exist. It is thought we so entirely change, that in a few years every part of the original matter composing our body is consumed, its place being occupied by entirely new formations. This constant loss must be supplied by elements similar to those already exhausted, or wearied nature, unable to do its appointed work, retires in disgust, leaving premature age, or death, master of the field. There is a continual war between the oxygen of the air and the body; every breath we breathe, or muscle we exert, a portion of our blood is used up by this oxygen. It does not, however thus exhaust without a return: it is by this battle between the oxygen of the air and the carbon of the blood, that animal heat is evolved; when this ceases entirely, death is sure to be the result. This it is that kills the frozen man; as long as any carbon remains in the system, heat will certainly be evolved. A man with a hearty breakfast can much better withstand the piercing blasts of winter than one with his stomach empty. The oxygen, in the case of a freezing man, first consumes the fat, then the lean, and lastly the brain; when all the carbon is destroyed, or consumed, the body soon sinks to the temperature of the atmosphere, and death ends the strife. In the words of Liebig, "the animal body acts as a furnace, which we supply with fuel. It signifies nothing what intermediate forms food may assume, what changes it may undergo in the body, the last change is, uniformly, the conversion of its carbon into carbonic acid, and of its hydrogen into water; the unassimilated nitrogen of the food, along with the unburned, or unoxidized carbon, is expelled in the urine, or in the solid excrements. In order to keep up in the furnace a constant temperature, we must vary the supply of fuel, according to the external temperature—that is, according to the supply of oxygen. In the animal body, the food is the fuel: with a proper supply of oxygen, we obtain the heat given out during its oxidation or combustion. In winter, when we take exercise in a cold atmosphere, and when, consequently, the amount of inspired oxygen increases, the necessity for food containing carbon increases in the same ratio; and by gratifying the appetite thus excited, we obtain the most efficient protection against the most piercing cold. A starving man is soon frozen to death; and every one knows that the animals of prey, in the arctic regions, far exceed in voracity those of the torrid zone. In cold and temperate climates, the air, which incessantly strives to consume the body, urges man to laborious efforts, in order to furnish the means of resistance to its action; while, in hot climates, the necessity of labor to provide food is far less urgent." "According to the preceding exposition, the quantity of food is regulated by the number of respirations, by the temperature of the air, and by the amount of heat given off to the surrounding medium."—See Liebig's Animal Chemistry, p. 16. But heat is not all that is wanting to repair the wastes of the system; we need food, not only to create heat for warmth, but to renew the wastes of the body caused by the labor of each day. The food best adapted to give strength furnishes the least heat, and that which the soonest furnishes heat strengthens the least. Blood is the same heat at the frigid zone as the torrid. The same proportion of the heat-giving properties united with the oxygen, is necessary for all climes. The more oxygen we inhale, the more food is needed; the warmer we dress, the less heat does our body give off to surrounding objects. The blood flows through the lungs at the rate of fifteen hundred pounds every hour, or twenty-five pounds each minute. It meets there the air, takes up its oxygen, and rushes on its way, carrying and equally distributing warmth to every part of the body. But although, as has been stated, the gastric juice is capable of reducing to paste, and the other juices to blood, every digestible article taken into the stomach, it is not capable of converting the properties of any food to the properties of any other. It cannot make fibre-creating substances heat-giving, or heat-giving fibrous. It cannot change poison to healthy nutriment, or make healthy food injurious. Our stomachs have not the power to choose what shall flow through the veins of our body, and what shall be discarded. Many imagine, if food digests, it is all that is needed to produce the desired result; when often the food is of such a nature as to seriously inconvenience the body for days and weeks. The brain is as seriously affected by our method of living as any other part of the body. The irritability of children often arises from improper food, and many nervous persons are thus affected by the same cause. The amount of nourishment absolutely necessary to sustain in health the animal body, is varied, as has been seen, by the amount of oxygen respired, and otherwise taken into the system through the pores of the skin; more oxygen being taken into the system in cold weather than warm, as the atmosphere in summer, containing more moisture than during the cold of winter, is received by the lungs, filling the same space which in winter is occupied by pure air alone. Thus the amount of oxygen consumed in cold weather must be proportionably greater than during the warm months of summer; consequently more nourishing food, rich with carbon, is needed during winter to sustain health than during the warm season. Here is seen the wisdom and goodness of our Creator, as is expressed most beautifully by the Psalmist, when he says: "These all wait upon thee, that thou mayest give them their meat in due season." During the warm months of summer, while most of the animal creation are rearing their young, and consequently out of season, vegetables are in their prime, affording nearly or quite all the food absolutely essential to man. Comparatively few of the esculent vegetables can be preserved in perfection for a great length of time, while the grains and a few seeds most rich in the principal elements, can be preserved, with proper care, in any climate, for an indefinite period. To the inhabitants of the frozen regions, where vegetation is almost unknown, animal food is found to be most conducive to health and comfort, containing a very large percentage—over sixty per cent.—of carbon; while the natives of the south, feasting on their delicious fruits, containing not over twelve per cent. of this heat-giving property, enjoy health and happiness on a diet that would soon destroy the northerners. Should the natives of the warm regions follow the example of travellers, creating artificial appetites by stimulating condiments, so that the use of animal food would become universal, diseases more terrible than any that have yet visited our globe, would, undoubtedly, be the consequence of this transgression of the laws of nature. The inhabitants of the extremes furnish to us an example in respect to diet it would be well to follow. We have, to be sure, more latitude in the selection of food, yet we should remember that our food is prepared for us by the Almighty with particular reference to each season, and were we to follow the dictates of reason, from infancy to old age, all things being equal, a perfect organization of the body, with strong nerves and vigorous intellect, unshackled by dyspeptic hypochondria, with a healthy, happy old age, would be the result. It is not only important that the proper food is chosen, but that it is taken at proper intervals. No doubt the old fashion of twelve o'clock dinners is, to persons taking exercise, most conducive to health. If late dinners are the most convenient, lunches should be taken at eleven or twelve. Infants and children need food oftener than adults, as they breathe oftener, and therefore consume more oxygen in proportion to their size than adults. Persons, whose respiratory organs are debilitated by disease, or are naturally weak, consume less oxygen than those of a contrary formation, and consequently require less food containing carbon.

In selecting food, avoid too much sameness, not only as to the articles of food, but to the elements of which they are composed. Variety is necessary, as a want of appetite for one kind of food, used constantly for a length of time, fully shows; nature craves, usually, what it requires. The brute creation understand this law of the system, seeking change, often wandering to different parts of the pasture for new herbage, eating sand, visiting salt licks, sulphur springs, etc.

The chapter following will, we hope, with what has already been stated, enable the housekeeper wisely to select such food as will best secure the health and comfort of each member of her family, according to their different occupations, ages, and state of health. Food can be so varied, in the arrangement of the several courses, as to furnish at each meal all the essentials needed by the family. But, too often, this is entirely lost sight of, and the several dishes served, though differing much in taste, possess in themselves the same elements, furnishing to the body but a small part of the food needed to enable nature to carry out in perfection the purpose for which the several elements of food were created.

CHAPTER II.

ELEMENTS OF FOOD.

It is as absolutely necessary to the healthy growth of vegetables as animals, that the waste going on without interruption in all growing vegetation should be supplied by elements corresponding to those constantly exhausting; and here we see the wisdom and goodness of the Creator in adapting one part of his creation to meet the wants of the other, having formed animals and vegetables sufficiently analogous to possess independently in themselves all the nutriment needed for each other, except that to which each has access, namely, air and water; the latter, however, is furnished in some measure to each by the combination of the oxygen and hydrogen received with their aliment. All animal food is rich in the four most essential elements to man, namely, carbon, oxygen, hydrogen, and nitrogen; it also contains many other very important elements to our well-being; as phosphorus, sulphur, chlorine, potassium, lime, iron, and water, which is a compound. Phosphorus is to be found in all animals in the state of phosphoric acid. This, united with lime, forms the phosphate of lime, never absent from bone. Sulphur is to be found in all animal substances; it is this that in the egg blackens silver. Chlorine is one of the parts of salt, which is composed of chlorine and sodium. Potassium is found in a very small degree in animals, and is the base of potash. Lime united with phosphorus has been noted. Iron, in the state of oxide, is found in minute portions in all animals. Water, composed of hydrogen and oxygen, is found ready formed. Blood contains 80 per cent. of water, and flesh 75. It is calculated that the human body makes up three-fourths of its weight in water. These are called the elements, and the four first named are the principal, or essential elements. The following are called the proximate principles of animals: fibrine, gelatine, albumen, oils and fat, osmazome, casein. Fibrine is the fleshy part of meat when freed from fat; it is the basis of the meat, and when boiled only sufficiently long to become tender, united with its gelatine, it is nutritive and strengthening. Gelatine is that part of the animal which, when dissolved and extracted by long boiling, forms a jelly. It is found in all animals in the form of membranes surrounding the fibres of the muscles, in bones, and in the skin. It does not unite with fat, but causes oil to unite with water, forming a milky liquid. When fat rises to the top of soups, it is because the soup is too weak. Albumen is found the most pure in the white of egg. There are in animals a solid and fluid albumen. It contains carbon, hydrogen, oxygen, and nitrogen. Oil or fat consists of carbon and hydrogen, but little, if any, nitrogen. Osmazome is procured from an extract of meat. It is this that gives flavor to roasts, soups, etc. Casein is found in curds of milk, coagulated with rennet; it is easy of digestion, and nutritious. As a general thing, large animals are of coarser grain than small. Young animals contain more gluten than old. This is the reason why a young chicken boils tender sooner than an old hen. The flesh of the female is more delicate than the male. Beef are never considered prime before they are six years old. Each animal, unless stall-fed, is out of season when herbage is poor, or when rearing their young. No flesh is as sweet and healthy as that from animals fattened on grasses. The mode of killing has a great influence on the beef. Whatever tends to destroy or exhaust the irritability of the muscular fibre suddenly, hastens decay. This will be found to be the case when animals are heated by exercise just before killing. Animals should be well bled; they should be kept fasting until the stomach is entirely empty of undigested food. Beef should fast a day or two; smaller animals one day. Fowls from noon until morning, and others in the same ratio. Vegetables contain always carbon, oxygen, hydrogen, and generally more or less nitrogen, though often in minute quantities. They also possess in themselves many other important substances ready formed, called the proximate principles of vegetables. Esculents are rich in the first five of these principles, starch, gluten, albumen, sugar, oils, tannin, acids, alkalies, jelly, and many others not connected with our subject. Jelly, as all housekeepers well know, is to be found in all fruits, but more particularly in the currant, apple, gooseberry, cranberry, and quince, of the American fruits. Oils are found in the olive, almond, peach, nectarine, the outer peel of the

ELEMENTS OF FOOD. 49

lemon and orange, in aromatic herbs, etc. The acids give flavor to fruit; they are, the malic of the apple, citric of the lemon, tartaric of the grape. Acetic is found in many fruits: the acid of common vinegar, tannic, is found in tea, coffee, and the barks of several trees. In tea, it is united with theine. Besides, the poison acids, oxalic of the sorrel, and prussic of the cherry. The two latter are never found in a pure state, and are extremely poisonous. The apple and pear are considered useful with other food; when cooked are slightly laxative. The quince is cooling, astringent, and strengthening to the stomach. The peach is healthy and agreeable when fully ripe. Cherries should be used sparingly, unless very ripe, and even then prove injurious to weak stomachs in a raw state. Oranges are agreeable, cooling, and healthy. The lemon is cooling and grateful. The pineapple has, in its juice, caustic properties, and is less healthy, especially in this country, where it is never found in perfection, than either of the abovementioned fruits. Grapes are very delicious and nutritive when ripe; they stimulate and strengthen the stomach, fresh or dried as raisins. Currants are very cooling and useful to the stomach with other food, either fresh or in jellies. Muskmelons are not considered very healthy; watermelons more so. Cucumbers are cold, and not easy to digest; they should be highly seasoned, and served with other food if eaten; weak stomachs should avoid them entirely. Figs are very nutritive and agreeable if fresh. Tamarinds contain potassa, gum jelly, citric acid, tartaric acid, malic acid, and are useful in cooling drinks. Cabbages are difficult to digest for weak stomachs, but to most persons are wholesome when cooked perfectly tender. Peas are highly nutritive, though, when ripe, more difficult to digest than ripe corn. Beans are more nutritive than most vegetables; they are too much so for weak stomachs; dyspeptics should avoid them. Potatoes are wholesome, they contain a great amount of starch, and are relished by all. Turnips contain but little nutriment. Carrots contain a great amount of sugar and little starch. Parsnips contain more sugar than any of the roots mentioned; they are the best flavored when grown on poor or rather light soil. Beets are not considered wholesome unless used very young; old beets are stringy and hard to digest. Onions contain nutritive mucilage; they are also strengthening to the stomach. Asparagus is light, and digests with ease, but is not particularly nutritive. Lettuce is a cooling vegetable, and useful in correcting other food; should be used as salads. Celery is not considered nutritious, but can be used with moderation without injury. The herbs are all useful in their places,

3

in the preparations of various dishes which would be insipid without them. The two following tables will give some idea of the value of the different kinds of food mentioned by them. The first is by Liebig, and the other by Sir H. Davy. Not all the vegetables used can be mentioned in this work; only those in general use have been touched upon, not scientifically, but merely statements drawn from science, showing how they range as nutritious food.

Liebig's Table for every ten Flesh-giving parts.

	Flesh-giving.	Warmth-giving.
Human Milk,	10	40
Cow's Milk,	10	30
Lentils,	10	21
Horsebeans,	10	22
Peas,	10	23
Fat Mutton,	10	27
Fat Pork,	10	30
Beef,	10	17
Hare,	10	2
Veal,	10	1
Wheat Flour,	10	46
Oat Meal,	10	50
Rye Flour,	10	57
White Potatoes,	10	86
Black Potatoes,	10	115
Rice,	10	123
Buckwheat Flour,	10	130

	Whole Quantity of Soluble or Nutritive Matter.	Starch or Mucilage.	Saccharine Matter.	Gluten or Albumen.	Extract or Matter rendered insoluble during evaporation
Wheat,	955	739	—	225	—
Barley,	920	790	70	60	—
Oats,	743	641	15	87	—
Rye,	792	645	38	109	—
Beans,	570	426	—	103	41
Dry Peas,	574	501	22	35	16
Potatoes,	250 to 200	From 200 to 155	From 20 to 15	From 40 to 30	—
Beets, red,	148	14	120	14	—
White Beet,	136	13	119	4	—
Parsnips,	99	9	90	—	—
Carrots,	98	3	95	—	—
Turnips,	42	7	34	1	—
Cabbage,	73	41	24	8	—

The above is but a part of the table drawn up by Sir Humphry

Davy, published in his work on agricultural chemistry; but it is sufficient, as we think, to guide housekeepers in selecting such articles of diet as will suit their respective families. Those who wish farther to consult this table, are referred to the original work.

CHAPTER III.

MARKETING.

GOOD OX BEEF is known by its having a loose grain, red meat, and rather yellowish fat. Beef from the cow has firmer grain, whiter fat, and less color to the meat. When the animal is too old or ill-fed, the lean part is a dark red, and the fat hard and skinny, and in very old animals there will be seen running through the ribs a sort of horny substance. When meat rises quickly after being pressed by the finger, it may be considered prime; on the contrary when the dent made by pressing rises slowly or not at all, the beef is poor.

VEAL, to be fine, should be white, though dark-colored veal is often good. It is said butchers bleed calves to make the flesh white. If the fat enveloping the kidney be firm and white, the meat will in all probability be good. Overgrown calves are not considered as delicate for veal as small fat ones. Veal will keep but a short time, and to be healthy must be used fresh. When decay commences, the fat softens and the meat presents a spotted appearance, losing its solidity of grain, and the dent remains when pressed with the finger.

MUTTON.—Sheep should be slaughtered about five years old, though often killed younger. In young mutton the flesh is quite tender, and when very old it wrinkles. To be prime the flesh should be red and firm, the grain close, and the fat white. Great care should be taken in dressing sheep or lamb. If the wool touches the flesh, it imparts an unpleasant taste.

LAMB must be used very soon after being killed. When the large vein in the neck is bluish color, the fore quarter is fresh, becoming green when too old. The first indication of decay in the hind quarter is an unpleasant smell in the fat of the kidneys.

PORK, when prime, has a thin, smooth rind, quite cool to the touch. When changing, clammy, the dent remaining when pressed.

When pork shows kernels in the fat, the hog was either ill-fed or diseased.

Venison is generally kept some time. When good there is considerable thickness to the fat, which is clear and bright. It should be cooked before the meat shows the least taint.

Poultry.—It is important in choosing poultry to ascertain, if possible, its age. A young fowl has smooth legs and combs. When old they are rough, and have long hairs on the breast. They should be plump breasted, with fat backs, and have white or light yellow legs.

Turkeys when young have smooth black legs, becoming rough as they grow old. When too long killed they become dark around the vent. A young turkey has a full, bright eye, and an old one a dull, sunken one. An old turkey's legs are reddish and quite rough, a young one's smooth.

Geese.—A young goose has yellow feet, old geese red. A gosling of two or three months is called a green goose. When long killed, the feet are stiff; when fresh, pliable.

Ducks.—Tame ducks have yellow fat, wild ones red. They should have pliable feet, with firm, plump breasts.

Pigeons.—Tame pigeons are considerably larger than the wild, and more desirable. Pigeons are good for nothing when long killed. The flesh becomes soft, and is often tainted, not showing it until cooked. The feet of a young pigeon are soft and pliant.

Partridges are miserable eating when old, but very fine when young; particularly relished by invalids. They are known to be young when the bills are dark, and legs yellow.

Prairie Chickens resemble the tame somewhat, but are by epicures more highly esteemed. They should never be killed while setting.

Quails are the very finest wild game at the West. The flesh resembles the chicken, but is as much finer as the bird is smaller. They are used during the early fall and winter; it is cruel to kill them when taking care of their young.

Woodcock and Snipe should be used young. It is easy to know when they are young by observing their feet, which will be soft and tender, becoming thick and hard as they grow old. When too long killed the feet become hard, the bills moist, and throat discolored, having a sort of muddy appearance.

BLACKBIRDS when fat are superb eating. They should be killed when feasting on green corn and wheat. The flesh is very sweet; none is better; and the bones being small, there is more eating on a bird than would at first be supposed.

HARES AND RABBITS.—Examine the ears; if pointed and tender, they are young; if the reverse, old. A young hare may also be known by a narrow cleft in its lip. To distinguish one-year old hare, examine the leg, and a small bone will be found near the foot.

OYSTERS.—If fresh the shell will be firmly closed.

LOBSTERS.—Press the eyeball; if fresh, some muscular action will be seen; if not perceived, it has been kept too long. When boiled, if the tail is elastic it is fresh. Select heavy lobsters; the light ones are poor and watery.

CRABS AND CRAWFISH.—Observe the same rule in selecting these as in lobsters. They smell pleasantly when fresh.

PRAWNS AND SHRIMPS.—These are firm and crisp when fresh.

FRESH WATER FISH must be used fresh to be wholesome. When so, the flesh is firm and the eye clear; when too long kept, the eye becomes dull and the flesh soft.

MACKEREL AND HERRING to be good must be used fresh. They must not be kept many hours out of water. When brought a distance are very poor eating. A fresh mackerel or herring has bright eyes.

SALMON.—This fish loses flavor as soon as dead, and must be used immediately to be in perfection.

COD when fresh have rigid muscles, clear eyes, and reddish gills.

TURBOT.—The underside of this fish when fresh is a cream color. If too long kept, it turns a bluish white. The flesh should be firm, indeed quite rigid, and the eye bright and clear.

TROUT.—These are in season from the first of March until August, but are the most esteemed in May and June. When in season the scales are bright and glossy. Cook as soon as possible after they are caught.

PIKE.—This is rather a dry fish. It is the best stuffed and roasted.

PERCH.—This is a fine fish, and on account of its great tenacity to life can be carried a long distance.

BULL'S HEAD.—Smoked resembles the salmon.

EELS.—These fish can be kept alive several days in wet sand. They are rather too oily to be very wholesome, but are considered a great delicacy. If the head of the eel is cut off before skinning, much of the cruelty usually attending the dressing will be avoided.

HALIBUT.—A very large fish weighing from one to three hundred pounds. The flesh of the largest is coarse and dry, but the small-sized has white, tender flesh, and is considered a rarity.

TURTLE.—The green turtle is the best for cooking, so called from the color of its fat. It should be killed as soon as possible when taken from the water.

VEGETABLES.—These should always be fresh if bought during the growing season. Wilted vegetables are very unhealthy.

ASPARAGUS.—The part that is tough is good for nothing: select bunches with close heads and tender stalks.

STRING BEANS.—Observe that they are not wilted and break brittle.

CAULIFLOWER.—The heads should be firm, white, solid, and crisp.

CABBAGE.—Select small-sized, firm, hard heads.

CARROTS.—Do not buy large roots; the small orange variety with round bottoms are the sweetest.

CUCUMBERS.—These should be good-sized, but not large enough to show seed; of a bright green color.

EGG PLANT.—The long purple is much better for the table than the round. Press the skin; if wilted it will give considerably. When not fresh it is apt to be bitter.

GREEN CORN.—Sweet corn is the best for the table: do not buy any that is wilted or dried.

BEETS.—Small-sized roots are the most tender and sweetest; the earliest are turnip-shaped. The blood beets are the best, let the roots be shaped as they may.

LETTUCE.—Select firm heads with thick leaves not wilted.

MELONS.—The small green are the highest flavored of the muskmelons. Press watermelons; if ripe, they will crack so as to be plainly heard. White-cored mountain sprout, Long Island, and Imperial are the best.

OKRA.—Run a pin's head through the pods; if young enough, it will go through readily.

ONIONS.—Select undersized onions perfectly dry. The white look the best, but the red are the sweetest.

PARSLEY.—The double curled is the finest; select such bunches as are not wilted.

PARSNIPS.—The largest are coarse and strong. Hallow or sugar crown, rather undersized, are the finest.

PEAS.—The June peas are a tasteless variety. Buy marrowfats fresh picked, and always in the pods.

POTATOES.—For the summer select such as can be peeled by rubbing with the hand, without scraping with a knife; for winter, firm skins, clear from clay, and well dug, instead of being hacked by the hoe, as is often the case. Pink-eyes are very good, also Mercers.

SWEET POTATOES.—The yellow are the driest and sweetest.

RADISHES.—The small, tender roots are much better to buy than large, overgrown ones.

RHUBARB.—The largest is not always the best. Select tender skinned stalks; the red is the earliest.

SALSIFY.—Select smooth tubers, and as large as possible.

SPINACH, when fresh, is an excellent green; see that it is not wilted.

SQUASH.—For summer the scallop is much esteemed; for winter there are many excellent varieties. Boston marrow among the best.

Tomatoes.—The large smooth red is the best flavored and least trouble to dress.

Turnip.—For summer, use the round white, known as "Early Strap leaved." Winter turnips should be slightly frosted.

Flour should be white, and when pressed in the hand remain in a lump, leaving the marks of the fingers, and even the skin, on the flour.

Coarse or Graham Flour.—The wheat should be washed and ground coarse; if it remains in a lump after pressing in the hand, the wheat is good.

Buckwheat Flour.—Select flour free from grit, and light-colored. Buckwheat is often very dirty, being generally threshed on the ground.

Indian Meal.—Yellow corn makes the best meal. It should be well dried before grinding, not ground too fine, and the sack be emptied as soon as brought from the mill, or it will heat.

Sugar.—Before buying sugars dissolve a little from the barrel. It is often adulterated, the brown with sand, and pulverized with flour. The best sugar is the cheapest.

Tea, (*see* Tea.)—Select a chest and try it before purchasing, unless you can judge by chewing the leaves.

Coffee, (*see* Coffee.)—Examine the sack to see how much waste there will be in the refuse coffee. If possible try the quality.

Raisins.—Raisins should be fresh. If a box is wanted wait until the current year's crop has been received, and the same with currants and prunes.

Dried Peaches should be dark, clear looking, without skins, and free from vermin. Be sure they are not baked so much as to make them tough.

Dried Plums and Cherries should look clear and bright; are the best dried with sugar without pits.

Dried Berries.—The only trouble in purchasing these is the danger of vermin. Examine well the inside of a handful below the surface. Vermin are never in sight.

DRIED APPLES.—Dried apples should be light-colored, plump, acid, and free from vermin. Examine the cores to know positively in regard to vermin.

RICE.—This is sometimes infested with vermin, as well as fruits, but they are soon seen if notice is taken.

ORANGES.—The sour oranges are used for jellies and syrups. They are the cheapest in March and April. The Seville are the best for marmalades; these are best in February and March.

PINEAPPLES.—If to be taken into the country must be purchased green. It is said they keep longer if the leaves are twisted out. When they can be immediately used they should be yellow and free from spots.

FIGS should be fresh and moist. These are often filled with vermin. In buying by the drum be sure they are fresh.

GRAPES, if bought by the box, should be examined before purchasing, as they will often be found decayed badly.

3*

PART III.

GENERAL COOKERY.

CHAPTER I.

SOUPS, SAUCES, AND GRAVIES.

REMARKS.—In making stock for soup, care must be used, or much of the flavor of the meat will be lost. It should boil up once to throw up any impurities in the meat or water; let it then be thoroughly skimmed, and the pot covered tight, and kept so while the soup is slowly boiling; while the steam, which will be constantly condensing on the cover, falls back in the soup; thus retaining all the flavor of the joint. The same rule applies to stews and sauces formed of meats. People usually hurry soups too much; but in this case, "haste certainly makes waste," according to the old maxim. If a little forethought is used, this can be avoided, and some fuel saved at the same time. It is certainly far less trouble to remove the fat from soups cold, than when boiling as furiously as possible. Meat for soups should be boiled long and slow. Salt should be rubbed on the meat to draw out the juices; the water should be cold when the meat is put in. Bones, as well as meat, are important to soup, as from them the gelatine is extracted. When the meat is wanted to serve in other forms, it should not be boiled to pieces; but if the soup is desired superior, the finer the meat the better. Shreds of meat, and bits of bones, must always be strained from soup, if desired to present a good appearance at table. A soup cannot be prepared for the table, unless the dinner is very late, the same day the knuckle is procured from market. Buy the bone the day previous; boil and strain the liquor; when cold, take off the fat. Most persons imagine that fat is what gives richness to soup; the

French, who are far before us in the manufacture of soups, always remove every particle of the fat not combined with the gelatine before adding the seasonings: it is the juices and gelatine that impart richness to soup. Physicians do not now consider soups as nourishing as formerly. Teas, made from meats, are much more so; indeed, nothing in the form of food can be found more stimulating than the essence of beef when properly prepared in the form of tea. Herbs can be used, dried or green; when the former, they should be finely pulverized and sifted, that no sticks may be left floating in the tureen.

PLAIN BEEF SOUP No. 1.—Procure from market a beef-shank, familiarly called a soup-bone; wash clean, and saw it nearly through the bone several times, and rub it with salt; after an hour put the bone into a kettle of cold water. A large shank will make six quarts of soup. If the soup is to be served the same day the bone is boiled, put it on by seven in the morning. Cover tightly, only lifting the lid to skim off the fat, which must be thoroughly removed before adding seasoning and vegetables. If the meat is to be used again, take it out before it boils in pieces; slip out the bone, and return it to the soup. Taste the broth before salting—it may have sufficient; always remember that pepper and salt can be added at table, but cannot so easily be taken out if too much is used. In seasoning dishes before serving, therefore, it is better they should lack than be overseasoned. Take out a bowl of soup and stir into it a heaping table-spoonful of flour, mixed with cold water, quite smooth; add pepper and summer-savory, if dried, finely powdered, and sifted. For six quarts allow six potatoes cut in halves, about a half of a small loaf of bread, (when there is none on hand dry, which is better than fresh;) when fresh, cut the bread into chunks, and let the crust remain on each piece; put the potatoes and bread in the pot at the same time, allowing twenty minutes for them to boil; then cut finely two large onions, and add to the soup; cover tight, and take up as soon as the potatoes are done. It should only boil: if it does more, the bread will break in pieces, and thicken the soup too much. When the bone is boiled the day previous, remove the meat, and leave the liquor to become cold; the next day remove the fat and prepare the soup as directed. If the meat is boiled to rags, the liquor should be strained while hot, fat and all, through a wire sieve.

BEEF SOUP No. 2.—Prepare the stock as already described in Plain Soup No. 1. To six quarts of soup, seasoned with pepper and salt, put a coffeecup of washed rice, six potatoes, three turnips, two carrots, three onions, parsley, and summer-savory.

BEEF SOUP No. 3.—Prepare stock as in No. 1; season with pepper, salt, summer-savory, and onion; make a paste of three eggs, a little salt and flour as stiff as possible, roll it out as thin as wafers, let it dry two hours, then roll it up quite tight, and cut it in shreds; add it to the soup while boiling; let it boil fifteen minutes. Parsley and celery can be added if desired.

BEEF SOUP No. 4.—Make the stock as for No. 1; season with pepper, salt, summer-savory, two onions, one carrot, one turnip, one quart chopped gombo, and one-half teacup of *macaroni;* parsley and celery, if relished.

ECONOMY BEEF SOUP No. 5.—Take the bone left from steak, boil it two hours; skim off the fat, add half a table-spoonful of shred gelatine, one onion, pepper, salt, parsley, summer-savory, a table-spoonful of tomato catsup, and a teacupful of washed rice; then peel three potatoes, cut in halves, or quarters, if very large; throw them in the soup; with crusts of bread, or biscuit. If the bone is large, the gelatine can be omitted; it adds richness to the soup. This recipe is calculated to make three quarts, with the vegetables.

VEAL SOUP No. 1.—Boil a knuckle of veal and four calves' feet, in six quarts of water, until the meat is boiled to shreds, and the gristle dissolved; add a teaspoon of salt, and one table-spoon of whole peppercorns, and sweet herbs tied in a bunch, consisting of equal parts of thyme, summer-savory, and parsley; strain it in a stone jar or earthen dish; the next day remove all the fat, and gradually dissolve the jelly in a clean pot; add a teacup of vermicelli; when this is dissolved, take the soup from the fire, but leave on the cover; break up two light rolls, and put them in the tureen, with a pint of rich cream, quite fresh; add a little soup and stir gently, then fill with hot soup, and mix all together; taste and see if the seasoning is as it should be; if not, add pepper and salt to suit. The French add mace or nutmegs, but Americans generally prefer those spices in cakes, puddings, and pies. There ought to be about five quarts when finished.

VEAL SOUP No. 2.—Prepare the stock as in No. 1; the next day, mince the veal fine, and season with pepper and salt; make it into small ballls, with eggs and bread moistened a very little; make them about the size of half-an egg, and quite firm; flavor the soup with onion, pepper and salt, thicken with a little flour, stirred in water, say one table-spoonful to four quarts; add a half teacup of rice well washed; boil slowly. Ten minutes before time to serve the dinner, add the balls; let the soup only simmer after they are put in, or they will break.

VEAL SOUP No. 3.—Prepare the stock as described in No. 1; the next day, melt the jelly, add pepper and salt; if desired, potatoes, celery, parsley, and two table-spoonfuls of tomato-catsup; make a paste with flour, one egg and salt, (as described in Beef Soup No. 3,) roll thin and cut in strips; thicken with a heaping table-spoon of rice-flour well mixed in milk, and stirred into a bowl of soup, and afterwards into the kettle.

ECONOMICAL VEAL SOUP No. 4.—Boil a bit of veal that will make a fricassee, pie, or hash; when tender, take out the meat, and slip out the bones; put them back in the kettle, and boil gently two hours; then strain the liquor, and let it remain until next day; when wanted, take off the fat, put the soup into a clean pot, add pepper, salt, an onion, a half teacup of rice, a table-spoon of flour mixed in water, dry bread, and potatoes.

LOBSTER SOUP.—Boil three large young hen-lobsters until tender, in boiling water strongly salted. If the heads of the fish are put in first, and the water is boiling hot, they will live but a moment; when cold, split the tails, take out the meat, crack the claws, and cut the meat in very small bits; bruise a part of the coral in a mortar with a part of the meat, season this with Cayenne, salt, nutmeg, mace, anchovy, grated lemon, and yolk of eggs; make it into small forcemeat balls; have ready three quarts of nice veal stock, bruise the small legs and chine, and boil them in the stock twenty-five minutes; then strain the stock; to thicken it, take the fresh coral and butter, bruise it with a little flour, and pass it through a sieve; add it to the soup with the force-meat balls and remaining coral; simmer gently ten minutes; if it boils, it will lose its bright color; pour it in a tureen, add lemon-juice, and anchovy sauce, if relished. *This recipe was communicated.*

EEL SOUP.—Put two ounces of butter in a saucepan, a couple of onions cut once, and stew them until lightly browned; remove the onions, and put into the pan, cut in pieces, three pounds of unskinned eels, shake them over the fire a few minutes; then add three quarts of boiling water. When it boils, remove the scum; add a quarter of an ounce of green, not dried, summer-savory, the same of lemon, thyme, twice as much parsley, two drachms each of allspice and black pepper; cover close, and boil gently for two hours, then strain it through a fine sieve; put in a stew-pan three ounces of butter, melt it, and stir in flour, until it thickens considerably, and add the soup gradually to it, stirring constantly. If the spices are not relished, omit them; cooks should always be governed by the tastes of the family. Put the soup in a stew-pan, and add nice bits of eel, fried brown in butter, ten minutes before pouring it in the tureen. *This recipe was communicated.*

CLAM SOUP No. 1.—Wash clean as many clams as are needed for the family; put them in just boiling water enough to prevent their burning; the water must be boiling hard when the clams are put in the kettle; in a short time the shells will open, and the liquor in them run out; take the clams from their shells and chop them very fine; strain the liquor in which they were boiled, through a thin cloth, and stir into it the chopped clams, season with pepper, add salt, if needed; thicken the soup with butter rolled thin in flour, let it boil fifteen minutes; toast bread and cut it in small squares, lay it in the tureen, and pour over the soup; if the family like onions, a little juice of onion can be added; if celery, it can be varied by the addition of a little celery cut fine; another change can be made by adding the yolk of well beaten eggs stirred slowly into it, or rich cream can be added. Persons living on the sea-shore can make several dishes with these changes with little expense.

CLAM SOUP No. 2.—Boil well cleaned clams in boiling water, until the shells open; there should be only water sufficient to cover them. When the shells open take out the clams, chop them fine, strain the liquor into the soup pot, and boil the minced clams two hours, or until the flavor is extracted. Then strain them from the liquor, add pepper; and salt also, if needed, but generally there is sufficient salt in the clam. Make a dumpling like a short biscuit, but very soft and rich, roll it out quite thin, and cut in small pieces with a cracker cutter. Work into a teacup of butter a large table-spoonful of flour, stir into it enough hot soup to make a batter, then add the batter to the soup, stirring constantly until it boils up; then put in twelve of the dumplings, cover tight, and let it boil fifteen minutes steadily; then take it from the fire, skim out the dumplings and lay them in the tureen; have ready the beaten yolk of three eggs, stir into them a coffee-cup of the soup, and strain the soup and egg through a wire sieve; after which it must be gradually stirred into the soup, which should not boil after the egg is added. This soup will require one hundred small, or sixty large clams. Care must be taken that too much water is not used, as the soup requires a strong flavor from the clams. If weak it will be insipid.

OYSTER SOUP FOR THE CITY.—Have ready two quarts of boiling water, into which put three quarts of fresh oysters, and their juice. Let them come to a boil, and skim thoroughly; have ready a teacupful of sweet butter, with a large table-spoonful of flour worked into it; add to it sufficient hot soup to melt the butter, and stir the whole into the soup; let it boil up once, and take it off immediately. The oysters should not be on the fire over fifteen minutes; they only want heating through. Have fresh crackers or toasted bread; if the first, split them; if the latter, cut in small squares; put them in the tureen, and pour over the soup. Let each person add pepper and salt to suit the taste. Celery, and ground horseradish, are both excellent relishes for oysters. Pickles can also be served with them.

OYSTER SOUP FOR THE COUNTRY.—Throw two quarts of oysters into three pints boiling water. Let it boil up and take off the scum. Have ready a small table-spoon of sifted flour, worked in a teacup of fresh butter; stir this into the soup, and as soon as it boils remove it from the fire. If the soup is preferred quite thick, add a teacupful of crackers rolled very fine. Serve with toasted bread or crackers. Many persons are fond of cream in oysters. If used, heat it over water, and stir it in the soup when dishing; a pint of very rich cream will make three-fourths of the butter superfluous. Pepper should be added at table; many persons never use it in oysters. We never use mace or nutmeg; in our method of cooking, we aim to preserve the principal flavor of every dish, and consider when this is accomplished, the perfection of cooking is attained.

MUTTON SOUP.—Boil a neck of mutton in as many quarts of water as there are pounds of meat, until the meat drops from the bone. Strain the soup into the pot, if to be served the same day; if not, into a stone or earthen dish. If the meat is wanted in other forms, use half the water, and boil any piece of mutton on hand. Remove all the fat, season with salt, pepper, onions, thyme, and parsley. Boil a pint of green peas, mash them fine, and add to the soup. Roll a half teacup of butter in flour to make a paste, (*see* ROLLED BUTTER,) and ten minutes before dishing add it to the soup. This can be varied, for those who are fond of vegetables in soup, by adding potatoes, turnips, Lima beans, cauliflower, carrots, or cabbage. Lima beans can be used instead of peas, but the latter are the best.

FRENCH VEGETABLE SOUP.—Boil a beef soup bone as directed in Beef Soup No. 1, straining the liquor. For six quarts of soup, take four large, or six small potatoes, one large or two small parsnips, two large or four small onions, one large or two small carrots. Peel the vegetables, and put them in the pot to boil. When tender, skim them all from the soup, and pass them through a wire sieve, beat them well together, and stir them in the soup. Season with pepper, salt, French mustard mixed, and tomato catsup; the two last to be added just before dishing. The soup should be as thick as good water gruel, when finished. Be careful not to scorch it.

BROWN CHICKEN SOUP.—Cut up a nicely dressed chicken. Put it in the pot with water to cover it, which must be measured, and half as much more added to it before the soup is dished. Keep it covered tight, boiling slowly, and take off the fat as fast as it rises. When the chicken is tender, take it from the pot, and mince it very fine. Season it to the taste, and brown it with butter, in a spider, or dripping pan. When brown, put it back in the pot. Brown together butter and flour, and make rich gravy, by adding a pint of the soup; stir this in the soup, and season it with a little pepper, salt, and butter. Be careful the chopped chicken does not settle, and burn on the pot. It will be well to turn a small plate in the bottom of the kettle, to prevent this. Toast bread quite brown and dry, but don't burn it, and lay the toast in the tureen, and serve it with the soup; stir the chicken through it, and pour it in the tureen.

WHITE CHICKEN SOUP.—Prepare the fowl, as in brown chicken soup, with the same quantity of water. When tender, remove it from the pot, and put into the soup a half teacup of washed pearl barley. Mince the meat fine, season it, and make it into balls with egg and flour, the size of marbles. Season the soup with salt, pepper, and butter. If the barley has not thickened the soup sufficiently, add a little flour stirred in water. Ten minutes before dishing, drop in the meat balls. The soup must be kept only boiling hot, or the balls will break in pieces. Toast bread lightly, or use cracker to crumb in the soup at the table. Celery and sour pickles give relish to chicken soups. Rabbits, squirrels, or birds, can be made into either white or brown soups.

MOCK TURTLE SOUP.—Procure from market a calf's head. Take off the scalp; separate the tongue and wash it, first in cold, and then in warm water, to draw out the blood, and put it to stew in not over two quarts of water and a little salt. At the same time the head (which should be divided, and the brains taken out) must lie in lukewarm water to draw out the blood. Break the bones of the head, and cleanse those of the nose well. Put some pieces of ham or bacon in the bottom of the pot, and then lay the bones in the soup kettle, with water to cover them, and let them boil. While the head and tongue are boiling, the vegetables must be cooking in another pot. Slice two turnips, two good-sized onions, a table-spoon half full of peppercorns, a quarter of a teaspoon of whole cloves, a chopped lemon peel, six chopped mushrooms, a bunch of parsley, the same of thyme, and a branch, not a whole head, of celery. The day before, a stock, as it is called, should have been made, as directed in Veal Soup No. 1. Remove all fat, and put in with the vegetables enough of the stock to cover them, let them simmer until tender, be careful they do not boil dry, as it is only the soup in which they are boiled which is used; they must not be mashed, merely boiled to abstract the flavor. When this is accomplished, strain off the liquor, and examine the head and tongue; if tender, remove all the fat, and add the liquor to that in which the vegetables are boiled. Let the soup simmer for an hour, and add veal stock to make the whole about three quarts. Take a teacup three-quarters full of butter, beat in it three table-spoonfuls of sifted flour, add enough of the hot soup to it, to melt and thicken it a little at a time; then stir the whole in the soup. Chop some lean veal as fine as possible, rasp some bread, and beat up as many eggs as will moisten the whole; mix thoroughly, add a little Cayenne pepper, an onion chopped fine, the yolks of two hard-boiled eggs worked to a paste, a little powdered parsley, and thyme. Mix well, and make this into small balls; have a kettle of boiling salted water ready, put the balls in a colander, and set it in the water three minutes, then take it out and let them drain. Divide the head, skin the tongue and divide it, put them into the soup, and when boiling add the balls of force-meat. If not seasoned sufficiently, add pepper and salt. Those not fond of onions cannot use this soup, for if these are left out, it would be another thing entirely. Some add the juice of lemon. The brains can be cooked in the following manner: let them steep in cold water until the blood is extracted, separate all the filaments and membranes. Then lay them in boiling water set on the stove, and allow them to simmer only for fifteen minutes, after which drain well, fry them in butter, and serve with drawn butter.

TURTLE SOUP.—Procure a turtle fresh from the water: if in winter, cut off the head the night before cooking, and hang it up by the fins, neck down, until morning. If in summer, as early as possible in the morning. It should bleed at least three hours. Cut off the forefins and callipee or under part, take out the entrails, and very carefully remove the gall; if broken, the whole is ruined. Remove all the meat from the bones, both callipash or upper, and callipee or under parts. Divide it in convenient pieces and scald them, being very careful not to set the scales. When cleansed, chop the fins in pieces four inches long, and put them with the meat in the pot, with water sufficient to cover them. Add three whole onions and a bunch of sweet herbs. Remove the scum as fast as it rises. When nearly done, take them from the pot. Remove the bones from the fins, strain the liquor, and reduce it by boiling to about one-third of its original quantity. Cut the pieces of meat quite small, not larger than half an inch square. Chop fine some parsley, onions, thyme, savory, and marjoram. Pound some mace, cloves, allspice, black pepper, and salt; put these with the chopped meat in a pot. Pour over them the soup, and some good veal stock. Boil gently until three-fourths done, then remove the meat, and strain the liquor free from the herbs, spices, etc. Thicken with butter and flour, add the meat, and lastly, the juice of five or six lemons. When served, have force-meat balls, and some of the real green fat previously prepared to dish with it. When turtle is plenty, the veal stock need not be added. This and the mock-turtle soup are communicated recipe. The writer thinks, from the source received, they must be good, but has no knowledge of them from her own experience. Try a small soup at first if they are used.

FRENCH VEAL STOCK FOR SOUPS.—Cut up a knuckle of veal, of lean ham one pound; add a peeled carrot, turnip, onion, celery, and one quart of water. Put in a cut-up fowl, and as much beef soup as will cover the whole; boil gently one hour, salt, and strain it; let it become cold, and remove all fat. Be very careful not to scorch, as, if so, it will not do for white soup.

VERMICELLI SOUP.—Take two quarts of the above stock, heat it, add half a pound of vermicelli, and cook slowly until it is tender. If boiled hard, it will burst the vermicelli, and make the soup too thick.

MACARONI SOUP.—Boil until tender a pound of macaroni, in a quart of good stock, being careful not to burn. Then remove about half of it, add a little more stock, and boil until the macaroni can be passed through a sieve. Mix with it as much stock as will make the soup of the proper thickness, and add to it in the tureen a pint of sweet cream; flavor to suit. Serve with biscuits or crackers. Rice and barley soup can be made in the same manner, without straining the barley or rice through the sieve.

To MAKE LEASON.—Beat the yolks of five eggs until light, with half a pint of sweet cream with a little salt. This is very nice for thickening veal soups of any kind that are to be white. It is sometimes made with blanched almonds pounded to a paste, and mixed with the cream and eggs. The latter would be the best in fancy soups made with game, etc. For dark soups, brown butter and flour, and add some of the stock; it should be as thick as cream, and free from lumps.

GRAVIES FOR MEATS.

DRAWN BUTTER.—Take two ounces of sweet butter, a heaping teaspoonful of flour, and two of sweet milk. Work the butter and flour together, then add the milk. Put it in a small saucepan on a slow fire; when melted, add a table-spoonful of sweet milk, mixed in six of water; keep the saucepan moving, managing it so that the contents always move the same way. When it commences to simmer and looks thick and creamy, set it down and allow it to gently boil up. Pour it in the tureen as soon as boiled. This is a proper sauce for boiled fish, mutton, lamb, turkeys, and game of all kinds, but should never be used for roasts. It can be varied by the addition of celery, or any spices desired. When intended to be mixed with catsups or essences, it must be nearly as thick as thin batter.

To CLARIFY BUTTER.—Put sweet butter in a clean saucepan, let it melt slowly, and skim off the buttermilk as it rises to the surface; when entirely melted, let it stand a few moments to settle, and then strain it into a clean pot. If strong, the best plan is to heat it hot enough to fry, and slice raw potatoes very thin, and fry them brown in the butter. Skim them out, and let it settle, and strain it in a crock.

To Oil Butter for Frying Fish.—Melt butter over steam until very hot. The water should not be boiling when the pan is set on the kettle. Allow it to stand quiet until the salt has settled, then pour it off, leaving the sediment which settles in the pan. When butter is used with the salt in it, to fry meats or fish, it is apt to burn, but when oiled there is no more danger of scorching than when frying in lard.

Brown Butter.—Put into a spider as much butter as needed. Let it melt slowly at first, then allow it to cook slowly until quite brown. If wanted immediately, add to it any gravy desired. If not, add a little vinegar and pepper, and pour it in a pot until wanted.

Gravy for Roast Beef, No. 1.—Take the drippings and water in which the beef was basted, remove as much of the fat as possible, pour off most of the water with the oil, set the dripping-pan on the stove, with the sediment of the drippings, let it brown; put a little of the gravy in the pan, and thicken it with a trifle of flour. The flour should not be perceived in the gravy.

Gravy for Roast Beef, No. 2.—Melt a little salt in a gill of water, pour it over a roast when put in the oven, place under it an earthen dish to catch the drippings. Baste often for a half hour, then set it to cool. When cool, remove all fat, heat the gravy, and pour it over the roast. For a-la-mode beef add wine.

Veal Gravy for Roasts.—For roasts, make a gravy of the drippings in the same manner as for beef. Or brown butter, and add water, pepper, salt, and a little flour.

Gravy for Mutton, Roast Lamb, and Venison.—Stew a little mutton, cut in bits, in as little water as will cover it, for an hour. Then drain off the gravy, and season with pepper and salt; rub a little butter and flour together to thicken it. This is proper for venison also.

Green Mint Sauce.—The French use this for boiled lamb. It is made by putting green mint, chopped fine, and parsley, in vinegar.

Oyster Sauce.—Prepare a nice drawn butter, quite thick, scald sufficient oysters in a little water, and stir them in the butter; mix well, and let the sauce nearly boil, after which pour them into the tureen.

Gravy for Beef or any other Steak.—Put on a platter, for

two slices of steak, a piece of butter the size of an egg, cut in small pieces. Add a little salt, a dust of pepper, and two table-spoonfuls of hot water. Do not let it boil, but just melt and keep warm.

LOBSTER SAUCE.—Mash the eggs of the hen lobster, squeeze them through a muslin bag. Divide the flesh of a boiled lobster into small bits; roll them in flour; put them in a saucepan, with enough butter and sweet cream or milk to make the sauce needed; let it simmer two or three minutes, then add the eggs. Remove it as soon as it turns a brilliant red.

EGG SAUCE FOR SALT FISH.—Boil eggs hard, allow three to half a pint of thin drawn butter, use all the yolks, but only half of the whites, which must be chopped fine; mix well.

CATSUP SAUCE FOR FISH.—Mix half a pint of walnut catsup with a gill of grated horseradish, two teaspoonfuls of made mustard, and a gill of vinegar from nasturtiums. This is not to be poured over fish, but used as a catsup.

WINE SAUCE FOR VENISON.—One gill of mutton broth, the same of port wine, and one table-spoonful of currant jelly; heat them nearly boiling hot, then thicken with the yolk of one egg.

SOUR SAUCE FOR VENISON.—Brown, not burn, a coffee cup of sugar in an iron kettle. Take it out, and dissolve it in half a pint of strong vinegar; heat it, and add a gill of cranberry juice or jelly; serve hot.

MUSHROOM SAUCE.—Pound fine a pint of mushrooms with a table-spoonful of butter, and a little flour, work it well together over hot water, and moisten with cream, or the gravy from veal or poultry; season high; add lemon juice, if desired, if no cream is used.

GOOSEBERRY SAUCE FOR BOILED LAMB.—Stir a half pint of gooseberries, after they have been scalded, into a pint of drawn butter—and serve hot.

BREAD SAUCE FOR POULTRY AND GAME.—Pour boiling water on bread crumbs, mash them fine, season with pepper, salt, and summer savory. Beat well, add water to thin the sauce, and, lastly, stir in butter the size of an egg. Or make the sauce thick without butter, and thin it with drawn butter.

GRAVY FOR GAME.—Take the stock of beef or veal soup, boil the hearts, livers, gizzards, and lights, in the soup. When done, chop them fine, and season with butter, pepper, and salt; thicken with the yolk of an egg.

LIVER SAUCE.—Boil liver in very little water, until tender; mash it, and pass it through a sieve; season very high with pepper and salt. Take what is needed of the water in which it was boiled, mix in the mashed liver, add to a pint of the sauce a piece of butter the size of an egg, let it boil, beat up the yolk of an egg, remove the sauce, stir it well, then stir in the egg. This can be made of any liver. If of fish, it can only be used as a sauce for them. It is fine with steamed or roasted liver. The same liver that forms the sauce, is the proper dish to serve it with.

GIBLET SAUCE.—Take the livers, lights, gizzards, and hearts, from fowls. Boil very tender, chop them fine. Make a nice thin drawn-butter, and stir them in; or boil and chop them, and use the water in which they were boiled; season with butter, pepper, and salt; beat up the yolks of two eggs, add them, and keep the sauce stirring until it thickens. *This sauce is best for roast fowls.*

FORCEMEATS, OR DRESSINGS FOR PIGS.—Soak bread, until it can be mashed fine, work into it butter, pepper, salt, thyme, or savory and sage, ground and sifted.

DRESSING FOR FOWLS.—Prepare bread as above, omitting the sage.

DRESSING FOR VEAL.—Prepare as above, seasoning with pepper and salt only.

DRESSING FOR DUCK AND GOOSE.—Use all the seasonings except sage, and chop an onion fine for each duck.

DRESSING FOR RABBITS.—Boil the liver, chop it fine, chop bread fine, mix it with the liver; season with pepper and salt; wet it with egg.

DRESSING FOR BOILED TURKEY.—Make a dressing of chopped bread and oysters, season with pepper and salt, dampen with hot water in which a quarter of a pound of butter is melted.

BOILED FISH DRESSING.—Crumb the bread, season with pepper and salt, and wet with drawn butter or egg.

DRESSING FOR A-LA-MODE BEEF.—Prepare bread crumbs, work in plenty butter, add pepper, salt, cloves, allspice, and nutmeg; mix it with egg.

DRESSING FOR PIGEONS, BOILED.—For boiled pigeons, soak bread crumbs, and season with pepper, salt, and butter.

FOR ROAST PIGEONS.—Boil and mash the livers fine, and mix them with soaked bread; season with pepper, salt, and summer savory.

DRESSING FOR BLACKBIRDS.—Toast bread lightly and mix with it butter, pepper, salt, and enough egg to moisten the dressing without softening it.

DRESSING FOR PARTRIDGES, QUAILS, ETC.—Prepare a nice dressing with crackers soaked soft in sweet milk, beat up an egg and mix with it, add pepper, salt, butter, and a mashed potato free from lumps; mix all well together; if too soft, add rolled cracker. It should be quite firm.

PUDDING SAUCES.

ROSE HIP SAUCE.—Open and remove the seeds from rose hips. Soak them and boil until tender, reducing the hips to paste, pass them through a sieve, stir them in boiling, wine, and sweeten to taste. The sauce should be as thick as thin cream.

CHERRY SAUCE.—Bruise one pound of cherries, with the pits, in their own juice until the meat of the pits is tender, then pass as much of the mass through a sieve as possible, add a pint of wine, sugar to the taste, and boil until of the consistency of thick cream. (This and the preceding receipt are from the German.) Spices can be added, if desired.

HARD SAUCE.—Stir to a light cream one cup of sweet butter, and two of pulverized loaf sugar; grate over it a little nutmeg after it is turned into the dish to send to the table. This can be varied in many ways, adding spices, extracts, etc. For all apple-puddings the nutmeg flavoring is the best. For cream and plain batter-pudding, flavor with vanilla, and thin a little with a few spoonfuls of boiling water. For rice-puddings the addition of a little lemon juice, wine, or brandy is proper. For dumplings no spice should be used.

SOUR SAUCE.—One cup of butter, two of sugar, and one of strong vinegar; stir the butter and sugar to a cream; heat the vinegar boiling hot, beat an egg very light, stir the egg into the butter and sugar; mix well, grate in a little nutmeg, and pour the boiling vinegar, little by little, in the sugar, egg, and butter; when well mixed, pour the sauce into the saucepan, and heat nearly to boiling, without allowing it to boil, stirring constantly. If the sauce is prepared before the dinner is served, set the saucepan in hot water on the hearth, where it will keep hot without congealing.

BRANDY SAUCE.—Heat over steam, in a covered saucepan, a half pint of brandy, beat two eggs light, and cream a cup of butter with two of sugar; beat the eggs into the sugar and butter, take off the brandy, and beat the eggs, sugar, butter, and brandy together, stirring the brandy into the other ingredients slowly, beating quickly while mixing; continue to beat the sauce until the whole is well mixed, After which keep it in hot water until needed. Brandy should be covered tightly, as it not only evaporates, but is in danger of taking fire. It must always be heated over steam.

SWEET SAUCE.—Stir to a cream one cup of butter, with two of sugar; pour into the butter and sugar a teacup of boiling water; beat an egg light, and mix it gradually with the other ingredients before they become hot; mix half a teaspoon of flour in a little cold water, free from lumps; stir it into the sauce, and beat the whole constantly until hot enough to thicken; add nutmeg. This is proper for all boiled puddings, especially berry, and also baked berry-puddings.

PEACH SAUCE.—Cut fine six juicy peaches; crack the pits, and put the kernels with the fruit in a porcelain-lined stew-pan; lay the fruit flat on the bottom of the pan, half cover it with water, and cover tight. Set the pan in hot water, and let it steam one hour. Then pour the fruit and juice in a hair sieve, to drain; when it ceases to drop, take the juice, and use it exactly as the vinegar in sour sauce, with the same proportions of sugar and butter, omitting the egg, and spice, and thicken with very little flour. Any other fruit can be used in the same manner.

MAPLE SYRUP FOR PUDDINGS.—Boil maple-sugar with very little water, clarify with egg, and strain the syrup. Vary by melting a little butter in it after straining. When maple-sugar is expensive, use half coffee-sugar. Coffee-sugar syrup, made as above, is the next thing to maple-syrup.

COMMON WEST INDIA MOLASSES is much improved by heating, and skimming. If butter is added, it makes a good sauce for children to eat with rice; sugar-house, Stewart's, and other syrups, are improved by heating.

CREAM SAUCE.—Cream and sugar is very nice on many puddings. Cottage and boiled Indian puddings are better with sweet cream. For rice plain boiled, many prefer cream a little sour. Cornstarch is best with cream beaten stiff, sweetened and flavored with vanilla or bitter almonds.

WINE SAUCE, No. 1.—One cup of butter, and two of sugar beaten to a cream, beat four eggs as light as possible, without separating, and add them to the butter and sugar, heat a pint of wine boiling hot, and stir it in the mixture; beat well, heat nearly boiling hot, and set it in hot water until wanted for the table.

WINE SAUCE, No. 2.—Beat together two coffee-cups of sugar and half a cup of butter; add a cup of wine slowly to the sugar and butter; beat it well, and melt it over steam, but do not stir it while melting. Brandy sauce can be made as above.

WINE SAUCE, No. 3.—Beat together half a cup of butter, and two of sugar; beat light two eggs, and stir them in the sugar and butter; heat boiling-hot half a cup of wine, and stir it into the other ingredients. Let it become hot, constantly stirring, when it may stand in hot water until wanted.

PLAIN SWEET SAUCE.—A half pint of boiling water, a half teacup of butter, one of sugar, an even teaspoon of flour stirred in a little water, and freed from lumps; beat the mixture while heating until it boils; add nutmeg.

PLAIN SOUR SAUCE.—Ingredients as above, substituting vinegar for water; if not sufficiently sweet, add sugar.

ORANGE SAUCE.—Half a cup of butter, one of sugar, beat light, and a teacup of fresh orange juice.

EGG SAUCE.—Beat the yolks of three eggs very light. Froth a teacup of cream, and stir it in the eggs; sweeten to suit the taste. This is a good sauce for rice; flavorings can be added.

DYSPEPSIA SAUCE.—One pint of sweet milk, a piece of butter as large as a butternut, the yolks of two eggs well beaten, a little vanilla, bitter almond, lemon, or nutmeg, as fancied; melt the butter in the milk, constantly beating it; take the milk from the fire, and beat it until cool. Stir a little of the milk in the yolks; beat it well, and add them to the milk, beating the milk briskly; when the egg is mixed in, put the sauce on a slow fire, and beat it constantly until it thickens a little, remove it from the fire, add sugar to suit the taste, and beat it until the sugar is dissolved, add spice or flavoring. Set it where it will not cook or cool. It should be as thick as rich cream, without settling on the bottom of the pan.

CHAPTER II.

FISH.

To CLEAN FISH.—Fish should be cleaned as soon as possible, after being taken from the water. Be very particular to remove the scales without mangling the fish; lay the fish flat on the fish-board, hold it firmly down with the left hand, and remove the scales with a round pointed knife; rinse the fish, by dashing cold water over it, to remove all loose scales; lay it in water while rinsing the fish-board, that the loose scales on fish and board may not adhere to the fish while being drawn; draw the fish without splitting it down any farther than necessary to effect the removal of the entrails; be careful that every part of the entrails are removed; scrape the back-bone clean, and rinse out all the blood; lay the fish on ice as soon as cleansed, and keep it there until the moment for cooking, to preserve the fish firm; fish soften very soon, and the perfection of them is firm flesh; fresh-water fish are soft after the water becomes warm, and unfit to eat. They should be taken as soon as the ice can be broken, to be of first-rate quality; indeed, it is doubtful about fish being healthy, when softened by warm running water. The best fish, peculiar to our lakes, are the white and Mackinaw trout; these are seldom taken in the southern part of the lakes, except very early in the spring; they frequent cold or deep water; the farther north they are taken, in the summer season, the better the fish. Many varieties are common both to the lakes and rivers; but the greater purity of the water always give the lake fish the advantage as to quality.

GENERAL DIRECTIONS FOR BOILING FISH.—An oblong kettle with a tin strainer, is the proper vessel in which to boil fish: they are called fish-kettles; when this is not to be had, dredge a towel with flour, and wrap the fish in it evenly, so that when unrolled, it can be dished without breaking. Select fish with lively prominent eyes, red gills, firm flesh, and stiff body, have them well cleansed, and rinsed before boiling, and if stuffed, bind them firmly with strips of cotton or tape; cover the fish with cold water; throw in a little salt, and boil gently and constantly; do not let the water get too low, and see that each part of the fish is constantly covered; do not allow the water to boil unevenly, but let the heat be strongest under the middle of the kettle, otherwise the fish will break; remove the scum as fast as it rises. It takes the same length of time to boil a pound of fish as the same weight of flesh. To try if the fish is done, run a thin sharp knife through it, touching the back-bone; if it adheres, it is not done; do not let the fish lie in the water a moment after it is done, as it will soon lose its flavor, besides presenting a poor appearance. Drain the water through the strainer, or if in a cloth, lay it on a sieve, where it will keep hot; cover the fish with a napkin folded thick, heat the fish-platter, lay it on carefully without breaking, and keep it hot and dry until the soup is served; do not place it on the table until wanted, as it cools very quickly. Most cooks add a little vinegar to fish while boiling, when nearly done. If fish are underdone, they are very disgusting; if overdone, tasteless and insipid. Serve with sauces composed of drawn butter; potatoes mashed should be the principal vegetable. Horseradish is always a good relish for boiled fish. Milk and water is better than clear water to boil fish in.

To Boil Lobsters.—Put them in a kettle of boiling salted water, allowing four table-spoonfuls to each gallon; boil from a half to one hour.

To Boil Crabs.—Boil the same as lobsters.

To Boil Sea Fish Fresh.—Soak, some time before dressing, in cold water, in which throw a handful of salt; always notch the back before putting them in the kettle; salt the water, and let it heat gradually, boil gently, or they will break in pieces. A fish weighing eight pounds, will boil in half an hour.

To Boil Cod's Head and Shoulders.—Tie them in cloth, and put them in cold salted water; they will be done in half an hour.

To Boil Mackerel Fresh.—Boil gently; the fish should be fresh, and boiled in salted water.

Rock Fish.—Rock fish, bass, and some other kinds of fish, are boiled plain, leaving on the head and tail. It will take a half-hour steady boiling; serve with drawn butter, in which mix hard-boiled eggs chopped fine; the eggs should boil one hour. This may seem strange, but for some reason, an egg boiled an hour is quite different from one boiled five minutes.

To Boil White Fish, Pike, etc.—Prepare a dressing with bread-crumbs, boiled eggs chopped fine, pepper, salt, and butter. Fill the body of the fish, and bind it firmly with slips of cloth; boil gently, until thoroughly cooked; remove it to the platter, and set it in the oven a few moments to dry; boil eggs hard, slice and lay them in the platter, around the fish, and just before serving pour over the fish a little drawn butter; prepare a sauce in this manner, namely, boil six eggs one hour, work the yolks, until they become a paste, with a wooden spoon; take a teacup nearly full of sweet butter, mix in it a heaping table-spoonful of flour, work in the yolks of the eggs, and then stir gently, little by little, half a pint of boiling water; add a little salt, if needed, and pepper; but, if the butter is salted much, no salt will be required.

To Boil Fresh Salmon.—Salmon should be plunged in boiling water; the water should be put in the kettle, allowing a handful of salt to four quarts water; let the water boil until all the scum, arising from the mixture of the salt with the water, has been removed, before putting in the fish. Salmon should be dressed as soon as taken from the water to be perfect, the flesh becoming soft very soon. The German method of treating fish, besides being less cruel, renders the fish firmer: As soon as caught, instead of leaving the poor fish to struggle and die by inches, they take it by the tail and knock it on the head, killing it instantly. It is said, fish treated thus, remain firm longer than those that die a lingering death.

A salmon should be of a bright color, scales clear, eyes bright, and gills very red. Allow, in boiling, a quarter of an hour to every pound of fish; serve with drawn butter, or simply cover it with sweet butter; serve for vegetables, mashed potatoes, and cucumbers sliced in vinegar, or for a dinner party, the cucumbers only. Cook in the same manner the salmon trout from the upper lakes. When salmon are transported, pack them in ice as soon as out of the water, killing them after the German method.

To Boil Fresh Shad.—If you wish to keep shad for a day or

two, scald and dress it when perfectly fresh; split open the belly, wipe it quite dry, and scatter a table-spoon of sugar, and a teaspoon of salt, and one of pepper, and keep it on ice; and before cooking, wipe off all the seasoning; fill the body of the fish with a dressing of bread and butter, seasoned with salt and pepper, moistened with water; put the fish in cold water, and boil until quite done; or boil without the dressing, and serve with drawn butter, or sweet butter laid on the fish.

To BOIL SALTED SHAD.—Soak them, and change the water once; remove the scales and boil until well done; lay them on a heated platter, and pour over them fresh sweet butter.

To BOIL SALTED SALMON.—Soak them over night, cleanse them thoroughly, and boil gently; serve with plain drawn butter.

To BOIL A SALTED MACKEREL.—Soak in milk and water, over night, and boil gently; for sauce use drawn butter, and serve with it mashed potatoes.

To BOIL SALTED COD.—Cut a thick nice piece of the fish, soak it over night, in the morning change the water, and stand the pot where it will only keep warm; change the water again about ten in the morning; cover it with fresh tepid water, and let it become so hot that it is uncomfortable to the hand; keep the water evenly hot, but on no account let it boil, for two hours, when it will be done; remove all the skin, cut hard eggs and place them on and around the fish, and pour over it nice drawn butter. Boil nice white potatoes without the skin, and dish them plain; have a gravy-boat of drawn butter on the table to add, when serving the fish and potatoes, as most persons prefer to mash them with the fish; serve cucumbers, or if out of season, pickles or nasturtiums. The cold fish will make a fine hash for breakfast, mixed with mashed potatoes and drawn-butter; dried codfish, if boiled, is hard and very poor eating; but prepared in this manner, it is as good as the cod that is transported on ice, although much inferior to the fish when fresh caught.

To BOIL STURGEON.—This fish should be parboiled before being cooked in any form, in plenty of water once or twice, according to the tastes of the family. To many its strong fishy taste is very disagreeable.

BOILED TURBOT.—After the fish is dressed, soak it two hours in salted water, and half an hour in cold ice-water; score the back, rub it dry, and bathe it in lemon-juice; have a large fish-kettle ready, lay it on its back, cover with cold water a little salted, and boil gently, remove all scum as fast as it rises; the last hour it should simmer gently, without boiling. Some cooks advise keeping turbots two or three days before cooking.

BOILED CODS' TONGUES AND SOUNDS.—If salted, soak them all night, change the water in the morning, and simmer gently, until well done; serve with drawn butter or egg-sauce.

TO BAKE A LARGE FISH WHOLE.—Cut off the head, and split the fish nearly down to the tail; prepare a nice dressing of bread, butter, pepper, and salt, moistened with a little water. Fill the fish, and bind it together with small cotton cord or tape, so as to confine it; the bindings may be three inches apart; lay the fish on a grate in a bake-pan, if you have one; if not, in the dripping-pan, and pour around it a very little water with butter melted in it; and baste it frequently. A good-sized but not over-large fish will bake in an hour; serve, with the gravy of the fish, drawn butter or oyster sauce. Those who are accustomed to wines in fish will relish a baked fish basted in wine and water, but this will suit but few tastes. Choose the middle of a cod, haddock, or any fish too large to bake whole. Serve baked cod with oyster sauce.

TO ROAST A LOBSTER.—When the lobster is more than half boiled, take it from the water, set it before the fire, and baste it with butter until well done.

TO BAKE A SHAD.—Clean the fish, wash and wipe it dry. Split the fish, and fill it with dressing of bread and butter seasoned with pepper and salt; bind the fish with cord or tape, rub it with salt, and put it to bake; when in the bake-pan, lay on the fish bits of butter; let it bake slowly until well done. Fish are often baked without any dressing. Shad and other fish are sometimes roasted before the fire on planks for the purpose; they are very nice, and when roasted in this manner, no stuffing is used. In dishing baked fish, be careful to leave them whole; a mangled fish looks very badly on the table.

TO FRY FISH.—The secret of frying fish well, consists in having enough fat in the spider; let them fry very slowly over a moderate and steady heat.

TO FRY SALMON CUTLETS.—Cut slices from a salmon half an inch thick, rub them over with pepper and salt, dip them in the beaten yolk of eggs, and fry in plenty of fat slowly. They should be put in the fat while it is hot, and turned immediately and often until done; serve plain.

To FRY SHAD.—Cut the fish in pieces, rinse and wipe dry; rub over the fish a little salt; and when it has melted roll them in flour; heat the fat, tried from salt pork, or oiled butter, nearly boiling hot; lay in the fish the skin side up; fry until brown, and then turn them; cook slowly without burning; serve plain. Horseradish makes a fine relish for fish.

To FRY TROUT.—Dry them thoroughly, and fry in hot oiled butter without scorching, or in pork fat; if the latter, rub salt on the fish. Lay on the fish, before serving, lumps of sweet butter.

To FRY EELS.—The sensation of eels can be destroyed by giving them a hard knock on the head. After they are cleaned and skinned, roll them in yolk of egg and thin rolled crackers, bread crumbs, meal or flour, and fry in pork fat or oiled butter slowly until a pale brown.

To FRY ROCK BASS OR ANY SMALL FISH.—Clean them; rub the fish with salt, and let them lie an hour; have a sufficient quantity of fat hot to cover the fish, and fry slowly until the fish is crisped entirely. Some very small fishes may be crisped, so that the bones can be eaten without inconvenience.

To FRY MACKEREL.—Take as many mackerel as are needed for the family; remove the skin, dip them in beaten egg and bread crumbs, fry them slowly until done. For a sauce, pound the soft roes with sweet thick cream, and pass them through a sieve; melt some butter in a little veal *consommé*, or water if no *consommé* is at hand; stir in the cream and roes, add a little lemon juice and mushroom catsup, heat it hot, and pour it over the fish after it is dished.

To BROIL FISH.—The fire should be hot and bright; the gridiron smooth and clean. If fish is oiled, it will not stick to the gridiron. If fresh oil cannot be had, oiled butter free from salt answers nicely. To prepare the butter, pursue the following plan: boil the butter, skim it, and strain it through a fine cloth, keep it warm, without cooking, half an hour, to precipitate the salt; then cool it, and use the top; most of the salt will be found at the bottom. Melt it for oiling fish.

To Boil Fresh Mackerel.—Split the fish down the back, wash and dry it thoroughly; with a feather oil it all over with fresh salad oil or oiled butter; season it with salt and pepper; lay it on a cold gridiron inside down; when browned slightly, turn it on the back; when the back is browned, wipe the oil from the gridiron as clean as possible, lift and turn it over so as to place the fish with the inside down on the platter. The platter should have been standing over hot water, with a bit of butter melting on it, to lay the fish in; lay bits of butter on the back to melt. Broil all fresh fish in the same manner; a person that can broil one fish well can broil any other as well. Large fishes, as salmon, cod, halibut, haddock, etc., are never broiled whole but in steaks.

To Broil Eels.—Eels when broiled are either wrapped in buttered paper, or dipped in egg and bread crumbs.

To Broil White Fish.—White fish is thought by some to be improved by making a very little smoke from sawdust, or a bit of wood under it when broiling.

To Soak Salt Fish.—Salted fish require to be soaked from twelve to twenty-four hours; they should be drained after soaking, until they are as dry as fresh fish; oil the fish before broiling, the same as fresh.

To Soak Mackerel.—Soak salted mackerel in milk and water; it gives them a better taste as well as improves their color; change the milk and water once, and drain well.

To Broil Salt Mackerel.—Oil the gridiron, and broil the same as fresh mackerel; lay over the fish sweet butter and very little pepper. Shad is broiled in the same manner; also white fish.

Picked-up Cod Fish.—This is an old-fashioned dish and name, but none the less to be admired on that account, being, with most persons, when properly prepared, a great favorite. Pick up the fish in small particles, separating the fibres as near as possible, the finer the better. Freshen by leaving it in water one hour; pour off the water, and fill up with fresh; bring it to a scald, pour it off, and put on the fish just enough water to cover it; add, to a quart of the soaked fish, a bit of butter the size of half an egg, a very little flour, and a dust of pepper. Beat up two eggs, and after taking off the fish, thicken it by stirring in the egg. Some let it boil after the egg is added, but if this is done, the egg will be curdled. Another way is to boil eggs, chop and mix them in the gravy. (*See* COD FISH HASH AND TOAST.)

MRS. W.'s SCALLOPED OYSTERS.—Eight square soda-crackers rolled fine, seven onces of butter, one quart of oysters; drain the oysters; put the crackers and oysters in alternate layers; divide the butter equally, putting it on the oysters at each layer, with a dust of pepper, and, if shell oysters, very little salt; be careful not to salt too much, leaving the bottom and top layer crackers. A moment before baking add a coffee cup of the liquor from the oysters; bake a light brown. This receipt will be found perfect.

TO SCALLOP FISH.—Pick the fish in flakes, mix it with rolled crackers or rusked bread; moisten with melted butter, pack it in shells, and bake in the oven.

CASSEROLE OF FISH.—Take any cold fish, divide it into small bits; have ready as many eggs as needed, boiled hard; work the yolks fine, chop the whites and mix the eggs and fish together; mash potatoes, and work the fish, egg, and potatoes together; moisten with butter, season with pepper and salt; put the whole in a mould, and boil; when done, turn it out.

KEDGEREE.—Boil rice; add any picked-up fish; heat it together, and while hot stir into the mixture a beaten egg; serve hot.

CROQUETTES OF FISH.—Mince cold fish; mix in the fish, egg, a little flour, a spoonful of cream; make the fish in balls or small cakes, and fry them brown. Lobsters make the best croquettes.

FISH CUTLETS.—Take steaks of any large fish; dip them in egg and bread crumbs, seasoned with pepper and salt, and fry slowly, until done, a nice brown.

SOUSED FISH.—Any fish can be soused. After it is boiled, put it in strong spiced vinegar; shad and mackerel are very nice soused for tea.

ANCHOVY BUTTER.—Beat fine as many of the fish as will be wanted, with sufficient fresh butter to moisten them; pass it through a wire sieve, mould, and cut it in slices.

SANDWICHES OF FISH.—Pick clear from bone any fish, spread the

4*

picked fish between two slices of bread and butter; and add mustard or catsups if desired.

FRIED OYSTERS WITHOUT EGG.—To fry oysters: select the largest oysters, simmer them in their own liquor a few minutes, and dry them with a towel; dip them in rolled crackers, and fry a light brown. Many cooks recommend bearding oysters, that is, removing their respiratory organs; where they are cheap it is well to do so, but in the country would be very extravagant. Oysters are also merely dipped in flour and fried, either after being scalded in their own liquor or not; fry them in butter.

BROILED OYSTERS.—Oysters are nice broiled in their shell, or laid in shells for the purpose; they must be laid over a bed of hot coal, and butter and pepper added in the shell; serve hot.

TO STEW OYSTERS.—Have, in a porcelain kettle, sufficient boiling water to cover the oysters; as the water heats remove the scum, add butter and pepper if relished; many persons never use pepper on oysters. This stew can be varied by the use of cream in the stew, when very little butter will be necessary.

SCALLOPED OYSTERS.—Select a dozen nice large oysters; if they are plenty beard them, if not use all of the fish; spread rolled crackers or rusked bread on the bottom of a shell; lay in some oysters and some bits of butter, then strew over them more crumbs; add oysters and butter, with layers of crackers or crumbs, until the shell is filled. Pour over the whole the liquid from the oysters, and bake brown; serve hot. If any are left, they are very good cold.

OYSTER PATTIES.—Cover small shells or patty-pans with nice puff paste, bake them well, when done turn them out on a plate; stew oysters, season them to suit the taste, thicken their juice with egg, and when cold, fill the patties with the oysters.

OYSTER PIES, VERY NICE.—Cover a deep plate with puff paste; lay an extra layer around the edge of the plate, and bake nicely; when quite done, fill the pie with oysters, season with pepper, salt, and butter, dust over a little flour, and cover with a thin crust of puff paste; bake quickly; when the top crust is done, the oysters should be; serve as soon as baked, as the crust soon absorbs the gravy.

TO BOIL HARD-SHELLED CLAMS.—Wash the shells very clean, put

them in a pot with as little water as will keep the pot from burning, with their edges down; and boil constantly. When the shells open they are done; remove them; have ready nice butter toast, and pour the clams on the toast, with as much of the juice as the toast will absorb; add pepper if desired.

To Fry Clams with Egg and Crackers.—Procure large sand clams; dip them in egg, bread crumbs, rolled crackers or meal, and fry brown in sweet butter.

Stewed Clams.—Put the clams in a stew-pan, with about the same quantity of water as the juice of the clams, boil from twenty-five to thirty minutes, remove all the scum that rises, and season with butter and a dust of pepper.

Hashed Clams.—Chop clams fine; stew them in very little water, add their own juice; boil fifteen minutes, and season with butter and pepper; after taking up the hash, thicken the gravy with a yolk or two of eggs.

Musoles Stewed.—These are stewed in their own liquor, and seasoned with parsley, and, if desired, onion and a little lemon juice.

Scallops, Crawfish, Spawns, and Shrimps.—These are first boiled in salted water until nearly done. They are then taken out, and stewed in their own liquor with a little wine, lemon juice, or vinegar; add some butter and grated bread, and after dishing, thicken with the yolks of eggs without boiling.

Turtle Stew.—Select the best of the meat, cut it in bits, season with salt, Cayenne, and sweet marjoram, nutmeg and mace; add sufficient butter rolled in flour, stew for an hour, and add a part of the green fat cut in small bits, the juice and grated rind of lemon, and wine; stew for an hour longer, very gently; serve hot.

Turtle Patties.—Scrape the back shell clean, line it with puff paste, fill it with the stewed turtle, cover with puff paste rolled thin, and bake as soon as possible, (or the paste will soak in the liquor,) in a moderately quick oven; serve as soon as taken from the oven. To dress and prepare the soup, *see* Turtle Soup.

To Dress Lobsters.—To boil a lobster, the pot should be full of strong salted water, boiling hot. Put the fish in the pot, alive, while boiling hard, with its head downward that it may die as quickly as possible. Boil steadily, and it will be done in half an hour, if not very large. Before dishing, remove the large claws and lay them on the platter by the side of the fish; separate the head, leaving it in its place; split the body to the tip of the tail, and send it to the table plain. For lobster salads, *see* SALADS.; for soup, *see* SOUPS; for sauce, *see* LOBSTER SAUCE.

LOBSTER BALLS.—Mince the meat of the fish with the coral very fine, season to suit the taste, add bread crumbs, butter or sweet oil; make it in balls, dip them in yolk of egg and flour, and fry, in hot lard, until brown.

LOBSTER PATTIES.—Cover shells with puff paste, fill them with minced lobster, seasoned as desired, cover and bake.

CHAPTER III.

BEEF.

GENERAL DIRECTIONS FOR ROASTING AND BOILING MEATS.—All salt meats should be put into cold water, heated gradually, skimmed as long as a particle of scum rises to the surface, and boiled gently without ceasing, until tender. The pot should be often filled with boiling water, that the meats may not be too salt. If the water is very hard, put into the pot a large teaspoon of soda, before putting in the beef or ham; for fat salt pork it is unnecessary. To boil fresh meats, have the pot boiling hard when the meat is put in; boil steadily; remove all scum; do not let it either soak or boil so hard as to make it necessary to leave off the pot-cover. For soups, put the meats in cold water, simmer gently a long time; soups ought never to boil furiously. In roasting joints, heat the surface as soon as possible, and afterwards roast more gently. The sooner the outside pores are closed, the less juice of the meat will be lost. A roast is in perfection when juicy in the middle and brown on the outside. To roast a fowl well, the skin should be protected at first; if it blisters and cracks, it presents not only a poor appearance, but loses much flavor. To boil a fowl, put it in boiling water, unless the broth is desired for soup; if so, use cold, and simmer gently. To broil well, the fire must be bright, not over hot, but brisk. To fry, the fire should be moderate and steady.

To stew, the fire should be slow, but steady. There is great waste in boiling fast. It not only takes more wood, but wastes the flavor of the meat, or vegetables, besides giving disagreeable notice to all in the house what is to be served for dinner. Old fowls should never be roasted, or, if so, very gently; allow an hour longer to roast an old turkey than a young one. It is better, if possible, to boil or stew an old fowl, than to either roast, fry, or broil them; give them half an hour more time than a young fowl. The same rule applies to all game. Old meats boil, roast, fry, broil, and stew in less time than the beef of a young creature. Too young cattle make poor beef. The finer the beef, the sooner it roasts, and the more juicy the joint.

To Boil Corned Beef.—If the beef is very salt, put it in a pot filled with cold water, and when nearly but not quite boiling, change it for cold water. As soon as the second water boils, skim it until no impurities arise. If boiled in hard water, throw in a teaspoon of soda before putting in the meat. Keep the pot closed, that it may keep full by the condensing of the steam on the cover. If the lid allows the steam to escape, and the water boils low, fill up with boiling water. Let it boil slowly until tender, so that the bones will slip out. If the meat is not too salt, put in only sufficient water to cover it; remove the scum as it rises, and, when the liquor is clear, close the lid tightly, and boil, as gently as possible, until very tender.

Superior Beef to Use Cold from Poor Pieces.—Soak in warm, not hot water, until as fresh as desired when boiled. Then cover it with water, and boil slowly; skim the pot as long as any scum rises, after which cover the pot closely, that the condensed steam may fall in the pot, and boil steadily, until the meat will break in bits if lifted with a fork; when sufficiently tender, skim it out, remove the bone, and mix the fat and lean together; put it in a wide earthen dish, deep enough to hold it; skim the fat from the liquor, and boil the liquor down; when sufficiently reduced, pour it over the meat; lay over it a flat cover, and put on a weight of fifteen or twenty pounds, and let it stand all night. When wanted for the table, cut it in thin slices, as you would head-cheese. The jelly of the liquor will make it firm, and, if properly mixed, the fat and lean will be in right proportion through the whole. This is an excellent way to manage the poor pieces of corned beef—the gristle will be tender, and every part good. The gelatine of the muscles will be saved; though not considered particularly nutritious when used alone, it will assist in forming the meat into a solid mass, making it both agreeable to the eye and taste. If the beef is much salt, it should be soaked forty-eight hours, or longer if not sufficiently freshened, to allow all the water to evaporate, and the jelly to solidify, without tasting too much of the brine.

REMARKS ON ROAST BEEF, ETC.—Most cooks advise heating meat slowly at the first, and afterward, more particularly in roasts, with more rapidity; but our experience is, that if the juices are wanted in the roast, it should be suffered to brown as quick as possible without burning, and afterwards roast as slowly as possible, and have the roast finished by a given time. Boiled fresh beef we put first in hot water; let it boil up once, skim thoroughly, and boil gently until tender.

TO ROAST A SIRLOIN OF BEEF WEIGHING TEN POUNDS, RARE.—Wash the beef quickly, not allowing it to soak; put no salt or pepper on it before it commences to roast. To have roast beef in perfection, it must not only be well seasoned, but its juices retained within itself, so that when the knife is drawn through in carving, the juice will immediately follow. This can be attained by following the given directions. Put the beef to roast two hours before the dinner hour, if roasted before the fire; or, if in a hot stove, an hour and a half. Brown a little suet in a dripping-pan, add sufficient boiling water, a little salted, to baste the meat conveniently, and place it under the roast. Never lay a roast in a pan; if in water, it will be stewed—if without, it will burn. The bone side should be turned before the fire at first, and afterward the other. When the beef is heated on the surface on all sides, so as to look a little brownish, and the water in the pan is boiling hot, baste it well, and repeat the basting once every fifteen minutes for an hour, if before the fire, and half that time if in a stove-oven, and the remainder of the time it is roasting, every five minutes. When it is fairly roasting, baste with flour and water; place bits of paper over the fat and thinnest part of the beef, to prevent its getting over done. Most cooks say, roast slowly at first; we prefer to heat quickly, and roast more slowly at the last; but care must be taken not to burn at the first outset, as this would ruin the whole operation. Thicken the gravy with flour or not, as desired. Just before the beef is taken from the oven, or fire, dredge it with flour, and allow it to brown without burning. Serve currant, or some other acid jelly, with all roasts of beef. Mash and season potatoes, turnips, and squash, when served with roasts of any sort. Plain boiled vegetables with these meats are decidedly improper. Roast the rump of beef in the same manner; sirloin is the finest roast in the creature, but the rump is considered good.

A-LA-MODE BEEF.—Prepare a dressing with bread or crackers, moisten with water seasoned with butter, pepper, salt, and nutmeg, cloves, and, if relished, allspice; add two eggs, and mix the whole well together. Have ready a round of beef of the proper size for the family; cut gashes in it, and fill them with the dressing. Bind it together with skewers, and put it in a bake-pan with water enough to cover the bottom of the pan, in which is dissolved a little salt. Baste it three or four times with the salted water while cooking. Let it stew gently. When nearly done, cover it with dressing reserved for the purpose. Heat the lid to the pan sufficiently hot to brown it, cover and stew until done. It can be stewed in a dripping-pan, in a stove-oven, and browned when done by holding over it, if not already browned, a heated shovel. The dressing should be poured over it half an hour before taking it from the oven. If the gravy is too thin, add a little flour worked free from lumps.

FRENCH BEEF.—Remove the bone from a circular piece of the round, cut away all fat and skin. Lard it all over with a larding-pin, which is an instrument made for the purpose, consisting of iron, sharpened like a needle at one end, and resembling a pencil-case at the other. The strips of pork or larding are entered at the square or hollow end, and the pin is pushed through the meat, the sharp end entering first. It is so contrived that the larding will be left in the meat when the pin comes out. Make a nice force-meat of chopped suet, bread, or crackers rolled fine, highly seasoned, and wet with egg; fill the cavity made by the bone with this dressing; wind it with twine to keep it in shape, and put it in a broad earthen jar with a tight cover, and set it in the oven until done; or put it in an iron bake-pan; put in the jar, with the meat, a quarter of a pound of butter rolled in flour, a teaspoon half full of whole pepper, and half a pint of port wine. Add, if relished, an onion and cloves; stew slowly, five or six hours, in proportion to its size. If in a jar, set it in a brick or stove oven; serve hot with its own gravy as it is.

STEWED BEEFSTEAK, No. 1.—Take a slice of good sirloin beef; put it in a dripping-pan without water, cover tight, and set in the oven; when heated, take it out, add pepper and salt, and return it to the oven. Let it cook without the cover, long enough to heat through, then turn it, and lay on small bits of butter rolled in flour.

As soon as the butter is melted, it is done. It should be not over fifteen minutes cooking, and the oven should be very hot before it is put in.

Brown Stewed Beefsteak.—Be sure the oven is hot enough to burn flour, before the beef is put in. Put the dripping-pan in the oven with enough suet from the beef to grease it well, and leave a little floating. Do not remove all the fat from the beef. Lay it in the dripping-pan; set it in the oven for five minutes. Take out the pan, and turn over the beef; sprinkle with a little salt and pepper the side turned over. Set it in again, and let it remain five minutes. It should then be done; but if not, leave it longer; mix as much butter as is needed, with a very little boiling water; pepper and salt to the taste, and a pinch of flour; mix all together, and heat, but not boil it. Take the beef from the pan, lay it on a platter, and mix the gravy with the juice of the meat, (if it is not scorched, if so, do not use it,) and pour it over the beef. It will take half a teacupful of butter, and two table-spoonfuls of boiling water, for a small slice. This manner of cooking is not as good as broiled; but, as it is often more convenient to stew than to broil, it will be found a good recipe, and much better than a fried steak. Serve with mashed potatoes.

Fried Beefsteak.—Heat the spider before putting in the beef, cut off most of the fat, season the fat with pepper and salt, before frying; put the steak into the hot spider, and fry as quickly as possible; when the beef is turned, sprinkle on a little salt and pepper; mix a little flour and water together in the proportion of half a teacupful of water to a half teaspoonful of flour; take out the meat and scraps of fat, and stir in the flour and water; let the gravy brown a little, and pour it over the beef. Serve with fried potatoes, if convenient; if not, with mashed.

Beefsteak Gravy.—For one slice of sirloin steak, take half a teacup of butter; set the platter over a kettle of hot water; cut the butter in bits, if very salt, very little if any salt will be needed; dust on a little pepper, and add two tablespoons of hot water. Save all the blood from the steak possible to add to the gravy, without pressing the beef. Be careful it does not boil, as it would become oily, and taste like stewed steak more than broiled. If the gridiron is bright, and the juice of the meat caught by it is not burned, add it to the gravy; but it is seldom, indeed, that it is in a fit state for any thing. Use the sweetest butter for steaks: there is no cooking injured more by poor butter than steak, as the gravy does not boil to throw off its imperfections, as in most other preparations for the table.

TO BROIL BEEFSTEAK RARE.—When beef is desired very rare, have a good bed of live coals ready, lay the beef on the gridiron, and put it on the coals. It should be ready to turn in three minutes. When it is turned, take it up carefully with two forks; roll it up, so as to save the juice of the meat which has collected in cooking; do not squeeze the steak, but merely drain off the juice on the platter; put it back as quickly as possible, that it may lose no heat in turning; add to the juice of the meat pepper, salt, and considerable butter, and set the platter over a kettle of boiling water. In three minutes, if the fire is right, it will be done. Lay it on the platter; let it remain a moment, and then turn it over, but on no account press it; add to the gravy two or three tablespoonfuls of hot water after the meat is well seasoned. Turn the platter two or three times, to mix the water with the gravy, and serve immediately. The platter should be sufficiently large to hold the steak, spread its full size, without touching the edge. If any of the gravy has soiled the edge of the platter, wipe it with a clean towel; nothing looks more untidy than a spattered platter. Serve with potatoes, turnips, and cauliflower, dressed. Relishes, cold or hot slaw, if no cauliflower is served; pickles and jellies are always fine with beefsteak.

TO BROIL A BEEFSTEAK TO SUIT ALL.—To broil a steak to suit all, it is necessary to cut it in as many pieces as there are tastes to suit. The part desired rare, should be put on with a bright bed of fresh coals, when the piece desired nearly done is about ready to turn, broil as described for rare steak. That to be partially broiled, should be laid on, when the part to be thoroughly cooked is ready to turn. When this part of the steak is ready to turn, dip the broiled side in the gravy, (see GRAVY,) and turn the raw side down. When the other side is browned, if not sufficiently done, dip again, and turn the first side to the fire. The piece which is to be well done, should be dipped, the broiled side down, as soon as it has cooked sufficiently, to close the pores. Dip it again, when the other side is in the same state, and so do for three or four times, according to the heat of the coals. It should be brown when finished. This plan will render the steak juicy and good. If salt and pepper are put on at first, the juice will be in the gravy, or lost in the fire; but after it has partly congealed, the salt will neither harden nor dissolve the fibre. The tenderloin makes the most tender steak. The sirloin is very fine; and the rump, though not very tender, is sweet and juicy. Vegetables should be dressed, if the steak is for dinner; but for breakfast, a baked potato is considered proper. Butter, for steak, should be as sweet as for table use.

BEEFSTEAK AND OYSTERS, OR CLAMS.—Get very tender sirloin steak; remove the bone, and lay it on the gridiron over hot coals. Have ready large fat oysters or clams. When the steak is browned a little, dip it in the gravy prepared as directed, with the addition of the oyster juice; which, if as salt as usual, will salt the gravy sufficiently; lay the beef on the gridiron again, and when a little hot, put the oysters on it, pressing the meat a little to make hollow spots, to retain their juice; cover the whole gridiron with a bright tin pan or cover; when the oysters are heated a little, turn them over, and when heated through, remove the steaks to the platter; lay the oysters round the edge of the meat in the gravy, and serve immediately.

BEEFSTEAK PIE.—Cover the bottom of a deep plate with paste, as directed in PASTRY. Cut the beef in pieces, convenient for the mouth; spread them evenly over the paste; then add butter, flour, pepper, salt, and water; cover with paste, press the edges firmly, and cut a gash in the centre of the pie; it is good cold or hot. If to be used cold, make a gravy by boiling a bit of the bone, seasoning it the same as the pie; heat the gravy, and serve it with the pie. Potatoes are all the vegetables needed—they should be mashed. These pies can be made from cold beefsteak left the day before, but are not quite as good.

To COOK DRIED BEEF.—Slice it as thin as possible, and let it lie in water, over night, or less time, if not very salt. Stew it in water sufficient to make the gravy needed, until tender. Beat up an egg with a little flour; add a lump of butter to the beef, and stir in the egg and flour. Toast bread; lay the beef nicely on it, and pour the gravy over it; add a trifle of pepper at the table, if relished.

MOCK VENISON OF CORNED BEEF.—Cut the beef in thin slices, and freshen it well, it should lie in tepid water three or four hours. When sufficiently fresh, lay it on the gridiron, and let it heat through quickly. Make a gravy of drawn butter; add a little pepper, and the yolk of an egg chopped fine, and pour over it; or put butter, pepper, and salt on it, as you would a beefsteak. This will be found a good dish, in the country where fresh beef is seldom to be obtained, but not equal to fresh beef or venison.

FRIED BEEFSTEAK TO RESEMBLE BROILING.—Heat a spider so very hot, that flour will burn on it instantly; wipe it free from dust, and lay in the steak; it should brown immediately; take it from the spider before it has had time to cook any part except the browning of the side that came in contact with the spider; lay it on the platter, which should stand over hot water; heat the spider again; wipe it free from fat, and brown the other side in the same manner as the first. Have butter, pepper, and salt, for the gravy, laid on the platter to melt, while the last is browning; remove the steak to the platter, and soak it in the gravy, add a table-spoon of boiling water to the gravy, and serve immediately. When these directions are followed to the letter, there are but few, that would imagine the beef otherwise cooked, than broiled. It is far before a poorly broiled steak. If desired well done, the process must be repeated, not left in to fry, until cooked through, as that would give a taste like fried beef to the whole dish. If the juice of the meat stands on the steak, when the first side is browning, lift the beef carefully, so as to pour it from the beef into the platter. If any escapes to the spider, it will be worse than wasted if added to the gravy.

CHAPTER IV.

PORK.

TO BOIL SALT PORK.—Allow one-third for shrinking; change the water as soon as it boils. Have ready a kettle of boiling water to fill the kettle. Let it boil very slowly. When tender take it up; remove the skin and bones, and dot it with ground pepper. Serve with plain potatoes, turnips, and cabbage, each boiled by itself. Indian pudding boiled with the pork is a proper dessert, with a sauce of cream and sugar, or maple syrup. Cold boiled pork is nice frozen stiff, cut thin, and laid between bread for lunch.

The same dessert is proper for boiled ham, bacon, and pork; but the vegetables of pork and bacon should be plain, while those to be used with the ham should be dressed. For baked ham, the pudding should be baked.

BOILED HAM.—Soak the ham over night if dry; if moist omit it. Boil slowly in plenty of water. At no time allow the water to get lower than when first put on. A large ham will take about six hours to boil tender enough to eat well cold. If the ham is too salt, the water should be changed once, but cold water must never be put on the ham after it commences to boil. No vegetables should be boiled with it; if the flavor of ham is desired in them, take out some of the liquor and boil them in it. If the water is hard, add a little soda. Filtered rain water is the best to boil salt meat in.

To Boil Bacon.—Wash it clean and put it on in cold water; if too salt, change the water; keep plenty of water in the pot until it is tender. Pork, ham, and bacon should be skinned as soon as taken from the pot, and ornamented with ground pepper put on in spots at regular intervals. The bones should be removed from pork and bacon, after it is boiled, but not from ham; horseradish, or catsups and mustard, should be on the table for relishes.

Baked Ham, No. 1.—Soak over night a small ham, and cover it with a paste of flour and water. Bake gently five hours, remember, gently; not a hot fire one hour, and none the next. When done, remove the skin. Serve as boiled ham.

Baked Ham, No. 2.—If you have an old-fashioned bake-kettle, line the inside with paste made as above; cut off part of the fat from the ham, and the bone close to the flesh; lay in the ham, and cover over the top with the same crust as the sides; place coals under and over the bake-kettle, keeping the ham stewing in its own steam for five hours. Then remove the skin, and serve as above. The ham should be small and rather lean. This method is said to be very fine, much better than boiling.

Pork a la mode.—Fresh pork can be dressed as a-la-mode beef, seasoned with sage, savory, thyme, sweet marjoram, pepper, and salt; and as French beef, with the same seasoning as above. It can also be gashed, and stuffed with dressing before roasting, as already described. It is much more healthy and quite as palatable cold. Cold roast spare ribs are excellent.

Fresh Stewed Pork.—Put into the pot just enough water to cover the pork; season with pepper and salt; when nearly done, thicken with a little flour.

Fresh Pork Stew.—Boil as above, season when half done; add potatoes and light crust. (*See* Pot-Pie.) There should be plenty of gravy, and the seasoning should be added and gravy thickened before the potatoes are put in.

FRESH PORK PIE.—Boil lean, fresh pork, and make the paste as for beefsteak pie; add to the pie, after putting in the meat, two potatoes cut fine, which have been before boiled; season with pepper, salt, and a dust of summer savory. If there is not fat enough in the pork, add butter; thicken the gravy with a little flour. The pie should contain as much gravy as possible. It is good cold or hot.

PORK STEAK BROILED.—The tenderloin is the best for steak, but any lean white meat is good. Broil slowly, after splitting it so as to allow it to cook through without drying or burning. When ready to turn over, dip the cooked side in a nice gravy of butter, pepper, and salt, which should be prepared on a platter and kept hot without oiling. It must be well done; there should be no sign of blood in the meat when cut. It requires slow broiling, it will take at least twenty minutes to broil a pork-steak.

FRIED PORK-STEAK.—Cut off the rind, and if there is enough fat on the pork to fry it, rub it with salt, sage, and pepper, and fry until thoroughly done; keep the spider covered while cooking, and be careful not to burn it; it should fry slow, and a long time; serve the gravy as it is, or add water and a little flour.

TO BAKE SALT PORK.—After the pork has boiled until quite tender, take it from the pot and cut the rind in gashes of the right thickness to slice, and bake until brown.

SCRAMBLED PORK.—Freshen nice salt pork, cut it in mouthfuls, and partly fry it. Just before it is done break into the spider with the pork from six to twelve eggs, break and mix the yolks with the whites, and stir them quickly with the pork. If the pork is fried brown before the egg is added, there may be too much fat for the egg; if so, put it in a gravy-boat if needed for the table, or save it for shortening. Baked potatoes are excellent with salt meats that have a gravy of their own.

SALT PORK PANCAKES.—Make a light batter of milk, flour, and egg. Freshen the pork, which should be cut as thinly as possible, and fry it until thoroughly done; then dip it in batter, and turn it as you would a pancake when fried on the under side.

PORK AND APPLE FRITTERS.—Prepare a light batter, freshen or use cold boiled or baked pork; cut it fine enough for hash, and fry it a little to extract some of the fat for frying the fritters. Peel sour apples, and cut or chop them not quite as fine as the pork; mix first the pork and then the apples in the batter, and fry them brown. Potatoes, parsnips, salsify, or any vegetable desired, can be used in the same manner.

PLAIN FRIED SALT PORK.—Cut the slices thin, and gash the rind, so that it will need but little masticating. Parboil, and fry slowly without burning the fat. It can be varied by dipping it in flour and browning. Some dip dry bread in water, and fry after the pork to serve with it.

Apples are excellent fried after pork, also potatoes. When these are fried for dinner, the potatoes must be put over before the pork in fat left from a previous frying, and the apples in another pan at the same time. Fried pork, fried apples, and fried potatoes together make an excellent meal. Some persons fry onions with pork; they should be cut evenly and fried brown. They are more pleasant to eat than to cook. If possible, they should be fried on a coal furnace in the air, as the odor of them will remain for days in the house after frying. Apples for frying should not be very acid, as they break too much; wash them clean, and do not peel them. The cores should be removed with a corer, and the slices cut round, with a hole in the centre of each slice. In stirring them do not mix the apples in a mass, but leave the slices as entire as possible. The fat should be hot when they are put in, and when fried they should be nicely browned.

SALT PORK WITH CREAM OR MILK GRAVY.—Slice the pork very thin, freshen, and fry without browning; when done, take the pork out of the spider and keep it hot; the best plan is to lay it on a pie-plate and set it in the oven. Pour off the fat, and rinse the salt from the bottom of the spider; for a common platter of pork allow about one table-spoonful of fat and a large pint of sweet cream; add salt and let it boil up. If milk is used, three spoons of fat and a little flour to thicken, so as to resemble cream as much as possible. The rule is to allow as much fat as will boil in without standing on the gravy. The richer the cream the less fat will be needed, and even if very thin a very little will suffice. Baked potatoes are the best with this dish. Children are generally fond of this gravy with bread broken in it.

PORK AND PARSNIPS.—After the pork is fried it should be cut in small bits, and boiled parsnips mixed with it cut in small bits and rolled in flour; let them heat through together. Some make a sort of parsnip stew with pork boiled in small pieces with parsnips. The pork should be well freshened before adding the parsnips.

To FRY HAM.—It is an excellent plan to use a ham and shoulder together; if not, the fat and lean of ham should be equally divided. Cut the slices thin and straight, do not haggle the ham, remove the rind, lay the fat in the spider, and fry slowly until well done. If the ham is too salt, lay the lean slices in milk-warm water while the fat is frying. When nearly done, remove the fat to one side of the spider, and lay the lean ham flat on the bottom; brown as quickly as possible, turn it on the other side, and take it up as soon as browned. If cooked hard it is poor eating. Serve with fried eggs, fried or baked potatoes, grated horseradish, or apple sauce.

SUPERIOR BROILED HAM.—Select the leanest part, and cut the slices evenly about one-eighth of an inch thick. Have ready a bed of nice bright coal, and warm the platter over a kettle of boiling water; lay the gridiron over the coals until nearly hot enough to hiss; then rub it off, lay on the ham, and broil quickly. It should be browned a trifle where it touches the bars of the gridiron, so as to look striped. When broiled both sides lay it on the platter, place a piece of sweet butter on each slice, and dust on a trifle of pepper. Serve with mashed potatoes, boiled eggs, and grated horseradish. If too salt it will be necessary to lay the slices in tepid water to freshen, although much of its flavor will be lost in the freshening. Dessert for fried and broiled ham, apple or tart pie; in winter, mince pie.

PLAIN BROILED SALT PORK.—Cut the pork thin, gash the rind, and parboil until freshened. Broil until brown, lay it on a hot platter, and make a gravy of a little butter, a table-spoonful of hot water, and a dust of pepper. Serve with baked potatoes, boiled eggs, and cold ham.

SUPERIOR BROILED SALT PORK.—Cut the pork very thin, lay the slices on the gridiron, commence on one side of the gridiron, take up each piece of pork separately and dip it in a bowl of water, laying it down on the opposite side each time; continue to do this until the pork is broiled quite brownish, then roll it in flour, and lay each bit on the gridiron. Brown the flour a trifle on one side, and then turn it to brown the other; it must not burn, or it will be bitter. Prepare a nice butter gravy with a little pepper and a spoonful or two of water, heat it over water, and lay the pork on the platter in nice order. Serve with boiled potatoes, mashed; peas or asparagus toast; cucumbers or pickles. If the potatoes are new, plain boiled is best.

To Fry Bacon.—Bacon should be nicely browned without burning. If too salt, freshen it by laying the slices in warm water. Serve with eggs and baked potatoes. For relishes, pickles, or any acid fruit, stewed, is proper.

Superior Pork and Beans.—Look over the beans, and put them in soak the evening previous to cooking, in soft water. Parboil, and throw off the water twice; prepare a piece of pork and put it in the beans with the third water. Let the water boil up, skim, and boil five minutes, and drain both pork and beans thoroughly. Have ready boiling water, put the beans and pork in the pot with as little water as will cover them, simmer gently until tender. The water should all be evaporated when done, leaving the beans nearly dry. Taste, and if not sufficiently salted by the pork, season with more, but be careful not to get too much salt. Spread the beans evenly in a baking dish; slash the pork, and put it on a pan by itself to bake; it should be handsomely browned. Stir up the beans often until within twenty minutes of dinner-time, then spread them evenly, and let them brown. If they do not look sufficiently brown, wet them over with egg, and brown with hot iron or any other manner convenient. Lay the pork in the middle, without the fat which dripped from it in roasting. This will be found much more healthy than when prepared after the old rule of baking pork and beans in the same dish. Serve as dessert a baked Indian pudding. Horseradish, catsups, and pickles, are the best relishes. Stewed beans are prepared as above, and gently boiled in the last water with the pork, until nearly dry. Beans should be cooked in soft water, or, if hard, with a small bit of soda in the water.

To Boil a Fresh Ham.—This is very excellent when well prepared; cut off all the fat, and skin with a sharp knife, leaving the ham in good shape for the table; put it in cold water well salted, and seasoned with two table-spoonfuls of ground mustard, and one of pepper; skim the pot carefully, and keep the ham under the water; boil steadily three hours; serve cold, and garnish with parsley or celery.

To Serve Cold Roast Pork.—Cut the slices very thinly across the grain, dust on, if not sufficiently salt, a trifle of fine salt on each slice as it is cut; if for breakfast or dinner, serve with it hot slaw and mashed potatoes.

To Serve Cold Boiled Ham.—Cut the slices very thin across the grain, and lay them evenly on the platter, or put the ham whole on the table before the carver; serve with potatoes, poached, scrambled or boiled eggs, and grated horseradish; the potatoes should be mashed and nicely seasoned, or baked. To prepare a boiled ham for the table: (*see* To Boil Ham) remove the skin without tearing the flesh, and garnish with pepper put on in spots, cloves, and parsley; the cloves can be used to fasten sprigs of parsley; cold boiled eggs cut in slices laid on the edge of the platter, with sprigs of double curled parsley, make a good appearance. Baked or roasted hams are said to be superior to boiled. Boiled pork is garnished much in the same manner, omitting cloves and eggs.

To Roast a Pig.—After the pig is well dressed, and every part in proper order, wipe it clean and dry, and proceed to make the dressing; it should be seasoned with pepper, salt, a little sifted sage, and thyme; crowd the pig as full as possible, put a potato in the mouth, bend the legs that it may lay strong upon its knees; rub the skin all over with sweet butter, and bake or roast three hours steadily; if the skin blisters, prick it and wet the spot with the drippings. The beauty of a roasted pig consists in browning the skin evenly all over without burning, and having it thoroughly done through. As this book may fall into the hands of persons in the country, it may not be amiss to give some directions for dressing pigs. The pig should be from four to six weeks old, fat and healthy. After the pig is stuck, examine the temperature of the water, this is the most important thing in the whole operation; if too hot, so as to cook the skin, it will be rough and difficult to clean, or if not hot enough it will not start the bristle from the roots; drop a few drops of fresh blood in the water; if instantly changed to a whitish color, it is too hot; if it retains its color, and tints the water, it is too cold; but if it changes to a milky color in a few seconds, it is the proper temperature. After the pig is once dipped in the water, rub it over with a little pulverized rosin; this will melt and mat the hair together, greatly facilitating its removal; a small opening as possible should be made for the removal of the inwards, always avoid opening the breast, as it makes the stuffing

5

it more troublesome. Particular pains should be taken with the nose, ears, and feet; the liver and heart should be saved to boil for thickening the gravy. Never serve roast pig without sour apples stewed plain, without sugar, or other sour sauce.

SAUSAGES.—The proper seasoning is salt, pepper, sage, summer-savory, or thyme; they should be one-third fat, the remainder lean, finely chopped, and the seasonings well mixed, and proportioned so that one herb may not predominate over the others. If skins are used, they cannot be prepared with too much care; but they are about as well made into cakes; spread the cakes on a clean whitewood board, and keep them in a dry cool place; fry them long and gently; serve with potatoes, cider-apple sauce, plain stewed apples without sugar, baked sour apples or sour pickles.

LARD.—Leaf lard is the nicest for all cooking purposes; skin all the fat that is to be tried into lard, and commence by frying gently a little leaf lard, or your fat will scorch; let it cook slowly, and dip off the fat as fast as it is liquefied, and strain it through a cloth; when all is strained that can be dipped off, squeeze the remainder by itself in the cloth. If the lard is to be used for cooking, salt it a trifle when first put on; but if for burning in lard lamps, salt would be injurious. If the fat is not skinned before trying, the gluten in the skin will make the lard impure and frothy. Save the scraps and skins for soap grease.

SOUSE.—Cleanse well the feet, legs, nose, and snout of the hogs, scald, scrape, and singe them; then boil them in water in which has been thrown a handful of salt, until tender, when it will fall to pieces, take it up, pick out all the bones, and set it in a cool place until wanted for the table. To prepare it for the table in the best manner, cut it in small bits, lay it in a spider, and fry it brown in its own fat, then add, if needed, salt, a bit of butter, a dust of flour, a little pepper, and sufficient strong vinegar to make a floating gravy; let it simmer in this three minutes, and then dish it; serve with mashed potatoes. It is considered a breakfast dish; if used for dinner, a sweet dessert should be provided.

PICKLED PIG'S FEET.—Boil until a straw can be run through them in water in which a little salt has been thrown, pack them in jars, and pour over them very strong vinegar, with or without spices to suit the taste.

HEAD-CHEESE.—Boil the head of a hog, after seeing it well cleansed and the eyes removed, tender. When it is boiled to rags, drain it in a colander, chop it as fine as possible, season to taste with pepper, salt, sage, and thyme; press all the water from it, put it in a form, and press it until cold; to use, cut it in thin slices like cheese; if properly prepared, will keep all winter.

FRESH PORK POT-PIE.—Boil a spare-rib, after removing all the fat, and cracking the bones, until tender; remove the scum as it rises, and when tender, season with salt and pepper; half an hour before time for serving the dinner, thicken the gravy with a little flour, have ready another kettle into which remove all the bones and most of the gravy, leaving only sufficient to cover the pot half an inch above the rim that rests on the stove; turn a small plate upside down in the kettle, and put in the crust; cover tight, and boil steadily twenty-five minutes. To prepare the crust, work into light dough a small bit of butter, roll it out thin, cut it in small square cakes, and lay them on the moulding-board until very light; if made with brewers' yeast, the butter should be melted in the wetting of the crust, and rolled out before rising, as the first effervescence of brewers' yeast is the strongest; work the dough well before making up the cakes.

TENDERLOIN OF PORK TO BROIL.—Broil until perfectly cooked, over bright coal, and season with butter, pepper, and salt.

PORK CUTLETS.—Dust over some slices of lean, white fresh pork, a little salt, and pepper; fry it slowly in pork fat, until well cooked, but not browned; have ready a batter of egg and flour, and just before serving dip in the pork, and fry until the egg is fried, but not browned.

A NICE WAY TO FRY FRESH PORK.—First cut the fat in small bits, dust on pepper, salt, sage, and thyme, or summer savory; fry until nearly brown enough, then cut the lean a little smaller than the fat, season the same, and fry without hardening until thoroughly done; serve with plain apple-sauce without sugar. Fresh pork can be fried to imitate broiling. (*See* FRIED BEEFSTEAK, No. 2.)

CHAPTER V.

VENISON, LAMB, MUTTON, AND VEAL.

REMARKS.—Venison should be well done without being dried. A haunch of buck venison, weighing twenty pounds, will require five hours to roast, allowing fifteen minutes to the pound; the doe-haunches are not quite as large, one weighing about eighteen pounds will require about three and a half hours, allowing about thirteen minutes to the pound. Before roasting, cover the fat with white buttered paper, and the paper with a coarse paste made of flour and water, this will prevent the fat from burning; baste the joint as soon as it warms with salted water and butter, and continue to do so as long as it is roasting; about twenty-five minutes before it is done, remove the covering from the fat, cleanse the dripping pan, and prepare some melted butter, and baste the haunch after it has been dredged lightly with flour. Garnish with white paper, ruffled round the knuckles. Prepare a gravy with the browned butter left in the pan, or make any fancy gravy prepared with wine or acids; serve with currant-jelly, cold or melted, or cranberry-sauce hot or cold.

TO ROAST A NECK OR SHOULDER OF VENISON.—Roast without covering; it requires less time than a haunch; baste as directed for a haunch; prepare a sauce with wine, jelly, or of the juices of the meat alone.

STEWED VENISON SHOULDER.—Remove the bone, and beat the flesh until tender, soak a part of the fat in wine: port is considered the best for this purpose; lay it upon the under side of the shoulder, dust them with a little salt, pepper, and, if relished, finely pulverized nutmeg, and cloves; the latter in very small proportion; then roll up the shoulder, leaving the fat on the inside, and bind it lightly together; put it in a small-sized stew-pan, pour over it a pint of veal broth mixed with a pint of wine; if the shoulder is not covered, add more broth; cover closely and stew gently for four hours; when done, open it, spread the meat neatly on the platter, strain the gravy, and pour it over the shoulders; if very fat, use but a small part of the fat, or it will be too rich to be agreeable; if the wine is disliked, omit it and the spices, and thicken the gravy a trifle with flour, or, if relished, melt currant or cranberry jelly in the gravy.

SUPERIOR VENISON STEAK.—This manner of cooking venison is the most healthy, and perhaps the most universally agreeable; the recipe was obtained from an old hunter, at the west. Broil, as you would a rare beef steak; have ready a gravy, prepared with butter, pepper, salt, and a very little water; heat the gravy, without boiling or frying the butter; cut the steak in small bits, not larger than a ten-cent piece, put it in the gravy, and cover tight, keep it hot enough to steam the meat sufficiently to coagulate the blood, but no hotter; serve in a covered dish, well heated.

DIRECTIONS FOR ROASTING A QUARTER OF LAMB.—Paper the roast all over, baste frequently, and cook thoroughly; if underdone, it is not fit to eat; when sufficiently roasted, the gravy which drops from it is entirely free from color; remove the paper half an hour before taking it from the fire; dredge it with flour, and baste it with butter, until it has penetrated the meat; brown nicely. The first basting liquid should be prepared with a little butter, salt, and pepper, to season the meat; some advise to cut off the fore shoulder and lift the flesh with a fork, and season it with pepper, salt, butter, and a little lemon-juice; if done, the shoulder must be replaced neatly, so as not to mar the quarter. It is easier to run a knife in the flesh in several places, making openings, without removing any of the flesh, and dust in pepper, salt, and lemon-juice, if relished. Serve with mint-sauce, the gravy of the quarter, or plain. Asparagus, peas, and potatoes, are the vegetables proper for serving with lamb; for relishes use salads. For dessert serve a light pudding, easy of digestion, and fruit.

LAMB CHOPS.—Fry them a light brown, in butter, then add a little water, flour, salt, and a dust of pepper, to the gravy, let it brown and pour it over the chops.

BROILED LAMB STEAK.—Broil slowly until quite done, then make a gravy with fresh butter melted by the steak, add a dust of pepper, and a little salt dissolved in a table-spoon of water; serve with peas, potatoes, and salads.

TO BOIL A LEG OF LAMB.—Wash and trim the leg nicely, have ready water that has boiled, and been skimmed, soft water is the best; put in the leg, when the water is nearly or quite boiling hot, and remove the scum as fast as it rises; when it has boiled five minutes, throw in the pot sufficient salt to give the water a saline taste, and boil the water briskly until the scum is all removed, then simmer until tender; the water should be kept to nearly boiling heat, and the pot tightly covered all the time. If the amount of water decreases, fill the pot with hot water from the tea-kettle; serve with nice drawn butter, flavored with celery, parsley, lemon-juice, or mint if preferred. The vegetables should be peas, potatoes, celery, and lettuce. The pudding a boiled fruit, or plain, with a third course of fruit.

LAMB CUTLETS.—Trim the slices free from fat, beat up the yolk of egg with rasped bread or crackers, season with pepper and salt, dip in the cutlets and fry in butter gently, until thoroughly done.

To BOIL A LEG OF MUTTON.—Cut off the bone close to the flesh, and nicely trim the knuckle. Pour over it milk boiling hot, and let it lay until the milk is cold. Cover it with cold water in the stewpan, add salt, and simmer gently until done. Remove the scum as fast as it rises to the surface of the water. It will take from two to two and a half hours to boil. Serve with boiled turnips, onions, potatoes, and caper sauce; if the caper sauce is not to be had, make a sauce of drawn butter flavored with celery.

To BOIL A NECK OF MUTTON.—Boil it with the skin on, after it has soaked in hot milk and water. Remove the skin before it is served. Make a sauce of drawn butter and celery.

STEWED LOIN OF MUTTON TO RESEMBLE VENISON.—Take out the bones and boil them for the gravy. Season the fat and lean before rolling up. In every other respect, proceed as in Stewed Venison. Add to the gravy mushroom catsup, whether the wine is used or not, and thicken with butter and flour. Serve with onions, parsnips, turnips, and potatoes.

To ROAST A HAUNCH OF MUTTON.—Have a brisk fire. Soak the haunch in hot milk and water, rinse off the milk and wipe it dry. Rub it over with salt, pepper, and butter, then cover it entirely with paper, baste frequently, and half an hour before serving remove the paper, and brown the roast. Prepare a nice gravy of the juices of the mutton. Serve with sour jellies of any kind, cauliflower or cabbage boiled to imitate cauliflower, onions, squash, turnips, and potatoes. The dessert should be delicate.

BROILED MUTTON CHOPS.—Cut the chops from the loin, or best part of the neck, trim them, and remove a part of the fat, pepper lightly, and broil over a clear fire, turning them often until quite done.

Have a platter over hot water, dish the chops, and lay on them bits of butter, add a spoonful or two of boiling water, in which is dissolved a little salt, and serve immediately.

FRIED MUTTON CHOPS.—Prepare the chops, season with pepper and salt, and fry gently in pork fat, turning them very often. When done, remove them to a hot platter, cleanse the platter, brown a little butter and flour, add a little water, and pour the gravy over the chops.

To BOIL A FILLET OF VEAL.—Remove the bone, and fill the cavity with a dressing of bread and butter, seasoned with salt and pepper, but not moistened, crowd it as closely as possible, and sew it firmly, so that none of the dressing can escape. Boil, and skim the water, then put in the veal, and keep the water to within twelve degrees of boiling until tender. (*See* USES OF THERMOMETER IN THE KITCHEN.) Remove all the scum that rises to the surface. When done, strain some of the gravy, season and enrich it with butter, and thicken with a little flour. Sweet cream may be used, in place of butter, flavored with mushroom powder or the catsup. Egg sauce is also fine with veal; beat the yolks of two eggs, and stir them into the veal gravy, after it is taken from the fire, and the butter and flour added to it. The sauce must not boil after the egg is added.

To ROAST A FILLET OF VEAL.—Fill the space, from which the bone is removed, with a dressing of bread and butter seasoned with pepper and salt, and moistened with water or sweet milk. Roast thoroughly, and baste with water and melted butter, seasoned with a little pepper, and salt frequently. Make a gravy of the drippings. Serve with potatoes mashed, squash, and pickles. For dessert a whortleberry or blackberry pudding, or pie.

LOIN OF VEAL.—To ROAST.—Roast as a fillet, with or without stuffing. Cover the fat with paper.

To ROAST A BREAST OF VEAL.—Cut off the thin end, and roast until thoroughly done. Baste constantly, or the skin will become hard and dry. Toast bread, and lay it under the kidneys. Make a gravy of melted butter, and pour over the whole breast. Serve with peas, cauliflower, squash, turnips, and potatoes.

To ROAST A SHOULDER OF VEAL.—Take off the knuckle just above the joint, fill the loose skin with dressing, and bind or skewer it down.

Roast thoroughly, and baste frequently; serve with the gravy of the roast, browned and thickened.

BREAST OF VEAL WITH OYSTER SAUCE.—Rub the veal all over with salt and pepper. Cover it with buttered paper, and then with coarse paste, baste frequently, to prevent the paper and paste from burning; half an hour before serving, remove the paste and paper. Beat the white of an egg, add a very little loaf sugar, and wet the veal with the egg and sugar, without leaving any lumps of the glazing, and brown it nicely. Prepare a drawn butter with oysters, and serve the sauce in a tureen. This sauce can be used with roast or boiled veal, to good advantage, if oysters are plenty. Serve with mashed potatoes, and celery.

STEWED VEAL.—Cut the veal in small bits, stew in a little water with butter, pepper, and salt, until tender; thicken with a little flour.

FRICASSEE OF VEAL.—Cut in bits lean veal, and parboil in salted water. Drain off the water, dust the veal with flour and brown in butter; add sufficient of the broth for the gravy to the browned butter, and thicken very little with flour. Toast bread, lay the slices on the platter, lay on each slice a part of the veal, and pour the gravy over the whole. Serve with mashed potatoes.

VEAL CUTLETS.—Trim free from fat, slices of nice veal, beat up the yolks of eggs, and mix in rolled cracker or rasped bread, and season with pepper and salt; roll the cutlets in the preparation, and fry gently in butter, without burning, until thoroughly cooked. Serve with the oiled butter remaining in the spider.

VEAL PIE.—Prepare a plain paste, cover a deep plate with it, set it in the oven until baked. Have ready veal that has been parboiled, cut in small bits, lay the meat on the crust, until it is evenly full, put in each pie a piece of butter as large as the bowl of a tablespoon, broken in small bits, a little salt and pepper, a spoonful of flour, and a little of the broth in which the veal was boiled. Put on the top crust, which should be made rather richer than the bottom, and rolled thin, Bake immediately in a quick oven. Serve with potatoes, and any other dressed vegetables; sponge-cake, or any other cake pudding is a proper dessert.

VEAL POT-PIE.—Boil the veal, and proceed exactly as directed in chicken pot-pie.

To Boil Calf's Head.—Split the head in two parts, and remove the brains, wash the brains in three waters, and lay them for an hour in cold salted water. Wash the head clean, and soak it in tepid water, until the blood is well drawn out. Put it in cold water; when it boils remove the scum, and simmer gently, until a straw can be run through it. A head with the skin will take three hours, if large, and without the skin two. Scald the brains, by pouring over them boiling water, take them out and remove the skin or film, put them in plenty of cold water, and simmer gently fifteen minutes. Chop them slightly, stew them in sweet butter; add a teaspoon half full of lemon-juice, or not, as desired, and a little salt; when done, skin the tongue, lay it in the centre of the dish, and the brains round it. Send the head to the table very hot, with drawn butter poured over it, and more in the tureen.

To Stew Calf's Head.—After it is boiled tender, remove all the bone without disfiguring the head, season with Cayenne or black pepper, salt, and if relished, nutmeg; most persons not accustomed to French cookery, dislike spices in meats and fish. Fry gently in sweet butter until slighty browned, then make a gravy of the liquor enriched with sweet butter, and thickened very little with flour. In the mean time, prepare the brains after they are boiled in the following manner: mash and season them with pepper and salt, or with whatever the head is seasoned with, beat the yolks of one or two eggs, mix them with flour, and stir them into the brains; incorporate the egg and brain into one mass, make it in balls, brown them in butter, and serve the balls with the head.

Hashed Calf's Head.—After it is boiled well, but not as tender as it could be made by very long boiling, remove the bones from half of the head, cover it with yolk of egg and bread crumbs, and brown it before the fire; slice the remainder of the head, after peeling the tongue. Put a pint of the gravy in which the head was boiled in a pan, with oyster liquor, salt, and Cayenne, and, if relished, an onion and a glass of sherry. The two latter can be omitted. Boil these ingredients a few moments, and strain it on the meat, having previously dredged it with flour. The addition of mushrooms, and two spoons of catsup, will improve the dish. Beat half of the brains with flour, add it to the hash, and simmer all together; garnish the dish with balls composed of yolks of egg, and the other half of the brain, fried oysters, and force-meat balls.

CALF'S BRAINS.—After removing all the large fibers and skin, soak them from four to five hours in water, lay them in boiling water with a little salt and vinegar in it, afterwards soak them in a strong white vinegar, a solution of citric acid, or lemon-juice. Dry them well, dip them in nice butter, and fry slowly in butter until done, and nicely browned. Serve with drawn butter, or a sour sauce.

CALF'S FEET AND EARS.—Boil tender, and serve with drawn butter. These can be fricasseed, if desired.

CALF'S KIDNEY.—Chop calf's kidneys after being boiled tender, season with pepper and salt, and serve as hash, or make it in balls with egg, and fry them in butter.

CALF'S LIGHTS AND LIVERS.—Parboil and chop them, season with pepper and salt, and stew them with butter.

SWEETBREADS.—Trim them carefully, soak them first in cold water to extract the blood, and afterwards put them in boiling water to blanch them. Boil and serve with drawn butter or lard, and roast them till thoroughly done, and serve on toast with a nice veal gravy, or slice thin, dip them in egg, and fry in butter until well done, and nicely browned.

CHAPTER VI.

POULTRY AND GAME.

TO DRESS FOWLS FOR MARKET.—Give no food for twenty-four hours. Instead of wringing or cutting off the neck, stick it with a penknife. If the head is cut off, the skin recedes and looks revolting. Pick them immediately, without scalding, and carefully remove all pinfeathers, particularly from the legs and neck. Do not tear the skin in removing the feathers; singe, and then draw the intestines; cut off the head; draw the skin above the neck bone and tie it. Have ready water nearly boiling hot. Rinse out the fowls, wipe them dry, and then plump them, by dipping them two seconds and no more in the hot water, and then immediately into cold (if ice-water so much the better) for the same length of time.

TO TRUSS FOWLS AND GAME.—To truss a fowl for roasting, draw

the skin over the bone of the neck, which should be cut close to the body, leaving the skin much longer than the neck bone. Break the back bone and the two leading to the pinions. Cut off the first joint of the legs, turn them down close to the sides towards the vent, and fasten them in place by a game skewer passed from one to the other. Place the gizzard under one wing and the liver under the other, and fasten the wings close to the body with a slender skewer passing through the joint of one wing and through the body and opposite wing.

To Truss a Fowl for Boiling.—Cut off all the leg except the thigh; cut a slit in the apron, or fat skin covering the belly of the fowl, and tuck in the ends of the bone. Stuff the breast out very plump; tie down the neck, and fasten the wings, gizzard, and liver as directed in roast fowls.

To Truss Fowls in French Style.—Make a hole above the joint of the leg, and skewer the claws into the body. Pass a string from the head to the skewers, draw the chicken in shape, and remove the string and skewers before serving. The claws, when left on fowls, should always be *skinned*, and the toes cut off.

To Truss Woodcocks, Snipes, and all Birds Living by Suction.—Remove the feathers with great care, as the skin is easily broken. Do not draw them; the trail is considered the most delicate part of the bird. Wipe them carefully; tuck the head under the wing; bend the knees, and fasten them in place with a skewer passed through the body.

To Truss Moor Fowls.—Truss the same as a domestic fowl, except the head and feet; tuck the head under the wing; and lay the bill close to the body; bend the knees, fasten them with skewers; cross the feet at the tail end, and fasten them in place. The feet should be skinned, and the toes removed.

To Truss Partridges.—Turn the head under the wing; bend the knees; pass a skewer through the body; put the liver and gizzard under the wings; cross the feet in front, and fasten them at the first joint of the leg.

To Truss Pigeons.—Prepare them exactly as partridges. Pick the head clean, or remove it entirely.

To Truss Canvas-back Duck.—Truss the same as the domestic fowl, except the head, which is tucked under the left wing.

To Truss Reed Birds.—Pick and draw them carefully without breaking the skin; fasten the wings and legs in place with skewers.

To Truss Wild Duck.—Proceed in exactly the same manner as directed to dress and truss poultry.

To Truss a Goose.—Proceed as in the directions for turkey, except that the liver, legs, heart, and most of the neck, are boiled together to make a giblet sauce.

To Prepare Hares and Rabbits.—Remove the entrails as soon as dead, and the skin just before cooking. Epicures keep them until the fibre begins to soften before dressing. The inside of the body must be kept dry, and it is well to dust it with pepper and salt. To skin them proceed in the following manner: Cut off the legs at the first joint, raise the skin on the back, draw it over the hind legs, and strip it from the tail, then slip it over the fore legs, and cut it away from the head and neck, leaving the ears on the head as perfect as possible. Wash them well, dry with a towel inside and out, and proceed to truss them. Cut the sinews of the hind legs, turn them towards the head, and fasten them to the sides of the hare or rabbit; then turn the fore legs to meet the hind legs, and fasten both with skewers. The head is crowded a little back, and fastened in place with skewers. The body is filled with dressing, the skin sewed up, and the whole bound firmly in shape with a string; the skewers and string must be removed after it is on the platter before sending the dish to the table.

To Truss Blackbirds and other Small Birds.—Pick them carefully; cut off the head, leaving the neck long; bend the neck bone, draw over it the skin, and fasten it under the left wing, with a small skewer; stuff the birds, sew them up, and fasten the legs the same as a partridge.

To Boil a Fowl, No. 1.—Boil a pound of fat salt pork for half an hour after changing the water the last time, then put in a fowl with the pork, boil gently until tender, and serve with plain drawn butter.

Boiled Fowl, No. 2.—After the fowl is prepared, fill the body with a dressing of bread crumbs, seasoned with pepper, salt, and butter. Put it in just enough water to cover it well, and stew gently until tender; serve with drawn butter.

Boiled Fowl, No. 3.—Boil the liver, gizzard, heart, and lower part of the legs, in very little water. Chop them fine, mix them with drawn butter and bread crumbs; season with pepper, salt, and summer-savory. Stuff the fowl, truss properly, and boil as above; serve with drawn butter.

SUPERIOR BOILED FOWLS, No. 4.—Stew a pint of oysters in their own juice, mix them with half a pint of drawn butter; soak dry bread in sweet cream until soft, and season it with butter, pepper, and salt; mix the bread and oysters well together, and fill the fowl. Tuck the liver under one and the gizzard under the other wing, and boil gently in veal stock until tender; serve with oyster sauce.

STEAMED FOWLS.—Fowls are better steamed than boiled, especially when there is no veal stock on hand to boil them in. When steamed, the juices should be saved by placing a pan under the strainer to catch all the drips. Drawn butter, plain or seasoned with parsley or celery, is the most common sauce used for boiled fowls. Liver sauce is good; but when oysters can be had, oyster sauce is to be preferred above all others.

BOILED TURKEY.—Turkey is boiled in much the same manner as the fowl. A large turkey will take two hours to boil, if tender; if old, it must have more time. If steamed, allow three hours. A tough turkey will be better boiled than steamed or roasted. The vegetables served with boiled fowls should be potatoes and turnips mashed, and boiled onions. The relishes, celery, sour pickles, jellies, or cranberries. The pudding should be boiled, and the sauce decided to give variety. Fruit would form a nice and appropriate third course.

TO BOIL A GOOSE.—After it is well dressed, singe it thoroughly. Put it in a deep dish, and cover it with boiling milk until morning. Early in the morning wash off the milk, and put the goose into a large kettle of cold water; let it remain until nearly or quite boiling hot; it must not cook or you cannot truss it. This is done to remove the strong taste of the oil; wash it again in warm water, and dry it with a towel. Have ready a dressing prepared as for BOILED FOWL, No. 2, with the addition of two finely-chopped onions, a little sage, and more pepper than would be used for turkey. Fill the body, and close it firmly; put it in cold water, and boil gently an hour, if tender; if not, longer; serve with giblet sauce. The onion can be omitted if not relished. For a goose the relishes should be decided; sour pickles, plain sour apples stewed without sugar, or acid jellies, are the most proper; beets, turnip, and cauliflower, are proper vegetables.

To Roast a Fowl.—Having nicely dressed the fowl, have ready a dressing seasoned with pepper, salt, and summer-savory; fill the body of the bird, sew up the opening, truss it nicely, oil it with butter, and put it before a moderately hot, but bright fire; heat the skin evenly as soon as possible, cover it with paper if there is the least danger of its browning too soon, roast pretty fast without scorching the first half hour, and baste the fowl all over every five minutes; after this let it roast steadily, but rather slowly, three-quarters of an hour, when, if young and tender, it will be done quite through. Stick a fork through the breast and thighs, and if the fluid which follows the fork is entirely free from blood, it is done. If not browned, replenish the fire, wet the fowl over with very little yolk of egg, dust it lightly with flour, and let it brown evenly all over. Remove the skewers and strings before sending it to the table.

To Bake a Fowl.—Prepare a fowl as for roasting; have the oven of good but not a raging heat; you should be able to count twenty slowly, while holding your hand in the oven. Lay the fowl on skewers if you have no hooks to hang it by in the oven; baste every five minutes, and manage the same as the roast. If young, it will bake in one hour.

To Roast a Turkey.—Proceed as directed in roast fowls; allow from two and a half to three hours for a good-sized tender turkey. The dressings of fowls can be varied by using oysters, &c. (See the chapter on Gravies and Sauces.)

To Bake a Turkey.—Follow the directions for baking fowls, and allow from two to two and a half hours steady baking for a common-sized young turkey; serve with a browned gravy. All roast fowls should be served with dressed vegetables, currant, grape, or cranberry jelly, and a baked pudding or pie.

To Roast a Goose.—Having prepared a goose as already directed for boiling, truss it nicely, and put it before a moderate fire. Let it lose all the oil it will, and baste it with a preparation in another dish of browned butter, salt, pepper, a little water, a teaspoon of the extract of sage and summer-savory. If not offensive, add a drop or two of garlic. (*See* Extracts of Herbs.) Keep the drippings separate from the bastings until nearly done, when the basting-pan may be set underneath the goose. In making the gravy use the basting, or make a fresh gravy of browned butter flavored with the extracts or not, as desired. If no extracts are used, add a little lemon juice to the sauce. Geese are so strong as to require additional seasoning to overcome their natural flavor.

NATURAL ROAST GOOSE.—Scald the goose in milk, and let it lay all night; stuff it with a dressing seasoned with sage, pepper, salt, summer-savory, and, if not disliked, half an onion. Roast slowly; baste with prepared gravy of browned butter, a little water and pepper, and make a gravy of the bastings without using the drippings, or port wine gravy, seasoned with mustard, salt, Cayenne, browned butter, and slightly thickened with the yolk of an egg. Serve with hot slaw, dressed potatoes, boiled onions, and dressed turnips.

GREEN GOOSE ROASTED.—Put in the inside sage, onions, salt, Cayenne, and butter; roast well; baste with butter, and brown; serve with a nice rich gravy.

TO ROAST MOOR FOWLS.—After they are dressed and singed, fill their bodies with bread crumbs, seasoned with pepper, salt, and butter, sew up the opening, and truss them as already directed; hang them before a clear but not fierce fire, and roast until done through, basting frequently. Young birds will roast in three-fourths of an hour, and a full-grown bird will take from fifty to sixty minutes; serve with a brown gravy, currant jelly, and dressed potatoes.

TO ROAST A PARTRIDGE.—Prepare the bird and roast it in every respect as the moor fowl. When quite done, remove it from the fire; game is ruined if overdone. A young partridge will roast in from twenty to twenty-five minutes, and an old one may take forty minutes.

TO ROAST A PHEASANT.—To roast a pheasant proceed exactly as in roasting a moor fowl; allow from forty to fifty minutes for a full-grown pheasant; serve with browned gravy, acid jelly, and dressed potatoes.

TO ROAST WOODCOCK.—Pick out the gall and gizzard, but do not remove the remainder of the trail. This is not usually done, but as this part of the intestines are filled with pebbles and sand it is better to do so. Toast bread, and lay a slice under each bird, to catch the drippings of the trail, which is considered the best part of the bird. Baste with butter, brown nicely, roast from twenty to twenty-five minutes, and serve with currant jelly.

To ROAST A PRAIRIE CHICKEN.—Dress and truss as a partridge, roast before a clear fire half an hour, baste often, and serve with brown gravy, currant jelly, and dressed potatoes.

To ROAST WILD DUCK.—Stuff it with bread moistened with water, seasoned with butter, pepper, salt, sage, and chopped onions. Truss properly (*see* To TRUSS DUCK), and put it to roast before a clear fire; baste frequently with butter, leave in the dripping-pan a piece of butter, roast brown, serve with rich brown gravy of butter, or a port wine sour sauce, (*see* SAUCES,) or the red gravy from the duck. Or, after the duck is nearly done, carve it, put the pieces in a porcelain stew-pan, cover the meat with the gravy, cover tight, and set the stew-pan ten minutes in a kettle of boiling water; keep the water boiling until the duck is removed; lay it in order on the platter, add the gravy, and serve very hot. The relishes for duck should be decided; if a jelly is used, let it be tart; if apples, very sour, stewed plain without sugar; dress onions, turnips, and potatoes.

To ROAST A CANVAS-BACK DUCK.—Dress and stuff it with a nice dressing of bread, butter, sage, and a little onion. Roast before a brisk fire, baste with butter, serve with its own gravy, or a sauce made with port wine, etc. (*See* SAUCES.)

To ROAST QUAIL, BLACK AND ALL OTHER SMALL BIRDS.—Pick them with great care, and draw them so as to leave all the fat in the bodies of the birds, wash and dry them nicely. Stuff them with bread moistened with melted butter and very little water, seasoned with pepper and salt. Truss them nicely, and fasten the wings and legs in place with very small skewers; roast or bake them fifteen or twenty minutes, basting frequently. Toast some nice bread quickly on both sides without burning, make up the gravy from the drippings; soak the toast; lay the slices in order on the platter, allowing half a slice to each bird, remove the skewers and strings; set a bird on each half slice of toast, and dip the gravy over them; serve hot. When the birds are roasted without stuffing, they will cook in from ten to fifteen minutes.

To ROAST SNIPE.—Snipes are roasted like woodcock, but require seven minutes less time to roast; serve with jelly and a rich gravy flavored with lemon, or port wine if desired.

To ROAST WIDGEONS AND TEALS.—Roast exactly like wild ducks, but in much less time.

ROASTED HARE.—After the hare is dressed, parboil the liver, and then boil it with a slice of fat ham until quite tender; then mash it fine; soak bread in milk, mix the liver with the bread, add a quarter of a pound of butter, sweet marjoram, Cayenne pepper, black pepper, salt, and the ham chopped fine; mix the ingredients well, fill the body of the hare, and sew it up. Truss the hare. (*See* To TRUSS HARE AND RABBIT.) When the hare is first put before the fire, baste with boiled milk half an hour; then remove the milk, and baste with butter until done. Just before it is done froth with butter and flour; this is done by merely dredging the whole surface with flour, and immediately basting with fresh hot butter. A common-sized hare roasts in an hour and a half. Serve with nice drawn butter or brown gravy, and melted currant or cranberry jelly.

To ROAST RABBITS.—Prepare them exactly like hare. Boil the liver, chop it, mix it with the gravy, and season with parsley if relished. The foundation of the gravy should be drawn butter; serve the gravy in a tureen. A rabbit, if young, will roast in from thirty to forty minutes; an old rabbit in from fifty to sixty; they will bake ten minutes sooner than roast. The hare and rabbit both being very dry, will be improved by the basting of milk; it should not be omitted. Hares, rabbits, and roast pigs look pretty on the table laid on a bed of double curled parsley, the stems all under the body, and the leaves entirely covering the platter; cut flowers from beets, turnips, and carrots, and lay on the parsley; roses, lilies, morning glories, and spiderwort are very easily imitated.

To BOIL RABBITS.—Soak them in warm water ten minutes, stuff and truss them as already directed; put them in cold water and boil very gently; if young and small they will require half an hour, if large three-fourths of an hour to boil. Pour over the rabbit drawn butter, and send some to the table in a tureen.

To BROIL A FOWL.—The fire should be clear but not scorching, the gridiron several inches from the coals, and rubbed over with the oil of the fowl, a small bit of which should be reserved for the purpose. Split the fowl down the back-bone, roll it to break down the breast bone, dust it slightly with salt and pepper, place it on the gridiron before it is hot, merely warm enough to melt the oil in greasing. Put the chicken on the gridiron breast down, and let it broil very slow. Cover the gridiron entirely with a shallow pan, and put a weight on the top to press the fowl to the bars; as soon as it has browned a little take it up, dip the side broiled, in butter, pepper, and salt, melted but not oiled over hot water. Turn the juice, if there is any standing on the fowl, into the gravy, turn the chicken over, broil slowly until nearly done, then turn it; dip on to it a little of the gravy, and broil gently until done. It takes full half an hour to broil a chicken well; if hurried it will be worthless, either half done or burned bitter. When done, dip it in the gravy both sides; add two table-spoons of boiling water to the dish, mix it with the butter, and serve hot with mashed potatoes and cold slaw. If you can broil one fowl well, you can broil all birds, whether domestic or wild.

To ROAST PIGEONS.—Pigeons are usually seasoned with chopped parsley, but they may be stuffed and roasted to suit the taste. If scalded in milk, the flavor will be improved and the flesh will not be as dry as it will without.

To BROIL QUAILS.—A quail is better broiled than roasted, boiled, or fried. Broil a quail exactly like a chicken, and serve with toast.

To BOIL A PRAIRIE CHICKEN, PARTRIDGE, OR PHEASANT.—Broil either exactly as you would a chicken, but very slow, so as not to burn.

To MAKE A PIGEON OR QUAIL PIE.—Cover the pudding baker with puff paste. (*See* PUFF PASTE.) Parboil the birds until nearly done. Cut them through the back or leave them whole, as suits the fancy; place the birds in the pie breast to back if whole, and flat, with the skin side down, if cut; sprinkle over pepper, salt, a dust of flour, and add for ten quails a teacup of butter. If the pie takes more than one layer of birds, divide the butter equally between the layers, and add flour, pepper, and salt to each layer. Pour in as much of the broth in which the birds were boiled as the dish will hold, if it is a quail pie; if a pigeon, use veal or chicken soup, or water with more butter. Put over the top crust, cut a gash in the top, and bake it in a brisk though not over-hot oven; cover the paste with paper before it commences to brown, to keep it white while baking.

CHICKEN PIE.—This is made as above, except the chicken is cut at each joint before it is parboiled. To make a chicken pie extra nice, cut the meat from the bones, boil the livers and hearts, mash them, put them in the gravy, and bake the pie in a dish not deeper than a large soup-plate. Oysters mixed with the chicken makes a delightful pie.

CHICKEN OR ANY BIRD POT-PIE.—Cut the chickens at each joint, and boil until tender; prepare a crust as directed in biscuits made of hop yeast. (*See* Part III. Chap. X.) When the chicken is half done, take the dough, which should be light for the third time, including the sponge, to the paste board. Cover the board with plenty of flour, roll out the dough with the pin, about one-eighth of an inch thick, cut it in cakes about three inches square; separate them from each other so that they will not run together to form one mass in rising, and let them remain in a warm place until wanted. When the chicken is nearly tender, season the broth, add butter, and thicken a little with flour stirred first in cold water; after a few moments skim out all the chicken into another kettle, and all the gravy except sufficient to reach one inch above the place where the fire comes in contact with the pot. Turn a plate of the right size to fit the pot below the rim which sets on the stove in the bottom of the kettle, put in the biscuit dough when very light, while the water boils, piece by piece, as quickly as possible, being careful not to let the cakes touch each other when first dropped in; (the biscuit will not adhere if they are slightly scalded before they come in contact;) as soon as the dough is in the pot, close the cover tightly and boil gently, without crowding the fire, thirty minutes, when it will be ready to dish; do not lift the cover unless you think it is in danger of scorching from the evaporation of the gravy. Keep the chicken and gravy simmering on the stove until the crust is boiled. If the crust should become light too soon for the dinner hour, knead it thoroughly and keep it cool until time to make into cakes. If pot-pie is made in this manner it will never be heavy.

To FRY CHICKENS OR OTHER BIRDS.—Joint a chicken; melt in a spider sweet butter, rub the fowl with salt and pepper, and fry as slowly as possible without either drying or burning the fowl.

COLD FOWL.—Cold fowls are always palatable, cold or warmed over.

FRICASSEE OF FOWLS BROWN.—Boil as for pot-pie. Then fry slowly in butter until browned, toast bread, lay it on the platter under the chicken. Pour a little of the broth in the spider with the browned butter, thicken with flour, season to suit, and pour it over the chicken; or, if you want it very nice, add the butter for the gravy to the butter in which the chicken was browned, dredge with flour, add salt and pepper, brown well, and, lastly, add the chicken broth.

WHITE FRICASSEE OF CHICKEN.—All the difference there is from the above is, that the chicken is not browned; the gravy is thickened with flour and is left white. It is the poorest manner of cooking fowls.

CHAPTER VII.

VEGETABLES—PRESERVATION, HERMETICALLY SEALING, AND COOKING.

ARTICHOKES.—Artichokes are first boiled till tender, in clear water with a little salt, and served with drawn butter, or browned after boiling in butter, and served with brown butter gravy.

ASPARAGUS.—Use it as soon as possible after cutting; there are several ways of cooking this, each of which is good. Discard all not brittle enough to break easily, tie it in small bunches, and boil it in very little water, slightly salted, until tender; take off the strings, put it in a covered dish, add butter to the water sufficient to make a rich gravy, and thicken it with very little flour, and pour the gravy over the asparagus; be careful to lay the heads all one way.

ASPARAGUS SOUP.—Cut the asparagus in pieces a half-inch long, boil in water with a little salt, and add rich sweet cream to thicken the soup.

ASPARAGUS TOAST.—Tie the stalks in small bunches, boil them in very little salted water until tender; toast as many slices of bread as there are bunches of asparagus, butter them while hot, lay a bunch on each slice of toast, add a little butter to the water, and pour it over the whole.

ASPARAGUS GREENS.—Boil the stalks with a slice of salt pork, in barely water enough to cover them, so that, when tender, there will be scarcely any left. Drain it and serve with vinegar; this is an excellent green, but it will be found too expensive, unless grown by the consumer.

To HERMETICALLY SEAL ASPARAGUS IN CANS.—*Directions from the French.*—First dip the asparagus into water while boilling, and immediately after into cold water. Pack the stalks in the jars or cans head down, without water or seasoning, seal tightly, and let them remain in the bath until the water boils. (*See* WATER BATH FOR PUTTING UP FRUITS.) The writer has no personal experience in regard to this rule. It may prove a good recipe. If the can is drawn in at the ends, it is probably perfect, though not positively certain. Cans often burst after laying months apparently perfect. Mark each can with Nitrate of Silver. (*See* HERMETICALLY-SEALED CAN.)

To BOIL BEETS.—Beets must not be cut before boiling, as the juice will escape, and the sweetness of the vegetable be lost. Select small-sized smooth roots, wash them nicely, and boil them in clear water until tender. When sufficiently cooked, skim them into a pan of cold water, and slip off the outside; cut them in thin slices, and while hot season with butter, salt, a little pepper and sharp vinegar, and serve hot. They can be sliced lengthwise, and put in strong vinegar to use cold. Beets soon kill vinegar; it should, therefore, be very strong.

BEET GREENS.—Young beets the size of a pencil, make, with the exception of asparagus, the best greens; the leaves must be examined for fear of insects, and well washed; boil with salt pork, beef, or ham; the latter is preferable; drain free from water, and serve with vinegar. They may be boiled without pork, and buttered.

BOILED BEANS.—Soak over night any small white beans in soft water, put them in a strong bag, leaving room to swell; let them boil in a potful of water, until done; hang them up to let all the water drain off, and season with butter, pepper, and salt, to the taste.

STEWED BEANS.—Soak them over night in soft water; put them, after breakfast, in enough water to cover them; when it boils, skim out the beans, empty the water, and put them on again; proceed as before; and in the next water, parboil a piece of salt pork, according to the quantity of beans, say a pound to one quart of beans; when this water has boiled ten minutes, change it again, and boil the pork and beans together until tender; the water should all be evaporated before dishing the beans.

BAKED BEANS.—These are prepared as above, and then set in the oven in a dripping-pan, to brown. Most persons lay the pork in the middle of the beans to crisp; but a better plan is to bake it on a separate dish. The pork should be nicely gashed before baking.

DRIED LIMA BEANS.—Soak in soft water over night, if wanted by noon; but if for a late dinner, only from early morning; drain off the soft water, and boil gently, without bursting, in water in which a little salt has been dissolved; when tender, drain them, and stew gently in sweet butter or cream, without scorching.

WINDSOR BEANS.—When young, boil until tender, and serve with butter, pepper, salt, and chopped parsley if relished. When old, boil until the outside skin slips off, after which boil until tender; mash fine, season with butter, pepper, and salt.

STRING BEANS.—Gather them while young enough to break crispy; break off both ends, and string them; break in halves, and boil in water with a little salt, until tender; drain free from water, and season with butter.

TO PRESERVE STRING BEANS FOR WINTER.—Gather them when just right for cooking, wash clean, and fill the can with beans without crowding; fill nearly full with soft water, seal the can, and cook until you are sure the beans are well done; then seal the small hole as directed for can fruit. It is, however, a very difficult matter to put these up, as experience has fully shown to the writer, yet she has succeeded, though sometimes failing.

BROCCOLI.—Soak an hour in salt water, then boil in a little water until half done, after which, add as much milk as water, and finish cooking; cut it up, and season with butter, salt, and pepper, or serve whole with vinegar.

EARLY YORK CABBAGE.—Early York is the best of all cabbages; it can be cooked like Broccoli, if desired, and is nearly as good.

BOILED CABBAGE.—Examine each leaf to see there are no insects, and boil in clear water without salt until tender; drain off all the water, put it in a deep dish, and with a round pointed knife chop it in small pieces; season with butter, salt, and a trifle of pepper.

CABBAGE BOILED WITH MEAT.—Select for boiling, small white cabbages with firm heads; cut the heads in quarters, and examine carefully that there is no vermin lodged in them, lay them for an hour in salted water to draw out any that may have escaped observation; skim the fat from the pot, and put in the cabbage while the water boils; drain well before serving; leave it as whole as possible. Should the meat be wanted cold, take some of the liquor from the pot to boil the cabbage, filling the pot with boiling water, as the cabbage imparts a disagreeable flavor to meat when cold.

HOT SLAW.—Cut cabbage in fine shreds, boil in clear water until perfectly tender, allowing so little, that when it is cooked sufficiently there will be scarcely none left in the spider; just before dishing, add to a common sized spiderful, a teacup of sharp vinegar, a piece of butter half the size of a common hen's egg, a little salt, and a dust of pepper; the latter can be added at the table if desired. Many persons dislike pepper, therefore as little as will answer had better generally be used in all cookery. Dish in extra plates at the table.

COLD SLAW.—Cut the cabbage very fine, dissolve in a cup of vinegar a teaspoonful of sugar, the same of salt, add a little pepper; pour it over the cabbage, and add another half cup of vinegar.

CHICKEN SALAD.—Chicken salad can be made with cabbage without celery; if the flavor of celery is desired, add extract to the taste. (*See* CELERY.)

CAULIFLOWER.—Soak the head two hours in salt water, and cook until tender in milk and water; drain, and serve whole with drawn butter; this makes the best appearance, but it will be found to suit the taste better cut up and seasoned richly with butter and a little salt and pepper. In either case it must be well drained.

CARROTS.—Boil and season as directed in boiled beets, or boil and serve with drawn butter. They can also be jammed, when they somewhat resemble squash. They are used in soups cut in small pieces. Stewed, and treated as pumpkins, they make an excellent pie, hardly discernible from pumpkin.

CELERY.—Dress it nicely, leaving on the green stems. It is also used in compounding salads.

CHICKEN SALAD, No. 1.—Boil, until tender, two nice fowls; take the best part of a small cabbage, discarding all the pith or green, chop it finely—there should be less than a quart when chopped; chop well blanched celery free from rust, say four large bunches; the celery should not be quite as fine as the cabbage; there should be about half as much celery as cabbage; when more is used, diminish the quantity of cabbage; pick the fowls in small pieces of a half-inch each, leaving out the black meat or not, as desired; it looks better out; mix the chicken, cabbage, and celery together. Boil four eggs one hour. (*See* BOILED EGGS.) Take out the yolks, and work them with a wooden spoon until they form a paste. If you can procure the best of sweet oil fresh, take half a gill—if not, a gill of melted butter; mix a little at a time with the egg until all is mixed, add a table-spoonful of superior black pepper, sifted through a fine bolting cloth sieve, and two table-spoonfuls of mixed mustard, (*see* MUSTARD,) stir this in the paste, then add a teacup of strong vinegar, half as much grated horseradish, and a table-spoonful of salt. Mix the sauce into the cabbage, etc., a half-hour before serving. It is always well to mix a little before for tasting; as there is such a difference in the strength of spices and vinegar, there may need some alteration to suit the taste.

CURLED CRESS.—Wash clean, and lay on a dish; let each season to suit themselves, at table.

CORN.—The sweet is the most desirable variety of corn for the table, when used in the green state. It should be gathered when quite young, before it begins to glaze, and be cooked soon after, as it not only loses flavor but becomes unhealthy by long keeping. Boil only long enough to cook through; every moment's exposure to heat after this is accomplished only hardens it, besides extracting its sweetness. To boil on the cob, all that is necessary is to throw the corn, after husking and silking, into boiling water for about fifteen minutes, allowing five for the cooling of the water and ten for boiling the corn.

CORN: AN EXCELLENT METHOD.—Cut the corn from the cobs, have ready just enough water to cover the corn, throw in the cobs and let them boil until within fifteen minutes of the time to serve dinner. Remove the cobs, and stir in the corn; let it come to a boil, which will take about five minutes. After it has boiled for ten minutes, add butter, salt, and pepper, if relished.

CORN, No. 2.—Proceed as above. When the corn is ready to dish, stir into a quart of corn a pint of rich, sweet cream, that is not old enough to curdle, add a little salt but no pepper.

CORN, No. 3.—Cook corn in its own juice slowly for fear of burning. The best method to do this is to set the pan or kettle containing it over steam. It will take a half-hour to cook, and must be kept tightly covered while steaming; this is superior to the others, but takes more time; season with fresh butter or cream; if the latter, add salt.

GREEN CORN CAKES.—Grate the corn; make a rich batter with cream, or according to directions given for batter cakes. Use just enough of the batter to hold the corn together, and lay the cakes on the griddle, as you would a common griddle-cake; serve with butter.

CORN MUFFINS.—Prepare as above, baking the muffins by setting the pan containing the rings in the oven; serve with butter.

CORN OYSTERS.—Grate the corn; to every pint take three well beaten eggs, sufficient flour to make the corn hold together in the shape of fried oysters. Season with pepper and salt, and brown on a griddle until cooked through; serve with butter. They must be quite flat, or they will not get thoroughly cooked.

SUCCOTASH, OR CORN AND BEANS.—If old beans are used, they must be soaked over night, and parboiled in two waters before putting in the pork. (*See* STEWED BEANS.) The corn should be added to the beans and pork about fifteen minutes before the hour for serving the dinner. It is well to boil the cobs with the beans and pork in the last water. Remove them before adding the corn. For using beans not fully ripe, one change of water is sufficient; the pork can be parboiled at the same time. Beans for succotash should remain whole; care must be taken that they boil gently, so as not to break them. Considerable water is generally used in boiling the beans, that no more need be added when the corn is put in; most persons like considerable soup in this dish. Families can be governed by taste in this. Dish the corn and beans in a deep dish with the broth, and season with butter and a very little salt; use no pepper; if any person desires it, it is easily added. Serve the pork on a platter, after taking off the skin and dotting it with pepper, by dipping the little finger in ground pepper and pressing it on the pork.

To PREPARE DRIED CORN FOR SUCCOTASH.—Look it over carefully to see there are no vermin or sour corn among it. Throw it in cold water, and stir it up; pour off the water, and add more, and let it remain soaking until within ten minutes of the dinner hour; then add it to the beans and pork, with the water in which it was soaked.

If boiled it will become very hard; as it has been cooked before drying, it only wants heating through. Add a teaspoonful of loaf sugar to a tureenful of succotash, to give it as much sweetness as green corn. About one-quarter beans and three-quarters corn is a good proportion for this dish, with half a pound of pork to a pint of dried, or a quart of green corn.

DRIED CORN.—Soak as above one hour before dinner, set the pan over steam, and let it simmer in the same water soaked in, which should be only just sufficient to cover it; let it become boiling hot by setting it on the stove three minutes before dishing; season with butter, salt, no pepper, and a very little sugar. Cream can be added if relished.

HERMETICALLY-SEALED CORN.—This is extremely difficult to put up; it cannot be done unless the corn is perfectly fresh, and even then it often fails. It is necessary to boil it, to destroy its fermenting properties. Split the kernels, cut it from the cob, add water, and boil half an hour; then fill the cans within one inch of the top; solder on the caps while hot; test the cans (*see* TESTING CANS); make a small hole in the top with an awl; place them in the bath, and let the cans boil three-fourths of an hour; and stop the hole with solder while in the bath. If perfect, the cans will be drawn in at the end; if swollen, they cannot be saved. The same may be said of peas, asparagus, beans, and pumpkin. All cans should be marked. As convenient a method as any is to write with a sharp-pointed stick dipped in rain water in which a little nitrate of silver is dissolved.

TO DRY SWEET CORN FOR WINTER USE.—Boil, in the after part of the day, until it is heated through, young sweet corn freshly gathered, spread it thinly in some convenient place until morning. As soon as possible, the next morning, cut it from the cobs, and spread it thinly in the sun to dry. If the day is favorable, it will dry so as to be out of danger of souring in one day; if so, take in the corn before the dew falls, and spread it on a table overnight. If, on the contrary, it has dried but little and there is no danger of rain, it will be less likely to sour if left spread in the air all night, than if spread in a close room. It will take three hot, sunny days to dry perfectly, when it must be put in a dry, tin pan, and heated very hot over steam, to destroy any insects' eggs which may have been laid in it. Hang it away, out of the reach of mice, in strong paper bags; there is almost as much danger of vermin in corn as in fruit. There is no corn fit to dry but the old sweet corn, the Stowell is too hard when dry; we speak from experience. There is an early corn perfectly white which is often dried and passed on people as sweet corn. It is so much more prolific, that growers prefer to raise it. It can be told from sweet corn by chewing. The sweet resembles the taste of chestnuts, is soft and easily chewed, while the other is hard and not very sweet.

CUCUMBERS.—Select half-grown cucumbers, peel, and lay them in cold water; just before they are wanted, slice them thinly, and season with salt, pepper, and vinegar.

To FRY CUCUMBERS.—These resemble egg plant, though not as good. Lay them in salt, after they are sliced, fifteen minutes, and fry in pork fat or butter. (*See* PICKLES and CATSUP.)

To COOK EGG PLANT, No. 1.—Select long purple if possible; the next best is the round kind with prickles on the stem. Peel and slice them, spread salt on each separate piece, and lay them in a colander to drain; let them lie one hour, parboil, and fry them, until thoroughly cooked, in pork fat or butter; egg plants, unless well cooked, are insipid, and even disgusting; they must be cooked through and browned.

To COOK EGG PLANT, No. 2.—Parboil, after laying in salt, roll in flour, and fry until thoroughly cooked.

To COOK EGG PLANT, No. 3.—Parboil until tender, dip in nice butter and fry brown.

To COOK EGG PLANT, No. 4.—Omit the laying in salt, boil in water until perfectly tender, make a batter, and beat the plant in it; there must be but little batter, just enough to hold the egg plant together; the cakes should be rather salt, but after the first cake is baked, if not sufficiently seasoned, more can be added; bake on a griddle. These are all excellent methods for cooking this vegetable, and make variety; there is no vegetable as poor as the egg plant when half cooked.

BAKED EGG PLANT.—Leave on the skin, take out the seeds, fill with dressing prepared as for a turkey, sew in the piece taken out, and bake until thoroughly cooked.

Lettuce, Dutch Method.—Heat quite hot pork fat or butter, add a little vinegar, pepper, and salt, and fry the tender leaves of lettuce until entirely wilted.

To Dress Salads for Dinner.—Look over, carefully, the tender half-blanched leaves of head lettuce, cut them slightly; make a dressing of the yolk of hard-boiled eggs, mixed mustard, (*see* Mixing Mustard,) black pepper, butter, and vinegar. Boil two or three eggs more than is needed for the sauce; slice the whites and yolks together, lay them on the dish, and pour over the whole the sauce.

Lettuce, No. 2.—Cut the lettuce and eggs fine, and make a dressing of melted butter, hot vinegar, mustard, and pepper, and pour over the whole.

To Serve in Heads.—Look each leaf carefully over inside and out, to see that no vermin are lodged in the creases of the leaves; lay them on a dish, and ornament it with slices of hard-boiled eggs or not, as suits the fancy. Or lay it on a platter, and lay around the edge a wreath of young peppergrass. Some use sugar and vinegar only, on lettuce. When each seasons to suit themselves, sugar should be near the salad, as well as the caster.

Mustard Greens.—Mustard, dock, and dandelion, when very young, all make excellent greens, boiled with a ham bone.

Okra.—This is much used as a thickening for soups, also for stews; the pods must be gathered when young and tender. It is dried by cutting in thin slices, and exposing it to a gentle heat, or hung in the sun, in the same manner as peaches and apples on strings.

Okra or Gumbo Soup.—Boil a chicken and a slice of ham in sufficient water to make a tureen of soup. When the fowl is thoroughly done, take it with the ham from the broth. Flavor the soup with onions, pepper, salt, and sweet herbs; make a paste with eggs and flour, roll it as thin as wafers, dry a little, then roll it as tightly as possible, and slice in thin shreds; put in the soup a teacupful of this, a teacupful of chopped okra, and a pint of oysters.

Stewed Okra.—Chop finely two quarts of okra pods, stew them in a very little water until cooked through; season with butter, pepper, and salt. The taste for this vegetable is acquired by habit; few relish, when first eating it. The French use it more than Americans, although Southerners make much use of it in thickening soups. The seeds are said to make possible coffee.

ONIONS.—The red onion is thought much sweeter than the white in its raw state, but the latter is preferred for boiling on account of its beauty.

BOILED ONIONS.—Take the outside skin from white onions as uniform in size as possible, lay them in cold salt and water one hour, boil them in milk and water until thoroughly tender; lay them in a deep dish, and pour over them melted butter.

FRIED ONIONS.—Some think this a great dish. Take onions, before they commence growing, that the natural sweetness of the vegetable may not be destroyed; peel, slice thin, and fry them brown in hot pork fat. If this dish is cooked, it should be done on a coal furnace, at a little distance from the house. It is almost impossible, for days, to remove the unpleasant odor arising from them. The best deodorizer to use in the kitchen is a little ground coffee burned on the stove, the smoke being allowed to penetrate to other parts of the house. Cabbage and turnips are almost as unpleasant as onions; a teaspoonful of cheap coffee would be well used in cleansing the house from any disagreeable odor.

PARSLEY.—The curled is the most beautiful, and could be kept in a growing state all winter with slight protection. It is used as seasoning to different soups and meats, and also to ornament different dishes at table. It can be dried as other herbs, and used pulverized in soups, broths, etc.

PLAIN PARSNIPS.—The sugar or hallow crown is the sweetest for table use. It is generally used in the winter and spring, but is eatable as soon as sufficiently grown. Boil them until tender in water in which a little salt has been thrown, split them, and serve with drawn butter; or, if boiled with corned beef or pork, serve whole without dressing.

BROILED PARSNIP.—After they are boiled tender, let them become perfectly cold; slice thin lengthwise, and broil until nicely browned; spread them with butter, and season with pepper and salt. To be served with roast, broiled, or fried meats.

FRIED PARSNIPS.—Boil and slice thinly, have ready hot pork fat, put them in, and brown without burning. Serve with fried meats.

PARSNIP FRITTERS.—Boil the parsnips in salted water so as to flavor them through, make a light batter, cut them round, and dip them in the batter. Have ready hot lard, take them up with a tablespoon, and drop them in while the lard is boiling; when they rise to the surface turn them; when browned on both sides, take them out; let them drain, and set them in the oven to keep hot. Serve with broiled, fried, or roast meats or fowls.

PARSNIP CUTLET.—Slice boiled parsnips lengthwise, and brown them in lard, after rubbing them with pepper and salt. When browned on both sides, dip one side in batter made of egg and flour; let them only brown, not burn; then dip the other side, and brown in the same manner; spread over them a little butter, or not, as desired. Serve with roasts, etc.

FRICASSEE PARSNIPS.—Cut the parsnips in chunks about two inches square, or as near square as convenient, boil until tender in salted water, skim them out, and brown gently in butter; when nearly brown, dust over them some flour, and let it brown, but not burn. Take them from the spider, and add to the butter a little of the water in which they were boiled; if there is not sufficient butter in the spider to form a gravy, add more; if not as thick as brown gravies usually are, add a little flour mixed, free from lumps, in a very little of the water from the parsnips, stir it in, and pour the gravy over them.

PEAS.—These should be gathered young and used immediately. It injures them to lie an hour. If the pods are sandy, wash and dry them before shelling, as they should never be washed after being shelled. There is a peculiar sweetness lost by washing or long keeping which is the beauty of the pea. June peas are poor things, hardly worth shelling if presented. Marrowfats are all good, some better than others. (*See* KITCHEN GARDEN.) Have ready a pot perfectly clean, and free from the peculiar odor of other vegetables. Put the peas in the pot with enough water to cover them, throw in a little salt, and cover tight. Watch them that they do not boil dry, they will cook in fifteen minutes if the peas are in a right state. Take out two or three table-spoonfuls of the peas, mash them fine, and stir them in the pot. Dish in a deep covered dish, and season with butter. Never put pepper in peas; it is easily added at table, if desired.

PEAS STEAMED.—Put the peas in a tin pail, or some other article with a tight cover, without water. To every quart put a piece of butter as large as a quarter of a common-sized hen's egg; set it in boiling water until the peas are cooked tender. This is said to be superior to any other mode, as they retain their whole flavor. Peas are generally served when lamb is cooked, if they are to be had; yet they are a proper dish with all roast, broiled, or fried meats, and with fowls in any form.

PEA SOUP.—Boil the peas until tender in sufficient water for the soup, then mash one-third of them, and stir them in the broth; season with butter and salt. Some use sweet herbs with peas, but we think the flavor of each vegetable should be retained separately, if possible. One reason why there is such sameness at public tables is, that all kinds of meats and vegetables are seasoned with the same herbs and spices.

DRIED PEAS.—These must be soaked until soft, and then cooked as other peas; a very little sugar added will give them more of the natural flavor of green peas.

HERMETICALLY-SEALED GREEN PEAS.—The peas must be fresh picked, and shelled as directed; boil them until tender, and fill each can nearly full without crowding; while hot add a very little hot water, and seal on the caps. Place them in the water bath while hot until they have become boiling hot, make a small hole, boil half an hour, and then solder the small aperture. This is a very difficult thing to manage; corn, peas, and asparagus are the most troublesome of all vegetables to preserve in this manner, as they sour almost while heating. Still it is accomplished, though many cans burst and are lost. Mark all cans, or you will be unable to designate them. If the ends of the cans remain drawn, it is supposed they are perfect. (*See* TESTING CANS IN BOILING WATER, Part V., Chapter VI.)

EARLY POTATOES, BEFORE THEY ARE RIPE.—When fresh from the ground, never use a knife, but rub the skin off with the hand. Put them in hot water with a little salt, take them up as soon as thoroughly cooked, lay them in a deep dish, and spread butter over them so as to form a gravy.

TO BOIL RIPE POTATOES.—Wash them very clean, and put them in cold water, let them boil slowly so as not to break; as soon as a fork can be put through them, take them up; peel immediately, and put them in the steamer to keep hot. Plain boiled potatoes are proper with any dish, but are generally served with roast and boiled meats.

MASHED POTATOES.—Peel the potatoes and cut them in quarters. Throw into a kettle of boiling water a spoonful of salt; let them cook, not too fast, but evenly; when tender, drain off all the water, and let them steam, that all the extra moisture may pass off. Mash them in the kettle, working them into a light paste without a lump. More depends on this than is supposed in giving mashed potatoes the superior flavor they should possess to be prime. After they are worked into a paste, which must be done quickly, set the kettle on the stove, working them all the time to prevent burning. Put into a common covered vegetable-dishful a piece of butter half as large as an egg, work it in well, then add a half-cup of sweet milk well worked in; taste, and if not sufficiently salted, add more. If you have cream, a teacupful will do instead of butter and milk; indeed, it is better. Dish the potatoes in a covered dish, smooth them nicely with a knife dipped in butter, and shake a trifle of pepper over the top. This dish can be varied by browning. Beat an egg and cover the top, and set them in the oven a few moments. Be careful not to spill the egg on the dish. Serve with fowls or roasts.

FRIED POTATOES CRISP.—Peel and wash nice white potatoes, slice them very thin, and fry in boiling lard a few at a time. Salt them as fast as fried, and set them in the oven to keep hot until all are finished, when they should be put in a covered dish for the table. Serve with fried meats.

FRIED POTATOES.—Peel and slice thin nice potatoes. Heat in a spider a lump of butter, fill the spider half full of potatoes seasoned with salt and pepper, lay on the top small pieces of butter, and pour into the spider a few spoonfuls of water. Cover them tightly and let them steam. When they have browned on the bottom of the spider, stir carefully so as not to break them, and so continue until the whole are browned. The fire must be rather slow, or they will burn, which would spoil the whole.

BROILED POTATOES.—Boil potatoes until nearly cooked through. When cold, slice them lengthwise and broil, after first seasoning with a little salt and pepper. Spread them with butter. Serve with broiled meats.

FRICASSEED POTATOES.—Boil, until nearly done, with a piece of salt pork; when cold, cut in small chunks, and brown in pork fat or butter.

HASHED POTATOES.—Peel and hash fine uncooked potatoes. To each quart allow a piece of butter, half as large as a common-sized egg; a half teacup of water, a half-teaspoon of salt, a dust of pepper only, if any; it can be added much easier than taken out; put water, butter, salt, and pepper in the spider, until it becomes hot; then stir in the potatoes, let them cook slowly so as not to burn; stir often, but do not mash them; sweet cream can be added, if desired, when taken from the fire; this is nice for breakfast.

WARMED POTATOES.—Cut in small chunks; season with butter, salt, a dust of pepper, and sweet milk; let them become heated through. Cold mashed potatoes can be made into small round cakes, and browned on the griddle. These are both excellent breakfast dishes.

BAKED POTATOES.—Irish and sweet potatoes are both excellent baked. The sweet requires more time than the Irish, which will bake, in a quick oven, in from twenty-five to thirty minutes. They should be served as soon as thoroughly cooked.

STEAMED POTATOES.—Both these varieties are excellent steamed. The sweet should never be boiled. Cold sweet potatoes are very good fried, but in no way are they as delicious as baked or roasted in the ashes.

PUMPKINS.—Some persons are fond of stewed pumpkins, which takes the place of squash. It should be cooked slowly, with as little water as possible. When finished, there should no water or juice of the pumpkin be seen; add a very little salt, but not so much as to have it perceptible. (To preserve hermetically, *see* SQUASH.)

RADISHES.—The finest are the long scarlet, or early scarlet short top. They should be nicely washed, the tip ends of the roots pinched off, and about one inch of the green stalks left on. Place them in deep glass bowls or goblets. They look very pretty on the table, when well dressed. All wormy ones should be discarded.

RHUBARB.—This is generally used for pies and tarts, though sometimes it is stewed and sweetened for sauce.

RHUBARB HERMETICALLY SEALED.—This is very easily put up.

6*

Gather the tender stalks, cut them in pieces about one inch long. Pack in bottles. Fill each bottle within an inch of the cork; pour into each bottle sufficient water to fill the vacuum between the pieces of rhubarb; cork and wire well. Put them in the water bath, and let them boil a half hour. Then seal tightly, as directed in CHERRIES, etc.

SALSIFY OR VEGETABLE OYSTER.—This is eatable both fall and spring. Scrape the roots clean, cut them in small pieces, and boil in clear water until tender. Take them up and mash fine, season with butter, pepper, and salt; make in small cakes, and fry like oysters. These are called salsify patties.

SALSIFY SOUP.—Prepare the salsify as above; boil until tender, then season the soup as for oyster, with butter, salt, and pepper. Toast bread, lay it in a deep dish, slice by slice; spread the salsify on each slice; when the whole is in, pour over the soup and serve immediately.

SALSIFY CAKES.—Boil, until tender, the scraped salsify. Then mash, and beat it up in light batter; drop the cakes on the griddle, and fry brown; serve with butter.

SPINACH.—For greens, this vegetable is esteemed next to young beets, and should be cooked in the same manner, using only the leaves. It is almost the first green to be obtained, if rightly managed in the fall. (*See* KITCHEN GARDEN.)

SQUASH.—Gather the summer squashes when young and tender. If the scallop, the seeds will do no harm. Cut it in quarters, and boil in a bag until tender. Squeeze out all the water, and season with salt and butter; pepper can be added at the table.

BAKING SQUASH.—These are sliced and baked like potatoes, and served in the same manner.

HERMETICALLY-SEALED SQUASH AND PUMPKIN.—Stew and strain ready for use, fill the cans nearly full while hot, seal hot on the cap, make a small aperture as directed for all other can fruits. Place in the water bath until they become boiling hot, let them boil half an hour, then close the aperture with solder. Mark the cans, that the contents may be known.

TOMATO.—The large smooth red, is, perhaps, the best on the whole, for family use.

To Stew Tomatoes.—Pour boiling water over ripe tomatoes; remove the skin, and cut them in small pieces. If very seedy, squeeze out all the seeds possible, without losing too much juice; cook them in a bright tin or an enamelled kettle; season with butter and salt. Let each add pepper at the table, to suit themselves.

Tomato Toast.—This is a nice breakfast dish; prepare the tomatoes, and stew them as directed. Toast a slice of light bread for each member of the family, and spread the stewed tomatoes evenly on each slice. If any is left, pour it over the whole; serve immediately.

Hermetically-sealed Tomatoes.—Peel as directed; let them become boiling hot, fill each can nearly full; seal on the caps; make a small hole in each, and place them in the water bath. Let them remain until the fruit becomes boiling hot, and the air exhausted, which can be told by placing a drop of water over the hole; while there is air in the can it will blubber; as soon as it is all expelled, the water will draw in, when the aperture must be closed. Mark the cans as soon as taken out. If the next morning any cans are not draw in, (*see* Peaches,) the cans are either imperfect, or the air not fully expelled; in either case, the fault must be, if possible, corrected. If no leak appears, place the swollen cans again in the water bath, to go through the same process before explained.

Turnips.—The early white Dutch, and green, and red strap-leaved are among the best for family use. The flavor is improved by slight frosts, although it is not well to let them freeze and thaw.

Plain Boiled Turnips.—Boil in water, with a little salt, until tender, or with corned beef, or pork. Serve whole with boiled dinners.

Mashed Turnips.—Boil in clear water, until very tender. Drain them well, mash free from lumps, season with butter and salt. Send them to the table in a covered dish, nicely smoothed, and dotted over with pepper. Serve with baked, roast, fried, or broiled meats, and with fowls in every form. They should always accompany duck, goose, and mutton.

TO PRESERVE VEGETABLES THROUGH WINTER.

Artichokes can be left in the ground, from one season to another; though it is well to throw litter over them.

Beets.—These do the best, for winter use, packed in sand in the cellar. For spring use, small roots not fully grown, should be selected, (*see* Kitchen Garden,) and buried below frost. An overgrown, tough beet is a poor vegetable.

Cabbages and Cauliflower.—These had better be buried in a pit below frost. They can then be removed at pleasure.

Celery.—A quantity can be packed in the cellar for winter use, in sand. The remainder will do very well left in the trench, with boards put over to form a ridge; cover these with coarse litter, to keep out the frost. When a large quantity is to be kept over, make the plan in the spring, and plant the trenches so that the middle trench shall be a half-foot higher than the two outside ones; pack the soil well around this, and fill up the other trenches. Saw boards just the right length, to place together, and cover the three trenches, meeting in the middle of the trench to form a ridge; cover it with litter, packing it ridge-shaped, to shed the rain. It must have sufficient litter to keep out the frost, and never be opened in severe weather.

Parsley.—Take up some roots, and pack them in a barrel filled with soil, with large holes bored at regular distances. Put the roots through the holes, leaving the crowns nearly outside; set the barrel in a warm light cellar, and moisten the soil once or twice every week. It can also be kept growing, by making a cold-frame over it, thus protecting it from the frost; but unless it has some light, it will blanch, and lose much of its beauty.

Parsnips.—Fill a barrel with them before the ground freezes; pack tight, and fill the vacancies with sand; let them freeze, and then put them in a cool cellar. They can also be left in the ground until spring, which is the old but not best mode.

Winter Radish.—Store them in the cellar, where they will neither grow nor freeze.

Potatoes.—Pack in barrels or boxes what are needed for winter use; scatter plaster over each layer, to absorb moisture; it is also a preventive to the rot, although not always certain, yet they keep better with than without it. If they grow, the sprouts must be rubbed off, and all decayed potatoes picked out. It is better to bury in the old-fashioned manner all potatoes wanted for spring use. It is a good plan too to sprinkle plaster in among them. The hills should not be uncovered in severe weather.

Turnips.—Store all wanted for winter consumption in the cellar, where they will be too cool to grow, but not cold enough to freeze. For spring use, bury below frost.

Salsify or Vegetable Oyster.—Pack in barrels in sand, as directed for parsnips for the winter. The remainder leave where they grew.

Winter Squash.—Hang them up by the stem in a cool place free from frost; or lay them on shelves where they will touch nothing.

Onions.—Gather them as soon as the tops are dead. Dry thoroughly, and spread thinly in a cool dry place. They are very apt to grow, which injures them much. If spread thinly they will remain dry, and keep much longer without sprouting than when laid in heaps.

Vegetable Cellar.—This should be cool and dark, yet so arranged that it can be ventilated without trouble. No imperfect, half-decayed vegetables should be allowed to remain, as it is not only unhealthy for the family to breathe the air which rises from the cellar, but they also promote decay in other vegetables, whether they come in contact with them or not. In the preservation of vegetables, we should, as far as possible, imitate nature. A cool dark cellar seems next to burying the roots, which would seem to be the nearest to the natural mode. Chloride of lime is an excellent purifier for a root cellar. The best method is to place a crock similar to a common filterer, on a bench in the centre of the cellar, with another dish to catch the droppings from it as it dissolves. There will be sufficient dampness arising from the vegetables to moisten it. When the dish is full, it can be dried, and used over and over again. This not only purifies but exhausts the air; making the cellar more healthy for the family and vegetables.

CHAPTER VIII.

PUDDING AND DINNER DESSERTS.

Directions to Boil Puddings.—To prepare a pudding-bag, sew firmly strong canvas in the shape of a sugar loaf, sew within four inches of the top a strong string. Before putting in the pudding, dip the bag in boiling water, turn the bag on the wrong side, and dredge it well with flour. Have ready a pot of water boiling hard; put in the pudding, allow room for swelling, and tie firmly. Turn a plate in the bottom of the pot, and be sure that there is enough boiling water to completely cover it. Keep the tea-kettle boiling all the while the pudding is in the pot, and fill up often. Fifteen minutes after the pudding is put in, turn it over in the pot, and after half an hour turn it again. When done, dip the bag in a pail of cold water and turn it out. A boiled pudding should be served as soon as dished. A pudding form or tin boiler should be greased with butter before putting in the pudding; the water should be above the pudding but not over the form, and the same quantity kept in the kettle constantly.

BAKED PUDDINGS.—All batter puddings fall soon after they are baked. They ought to be served immediately after they are done. Indian puddings require long and slow baking. Rice should be baked quickly. Tapioca and other puddings of the kind should bake in a moderate oven, like custards. All cake puddings should be baked in the same manner as cakes of nearly the same composition; as, for instance, sponge puddings quick, and plumb puddings a long time.

COTTAGE PUDDING.—One cup loaf-sugar, two eggs beaten separately, two table-spoons of melted butter, two teaspoons of cream of tartar, and one of fine salt mixed in three cups of sifted flour, and the flour again sifted; one teaspoon of soda, dissolved in one cup of milk and strained; stir the butter and sugar together, add the yolks of the eggs, afterwards the whites and flour, and lastly the milk. Prepare the pudding when convenient, leaving out the milk until the dinner is ready to serve; have the oven heated to a quick but not burning heat. The pudding baker should be of earthen, and shallow; grease it with sweet butter, stir in the milk and soda with a quick movement, and bake immediately. It will be ready for the table in twenty minutes, or less if very thin. Serve with sweet cream, sugared with loaf sugar, and flavored with a drop of any extract fancied by the family. (Wine sauce, or Dyspepsia sauce, *see* SAUCES FOR PUDDING.)

LEMON PUDDING.—Take two large fresh lemons, roll them on the table under the hand; grate the thin yellow part of the peel, and mix it with half a pound of pulverized loaf-sugar; mix with the sugar, until light and creamy, six ounces of sweet butter; separate and beat as light as possible six eggs, beat into the sugar and butter, first the yolks and afterwards the whites, and lastly the juice of the lemons strained through a sieve; beat the whole well together, and pour it in white shallow pudding-bakers with broad rims. Cover the rims with puff paste, but do not line the dishes. After the pudding is done, have ready the whites of two eggs beaten light, with a quarter of a pound of sugar worked slowly in it, as directed for SUGAR KISSES; cover the top of the custard with the egg and sugar, lay paper on the puff paste to prevent its scorching, and set the pudding in a coolish oven, until the frosting is dried over the top. Serve cold, without sauce, cutting in equal parts. Any other juicy fruit can be used in place of the lemon.

STRAWBERRY PUDDING, ETC.—Take sufficient strawberries to make a half pint of juice, six table-spoons of sugar, two table-spoons of melted butter, four eggs; beat it well together, and bake and ornament it as described in LEMON PUDDING. Orange, raspberry, cherry, cranberry, currant, or any other fruit can be used in the same manner, varying the amount of sugar.

PINEAPPLE PUDDING.—Prepare ripe pineapples by grating them very finely. Prepare a custard with cream and egg. Heat the custard over steam until sufficiently hot to congeal the cream. Having drained the pineapple free from juice, and sweetened it one hour before, it will be ready to mix with the cream; pour in a fancy dish that has been heated, so that it will not break, a layer of the cream, then a layer of the pineapple, until the whole is in the dish. Beat sweet cream stiff, sweeten with loaf-sugar very sweet, and just before the dessert is served add the juice of the fruit, and pile the beaten cream on the top of the pudding. The only care in making this dessert is the danger of the custard and cream becoming sour. Cocoa pudding can be made in the same way, adding the cocoa milk to the cream.

COCOA SNOW.—Grate the white part of a cocoa-nut and mix it with white sugar; serve with whipped cream or not, as desired. This is called cocoa snow. It looks beautifully on the table, it is proper for dinner or evening parties.

A BEAUTIFUL CHARLOTTE RUSSE, No. 1.—Cut the inside from a nice sponge-cake, leaving the sides whole; prepare blancmange, and let it remain over steam until wanted; spread on the bottom of the cake a layer of the blancmange, moving it around until a little thick;

spread in a thin layer of any marmalade, then a layer of blancmange, and a very thin layer of marmalade, until the cake is full; the marmalade should be much thinner than the blancmange, and the last should be blancmange, to look well.

CHARLOTTE RUSSE, No. 2.—Prepare a ladies' cake as above; have ready nice calf's foot jelly, blancmange, and the white and yolk of an egg beaten separately, and made stiff with pulverized loaf-sugar; into the whites squeeze the juice of a lemon, and add the thin grated rind to the yolks; spread the yolk over the bottom of the cake, let it dry a little, and spread a thick layer of blancmange; on this put another layer of yolk, then blancmange, on this the whites very thin, then the calf's foot jelly, blancmange next, and last the top of the cake; let it stand until solid, turn it out, and frost its top and sides, or cover the whole with calf's foot jelly.

IMPROVED BOSTON APPLE PUDDING.—Eighteen fine acid apples stewed with very little water, with half a nutmeg; rasp the yellow rind of a lemon, sweeten to taste, and pass the whole through a sieve; add, while the pulp is warm, one-quarter of a pound of butter, with the juice of the lemon, the beaten yolks of four and white of one egg; beat fifteeen minutes hard; line a shallow pudding baker with puff paste, set it in the oven until baked, pour in the custard, and bake half an hour; while baking, which takes half an hour, beat the whites of two eggs stiff, allow a quarter of a pound of loaf-sugar, and beat thoroughly; spread the sugar and egg over the top of the custard, and set it in the oven until browned; no sauce is needed, but plain cream would be an addition.

FRUIT BLANCMANGE.—Prepare blancmange as directed; have ready any fruit not too juicy, nicely sugared; stir the blancmange until it thickens, then put a layer of pulped fruit and a layer of blancmange into a deep glass dish until quite full. Serve with cream.

DINNER CREAM, No. 1.—Beat sweet cream stiff, sugar to the taste, and add any sweet fruit pulped; soak ladies' fingers or slices of any nice sponge-cake in wine, and serve it with the fruit; or the cake may be steeped in the juice of the fruit; and beat with the cream, in which case sweeten the juice.

DINNER CREAM, No. 2.—Cream beat stiff, sweetened, with no fruit, is very nice to serve with blancmange jellies, or fresh fruit; a coffee-cupful of good cream will beat to a common-sized bowlful; when cream is scarce, it is economy to beat it.

COCOA CREAM.—Whip sweet cream stiff; mix with it as much grated cocoa as convenient; about half as much by measure, after it is grated, as the cream was before whipping, is a good proportion; sweeten to suit the taste. Sweet almonds, pounded with rose-water in a marble mortar, with a few bitter ones, are very nice prepared in the same manner as cocoa.

CALF'S FOOT JELLY DESSERTS.—Take four nice large calf's feet; the hair only should be removed, not the skins; having cleaned them perfectly, split them as far as convenient, and boil in filtered rain-water, allowing, if the feet are large and the skins on, one quart to each foot; boil until the water will measure two quarts, and the flesh reduced to pieces. They want slow but steady boiling; strain the liquid through a sieve; heat it over, and strain it through a bag; if grease still appears on the surface, remove it carefully; turn it out and remove all impurities; after this is prepared, it can be flavored to suit the fancy; and according to the flavor, it is called wine, lemon, or any other jelly. Cut up the jelly, put it in a porcelain kettle, and set it over steam to melt; mix with the melted jelly, five gills of pure grape-wine of the best quality; sherry is probably the best, as it is decided and light colored; the grated rind of five large or six medium-sized fresh lemons, not allowing any part of the under or white part of the lemons to be used, as it gives a bitter taste; squeeze all of the juice from the lemons, and strain it in the jelly, with a pound of loaf-sugar; beat up slightly, merely enough to mix the eggs, the whites of six eggs with their shells well washed and pounded fine; mix the ingredients and boil about a quarter of an hour, and let it stand and settle a few moments where it will not cool nor boil; have ready a flannel jelly bag, (see JELLY BAG,) pour in the jelly, and let it drip through by the fire; if too cool, it will congeal. If the jelly is to be moulded, it will need a quarter of an ounce of isinglass melted with the other ingredients. It is fashionable now to break up jelly, and serve it in glass dishes; it looks very pretty in this way, and we think the isinglass no improvement to jellies, where they can be set without it: this can be varied to suit the taste: if moulded, set it on ice, if the weather is warm; it is nice frozen as you would ice-cream; the rule for isinglass jellies is an ounce to a pound of sugar and a pint of liquids; the isinglass should be soaked and dissolved in as little water as possible, the pint of juice mixed with it after it is melted, and afterward the sugar, when it must be strained until clear; calf's foot jelly and isinglass jellies often require straining several times before becoming clear; the bag should be washed each time it is used before repeating the straining. Pig's may be substituted for calf's feet, if the latter cannot be obtained.

BLANCMANGE CALF'S FEET.—The jelly being prepared from the calf's feet according to former directions, melt it over steam; after it is melted, boil and skim it as long as any grease remains; pass it through the jelly-bag, if not quite clear; after it is quite solid, turn it out and scrape off all impurities that may yet be left; cut up the jelly and melt it again; boil a pint of rich cream from the morning's milk if used in the afternoon, or the night's milk if in the morning; when the cream boils, add half a pound of loaf-sugar; flavor with vanilla or bitter almond, not stirred in until partly cool; mix the cream and sugar gradually with the jelly, and transfer to the moulds, which should have been dipped in cold water, stirring constantly until it thickens; add the flavoring when it is so thick as to stir with difficulty, and set the moulds on ice until wanted; to turn it out, dip the moulds in warm water, and turn them bottomside up; serve with cream, if for dinner.

GERMAN BOILED RICE PUDDING.—Scald in water eight ounces of rice, after which boil it in one quart of milk until it forms a mass or jelly; stir into it one-quarter of a pound of butter, let it become entirely cold, then stir in the yolks of ten well-beaten eggs, and beat well until the eggs and rice are thoroughly incorporated; add a little cinnamon, the yellow rind of a lemon, and a little salt, and beat thoroughly; beat the whites of the ten eggs to snow, and stir them into the rice; grease a pudding form, and fill it, allowing four inches for the swelling of the pudding; boil it three hours without ceasing; the water must not cover the pudding, nor be allowed either to cool or boil away; fill often with boiling water from the tea-kettle. Serve with wine sauce or rosehip sauce.

GERMAN RAISED PUDDING.—Stir into a pint of milk half a pound of flour; mix in the middle of the dough two large spoonfuls of lively homemade hop yeast, let it rise; when light add two ounces melted butter, six ounces blanched almonds, pounded with a little white of eggs, or chopped very finely, a little salt, half a pound of Zante currants, and five eggs, the whites and yolks beaten separately; mix all together, and let it stand until light; it will take three hours to boil; put it in boiling water; do not cover the pudding with it or allow it to boil away; keep the tea-kettle boiling to fill the pot; serve with a sweet liquid sauce.

GERMAN RYE BREAD PUDDING.—Six ounces of rye bread, finely pounded, and weighed after drying; brown without scorching, and wet the bread with red wine, allowing it to soak all it will; add six ounces of melted butter, not oiled; mix well; then add six ounces of pounded almonds, six ounces of sugar, and cinnamon and nutmeg to the taste; separate and beat twelve eggs as light as possible, mix in the yolks, and lastly the whites. Boil the pudding in forms or a bag, from two to two and a half hours; serve with any sauce that suits the taste. The German rules for cooking in this book are very superior, they were obtained from a superior German cook, and may be relied upon.

FOURTH-OF-JULY PUDDING.—Flavor very highly three pints of cream from the last night's milk, with equal parts of extracts of vanilla and lemon; slice a pound of sponge-cake (almond sponge is the finest) in a deep dish, and pour over it the cream; let it stand until the cake is dissolved; blanch two ounces of bitter almonds, and pound them one at a time, fine, with rose-water, in a marble or glass mortar; when finished, set them in a cool place; if the almonds are too much trouble, add a little extract of bitter almond to the cream; beat eight eggs, the whites and yolks separate, put in the yolks a half pound of loaf-sugar, beat up the cream and cake, then stir in gradually the almonds and eggs; the yolks first, and whites last; butter a deep white dish, and pour in the mixture; bake in a brisk oven; when baked, grate over the top loaf-sugar until it is white, and ornament the top with citron cut in stars and stripes, to resemble the American flag; or the same may be done with red sugar sand; another way is to form a large star in the centre and small stars near the edge. There should be the same number of stars as there are States in the Union. Preserved citron melon looks better than dry citron, if you have it; this is good as well as fanciful, and will be found economical, after a party, when bits of cake, nuts, and ice-cream are left, which can be used in place of the cream.

QUICK PUDDING.—Soften light sponge-cake, or any other kind, made with little butter, in sweet cream or rich milk, heated and poured on hot; make a rich boiled custard, and pour it over the cake and cream while hot, and beat the whole well together; flavor with the same flavoring used in the cake; if it has none, with lemon, vanilla, or bitter almond; it can be eaten hot or cold; use a sauce of butter and sugar, beat together until light, and thin it with wine. The pudding should be as thick as baked custard.

WINE PUDDING.—Moisten sponge or lady-cake with wine, add a little lemon or vanilla, nutmeg and powdered sugar; beat separately four eggs, and stir them in a pint of rich cream; mix the whole together, beating it well, pour it in a deep dish well buttered, and bake a light brown; when cold, cover it with a light frosting and dry it without scorching; the frosting can be flavored with lemon or strawberry juice; the latter gives a pinkish tinge, but little must be used, or the frosting will be too thin. This is a beautiful-looking pudding; serve with egg wine-cream sauce, made as follow: beat thoroughly three eggs; heat a half pint of wine over steam until nearly boiling hot, strain the egg through a wire sieve, and mix it gradually with the wine while hot; when cool, add half a pint of rich sweet cream beat stiff, and a little nutmeg.

PLAIN RAISED BATTER PUDDING.—Warm a pint of rich milk, melt in it a large heaping table-spoonful of butter; add a pinch of salt, a half teaspoon of soda, a table-spoon of good yeast, three well-beaten eggs, a teacup of sugar, a little nutmeg, and enough sifted flour to make a batter as stiff as it can be mixed, and beat it with a spoon; let it stand in the pudding-dish until light; fruit can be added if desired. When baked, turn it bottomside up, and serve with a rich sauce.

FRUIT RAISED PUDDING.—When baking take two and a half cups of light dough, one of sugar, hardly three-fourths of a cup of butter, two eggs, half a teaspoon of soda, one glass of wine or brandy, cinnamon, cloves, and nutmeg, being careful not to let one spice predominate; a half pound of washed currants, the same of stoned raisins, and a quarter of a pound of citron chopped fine; let it stand until light, in the pudding-dish; bake carefully so as not to form a heavy crust; turn it out when baked, and pour over it while hot a rich wine sauce; this will be found excellent; it must be started very early in the morning. If homemade yeast is used, the dough can be saved until the next day; sweeten it with soda, before mixing in the other ingredients, and allow it to rise again.

COUNTRY RAISED PUDDING.—Take two cups of dough, a quarter of a cup of butter, a half teacup of sugar; any dried fruit on hand, or none, as desired; equal parts of caraway and coriander seed ground and sifted, one teaspoon each, a pinch of salt, two eggs, and half a teaspoon of soda; let it rise; when baked, turn it out, and serve with sweet cream and sugar. If the pudding is too late for the dinner the same day baked, steam it the next day one hour over milk, and if any thing it is better than at first.

RAISED GRAHAM PUDDING.—Take unbolted flour, and mix it with milk sweetened with two table-spoonfuls molasses as thick as it can, possibly be stirred with a spoon; stir in it a table-spoon of yeast, and let it rise; when light bake it; let it remain in a dry place two days; then take off the top and side crust, and steam it over milk three hours; serve with cream and sugar, or maple syrup. If home hop yeast is used, take two spoonfuls.

PENNSYLVANIA PUDDING.—One pint of milk, a table-spoonful of washed rice, half a cup of raisins; sugar to the taste, a little salt and nutmeg; mix all together and put it in to bake; stir it up after it has skinned over four times, mixing up raisins and rice with the milk each time; let it bake until the rice is cooked; serve cold, with cream and sugar.

A BAKED PUDDING OF BOILED RICE.—One teacup of boiled rice, three beaten eggs, a large pint of milk, a teacup of raisins, nutmeg, a little salt, and sugar to suit the taste. If it is to be served without sauce, it will take more sugar than if with; if served hot, a sauce of sugar and butter worked together; if cold cream and sugar, beat well and flavor with nutmeg.

BAKED RICE FLOUR PUDDING, No. 1.—Boil a pint of rich milk, and while hot, stir in it a half teacup of rice flour, mixed smooth in sweet milk; let it scald to thicken, add a piece of butter the size of a pigeon's egg, and stir into the butter a pint of milk; beat three eggs, and stir into the mixture when cold; add salt, sugar, and nutmeg; bake twenty minutes, stir it up once after it skims over; if quite sweet, serve with butter alone; if not, add sugar.

BAKED RICE FLOUR PUDDING, No. 2.—Boil one pint of milk, thicken with a table-spoonful of rice flour; let it become cool, add five eggs well beaten, with sugar, salt, and nutmeg; stir in a cup of raisins, and lastly a pint of sweet cream; bake twenty minutes, stirring the whole of the ingredients together after it becomes hot; serve with sweet or wine sauce.

GRAHAM RICE FLOUR PUDDING, No. 3.—Boil a quart of milk, stir into it while hot a teacup of rice flour mixed in milk; sweeten quite sweet with sugar, and add a little salt; then stir in a pint of milk, and put it in the oven; when quite hot stir it up from the bottom, and once again after it skims over; serve hot with loaf sugar, if not very sweet; if sweet, use cream or butter.

RICH RICE FLOUR PUDDING, No. 4.—Boil a table-spoonful of blanched bitter almonds or peach kernels, in a pint of milk, until it is reduced one-half; strain it, stir into a gill of milk five heaping table-spoonfuls of rice flour, making a smooth paste, then add the boiled and another gill of rich milk; beat the whole well together, and heat it over steam, until it becomes quite thick, stirring all the time; after which stir into it a quarter of a pound of sweet butter, and the same of powdered sugar; add nutmeg and a pinch of salt, unless the butter makes it sufficiently salt; beat eight eggs as light as possible, and stir them in the mixture as soon as it is too cool to cook them; beat well together, and bake steadily three-fourths of an hour; the top must not be allowed to scorch or blister; it may be eaten either warm or cold. Serve with wine sauce, or butter and sugar worked together. If eaten cold, cream and sugar is better.

TAPIOCA PUDDING, No. 1.—Soak three table-spoonfuls of tapioca in a quart of milk; flavor with nutmeg, add salt and sugar, to the taste; beat four eggs and stir into the mixture; and bake three-fourths of an hour very steadily; serve with sour sauce.

TAPIOCA PUDDING, No. 2.—Soak in one quart of night's milk four heaping table-spoonfuls of tapioca; in the morning, boil it over steam until quite thick, stirring it from the bottom several times; add a piece of fresh butter as large as an egg, one-quarter of a pound of sugar, and four well-beaten eggs, and lastly, a gill of sweet thin cream from the morning's milk; flavor with nutmeg; if the butter does not make it sufficiently salt, add a little salt. Bitter almond can be used in place of nutmeg if relished; bake a half-hour, serve with butter and sugar worked to a cream, and thinned with a gill of hot wine.

ICE CREAM PUDDING.—To one pint of cream left over from ice cream add the whites of eight eggs beat stiff, into which work gradually six ounces powdered sugar. Stir the egg and sugar into the cream, alternately with four ounces of sifted flour, beat the whole very hard;

butter well a deep dish, pour in the pudding, and bake thoroughly. Serve hot, with sweet or wine sauce.

ENGLISH BREAD PLUM PUDDING, No. 1.—Crumb a small loaf of bread fine, mix with it one and a half pounds of raisins, the same of washed currants, and half a pound of citron; add one pound of suet chopped fine and free from strings, a little salt, and three quarters of a pound of sugar. Flavor with a little nutmeg. Mix this together and let it stand all night to dry the crumbs that it may not be clammy. In the morning beat twelve eggs as light as possible without separating, and stir them in the mixture; beat well, and when thoroughly incorporated with the bread and fruit, stir in enough morning's milk to moisten the whole; add a little salt, a little grated nutmeg, and three quarters of a wine-glass of brandy. Boil five hours. Serve with brandy, wine, or rich sweet sauce.

COCOANUT PUDDING.—Grate cocoanut and mix it with sugar, discarding the black part. Make a nice boiled custard without sugar, boil it over steam until too hard to use as boiled custard, strain it in the cocoanut and sugar before it becomes solid, and beat it together lightly. When cold it should be quite stiff. Serve with sweet cream.

ENGLISH PLUM PUDDING, No. 1.—Roll three-quarters of a pound of soda crackers, and mix them in two quarts of milk. When they have soaked soft, put in a quarter of a pound of melted butter, the same quantity of loaf-sugar rolled, two gills of flour, measured after sifting, one wine-glass of wine, and one-third of a nutmeg. Beat ten eggs as lightly as possible, and stir them in the mixture. Beat the whole well; then rub in flour, half a pound of seeded raisins cut once, the same quantity of Zante currants washed and dried, and half as much chopped citron; and mix the fruit well in the pudding. Bake or boil two hours. Serve with brandy or wine sauce. It can be eaten hot or cold.

ENGLISH PLUM PUDDING, No. 2.—One pound of beef suet finely shred and free from strings, one pound and a quarter of flour. Mix these together with a little salt; add one cup of sugar, six beaten eggs, one-third of a nutmeg, half a pound of seeded raisins, and the same of Zante currants washed and dried. Mix all well together, and add enough sweet milk to make a stiff batter. Boil four hours. Serve hot or cold with a rich liquid sauce.

RICH PLUM PUDDING.—One cup of beef suet chopped very fine and free from shreds. Mix with it a cup and a half of flour, and one cup of sugar. Beat three eggs very light, and mix them with the beef suet, etc. Add half a wine-glass of brandy, a little nutmeg, and salt; and lastly, stir in first one cup of washed Zante currants, the same of stoned raisins, and half as much of chopped citron. Mix them well, and add sufficient sweet milk to make a stiff batter. Boil three hours. Serve hot or cold with rich liquid sauce.

APPLE PUDDING, No. 1.—Take six tart apples, pippins or greenings are the best; steam them without peeling, after washing them quite clean; strain them through a sieve. Add six spoons of melted butter and the same of sugar, six eggs, half a wine-glass of brandy, and the juice of one lemon. Line a pudding dish with puff paste, and bake it. Serve hot or cold with sweet cream without sugar.

APPLE ROLL OR APPLE PUDDING, No. 2.—Make a paste with one-fourth of a pound of butter to one of flour mixed with water, not very stiff. Peel and slice rather thick tart apples, roll the paste very thin, or as thin as the bottom crust of a pie, spread the apples on the crust, so as to cover it, dredge on a little flour, and roll it as tight as possible. Cut the ends even, and put it in the steamer, or wrap it in thick cloth and boil it. It will take one hour steady cooking. Serve with butter and sugar; cut it in thin slices from the end when serving.

BERKSHIRE PUDDING.—Peel large tart apples free from blemishes, take out the cores with a corer, or if you have none, with a three-pronged fork, turning it round until it takes out the core on the opposite side, leaving the fruit whole. Prepare a nice batter, (*see* BATTER PUDDING,) beat it well. Butter a deep dish, place as many sour apples as there are persons to be served in the dish, and pour over them the batter. If the apples rise when the pudding heats, push them under the batter once. It will bake in twenty minutes. Serve as soon as baked or it will fall. Make a sauce with butter and sugar in equal parts, beat to a cream. To serve it, put on each plate an apple and the crust that surrounds it.

SAGO PUDDING.—Cleanse a half pound of sago in boiling water, put it in a quart of milk, and boil it over steam until dissolved, stirring often. When soft, take it from the fire, and stir in a half-teacup of butter, four large table-spoonfuls of powdered sugar, one wine-glass of wine, and when cold four beaten eggs. Grate in a little nutmeg, and add salt. Bake immediately, and serve cold or hot.

CUSTARD PUDDING.—Stir a half-pint of flour into a pint of milk, when free from lumps add another pint, seven beaten eggs, three table-spoonfuls of white powdered sugar, a teaspoonful of salt, and a little nutmeg. Bake steadily a half-hour. Serve with sweet sauce.

BIRD'S NEST PUDDING.—Peel tart apples, take out the cores, leaving the apples whole; make a custard of eight well-beaten eggs, half a pint of cream, and a pint and a half of scalded milk thickened with a heaping table-spoonful of flour and a little salt, but no sugar. Pour it over the apples. Bake twenty minutes. When the apples are tender the pudding is done. Serve immediately with butter and sugar stirred to a cream.

RICH PEACH PUDDING, No. 3.—Drop ripe sweet freestone peaches into boiling water a moment; take them out, and slip off the skins, place them in a deep dish, and make a boiled custard without sugar of the cream from the morning's milk, or a pint of sweet milk and cream mixed, add a little salt, not so much as to taste, only sufficient to remove the freshness of the custard. Strain it over the peaches while hot, and set it away. Serve with cream beat to a froth, slightly flavored with bitter almond, and sweetened. Serve cold.

QUINCE PUDDING.—Peel quinces and take out the cores, leaving the fruit whole; boil them in just sufficient water to cover them, by setting the preserving kettle over hot water until quite tender. Place them in a deep dish, and make a custard and pour over the quinces. Bake just long enough to have the custard become solid. Serve cold, with sweet cream and no sugar.

RICH PEACH PUDDING, No. 4.—Rub free from the down, or take off the skin from as many peaches as there are persons in the family, cover a deep pudding-dish with nice light puff paste, set it in the oven until quite baked through; then lay in the peaches, filling the dish full; add a piece of butter the size of a pigeon's egg, sift in some flour, and dissolve in a teacup of water sufficient sugar to sweeten it. If the peaches are sweet it will take but little; pour it in the dish, sift in more flour, and cover it with puff paste. It is good without sauce, but sweet cream without sugar is an improvement.

CHERRY PUDDING, No. 1.—Pit the cherries, and save the juice.

Line a shallow pudding-dish with paste, and bake it. Cut paste for two covers to fit the inside of the dish, and bake that. If the dish is deep it will take three or four. The easiest way to do this is to make a paper or pasteboard pattern to cut by. When the paste is well baked, spread a layer of cherries on the bottom of the dish, put at equal distances pieces of butter the size of Lima beans, cover with sugar, dredge on flour, and lay in a cover of paste; on this put another layer as before, and so continue until the whole is used. Lastly, put on a paste cover not baked, press it over the edge of the dish, and cut a slash in the centre. The fruit should have been drained on a hair sieve, and the juice saved in an earthen dish. Take the juice, add to each pint a half-pint of loaf sugar, let it boil up, and skim it. If there is not a sauce-boatful, add hot water and the same proportion of sugar. Serve both pudding and sauce before it is cold, but not burning hot.

CHERRY PUDDING, No. 2.—Pit the cherries; for every pound of fruit allow half the quantity of good sugar, poor will not do; let them lie all night on a hair sieve to drain, and save the juice in an earthen dish. Make a nice batter in the morning, and stir in the drained cherries, as free as possible from juice. Boil or bake. It will take one hour to bake and two to boil. When ready to serve, heat the juice, add sugar and a small bit of butter rolled in flour, to serve as sauce. It will be found superior.

BERRY PUDDINGS.—Sweeten the fruit if acid, and drain off the juice without pressing. Mix the fruit in rich batter, and either bake or boil. For sauce, beat to a stiff froth sweet cream, and stir in it the juice of the fruit. Serve cold or hot.

WHORTLEBERRY PUDDING.—Make a light batter and stir in enough berries to make the pudding black. It may be boiled or baked. Serve hot, with rich sweet or wine sauce.

GINGERBREAD PUDDING.—Make a light soft gingerbread, and serve, while hot, with rich wine or sweet sauce.

BARLEY PUDDING.—Wash pearl barley in boiling water, and boil it in milk until tender; add salt. It can be eaten plain with cream and sugar, or mixed with custard and baked.

BOILED RICE, No. 1.—Wash the rice clean, and put it in cold water; when it boils, throw it off and add more; let it boil until nearly tender and the water about evaporated, then salt it; stir in milk, and let it simmer until done. Be careful not to break the kernels more than is necessary. If it burns it is ruined. Serve with sour wine or sweet sauce, it is also good with butter and sugar, maple syrup, or sweetened cream. Raisins may be added.

BOILED RICE, No. 2.—Wash the rice thoroughly, and throw it in a pot of boiling water. Let it boil twenty minutes, skim it out, and drain it. This is used as a vegetable or dessert; add salt. Serve with cream and sugar, or as a vegetable.

RICE BOILED FANCY.—Boil according to method No. 1; when done, while hot, pack it in small cups partly filled; when cold turn them out into the centre of a deep dish. Make round holes in each, and fill them with jelly. Make a boiled custard with yolks only, pour it in the dish, leaving the rice above it. It should be stiff enough to be solid when cold, and poured on hot. Beat the whites stiff, then beat with them some of the same jelly on the rice, and lay it in even spoonfuls round the edge of the dish. Serve cold, it makes a pretty dish. The rice, which is tasteless, can be flavored with lemon juice or any thing desired. Strawberries or raspberries can take the place of the jelly.

MINUTE PUDDING.—Beat up the flour in as little milk as will mix it, freeing it perfectly from lumps, add to every quart of milk two well-beaten eggs, beat them thoroughly through the batter, and add salt. Boil two quarts of milk, and stir the batter in the milk very gradually, while off the fire; stir in a half-teacup of butter just before it is finished, and let it boil fifteen minutes. If it scorches it is ruined. It is a good plan to butter the kettle before using it. Serve with sour, sweet, or wine sauce, cream and sugar, or maple syrup. It is good for nothing if it stands after boiling. If every thing is ready it can be made just as the dinner is served. The sauce should be made before the pudding.

MUSH, OR HASTY PUDDING, OF INDIAN MEAL.—Good mush cannot be made of poor meal. Yellow corn is the best, not ground so fine as to kill the meal. Sift it, and make a batter of meal and water. Heat water boiling hot, and gradually stir in the batter until just thick enough for the mush to hop and sputter while boiling hard. Do not forget the salt. Let it boil two hours over a slow fire, it burns easily, and is spoiled if scorched. It is best when hot; never add meal after the batter is all in. If wanted to fry, pour it in a deep earthen dish to cool; in the morning cut it in slices one-fourth of an inch thick, and fry in lard, or pork fat, until it is not only brown, but crispy. Maple syrup is the very best to use on it, if made fresh from the sugar.

BAKED INDIAN PUDDING.—Take one quart of milk, dip out a teacupful and scald the rest, stir five table-spoonfuls of sifted meal in the hot milk; add salt, nutmeg, a spoonful of ginger, two of sugar, half a cup of molasses, and lastly the cup of cold milk. Bake two hours. Serve with butter as soon as taken from the oven.

CORN STARCH PUDDING.—Heat a quart of milk, and when boiling stir in three table-spoonfuls of starch, wet with milk; add salt, sugar, two eggs, a lump of butter as large as a walnut, nutmeg, and sugar to suit the taste. Bake slowly, and serve hot with liquid sauce.

CORN STARCH BLANC-MANGE WITHOUT EGGS.—Boil one quart of sweet milk over steam, stir into it gradually five table-spoonfuls of starch mixed in milk; add salt, and only two large spoonfuls of loaf sugar, stir until thoroughly cooked. When done take it from the fire, and when cooled add lemon and vanilla, beat it well together, and pour it into moulds. If used for pudding, serve with jelly or fresh fruit, and whipped cream sweetened and flavored like the pudding.

MRS. W.'s SPONGE CAKE PUDDING.—Pulverize a teaspoonful of cream of tartar, and mix it in a teacup of flour, measured after sifting, sifting the flour again after adding the tartar. Mix a teacup of pulverized loaf-sugar with the beaten yolks of three eggs, beat until very light, then add the whites beaten stiff. Stir in the flour as quickly as possible, then strain in the pudding a half-teaspoonful of soda dissolved in as little boiling water as possible, and as much salt as would lie on a three-cent piece. Bake in a slow oven. Serve with WINE SAUCE No. 1.

MRS. F.'s BREAD PUDDING.—One pound of bread or biscuit soaked in a quart of new milk and run through a colander, one-fourth of a pound of melted butter, not boiling hot, but just soft enough to flow, three-fourths of a pound of nice sugar, seven beaten eggs, a little salt, one-fourth of a nutmeg, one pound of seeded raisins, half a pint of milk. Bake three-fourths of an hour in a middling oven.

PUDDING AND DINNER DESSERTS. 149

APPLE DUMPLING, No. 2.—Peel tart apples free from blemishes, take out the core, and make a paste according to No. 1. Roll the paste one-eighth of an inch thick, and roll each apple in it. Tie each in a separate cloth, and put them in a pot of boiling water; let them boil half an hour, or until the apple is tender. If baked, follow directions in No. 2. Serve with butter and sugar. If steamed, omit the extra salt in the paste. (*See* No. 1.) We consider this rule the best of the two, though the cream paste may be more healthy.

BOILED BATTER PUDDING.—One quart of new milk, eight well-beaten eggs, one pint of flour, and a little salt. Beat it well to break all lumps, and thoroughly incorporate the ingredients. Allow one-third of the bag or boiler for swelling. Let the milk and flour soak fifteen minutes before adding the eggs. The pudding should be turned over, if boiled in a bag, after it has been in the pot ten minutes. Puddings should be put in boiling water, and kept steadily boiling for two hours if large. Keep a tea-kettle of water on, to replenish the pot, as it should be constantly covered with water, and to put cold in would make it heavy. Serve with rich liquid sauce. It should be served as soon as boiled, or it will fall.

BAKED BATTER PUDDING.—One quart of new milk, eight well-beaten eggs, nine large spoonfuls of sifted flour, and a little salt; mix the flour in a stiff paste, and work out the lumps, then gradually mix in the milk and let it swell a half-hour, then stir in the beaten eggs, and thoroughly incorporate the ingredients by quick beating until it foams. Bake in a quick oven twenty minutes if a small pudding, and thirty if large; serve as soon as baked, or it will fall. A nice liquid sauce, or butter and sugar worked to a cream, are either proper.

CREAM PUDDING, No. 1.—One pint and three gills of new milk, and nine table-spoonfuls of sifted flour; mix it in a batter free from lumps, and let it stand a half-hour to swell; then add nine well-beaten eggs, and a little salt; it should taste of the salt. Beat until very light, and then stir in a gill of sweet cream not richer than what would rise on a good cow's morning's milk by noon; bake quickly, and serve as soon as baked. It will take about half an hour for a good-sized pudding; serve with a rich liquid sauce.

CREAM PUDDING, No. 2.—Beat six eggs to a froth, mix a pint of milk with a pint of flour and two small teaspoonfuls of salt, and just before baking stir in a pint of sweet cream.

CREAM PUDDING, No. 3.—Mix a pint of flour in a half-pint of new milk, add salt, let it swell fifteen minutes to half an hour, beat seven eggs very light, the yolks and whites separately; mix in half a pint of new milk, first the yolks and beat them well, afterwards the whites, and beat it again; then stir in the milk and flour, and lastly a pint of rich cream.

CREAM PUDDING, No. 4.—Make as above, adding three table-spoonfuls of white sugar, and a little nutmeg; serve with wine sauce. It should be served as soon as baked, as well as all other flour batter puddings, as they fall immediately on being taken from the oven.

FANCY DESSERTS FOR DINNERS, ETC.

FLOATING ISLANDS.—Beat to a stiff froth the whites of fourteen eggs, cook them by spoonfuls on boiling milk until they can be lifted with a fork, skim them out, and let the milk drain from them; beat the yolks, and stir them into two quarts of the milk when a little cool; add sugar to the taste, a pinch of salt, and as much loaf-sugar as suits the taste. Do not let it boil, only thicken; it should be about as thick as morning's cream at noon; pour the custard into a deep dish and lay the whites on the top, sift on a little red sugar sand, and nutmeg or not, as desired.

BOILED CUSTARD.—Heat a quart of milk over hot water, beat four eggs with sugar as light as possible, stir them in the milk; when a little cooled, add a pinch of salt, set it over the fire and stir it until it thickens—it should be as thick as cream only; flavor to suit; pour in cups while hot.

THICKENED CUSTARD.—Prepare a boiled custard as for floating islands, and stir the whites in as soon as taken from the fire; it should cook but not toughen them; flavor to suit.

BAKED CUSTARD.—Beat eight eggs as light as possible, with three table-spoonfuls of loaf-sugar; as fast as the foam rises on the eggs, skim it off into a quart of cream; when nearly all is in, strain the remainder into it, add a little salt, and bake until it is just solid.

CUSTARD AND WHEY.—Beat six eggs with sugar and add them to a quart of milk, bake hard until the custard separates; pour it into cups, and serve warm.

CREAM CUSTARD.—One quart of sweet cream, one half-teaspoonful of salt, four eggs beat as light as possible and strained into the cream. Do not beat the cream, but merely mix the egg in it, stirring lightly. Bake until solid, but do not scorch; a nice way is to set cups in hot water in a pan in the oven or on the stove until the custard is solid; but in this case it had better be allowed to thicken over hot water before putting it in the cups; flavor to suit.

WHIPPED CREAM.—Sweeten rich cream to suit the taste, put it in a bowl, and stir it quickly with a beater until the whole is stiff; when much is wanted, it will be found the least trouble to prepare a jar with a dasher, and churn it until stiff, but care must be taken that it does not separate.

Prepare a cream in the following manner: beat light six eggs, add the froth to a quart of cream until all or nearly all is beat up, then strain the remainder and add that, beat it well and sweeten to the taste, after which add one gill of French brandy or two of wine, mix it all together, and fill the glasses half full and pile the cream on the top.

SYLLABUBS AND WHIPS.—One quart of sweet cream, a half-pint of white wine, and three-fourths of a pound of pulverized loaf-sugar; beat the mixture with a whisk, and take off the cream as fast as it rises, and lay it on a thin muslin over a sieve; when all is whisked that will froth, and the froth is drained, add to the remainder what has drained from the whips, grate in a little nutmeg, and half fill the glasses, laying the froth on the top.

STRAWBERRY WHIPS.—Beat cream as described in whipped cream. Sweeten and strain strawberry juice, fill the glasses half full, and pile up the cream; lay on each glass a large strawberry. This is a beautiful country dessert.

JELLY FLUMMERY.—Beat the whites of eggs stiff, sweeten to taste; mix with the egg any jelly desired, and beat it well; make a thin boiled custard or a syllabub, and partly fill a deep glass dish with it, and lay the egg on the top; or have two dishes, one for the float, and another for the custard or syllabub.

VANILLA FLUMMERY.—Make a thin boiled custard with the yolks of well-beaten eggs, flavor with vanilla; beat the whites stiff, mix in sugar and vanilla; line a deep glass dish with sponge cake, dipped as quickly in wine and out as possible, pour over the cream and lay the egg on the top; put a drop of jelly on each bit of egg. This is a dinner dessert.

Cocoa Whips.—Beat sweet cream until solid; have grated the white part of a cocoa-nut, mix it with pulverized sugar; take a pint of thin cream or rich milk, heat it boiling hot, have ready two beaten eggs, take it from the fire and stir them in the hot milk, when cool stir in the milk from the nut, fill the glasses half full and set them to cool; when cold, mix the cocoa and whipped cream together and lay it on the top.

Cocoa Flummery.—Beat the whites of eggs stiff, grate the white part of a cocoa-nut, mix the nut and egg together, sweeten to the taste; prepare a boiled custard, pour it over sponge cake, and lay the egg and cocoa on the top.

Jelly and Whips.—Fill glasses one-third full of jelly and fill up with whipped cream, flavored to suit the taste.

A Charlotte Russe, No. 3—Prepare a rich boiled custard with half a pint of rich new milk and half a pint of sweet cream, flavor with vanilla; dissolve half an ounce of isinglass in half a pint of water; when both have cooled, mix them well and add four tablespoonfuls of powdered loaf-sugar. Then take half a pound of loaf-sugar in lumps, and rub on them the yellow rind of two lemons, strain the juice, and mix it with two wine-glasses of sherry, and one of brandy, pour it over the sugar, and when dissolved mix it with a quart of rich cream, whisk it, and add the froth to the custard, stir it very hard constantly while adding the froth, and beat it well after it is all in. Have ready a sufficient number of small sponge cakes, or one large one to hold the custard; take out neatly all the inside of the cake, and fill it with the custard; set it on ice until cool, then ice it with a frosting made in the usual manner, flavored with lemon; ornament it while soft with strawberries without jamming, white grapes, or in any other way fancy may dictate; keep it cool until wanted for the table. This is a beautiful as well as excellent flummery or trifle, is proper for evening parties, etc. The bits that come from the centre can be soaked in cold custard beat up together, and the beaten whites of eggs flavored with jelly laid over it, and served for the family at dinner as dessert; any old dry cake can be used in the same manner.

Isinglass Blanc-Mange.—Dissolve shred isinglass in the proportion of one ounce to the quart in new milk; if in the winter, you can add another pint of milk; melt it over boiling water, constantly stirring it; when dissolved, flavor with vanilla and lemon or bitter almond, add sugar to the taste, and as much salt as will lie on a three-cent piece, and no more; let it boil five or six minutes, stirring constantly. Dip the moulds into cold water, strain in the blanc-mange, stir until thickened, and set it on ice until needed for use.

SNOW CREAM.—Beat to a stiff froth the whites of six eggs, beat in powdered loaf-sugar to suit the taste, two table-spoonfuls of sweet wine, and a trifle of nutmeg; beat well, then add a pint of sweet, thick cream, beat stiff; serve with sweetmeats or ripe fruit.

ORANGE CREAM.—Peel nice oranges and slice them, lay them on a hair sieve to drain; when all the juice has run off that will without pressing, lay the fruit in a deep dish and sugar it. Beat sweet cream stiff, sweeten and flavor with the orange juice, and serve with the fruit; the juice must be added just before serving, or the cream will curdle. Strawberries, raspberries, or any sweetish fruit can be prepared in the same manner; sour fruits would curdle the cream.

FRUIT PUDDINGS.—*See* Part V. Chapters I. II. III. IV. V. VI.

CHAPTER IX.

PASTRY AND PIES.

REMARKS ON PUFF PASTE.—The flour must be white and cold, the butter sweet, the rolling board or marble slab even, the rolling pin of equal thickness with handles, the water ice cold, the mixing room cold, the person who makes it must be able to move with rapidity, and the oven should bake quickly without burning.

To PREPARE FOR MAKING PUFF PASTE.—Sift all the flour needed, and set it on the table, wash the butter, press it in a coarse towel to remove all the water and buttermilk, and lay it on ice. Put a lump of washed ice in a pitcher of water. Get the plates ready, dust them with flour, and then wipe off nearly all of it. Now decide the amount of paste wanted, measure the flour, and weigh the butter. If tarts

7*

are to be made, have the filling ready. If meat pies, let the meats be cooling, while the paste is being made.

PLAIN PASTE.—This is a proper paste for apple, cherry, rhubarb, whortleberry, peach, plum, or any other fruit pie which has a top and bottom crust. Measure one quart of flour, allow a little for rolling. Weigh five ounces of butter, after it is pressed and cooled on the ice. Cut the butter quickly in thin slices, not over one-fourth of an inch square, and as thin as possible; into the flour, with the forefinger, stir the butter and flour together without incorporating them; now wet it with sufficient ice water to moisten the paste, stir it with one finger, leaving it a rough mass of flour, butter, and water, mingled but not united; dredge the paste-board with considerable flour, take up a handful of rough dough, place it on the board, dust it over with flour, roll it, quickly but lightly, as thin as it is possible, and allow the paste to be lifted without breaking; roll it over the pin and lay it on the plate without handling; press it lightly in place, and cut the edges with a sharp knife, use the cuttings and a portion more of the paste for the under crust of the next pie, and so on until all the plates are covered; then use fresh dough, taking as little as will cover the pie for the top crusts; fill the pies, cover and bake quickly without browning. (*See* Part V. Chap. I. APPLE PIE, Chap. II. PEACH, and Chap. V. CHERRY PIES.) Paste managed in this way will be nearly as flaky as puff paste, and not too rich for health. Lard is not as healthy or as good for pie-crust as sweet butter, but those who prefer it for the sake of economy, can substitute lard for butter, or what is better, use half lard and half butter. If lard is used, don't forget the salt.

PUMPKIN OR CUSTARD PIE PASTE.—Take four ounces of butter to a quart of flour, rub them well together, but do it quickly, wet it with cold water, and incorporate it into one mass. The paste for pumpkin and custard pies needs to be firm, not flaky, to hold the contents of the pies.

To MAKE A NICE PUFF PASTE.—Weigh one pound of flour, and one pound of worked butter, freed from water as already directed. Reserve half a teacup of the flour, make the flour into a stiff paste with ice-cold water. Roll it out thin four times with a light brisk movement, without handling the dough. Divide the butter in four parts, and each part again in four parts, leaving them in one-ounce parts. The dough should be left spread on the board when rolled out the fourth time; now with a knife spread on one ounce of the butter, fold over the paste and roll lightly, without breaking through to the butter; fold again, and roll as before, and again; the third time leave the paste spread on the board, and add another ounce in the same manner, and so continue until the sixteen ounces are all rolled in, giving the paste fifty-two turns, including the four before the butter was added. This seems a hard job to undertake, but as the dough rolls easier each time, it is soon done. For a common puff paste use half the butter, and turn twenty-eight times. This will cover a large quantity of pies, or make as many tarts as would be wanted for a large party. In our family, we divide the paste when one-half of the butter is used, in which case four ounces less butter is needed. Roll into one part four ounces, half an ounce at each fourth turn, and no more in the other. When all the butter is in, roll up the paste and cut from the ends of the roll to form into tarts. That part which has only the half of the butter, we use for the under crust to tarts and mince pies, and cover the top with the richer; when this is done, put half an ounce into each turn, that the paste may have the proper amount of turns. Use the reserved flour to dredge the board and flour the pin, but work no more flour into the paste. *Remarks.*—This paste cannot be made in warm weather, unless rolled in a refrigerating room; neither can it be made in a hot kitchen in winter; the cook should be brisk enough to keep her blood circulating, and she may stand on a heated plank or soapstone while making it. For tarts place four layers of the paste rolled as thin as paper, first the bottom, then three rings, place them on paper, on dripping pans, and set them in the cold air a few moments after they are ready, have the oven of a quick but not deep heat, and protect the tops with paper. If the oven inclines to burn on the bottom, either put two thicknesses of paper under them or raise the pan with brick. For tart pies, cover the bottom of the plate with the poorest paste, or make a good plain paste for that purpose, and roll the three layers so thin that the board can be seen through the paste, the thinner the better. Cut the strips of even width, and lay them on neatly. For mince pies use two layers only, as thin as possible. For oyster pies, the poorest paste is rich enough, for all but the layers. For chicken pie, use a plain paste under, and the best for the layers and covering. For meat pies, the poorest of the puff paste is good enough for the top and layers, and the plain paste for the bottom. For common use, the plain paste is as good as is necessary for top, bottom, and layers.

French Puff Paste.—To one pound of flour, take one pound of butter washed free from salt, and pressed in a cloth to extract the water; make the butter in a square cake, and lay it on ice. Mix the flour into a pretty stiff but not hard paste, roll it out four times, make it into a square lump and roll it out. Cool the paste by placing the paste-board in a cold place, now lay the butter in the centre of the paste, fold over the paste, and roll it gently without breaking through to the butter; when rolled as thin as possible without breaking through to the butter, fold it in three, dust the board and roller, and roll the paste again to its utmost extent; repeat this, then set it to cool fifteen minutes; then fold it in three folds, roll again and again, let it cool fifteen minutes again, and roll it the fifth and sixth, which is the last time. If three-fourths of a pound of butter is used, fold and roll it five times. If half a pound, fold and give the paste three turns, in the same manner as directed for one pound. The butter must not be too hard at first, but about the same temperature as the paste. If too hard it will break through the paste while rolling, which must be avoided.

Dumpling Paste.—Make dumpling paste as directed to make paste for pumpkin and custard pies, allowing three ounces of butter to the quart of flour.

Pumpkin Pies.—Select fine sweet pumpkin, stew it slowly until reduced to paste with no standing juice. Pass it through a colander, and thin it with milk to the consistency of batter; add to a six-quart pan a teaspoon of salt, and sugar to suit the taste, ginger, and if relished, nutmeg. If pumpkin is plenty, use no eggs; if not, three may be used to the pan, and milk added; a little thin cream is an addition. Cover the plate to the edge with the paste, pack it to the rim of the plate, and prick it two or three times with a needle or pin, then bake the crust, and while it is baking roll out a piece of dough, measuring in diameter as much as a small finger, and long enough to reach around the plate; when the crust has cooled, lay this roll around the edge of the plate; pinch it or leave it round, according to fancy; fill the paste or shell with the pumpkin, and bake it in a hot oven, without burning or blistering. In filling the shell be careful not to drop any of the pumpkin on the edge.

Custard Pies.—Prepare two shells as described for a pumpkin pie, beat four eggs without separating, and add the foam, as fast as it rises, to one quart of rich new milk, sweeten to taste, add a salt-spoon of salt, and fill the shells after the bottom crust has baked, etc. Bake until the custard is solid; serve cold—a hot custard is a poor pie; flavor, if desired, with nutmeg, vanilla, bitter almond, or lemon. Use the same day baked.

CREAM PIE.—This is baked like a custard, but to be very nice, the edge of the plate should be layered with puff paste; make a custard of thin cream instead of milk, and bake it as a custard. It must be eaten the same day it is baked.

RASPBERRY PIES WITH COVERS.—Cover the plate with the plain paste, fill the shell with raspberries, add sugar, butter, and a little flour, cover the pie, cut a slit in the centre, and bake gently until quite done. Send it to the table when warm, it is not as good the second day. The sealed fruit is used in the same manner.

WHORTLEBERRY PIES.—After the plate is covered, spread in the whortleberries, add a little citric or tartaric acid, dissolved in a tablespoon of water, sprinkle over sugar, add a piece of butter as large as a teaspoon, and flour to thicken the juice. Cover the pie, cut a slit in the middle of the top crust, and bake gently. Use the day it is baked, if possible. Use the can fruit in the same manner.

BLACKBERRY PIE.—Make a blackberry pie exactly like a whortleberry, adding one gill of water, instead of a table-spoonful. Serve the day it is baked, barely cold. Make the hermetically-sealed fruit in the same manner.

GREEN CURRANTS.—Those preserved for winter make better pies than fresh currants—they part with the flavor of the leaves which they have when fresh, which is a great improvement. Fill the pies with currants; when baked, take off the top crust, and add sugar, butter, a little flour, and a piece of soda as large as a pea; mix the ingredients together, and set the pie in the oven five minutes with the door down. The pies made from the hermetically-sealed currants, are sugared and seasoned before baking. Use all the water in fruits preserved for pies. Use no soda in the preserved fruit; they will require less sugar than pies of the fresh fruit.

PLAIN GOOSEBERRY PIES.—Stew gooseberries, add sugar, break the fruit, and put them in the pie; add a little butter and flour, and bake until the paste is done. Make the hermetically-sealed fruit pies in the same manner.

GOOSEBERRY TARTS.—For directions to cover the plates, or make the shells for small tarts, *see* PUFF PASTE; stew the berries with sugar until they look clear, then pass them through a colander, and fill the shells for the tarts; after they are baked, the fruit may be covered with the whites of egg beat stiff, and mixed with sugar, in the proportion of one egg to two ounces; beat half an hour briskly, and cover the centre of the tarts, and place them in the oven until slightly browned. Prepare the sealed fruit in the same manner.

RHUBARB PIES.—If the skin is tender do not peel it; if not, remove the skin, cut the stalks in small bits, and place them in the pie, add a salt-spoon of soda and a little flour. When the paste is done, remove the top crust and add sugar and butter; mash the rhubarb fine, and incorporate the sugar, butter, and fruit perfectly. Put the top crust on the pie, and serve warm. If nutmeg is relished, grate over the top of the fruit a little before putting on the crust, but do not mix it through the pie. Rhubarb may be put up in the spring for winter use in bottles, as directed in plums.

CRANBERRY PIE.—This may be made exactly like a gooseberry pie.

CRANBERRY TARTS.—Make them like a gooseberry tart. Cranberries are very nice stewed and made in an open pie without straining.

LEMON PIE.—The proportions are two lemons, four eggs, two table-spoons of melted butter, ten table-spoons of loaf-sugar. Grate the yellow rind of the lemon, beat together the rind, juice, sugar, and the yolks of the eggs until very light. Prepare a large tart pie, fill the pie with the mixture before baking the paste, and bake until the paste is done. Beat the whites stiff, and stir into them little by little one-fourth of a pound of sugar, spread it over the top, and bake a light brown. Cranberry, strawberry, or any juicy fruit can be prepared in exactly the same manner, and will be found superior.

STRAWBERRY PIE OR SHORT CAKE.—*See* Part III. Chap. X. Make a nice short cake; while hot, split it as many times as possible, and spread each layer with butter, strawberries, and sugar, put on the top crust, wet it over with egg, sift over sugar, and serve hot. Raspberries, blackberries, and whortleberries can be used in the same manner.

MINCE PIES.—One part of beef suet finely chopped and freed from skin to two of lean chopped beef, and four of sour chopped apples. Mix the suet and beef together, and rub salt through it, then add the apples and mix thoroughly, add sugar, sweet cider, a little nice syrup, raisins, currants, cinnamon, mace, a few cloves. Work all together, and let the mince remain until morning—then taste; if not sufficiently spiced, add more, but be careful not to overspice with cloves; add sugar and cider if needed; if too much seasoned, chop more suet, meat, and apple, and add to the mince. If properly made in December and kept cool, it will keep three months. Sugar and cider must be added to the quantity used at each baking, stir up the whole once each week, and cover it tightly, to prevent mice or insects from troubling it. Currant wine is excellent in mince pies. Cover a plate with good plain paste or half-turned puff paste, (*see* PUFF PASTE,) fit three layers of the best puff paste to the edge of the plate one and a half inch wide, fill the pies even with the layers, put in each four pieces of butter the size of hazlenuts, add a little nutmeg, dredge with flour, and cover with thin puff paste; bake rather quick without browning the paste. A mince pie should be juicy, rich, sweet, the spices well balanced, and, to be perfect, should be two weeks old before cut; they are better one month old, if kept where they will not mould. Always warm, not heat, mince pies, before sending them to the table.

FRUIT PIES.—*See* Part V. Chapters I. II. IV. V. VI.

CHAPTER X.

YEAST, BREAD, BISCUIT, ETC.

REMARKS.—In order to make good bread, the cook must be furnished with good flour from sound wheat, white and dry; fresh yeast, a good oven, and strength to knead the dough. If a poor barrel of flour is sent, return it; flour is usually warranted, and the only extra expense will be in the drayage of the barrel or sack, to and from the mill or flour store. To know the state of yeast, either brewer's or homemade, before making bread, is very important. If the yeast is lifeless or partially so, it will not raise bread to a proper lightness. Bread that is a long time rising, will be either heavy, sour, or very dark colored. Stir in a little yeast, flour to make a batter; if brewer's, it will rise in three minutes, if quite fresh and of sufficient strength. Homemade yeast will take from five to ten minutes, according to its strength. Brewer's yeast, when very bitter, is improved by washing in cold water; the lively part settling to the bottom, and the bitter part mingling with the water, which is drained off from the yeast. It may need washing several times, especially if it is the yeast from lager beer. Yeast, from strong beer, is usually in a fit state to use without washing. The rule for using the yeast of strong beer, is a teaspoonful to one loaf of bread. For homemade yeast, a tablespoonful if not too bitter. For dried yeast, a tablespoonful to a loaf is about the proper proportion. If a brick oven is used, it should be nearly hot before bread raised with brewer's yeast is mixed; but for baking with homemade yeast, make the fire when the bread first shows signs of rising in the mixing pan, which ought to be from five to ten minutes after mixing.

To MAKE BREAD WITH HOP YEAST.—Sift into the bread-pan three quarts of flour. Having tried the yeast, take three tablespoonfuls. Dissolve a piece of soda, as large as a green pea, in half a pint of warm water, and stir in the yeast; make a hole in the centre of the flour; mix the yeast and half a pint of warm water into a batter in the centre of the pan, and cover the batter with flour. Set the pan where it will keep about blood heat; when it commences to rise, the flour will rise and form cracks; and when the batter or sponge breaks over the flour, it is fit to mix; if it remains too long it will sour. When the sponge shows signs of being soon ready, warm one quart of sweet milk and half a pint of water to a little more than blood heat; dissolve in the milk and water as much soda as was used at first, unless the sponge is soured, when more will be needed; add the wetting gradually to the flour and sponge, mixing it well together; rub the dough from the hands with the flour; dredge the paste-board with flour reserved from that measured; turn out the dough; rub the pan entirely clean with some of the flour, add the cleanings of the pan to the dough, and knead all together. Kneading is best performed by doubling the hand, and pressing the knuckles in the dough with all the strength of the arm; it should be performed with a quick shoving movement, and as quickly as possible; work the dough until it cleaves from the hand without sticking in the least to the hand when entirely free from flour; make it up in a large smooth lump; flour the bread-pan, put back the dough, dredge the dough with reserved flour, warm the bread cloth, cover the pan, and set it where the dough will keep a blood heat. Now arrange the wood in the oven, take twelve long sticks of dry bass, or some other light wood, lay them across each other, keeping them near the centre of the oven, and put light kindlings near the mouth. When the dough has a puffy appearance, light the fire, and let it burn slowly; some ovens will heat with one dozen sticks of bass wood, and others take more; the cook will learn to manage her own oven after heating it a few times. Watch the bread; when light, take the pan to the table; if there is danger of the bread being light too soon for the oven, knead it down thoroughly, and let it stand where it will not chill or be very warm; if the oven is in the right state for the bread to be put into loaves, the wood will be mostly reduced to large brands, and the roof of the oven will have burned white. Make the dough into three loaves; set it where it will keep warm, and cover it with the bread blanket. Now stir the coals over the oven, so that it will heat regularly; when the brands cease to blaze and smoke, shut the iron door of the oven until the bread is nearly ready. Then clear the oven, sweep it with a damp broom free from ashes, throw in a little flour; if it burns immediately, the floor is too hot; hold in your hand, count twenty seconds; if you can do this, the oven is of the right heat; and if the flour browns, instead of burning, the floor is also of the proper heat. If too hot, swab the floor with a wet broom until it is the proper heat; put in the bread, examine it in five, ten, and again in fifteen minutes; if baking too fast, leave down the door; if too slow, add coals to the mouth of the oven; if baking right, give it forty-five minutes' time, then take it out, and turn out the bread. If the crust is rather hard, dampen it very slightly; wrap it in the bread-towel, and let it steam until cold. When entirely cold, put it in the bread-box, but not while the least warm. Although we give an exact measurement of wetting for bread, it will not always make bread of the proper consistency; some kinds of wheat make flour which takes up more fluid than others. The bakers know this, and for this reason select the red winter wheat for making bread. Bread to be of the right consistency, should be as soft as it is possible to knead; at first, soft dough will be sticky, and trouble the uninitiated cook; but she will soon learn to manage her bread-pan dexterously, when her labors will be much lightened. When a new barrel of flour is first baked from, measure the wetting accurately, and the proportion proper for the future bakings while that flour lasts will be ascertained. When milk cannot be obtained, add to three pints of water a bit of sweet butter, as large as the bowl of a teaspoon. The crust of bread is improved by oiling the top of the loaf, before putting it in the oven, with very little sweet butter. Grease bread-pans with sweet butter, or fresh pork fat. Rancid grease will ruin the bottom crust.

BREAD RAISED WITH BREWER'S YEAST.—Sift into the bread-pan three quarts of flour, and reserve half a pint. Warm the flour by setting it in the stove oven a few moments, but do not let it scorch or become hot. Heat equal parts of milk and water, allowing one pint of wetting for one quart of flour. Dissolve in the wetting a salt-spoon of soda. If no milk is used, omit the soda. When the wetting is a little more than blood-heat, but not hot enough to scald flour or yeast, take it from the fire. Having tried the yeast, and found it good, take three teaspoons of the yeast from strong beer, or four from lager bier, (after it is washed nearly free from its bitter properties;) mix it in the wetting, and add it to the flour. Knead the bread briskly; rub some of the reserved flour on the pan; roll off all the dough, and rub your hands the same way. Continue to knead the bread until it can be handled, and cut without adhering to the knife, paste-board, or hands. Rub over three common sized bread-pans with sweet butter, or fresh lard. If the paper or rag with which the pan was rubbed is at all discolored, rub off the butter entirely with a clean cloth, and grease the pans over. Cut the dough in three equal parts; knead each part briskly for several minutes, and put them in the pans. Run the point of a knife blade through the centre of each loaf until it touches the pans; press the loaf in shape; set them where they will have equal heat; cover with the bread-blanket, and let it rise. Keep a little watch of the bread, and as soon as it appears puffy, clear the oven. When the oven is properly tempered, the floor will brown flour, and you can hold your hand in the centre twenty seconds. By this time the bread should be light. If too light, it will dry very soon. Oil the top of each loaf with a trifle of sweet butter, and place it in the oven. After five minutes look in the oven; if too hot, leave down the door one minute. In ten minutes look at the bread again; and examine, lastly, when the bread has been in the oven fifteen minutes. It will take three-quarters of an hour to bake, if the oven was a proper heat from the first. Bread, baked in a brick oven, is much better than that baked in a stove oven. If the bread is baked in the stove, the cook can easily determine when it is done. If the oven is regular, bread will bake in from ten to fifteen minutes less time than in a brick oven, where the heat is constantly decreasing. If the yeast is good, it will rise in half an hour.

GRAHAM BREAD.—Graham flour. The wheat must be of the best

quality, and either run through a smut mill, or washed and dried before grinding. It should be ground rather coarser than common flour, and used without bolting. It takes more wetting than fine flour. For every loaf allow three large table-spoons of molasses, one quart of wetting, a teaspoon of salt, yeast in the same proportion as in the two preceding rules. Mix the yeast, molasses, and salt, in the wetting; add a half-teaspoon of soda, and mix in as much coarse flour as can possibly be stirred in with a spoon. Now knead the bread briskly, until it cleaves from the hand. If made with brewer's yeast, put the loaves in the pan, and pat it in place and shape. If made with homemade yeast, sponge the bread as in the directions for sponging bread; and add the molasses and other wetting after the sponge rises. Knead until the dough cleaves from the hands. Set it in a warm place until it rises; when light, knead it again as before, and put it in the pans to rise. Add no flour after the first mixing; the dough will not be stiff enough to form into loaves; shape the loaves after they are in the pan with the hand.

BRAN YEAST BREAD.—Just before retiring, heat a quart of water hot, but not scalding; stir into it bran, until the spoon will stand upright; be careful not to get the yeast too thick, add a little salt; take up hot ashes, not coals, place a kettle of warm water on the ashes, and the yeast in the water, where it will keep warm all night. When the bran rises above the water, it is light and fit to strain. If not light in the morning, put the yeast in warm water until the bran rises to the surface. Allow for each quart of flour a pint of wetting, including the yeast; dissolve half a teaspoonful of soda in the milk; sponge the bread with milk and the yeast, mixing in the centre of the pan one-fourth of the flour to a batter, and let it rise. As soon as light, mix the sponge and milk into a loaf, knead it until the dough cleaves from the hands, and put it into the pans immediately. Let it rise again, and bake as soon as light. It takes less time to bake than other bread, and requires a moderate oven. It will not remain fresh as long as hop yeast, but is a good healthy bread. It will resemble hops if a little of the flavor of hops is added to the wetting, and can be made, when by any accident the hop yeast has either frozen, scalded, or been in some other manner spoiled.

BISCUIT RAISED WITH HOP YEAST.—Sift into a pan one quart of flour; warm a pint of milk; make a sponge with one half the milk, add a bit of soda as large as a pea. Stir in the sponge one table-spoonful of good homemade yeast; cover the sponge warm, and let it rise. When the sponge breaks over the flour, add the milk, in which is dissolved a piece of soda as large as a pea, and a salt-spoon of fine salt. Knead the biscuit until it feels smooth, and cleaves from the hand, and let it rise; when very light, but not sour, take the pan to the table, soften two-thirds of a teacup of sweet butter, and work it by degrees into the dough, until the whole is thoroughly incorporated with it; then knead, until the dough cleaves from the hand. If there is the slightest tendency to acidity, dissolve and strain a little soda, and add it with the butter; probably one-fourth of a teaspoon will be all that will be needed. If possible to knead the biscuit, add no more flour, and, at all events, as little as possible. Let the biscuit rise again, and knead it once more; butter the pans, (it will take two common bread-pans,) make the biscuits in small round loaves, turning in the dough to the middle of the biscuits. When finished, before rising, the loaves should be as large as a dollar and nearly round; place them in the pans; butter each biscuit slightly where they press each other, prick them entirely through, so that the fork will touch the pan in three different places, cover warm, and let them rise. Examine often, and do not allow them to sour. As soon as light, bake them in a moderate oven. The top and bottom crusts should neither be hard baked nor moist. Wrap them in a towel to steam, if the crusts are baked too hard; if not, turn them up, so that the bottom crust will not steam-soak. If not to be used warm, do not separate them until entirely cold.

BREWER'S YEAST BISCUITS.—Sift into the bread-pan one quart of flour; melt a large table-spoonful of cold butter in one pint of sweet milk, dissolve a salt-spoon of salt, and as much soda in the milk; reserve a handful of flour to knead the dough; cool the milk to blood heat, and stir in one teaspoonful of brewer's yeast from strong beer or two of washed lager beer; knead the dough fifteen minutes briskly, then make it up in small round loaves no larger than a half-dollar. Have the tins well buttered, lay in the biscuit, dredge them with flour where they join, and prick them several times through to the pan, let them rise, and bake in a moderate oven as soon as light. Bake without browning till thoroughly done; do not separate the biscuit until quite cold, unless used hot, in which case break them apart just before serving.

SODA AND CREAM OF TARTAR BISCUIT, No. 1.—Sift one teaspoon

of soda and two of cream of tartar, with one quart of flour in the bread-pan. Cut in bits not larger than a three-cent piece, and as thin as possible, one quarter of a cup of butter; mix quickly, without rubbing or working the butter with the other ingredients. Have ready a pint of sweet milk, wet up the biscuit quickly, roll the dough half an inch thick, cut it with a small biscuit cutter, and bake immediately in a brisk oven.

SOUR CREAM BISCUIT.—Sift a teaspoon of salt and one of soda with a quart of flour in the bread-pan; have ready a large pint of sour cream, beat one egg, add it to the cream, mix, roll, cut, and bake the biscuit as quickly as possible.

SOUR MILK BISCUIT.—Sift one teaspoon of soda, one of salt, and a quart of flour in a pan; rub into the flour one-quarter of a cup of butter, mix quickly, knead briskly, and bake as soon as possible in a brisk oven.

CREAM OF TARTAR BISCUIT, No. 2.—Sift two teaspoons of cream of tartar, one of soda, and one quart of flour in a pan; mix in the flour one-third of a cup of butter as lightly as possible, without rubbing the butter to warm it in the least. Mix up the biscuit with a large pint of water, knead briskly, and bake quickly.

BUTTERMILK BREAD.—With one quart of buttermilk mix two quarts of flour, and two even teaspoons of soda; knead well, make the dough into two loaves, let it rise ten minutes, and bake.

FRENCH BREAD OF BREWER'S YEAST.—Take one pint of milk, two ounces of butter, and a salt-spoon of salt; warm the milk until the butter is softened; beat three eggs light; mix into the milk one pint of flour, add a teaspoon of strong beer yeast; let it stand ten minutes, or until it has slightly risen, add the eggs, and sufficient flour to make a soft dough, knead it ten minutes briskly. Roll it out in strips, and either braid the strips or make larger rolls the width of the pan it is to be baked in, and bake when light.

FRENCH TWIST BREAD.—Take one quart of light dough raised with homemade yeast; mix in it a large table-spoon of sweet butter, a salt-spoon of salt, and one egg; add flour, and knead well. Let it rise until light, then knead very gently; roll the dough in thin strips, measuring an inch in diameter; dredge lightly with flour, and braid loosely; let it stand a few moments, and bake quickly without burning.

GERMAN STEAMED NEUDLES.—Three gills of sweet milk made into a sponge with a teaspoonful of brewer's yeast, or a table-spoon of fresh homemade, and a teaspoon of salt; let it rise until quite light, then add half a teacup of butter, three eggs, and flour to make a soft biscuit dough; knead it well; if made with homemade yeast, let it rise before making up the neudles; if brewer's, make up the dough as soon as mixed in small balls, the size of half a small egg. Melt in a deep spider with an iron or close-fitting tin cover, half a table-spoon of sweet butter; lay the neudles in the spider, and let them rise; when quite light, fill the spider half full of boiling water, or until it reaches to about the middle of the neudles; place the spider over a steady but not too brisk fire, and steam them half an hour without lifting the cover. Be sure the cakes do not boil dry too soon, so as to scorch the bottom crust. When quite done, the water should be evaporated, leaving the neudles dry. These are an excellent breakfast cake, and when managed properly, are as light as a sponge. Serve hot.

HOP YEAST.—Boil four potatoes; mash them fine, mix them with one pint of flour, boil a pint of hops in a quart of boiling water five minutes, add a teaspoon of salt, strain the hop water gradually on the flour and potatoes while it is boiling hot, so as to scald the flour; beat it well, and let it cool to blood-heat; then add one teacup of good homemade (not brewer's) yeast, and half a teaspoon of soda; beat it well, and let it rise. To make dry yeast, mix in this yeast, when about two-thirds light, as much Indian meal as can be dampened with the yeast, leaving it in dry crumbs; spread it thin where it will dry quickly without feeling the sun or stove heat; it dries best in the wind. To make yeast cakes, let the yeast get light, but no more than light; mix up the dough with Indian meal in a round long roll, four inches in diameter, cut off the cakes as soon as mixed, without letting it rise, one-fourth of an inch thick, dry in the wind, and turn them frequently; when quite dry, put the dried yeast or cakes in a tight paper bag. Be sure the meal is sweet, free from a bitter taste, and made from sound corn. If kept dry, it will last months. To use it, soak the cakes or crumbs quite soft, mix a sponge, add a little soda, set it in a warm place, and let it stand until morning; use it as the sponge of home yeast bread without sponging again. If hops cannot be had, use peach leaves for making homemade yeast, though fresh hops are the best.

WHEAT AND INDIAN BREAD.—Sift into a pan four quarts of Indian meal, have ready boiling water; stir into the meal boiling water until the spoon will stand nearly upright in the mush; let it cool to blood-heat, then stir into the meal two quarts of wheat flour, a little salt, and a small teacup of fresh homemade hop yeast; mix well, grease an old-fashioned bake kettle, and put in the bread; let it stand until it shows signs of cracking, then set the bake kettle on coals, heat the cover, put it on the kettle, and cover with warm ashes; bake gently three or four hours. Or, what is much better, put the bread in a large pan; when it shows signs of cracking, put it in a brick oven, bake gently, cover the top with paper to prevent the crust becoming hard, and leave the bread in the oven all night; or bake two hours in a stove-oven, cover the top with paper, and when done, close the damper and let the bread remain in the oven until morning; add two table-spoons of molasses, if desired very sweet.

RYE AND INDIAN BREAD.—Sift three pints of rye flour, with four quarts of Indian meal; add a little salt, stir in boiling water until the spoon will stand upright; let it cool, add a small teacup of home hop yeast quite fresh; let it rise in the pan in which it is to be baked, until it shows signs of cracking; then bake as directed in the above recipe.

PUMPKIN BREAD.—Pumpkin bread is made according to the two preceding recipes, except that instead of using flour or rye, one quart of stewed and strained pumpkin is used, with three quarts of meal; add little salt.

BUNS.—Take three teacups of light dough from homemade yeast bread, mix into the dough three teaspoons of melted butter, a little salt, one and a half ounces of sugar, three well-beaten eggs, and half a teaspoon of dissolved and strained soda; mix all together, and add flour to make the dough stiff enough to knead; knead well, and let it rise; when light, make the dough up in rather high cakes, the size round of one dollar; pack them closely in the pan, and dredge lightly with flour to prevent their becoming one mass. Bake as soon as light, and when done, brush over the top with yolk of egg and sugar; do not separate them until cold.

CARAWAY BREAD.—Take one quart of light hop yeast raised dough, mix into the dough a table-spoonful of cold butter, half an ounce of caraway, two ounces of sugar, a salt-spoon of soda, and one of salt; work the ingredients well together, add flour to make a loaf, butter a pan, put in the dough, and let it rise; when quite light, bake slowly but thoroughly; when it comes from the oven, wet the top crust with egg and sugar; when cold, cut the bread in slices. It is plain and excellent food for children; if it is intended for young children who have not all their teeth, grind the caraway-seed. Caraway and coriander united and ground, makes an excellent spice for such breads.

RYE BREAD.—Make rye bread like wheat, but be careful it does not sour; it sours more readily than wheat or Indian; the same may be said of oatmeal; Indian sours sooner than wheat after it is light.

RICE BREAD.—Scald thoroughly one pint of rice flour, add to it three pints of wheat flour, and sufficient water to make a dough; mix in the water two teaspoons of brewer's yeast, or a table-spoon of homemade; let the bread rise in the pans but once, if made with brewer's yeast; but if of homemade, once in the bread-pan, and again in the bake-pans; add a little salt.

POTATO BREAD.—Sponge wheat flour as for wheat bread; while it rises, boil one large potato for every pint of flour; mash fine, and pass them through a sieve; when the sponge is light, mix the potatoes with the sponge, add the wetting and mix up the bread, knead well, and let it rise; when light make up the loaves, and bake when they rise.

CRUMPETS.—Half a pound of flour, one table-spoon of fresh brewer's yeast, a salt-spoon of soda, half a teaspoon of salt, and sufficient rich milk to form a fluid paste; let it rise, and bake like pancakes.

HOE CAKE.—Have ready two quarts of boiling water, mix in one quart of the water half a cup of sweet butter and one large teaspoon of soda; in the other quart dissolve half a teaspoon of tartaric acid; sift in two pans a pint each of Indian meal; stir into one the soda water and butter, boiling hot, and beat it ten minutes hard; in the other, stir the other quart, also boiling, beating it the same time. If the meal does not make the dough stiff enough to handle, heat it and add more; have the griddle ready, take a table-spoonful of each of the mixtures in the hand, work it together quickly, form it in square cakes, one-fourth of an inch thick, and four inches square, and brown them on the griddle; serve hot.

INDIAN MUFFINS.—Take one quart of sweet yellow corn meal, add a teaspoon of salt, have ready one quart of boiling milk; mix the meal to a stiff dough, add nearly a cup of sweet butter merely warmed and a little soda; beat the mixture hard fifteen minutes. While the cakes are making, have six eggs beat separately till very light, add them gradually to the muffins, and beat them hard five minutes; the dough should be thin enough to beat well; heat the dripping pan and muffin rings, grease them, fill the rings full, and bake thoroughly until done; serve with maple syrup. These are excellent, if well beaten.

MILK RISING BREAD.—Take one cup of milk, one of water, a teaspoon of salt, and flour to make a batter; keep it warm until light, then warm milk, and mix the rising and milk with sufficient flour to make a soft dough; knead it thoroughly, put it into the pans, and bake as soon as light. Milk rising managed in this manner, has no offensive odor.

MRS. P.'s CRACKERS.—When the above dough is light add to one quart a small teacup of butter; work it well and pound in all the flour possible; beat the crackers until the dough feels smooth as glass; then break off small lumps; roll very thin, and bake a long time without browning. The crackers should be about as large as a dollar. Prick them several times before baking.

CHAPTER XI.

CAKES.

REMARKS ON MOLASSES CAKES.—Cakes that depend on molasses for lightness, should be made of real West India molasses; syrup will not do. They should be put in the oven immediately after adding the soda; bake in a quick but not over hot oven, without burning, until well done; they must be used fresh, unless made hard, when they will keep some time; if shortened with lard, don't forget the salt; pork fat is better than lard, and is equal to butter for spiced molasses cakes; alum is an addition; when used, more soda is needed; spice with ginger and cinnamon; if used warm, break instead of cutting; bake in shallow pans, the more surface the better, most persons preferring the crust. Warm gingerbread with sauce makes a good dinner dessert.

GINGERBREAD, No. 1.—One cup of melted (not heated) butter or lard; if the latter, add salt, stirred into two cups of molasses, a table-spoonful of ginger, and a teaspoon of cinnamon; sift the flour, and stir in enough to make a very stiff batter, dissolve a piece of alum as large as a kidney bean in half a cup of water, and stir it in, then add as much flour as will make it thick enough to nearly roll on the board;. have the pans greased and the oven hot, then stir in one heaping tea-spoonful of soda, dissolved in half a cup of boiling water, mix it well and as quickly as possible, and put it immediately in the oven; use it while fresh; after it is put in the pans, slash the cake as bakers do theirs, and when it comes from the oven, wet it over with syrup.

GINGERCAKE, No. 2.—One cup of melted butter, two of molasses, one of sour milk, one teaspoonful of soda,—if the molasses is quite acid a half spoon more than this will be needed,—three eggs, five cups of sifted flour, and a spoonful of ginger and cinnamon; dissolve the soda and stir it in last, and bake in an oven with steady heat imme-diately. No cake burns as easily as molasses cake.

GINGERCAKES, No. 3.—One cup of butter, two and a half of sugar, half a cup of sour milk, two eggs, ginger and cinnamon to suit the taste, and sufficient flour to make a stiff batter, and lastly, half a tea-spoon of soda.

SUPERIOR GINGERBREAD, No. 4.—Stir until light, one-quarter of a pound of fresh butter, and the same of sugar; then add half a pint of West India molasses (not syrup); beat four eggs very light, and stir them in the cake; add a table-spoonful of ginger, and a teaspoonful of ground cinnamon; beat well and mix in a pint and a half of sifted flour; dissolve a teaspoonful of soda in hot water, and strain it in the last moment before putting in the oven. No cake requires more care in baking than molasses cakes; they require a brisk oven, but burn very easily, and if burned, are entirely spoiled. Use while fresh.

MRS. L.'s GINGERBREAD, No. 5.—Mix together half a cup of butter, and half a cup of sugar; melt half a cup of lard, in one of West India molasses, one cup of sour milk, two beaten eggs, one teaspoonful of salt, five cups of flour, a table-spoonful of ginger, and a heaping tea-spoon of soda dissolved in hot water, and strained in the cake.

HARD GINGERBREAD, No. 6.—Three-fourths of a cup of shortening, one cup molasses, one cup sugar, three-fourths cup hot water, a tea-spoon of salt, table-spoon of ginger, a bit of alum as large as a hazelnut dissolved in the water; a dessert spoon of soda, sifted with a coffee-cup of flour; mix the ingredients, and half flour, enough, without soda, to make it stiff; then work in quickly the cup of flour, in which the soda is mixed; it must not be quite stiff enough to roll out; put it in square pans, pat it smooth, and mark it in strips.

Mrs. W.'s Gingerbread, No. 7.—One cup of butter, two of sugar, half a cup of sour milk, two eggs, a small teaspoonful of soda, ginger to the taste, and flour to make a stiff batter; bake as soon as mixed.

Hard Gingerbread, No. 8.—Melt butter as large as a hen's egg, and mix it in a pint of West India molasses; add a teaspoonful of cinnamon, and a table-spoonful of ginger, then mix in flour to make a stiff batter; dissolve a small piece of alum, and mix in; then add a table-spoonful of soda dissolved in half a pint of milk, and strained, work it in well, and quickly, stirring in, at the same time, more flour, until it can be rolled out easily; roll it about half an inch thick, and cut it in squares; bake quickly on flat tins well buttered; it is soon dry. None but West India molasses will do for this.

Mrs. F.'s Soft Gingerbread, No. 9.—One cup of sour milk, four eggs, four cups of flour, a teaspoonful of cinnamon, and a table-spoonful of ginger, one teaspoon of soda, dissolved in a little hot water, and strained. Put the ingredients together like cup cake.

Gingersnaps.—One-fourth of a pound of butter, and the same of lard, mixed in a quarter of a pound of brown sugar, a pint of West India molasses, ginger according to its strength, and cinnamon according to taste; add one quart of flour, two teaspoonfuls of soda, dissolved in a wine-glass of milk and flour, to enable you to roll it thin. Bake in a moderate oven.

Soft Gingerbread, No. 10.—Melted butter half a coffee-cup, molasses two coffee-cups, one egg, one table-spoon of ginger, one coffee-cup of sour milk, two heaping teaspoons of soda, added the last thing before baking, and flour to make a stiff batter. Bake quickly.

To Beat Eggs.—Separate the yolks very carefully; put both whites and yolks in shallow earthen pans, or platters; beat in long strokes from one end of the dish to the other, with long wooden rods made quite light; never move the elbow, but keep it pressed to the side, moving only hand and wrist. Eggs beat more quickly that have been laid two or three days, than those laid the same day. A three tined fork where no rods are to be had is better than spoon, or knife. When the whites are perfectly beat, they will remain on an inverted dish without slipping; they sometimes go back and should be used as soon as ready. The yolks when perfectly beaten are light, with no stringy appearance; it takes as long, if not longer, to beat them as whites. The lightness of the cake depends almost entirely on the whites; the yolks enrich it.

To PREPARE FOR CAKE-BAKING.—Sift a pan of flour, if butter is too salt, wash and squeeze it in a cloth; if spice is wanted, grind it; if fruit, prepare it; if currants, wash them thoroughly and dry them; if soda, measure and dissolve it; if cream of tartar, mash it; if sugar is lumpy, roll it; if milk is to be used, measure it; if extracts, have them ready; if eggs, wash them, and see that they are fresh; if a brick oven is to be heated, have ash-wood ready, and the oven nearly hot before commencing; if the stove-oven, see that the fire is right and damper turned as it should be, to heat the oven properly; see that the cake-pans are clean, and butter them, etc. Never put in cake half an ounce over-weight of flour; the best cooks advise full-weight butter, and light-weight of flour; sometimes the sugar is mixed with flour by the grocers; if this is the case, the cake will be spoiled. Dissolve a little and see if it is pure before making very nice cakes.

CORN STARCH CUP CAKE.—One cup of butter, two of sugar, one of milk, one of corn starch, two of flour, the whites of seven eggs beaten stiff; mix in the flour and starch two-thirds of a teaspoon of cream of tartar, and half a teaspoon of soda; put together like bride's cake; bake quickly.

BRIDE'S CAKE.—Mix in half a pound of corn starch, half a teaspoon of soda, and one of cream of tartar, pass it through a fine sieve, stir until light half a pound of best powdered loaf-sugar, with a quarter of a pound of sweet butter, beat the whites of eight eggs stiff, add them to the butter and sugar, mix in the starch the soda and tartar, and flavor with vanilla and bitter almond, and bake quickly.

CREAM CAKE.—One pint of very rich sweet cream if convenient, if not, sour; old cream will not do; one teacup of sugar, four well-beaten eggs, a little salt, and enough flour to make a batter, nearly as stiff as it can be stirred, and well beaten with a spoon; if the cream is sour, dissolve a heaping teaspoonful of soda in hot water, and strain in the cake; bake as soon as well mixed in a rather quick oven; serve hot; it is to be eaten with butter; bake in shallow tins.

VERY PLAIN TEA CAKE.—A half cup of butter, two of sugar; work the sugar and butter together, add four beaten eggs; three tea-cups of sifted flour, an even teaspoonful of soda dissolved and strained, ground coriander-seed, and lastly a teacup of sour milk.

MRS. F.'s POUND CAKE, No. 1.—One pound of pulverized loaf-sugar, the same of sweet butter worked free from salt; beat the sugar and butter to a cream with the hand; separate and beat ten eggs as light as possible; mix the yolks with the sugar and butter, and afterwards the whites alternately, with one pound of sifted flour; beat well and bake without burning in round basins. It used to be thought vulgar to use pound cake when fresh; it ought to be three days old before cutting to serve with fruit cake at parties. A glass of wine improves it. Pound cakes should never be flavored; it is generally mixed with other cake, and if spiced there is too little difference in the cakes.

POUND CAKE, No. 2.—One pound of sugar, three-fourths of butter, eight eggs, the whites and yolks beat separately, and one pound of flour. Mix as No. 1.

CAROLINA CAKE.—Two coffee-cups of pulverized sugar, one of cream, two table-spoonfuls of butter, and the whites of eight eggs, beat stiff; if the cream is sour, use one teaspoonful of soda; add two coffee-cups of flour, mix quickly, and bake as soon as mixed; flavor to suit the taste. Put together like white cake.

WHITE CAKE.—One cup of butter, two of sugar, beat to a cream the whites of eight eggs, beat stiff three cups of flour mixed in the cake, one even teaspoonful of soda dissolved, and strained into the cake, and lastly a cup of sour cream; bake immediately.

BOSTON CAKE.—One pound of sugar, and half a pound of butter stirred together, three eggs beat lightly, one glass of wine, half a pint of milk, mixed with the wine, and an even teaspoonful of soda sifted with a pound of flour; bake in rather quick oven.

MRS. F.'s CUP CAKE.—One cup of butter, and three of sugar, worked to cream, a half wine-glass of wine, five eggs beat separately, one teaspoonful of soda sifted with five cups of sifted flour, a little nutmeg, and lastly a cup of sour cream; bake in round tins, in a moderately quick oven; fruit may be added if desired; frost while the cake is warm, and it will keep some time without becoming stale. This cake is rich enough for any company.

WHITE CUP CAKE.—One cup of butter and two of white sugar beat to a cream; beat five eggs as lightly as possible, and stir them in the cake, stir in four teacups of sifted flour, grate in a little nutmeg, dissolve a very small teaspoonful of soda in as-little hot water as possible, and strain in the cake, stir it in, and add lastly a teacup of sour cream, stirred in as quickly and lightly as possible; bake immediately.

DELICATE CAKE, No. 1.—One pound pulverized loaf-sugar, and one pound of sweet butter free from salt and water, worked with the sugar to a light cream; one teaspoonful extract of lemon, and the same of vanilla, the whites of twenty eggs beat stiff, and lastly one pound of flour stirred in lightly; bake immediately in round pans, and frost it before cold; the frosting, if flavored, should have the same extracts as the cake; it should not be cut fresh.

DELICATE CAKE, No. 2.—Three-fourths of a pound of butter, one pound of pulverized loaf sugar, the whites of sixteen eggs beat stiff, and one pound of flour. Put together as No. 1.

SODA DELICATE, No. 3.—One pound of pulverized sugar, half a pound of butter, the whites of sixteen eggs put together as in No. 1, one teaspoon of soda dissolved in a cup of sweet cream, and two teaspoonfuls of cream of tartar, sifted with a pound of flour. Add the soda and cream just before baking. Bake as soon as possible, in a quick oven.

DELICATE CUP CAKE, No. 4.—One cup of butter, three of loaf-sugar pulverized, the whites of ten eggs, five cups of flour, in which two teaspoonfuls of cream of tartar have been mixed and sifted. The flour must always be sifted before measuring; and then again, after the tartar is in, and lastly, a cup of sweet cream with a teaspoonful of soda dissolved in it and strained. This can be varied by mixing through it a few currants. Delicate cake is now the fashionable cake for bride's loaves at weddings. The richest should be used for that purpose.

RICH SODA CAKE, No. 1.—One pound of pulverized loaf sugar, mixed with three-fourths of a pound of sweet butter. The beaten whites of fourteen eggs, and two teaspoonfuls of cream of tartar, sifted with a pound of flour, and lastly, a teaspoonful of soda dissolved in half a teacup of sweet milk and strained. Bake immediately.

YELLOW SODA CAKE, No. 2.—One pound of sugar, a half-pound of butter. Mix them together, then stir in the beaten yolks of fourteen eggs after which mix gradually one pound of flour, in which two teaspoonfuls of cream of tartar have been mixed before sifting; and lastly, a teacup of sweet cream, in which a teaspoonful of soda has been dissolved; strain the cream for fear of lumps of soda, and stir lightly. Bake immediately in a rather quick oven.

SODA CAKE, No. 3.—One cup of pulverized loaf-sugar, two and a half table-spoonfuls of melted, not heated, butter. Mix these well, then add a teacup of sweet milk in which is dissolved two teaspoonfuls of soda, strained in the cake. Beat two eggs and mix them in the cake. Beat hard until all the ingredients are well incorporated. Measure a pint of flour, stir half in the cake, mix in the remainder one teaspoonful of cream of tartar, pass it through a sugar sieve; be sure the oven is ready and the pans buttered. Grate in a little nutmeg, and lastly, stir in the flour and cream of tartar as quickly as possible; when well mixed, pour it into the pans and bake immediately. Use the same day it is baked, as it is very poor when old.

SODA CAKE, No. 4.—Mix together thoroughly half a teacup of butter, and two of pulverized loaf-sugar; then add the yolks of two well-beaten eggs, and beat well. The whites should be beaten separately and added. Mix in three teacups of sifted flour, one teaspoonful of cream of tartar mashed fine, and passed with the flour through a sieve; stir it in the cake, and lastly, add half a teaspoonful of soda dissolved in half a teacup of milk and strained. Flavoring to suit. Bake immediately in a moderately hot oven.

CONVENIENT SPONGE CAKE, No. 5.—Take a common bowl for the measure, fill it within an inch and a quarter of the top with powdered loaf-sugar, beat nine eggs well without separating, add a little salt, measure a trifle more flour than sugar, and bake as soon as mixed. Flavor as you choose. This is a good common cake to eat soon.

SPONGE CAKE, No. 1.—One pound of pulverized loaf-sugar, twelve eggs, and half a pound of flour. Separate the yolks from the whites and put them in the sugar. Beat the whites separately, as stiff as possible, while another person beats with the hand the yolks and sugar; add the flour, a pinch of salt, and what flavoring is to be used, and bake immediately.

MRS. F.'s SPONGE CAKE, No. 2.—One pound of pulverized loaf-sugar, ten eggs, and three-fourths of a pound of flour. Mix as No 1. When the cake is in the pan, sift a little pulverized loaf-sugar over the top before baking, and cover the cake with white paper to keep the crust from scorching. Sponge cake being rather tasteless, requires flavoring. Lemon, vanilla, bitter almonds, or equal parts of coriander and caraway seed ground and sifted, can be used. This variety of cakes bakes quickly, but the oven must not be hot enough to scorch.

EXCELLENT SODA SPONGE CAKE, No. 3.—Half a teacup of butter, two of sugar, three of flour, and four eggs. Mix the butter and sugar, then add the yolks of the eggs, well beaten, and afterwards the whites. Mix one teaspoon of cream of tartar in the flour, and pass it through the sieve; stir it in the cake, and lastly, dissolve a half-spoonful of soda in half a cup of milk, and strain it in the cake. Mix quickly, and bake immediately in a quick oven without scorching. This cake should be used fresh, and but little baked at once. It can be flavored as desired, though not needing extracts as much as sponge cakes without butter, having a much more decided taste.

ARROWROOT SPONGE CAKE, No. 4.—Separate and beat twelve eggs, they should have been laid just three days. Add to the yolks gradually one pound best pulverized sugar, beat half an hour, then add gradually the whites, beating another half-hour. Add the juice of one large lemon, the flavor of the skin should have been rubbed on the sugar. Now make the bake-pan ready, line it with buttered paper sides and bottom, then add gradually, stirring lightly, half a pound sifted arrowroot. Sift pulverized sugar over the top.

LADIES' FINGERS.—Beat the whites of six eggs lightly as possible; beat the yolks the same, add to the whites, little by little, half a pound of best pulverized sugar; have the yolks beating all the time, when the eggs have been beaten one hour, mix them very gradually, by using the top of the yolks, until the whole is added. Squeeze in half the juice of a lemon, and add gradually, beating lightly, one-fourth of a pound of arrowroot or flour, (the arrowroot is the best.) Have ready buttered paper, spread the batter in small oval cakes, joining in the middle to represent the joint of a finger. Bake quickly, and leave the cakes on the paper until wanted. For parties frost them.

GERMAN LADIES' FINGERS.—Beat one hour the yolks of five eggs with half a pound of sugar; add half a pound of blanched almonds pounded fine, the yellow part of one lemon grated. Mix well, add half a pound of flour very gradually Roll out the paste, and cut it in strips the length and size of the fore-finger; beat lightly the whites of two eggs, and wet the fingers.

GERMAN PEPPER NUTS.—Half a pound of loaf-sugar and three eggs, beat together half an hour. Pound two ounces of blanched almonds very fine, chop an ounce of citron as fine as possible, grate in the yellow rind of a lemon, add cinnamon, nutmeg, and a quarter of a teaspoon of black pepper, half a teaspoon of cloves, and seven and a half ounces of flour. Measure and shape the dough in a teaspoon, and bake in a moderate oven. They are very nice.

GERMAN CORNUCOPIA CAKES.—Beat the whites of four eggs to snow, add gradually one pound loaf-sugar, and beat one hour. Mix in half a pound of blanched almonds pounded fine, with the white of an egg, to prevent their oiling; add half an ounce of cinnamon; grease the paper with butter, put for each cake a heaping spoon of the mixture, and spread it round until it is as large as the top of a half-pint tumbler; as soon as they are baked a light brown take them up, and while soft roll them in the shape of a cornucopia. Sift over them sugar and cinnamon mixed.

CLAY CAKE.—Stir together until light half a pound of butter, and one of best loaf-sugar. Mix in one pound of flour, one teaspoon of tartar, dissolve in half a pint of milk half a teaspoon of soda, add to the butter and sugar the yolks of six well-beaten eggs, mix well; add the beaten whites, mix in the flour, and lastly strain in the milk and soda, and bake quickly.

WHITE MOUNTAIN CAKE.—Bake the above as you would for a jelly cake, spread between each cake icing beaten one hour, flavored with lemon-juice, vanilla, or bitter almond, and ice the last cake over the top.

MRS. F.'s FRUIT CUP CAKE.—One cup of sweet butter, and three of nice sugar worked to a cream, five well-beaten eggs, the yolks, and afterward the whites, a glass of brandy or wine, half a nutmeg, half a dozen cloves, and a teaspoonful of ground cinnamon. Pulverize a teaspoonful of soda, and mix it in five cups of sifted flour, and stir the flour in the cake. Flour one pound of washed currants, and mix them in, and afterward one pound of seeded raisins cut once and rubbed in flour; stir it well, and just before baking add a cup of sour cream. Do not beat it much after the cream is in, but thoroughly mix, and bake immediately. It will take one hour to bake. Frost while a little warm. It will keep fresh some time. Do not cut it the day it is baked. This is an old but excellent receipt.

RICH FRUIT CAKE.—One pound of sugar, three-fourths of a pound of butter, worked together until very light; one wine-glass of brandy, one dozen ground cloves, half a nutmeg, a teaspoonful of ground cinnamon, ten eggs beat separately, the yolks to be used first, and afterwards the whites, one-fourth of a pound of sliced citron, two pounds of washed currants rubbed in flour and mixed in the cake with one pound of raisins cut fine, and one seeded and left whole or cut once, and one pound of sifted flour; stir in the citron, currants, and the chopped raisins, and lastly, the flour and whole raisins alternately; bake in a moderate oven in deep basins two hours. If the fire is strong, the heat should be decreased the last hour. Line the basins with buttered paper, and keep a piece over the top of the cake. Frost it and it will keep two months or longer if desired.

BLACK CAKE.—Commence the day previous to baking to prepare the fruit and spices. Wash the butter from most of the salt, and press out the water by wringing it in a cloth; seed the raisins; wash, dry, and pick over four or five pounds of currants. Weigh one pound of flour, and brown it, stirring constantly; dry brown sugar, and roll it until it is as fine as flour; seed three pounds of raisins, and chop them; cut in thin small slices one pound of citron; grate half a nutmeg; grind and sift a dessert spoonful of cinnamon, one teaspoon of mace, three-fourths of a teaspoon of cloves. The next day weigh one pound of the dried brown sugar, three-fourths of a pound of butter; and work them together until light; add a table-spoonful of molasses and the spices. Dissolve a teaspoon of soda in a wine-glass of milk; strain it, and mix it with a wine-glass of wine, and one of brandy, and stir it in the cake. Have beat ten eggs as light as possible; stir in the yolks, and beat well; and then the whites, and beat thoroughly; then add gradually the browned flour. The pans should be buttered, and lined with buttered paper; stir in first the citron, then the raisins chopped, and lastly three pounds of currants weighed when dry; stir a few moments to mix well, and bake immediately in a moderate oven; cover the top with paper; bake steadily, if in thick loaves, from two to two and a half hours. It should not be cut under two weeks, and it would be better left until four. Frost before cutting. The frosting becomes discolored by standing. This cake, if frosted while warm, will keep for a year. It should be kept shut in a tin box. As soon as cold, roll it in thick linen cloth, and pack it away. For weddings, it is considered indispensable, and is generally baked in a milk-pan; it will then take three hours steady baking. It tastes better to dry flour without browning.

WEDDING CAKE OF 1818.—Two teacups of sugar, two of light dough from hop yeast bread, and one and a half of butter. Mix these ingredients together; then add a quarter of a nutmeg, a teaspoonful of cinnamon, half as much mace, a pinch of cloves, eight well-beaten eggs, and one glass of wine. Beat it well; the longer it is worked, the lighter it will be; let it rise until very light. Then add two pounds of seeded raisins, one pound chopped fine, the other cut once, two pounds of washed currants, and a quarter of a pound of citron; mix in a teaspoon of soda dissolved in a very little water, and strained; let it rise again, and then butter some pans; line them with paper, buttered well, and once again beat up the cake to stir up the fruit; pour it in the pans, let it stand a while to rise, and then bake it in a moderate oven. Cover the top with papers; if this is baked in one loaf it will take three hours' steady baking in a very moderate oven. It must be hot enough to scald the dough very soon through, or it may run over. Frost while hot. Old-fashioned people always made this cake for weddings. It cannot be made with brewer's yeast, use hop.

MRS. S.'s LOAF CAKE.—Five cups of dough, three of sugar, one and a half of butter; work the ingredients well together; add a wine glass of brandy or wine, a half teaspoonful of soda dissolved, and strained in as little water as possible, and four eggs; work these in the mixture, and add a pound of seeded raisins, cut once. Spice to the taste; line basins with buttered paper, pour in the mixture. Bake as soon as very light in a moderate oven. Make the dough with homemade yeast.

CHILDREN'S LOAF CAKE.—Five cups of dough, two of sugar, one of butter, caraway seed ground, and two eggs. Line pans with buttered paper, and bake as soon as light, use homemade yeast.

QUICK LOAF CAKE.—One cup of butter, three of sugar, worked together, two beaten eggs, two teaspoons of cream of tartar, mixed in one and a half cup of sifted flour, and again sifted. Fruit and spices to the taste, and lastly strain in the cake one teaspoonful of soda dissolved in one and a half cup of sweet milk. Bake immediately in rather a quick oven.

FEDERAL CAKE.—One pound of sugar, a half-pound of butter mixed together, six well-beaten eggs, spices to the taste. One teacup of sweet milk, and one pound of flour. When these ingredients are well mixed, add a half-teaspoon of soda dissolved in wine, and bake immediately.

WASHINGTON CAKE.—Three-fourths of a pound of butter, and the same of sugar worked to a cream, five eggs well beaten, nutmeg, and cinnamon; one pound sifted flour, one gill of wine, a half teaspoon of soda dissolved in one gill of cream, one pound of currants or raisins. Bake in a moderately quick oven.

MRS. F.'s HARRISON CAKE.—One and a half old-fashioned coffee-cups of sugar, and the same of butter. One of molasses, not syrup. One gill sweet milk, one teaspoon of soda, cinnamon, and cloves, five beaten eggs, five cups of flour, and one pint of raisins. Dissolve the soda in the milk, and strain it in the last thing. Bake in a moderate oven. This cake can be made with the fat from fried pork.

THANKSGIVING CAKE.—Six pounds of butter, and six pounds of sugar, worked together; twelve eggs well beaten, three quarts of sweet milk, twelve pounds of flour, mace, cinnamon, raisins, and one quart of hop yeast, good and fresh. Let it rise once before putting in the pans; if the fruit settles, stir it up before pouring it in the pans. This is an old New England receipt.

MADISON CAKE.—One pound of fresh butter, and one pound of pulverized sugar, rubbed together, and beat light; add a teaspoonful of grated nutmeg, and a tablespoonful of ground cinnamon; separate and beat until light fourteen eggs; mix in the yolks, and beat them well with the sugar. Pulverize a teaspoonful of soda, and sift it with a pound and three-fourths of flour; seed two pounds of raisins, cut them once, dredge them with flour, and stir them in the cake, and lastly stir in a pint of rich sour milk. Bake immediately in a moderate oven, and ice when partly cold. If more fruit is desired, mix in the same quantity of washed Zante currants.

MARMALADE CAKE.—Take a thick pound cake, baked in a two

quart basin—it should be three days old; slice it horizontally, so that the slices will be one sixth of an inch thick, spread on any nice marmalade, and pile the cake very evenly; then make a nice frosting, and ice the top only; cut American citron in circular pieces; wipe it free from juice, and lay a border of half-moon-shaped pieces on the edge of the cake.

STRAWBERRY CAKE.—Prepare a pound cake as above; mash ripe strawberries, and drain them; spread the fruit evenly on the cake, and frost the top; stick large ripe berries on the cake, before the icing sets, sweeten the juice, and serve it with the cake; this is a proper dinner dish, but is good for tea also.

JELLY CAKE.—One pound of pulverized loaf sugar, half a pound of sweet butter, five eggs well beaten, and one glass of wine. Beat the sugar and butter together, then add the yolks; beat it well, and stir in the beaten whites. Dissolve a teaspoon of soda in half a pint of milk; stir in one pound of flour, and lastly the milk and soda. Butter round shallow pans, or square, if you have no round ones. Spread the cake evenly on the bottom, one-sixth of an inch thick, and bake quickly without burning; let them become entirely cold in the pan. Then remove one to the plate it is to occupy, spread it evenly with jelly; then lay on another, and so continue until all but the last one are spread, and ice with a thin frosting. The jelly should not be spread on the cake a long time before using, as it will absorb it.

GERMAN NEW YEAR'S COOKIES, VERY FINE.—Four fresh eggs beat with a pound of sugar one hour, the juice and rind of one lemon, one pound of flour, and one half-teaspoon of hartshorn. These cakes must be made in a cold room, or they will be too soft; roll thin, cut them in squares, and impress them with any fancy mould; lay on the pans anise or caraway seed, instead of buttering; let the cakes dry from twenty-four to forty-eight hours, and afterwards bake in a very slow oven without browning. They will keep a year.

SOFT COOKIES.—One coffee-cup of butter, three of sugar, one of thick cream, four eggs; mix the butter and sugar, then add the eggs and cream. Sift a pan of flour, and into a pint bowlful mix a teaspoonful of soda, and pass it through a sieve. Stir it in the cake, and enough more to make the dough just stiff enough to roll out; spice with caraway, nutmeg, or ground coriander seed.

MRS. CASE'S COOKIES, No. 1.—One coffee-cup of sugar, a piece of butter as large as a large egg, half a coffee-cup of water, in which is dissolved a half-teaspoonful of soda, and flour enough to roll. The quicker these are made, the better; spice with nutmeg, caraway, or ground coriander.

WINTER COOKIES, No. 2.—Four cups of sugar, one cup of pork fat, and one of butter, work together one cup of sour milk, and sufficient flour to roll, in which a teaspoonful of soda has been mixed; add coriander and caraway ground, a teaspoon of each.

WINTER COOKIES, No. 3.—Three coffee-cups of sugar, two of butter, mixed together, a tablespoonful of caraway seed, a half-teaspoonful of tartaric acid dissolved in a coffee-cup of water, one teaspoonful of soda pulverized and sifted in a part of the flour; mix in the water and acid, then a part of the flour without the soda, and lastly that containing the soda. Roll thin, and bake quickly, on buttered papers.

RICH COOKIES, No. 4.—Work together one teacup of butter and two of sugar. Beat two eggs separately, and stir in first the yolk, and then the whites. Dissolve in half a cup of water a third of a teaspoon of tartaric acid. Sift in a part of the flour a half-teaspoon of soda; mix in first a little flour without soda, and afterward that with the soda; spice with nutmeg; spread granulated sugar on the pasteboard and roll the dough on it instead of flour, and after it is rolled thin enough, sift sugar over the dough, and pass the rolling-pin lightly over it. Be as quick as possible in getting the cakes into the oven after the acid and flour is added; bake quickly. Bake them on buttered paper and cover them if there is danger of scorching with white paper. Let them cool a little, and then lift the paper with the cakes and let them become cold before taking them off.

POUND COOKIES, No. 5.—One pound of sugar and one of butter stirred together, one nutmeg, three eggs, a teaspoon of tartaric acid dissolved in a half-pint of water; one quart of flour, and two teaspoons of soda dissolved in half a pint of hot water; mix it in the cake, and as quickly as possible; add enough flour to just roll; scatter over some granulated sugar, and roll lightly. Bake quickly without scorching.

NEW YEAR'S COOKIES, No. 6.—One pound of sugar, three-fourths of a pound of butter, three beaten eggs, one teaspoon of ground coriander, two table-spoonfuls of caraway seed, one pint of flour, and a teaspoon of soda dissolved in half a teacup of milk; stir it in and add nearly all the flour needed, and lastly, stir in a half-cup of water in which is dissolved a half-teaspoonful of tartaric acid, and the necessary flour to roll it. Bake as soon as possible, in a quick but not burning oven.

JUMBLES, No. 1.—Put one pound of pulverized loaf-sugar and a grated nutmeg into two pounds of flour, pass it through a sieve. Beat four eggs as light as possible; melt over water three-quarters of a pound of butter, beat it and the eggs together, and mix them with the flour; roll the paste thin, and cut them with a jumble cutter; scatter over the top pulverized loaf-sugar, and bake on buttered papers, without browning.

POUND JUMBLES, No. 2.—One pound of sugar, one of butter worked until light, ten eggs beaten separately, add first the yolks and then the whites, with a little grated nutmeg, a teaspoon of lemon, and one of vanilla, and flour to make a paste that will roll well. Bake quickly.

SPONGE DROP CAKES.—Make a sponge cake, heat a dripping-pan hot enough to cook a griddle cake, butter muffin rings, and set them in the pan, and when the rings and pan are hot, drop a table-spoonful of cake in each ring, and set them in the oven a few moments. Have icing ready, and whiten them while hot.

ALMOND CAKES.—Make as the preceding receipt, and mix in a half-pound of blanched almonds, pounded separately with rose water in a marble or glass mortar.

GERMAN HARD CHOCOLATE CAKES.—Grate and sift half a pound of chocolate. Beat the yolks of two eggs and add the chocolate gradually; add the whites of six eggs beaten to snow, to the yolks and chocolate; beat well, and if not sweet enough add sugar. If the chocolate is good, they will be sufficiently sweet. Take off small bits with a teaspoon and bake on buttered paper.

SOFT CHOCOLATE CAKE.—One pound of sugar, twenty eggs beat half an hour without separating; half a pound of grated chocolate added gradually to the egg and sugar, with three-fourths of a pound of starch flour; the whole beaten half an hour. Butter the forms, and sprinkle them with pulverized crackers, and turn in the mixture.

CHESTNUT CAKE.—One pound and a half of boiled chestnuts mashed and sifted. One-fourth of a pound of loaf-sugar, the yolks of eight eggs beat light. Beat the ingredients well together, and spice to suit the taste. Line a shallow pudding-plate with puff paste, (*see* PUFF PASTE;) pour in the mixture. The Germans call this cake, but it is more like a pie or pudding.

PLAIN FRIED CAKES.—Melt a table-spoonful of lard in a quart of milk, add two coffee-cups of sugar, a teaspoonful of salt, and half a nutmeg. Dissolve a teaspoonful of soda in as little hot water as possible, and strain in the milk. Sift one quart of flour. Pulverize a half-teaspoonful of tartaric acid, and mix it in half the flour thoroughly; pass it again through the sieve. Have the fat ready hot, mix the milk, sugar, soda, etc., in the quart of flour without the acid; then mix in the remainder as quickly as possible, and fry immediately; the sooner they are fried the lighter they will be. Roll about a quarter of an inch thick, and cut them like jumbles. Try the lard to see if it is sufficiently hot or too hot; if right, the dough will rise and look a little brown; if too hot, it will sputter and brown the dough as soon as it is in. If too cold, it will remain on the bottom or rise slowly, with no appearance of cooking. These cakes will be good for two days only.

RICH FRIED CAKES.—Three cups of sugar, one cup of butter or lard—if the latter, a teaspoon of salt—half a nutmeg, five eggs, a teacup of sour milk, and a teaspoon of soda mixed in a small part of the flour and sifted, and just enough flour to roll nicely. Cut with a jumble-cutter and fry quickly.

MRS. F.'s CRULLERS.—Six eggs, six heaping table-spoonfuls of pulverized sugar, and six running-over table-spoonfuls of melted, not hot, butter, nutmeg, and enough flour to roll conveniently. Flour the paste-board well and evenly; roll the dough one-eighth of an inch thick, straighten it on each side, dipping the knife or dough-spur in flour; then proceed to cut out the cakes. Mark them off with a small light ruler in oblong pieces two inches wide and four long. Slash them width-wise every fourth of an inch nearly through, to the edge, making slits, fold them up, leaving the side next the board on the inside, pinch the two upper ends together, and then the two lower, leaving a slash where they join; fry in hot lard, sift loaf-sugar over them, lay them on plates in three layers, the first covering the plate, the next leaving one row on the edge, but one cake thick, and the third one cake in the middle. These are beautiful and excellent. They will keep fresh for months. They should be round with a hole through the centre resembling a mousetrap. If not made regular they look badly.

FRIED CAKES WITHOUT EGGS OR MILK.—Mix with flour a coffee-cup of sugar, one teaspoonful of soda, and two of cream of tartar freed from lumps; pass the flour, soda, and tartar through the sieve. Dissolve in a pint of hot water a heaping teaspoonful of salt, and melt in the same a small table-spoonful of lard; wet the flour prepared with the soda and tartar with the water and lard, work the dough quickly but thoroughly. Roll thin, cut the cakes with a jumble-cutter, and fry immediately. They will keep fresh two or three days. Nutmeg is an addition.

COFFEE CAKES.—Mix as for Mrs. W.'s Superior Fried Cakes, p. 190, without sugar, and let it rise. Fry in balls not over two inches thick. Serve warm for breakfast. It will have to be prepared to make up overnight if wanted for breakfast. The oftener it is kneaded over when made with hop yeast the better, and when sour add soda. If made with homemade hop yeast, the dough can be kept on hand a week, by adding soda every morning.

FRITTERS.—Make a nice batter of sweet rich milk, add salt. To every quart of milk allow three eggs beat separately. Mix in first the yolks, and after the flour the whites. Boil in hot lard. The batter should be just stiff enough to drop in without flying in pieces. Dip the spoon in the lard before putting it in the batter. Serve as soon as boiled. Some use sweet cider and sugar, but the best sauce for them is maple syrup. They should be fried in a deep spider.

VANITIES.—Take two eggs, beat without separating as light as possible; add a teaspoonful of salt, and wet up as much flour as will roll; they should be pretty stiff. Take small bits of the dough, not larger than a teaspoon bowl, roll them in the hand until quite round, dredge the moulding-board with flour, and roll as thin as possible. Fry in sweet lard that has not been used to fry in before.

BREAD FRIED CAKES.—Take five cups light dough from hop yeast bread, half a cup of butter, three of sugar, a teaspoon of salt, four eggs, a teaspoon of soda, a little nutmeg, and flour to knead well. Let them rise until very light, but be careful they do not sour.

Knead it down again after it rises; roll out the dough, cut it in small diamond-shaped cakes, let them rise, and fry as soon as light. These are the best fresh.

POUND WAFFLES.—One pound powdered loaf-sugar, three-fourths of a pound of butter, a short pound of flour, and ten eggs separated and beaten light. Bake in waffle-irons and eat them cold.

PLAIN WAFFLES.—One quart of sweet milk, nine well-beaten eggs, two table-spoons of butter, a teaspoon of soda dissolved in the milk and strained, and two of cream of tartar sifted with the flour. Make the batter as thick as pound cake. Serve with maple-syrup, or cream and sugar.

RICH GERMAN WAFFLES.—Half a pound of butter beat to a cream, the yolks of twelve eggs beaten light, and twelve heaping table-spoons of sifted flour. Beat well, add four table-spoons of sweet cream, lastly add the whites beaten stiff, and beat all together. Serve hot. Butter the irons with sweet butter, (see IRON WARE, PART II.) Serve with powdered sugar and cinnamon.

GERMAN RAISED WAFFLES.—One and a half pound of flour, six ounces melted butter, one pint of sweet milk, ten eggs beaten separately, a teaspoon of salt, two table-spoons of brewer's yeast, washed free from the bitter properties, (see PART III. CHAP. X.) Bake when light, and serve hot, with maple-syrup or sugar and cinnamon. These may be sweetened if desired. This recipe will make good muffins baked in rings.

GOOD WAFFLES.—A pint of new milk, the yolks of four beaten eggs, stirred in the milk, and afterwards the whites, a quarter of a pound of butter, melted and stirred in, a little salt, one teaspoon of soda dissolved in the milk and strained, nearly all the flour, one pint of sour cream, and sufficient flour to make the batter as stiff as pound cake. Serve as soon as baked. Grease the irons with sweet butter. Serve with pulverized loaf-sugar and strong cinnamon ground and sifted.

AMERICAN RAISED WAFFLES.—One pint sweet milk, one heaping teacupful of butter, three eggs, a table-spoonful of thick brewer's yeast, one quart of flour, and another teacup of sweet milk, in which is dissolved a quarter of a teaspoonful of soda. Let it rise until very light, then bake as other waffles. Serve hot with butter and sugar.

Mrs. W.'s Muffins.—One-fourth of a pound of butter, a teaspoonful of salt, three eggs, one pint of sweet milk. Melt the butter, stir it in the milk, beat the eggs, and add them with one quart of flour, and a heaping table-spoonful of brewer's yeast. Let it rise, then butter the rings, heat the griddle, and set the rings on it, dip in the batter, bake quickly, and serve hot.

Sally Lunn.—One pint of sweet milk, butter the size of an egg, melted and stirred in the milk, a teaspoonful of salt, three well-beaten eggs, a table-spoon of brewer's yeast, and a quart of flour. Let it rise in the bake pans, bake quickly, and serve hot. If any is left, heat it over the next day.

Cream Drop Cake.—A half pint of rich cream, and a half pint of egg, beat the yolks and whites separately, add a teaspoonful of salt, and as much flour as can be beat in with a spoon; it should be just thick enough to drop from a spoon; butter pans and drop the cake on it; let it bake hard. If the cream is sour, add soda.

Genuine Boston Cream Cakes.—Take one quart of sweet new milk, from which take three table-spoonfuls to moisten four table-spoonfuls of sifted flour, and put the remainder on to boil; separate four eggs and beat them as stiff as possible; add to the yolks five heaping table-spoonfuls of pulverized loaf-sugar; when the milk is boiling hot, stir in first the moistened flour, let it thicken but not boil, then stir the whites and yolks together and beat them well, pour a little of the boiled milk in the egg, stir it well, and then mix it in the hot milk, let it boil three minutes, then add the grated rind and juice of one lemon, and set it away to cool, then proceed to make the paste; take one pint of sifted flour and one-fourth of a pound of butter, set it over hot water until it melts, then add a quart of milk, and stir in three-fourths of a pound of flour, let it scald through; then let it become cold, beat all the lumps out, separate and beat twelve eggs, stir them in the paste, first the yolks and then the whites; butter twenty-four round tins, fill them not quite half full; bake thoroughly; when cold, open them a little with a knife and put in the cream; press the edges together and wet them over with egg. These cakes must be used the same day they are baked.

Sweet Milk Griddle Cakes without Eggs, No. 1.—Dissolve a teaspoonful of soda in a pint of sweet milk, strain it and add one heaping teaspoon of salt; sift with a pint of flour two teaspoonfuls of cream of tartar, mix the flour in a pint of sweet milk, and stir it well to get out all lumps; then mix in the milk and soda, and bake immediately; if too thin to suit, add more flour; some like thin and some thick cakes.

SOUR MILK GRIDDLE CAKES WITHOUT EGGS, No. 2.—One quart of sour milk, and one pint of flour, in which is mixed before sifting two teaspoonfuls of soda; mix the flour in the milk, beat out all the lumps as soon as possible, and bake immediately.

GRIDDLE CAKES, VERY NICE, No. 3.—One quart of sweet milk, two heaping table-spoons of butter, measured before melting; stir in the milk a teaspoon of salt, and one of soda; separate and beat five eggs and stir in the milk, first the yolks and then the whites; sift flour and mix in a part of it two teaspoonfuls of cream of tartar; stir in first the part without the tartar and afterwards the other; it will take about one pint; if not thick enough to suit, add more flour. Bake immediately and serve hot from the griddle.

CREAM GRIDDLE CAKES, No. 4.— One quart sour cream, four beaten eggs, one teaspoon of salt, two of soda, and one pint of flour; mix the soda in half the flour, and stir it in last; bake as soon as mixed, and serve immediately; add more flour if not thick enough to suit.

BARLEY GRIDDLE CAKES.—One teacup of boiled barley, one pint of sweet milk, two eggs, a piece of butter the size of a hickory-nut, a teaspoon of cream of tartar, flour enough to make the cakes into batter, and half a teaspoon of soda.

RICE GRIDDLE CAKES.—A pint of boiled rice, one quart of sweet milk, a teaspoon of salt, two eggs, a half-teaspoon of soda, one of cream of tartar and flour, to make them in a batter.

INDIAN MEAL GRUEL GRIDDLE CAKES.—Make a thin gruel with milk instead of water, and let it boil until it thickens; then thin it with sour cream, add a teaspoon of salt to a quart of the mixture, and a tablespoonful of molasses, stir in wheat flour until thick enough to bake well, and lastly, a teaspoonful of soda.

MOCK BUCKWHEAT CAKES.—Scald a teacup of rice flour in one quart of water; after it thickens, stir in a bowl of Graham flour unbolted, add just water sufficient to make a batter of right consistency, stir in a teaspoon heaping full of salt, and two table-spoonfuls of brewer's or half a teacup of home hop yeast; let it rise and bake when light.

QUICK BUCKWHEAT.—Dissolve in a quart of water two teaspoonfuls of soda, add salt and enough flour to make a batter; just before baking, stir in a teaspoonful of tartaric acid, dissolved in a teacup of hot water; bake immediately and serve as soon as baked, or they will taste of soda, which spoils them.

RAISED BUCKWHEAT CAKES, No. 1.—Warm a quart of water, and stir in a table-spoonful of molasses, and a teaspoonful of salt.; mix in enough buckwheat flour to make a batter, and stir in a table-spoonful of brewer's or two of hop yeast; let it rise; if it remains all night and becomes sour, add soda.

RAISED BUCKWHEAT CAKES, No. 2.—Soak enough dry bread to fill a pint bowl, make a batter with one quart of warm water, two even table-spoonfuls of molasses to make them brown, and enough buckwheat to make a thin batter; beat out all the lumps from the bread, add salt and a table-spoonful of brewer's or two of hop yeast, and let it stand all night; if it sours, add soda.

INDIAN MEAL GRIDDLE CAKES WITHOUT MILK.—One and a half coffee-cups of Indian meal stirred into two and a half coffee-cups of boiling water; beat thoroughly; Indian meal cakes need long beating. Add two cups of cold water, one and a half cups of sifted flour, two table-spoons of melted butter, a salt-spoon of salt. White meal is the best.

GRAHAM GRIDDLE CAKES.—Make a batter with one quart of sweet milk, the whites of four and yolks of two eggs, separated and beat very light, a little salt and two table-spoons of molasses.

JOURNEY OR JOHNNY CAKE, No. 1.—Four coffee-cups sour milk, two coffee-cups of Indian meal, three eggs, salt, and an even table-spoon of soda, dissolved and strained; beat the whole twenty minutes; unless well beat, it will not be light.

JOHNNY CAKE, No. 2.—Boil a pint of sweet milk, pour it on one and a half cup of Indian meal, and beat fifteen minutes; add salt, half a cup of sour milk, one beaten egg, a table-spoon of butter, or two of cream, a teaspoon of soda, and a table-spoon of flour, beat well together. This cake is best baked in a spider, on the stove; when browned on the bottom, turn it into another spider, or finish on the griddle.

Mrs. W.'s Superior Fried Cakes.—One pint of water, one quart of flour, and two table-spoons of brewer's yeast; knead the dough until it cleaves from the hand, and set it in a warm place until quite light, which should be, if the yeast is perfect, within twenty minutes; when sufficiently light, mix three well-beaten eggs with a coffee-cup of *good* sugar, beat well until the sugar is dissolved; work into the dough half a coffee-cup of butter, and when well incorporated with the dough, add the egg and sugar, working the dough until the ingredients are mixed evenly through the whole; put it back in the pan, cover it warm, and let it rise again; when quite light roll the dough lightly, cut the cakes with a ring shaped jumble cutter, and fry in hot lard a light brown; they should be used fresh; lard may be substituted in place of the butter, by using a trifle less and adding a teaspoon of salt; should the yeast be very bitter, wash twice the quantity in a quart of cold water; let it settle and drain off the water, and afterward measure of the thick part of the yeast, two table-spoonfuls.

Composition Cake.—Work together until light, three-fourths of a pound of butter with one and a fourth pounds of nice sugar, add four well-beaten eggs, half a pint of milk, one wine-glass of wine, one and three-fourths pounds of flour, one nutmeg, one pound of raisins, one-half pint of cream, and one teaspoon of saleratus; more fruit may be used if desired; when no cream can be had, use a pint of milk, and a teaspoonful more of butter. This will make three cakes.

CHAPTER XII.

CONFECTIONERIES, CREAMS, ETC.

Lemon Puffs.—One pound of pulverized loaf-sugar beat in the yolks of four eggs; add one table-spoonful extra for every spoonful of flavoring; beat the yolks and sugar as stiff as possible; then add the whites beat to a stiff froth; beat well, flavor with lemon-juice, and extract of the peel or citric acid, and extract of lemon; drop on buttered papers in small cakes, and bake quickly without browning; leave the puffs on the paper until entirely cold.

Cocoa Cakes.—One pound of pulverized loaf-sugar mixed in one pound of the white part grated of cocoanut; beat six eggs stiff, and mix them with the sugar and cocoa; if there is more than enough of the egg to just wet them, do not use the whole; there should be merely sufficient to dampen the cakes thoroughly; bake on paper without browning, in a moderate oven; leave them on the paper until entirely cold.

MACCAROONS.—One pound of blanched sweet almonds, and a handful of bitter; pound them in a glass mortar with rose-water, to prevent their oiling; beat to a stiff froth the whites of four eggs, stir into them one pound of powdered loaf-sugar, and then mix in gradually the almonds; drop them on buttered paper, sift over them some sugar, and bake quickly without browning; leave them on the paper until cold.

To PREPARE SYRUPS FOR CANDIES.—Confectioners purify the purest sugar. Dissolve two pounds of loaf-sugar in a pint of cold water, add the white of an egg, and beat the mixture well; when it boils up take it from the fire, and remove the scum; put it again on the fire, and when it boils up, throw in a little cold water; again take it off, and remove the scum; continue this until no scum rises; it will take but a few drops of water each time.

STRENGTH OF SYRUPS.—It is ascertained by experiments, that two pounds of sugar to a pint of water, is the proper strength for syrups; to prevent their working or candying. Of course the juice of fruit is to be taken into account in this rule; juicy fruit would need no water.

CANDYING SYRUPS.—After the syrup is clarified, which is known by a thin skin appearing on the surface, strain it; then put it again on the fire, boil slowly, trying it often, by taking a little between the thumb and finger; if in opening them a short thread forms, and quickly breaks, it is said the syrup has reached the strength of the little thread; if a longer thread of greater strength forms, it is called the "great thread;" it is said then to have reached the first degree. The second degree is called the pearl, it is obtained by farther boiling; in this the thread will bear being drawn as far as the thumb and finger can stretch; this makes candied sugar. By farther boiling we obtain the blow; this is known by dipping a skimmer with holes in the syrup; if it blubbers when blown, this degree is obtained; this is used in candying fruit; this is called the third degree; the fourth is the feather; it has more blubbers and the sugar flies off in flakes in tossing the skimmer quickly. The fifth is the ball; this allows the syrup's being made into balls, by dipping the thumb and finger into cold water, and rolling it quickly. The sixth is the crack; it will not stick to the fingers, and cracks when cold; this is proper for candies made at home, and is usually known by dropping it in cold water. The seventh and last degree, is called the "carmel;" this makes a beautiful ornamental covering for sweetmeats. After this it will burn. Confectioners use cream of tartar also to clear their syrups. The rule is half an ounce to every five pounds; both sugar and cream of tartar is dissolved in one pint of water; when it boils skim off all that rises. Too much cream of tartar makes the candy crumble.

To CANDY PLUMS, APRICOTS, ETC.—Boil the fruits in syrup, then dry them on the stove, or before a fire; the syrup must then be boiled to a candy height, the fruit dipped in it and again dried before the fire or in a slow oven; continue to dip the fruit until candied, then pack it in boxes and keep it dry; sometimes once dipping is sufficient. English method.

FRENCH METHOD OF CANDYING GREEN GAGES, APRICOTS, ETC.—The fruit must previously have been nicely preserved in syrup; provide two square boxes, one made of tin, about twelve inches long, and eight inches wide, and three or four inches deep; at one corner of this box there must be a hole and pipe through which the overflowing of the syrup may pass off, but which must be corked up while the fruit is in the oven; the other box must be made entirely of wire, and somewhat smaller than the first; to this last there must also be a cover; the fruit which is to be candied, is placed in layers, one above another, on wire frames, and when the wire box is completely filled, the cover must be put on to keep the fruit in place; the box is then placed within the tin box, the cover shut closely, and both set in a moderately heated oven.

Candying is produced by boiling syrup to the little blow, (*see* SYRUPS;) boil a pint of syrup to this degree; as it cools, candy will form on the surface, which must be skimmed off and poured in among the layers of fruit, after it is placed in the wire box; when the whole syrup is thus used, the box containing the fruit must be covered closely and be put into the oven, and suffered to remain there for twelve hours; when taken out, the wire case must be so placed as to allow all the syrup which has not candied to pass away; as soon as the moisture disappears, the fruit must be taken out with great care and put into tin boxes to be kept dry until wanted.

To MAKE MOLASSES CANDY.—Boil a quart of molasses slowly, until it reaches the sixth degree called the crack; this is known by dropping some of the candy in cold water; if it breaks brittle it is done; butter immediately some flat pans, pour out the candy, and set it to cool; when nearly cool, take it from the pans and stretch it until white; if the molasses is impure, skim it when it first boils; a piece of alum as large as a filbert, will make it more brittle. If desired it can be flavored, mixed with nuts or pop corn.

POP CORN BALLS.—Boil honey, maple, or other sugar to the great thread; pop corn and stick the corn together in balls with the candy.

MAPLE SUGAR CANDY.—Take five pounds of sugar and half an ounce of cream of tartar; break the sugar and add two tumblers of water; when the syrup boils up throw in a little water and take it from the fire, and skim it; continue to do this while any impurities rise, then boil slowly without stirring until it reaches the sixth degree or crack; drop a little in cold water often, to be able to decide when it is boiled sufficiently; have the pans ready buttered, pour but little in each pan, cool speedily by setting the pans on ice or floating in water, and stretch the candy as soon as it can be handled; if not stretched very warm, it cannot be worked, as it is very brittle. Pull it back and forth with the hands, or throw it over a stretcher until it is as white as possible, then twist it in small strings and break it into sticks. This candy requires great care to make and not have it grain, but is as good as any confectioner's when properly made.

TAFFY.—Three pounds of sugar dissolved in a pint of water, in which half a teaspoon of citric acid has been dissolved; remove the scum as fast as it rises. Boil until it will crack when dropped in cold water; remove from the fire, and add the juice of three lemons or four oranges. Mix it well and boil very gently, until it is as hard as before the lemon was added; pour it in square buttered pans. It should be about an eighth of an inch thick when cold. Before it hardens mark it off neatly in small blocks that it may break regularly.

LEMON DROPS.—Boil clarified syrup to the sixth degree, flavor with lemon, and drop the candy in small drops on buttered paper, and let it remain on the paper until cold.

9

COMFITS.—These are made by dropping cassia buds or coriander seeds in syrup, and then rolling them lightly in flour, shaking them in a sieve, letting them dry, and again repeating the process until they are as large as desired.

SUGAR HEARTS OR OTHER FANCY CANDY.—Boil syrup to the seventh degree, flavor to suit, and pour it evenly in moulds the shapes desired. The moulds should be buttered with fresh butter, as the salt will not taste well in the candies.

ICE CREAM CANDY.—Five pounds of loaf sugar, half an ounce of cream of tartar, and one pint of water; boil over hot water until the syrup is reduced to the sixth degree. When it cracks, take it from the fire, let it become half cold, and add the flavoring, which should be the same as for ice cream; butter a platter, and cool quickly; work it as soon as it can be handled without burning the hands; it cannot be made in the summer.

SUGAR KISSES TO MAKE QUICKLY, No. 1.—Beat the whites of four eggs stiff, flavor with vanilla; lay sheets of white paper on a board, beat gradually one pound of powdered loaf-sugar in the egg, and drop them in small half egg shaped piles on the paper, dry them in a moderate oven without browning; lay the board on bricks that it may not scorch; pine boards will not do. When stiff, take them up with a knife and lay the two together, making them egg-shaped.

KISSES VERY NICE MADE BY LONG BEATING, No. 2.—The whites of eight eggs beat stiff, and one pound of pure pulverized loaf-sugar, and flavoring to suit the taste. Beat the sugar in by the teaspoonful; after adding the sugar, beat half an hour. The kisses to be light and crisp should be beat at least one hour; the longer the egg and sugar are beat, after all the sugar is in, the better; bake as directed above.

ORANGE, COCOA, OR PINE APPLE KISSES.—Make kisses by the last rule; when cool scoop out the centre, and fill them with orange, grated cocoa, or pine apple; wet the edges with some of the sugar, and place them together, so that the edges will adhere.

STRAWBERRY MERINGUES.—Pour over a pound of fine powdered loaf-sugar the juice of strawberries, until it is all colored. Beat the whites of four eggs stiff, and work a pound and an eighth of sugar into them; bake, or rather dry them, in a moderate oven, on paper spread on boards, which contain no gum or sap, raised on brick. When done, lift them with a knife and place them together; they should be as uniform in size and form as possible.

LEMON CAKES.—Rub the rinds of four lemons with lump sugar, then powder it. To every pound of sugar, allow the whites of four beaten eggs; mix the sugar, after it is powdered, with the eggs, a teaspoonful at a time; add a table-spoonful of the juice of the lemon; bake on papers spread on boards, until dry; then place the bottoms together, and keep them in a dry place.

JELLY KISSES.—Make kisses as described before; after they are cold fill the cavities with jelly formed with isinglass, flavored to suit the taste, then place the cakes together.

FANCY JELLIES FOR PARTIES.—Dissolve one ounce of shred isinglass in as little water as possible; mix it with strawberry syrup, or any other fruit syrup, and strain it into moulds; set it on ice if made in the summer, or in a cool place for winter; a pyramid is beautiful on a table.

FROZEN JELLY.—Freeze calves-foot jelly in the same manner as ice cream; it will not mould but looks beautifully. *See* CALVES-FOOT JELLY.

TO MAKE A PYRAMID OF KISSES.—Make a pasteboard frame, and stick the kisses together as fast as they come from the oven; as soon as cold, or just before using, remove the form carefully.

ICE CREAM.—The freezer must be free from rust. It will take a peck of coarse salt to freeze two gallons. The ice must be pounded fine, mixed with salt and packed around the freezer, which must stand in a tub; the brine should be saved, and allowed to dry by evaporation, or be thrown in the garden where needed. It is also useful to throw on pavement to destroy the grass between the bricks. The freezer should be turned half round and back, until the whole is so nearly frozen as to remain stiff. Cut the cream every ten minutes from the sides of the freezer with a long thin shovel made of wood; if a knife is used, the tin is scratched, and the scrapings mixed with the cream; beat it well every time the cream is cut. If lemon or the juice of any acid fruit is added, it should be at the last cutting, as the cream will sour if it is put in before freezing. If it is to be moulded, put it in the moulds just before it becomes solid, pack it tight, and cover the moulds in ice and salt. When the cream is solid, cover the freezer with ice and salt until wanted; if there is an ice-house, it will keep any length of time. Great care must be taken, when opening the freezer, not to drop any of the brine in it, as this would ruin it entirely; when to be taken out for the table, wrap two or three towels around the freezer dipped in boiling water, or dip the freezer in and out a kettle of hot water quickly once or twice, and turn it on a platter. The faster the ice melts, the sooner the cream will freeze. In summer twenty minutes will be long enough after the freezer is packed; in winter it takes longer. With the old-fashioned freezers there is much more ice required than with the new patents. It would be economy to buy one of the new style if much cream is frozen in the family.

ICE CREAM, No. 1.—Boil two quarts of milk; thicken with three table-spoonfuls of arrowroot, and, when cool, add one pound of powdered sugar, and the whites of eight eggs well beaten; flavor with vanilla, or lemon, or both.

SUPERIOR ICE CREAM, No. 2.—Take three quarts of very rich cream, it must if possible all be of the same age, and perfectly sweet; beat it until it is as stiff as possible; the easiest way to do it is in a small churn. Boil two quarts of morning's milk over water, thicken with wheat flour to the consistency of thin cream, cook thoroughly; add one and a quarter pound of powdered loaf-sugar, lemon and vanilla, mixed or separate, as desired; strain this through a hair sieve, and mix it with the beaten cream. Mix thoroughly, then taste it; if too sweet to suit, add more milk or cream; if not sweet enough, more sugar. It should be much sweeter than would relish before freezing; it loses both flavoring and sweetness in freezing. Be careful not to beat the cream to butter, some cows' milk churns in a short time. This rule makes from eight to ten quarts, according to the lightness of the cream. If the cream is thin increase the quantity.

ICE CREAM WITHOUT CREAM, No. 3.—Take new milk, scald half of it, and thicken it with flour; let it boil until all the raw taste of the flour disappears, and the whole is smooth and as thick as the thickest cream; stir it while hot in the other part of the milk, little by little; flavor with lemon and vanilla, half and half; sweeten very sweet, and strain the whole through a sieve. The milk should be boiled over water for fear of scorching, and the flour thoroughly cooked in it, or it will be very poor. If this is made properly, it will be taken for rich cream; it freezes very smoothly.

FROZEN CUSTARD.—Prepare a nice boiled custard and freeze as ice cream; call it frozen custard, not ice cream.

QUICK ICE CREAM, No. 4.—Take a pint of rich sweet cream, sweeten very sweet, and flavor as relished with vanilla, lemon, or bitter almonds, very strong; beat the whole to a froth, and stir into it sufficient light dry snow to make it stiff, and serve immediately.

MRS. A.'s ICE CREAM.—Two quarts of new milk, two quarts of sweet cream, one quart of pulverized loaf sugar, four eggs, one tablespoonful of vanilla, two teaspoonfuls of bitter almonds, and two tablespoonfuls of wheat flour. Boil one quart of the milk, mix the flour in half a pint of cold milk, and add it to that boiling; stir constantly until well cooked, then thin the thickened milk with half a pint of cold milk; beat the eggs as light as possible without separating, stir into them half a pint of cold milk, beat the eggs and milk well together, and add them to the thickened milk; beat the thickened milk and egg briskly three minutes, add the remainder of the milk and the sugar; when the sugar is dissolved, strain the custard through a fine sieve, and when cool add the extracts. Beat the cream until light and add it to the other ingredients after they are in the freezer; this is an excellent rule. Freeze as usual; if patent freezers are used, the cream will not require beating.

COFFEE CREAM.—Take very rich cream, beat it well, and sweeten very sweet with powdered loaf-sugar. Prepare in the best manner a decoction of very strong coffee; it must be very clear; stir sufficient into the cream to flavor it highly and freeze; it will be a darkish color, but is highly esteemed by gentlemen.

CHOCOLATE CREAM.—This is made as above, using the chocolate instead of coffee.

BRANDY CREAM, A DESSERT OF 1818.—Heat one quart of good sweet cream from the previous night's milking, boiling hot; have ready three thoroughly beaten eggs, take the cream from the fire and stir in the eggs. Dissolve loaf-sugar to suit the taste in half a pint of French brandy; when cold stir in the brandy and sugar, beat well, and serve in glasses. It is proper for either dinner or evening parties.

ORANGE ICE CREAM.—Fill the freezer nearly full of rich cream, well beat and sweetened; do not flavor with any thing but orange peel. This can best be obtained by rubbing lump sugar on the outside of the oranges, and extracting from them the oil of the skin. When the cream is nearly congealed, add as much juice from oranges strained and sweetened as desired; mix it well, and let the whole freeze.

STRAWBERRY ICE CREAM.—Pine apple, raspberry, cherry, or any other juice, or syrup, can be used in the same manner, if not too acid.

FROZEN FRUIT.—Mash any fruit and freeze it; serve with ice cream; oranges are superior.

FRUIT ICE.—Make an ade of any fruit as you would lemonade, but much richer, and freeze it. It is very excellent. This can be prepared from syrups, if they are made from the fruits; many preservers make syrups from extracts.

FRENCH METHOD OF ICING CAKE.—Eight ounces of fine loaf-sugar beat in a mortar, with four spoonfuls of rose water, the juice of a lemon, and the whites of two eggs beaten stiff and strained. Beat the ingredients well together, and cover the cake, when half cold, with a paste brush; set it in a cool oven to dry the icing. It will become solid in one hour.

COMMON ICING.—Beat the whites of three eggs to a stiff froth, until they will remain on an inverted plate; beat into them, one tablespoonful at a time, twelve heaping table-spoonfuls of fine sugar, and one of powdered starch; the sugar and starch should be passed through a sieve made of bolting cloth, and by heaping is meant as much as can possibly be made to lie on a spoon without packing; if desired, flavor with lemon juice, a little extract of lemon, vanilla, bitter almond, or, if desired to color it, add a little juice from the strawberry or any other fruit. Allow three eggs for two common sized cakes; spread evenly with a knife dipped in cold water and shook, that no water can mix with the frosting. It is not considered genteel now to ornament with colored candies; the only kinds of candies now tolerated are the fine French sorts of fruits, birds, etc. Always spread frosting on cake when partly cold, and set it in the sun by the window to dry. It will take longer than in the oven, but it is often scorched, and for that reason it is better to avoid it if possible; if frosting is left, drop it on papers and bake it.

To PREPARE CAKE FOR FROSTING.—Turn it upside down, if very large, on a whitewood board; dredge it all over with flour, let it remain on fifteen minutes, then wipe it off. This removes the grease, and makes the frosting adhere better; commence by pouring a quantity on the centre of the cake, dip a knife in cold water, smooth it down, and let it dry.

CONFECTIONERS' ICING.—To every egg beaten stiff allow four ounces of fine powdered loaf-sugar, powder as much gum-arabic as will lie on a shilling in a teaspoonful of rose water, or any other light-colored extract, or lemon juice. We prefer the latter, as it makes the icing more adhesive. Strain the eggs to remove the stringy substance in them, beat until they will remain on an inverted plate, and then stir in gradually the sugar, gum-arabic, and lemon juice; ice as already described. When the cake is to be ornamented with the icing in wreaths, dissolve gum-tragacanth, and stir a little in the frosting. Pick the gum clean, and wash it; allow a quarter of an ounce to a gill of boiling water, if wanted for immediate use; it takes some time to dissolve. The icing can be made into forms by moulding, or can be put on with a small syringe. The ornamental icing is not put on until the covering of the cake is nearly dry.

LEMON MACAROONS.—Rub off the rind from a large fine lemon on lumps of loaf-sugar; roll the sugar, and add enough of powdered loaf-sugar to make a quarter of a pound. Then strain the lemon juice through a strainer. Beat light four eggs, stir the sugar in the eggs, and beat well. Then add the lemon juice, and three large heaping table-spoonfuls of flour; mix the whole thoroughly. It must be thick enough to form into balls; if not, add flour until it will. Moisten your hands with cold water, and form the paste into balls the size of a plum; lay them on buttered papers and bake without browning. You will be obliged to try one, to see if it is done. As soon as done, remove them from the paper with a knife.

ORANGE MACAROONS.—Make in the same manner, using the rind of half an orange, and the juice of one.

VANILLA MACAROONS.—Boil just as little milk over water in a small vessel as will cover a vanilla bean, and mix it with the egg. Make as LEMON MACAROONS.

ALMOND MACAROONS can be made in the same manner, making balls instead of cakes. Cocoanut can also be used in the same way, as indeed can any nut.

Pop-Corn Cakes.—Prepare the eggs and sugar as for lemon macaroons, and bake without browning; the balls must not be larger than plums.

WEST INDIA SWEETMEATS.

Pineapple. The best Way of preserving, when not Decayed in the Least, No. 1.—Select ripe pineapples entirely free from blemishes. Do not break them, or remove the leaves. Put them in a large pot filled with water, and cover tight. Boil, until tender enough to run a splinter through them. Take them from the water, let them cool, then peel and cut them in round slices, and take out the cores with a round tin tube. The slices should be one-fourth of an inch thick. Weigh the fruit, allow the same weight of the best sugar. It should be No. 1, Granulated. Spread a little on the bottom of the jar or dish which is to contain them. Lay in a layer of fruit, then a layer of sugar, and so on until the whole is in. Let it remain until the whole of the sugar is dissolved; then drain off the syrup, and strain it. Set the jar (it should be glass) in cold water. Let it remain until the water boils; then set it off with the water in which it was heated. Have the syrup on the fire heating, at the same time the jar is heating. Place the fruit in the jar, and leave it in the hot water; then fill up with the syrup boiling hot. Set the kettle on the fire again, until the water boils. Cork, and paste white paper over the jar, wet with the beaten white of egg, press the edges firm, and then put on another-paper covered inside and out with the egg; keep it in a cool place. The jar should be small, as it will soon work after opening. This is as fine as any India preserved pineapple.

Pineapples without Cooking, No. 2.—Peel very ripe pineapples, cut them in slices, take out the cores, and weigh the fruit; allow a pound of double-refined loaf-sugar to every pound of fruit. Spread the sugar evenly over the fruit; pack it in layers, and let it stand twenty-four hours; then drain off the syrup, and boil it as long as any impurities rise to the surface, skim it constantly, and pour it over the fruit boiling hot; seal as directed in Pineapple, No. 1.

Fresh Pineapple, Hermetically Sealed, No. 1.—Peel, and cut the fruit in circular pieces, about one-third of an inch thick. Cut these pieces in quarters. Pack them close in bottles, and fill up with filtered rain-water, so as to come within one inch of the cork. Put in the cork tightly, and wire it well; then set the bottles in the water-bath, until the fruit has heated through. The water must be cold when the bottles are put in the bath. They will need to boil about half an hour. Hermetically seal the bottles as soon as taken from the bath.

HERMETICALLY-SEALED PINEAPPLES IN TIN CANS, No. 2.—Prepare the fruit as directed in No. 1. Fill the cans as full as they can be packed, as the fruit would naturally lie. Add to each can a half-pound of loaf-sugar and a gill of water. Solder on the covers, and let them remain in the bath until the air is all exhausted, which will be in about half an hour after the fruit boils. Then solder up the small hole left in the can to let out the air. Mark the cans and set them away. If the ends of the cans are not drawn in, there is some imperfection; either the air was not exhausted, or the can is imperfect.

PINEAPPLE JELLY.—This is set with isinglass. To every quart of syrup allow one ounce of shred isinglass. To make the syrup, allow to a pint of juice a pound of the best loaf-sugar.

PINEAPPLE MARMALADE.—To every pound of grated pineapple allow a pound of double-refined loaf-sugar. Boil until thick; then pack in tumblers, and paste over them papers wet with the beaten whites of eggs. Keep in *a dry cool place until wanted.*

To PRESERVE GREEN GINGER, No. 1.—Scrape the root clean, weigh it, and allow the same weight in loaf-sugar that there is of ginger. Boil the ginger until it can be pierced with a splinter. To every pound of sugar allow half a pint of water, and half a teaspoonful of cream of tartar. Boil the syrup over boiling water, remove all the scum, and scald the ginger in the syrup. As soon as it becomes boiling hot, put it in bottles, and seal it with paper wet in the beaten whites of eggs.

PRESERVED GREEN GINGER, No. 2.—Prepare as above the ginger and syrup. Boil in the syrup one lemon peel and juice to every three pounds of fruit; allow a pound of sugar for every pint of lemon juice. Strain out all the seeds before putting the lemon in the syrup. It can be varied with pineapple or orange.

ORANGE MARMALADE.—Strain the juice, and rub the pulp through a wire sieve; add to every pound a pound of loaf-sugar. Boil until solid; try it often, to know when it is sufficiently cooked. When done, put it in tumblers, and paste papers over them with the whites of eggs. Keep it in a cool place.

AMERICAN CITRON.—Pare ripe citron melons, and cut them in any form desired; small half-moon-shaped pieces will cut to the most advantage from a melon. They should be about half an inch thick, before boiling. Boil in soda water until tender; when a straw will pass through them, skim them out, and lay them in weak alum water. Let them remain three or four hours; then throw them in cold water for another hour. Dissolve a tablespoonful of citric acid in a quart of water; lay in the citron. There should be just enough water to cover them. The next morning take them from the acid water, measure the water, and allow, for a quart, four pounds of sugar, and the same weight of citron, weighed after boiling, etc. Or weigh the citron, and allow the same weight of sugar and a pint of acid water, for every two pounds. Boil the syrup, and remove the scum. When it is clear, put in the citron, and let it remain until the sugar has penetrated it thoroughly; then pack it in jars. Boil the syrup until it will make a thread between the thumb and finger, (*see* SYRUP,) and pour it in the jars. If you have ginger sweetmeats, put two or three bits in each jar; if not, flavor with extract of ginger. Add to each quart jar a table-spoonful of strong extract of lemon-peel, and seal the jars, as soon as filled, with paper wet in egg. Keep cool and dry.

GREEN TOMATOES TO RESEMBLE INDIA SWEETMEATS.—Take small plum or pear-shaped tomatoes, when perfectly green. Weigh them. Allow a pound of loaf-sugar to one of fruit; add the juice of one lemon, and enough water with the juice, to allow a pint of fluid to every two pounds of sugar. Put in a preserving kettle the lemon-peel and pulp, chopped fine, but not the seeds, and a handful of ginger root; boil these until the water is highly flavored. Then, while hot, throw in a handful of peach leaves. Let it remain in the kettle, if a porcelain one, until morning; if brass, pour it into an earthen dish. The next morning strain the water; pick out the lemon and ginger, and throw it back in the water. Line the kettle with grape leaves, and lay in the tomatoes; cover with leaves, and add another layer, until the whole are in. Then pour over them hot, but not boiling water. Set the kettle where it will heat gradually; when hot, but before the fruit breaks, take it from the fire. Let them cool, and heat again and again until green. The best way to heat them is over hot water. Then strain the water containing lemon and ginger, and if not highly flavored, boil it again before straining. There should be a pint of water to every four pounds of sugar. If too much, boil it away. After it is strained, mix the sugar and lemon juice with it. Let it boil up and skim it. Then remove the tomatoes from the grape leaves; wash them, and roll in a towel gently without breaking. Prick them two or three times with a coarse needle. Cool the syrup, and put them in; set the kettle over water; let them simmer until the sugar has penetrated them. Remove the kettle, let them remain overnight in the syrup. In the latter part of the forenoon put them over again. Let them nearly boil, take them off the fire, and set them on hot water an hour. Then skim them out. Boil and skim the syrup; when no scum arises, put them back; let them boil up, and put them in the jars. Cover with paper wet with egg. If you have preserved ginger or ginger root, and a strong extract of lemon, put the peach-leaves in water, and scald them. Pour the water on the tomatoes hot; let them remain over a kettle of water an hour. Then put them in the grape-leaves, as directed. Heat the sugar and lemon juice over water. Blanch a dozen peach-pits to every jar; lay them in the syrup. Cook the tomatoes in the syrup, as directed; cut up the ginger, and put it in the jars, and add a table-spoonful, or more, if needed, of lemon extract to each jar. The syrup will be much lighter made with extract and preserves. Extract of cinnamon would do also, and tartaric or citric acid instead of lemon juice. This will be found a beautiful sweetmeat resembling the INDIA SWEETMEATS.

PRESERVED CITRON OR NUTMEG MUSKMELON.—Take melons that have a fine spicy flavor, nearly ripe, but before they mellow in the least. Cut them in halves; take out the seeds, and scrape off the outside rough skin. Cut them in quarters, and lay them in weak brine all night. The next morning throw them in alum water, for an hour. Then pack them in peach leaves, pour boiling water on them, and let them get cool. Boil the water again, and pour over them. Then boil them in water, strongly spiced with ginger, nutmeg, cinnamon, mace, a very few cloves, and a handful of coriander seed. The spices must be well balanced, so as not to taste of one more than another; to give the melon, as near as possible, its own spicy flavor, a dozen cloves will be enough for two quarts of water. Prepare a rich syrup. When the melons have become boiling hot in the spice water, take them from the fire, and let them cool in the water. Then simmer them in the syrup, until the sugar has penetrated them perfectly. The melon will be less apt to break, if simmered over hot water. There should be as many pounds of sugar as there are of melon, and a pint of water to every two pounds of sugar. Seal up the jars while boiling hot, and keep in a cool place.

PRESERVED MUSKMELON, No. 2.—Another method is, after soaking in the brine, etc., to boil them with ginger and peach leaves, until tender, but not so as to break; and afterward in syrup, made as described in No. 1, flavored with ginger and lemon. Seal the jars while hot, and there will be very little danger of fermentation. Some persons are very fond of these kinds of sweetmeats. They are convenient at the Far West, where it is difficult to get fruit.

PUMPKIN CHIPS.—Saturate as many pounds of sugar as you have prepared of pumpkin in lemon juice, (citric or tartaric acid, if you have no lemons.) Pour it over the pumkpin, which should be cut in any shape desired. The most convenient would be round, cut with a canister top, or cracker-cutter; let it remain twenty-four hours. Blanch a dozen peach-pits, or bitter almonds, to every pound of sugar. Drain the pumpkin and heat the syrup, put in the peach-pits; add for every two pounds eight cloves, a half nutmeg pounded, or a teaspoon of mace rolled, a table-spoonful of broken cinnamon, and a half of a vanilla bean. Put in the pumpkin; let it simmer over water until thoroughly saturated with the syrup, and quite tender. Then remove it to the jars, and keep them hot while the syrup cooks. Boil it until it will form a thread with your thumb and finger, then pour it on the pumpkin, straining it free from every thing except the pits and vanilla bean; seal up while hot, and keep cool.

CHAPTER XIII.

TEA.

DESCRIPTION OF PLANT, PREPARATION FOR MARKET, VARIETIES, STEEPING, ETC

THE plant which produces tea is grown in small plantations by natives, little above the class of peasants. It is a native of China and Japan, and belongs, in the Linnæan system, to the class and order of *Monadelphia Polyandria*, and, in the system of Jussieu, to the natural order of *Aurantiaceæ*. It has since been made into a new order called *Theasia*, which includes camellia and some other plants.

It is an evergreen tree or shrub, resembling the myrtle in its leaves and general appearance; the flowers, which are not unlike our wild rose, though smaller, are white and fragrant. The capsules, which contain from one to three white seeds, are soft and green, containing oil, which is obtained by crushing, and used generally in China. The black and green were once thought to be two distinct species, but botanists have decided them to be one, divided into several varieties, by cultivation, soil, etc., with only two of which we are familiar; the black with broad, and the green with narrow, leaves. The best black tea is grown in Tokien and Canton; the best green in the district of Hoey-chow-foo, in a soil of decomposed granite and feldspar, the same mineral from which the best porcelain cups are manufactured.

The finest black tea is manufactured from the youngest leaves, which are gathered at four different periods. The best black brought to this market is the Souchong; this tea is quite small, of a greenish color when steeped, and the flavor agreeable.

Congou is much more imported than the Souchong; the best kind is Campo Congou; it has an agreeable flavor, but the poorest much resembles Bohea, which is the worst of all black teas.

The Hysons are the best green teas brought to this market; when good, the flavor is superior, and the infusion a fine green. Pearl gunpowder stands first, Imperial gunpowder next, then the varieties of Hyson, and, lastly, Hyson skin. These are the best; but, of course, there are many sub-varieties not enumerated. Green tea depends more on soil and culture, than stages of picking, and there is a difference in the manner of curing, but there is no copper used in drying either. The English have endeavored to manufacture teas from other leaves, some of which are poisonous, and use copper to give them the color of green tea; it is easy to detect copper, if any exists, in the tea by the following method: Steep the tea, and put some into water, impregnated with sulphureted hydrogen; if the tea contains copper, it will turn black; if not, no change will be seen, the infusion remaining green as before.

To CHOOSE TEA.—Select tea as whole as possible, of agreeable odor, and that has not been exposed to the air; if bought by the chest, take out what is needed for present use, and close the chest as tightly as possible.

To PREPARE GREEN TEA.—There is as much difference in the preparation of tea as coffee. The best teas can be ruined by steeping, so that an experienced tea-drinker would be puzzled to distinguish gunpowder from Bohea. It is a poor plan to steep tea in the tea-pot; the pot is apt to receive injury by standing on the stove; if of metal, is likely to melt, or get bruised; if of earthenware, to be seared, or cracked by the heat; the inside will become coated, and is soon discolored by the steam settling in the hinge of the lid, looking any thing but neatly on the table; the spout, too, if as small as is usual, will close, so that the liquid will hardly pass through; and this coating can only be removed by boiling the pot in strong lye, which injures the metal much. Have made a tin pint cup with a handle, and tight-fitting cover on a hinge, in which to steep the tea. This little tea-steeper must be scalded and dried every time it is used, or it will soon rust, and give the tea a bad flavor. Pour boiling water into the steeper before putting in the tea, that the water may not cool, when poured over it. Allow one teaspoonful for three cups, that is about one spoonful to a person; fill the steeper half full of water, boiling hot; let it stand on the hearth from five to fifteen minutes, where it will remain hot, not boiling. Pour into the teapot boiling water to stand while the tea is steeping; throw out this water, pour in the tea-grounds and all; add one and a half cups of boiling water to every teaspoonful of tea. Have a water-pot filled with boiling water; fill each cup half full with the infusion, then add the boiling water until they are nearly filled. Sugar should be put in the cup before the tea, if relished, and cream after the water. Have the water-pot filled again, before replenishing the cups; pour into each cup a little hot water, and throw it, with the sediment from the previous filling, into the slop-bowl, which should always be on the tray, and fill the cups as at first; the same also with the third. This will equalize the tea, not giving the whole strength of the infusion in the first cup, and warm colored water for the other two. The tea-kettle should be boiling, while the tea is being served to fill up the pot. Spring is the best water for tea; filtered rain next; lime water, if used, soon crusts over the kettle; it is well to rinse it every time it is used, and absolutely necessary to do this once every day. Some tea requires more steeping than others; the housekeeper can determine by the appearance of the infusion; in green tea, the liquid should be greenish; if steeped too long, it turns a dark color; if in fifteen minutes the tea becomes dark, steep less time; fifteen minutes will be sufficient time for tea requiring the longest steeping; some teas requiring only three minutes, most requiring five. The tea-kettle should but just boil; do not use water that has boiled a long time for tea.

To PREPARE BLACK TEA.—Use a steeper as in green tea; black and green should never be steeped in the same vessel. Prepare both steeper and pot as described before, but black tea wants boiling from three to five minutes hard; three is usually sufficient. Some prefer steeping black tea in the same manner as green. Black tea is much lighter than green; and, of course, more by measure should be allowed to each person. The best loaf-sugar only should be tolerated in tea, and cream is as much better than milk, for those who relish it, as in coffee. There are so many persons now who use but one variety, that it is well, when company are present, to steep both black and green, that all may make a choice. Serve the same as green, putting the cream in the cup before pouring in the tea. There is an article, now sold by grocers, called BREAKFAST TEA; it is a mixture of green and black; prepare as black tea, as this has the most prominence in its appearance and flavor. Throw out the cold tea, rinse and scald the pot after using. It ruins teapots to stand with cold tea.

CHAPTER XIV.
COFFEE.

DESCRIPTION OF PLANT, PREPARATION FOR MARKET, VARIETIES, BROWNING, GRINDING, PREPARATION FOR TABLE, ETC.

DESCRIPTION OF PLANT.—The coffee tree is a native of warm climates. It belongs to the natural order of *Rabiaceæ*. Its height is from twelve to fifteen feet. The tree resembles the laurel, although the leaves are thinner and rather more pointed. The flowers, which are white, growing from the angles of the leaf stalk, resemble the jasmine, and are produced in such profusion and rapidity as in a single night to resemble a fall of snow; they are, however, very short-lived, lasting but a few days. When the blossoms fall, a berry appears, resembling, when ripe, the cherry; each of which contains, enclosed in a sort of parchment, two seeds or beans, the flat sides being pressed closely together. The fruit is known to be ripe when it becomes red, and falls to the ground, unless gathered immediately. The tree is grown from the seed, and commences bearing when two years old.

PREPARATION FOR MARKET.—In Arabia the fruit is allowed to fall on cloths spread for the purpose, but in the West Indies it is gathered by the negroes, after which it is left in the sun until fermentation takes place, and the sour moisture has passed off, which is generally accomplished in three or four days. The bean is then gradually dried, the process occupying about three weeks, after which the husk is separated from the seed by passing through a mill. The fruit is not always fermented, but the pulp is removed by passing it under rollers, and the parchment by another mill; the seed is then winnowed, and, after a thorough drying, is ready for market.

VARIETIES.—The best is the Mocha, a native of Arabia; the bean is smaller and rounder than any other. The next is almost as good, and by some preferred, called Old Government Java, a native, as its name implies, of Java. Rio (the poorest in general use) is a native of Rio Janeiro.

BROWNING, AND PRESERVING THE AROMA.—Wash coffee, rubbing it well with the hands, and rinse until the water is clear; drain on a hair, not wire, sieve, or shake it in a coarse towel, dry slowly without heat until free from moisture, then spread thinly, and keep it where it is just warm, until perfectly dry. It is well to wash and dry large quantities at one time, as it often happens to be wanted without sufficient notice to dry well before browning. Coffee dried in this manner can be quickly and thoroughly browned, which is of the highest importance, if a first-rate cup of coffee is desired. When the coffee is a long time browning, much more of the volatile oil is lost than when quickly done; it must also be browned to the centre, or much waste occurs from not getting the whole strength of the bean; when there is much haste in getting coffee ready to grind, partly brown it, and break the bean in two or three pieces by beating it in a mortar, after which it must be finished scorching. When sufficiently roasted, it will be a dark chestnut color from outside to centre. Before it becomes cold, put it in a tight vessel; glass or earthenware is better than metal. A vessel can be prepared with but little trouble that will answer all purposes. Procure a thick glass bottle, it must be strong to withstand heat; get a tight-fitting cork, free from air holes, four inches long, pass a large wire, heated red-hot, through the centre, whittle round a piece of strong hickory as large as a pipe stem, four inches longer than the cork, leave a square piece on one end to form a sort of nut, pass the stick through the cork, the largest end being inside the bottle when it is corked; seal over the top with sealing-wax; if any runs down the side scrape it off, as the cork should press the bottle closely; if the glass is dark, label the bottle. Coffee should be browned at least three times in a week, and no matter how much oftener. It matters little by what mode this is accomplished, so it be well done, whether in a moderately quick oven, spread thinly on iron pans free from rust, in a kettle over a brisk fire, constantly stirred, or in a regular roaster; the same object will be attained, with care, by either, and without, most certainly ruined.

To STORE COFFEE.—Coffee, even before it is browned, may be spoiled by leaving it where it can be affected by unpleasant odors, as it very quickly absorbs them; and yet, when kept in a dry, sweet place, it is constantly improving; brown sugars, teas, chocolate, spices, herbs, in short any strong flavored articles, as well as impurities, are injurious.

GRINDING.—Never grind coffee until wanted; the plan adopted by many of grinding for breakfast the evening previous is wasteful. It is impossible to cover it in a bowl or cup in such a manner as to prevent the escape of the volatile oil, which gives life and flavor to the coffee. Care must be taken to grind it rightly; if too coarse, it is wasted, and if too fine, is difficult to settle. The mill should be set to grind, not fine like flour, or coarse like hominy, but about as Indian meal, when ground right for mush. Every housekeeper should give this matter personal attention, and not leave it entirely to the care of servants.

MIXING AND BOILING.—Allow one heaping tablespoonful of ground coffee for each person, and one for the boiler. If eggs are plenty take half enough to wet the grounds; if not, add sufficient cold water to mix thoroughly; beat the coffee and egg until it shows foam; egg if used too freely congeals the coffee and retains the strength. Scald the boiler, and shake out all the water; pour on sufficient boiling water to serve the first table, allowing a cup for evaporation and waste; as soon as it boils, stir down the grounds that rise until all inclination to boil over has ceased; after this boil five minutes hard, with the pot closed; then take it from the fire, and drop a half-teaspoonful of cold water, *and no more*, in the pot; let it stand where it remains hot, but not boiling, from three to five minutes. Scald the urn, or coffee-pot, with boiling water at least five minutes; throw it all out, and fill with coffee from the boiler while hot; should the table urn, or pot, be too small to hold all that will be needed for the first table, another tin pot should be filled, without spout or air-hole in the cover, in which the extra coffee can be kept hot, not boiling. When the first coffee is poured off, fill the boiler again with hot water, and let it boil as before, this will be nearly as good as the first, and much better than coffee made in the old manner of boiling an hour or two before breakfast. This rule will be found to make a good cup of coffee, strong enough to suit most people; the whole strength of the grounds being used, it is best to throw them out, and make an entire new cup every morning, instead of leaving half the strength in the boiler until the next day, and then adding half as much more to make a tolerable cup of coffee, and in the end using the same amount, with an extra strong cup the first, and only a tolerable one the next, morning.

PROPORTIONS FOR AN EXTRA CUP.—For an extra cup, take one pound before browning of good Mocha coffee for fifteen persons, allowing three cups to each and three for the pot, or five quarts of water; make as above.

BOILED MILK TO REDUCE COFFEE.—Never weaken coffee by adding boiling water, a teacupful will spoil a whole boiler. When the coffee is desired with less strength, reduce with hot milk, or cream. Some are fond of coffee, but find it disagrees with them; such persons would find the following rule useful: Fill the cup two-thirds full of milk boiling hot, sugar to the taste, and half the space left in the cup fill with strong coffee. When cream cannot be had, the *yolks of eggs*, beaten to a froth, and stirred gradually into milk, in the proportion of three to a pint, is a good substitute; pour the milk and egg in the cup, and stir with a spoon while filling with coffee.

COFFEE SUGAR.—Use either number one coffee or loaf-sugar; always put sugar in first, cream next, and lastly coffee, when filling cups at the tea-board.

TO SERVE COFFEE.—When served for large companies, where every person's taste cannot be consulted, it is better that each suit himself to sugar, if not to cream.

REMARKS.—Lastly, a good cup of coffee cannot be made from poor material. Old Government Java is as economical as any for family use, and is also good-flavored; the older coffee is the better. Rio is inferior, and is seldom found at a table where good living is prized; even the steam is offensive to persons accustomed to good Java or Mocha.

AMERICAN CHOCOLATE.—Procure the best chocolate, grate it, and allow for one quart of water four table-spoons of chocolate; mix free from lumps with little water, and boil fifteen minutes. Then add one quart of rich milk, let it boil, grate in a salt-spoonful of nutmeg, and sweeten to the taste; add cream at the table.

GERMAN CHOCOLATE.—Four large table-spoonfuls of the best chocolate grated fine, two quarts rich milk added gradually to the chocolate, the whites of four and yolks of two eggs beaten light, but not separated; add one gill of cold milk to the eggs, beat well; add gradually a coffee-cup of the chocolate to the milk and egg while hot, beating constantly. Take the chocolate from the fire, keep it hot but not boiling, and add the egg and milk gradually; stir constantly, or it will curdle; flavor with nutmeg, vanilla, or cinnamon, as desired; sugar it to suit the taste. The Germans use no sugar. The egg is to be added just before serving. This makes a very delicious drink. Serve in chocolate bowls.

MOCK CREAM FOR COFFEE.—Heat a quart of new milk; work together a dessert-spoon of sweet butter, with a teaspoon of flour; thin it with a little of the hot milk, add the mixture to the milk, and beat it constantly for five minutes while boiling; then remove it from the fire, and continue to beat it for five minutes longer; have ready beat the yolks of two fresh eggs very light, and add them to the cream while hot; mix well, strain it through a fine sieve, and afterward beat it until very light. This is even better than good cream for coffee. One of the whites can be used for settling the coffee.

COFFEE-POTS AND BOILERS. — Scald them every morning after breakfast, and dry thoroughly outside and in. Rub the pot with wash-leather, if metal.

PART IV.

CHAPTER I.

BREAKFAST DISHES.

SOFT BUTTER TOAST.—Toast nicely stale bread, and keep it hot in the oven; have ready a square shallow pan, with one pint of water, one teacup of sweet butter, heated hot without boiling; unless the butter is quite salt, a little salt should be added, though this is a matter of taste. When the breakfast is ready to dish, dip each slice into the gravy, wetting it thoroughly: pour all the gravy that is left in a gravy tureen, to serve with the toast. If poured into the dish, as is usual, the whole is taken up by the bottom slices, and the remainder is too dry. The toast should be sent to the table the last thing; and the gravy-boat or tureen heated by boiling water, so as not to cool the gravy, which ought to be near but not quite boiling hot.

EGG TOAST, No. 1.—Make a nice butter toast as above, with only sufficient sauce to dip the bread; have ready some scambled eggs, (*see* SCAMBLED EGGS,) cooked very slightly, spread the egg on the toast, and serve while hot; if the toast stands, the eggs will harden.

EGG TOAST, No. 2.—Toast fresh but not new bread quickly, without drying; dip each slice in melted not oiled butter; have ready eggs poached soft, (*see* POACHED EGGS,) cut the slices of bread in the middle; lay on each piece of toast an egg without breaking the yolk, dust on very little pepper, and pour over each egg a half-teaspoon of melted butter; never allow butter to boil for toasts; it ruins the whole dish.

MOLASSES TOAST.—Boil nice West India molasses; remove the scum, and strain it through a hair sieve or thin cloth strainer; let it boil five minutes slowly with a bit of butter to a pint, as large as half an egg; if the toast is dry and hard, dip it quickly in hot water, and then in the molasses; if fresh, in the molasses only; if the molasses has thickened, so that when not boiling the basin is not as full as when put to boil, add sufficient boiling water to make up the deficiency; some molasses thickens rapidly, while other does not. This dish is much better than would be supposed; resembling in taste a buckwheat cake with butter and molasses; the author well remembers enjoying it much when a child.

CREAM TOAST.—Heat sweet cream over steam until hot, but do not allow it to boil; add a little salt, dip the toast in the cream, and send all that remains to the table in a gravy-boat. This toast is delightful when properly made; but if the cream boils or is cold, or the toast soaks or cools, it is insipid.

MILK TOAST, No. 1.—Add to one quart of milk perfectly sweet, a bit of butter as large as a small egg, a little salt, and a teaspoon of flour stirred free from lumps; beat the milk, butter, and flour until it boils, dip the toast, and send all the gravy left to the table in a gravy-boat. This is a very good toast if well made and served hot.

MILK TOAST WITHOUT BUTTER, No. 2.—Boil a quart of milk, and add to it while boiling, little by little, pork fat, letting the gravy boil a few moments each time; thicken a little with flour after the first fat has been added, and stir constantly; when the milk will not take up the fat, there is sufficient in the milk; add salt to suit the taste. It should show no drops of fat on the surface. Dip the toast and serve the gravy as directed in other toasts. When this is made properly, no person would know, unless informed, that the milk was not enriched with butter; this is excellent on baked potatoes also.

MOCK CREAM TOAST.—Melt in one quart of morning's milk, two ounces or one gill of butter measured without melting, a large teaspoon of flour freed from lumps, and the yolks of three eggs beaten light; beat these ingredients together several minutes; strain the cream through a fine hair sieve, and when wanted, heat it slowly, beating constantly with a brisk movement; it must not boil, or it will curdle and lose the appearance of cream; when hot dip the toast; if not sufficiently seasoned by the butter, add salt; send to the table hot, the cream not taken up by the toast, in a gravy-boat. This will be found superior if properly made.

SUPERIOR TOMATO TOAST.—Remove the skin and all the seeds from tomatoes, *ripe, but not overripe;* stew them to a paste without scorching; season with butter, and very little pepper and salt; toast fresh but not new bread quickly, without drying; dip the slices in hot water, in which very little butter is melted, spread each slice of toast with tomato, laying it two slices thick on the platter; before sending to the table cut the slices through, that each may have a top and bottom piece, serving each with two half-slices, otherwise, the carver will endeavor to lift one slice for each, and mangle the remainder.

DRY TOAST.—Toast nice fresh-sliced bread over hot coal, and send to the table as required, during breakfast.

DIP TOAST.—Toast bread; as fast as toasted, dip it in boiling water quickly, and spread it with sweet butter; stand it in the oven until all is ready; it should have plenty of butter.

DRY BUTTER TOAST.—Toast fresh-sliced bread by a bright fire, without drying, spread each slice after it is toasted with plenty of sweet butter, and set it in the oven until all is ready.

Indian, Graham bread, or crackers, can be toasted and served with any of the above sauces.

FRIED POTATOES are a nice breakfast dish, also warmed in cream; broiled and buttered, baked, or made into balls and browned. (*See* POTATOES.)

GRIDDLE CAKES are also not only nice, but proper for breakfasts. (*See* GRIDDLE CAKES, also COFFEE and PLAIN FRIED CAKES.) Dried beef, cooked nicely as already directed; soup meats, etc.; fricassee; cold fowls warmed over; cutlets of any meats; in short, any meats quickly cooked, and not too troublesome, are proper for breakfasts; but in many families coals cannot be obtained for broiling without great waste in the morning. Charcoal is the most economical coal for early broiling; green corn cakes, egg plant, parsnip fritters, salsify toast or fritters, among vegetables, are perhaps more in place at breakfast than at any other meal; also cod and oyster toast.

CODFISH TOAST.—Freshen nicely picked-up codfish, by laying it in water all night; add, if you have it, sweet cream and an egg, and heat it boiling hot; pour it over toast, or make a gravy of water and butter; beat up two or three eggs, and thicken the gravy without allowing it to curdle, and pour it over toast.

OYSTER TOAST.—Toast bread nicely, and spread it thinly with butter; have ready sufficient oysters to allow to each half-slice six; scald them in just enough water to moisten the toast; add butter and pepper to the taste; dip the toast in the oysters, and after cutting each slice in the middle, lay them regularly on the toast, and dip the liquor over them; it should not be piled up, as the bread disfigures the oysters; serve as soon as possible. If they are to be passed the second time, reserve a part of the toast; cover tight and place the dish over steam until required. In the cities of the sea-coast, where oysters are plenty and fresh, this is a cheap as well as excellent dish.

FRIED OYSTERS WITH EGG.—Select large oysters; heat them partially in their own liquor without allowing them to really boil dry; dredge them with flour; dip them in beaten egg and bread crumbs, (*see* DRY BREAD,) and fry brown in butter, without scorching; or make a batter of egg and flour, seasoned with pepper and salt; dip the oysters, and fry a light brown. Where oysters are plenty it is well to beard them—that is, remove the respiratory organs of the oyster; but in the country oysters are too expensive to use bearded.

CLAM FRITTERS.—Make a nice, smooth batter; dip the clams in the batter, and fry in hot lard until brown; or take the liquor from the clams, a little milk, an egg or two, and flour sufficient to make a batter that will not fry in bits; stir in the clams, and drop them one by one in hot lard; when browned on one side, turn them over; take care not to have the lard too hot. Oyster fritters can be made as above.

EGGS in any form are nice for breakfasts, (*see* EGGS,) omelets in particular.

OYSTER OMELETS.—Allow for every six large oysters or twelve small ones one large egg; remove the hard part of the oysters, and mince the remainder; take the yolks of eight and the whites of four eggs, beat them until very light, mix in the oysters and a little pepper, and beat them thoroughly; put in a frying-pan a large gill of butter, measured before melting, and move it around until melted; when it boils, if the buttermilk rises, skim it and turn in the omelet while boiling; stir it until it begins to stiffen, fry it a light brown; lift the edge carefully, and slip under a round pointed knife; be careful not to have it overdone; as soon as the underside is a light brown, turn it on to a hot plate by turning the pan upside down. Omelets used always to be folded over, but at the present time, the best cooks do not advise it, thinking it is apt to make them heavy. Serve immediately. If desired brown on the top, hold over it a red-hot shovel, or cover for a few minutes with a bake-pan cover, heated very hot; if turned while frying, they are apt to fall. (For omelet pan, see IRON WARE.) Clam omelets can be made in the same manner; also green corn, allowing to six eggs eighteen ears; add salt; the corn should be very young and finely grated.

ASPARAGUS OMELET.—Boil two pounds of tender, fresh-cut asparagus, in very little water, with a little salt, or, what is better, steam it without water until tender; chop and mash it finely, incorporate with it the whites of three and yolks of five well-beaten eggs; mix them thoroughly; if not salted sufficiently, add more; after these are well mixed, so as to form one mass, add two table-spoonfuls of sweet cream; fry as directed above, and serve hot.

MUSHROOM OMELET.—In gathering mushrooms, always examine the gills or under part; if of a pink or flesh color, you may be certain they are not the poisonous kinds. When young they are roundish like a button, the stalks and button white, the flesh white when broken, and the gills beneath livid; remove the stalks, and rub the heads with a very little salt and pure Cayenne; if not pure, use white pepper; stew them with hardly cream or milk sufficient to cover them; stir them constantly with a *silver* spoon, and as soon as the cream boils up take them from the fire, cool and chop them fine. To a pint of minced mushroom allow the whites of four and yolks of six well-beaten eggs; mix the mushroom gradually with the egg, and beat them well. Fry as directed. (For farther directions in regard to frying Omelets, *see* OMELET OF EGG.)

BREAD BALLS are a breakfast dish. (*See* DRY BREAD.) (For hashes, which are all breakfast dishes, *see* HASHES; for coffee, *see* COFFEE; for cream for coffee, *see* MOCK CREAM.)

Relishes for breakfast, to eat with meats, are tomatoes, sour pickles, mustard, and catsups; for hashes, raw onions for those who do not discard them, horseradish, cucumbers, &c.; for griddle cakes, syrups and sugar; for light breakfast, where the coffee is the principal article, plain fried cakes, coffee-cakes, and plain cookies.

CHAPTER II.

HASHES.

CORNED BEEF HASH.—The best hash is made from boiled corned beef. It should be boiled very tender, and chopped fine when entirely cold. The potatoes for hash made of corned beef are the better for being boiled in the pot liquor. When taken from the pot, remove the skins from the potatoes, and when entirely cold chop them fine. To a coffee-cup of chopped meat allow four of chopped potatoes, stir the potatoes gradually into the meat, until the whole is mixed. Do this at evening, and if warm, set the hash in a cool place. In the morning put the spider on the fire with a lump of butter as large as the bowl of a table-spoon, add a dust of pepper, and if not sufficiently salt, add a little; usually none is needed. When the butter has melted, put the hash in the spider, add four table-spoons of water, and stir the whole together. After it has become really hot, stir it from the bottom, cover a plate over it, and set the spider where it will merely stew. This is a moist hash, and preferred by some to dry or browned hash.

BROWNED HASH OF CORNED BEEF.—Heat the hash in a kettle, and mix through it two table-spoons of sweet butter, add seasoning to suit, add a spoonful of water only. Have ready two table-spoons of melted butter boiling hot in the spider, turn it up and round, that the butter may touch the whole surface of the spider. Put in the hash, press it tightly, and keep it cooking gently without burning. Run a knife under it now and then, to see that it is not scorching. When browned, place a platter over the spider, and turn it out without breaking. It will need two persons to dish it; one to hold the platter firmly on the spider, and the other to turn it out.

HASH BALLS OF CORNED BEEF.—Prepare the hash as above, omitting the butter; make it into flat cakes; heat the griddle and grease it with plenty of sweet butter; brown the balls first on one side and then on the other, and serve hot. The fault usually with hash is, that there is too much meat for the potatoes. It is not necessary that the potatoes should be boiled in pot liquor, but cold mashed potatoes will not make good meat hashes, and poor hashes are very poor dishes.

10

FRESH BEEF HASHES.—Chop very fine the meats left cold, and allow one-fifth of beef to four of chopped potatoes; season to the taste; add more butter and water than to brown hash, and cook it some time; let it slightly brown, and then disturb it, bringing the crisp to the top until quite dry, and mixed through with the crisped part. Dish it in a deep dish. Potatoes for fresh meat hashes should be boiled in clear water, without the peel. The fat of fresh beef should be discarded in hash, it gives a taste of fried tallow to the dish.

FRESH MEAT HASH WITH TOAST.—Some hash cold meat as fine as possible, season it highly, and stew it with butter to put on toast; but this dish would not, in our family, find many admirers. Others mix the meat with bread crumbs and brown them. In either case season highly.

PORK HASH.—Boil tender salt pork; when cold chop it fine, and mix one part of the chopped pork with five parts of the potatoes; season to suit; grease the spider with a bit of the pork, and fry brown. Or, chop raw potatoes fine, and mix six parts of potatoes with one of pork; add salt, and very little pepper, and fry brown. Or, prepare the hash as first directed, make it in cakes, and fry them brown on both sides.

PORK, PARSNIP, AND POTATO HASH.—Chop them when cold very fine, allowing two parts parsnip to one of potatoes; if the vegetables are mashed it is better; add one part of pork to four parts of the mixed potato and parsnip; fry brown in small cakes.

PORK AND PARSNIP HASH.—Boil the parsnips and let them cool; to four parts of parsnip allow one of pork; make the hash into cakes and fry brown. The whole should be chopped very fine. If mashed, so much the better.

CODFISH HASH.—Put in soak overnight a teacup of codfish picked up fine. In the morning boil some potatoes nicely, mash and work them until very light. Put the fish in the chopping-bowl and chop it fine, after which, before taking it from the bowl, mash and work it until as fine as possible. Work the potato in little by little, working it with the potato-pounder, until five parts of potato are thoroughly incorporated with the fish. This should be so perfectly done that the fish can neither be seen nor felt in the mouth separate from the potato. Season the hash a little richer than for mashed potatoes. Put it in the potato-kettle and heat it, constantly stirring. Have butter heated in the spider, press the hash into it firmly, and cook it gently. When brown, turn it out without breaking, and set it in the oven until the coffee is on the table. It is better, however, to leave it in the spider, if not scorching, until it is served. This is a very different dish from that called by many codfish hash. ·Always buy white codfish.

CODFISH BALLS.—Pick up as fine as possible a teacup of nice white codfish. Freshen all night, or if wanted for any other meal than breakfast, from the morning; scald it once, and drain off the water. Put it in the chopping-bowl, chop and work it until entirely fine; put it in a basin with water, a bit of butter the size of an egg, and two eggs; beat it thoroughly, and heat it until it thickens, without boiling. It should, when all is mixed, be about a quart. Have some potatoes ready prepared and nicely mashed, work the fish and potatoes thoroughly together as above, make it in flat cakes, and brown both sides. This is a very nice dish, as all who have tried it allow.

CHAPTER III.

EGGS.

To SELECT EGGS.—There are several ways of determining whether or not eggs are fresh. If they shake like water, they are not. If both ends of the egg, when put to the mouth, are of the same temperature, they are bad; but if a perceptible difference in the heat is perceived, they may be depended upon as good eggs. If eggs swim, they are bad; if they rise nearly to the top, not fresh; if they sink, they are newly laid. Eggs newly laid are the best for the table; but for beating it is better they should have been laid three or four days. The eggs of overgrown hens are not as delicate as those of the common fowls; there is as much difference in the eggs as in the flesh of the birds. White eggs look much better on the table than brown shells. Eggs that are badly stained in the nest cannot be entirely cleansed, so as to look neatly on the table. It is better to select clean-shelled eggs, brought to market by hand.

To Preserve for the Winter.—Obtain eggs newly laid, and brought to market by hand. If jolted, the yolks and whites mingle, and they will not keep as fresh. Dip each egg in hot suet, and drain them without wiping; dip them in diluted oil of vitriol a moment, or brush them over with gum-arabic. These methods are all good, the same effect being attained by each, which is the closing of the pores of the egg, to prevent evaporation. It is the evaporation of the moisture in the egg, and consequent filling of the space by air, which decomposes the egg; and whatever prevents this preserves the egg the most perfectly; but if eggs lie before this is done, there will be sufficient air already in the egg to spoil it. If they can be oiled or varnished fresh from the nest daily, their preservation will be complete, the eggs coming out in winter nearly as fresh as when first laid.

To Close the Pores of Egg-shells by the Use of Hot Water.—Select newly-laid eggs, put them in a frame, and dip them in and out three successive times quickly, while the water is boiling.

Another Mode.—Have a frame prepared to hold as many dozens as desired to preserve; place the eggs firmly in place, so that they will not move by turning the frame, and pour boiling water over them, so that every egg has felt the influence of the boiling water on every part of the shell; hang the frame in a cool cellar, where the air can circulate freely around them.

To Try Eggs by Looking through them.—Cover the sides with the hand, and look through the small end towards the light. If the egg is entirely fresh, it will be translucent, showing the color of the yolk through the white, giving the whole a reddish tinge. As soon as an egg commences to change, the color changes, and one spoiled will present a dark appearance. With a little practice, a dealer can select quantities in a short time with hardly a mistake. This is perhaps one of the very best tests known by which to determine the freshness of eggs.

ENGLISH RULE FOR KEEPING EGGS, SAID TO BE EXCELLENT.

Liquid to Preserve Eggs.—One bushel of quicklime, thirty-two ounces of salt, eight of cream of tartar, mixed in sufficient water to swim the eggs. Common lime-water, if too strong, will partially cook the whites.

To PACK EGGS.—Set the eggs with the small end uppermost, wedged tightly in bran, so that they cannot move. If to send to market, they must be packed with the utmost care, or they will break. If laid on the side, the egg will adhere; the cask must be kept upright. If packed in pine, or any other gum-wood sawdust, or shavings, the eggs will imbibe the flavor of the wood. Some advise turning the cask end for end once or twice each week. If this is done, it will prevent the yolk settling.

EGGS CONSIDERED AS FOOD.—As food, eggs are extremely nutritious. Those of the common hen are the most delicate. The eggs are affected by the food given the hen as certainly as is meat by the food of the ox. The white of egg is nearly all albumen; the yolk consists of an oil united with albumen, and contains a little sulphur and phosphorus. It is this that blackens silver spoons used in egg.

To BOIL EGGS.—An egg should be well washed in warm clear water and wiped dry before boiling. Have ready a kettle over a brisk fire partly filled with boiling water. Put the eggs in a skimmer, and lay them in the water carefully, without cracking the shell. Do not put in the pot at one time more than the skimmer will lift, and select those of a size. Have a watch open in the hand, or a clock near by; look at the clock as the eggs are being put into the kettle. For merely coagulating the white two and a half minutes are sufficient; for solidifying the white without cooking the egg, three minutes is the proper time; for partially cooking the yolk, three and a half; for solidifying the yolk, four; for boiling hard, five; and for boiling mealy, which is the most healthy next to the three minutes rule, one hour; for salads, always boil one hour. Stand by the egg kettle, skimmer in hand, with a dish of cold water near by; when it is two minutes, put the skimmer under the egg, and lift when the last second of the half-minute has passed. Be as particular with each mode of boiling, except the hard. As soon as the eggs are lifted, cool the shells by immersing them a moment in cold water; wipe them dry, and serve immediately. No dish on the table is more frequently spoiled in cooking than eggs. They ought never to be boiled by guess.

To FRY EGGS SOFT.—After the pork, ham, or bacon is dished, pour off the fat, clear and wash the spider free from sediment. Drain in the melted fat carefully; there should be sufficient to dip on the eggs while frying, as they ought never to be turned. Break carefully in a cup one egg at a time, (without breaking the yolks,) for fear some may not be quite fresh. If the yolks are mingled with the whites they will not fry nicely. When sufficient are broken to fry at one time, remove the boiling fat from the fire, pour in each egg by itself so that they may not form a mass; scatter over the yolks of each a pinch of fine salt and a dust of pepper, throw the white belonging to each egg over the yolk with a table-spoon, and as soon as it is nearly congealed remove the egg to the platter; if it cooks too slowly, dip over the egg some of the hot fat.

To Fry Eggs Hard.—Proceed as above, leaving the spider on the fire, dip the hot fat over each egg until sufficiently cooked.

To Poach Eggs.—Have in the spider water instead of fat; the water should barely cover the eggs. Remove the spider from the fire before putting in the eggs, and remove it as soon as the whites are congealed. Lay on each egg a small bit of sweet butter, and dust on a trifle of pepper; if desired hard, let them remain longer in the water. (*See* Egg Toast.)

Scambled Eggs.—Put in a spider enough sweet butter to oil the bottom of the pan; put in the eggs without breaking the yolks, add a bit of butter as large as a walnut to twelve eggs, season with very little salt and pepper; when the whites harden a little, stir the eggs from the bottom of the spider, and continue to do this until cooked to suit the family. The yolks and whites, when done, should be separate though stirred together, not mixed like beaten eggs. (*See* Egg Toasts.)

Omelet, Soft.—Put in a basin a teaspoon of water, a little salt and pepper, the yolks of six and whites of four eggs, and beat the mixture until very light. Have ready in an omelet or small frying pan butter very hot; pour in the mixture, move the pan constantly over the fire until the sides commence to harden, then roll it, and turn it out without soiling the dish; serve hot.

Omelet, Hard.—Proceed as above, using all the egg, and cook the omelet until the whole of the eggs are hard; serve hot. Omelet fall if they stand after being dished.

Omelet Souffle, French Method.—Beat the yolks and whites of six eggs separately as light as possible, season with sugar, a little grated rind of lemon, and a trifle of salt; mix slightly, and after it has stood long enough for the edges to harden, set it in the oven; apply heat to the top of the omelet and bake; it will rise considerably; it can be glazed, if you choose.

EGGS IN A MASS COOKED WHOLE.—Butter a dish, place the eggs in layers with small bits of butter, and season with very little salt and pepper; steam them, and when the whites are solid, serve in the same dish.

EGGS IN THE ITALIAN METHOD.—Moisten butter and flour in a stew-pan, stirring constantly; when the thickness of rich batter, thin with a little boiling milk, and season with pepper and salt; add about three ounces of butter and a little chopped green parsley, worked well together. Have ready eight eggs boiled one hour, slice and add them to the sauce, and serve hot.

SHELLS OF EGGS.—Wash the shells and dry them, to settle coffee in the winter. To use them, soak them overnight.

CHAPTER IV.

ECONOMY DISHES.

TO USE NICELY COLD FOWLS.—Pick the meat from bones; break the bones, and boil in very little water; stew the meat, gravy, and dressing of the cold fowls together, and add the soup.

TO USE THE MEAT AND GRISTLE OF A SOUP-BONE.—Cut all the gristle from the bone, boil until perfectly tender; if there is enough to serve for a dish, add vinegar, butter, pepper, and salt, and it will resemble souse; if not, mix the meat with it, fricassee brown, and add butter, salt, pepper, a dust of flour, and sufficient water to make the gravy, and serve with dry bread toasted; lay the bread on the platter, and pour over it the fricasee.

COLD EGGS AS EGG BALLS.—Take the yolks of the eggs, work them to a paste with a little butter; chop the whites as fine as possible, make them in balls or small flat cakes, and brown them in butter.

COLD BEEFSTEAKS.—Make a plain paste, cover a plate, and bake 't, put in the meat cut in small bits, put it in the pie, add seasoning to suit, cover and bake; it will bake in twenty minutes.

COLD FISH.—Take any kind of cold fish, pick it up finely, mix it with potatoes, make it in small cakes, and fry it brown.

TO MAKE A SOUP OF THE BONES OF STEAK.—Boil the bone and fat of beefsteak in very little water, season with onion, pepper, and salt, thicken with very little flour, add potatoes, bread, or any vegetable desired. Bones from two slices make a good soup for a small family. The bone, if left on the steak, wastes butter, and the fat burns in the fire.

COLD VEAL.—Either make a pie, a stew, or a fricassee; it is very nice cold, when it is fit to put on the table; but the broken bits can be used to advantage in either of the above dishes.

COLD, FRIED, OR BROILED HAM.—Cut the ham in bits, fry the fat part to a crisp, stir in the lean bits, and just before dishing add a few eggs; stir them with the meats, and serve all together; cold bacon and pork can be served in the same manner.

COLD RICE.—When rice is left cold, mould it in small cups, filling each cup half full, or less, according to the amount of rice; the next day turn the moulds bottom side up in a deep dish, and pour over them a boiled custard; serve cold; or use it in making puddings; it can be used also in griddle cakes and soups.

BROKEN CAKE PUDDINGS.—Soak the cake in domestic wine, and serve with cold custard; heavy cake can be used in the same manner.

HEAVY PLUM CAKE PUDDING.—Soak in milk, add soda and cream of tartar, and bake or boil as pudding.

COLD CABBAGE.—Chop fine and heat it in vinegar, season with pepper and salt; if not boiled with meats, add a little butter. It can also be fried; cauliflower and broccoli can be prepared in the same manner.

COLD MUSH.—Cut in thin slices, and fry brown; serve with syrup or molasses.

PIE CRUST, LEFT OVER.—When any is left after baking, work in all the flour possible, and form it in crackers.

REMNANTS OF PRESERVES, TO USE TO ADVANTAGE.—When several jars of preserves have been opened, and a little of each left without being enough of one kind for a dish, mash and cook them down to a jam with the syrups, and use the jam for tarts, or save the syrups to put in pudding sauces, and make jam of the fruit only.

COLD POTATOES.—These can be prepared in many different forms; the best are fried, broiled, and in hashes.

COLD CORN.—Grate it, and make in cakes with egg and a little flour, fry brown.

COLD PEAS.—Mash them; boil cream and thicken it with peas, or make a soup with water and butter thickened with peas; beans can be used in the last-described manner.

COLD EGG PLANT.—Egg plant may be heated over, as also squash, turnips, onions; beets are better used cold. Parsnips are better heated the second time than the first; cold sweet potatoes are nice fried or broiled; soup, if not left in iron, can be warmed several times, but to be kept sweet long, it must either be heated boiling hot each day, or be kept very cold.

DRY BREAD.—When bread has accumulated and there is danger of losing it, it is well to make a plain beef soup, and boil in it as much bread as the family will use. Bread left from the table each day should be thoroughly dried, and kept in a dry place where it can neither mould nor contract unpleasant tastes. For dressings, thoroughly dried bread is much better than when only moderately dry or stale.

RUSKED BREAD.—Dry and brown very gradually slices of old bread, it should be browned through without scorching; pound it in a mortar until as fine as Indian meal; use it in milk as a meal for children or lunch for adults. Use with clams, fish, cutlets; to thicken soups, in scalloped fish, or dressings for geese, duck, or pigeons. Dried bread without browning is nice for scalloped oysters, to make griddle cakes and puddings, etc.

BREAD GRIDDLE CAKES.—Soak the bread overnight, add sufficient milk for a batter, a little salt and soda, with a handful of flour, and one egg to every pint of soaked bread. A bowl full of soaked bread in a pan of buckwheat batter, is considered by some a great improvement, no doubt the cakes are rendered more healthy by it.

10*

Bread Balls.—These are made of soaked bread and egg, seasoned with salt and pepper.

Fried Bread.—Dip the bread in egg, and fry slowly until nicely browned; serve with ham or pork. Children are usually fond of fried bread, and if not too oily it is an excellent dish for them.

CHAPTER V.

COLD DINNERS.

Remarks, No. 1.—It is often very inconvenient to cook warm dinners. Where there is but one servant in the family it will be impossible to get up hot dinners in good style, on washing and other days of extra labor, unless the housekeeper herself does the work, which in families of much size is often more than she can well perform.

Cold Dinners, No. 1.—First course; cold ham, baked potatoes horseradish or jelly, bread and butter. Dessert; apple pie and cheese.

No. 2.—Cold corned beef nicely sliced, potatoes baked, mustard, bread, butter, and pickles. Dessert; mince pie and cheese.

No. 3.—Cold roast beef, jelly, baked potatoes, bread, butter, and crackers. Dessert; cherry pie with cheese.

No. 4.—Cold lamb, baked potatoes hot, cranberry sauce, bread and butter, lettuce with cold boiled egg and vinegar. Dessert; cold custard.

No. 5.—Ham boiled and sliced; each slice spread with mustard and a slice of cold hard egg, baked potatoes hot, bread and butter. Dessert; cold rice, with cream and sugar.

No. 6.—Corned beef sliced, with horseradish, baked potatoes hot, bread and butter. Desert; corn starch blanc-mange, cream, sugar, and jelly.

No. 7.—Chicken pie, celery, hot baked potatoes. Dessert; cake soaked in wine, served with cold custard.

No. 8.—Oyster pie, crackers, celery. Dessert; fruit.

No. 9.—First course, raw oysters with lemon and crackers; second course, cold veal with jelly and baked potatoes hot, bread and butter. Desert; mince pie.

No. 10.—Veal pie, baked potatoes hot, pickles, bread and butter. Dessert; cranberry tart.

No. 11.—Cold chicken, hot baked potatoes, cold slaw, bread and butter. Dessert, strawberries and cream.

No. 12.—Spare rib of pork, stewed apple without sugar, baked potatoes hot, bread and butter. Dessert; apple pie.

No. 13.—Fillet of veal, jelly, hot baked potatoes, bread and butter. Dessert; rhubarb pie.

No. 14.—Cold scalloped oysters, cold ham with baked potatoes, jelly, bread and butter. Dessert; pumpkin pie.

No. 15.—Cold fried chicken, jelly, baked potatoes, bread and butter. Dessert; cherry pie.

No. 16.—Beefsteak pie, baked potatoes hot, cold slaw, bread and butter. Dessert; custard.

No. 17.—Cold baked pork with beans, pickles, bread and butter. Dessert; pumpkin pie.

No. 18.—Cold stewed beans with boiled pork, pickles, bread and butter. Dessert; custard pie.

No. 19.—Soused pig's feet, baked potatoes, bread and butter. Dessert; cold rice custard.

No. 20.—Soused fish, with bread and butter. Dessert; mince or fruit pie.

No. 21.—Scalloped fish with mushroom catsup, bread, butter and pickles. Dessert; apples steamed, served with cream.

No. 22.—Casserole of fish, with catsup, bread, butter, and pickles. Dessert; apple pie.

No. 23.—Minced clams scalloped, salad, and bread and butter. Dessert; cranberry tart.

No. 24.—Cold tongue sliced, horseradish, bread and butter. Dessert; cold rice with jelly, and custard.

No. 25.—Cold turkey, hot baked potatoes, jelly, bread and butter. Dessert; apple pie.

No. 26.—Cold boiled fowl, hot baked potatoes, oyster sauce hot, jelly, bread and butter. Dessert; fruit and cream.

REMARKS, No. 2.—By proper management cold dinners can be prepared the day before they are wanted, and the family be made comfortable even when there is an unusual amount of work in the kitchen; potatoes can often be prepared the day before, and heated over in the oven with very little trouble; the meat pies, if set in the oven for fifteen minutes, can be nicely warmed; apple pies are better warmed than served cold, set them in the oven a few moments. If warm gravies are preferred with cold meats and fowls, they can be prepared and warmed before serving dinner. Cold dinners can be prepared with as many courses as desired, but as the object of this chapter is to lighten the work of the family, two have generally been thought sufficient.

TO PREPARE LUNCHES.

LUNCH, No. 1.—Cover a tray, or small table, with a napkin; place plates, napkins, goblets, a pitcher of ice-water, a plate of buttered bread, cut in thin half-slices; cold meats or fowl, seasoned to suit; crackers, pickles, and, if used, wine-glasses filled with iced wine, and a dish of fruit and nuts, arranged neatly and with taste.

LUNCH, No. 2.—Sandwiches of cold corned-beef, ham, or chopped tongue; cold strong coffee, reduced with thick cream, and cooled in goblets with pounded ice; pickles, crackers, or cookies; sugar, spoons, nuts, and fruit; the whole arranged tastefully on a small table, placing the plates, etc., ready for each person who is to partake of the lunch.

LUNCH, No. 3.—Chocolate iced, raw oysters, buttered bread, sugar, crackers, sliced lemon, pickles, fruit, ice-water, plates, knives, forks, spoons, napkins, goblets, table-spoon, and castor; arranged as No 2.

LUNCH, No. 4.—Sardines, sliced lemon, buttered bread, crackers, ice-water, fruit, castor, goblets, plates, knives, forks, and napkins; arranged as No. 2.

PART V.

CHAPTER I.

APPLES.

HERMETICALLY SEAL, COOK, ETC.

REMARKS.—Every housekeeper knows the value of this fruit in the family, while but few are capable of selecting the different varieties needed not only to prolong the season, but to use to the best advantage in desserts, jellies, sauces, etc.

SUMMER APPLES.—Early harvest best for pies and tarts, and earliest of all apples; golden sweeting excellent for baking; then comes early joe, early strawberry, and red astracan; all good.

AUTUMN APPLES.—Fall pippins, golden pippins, etc.

FOR EARLY WINTER choose yellow bellflower, Rhode Island greening, Spitzenburg, seek-no-further, etc.

LATE WINTER AND SPRING.—Yellow Newtown pippin stands first, red Newtown pippin next, Roxbury or Boston russet last; this keeps well, but is not as high-flavored as the others, becoming insipid by spring.

GATHERING WINTER APPLES.—Pick the fruit by hand; lay each apple in a small basket not holding over one peck; take them immediately to a cool, dry place; select sound perfect fruit; lay each apple on the floor one by one, so as not to touch; let them remain as long as there is no danger from frost. When winter sets in, lay them in barrels which have had lime or plaster scattered in them; if they have stood filled with lime so much the better, if the staves are not shrunk. Handle them as carefully as eggs, not even breaking the stem; then head up the barrels, and keep them as cool as possible without freezing. Those intended for spring use had better be wrapped in newspaper. Apples can be preserved in this manner until the early harvest varieties are large enough for pies and sauce. (*See* DIRECTIONS FOR PRESERVING APPLES FOR SPRING SHIPMENTS, ETC.)

CIDER.—If you wish to make superior cider, select apples that ripen about the same time. Leave the decayed and imperfect apples to make vinegar. Let the pomace remain without pressing as long as possible, but do not let it approach fermentation. Sweet apples make the richest cider; use no water. Keep the cider as cool as possible; even temperature is very important. Have ready a tub filled with alternate layers of coarse gravel and charcoal broken large; lay on the top a piece of coarse flannel. As fast as the cider comes from the press pour it into the tub; a hole must be bored in the bottom of the tub and a plug put loosely in, so that the cider may run through slowly. Pour it into clean white-oak casks as fast as it leaches through, and put it in a cool dark cellar of even temperature immediately. Leave the cask open until all fermentation has ceased; then put the bung in tightly. It is said cider made in this manner will keep sweet for a long time. Mustard seed is also used to keep cider pleasant to drink. If cider free from water is made after freezing weather sets in, and drawn into clean barrels, it may be preserved sweet all winter by being kept where the thermometer stands just above freezing point. If boiled down one-quarter, it will be better still.

To PREPARE CIDER VINEGAR FROM THE PRESS.—After the cider is pressed, pour half as much water on the cheese as there was cider; let it remain until it ferments, then press and barrel the watered cider; keeping it in a warm place facilitates the fermentation. Or, reduce cider one-half. It is a good plan to use the same barrels for years for vinegar, which can be done if iron-bound and well painted. The mother should be taken out before filling with the new vinegar, the barrel rinsed, the decayed mother thrown away, and the good washed and returned to the barrel. Cucumbers, green corn cobs, white paper wet in molasses, or a grape-vine sprout, will turn vinegar much more quickly than if left to itself, with nothing but the cider. Shake the barrels often and leave them in the sun; it will turn faster in half-filled casks than when full; keep a bottle in the bunghole of each barrel.

DRYING APPLES.—If you wish dried apples to retain their flavor, select very sour fruit, too acid to use green. If dried in the air, it will be necessary to heat the fruit to destroy any insects' eggs which may have been laid in it while drying. The safest way to do this would be to place a tin pan about half full of the fruit over a kettle containing boiling water until it has heated through. The usual method is to put the fruit in ovens, but a moment's forgetfulness often spoils the whole lot, while over steam there is no danger of scorching.

COOKING DRIED APPLES.—Look over the fruit to see if any insect eggs may have been left that have hatched; wash and rinse the fruit thoroughly; then cover over night with clean soft water. If in the morning it is absorbed add a little more; place the pan over steam until the fruit is tender, then sweeten to suit the taste. If quinces are relished, a few dried in the same manner as apples, soaked and cooked with them, will be an addition. Or the syrup left from preserved quinces can be used instead of sugar to sweeten them. Some persons add lemon and raisins.

BOILED CIDER.—Boil sweet apple cider as soon as it comes from the press to the consistency of thick molasses; bottle, cork, and seal it while hot. Keep in a cool place.

CIDER APPLE SAUCE.—If you like very sweet sauce, take only sweet apples; if not, one-third sour, and two-thirds sweet. Peel, quarter, and core the apples; lay them in the sun two or three days to prevent the fruit breaking. To every pailful of apples put one quart of boiled cider. Boil slowly until the fruit becomes a dark mahogany color. To those who like the flavor of quinces, two to each pailful cut fine, will be an addition.

APPLE BUTTER.—Take to every pailful of sour apples, after they are peeled, quartered, and cored, one quart of boiled cider; cook slowly until the whole becomes a jam of dark mahogany color with no separate syrup; spice with cloves, allspice, and cinnamon, if it is agreeable, being careful not to have one spice predominate over the other.

APPLE SWEETMEATS.—Select small-sized apples, pare them nicely, take out the core with a corer, so as to leave the fruit whole; if the apple is too large, quarter it. Take eight pounds of double refined sugar, one quart of filtered or clean rain-water, and two teaspoonfuls of citric acid dissolved in the water; put the water on the fire, and when nearly boiling stir in one-half of the sugar; as soon as it is dissolved, place the kettle over a boiler of hot water and stir in the remainder of the sugar. Let it remain until the syrup becomes perfectly clear, and all the scum or froth has been removed; then put into the syrup eight pounds of fruit; if the apples are not covered with the syrup, they must be frequently turned. Let them remain over the hot water until the fruit is clear. Have ready some glass jars which have been put into cold water and boiled; let them remain in the boiling water until wanted. Set the preserves on a slow fire until they boil up; put them back over the water to keep up the temperature to boiling heat. Have ready corks and a wax of rosin and beeswax melted together. Take out the fruit without breaking, and fill up the jars with syrup as soon as possible. Place a piece of cotton wadding wet in brandy on the top of the preserves; cork and seal immediately. If it is air-tight, and the fruit put up according to directions, it will never ferment; but as sometimes this is not the case, it will be best to put the jars where you can see without moving them; should mould appear, let them remain until wanted, and remove it with the cotton before shaking up the fruit. It will be no injury to the preserves. Always label preserves, writing out the name and date. Some persons flavor with lemon, others like quinces. Appleseeds pounded and tied in a piece of muslin, boiled in the syrup, gives the apple flavor.

APPLE JELLY.—Select any rich juiced apple, such as golden pippin, Newtown pippin, or belleflower, wash and wipe them, removing the stems, and any imperfections of the skin. Allow one quart of water to one peck of apples, and cover the kettle tight. Be careful not to burn the fruit. When perfectly tender, pour them into a jelly-bag, without pressing, and let it drain into an earthen dish until the next morning. Measure the juice, and allow for every pint one pound of Stewart's No. 1 granulated sugar, place the syrup on the fire in a preserving-kettle; as soon as it becomes hot stir in the sugar, when it is melted the jelly is ready for the moulds. It must not boil. Apple jelly can receive any flavor desired of fruit or extracts. The most appropriate are, lemon, quince, and bitter almond.

CRAB-APPLE JELLY is made in the same manner, except the addition of a little more water, say three pints to a peck of apples.

CRAB-APPLE PRESERVES.—The apples must be parboiled before putting in the syrup. The large kinds should be cored, not peeled; the small varieties, preserved whole, with the stems on. In every other particular follow directions for preserving apples.

APPLE MARMALADE.—Take either common, or crab apples; after they are washed and wiped clean, steam them by placing a preserving kettle, over a boiler of hot water, with a very little water, not over a pint to a peck of apples; cover tight; when perfectly cooked, pass the fruit through a sieve. Weigh the pulp; to every pound allow one pound of Stewart's No. 1 granulated sugar. Boil the pulp until quite thick, then add the sugar. It must be cooked until stiff enough to mould, and stirred constantly to prevent burning. The common apple can be flavored; but the crab is better without.

APPLE DUMPLINGS, No. 1.—Peel apples that will cook quickly as greenings, pippins, belleflower, etc., take out the core, leaving the apple whole. (*See* PASTE FOR DUMPLINGS.) Prepare a plain paste as you would for very plain pies; roll the crust about one-fourth of an inch thick; cover each apple separately; put them in a steamer; let them steam about half an hour; when boiled, put them in boiling water, and boil gently, without removing the cover, half an hour; if steamed they will require three-fourths of an hour, when they will be done. Serve with butter and sugar, or sweet sauce, if preferred.

APPLE PIE.—Take in the proportion of one pound of flour to one-fourth of a pound of butter; have the butter and flour very cold; cut the butter in small thin slices into the flour; stir it up quickly, not working the butter into the flour; add just enough water to moisten the paste; don't work it up in a lump, but take it up ragged, and put enough for a pie on the moulding-board; roll it out thin, and cover the bottom of the pie with the paste. Have ready sour apples sliced thin; fill the plate with them; roll out the top crust, and cover the apples; cut off the crust neatly without pressing down the edge, and put it in the oven. When the crust is baked, the apples will be soft; take out the pie, remove the cover, add sugar to the taste, and a piece of butter, the size of an almond; work it well through the apple, spread it evenly, and put on the crust. If nutmeg is relished, grate a dust over the apple, before putting on the cover, but don't mix it in. Apple pies should always be warmed before eating.

APPLE FRITTERS.—Make a batter in the following manner, and stir into it sour apples sliced thin: Take one pint of milk, a little salt, a pint of sifted flour, and two eggs; beat the yolks thoroughly, and stir in with the flour; after the batter is beat sufficiently to break every lump of flour, add the whites, which must be beat stiff enough to remain on an inverted plate. Dip one table-spoonful of batter at a time into boiling lard, turn them over when they rise to the top; when browned on both sides, lay them in a colander to drain. Serve hot, with maple syrup, or any sauce relished. Fritters should be boiled in a shallow kettle, or deep spider, as they will fly to pieces, if there is much depth of lard. Never stick a fork into cakes boiling in lard, it makes them soak fat. Apple fritters are a dinner dish. Common fritters are made in the same manner, omitting the apple.

BOILED OR STEAMED APPLES.—Wash rich flavored apples, take out the core, and leave the fruit whole. Lay them in a steamer until perfectly tender; take them out, and pour over them sweet cream and sugar, and serve for tea.

BAKED APPLES.—Prepare apples as above; lay them on baking-tins, fill the holes from which the cores have been taken with sugar, and bake without burning. Before putting the fruit on the table, sift loaf sugar over them, and serve for tea.

BAKED SWEET APPLES are nice with cream alone. Some are fond of them with bread and milk.

RICE APPLE DUMPLING.—Prepare apples as for apple dumplings; wash rice, and put it in cold water with a little salt; let it boil five minutes; take enough of the rice to cover the apple. Have ready pieces of cotton cloth, just large enough to hold one dumpling; cover the apples half an inch thick with the rice; tie up the dumplings, and boil or steam them half an hour, and serve with butter and sugar.

APPLE PUDDING.—Make a nice batter, (*see* BATTER PUDDING;) prepare apples as for dumplings; put the apples in a dish or basin, and pour the batter over them, cover with a cloth, and steam an hour; serve with butter and sugar worked together until light and creamy.

APPLE TARTS.—For apple tarts, the apples must be sifted after they are stewed. When eggs are added, they are called apple custards.

GREEN APPLES.—Pies can be made in the same manner as though the apples were ripe; it is not necessary to stew them, as many imagine, after they are half grown; they will cook in the crust. If very green, put into the pie a little water before baking. It often happens, that apples in the spring lose their flavor and become insipid; when this is the case, add to each pie a piece of citric acid as large as a filbert, dissolved in a little water. This must be done before baking.

HERMETICALLY SEALED IN CANS.—Have made air-tight tin cans; fill these with apples peeled, quartered, and cored, and seal them tight. Then perforate each can with a common awl; place them in a vat or boiler, with just enough cold water to rise to the top of the can while boiling. When the cans and fruit are the same temperature as boiling water; drop some solder on the small holes, and take them from the vat. If they are perfect, the ends will be drawn in, and remain so. If not, they are imperfect, either in the exhausting, or can, and will certainly burst the cans. If the leak cannot be immediately found, the can must be opened to save it. If found, the same process of exhausting must be gone over again. (*See* WATER BATH.)

HERMETICALLY SEALED IN BOTTLES.—Prepare apples as for cans. Fill nearly to the cork with apples, then put enough filtered water in each bottle to reach within one and a half inches from the cork. The cork must be very tight, and well wired down. Place the bottles in vats, containing sufficient cold water to reach the necks; heat the water gradually. When the fruit begins to crack, take out the bottles, and seal air-tight. If there has been no imperfection in sealing or exhausting, the fruit will remain the same for years; but the slightest amount of air will certainly burst the bottles. (*See* WATER BATH.)

DIRECTIONS FOR PRESERVING QUANTITIES OF APPLES FOR SPRING SHIPMENTS.—Gather carefully, as directed in the first part of this chapter, lay them as soon as gathered in a heap, eighteen inches deep, and cover them with a light cloth or straw, where they will soon sweat; when this has succeeded as desired, remove the covering, open the windows and doors, and cool them as suddenly as possible. When entirely dry, repeat this process exactly, and when perfectly dry, pack in barrels and ship. If apples, when bought, are found to be damp, empty the barrels and cool them suddenly, removing all decaying fruit. Fruit buyers would lose much less fruit, if they could spread and dry apples as soon as received, when they should be again repacked. Apples managed as above, can be sent to Europe with but little danger. The varieties, whose keeping qualities are the best, should be selected for long voyages.

CHAPTER II.

PEACHES.

HERMETICALLY SEAL, PRESERVE, ETC.

REMARKS.—It would be impossible to mention the many excellent varieties now grown for the dessert and table use of this delicious fruit. Among the very early, Large Early York probably stands among the first; then there is Early Tillotson, Early Purple, and many others. Later comes Early Crawford, Le Grange, Rare Ripes, Red, and Yellow; George, Old Mixon Free, and many others equally good. For brandy fruit, Morris White is preferred before all others, and Snow comes next; but these are often scarce; the trees being shy bearers. Old Mixon Free comes next for preserves, etc.; although not as white as the two last mentioned, it will do very well when the two first cannot be procured. Use Freestone peaches always for preserves; they are not only less trouble, but more tender, and not as liable to shrink.

BRANDY PEACHES.—Take one quart of water, a table-spoonful of citric acid, and eight pounds of the best sugar; put the whole in a preserving kettle, and set it over steam until the sugar is melted, and the syrup becomes perfectly clear; should any scum arise, skim it off when quite clear, let it cool until about blood-heat; then mix with the syrup the same quantity of the best quality of white French brandy; beat it well together, or the syrup will settle, being so very thick as not to mix readily with the brandy; take perfectly ripe, but not soft, Morris White, or some other white-fleshed peaches; dip them in boiling water, just long enough to make the skin slip from the fruit with ease. Pack as many peaches as possible without breaking, in wide-mouthed bottles or jars, and pour over them the brandy syrup, being careful to keep the fruit under the syrup, which must not quite reach the cork. Leave a little syrup until the next day, as the fruit will absorb so much as to make it necessary to fill the bottles again before sealing. Seal them perfectly, and keep them in a cool, dark place, if possible.

PEACHES PRESERVED IN SOUR SYRUP.—Take one quart of the best wine or cider vinegar, four pounds good sugar, a teaspoonful of whole cloves, one table-spoonful of mace, and two table-spoonfuls of rolled, not ground, cinnamon; melt the sugar in the vinegar and add the spices; do not let it quite boil, as that destroys the acid of the vinegar. Wash, and rub free from fur, perfectly ripe Freestone peaches, of fine flavor, and small pits; they must not be soft, or they will break; nor green, as then they will shrink; pack them in glass bottles or jars, and pour over them the vinegar syrup; cork the bottles and set them in water, about the same heat as the syrup is, after being poured over the cold fruit; let them remain until heated through, which will be after the water has boiled about fifteen minutes. It will be best to wire down the corks, as the heat will force them out; seal them when first taken out the water, and keep the jars in a cool place; they sometimes mould, which will do no injury unless mixed with the syrup, except to the top peach. Should the vinegar not seem sufficiently acid, add a teaspoon of citric acid to the syrup.

SOUR SPICED PEACHES.—Take hard peaches, of good flavor; wash them in hot water and rub the skins with a harsh towel to remove the roughness; stick into each peach three cloves, and pour over the fruit strong vinegar scalding hot, seasoned with cinnamon, ginger, mustard, mace, and nutmeg; do this three times; then take fresh vinegar, season as above, slightly; heat it and pour over the fruit, which must be kept under the vinegar, and corked tight; examine them often, as the vinegar may become lifeless, and spoil the fruit.

SWEET SPICED PEACHES.—Select large Freestone peaches with large pits, quite ripe, but not the least soft; remove the roughness of the skin by friction; then halve the peach, and take out the pit; fill the cavity with white mustard-seed, one pod of bird or cherry pepper very small, or if these cannot be obtained, two kernels of black pepper, a few cassia buds, and a piece of mace; sew them up, pour over them hot vinegar, three times; add to one quart of vinegar, one pound of sugar; heat the syrup and pour it over the fruit; cover tight and keep the peaches under the syrup; examine often, and keep them in a cold place; if the fruit is very hard, after being scalded, set the bottles in the bath until heated through.

PLAIN PEACH SAUCE.—Take five pounds of peaches, so ripe that the skin will slip off without scalding or peeling with the knife; mash them very fine; boil slowly one hour, stirring often; after which add one pound of sugar; continue to boil over a slow fire, often stirring, until the whole becomes a dark mahogany color, free from juice; pack it in jars that can be sealed tight while hot; dip a paper in brandy, and lay on the top of each jar; then cork and seal tightly; keep it as cool as possible. Use the sauce as soon as opened.

PEACH JAM.—Prepare the fruit as above; boil slowly one hour; then add a pound of sugar to every pound of fruit; when finished, it will be quite stiff. Pack it in wide-mouthed jars, and seal tight.

PEACH MARMALADE.—Prepare peaches as for jam, boil one hour; mix equal parts of sugar with the jam; when dissolved, pass the whole through a sieve; boil slowly two hours, being very careful not to burn; spread it on plates and set it in a cool oven, where it will dry but not burn, for a half-day, when it will be ready to pack into moulds; cover the moulds with paper dipped into the white of eggs, beaten as stiff as possible; it must be entirely free from juice, of a dark mahogany color and clear when finished, sufficiently stiff to cut with a knife; keep it cool; it is liable to mould, which can be the more readily removed if a piece of paper, closely fitting the edges of the jar, is pressed firmly on the marmalade before covering with the egg paper. No air should be allowed to remain in the fruit, which should be packed very closely; and as the marmalade is very thick, it will require some care to accomplish it.

PEACH JELLY.—This can only be made by setting the syrup of Peaches with isinglass or gelatine, as there seems to be but little natural gelatine in the fruit.

PEACHWATER ICE.—Sweeten the juice of peaches; blanch and pound fine the pits; stir them into the syrup; let the whole remain two hours; to every gallon of syrup add one quart of water; strain through a fine hair sieve, and freeze; should the ice be wanted in haste, the pits can be scalded in the water to extract the flavor, and strained into the syrup.

PEACH BUTTER.—Select very ripe peaches, peel, remove the pits, and mash them; have ready rich sweet cider, reduced by boiling to the consistency of molasses, (or four gallons to one;) add to each gallon, after boiling, one pound of sugar; simmer the peaches in the cider, and sugar until the whole is reduced to paste; allow a pint of the molasses and sugar to three quarts of the mashed fruit. This is a southern mode of preserving peaches, and is very excellent; it is used in the same manner as cider apple sauce.

BRANDY PEACH SYRUP.—Boil over steam until reduced to a mass, two gallons of peaches, with the pits cracked; pour over them two quarts French brandy; cover tight and leave them over night; then strain all the syrup from them, and add to every quart three pounds of sugar, and a salt-spoon of citric acid; bring it to a scald, pass it through a jelly bag, and bottle it, cork and seal tightly; use it for jellies or sauces.

DRYING PEACHES WITH SUGAR, No. 1.—Select rich flavored fruit, quite ripe; take off the skin, and slice the peaches quite thin; spread the fruit on plates, and scatter over it some coffee sugar; set the plates in the oven until the fruit becomes hot; then dry slowly, either in the oven, or sun; if the latter, heat it before packing away, to destroy any insect eggs which may have been laid in the fruit while drying. Pack in stone jars, and paste paper over the mouth; set the jars out of the reach of mice.

ANOTHER METHOD OF DRYING PEACHES WITH SUGAR, No. 2.—To five pounds of sliced peaches, take one of sugar, put them in a preserving kettle until heated through; skim out the fruit, leaving the syrup in the kettle; dry the peaches in the oven slowly, until the juice is all absorbed; boil down the syrup left in the kettle, as thick as possible without burning; pack the dried fruit in jars, and pour over it the syrup; paste paper over the mouth of the jar, and set it in a cool dry place.

COMMON DRIED PEACHES, No. 3.—Remove the skin from dead-ripe peaches of superior flavor; cut them in thin slices, string and hang in the sun, or spread them thin on clean white wood boards to dry. Fruit is best dried in kilns, but few have this convenience. Heat the fruit in the same manner as recommended for dried apples, and pack in paper bags.

STEWING DRIED PEACHES.—Follow the directions for stewing dried apples; those dried with sugar will need no sweetening; save the syrup left from preserved peaches, to use in seasoning dried peaches; the only way to do it is to scald the syrup and bottle it hot before it ferments.

PEACH LEATHER.—Take very rich sweet peaches, so ripe as to be near decaying, but before decomposition has commenced, peel and mash them fine; spread evenly on plates and dry, slowly in the oven; when dry, it will somewhat resemble sole-leather; roll it up and put it away in paper bags; when wanted, cut it in small pieces, and soak over night in only water enough to cover it. It does not need sugar if the peaches are as sweet as they should be; if not, sweeten to taste; it needs no stewing, and is excellent; it would be ready for tea if put to soak in the morning. This is the best way of drying peaches, as the flavor is retained almost perfectly; and not only this, but the fruit can be saved without the expense of sugar, when too far gone for the other methods of drying.

RICH PRESERVED PEACHES, HERMETICALLY SEALED.—Obtain, if possible, Morris White peaches; if these cannot be had, some other white-fleshed peach of fine quality; much depends on the variety of peach used in making high flavored sweetmeats; rather use yellow or red-fleshed peaches, than poor, tasteless whites; never use Clings, if you can obtain Frees. Make the syrup in the same manner described in the recipe Preserved Pears, allowing one pound of sugar to one of fruit; the fruit should be fully ripe, but not in the least soft; *stone hard* peaches, make a very poor preserve; scald the fruit in boiling water to remove the skin, but be careful it does not cook; when the fruit is in the proper state, dipping the fruit will be sufficient; care must be taken in this, or the fruit is ruined. Lay each peach in cold water as soon as peeled; when the syrup is in the clear state, put enough fruit in the kettle for two bottles, which must be prepared as described in preserved pears; let the fruit remain in the syrup over steam, long enough to become heated through; then lift each peach one by one, with a spoon or silver fork; fill the bottle two-thirds full of fruit, and fill with the syrup; blanch one dozen peach pits to every quart of preserves, and lay them in the top of the bottles; cover over the bottles, so that flies cannot get in during the night; the next morning, fill the bottles within one inch of the top with syrup left for that purpose; cork with close-fitting corks, of the best quality, and wire them firmly; set the bottles in cold water, and heat gradually; let the water boil five minutes with the fruit in, if cut in halves, and ten if preserved whole; have ready rosin and bees-wax melted together, to seal over the corks, which must be done very particularly; let them remain until perfectly cool, then turn them over the corks down, and examine closely; if no moisture escapes, they are well sealed, and will never ferment, even if kept for years. This sweetmeat is far too rich for common use. Don't forget to label and date the bottles. It is well to put them in a cool, dark, and dry place; they will be less apt to mould if kept in the dark.

NATURAL PRESERVED PEACHES, HERMETICALLY SEALED, No. 3.—Prepare the fruit in the same manner as for rich preserved peaches. Blanch the same amount of pits for each bottle. Weigh the fruit, and allow a half-pound of sugar to one of fruit. To every three pounds of sugar allow one pint of water, in which a half-teaspoonful of citric acid has been dissolved; prepare the syrup over steam in the same manner as described in PRESERVED APPLES. When melted, it will be about three pints. Have the syrup ready before the fruit is prepared. Halve the peaches, and put them in quart bottles, not so as to crowd, but pretty full; lay the hollow side down, as they will pack better. Pour over the syrup either cold or hot as convenient. Lay in the blanched pits, cork tightly, and wire firmly. As soon as the bottles are all ready, place them in the water bath, in cold water, which must be within three inches of the cork. After the water boils, let the fruit remain in the bath a half hour. Then seal immediately, and when cool turn them up to test the sealing. Set them in a cool, dry, and dark place, where they can be examined without trouble; label and date the bottles. This fruit retains more of the peach flavor than the former, and is a very fine sweetmeat; good enough for all occasions. (*See* WATER BATH.)

PEACHES TO PRESERVE ELEGANTLY, HERMETICALLY SEALED.—Select the fruit after it is colored and flavored, but perfectly hard. Rub them with a small brush without bruising the skin; do not peel the fruit. Put them in cold water in an enamelled kettle, set it over steam until the water reaches to the heat of 140°; have ready a weak syrup, lay in the peaches, heat to 140°, and keep the syrup that heat one hour without increasing. In the mean time make a rich syrup with one pint of water, half a teaspoonful of citric acid, and three pounds of the best loaf-sugar; heat it over water; when dissolved, bring it to a boil, skim and strain it through a fine sieve; put it back in the kettle, and place it over hot water. Have ready wide-mouthed jars, pack the fruit closely without breaking, fill the bottles to within one inch of the cork, pour over them the syrup while hot, cork them, and let them remain one day; press the fruit under the syrup, wire the corks, set them in the bath, bring the water to boiling heat, let them boil ten minutes, and seal tightly. This is the most elegant manner of preserving peaches; the fruit retains its color and flavor, and will remain perfect any length of time. The receipt originated with the writer, and is for the first time made public. *No person can preserve well without using a thermometer.* Dip it in the syrup, or water, above the bulb of quicksilver; it will not break. If used carefully, they will last for years; for culinary purposes, they should be cased in japanned tin.

VERY PLAIN PEACH PRESERVES, HERMETICALLY SEALED. — Proceed in every way as described in NATURAL PRESERVED PEACHES, except in the richness of the syrup, which has only half the sugar. Make it thus: Weigh for every pound of fruit a quarter of a pound of syrup. It will not be necessary to use the acid; the syrup being so thin, there will be no danger of the sugar becoming crystallized. To four pounds of sugar, take one quart of water, and divide the syrup equally with the fruit.

PEACH JAM FOR TARTS, HERMETICALLY SEALED, No. 1.—Take very ripe sweet yellow peaches, mash fine, and pass them through a sieve. Have ready quart cans air-tight; fill them within one inch of the top and seal up; after piercing the cans with an awl, place them in a water bath filled to within two inches of the top of the can with cold water, which must be gradually heated. Let them boil one hour, or until the jam is forced out the small aperture; then seal up, and take them from the bath; examine the cans as soon as cool. If the ends are well drawn in, they are thought to be perfect, although it is not always the case. (*See* TESTING CANS.)

PLAIN PEACH JAM FOR THE TABLE, HERMETICALLY SEALED, No. 2.—Mash fine good flavored peaches, put them into a preserving bottle over steam, and let them become very hot. To eight quarts of jam put four pounds of sugar. Stir it in the jam while hot, when entirely dissolved; fill quart cans to within one-quarter of an inch of the top. Have the caps sealed on while hot. Place them in the hot water bath, and pierce the caps before the water boils; let them boil ten minutes hard, if the cans are hot when put in—if cool, twenty; solder the aperture before taking them from the water. Examine when cold. This is very fine, the flavor is retained nearly perfect. Tin cans should always be marked in some way before the caps are sealed on. A good way to do this is to dissolve nitrate of silver in a little rain water, and with a sharp-pointed stick write the name, kind of fruit, and when put up, upon the side of the can, so that if they are packed one above the other, it will not be necessary to take the whole down to find the one wanted.

PRESERVED PEACHES IN CANS, HERMETICALLY SEALED, No. 4.—
Peaches can be preserved in cans just as well as bottles, but is more trouble to persons generally, as they must either send the cans to the tinner, or he must come to the house, to solder on the caps. Many of the self-sealing cans are used now, but are quite expensive, and no tin is certain more than a year. Those with lead caps are very dangerous to use; as the lead and acid often forms acetate, or sugar of lead, a deadly poison. No one can be certain in earthen that the fruit is free from air, and if not, it certainly will ferment, unless very rich and thoroughly impregnated with sugar.

FRESH PEACHES, HERMETICALLY SEALED, No. 1.—Take fine-flavored fruit, remove the skin by scalding, and lay them in water until wanted; fill the cans almost full, packing the fruit pit side down; put in each quart can a half-pint tumbler half full of water, and a quarter of a pound of the best sugar. After they are sealed and pierced, place them in the bath, filled to within two inches of the top of the can with cold water. Heat until the water becomes boiling hot, if heated in a kettle over a slow fire; if by steam, let them remain in the bath half an hour after the water reaches 170°, which can be known by testing with a thermometer. Solder the aperture as soon as possible after this takes place, as more cooking impairs the flavor of the fruit, and take the cans immediately from the bath, and turn them bottom side up. Notice if any of the cans make a noise; if so, they probably leak. To ascertain this, place the can on the stove a short time, and the juice will appear in the leak, which must be immediately soldered up. Be very careful that the can does not become too hot, as it will burst, and be apt to burn those near. When it looks at all swollen take it from the stove. If no leak is shown, set it aside for further inspection. Leaks can be often found by careful examination of the can without putting on the stove, and when this can be done, of course it is the best method. When the air is fully exhausted, and the can air-tight, the peaches will be just as good years after as when just put up. But if, on the contrary, the exhaustion or can is the least imperfect, sooner or later the fermentation will burst the can. So that, if the leaks cannot be found, it is the best policy to use the fruit immediately. This will save both can and fruit. (*See* TESTING CANS.)

Fresh Peaches without Sugar, Hermetically Sealed, No. 2.—Prepare the fruit and exhaust the air from the cans in the same manner as in Table Peaches. Put in each quart can half a gill of filtered rain, or clean soft water, but no sugar. If used for the table, add sugar to the taste when wanted. Peaches prepared in this manner make delicious pies.

Peach Pie.—Line a deep pie-plate with nice paste; peel and halve as many peaches as will fill the plate; add a piece of butter the size of a walnut and a little sugar, be careful not to get it too sweet, and dust over a little flour. Cover with the paste and bake in a moderate oven. When the paste is baked, the fruit will be. Some serve with cream, but it is good enough without. Serve fresh. They may be made as tarts, without heating the fruit.

Plain Peach Pudding, No. 1.—Line a pudding-dish with plain paste; peel as many peaches as the dish will contain whole; put the fruit in the dish; sift over a very little sugar; add two small pieces of nice butter, a half-pint of water, and a sifting of flour. Cover all with a nice paste, and serve with sugar and cream. (*See* Rich Peach Pudding, Nos. 3 and 4.)

Plain Peach Pudding, No. 2.—Make a nice batter, put whole peaches after peeling in a shallow pudding-dish; pour over just enough batter to cover them. Serve with sugar and butter worked together to form a cream.

CHAPTER III.

PEARS AND QUINCES, HERMETICALLY SEALING, ETC.

Plain Boiled Pears.—Take the common French, or any small-sized acid pear; wash and wipe them clean, leaving on the stems. Put them in an iron kettle. To about half a peck of pears put a quart bowl full of sugar, and a teacupful of water; cover them, and boil over a slow fire until thoroughly cooked. Maple-sugar is the best, but any other will do.

Preserved Pears.—Peel small-sized pears, leave the stem one inch long, weigh them, and allow one pound of sugar to one of fruit;

put one pint of water and one teaspoonful of citric acid to every four pounds of sugar. Melt the sugar and acid slowly over steam; when melted let it boil up once, then skim the syrup well and keep it over the steam until wanted. At the same time the syrup is in the process of preparation, have the pears boiling in a preserving-kettle in sufficient water to cover them, in which is dissolved citric acid sufficient to taste quite acid. When so tender that a straw can be run through them, take them out and put them in the syrup, where they must remain about twenty minutes. Have ready some glass jars or bottles with mouths large enough to take in the fruit without breaking; put them in cold water, and boil them; put the fruit into the bottles while they are hot. This is done for two objects: first, to prevent the hot preserves from breaking the bottles, and secondly to prevent the fruit from fermentation by the cold air. Cork tight, and seal up each bottle while the syrup is boiling hot. Be careful to seal perfectly tight; a hole no larger than a cambric needle will do as much mischief as one much larger. Put cotton wadding over the fruit, as described in the directions for PRESERVING APPLES. Label and date the jars; keep them in a cool, dry, and dark place, where they can be seen without disturbing the bottles. (*See* observations on mould in the recipe for PRESERVING APPLES.) Stewart's No. 1 granulated is not only the best, but cheapest sugar to use in preserving fruits of every description. All fruit should be thrown into water as soon as peeled, to prevent its turning dark from the rust of the knife.

BRANDY PEARS.—Prepare and boil the fruit as for preserves. Make the syrup in the same manner; let the pears lie in white French brandy over night, covered close. In the morning take equal quantities of the brandy and syrup; beat them together until thoroughly mixed; put the fruit in bottles, strain and pour over them the prepared brandy syrup; cork and seal tight. It is very important to keep the fruit under the syrup. Label and date; keep in a cool, dark, and dry place.

GINGER PEAR.—Prepare Virgaloo pears as for preserves, except they must be cut into about four equal parts. Make a syrup as rich and in the same proportion. Take green ginger, scrape it clean, put to every pound of pears one quarter of a pound of ginger, boil it with the pears, until tender, then put it in the bottles with the fruit, and the same number of slices in each bottle. Prepare the bottles and put up the fruit in the same manner as preserved pears.

LEMON PEARS.—Prepare and boil Virgaloo as for ginger pears; make the syrup as for preserves, and flavor high with lemon; superior extract, and citric acid are much better than the fruit, in giving lemon flavor, as the peel is apt to be bitter. Put up the fruit in the same manner as described for preserves.

PICKLED PEARS.—Prepare pears as for preserves, boil until tender; stick into each of them three or four cloves; take one quart of wine, or strong cider vinegar, four pounds of sugar, half an ounce of cinnamon broken into pieces two inches long, a quarter of an ounce of mace, and half an ounce of dry ginger scraped and washed clean. Put all into a preserving-kettle, let it remain over steam where it nearly boils two hours, then dissolve a teaspoonful of citric acid in a little of the syrup, and stir it in while hot. Put the fruit into the syrup a half hour, then bottle, cork, and seal tight. Keep in a cool place, the same as other preserved fruit. This is not a proper pickle for dinner, it should be served for tea and suppers. They can be pickled also with or without sugar or spices, for sour pickles.

HERMETICALLY-SEALED FRESH STEWED PEARS.—Wash and wipe dry small-sized pears; boil until quite tender. Make a light syrup of either maple, or No. 1 coffee sugar, to the proportion of four pounds to one quart of filtered or clean rain-water; add one teaspoonful of citric acid. Have ready tin cans perfectly air-tight, fill the cans nearly full of the boiled fruit, pour over it the prepared syrup, allowing a half-pound of sugar to every quart can. After the tinner has soldered on the caps, pierce the can with a small awl, set them in cold water, and heat gradually. Let them boil one hour, and then solder up the small holes. The water must only reach the top of the can while boiling. When cool examine the cans; if the ends are not drawn well in, the can is imperfect; if they are, they will generally prove perfect, though not always, as sometimes the leak is so small, and perhaps stopped by sugar for the time being, as not to show air until the fruit is soured, which is shown by the swelling of the can, which will burst unless opened. (*See* WATER BATH and TESTING CANS.)

TO PRESERVE PEARS WITHOUT SUGAR.—Prepare and exhaust the air from the fruit in the same manner as in fresh stewed pears, using a half-pint of filtered water to every quart, instead of syrup.

PLAIN PRESERVES HERMETICALLY SEALED.—Cheap preserves can be made and preserved by the same process as described. To every pound of pears, peeled, quartered, and cored, take a half-pound of sugar, and to every three pounds of sugar one pint of water; this will make three pints of syrup; divide it equally on the fruit, allowing a half-pint of syrup to every pound of fruit. Put the fruit in cans hot; put the cans in boiling water as soon as sealed, and let them remain one half-hour; then solder the small holes, and take out of the water immediately. Cans must be marked in some manner before sealing, or mistakes will often occur, as it is impossible to designate them afterwards.

BAKED PEARS FOR WINTER, HERMETICALLY SEALED.—First boil the pears, with the skin and part of the stem on, until tender; have ready a strong syrup of maple-sugar flavored with citric acid. To one quart of syrup add as much salt as will lie on a five-cent piece; put the pears into the syrup, let them bake until shrivelled a very little; dip the syrup over them often, and when ready can them, and exhaust the air. The syrup should be equally divided, and poured in the cans. These will be found superior. Bottles may be used instead of cans; cork and wire them before exhausting, and seal hot.

QUINCES.—The large orange quince is the best for family use. Let them hang on the bushes until after frost. If gathered and laid in a cool place they may sometimes be preserved several months, and in other seasons they decay soon. Never preserve them until a few show signs of decay.

To PRESERVE QUINCES.—Boil them in water slightly acidulated with citric acid; have ready a syrup prepared with one pound of sugar to one of fruit dissolved in water in the proportion of one pint to four pounds, and a teaspoon of citric acid. Place the quinces in the syrup when boiled perfectly tender, heat them to boiling heat, fill the bottles while the fruit and bottles are both hot, cork and seal immediately. They may be preserved whole, in quarters, or in rings. They will ferment badly if the sealing is the least imperfect. Turn the bottles upside down if the fruit rises.

To PRESERVE QUINCES HERMETICALLY SEALED IN CANS OR BOTTLES. —Proceed as directed for pears, except they must be peeled and cored. Quinces are pickled and brandied the same as pears. They may be put up without sugar for dinner desserts. In our opinion this is their best use. Use cans or bottles, as preferred. If in bottles, wire the corks before placing the bottles in the bath.

QUINCES FOR DINNER DESSERT.—Quarter the fruit, and boil or

steam them until tender, and serve with rich cream and loaf-sugar. They are also baked and used in the same manner.

QUINCE MARMALADE.—Boil the quinces, with the peels and cores, in as little water as will cover them. Press the pulp through a sieve, and allow one and a fourth pound of loaf-sugar for every pound of pulp; boil gently, stirring constantly, until it is reduced to a stiff mass, after which pack it in small jars and cover it with paper wet with the white of an egg. If of proper consistency it will cut like cheese.

QUINCE JELLY.—If quinces are high, a jelly may be made of the peels and cores; but if the fruit is plenty, boil the whole of it. Cover the fruit and boil until tender; then drain all the juice from the fruit, and allow a pound of the best sugar for every pint; boil a few moments, and put it in moulds. If the jelly appears cloudy, strain it through a flannel bag, after the sugar is dissolved, before it boils up. If the cores and peels are used alone, the jelly will be very stringy.

To DRY QUINCES OR PEARS.—Peel, and cut them in thin slips; string and dry them in the sun; soak them over night, and stew in the same water.

CHAPTER IV.

PLUMS.

HERMETICALLY SEAL, PRESERVE, ETC.

REMARKS.—Only the finest are fit for the table in their natural state, and even these should be served as a third or fourth course, and eaten with moderation. Among the most popular of these are the green and yellow gage, Washington, Coe's golden drop, purple favorite, Lombard, etc. Among the finest flavored for preserves, jams, jellies, tarts, etc., are the damsons. The winter damson is the finest of all, a very small purple plum, with small pit, fit only for preserving, being in its natural state very astringent. It is the very latest plum, and it is said to be the only variety not troubled with the curculio.

To PRESERVE WINTER DAMSONS.—After looking over the fruit, and throwing out all poor-looking plums, wash and wipe them clean, pierce every plum twice with a coarse needle; weigh the fruit, and allow for every pound, the same in weight of sugar of the best quality, rolled fine; begin with the sugar, and put alternate layers of it and fruit in an enamelled preserving kettle. Set the kettle over a boiler of hot water, cover tight, and let it heat gradually. When there is reason to think the sugar is dissolved in the juice, stir up the sugar and the fruit together, being careful not to break the plums any more than the steaming has already done; let the kettle remain over the steam covered tightly, until the whole is heated through, and the fruit completely saturated with the sugar. Bottle it while in a boiling state, according to directions given before in other preserves. Place cotton wadding of the best kind soaked in brandy on the top of each bottle, which should be pressed down so as to admit the syrup to rise a little above it, but no fruit. This is to prevent mould, should any form, from doing injury to the fruit. Examine daily; should any air bubbles form, either the fruit has not been heated through, and put up boiling, or not sealed tightly; in either case it would ferment. Take off the wax from the corks, place the bottles in cold water on wood; if placed on iron they would be apt to crack; heat gradually and boil slowly a half-hour after the water becomes boiling hot; have ready new corks, and seal tightly. If much sour, take the corks from the bottles before putting in the water, or they will burst; if any foam rises while heating, put the fruit in the preserving kettle, and boil hard a half-hour; it will only be fit for tarts, and most certain to ferment again if sealed ever so well, but if properly done at first, it seldom needs heating over. This preserve is not as beautiful as some others, but is probably the very best flavored of the plum, retaining its freshness, while it remains without fermentation for years. It is particularly relished by invalids. Should the preserve not be in a fit state for bottling the day commenced, it can be left in the kettle over night, and heated over steam in the same manner as at first.

PLUM JAM.—Take any variety of plum desired, steam them in an enamelled kettle until heated through; strain off the juice, and pass the pulp through a fine sieve, boil one hour, stirring constantly; if it burns it is ruined; weigh, before boiling, the pulp and juice, dissolve the same weight of the best sugar rolled fine in the juice; when entirely melted, add this to the pulp, beat it well together, and let it boil one minute; have the moulds ready, which must not be glass; pour in the jam, filling the moulds quite full, and set them in a slow oven

11*

twenty-four hours. Wooden moulds will do lined with paper; when the jam is used, wet the paper in a little warm water, and take it off.

PLUM PASTE.—Boil tart plums in their own juice until quite tender, take out the pits and pass the pulp through a wire sieve, boil gently, stirring constantly one hour; stir half the weight of the pulp, before boiling, of sugar in the pulp, and boil one minute; have ready shallow earthen plates, a square shape to be preferred; pour the paste in this, not over a quarter of an inch thick, and dry slowly in the oven, being careful not to burn it. When dry turn it out, and pack the paste away carefully; these are used to cut in rings, or any other form for ornament to cakes, ices, whips, etc.

PLUM COMPOTE.—Prick the fruit with a needle, and throw them in cold hard water, let them lie as long as it will take to boil a pan of water; into this they must be thrown as soon as it boils. When the fruit rises to the surface, skim it out, and throw it again in cold water. Prepare a syrup and boil them up in it, set it to cool, and boil again and again. If not wanted for immediate use, put it, while hot, in bottles, cork and seal as other sweetmeats.

GREEN GAGES, HERMETICALLY SEALED, No. 1.—Select quite ripe, not soft but perfect fruit, prick them with a needle on opposite sides, throw them in hot, not boiling water, off the fire, let them remain in the water five minutes; have ready cold water, skim them out, and throw them in it, and let them remain until cold; lay them on a hair sieve to drain, pack the fruit in strong bottles, holding about one quart, with mouths large enough to let the fruit in without bruising; leave a space between the fruit and cork, of two inches. Have a syrup prepared in the following manner: To one pound of water, take two of sugar, dissolve the sugar over steam until clear, use only the best sugar; add to each pound of water a piece of citric acid as large as a hazelnut; pour the syrup on cold; wire the cork well down, let the syrup cover the fruit well, leaving nearly two inches space in the bottle; place them in the water-bath cold, which must always have a wooden bottom for the bottles to stand on; heat gradually, and let them boil until the fruit shows signs of cracking, or (as it is sometimes the case that it does not crack) a half-hour is long enough to boil them, counting the time after the water becomes boiling hot; seal perfectly, and set them in a cool, dry, and dark place, not forgetting to label them. Examine for a week or so, to see if all is right, and turn them upside down three times each week for a month.

GREEN GAGES, HERMETICALLY SEALED, No. 2.—Prick sound ripe fruit, pack it in jars or bottles as above, without scalding. Make a light syrup in proportion of four pounds of sugar to one quart of water; pour it on the fruit cold, cork and wire as directed; boil in the water-bath three-fourths of an hour unless the fruit cracks, if so, less.

GREEN GAGES, HERMETICALLY SEALED, No. 3.—Throw gages in boiling water until the skin cracks and loosens; strip off the skin, pack in jars, and proceed as above, boiling twenty-five minutes, unless the fruit appears like melting. Make the syrup with five pounds of best sugar to a quart of water, and a small teaspoonful of citric acid. Any plum can be prepared in this manner, only observing, that the more juicy the fruit, the stronger the syrup should be, and the larger, the longer time in heating through.

BRANDY GAGES.—Wash and wipe dry green gages, prick them on opposite sides, pack in bottles or jars with large enough mouths to let the fruit in without pressing; pour over just sufficient good white French brandy to cover them, cork tightly, and let them stand two days; should the fruit absorb the liquor so as to leave any uncovered, pour on a little more brandy, but no more than is necessary. Then pour off the liquor, and stir gradually into every pint, a pound of sugar; dissolve it well, and when quite clear, fill the bottles as full as possible without touching the cork; cork tightly, and paste over the cork a paper wet with the beaten whites of eggs; put what syrup is left, if any, in a bottle; cork, and seal in the same manner; in a few days examine the bottles; if the fruit has absorbed the syrup so as to leave the fruit exposed, fill up again, and seal very particularly with wax, so as to be able to turn the jars up if necessary. Don't forget the labels.

BRANDY GAGES, FRENCH METHOD.—Pick the fruit when quite hard, but ripe, and pack it in jars. Take white French brandy; to every quart add five ounces best refined sugar, cork and seal perfectly tight, with brittle wax.

BRANDY GAGES, No. 3.—Fill the jars as above described, prepare very rich syrup, let it cool to blood-heat; mix in the proportion of one-third syrup to two of brandy, mix thoroughly; fill the bottles as for other brandy plums, cork, and seal perfectly. If any syrup is left, bottle and cork it for future use. If the skins are tough, remove them.

BEST BRANDY PLUMS, FOR FAMILY USE.—Weigh eight pounds of the best loaf-sugar, divide it in two equal parts; put half of it in a porcelain preserving kettle with one quart of water and a teaspoonful of citric acid; set it over steam until the sugar melts, then let it boil up once, take off the scum, and set the kettle from the fire; have ready about eight quarts of plums, (green gages are the finest for brandy fruit;) having looked them over carefully, washed, wiped, and pricked them, lay them overnight in the kettle, being careful that the fruit is wholly covered with the syrup; the next morning set the kettle over steam until the syrup is nearly boiling hot; take out the fruit, and add the other half of the sugar, and another teaspoonful of the acid; let it dissolve gradually over steam, and take off all the scum that rises. While the syrup is thickening, have the plums soaking in just enough white French brandy to cover them; let them be covered as tightly as possible; a bright tin pail with a tight-fitting cover, is as good as any thing for this purpose; when the syrup is clear, set it to cool; when it has become cold enough to prevent the evaporation of the brandy, mix with it three quarts and one pint of brandy; the brandy should be measured before it is put on the fruit. Mix the brandy and syrup thoroughly, passing it through a fine hair sieve, to prevent the syrup and brandy from separating; fill the jars or bottles, which have a mouth large enough to let in the fruit without bruising; fill up the bottles so as nearly to touch the cork; put in the corks, and let them stand until the next day; bottle and cork tightly the syrup left; if the fruit absorbs the syrup so as to uncover the fruit, fill the bottles again; cork and seal with brittle wax, so perfectly, that the bottles will not leak when turned upside down; label and set them away.

To HERMETICALLY SEAL AND PRESERVE EGG PLUMS.—Select fruit quite ripe, but not soft; wash, and wipe them dry; leave on a short piece of the stem; prick the skin, with a common-sized needle, in many places. Have ready water, boiling hot; take the kettle from the fire; throw in the fruit in the proportion of four quarts of fruit to eight of water; be careful to sink the plums, as they will be scalded only on one side if floating, and when they crack slip off the skins; prepare the day before, the syrup in the following manner: Take the weight of the fruit in the best loaf-sugar; and divide it in two equal parts; dissolve half the sugar in the same weight of water, with a little citric acid, and take off the scum as it rises; when quite clear, set it off to cool; if made in a porcelain kettle, it can stand in the vessel in which it was prepared overnight without harm; put the fruit in the syrup over steam until it feels quite hot, but do not boil it, as this will break the fruit; take off the kettle, and let them become cold, keeping the fruit constantly covered with syrup; set it on again, and again, in the same manner until the syrup has penetrated the fruit to the pit; then take it out; and after it has been well drained, pack it in a jar, with a mouth large enough to let in the fruit without pressing; add to the syrup the remainder of the sugar, and a lump of citric acid as large as a pea; to every two pounds of sugar, add the pits of peaches or plums blanched, in proportion of six pits to every pound of sugar, and let the syrup boil slowly five minutes; take it off, and skim it well; cool a little, and pass it through a fine sieve without pressing; fill the jars with the syrup nearly full, and cover them over to keep out insects; the next day examine the bottles, and if the fruit is not well covered with syrup, add more; leave less than two inches space, if the bottle is just large enough to admit the fruit, and less if larger; cork and wire tightly; place the bottles in the water bath to remain after the water boils one hour, unless the fruit looks like breaking; when this happens, take out the bottles, and seal them immediately. Any large plum, apricot, or nectarine, can be preserved in the same manner.

FRENCH METHOD OF PREPARING NECTARINES AND APRICOTS.—Take fruit not too ripe, make a small slit at the stem end and push out the stone. Simmer in water until about half done, and afterward throw them into cold water; when they have cooled, take them out, and drain them. Put the fruit into the preserving pan, with sufficient syrup to cover them; let them boil up three or four times, and skim well, remove the fruit from the fire, and pour it into an earthen pan until the next day. Boil it in this manner three successive days, and they will be finished. Examine the syrup; if too thin, add a little sugar, unless there is enough syrup for the fruit; in that case, boil it down until of the right consistency. Put the fruit up hot, and seal tightly.

TO PRESERVE THE COMMON BLUE PLUM.—After weighing the fruit, throw it a little at a time, in boiling water to loosen the skin, slip it off; weigh the same amount of sugar, granulated is the best, and pack the fruit in layers in a preserving kettle, as directed in preserving winter damsons. They will not need quite as much cooking, on account of the skin being off the fruit; put them up in the same manner as the damsons. Horse, or any other coarse plum, can be preserved in the same way.

PLUM SYRUP AND JELLY.—Heat damson plums over steam, until

scalded through; drain off the juice, add one and a half pound of sugar to every pound of juice; heat the juice to boiling heat, and stir in the sugar; let it boil a moment only. If it does not become solid, heat it over, and as soon as boiling hot pour it into bottles prepared in boiling water as before described, and seal them up while hot. When wanted for jelly, if not solid, dissolve in warm water, either isinglass or gelatine, in the proportion of four ounces to a pint of water, and strain it through a fine sieve; this will make four quarts of jelly, if dissolved in that quantity of the bottled syrup, firm, and hard; but it will melt in a warm room, or in summer heat. It makes nice syrup for ices, puddings, etc., and often jellies firm.

PLUM ICE.—Prepare the juice of the damson plum as described, allowing one pound of sugar to each pint of juice. When wanted, add as much water as syrup; blanch and pound to a paste a few kernels of the fruit; mix them well through, and freeze smoothly. Apricot ice, is made in the same manner.

PICKLED PLUMS, SPICED, No. 1.—Wash and wipe dry perfect plums, leave a short piece of the stem on the fruit. Prick them pretty thoroughly with a needle, about number six. Have ready prepared vinegar very strong, heated over steam to nearly boiling heat, in which is put cloves, cinnamon, mace, and green ginger root if to be had, if not dry, in the following proportions: one quart of vinegar, a teaspoonful of mace, half as much cloves, a table-spoonful of cinnamon broken about as large as cloves, and as much ginger scraped free from the bark if green, half as much if dry. Put a part of the fruit in the vinegar; let it remain a few moments, not long enough to crack them; take them out, and pack in jars; when all have been scalded, tie over the mouths of the bottles thin cloth, and turn them up to drain; measure the juice and vinegar, allowing three pounds of sugar to every quart; mix all together, and when the sugar is entirely dissolved, pour the syrup over the plums; let them stand until the next day; then cork and wire them, and put the bottles in the water bath. If small plums, let them boil ten minutes, and seal up. If egg, or other large plums, a half hour. To be served for tea or at supper, and parties, in pickle shells.

SOUR PICKLED PLUMS, No. 2.—Pour over pricked plums hot spiced vinegar, four different times, on successive days, and seal tightly. If the vinegar loses its strength, take fresh; the fruit should be very hard; serve with meats.

PICKLED PLUMS, No. 3.—Prepare the plums as for No. 1. Take one quart of ten per cent. vinegar; dry ginger root broken up; about two table-spoonfuls green, one half a teaspoon of cloves broken twice, a teaspoon of broken mace, and two table-spoons broken cinnamon. Heat the vinegar, and pour it on the spices hot; cover tight, and let it stand all night. In the morning strain it through a jelly bag, and add two pounds loaf sugar; let it gently boil and remove the scum. Take off the syrup, and when nearly cool, put the plums in it. Let it stand until the next day. Then remove the plums to the bottles; strain the syrup, and cover the plums with it. Cork, and wire the bottles; set them in cold water, and heat gently. When the water has boiled fifteen minutes, take them from the bath and seal tightly; serve for tea and parties.

HERMETICALLY-SEALED NATURAL PRESERVED PLUMS.—Prepare the fruit as for other preserves. Pack them in bottles; allow a half pound of sugar to one of fruit. To every three pounds of sugar, take one pint of water, and a half teaspoonful of citric acid, dissolved in the water; stir gradually the sugar into the water, which must be melted over steam; take off all the scum; when clear, pour it over the fruit, which must be equally divided in the jars, so as to portion the syrup alike; have ready blanched kernels of plums or peaches; put in each bottle a dozen, and let them stand until the next day. If the fruit absorbs the syrup, so as to uncover the plums, add more. Leave less than two inches space. Cork, wire, and place in the water bath; let them remain one hour at a temperature of 180°, unless the fruit appears like cracking, then seal tightly, etc., as directed for other fruits.

NECTARINES AND APRICOTS TO PICKLE.—Proceed exactly as in pickled peaches. Keep in a cool place, and examine frequently.

HERMETICALLY-SEALED PLUM PIE FRUIT IN BOTTLES.—Select quite hard fruit, (gages are the finest for this purpose.) Fill the bottles (which should be the kind designated Pie Fruits) to within two inches of the cork, shaking them down, so as to get in as many as possible. Fill up, with filtered rain-water, to within one and a half inch of the cork; wire the bottles well, and put them in the water bath. Let them remain a half hour at a temperature of 180°, unless the fruit shows signs of cracking. To ascertain this, examine those in the hottest place often, after the heat has been up to 180° ten minutes. The riper the fruit, the sooner it will heat through, which is all that is wanted. Seal very carefully. Examine often; for although fruit, put up in this way, cannot be recovered if imperfect, the bottles may be saved, and mischief to other fruits prevented, by timely opening, as they will certainly burst, if not perfect. See that the fruit is under the water, and turn them often. It often moulds by the action of light, the reason of which is unaccounted for by chemists. (*See* MOULD, in another part of this book.)

HERMETICALLY-SEALED PLUM PIE FRUIT IN TIN CANS.—Fill each can full without shaking much; put as much soda in a quart can, as will lay on a sixpence; add a half pint of filtered rain water. Solder on the cap, pierce each cap with a common awl; place the cans in the water bath; heat gradually; after the water reaches the heat of 180°, (which must not cover the cans,) let them remain from twenty to thirty minutes, after which time the fruit will be ready to close; drop upon the aperture solder, and take them from the bath. Examine the cans as directed for other can fruit. (*See* TESTING CANS.)

HERMETICALLY-SEALED TABLE PLUMS.—These are put up as above, without soda, and the addition of a pint tumbler full of granulated loaf-sugar. (*See* TESTING CANS.)

HERMETICALLY-SEALED NATURAL PLUM PRESERVES IN CANS.—Allow a quarter of a pound of sugar to a pound of fruit, made into a light syrup, divide it equally, cook the fruit in the cans a half hour at 180°, and seal up as directed.

PLAIN PLUM JAM can also be put up in cans and treated as described.

DRIED PLUMS WITHOUT SUGAR.—Plums can be dried in the same manner as peaches, using the sweet, and less juicy varieties, and are cooked in the same manner.

PLUM LEATHER.—Mash green gages, that are very ripe, quite fine; remove the pits, and dry on plates in the oven. Cook as peach leather, adding sugar.

PLUMS DRIED WITH SUGAR.—Cut open sweet plums, not removing the pits; scatter over them sugar; spread the fruit on plates, and set it in a slow oven. When the sugar is taken up by the fruit, add more, and continue to do this, while there is sufficient moisture to take up the sugar. Pack in jars, with paper pasted over them, and place them above the reach of mice; they will need no washing. Soak over night, and heat through in the same water. If not sweet enough to suit, add more sugar.

PLUM TARTS.—Prepare puff paste, as directed for tarts; bake the paste, and fill the cavity with jam or jelly; fruit should never stand in the paste; the tarts should be filled just before using. Shake over them powdered loaf-sugar, or ice them. (*See* PUFF-PASTE and ICING.)

APRICOT BISCUITS, FRENCH.—Reduce apricots to a paste; stir into it its weight in sugar; cook an hour, stirring constantly. Drop on paper, or in paper moulds, and dry in the oven; pack away in tight tin boxes, for winter use. Plums, being more juicy, require more sugar, probably one-third more.

CHAPTER V.

CHERRIES.

HERMETICALLY SEAL, PRESERVE, ETC.

HISTORY AND VARIETIES.—The cherry is a native of the north temperate zones, and has been cultivated since the year 1500. There are two or three hundred varieties. These are divided into classes. First, the heart-shaped fruit; these are the best for the dessert in their natural state; second, Bigarreau, with firmer flesh than the former, and, of course, better for brandy fruit, pickles, fancy preserves, and candying. Third, Duke, more acid, make better preserves, pies, and can fruits. Fourth, Morellos, more acid still; one of the finest of the last, is Pulm-stone Morello. This fruit, more particularly the Duke and Morello, are not considered very wholesome. The fact, that it is generally necessary to gather the fruit before fully ripe, to save it from the depredation of birds, is probably the great reason why the eating of cherries often produces such terrible results. It is also well known that they contain the essentials of Hydrocyanic or Prussic acid, as well as Hydruret of Benzule, a poisonous oil, to which the blossom, both of peach and cherry, owe their peculiar odor. Whether this has a deleterious effect on the fruit is not certainly known; it is, however, the firm opinion of many, that this is the case. Let it be so or not, it certainly is safe to use the fruit only in moderation. Experience shows, that they cannot be eaten by all, with impunity, in the crude state; but, when cooked and sugared, may be used as a relish, with comparative safety.

Fancy Preserves.—Pit the fruit, being careful not to break the cherries; weigh them; take as many pounds of the best loaf-sugar as there is fruit; put it in an enamelled preserving kettle; to every six pounds of loaf-sugar take one quart of water, and as much cream of tartar as will fill a teaspoon, finely pulverized: put the whole over a slow, clear fire, or what is better, a kettle of boiling water, until the sugar is entirely dissolved, so as to lose all the grain; let it boil up once, and skim it well; then lay the fruit in the syrup over night, being careful to have the cherries entirely covered with the syrup; in the morning, place the kettle containing the cherries and syrup over a kettle of boiling water, keeping the fruit constantly covered with syrup until nearly boiling hot; put it then on a slow clear fire until it boils up once, take it off immediately, and set the kettle away until the next day, when the same process must be gone over again; the third day after the fruit boils up, skim out, and drain it on a hair sieve; when well drained put the whole of the syrup on the fire, boil and skim it, until there remains just about enough to cover the fruit; while boiling the syrup, select the fruit, leaving out small bits, only using round looking fruit not broken; put it into the boiling syrup, set it over boiling water while the fruit heats through; when you are sure this is the case, let it come to a boil, and bottle in the same manner as before directed; seal tightly, etc. As white cherries do not have much flavor, they are used as fancy preserves; any other variety of cherries can be preserved in this manner if desired.

To Preserve Black Hawk, or any other large Black Cherry.—Pit carefully, so as not to break the fruit; weigh the cherries, allowing for each pound of fruit the same weight of number one granulated loaf-sugar; scatter a little on the bottom of an enamelled preserving kettle, then a few cherries, until the kettle is filled, or the fruit and sugar, in alternate layers, is all in; put the kettle over a boiler of hot water, and keep it there until the sugar is all dissolved, and the fruit heated through; stir it up carefully with a wooden spoon, and set it over a slow fire until it boils up; let it simmer three minutes slowly, keeping the fruit constantly under the syrup; then set it where it will keep boiling hot, and bottle it. Place cotton wadding saturated with brandy on each bottle, just below the syrup, that mould, if any forms, will adhere to it; seal, etc., as directed before. If there is too large a proportion of syrup, save a bottle or two out, which must be put up hot, with the same precautions, as preserves; it is a nice sauce for cherry puddings, and also makes a beautiful ice or cream for parties, etc.

DUKE AND MORELLO CHERRIES TO PRESERVE.—Follow the directions given for preserving black cherries, adding an extra pound of sugar for every eight of fruit. Particular care must be used in boiling; remember, three minutes on the fire is all they require after being heated over steam; if boiled too long, they will lose their color. The Duke and Morellos make altogether the finest flavored preserve.

HERMETICALLY SEALED NATURAL PRESERVES, No. 1.—Make a syrup with six pounds of sugar to one quart of soft water, and a teaspoonful of citric acid; be careful not to burn in melting the sugar (*see* SYRUPS); pit the fruit carefully, lay it a half-hour on a hair sieve to drain; after which fill strong quart bottles two-thirds full of the fruit; as it naturally falls in without shaking down, pour over it the syrup while hot, until it reaches to within four and a half inches of the mouth of the bottle; prepare the best of corks by soaking in hot water; drive them one inch and a half into the bottle, after the syrup is cool, and wire them well down; place the bottles in the bath filled as far as the syrup reaches with cold water; turn on the steam, and let them remain a half-hour, after the water reaches 180°; seal immediately, etc., as directed for other bottles; keep a good lookout for them, for a week or two; should any sign of fermentation appear, take off the wax and heat over; if neglected until they really work, there is no such thing as saving them; they will burst the bottles; in this case use them for puddings or pies, immediately. Measure what juice strained from this fruit through the sieve, which should have been set over an earthen dish, and add to every pint a pound of sugar; put it in a preserving kettle, let it become boiling hot, try it, if it jellies put it up in moulds—but this seldom happens; if not, skim and bottle it hot, sealing with care. Jelly can be made when wanted, by using gelatine or isinglass (*see* GELATINE), or the syrup can be used to flavor creams and sauces, or made into ices. (*See* CHERRY, ICE.)

HERMETICALLY SEALED NATURAL PRESERVES, No. 2.—Pick over the fruit carefully, see that no imperfect fruit is used; put it in bottles; cork and set the bottles in the water bath until the fruit shows signs of cracking; have ready a rich syrup hot; pour it on the fruit while boiling, and while the fruit itself is in the water bath, or just taken out; put the cork in as well as it can be, and let them boil fifteen minutes, then cork and seal tightly. If the stems are removed, it must be done so as not to break the fruit and let out the juice; it is better to clip them with the scissors, and leave a small part of the stem on the cherry.

BRANDY CHERRIES, No. 1.—The white cherries make the finest looking brandy fruit. Select the fruit carefully; clip off each stem so as to leave a little point on the fruit; pack the fruit in the bottles designed for them, and cover with white French brandy; cork tightly, and paste over the corks white paper wet with white of eggs; let them remain forty-eight hours, or longer if convenient; then pour off the brandy, and mix it with the same quantity of very rich syrup free from grain, pass it through a fine hair sieve, and pour enough on the fruit to cover it well; cork and let it remain overnight; the next day examine the bottles, and fill up with the syrup, just as full as possible without touching the cork; seal tightly with wax, so as to be able to turn the bottles cork end down, should the syrup be again absorbed by the fruit.

BRANDY CHERRIES, No. 2.—Prepare the fruit as above, pack it as closely as possible, without shaking down, in quart bottles; place them in the water bath until the fruit shows signs of cracking; then remove them, take out the cork, and tie a thin cloth over the mouth of the bottle, and turn them up in a clean dish; and let all the juice drain off. Measure the juice; to every pint take three pounds of sugar, and melt it together over boiling water; as soon as clear take it off; if it looks like graining, dissolve a teaspoonful of citric acid in a very little water, and add to the syrup; heat it again, and if any impurities arise, skim it; after which let it cool until about blood heat; add to the syrup three pints of white French brandy; beat it up well and pass it through a fine sieve; fill the bottles so as not to touch the cork, and seal immediately. Should any syrup be left, bottle it, and seal tightly for future use.

PICKLED CHERRIES, No. 1.—White cherries look the best pickled. Prepare the fruit as for brandy cherries, leaving the stems a trifle longer. Take two quarts of very sharp vinegar, free from unpleasant flavor, six pounds of the best sugar, one teaspoonful of cloves pounded, not ground, a table-spoonful of mace, two of cinnamon, and one of ginger-root pounded. Have prepared ten pounds of the cherries. Pack the fruit equally in quart bottles, cork and place them in the water bath; let them boil twenty minutes; have the syrup all ready, the sugar melted, and all the spices strained out by passing it through a sieve; put in each bottle six cloves, three or four pieces of mace, and the same of cinnamon. While the fruit is boiling hot pour enough syrup, also boiling, into each bottle to cover the fruit, and cork and seal immediately. As these are apt to mould, it is well to put the cotton wadding in as before directed, having first dipped it in hot syrup, or put it on the fruit, and pour the syrup through it, being careful to prevent its being carried too far down.

PICKLED CHERRIES, No. 2.—Prepare the fruit as before directed. To two quarts of vinegar, and spices to the taste, take four pounds of sugar, weigh eight pounds of fruit, and divide it equally in bottles; after the sugar is entirely dissolved strain it on the cherries; if it is not sufficiently seasoned, let the spices remain in the syrup; cork and wire well, and place the bottles in the water bath, let them boil fifteen minutes, or until they look like cracking, when seal.

PICKLED CHERRIES, No. 3.—Prepare the fruit, put them in jars, and fill with the strongest vinegar; let them remain in this, corked tightly, one month, or longer, as convenient. Then prepare a spiced syrup, take them from the vinegar, and put them in the syrup. Seal tightly.

PICKLED CHERRIES, No. 4.—Leave the stems on, just as the fruit grows, in clusters or single; put them in the strongest vinegar, let them remain for one month, then examine; if any mould appears, the vinegar is too weak; change it, and at this time add spices, and a couple of spoonfuls of sugar to each bottle; cork and seal. These make a beautiful garnish. Cherries can also be pickled in vinegar alone if desired. Proceed as follows: Leave the fruit in clusters, place them in an enamelled preserving-kettle; cover with strong vinegar; let them heat slowly, until nearly boiling hot, over hot water; allow them to remain in this vinegar until cold, after which pour over them some eight per cent. vinegar, and cover closely. Spices can be added if desired.

HERMETICALLY SEALED IN GLASS FOR PIES.—Remove the stems, and carefully select any acid cherry that makes a good pie in its season; fill quart bottles within one and a half inch of the cork (not one and a half inch from the mouth of the bottle, but from the inside of the cork); cover the fruit with filtered rain-water, leaving one and a half inch space for air; cork and wire tightly, after which place the bottles in cold water, which should reach the top of the fruit. Let them remain in the bath twenty minutes after the water reaches the heat of 180°. Test the water frequently to know when it has obtained the desired heat. If in a kettle instead of a bath, remove them as soon as the water is boiling hot. If heated on the stove instead of steam, let the fire be very low, so as to increase the heat slowly, or the fruit will not be heated evenly. Seal the bottles carefully, and shake them gently every day for two months to prevent mould. Or, lay them on their sides, and roll them each day. If sealed properly, they cannot fail to make as good pies in winter as fresh cherries. Use the filtered water with fruit when making the pies, they will be none too juicy. The fruit must be put up the day it is gathered, and should be hardly ripe; at least, let it not have been in its prime long enough to be what is called dead ripe, which is in fact the commencement of decay; no fruit arriving to that state should be put up to be used as fresh fruit. If preferred to pit the cherries, crack a handful of pits for each bottle, using the meats only, or boil a quantity of the cracked pits, shells and all, in the filtered rain-water that is to be used, until the flavor of the kernel is extracted. So much of the peculiar flavor of the cherry lies in the pit, that unless this is in some way preserved, the fruit is almost worthless for pies, or rather no better than dried fruits. Use a thermometer to test the water.

CHERRIES HERMETICALLY SEALED IN CANS FOR PIES.—Fill the cans within one inch of the top with acid cherries; add sufficient filtered rain-water to cover the fruit, and solder on the caps. Place the cans in a bath of cold water; if over the fire heat slowly as possible. When the water reaches 140°, pierce the cans, and let them remain half an hour after the heat is increased to 170°; or if over the fire only, until the water is boiling hot; seal with solder the small hole in the can before removing them from the bath. Examine the next morning, or as soon as cold; if perfect they will be drawn in at the ends. (If pitted add the kernels.)

FRESH TABLE CHERRIES HERMETICALLY SEALED.—Proceed as above, substituting syrup in place of water; if pitted, add the cracked kernels. Acid cherries only are fit for this receipt. The choice sweet cherry will be found tough and tasteless after being heated.

DRIED CHERRIES, No 1.—The best manner of drying cherries is to pit and stew them gently with a little sugar, after which spread them on tins, and dry gently in the oven. While drying boil down the syrup, and pour it over the fruit each day, a little at a time. When dry pack in jars, and paste a paper over the top.

DRIED CHERRIES, No. 2.—Pit the fruit, spread it thin on earthen dishes, scatter sugar over it, and dry in the oven; pack as above. Dried without sugar they hardly pay for the trouble.

To COOK DRIED CHERRIES.—If dried in the oven, and put immediately away, they will need no washing. Soak overnight in sufficient water to cover them; those that have been stewed will only need to be made boiling hot. If not before cooked, stew ten minutes, add the sugar needed while heating. Serve cold. Some use them in place of raisins in mince pies.

FRESH CHERRY PIES.—The fruit should be dead ripe for pies; they will take much less sugar and make richer pies than if barely ripe. Cover the plate, which should be deep, with a plain paste. If the cherries are pitted bake the paste without crisping before putting in the fruit. Mix the sugar with the fruit, remembering the cherry is very acid; spread the fruit evenly on the paste, add a piece of butter as large as the bowl of a dessert-spoon, cut in small bits, dredge with flour, cover with paste, and bake until heated through. A few pits will improve it. A perfect cherry pie is rich, juicy, and sufficiently sweet without tasting of the sugar or butter. On this account use none but good granulated loaf-sugar and sweet butter.

CHERRY PIES MADE OF THE SEALED FRUIT for winter use require less sugar than fresh cherries. Use the water in the fruit, which should be thickened with flour and enriched with more butter than fresh cherries. The bottom crust should also be baked before adding the fruit.

Cherry puddings will be found in another part of this work.

CHAPTER VI.

SMALL FRUITS.

HERMETICALLY SEAL, PRESERVE, ETC.

BARBERRIES, BEST METHOD OF PRESERVING.—Boil them in a jar without water, by placing the jar in boiling water for two hours, or until they are heated through. A small jar would take much less time than a large one; when quite hot remove them to a hair sieve, place the sieve over an earthen dish, and as soon as cold press the pulp through the sieve, leaving the seeds and skin behind; weigh the pulp and allow equal weight of sugar. Boil the pulp without the sugar fifteen minutes, then add the sugar gradually, and try the jelly as soon as the sugar dissolves, and constantly after until it shows signs of setting. When a drop forms readily on the spoon, put the jelly or jam in small jars until cold, then cover with a tissue paper dipped in brandy fitted to the jar, and pressed to the jam; cover the top with paper dipped in the white of egg, beaten stiff, and pasted with the egg to the jar; mark the preserve with the name and year, and set it in a dry, cool place. Jellies are ruined by long boiling; they should be dished as soon as set.

CURRANT JAM, No. 1.—Pick currants clean from the stem, weigh them and allow equal weight of sugar; mash the fruit, put it in a porcelain kettle, and boil gently three minutes, then add the sugar gradually, let it become boiling hot but no more, and put it in the jars; fill the jars to the top, and cover, while boiling hot, with paper dipped in beaten egg, press the paper to the jar so that there can be no air hole, cover the top with egg until it is perfectly air-tight; mark the contents and date of preserving on the cover, and set it in a cool, dry place, where the mice cannot get at it.

CURRANT JAM, No. 2.—Boil the currants gently one hour with the sugar, and put it in jars. This will be dark and very rich, it will not work, and can be used to advantage in large families, but is not as handsome as the first receipt. If boiled until very thick, it will keep years. If it candies, set the jar in boiling water until it heats through, and dissolves the sugar.

CURRANT JELLY.—Pick currants always for jam and jelly in a dry day, and before they are dead ripe; when very sweet and nice for table use, the gelatine has been converted by a process of nature into sugar. Currants must be scalded the same day they are picked, or they may not jelly; look them over, carefully removing all stems, and scald them over boiling water in an enamelled kettle, but do not allow them to reach boiling heat, and pour them in the jelly bag without bruising while hot; hang the bag over an earthen dish, and let them drip without pressing until the next morning. Then measure the juice, and allow eight and a half pounds of sugar to eight pints of the juice; put the juice in an enamelled kettle over a clear fire, remove all the scum that rises, and when boiling hot scatter in the sugar with one hand, and stir the jelly with the other; let the jelly become nearly boiling hot, slip in the skimmer, shake it in the cold if it appears like setting, dish it immediately into small moulds, tumblers, or jars. If the currants were in a right state, the jelly will set by the time the sugar dissolves. White currants do not make as pretty jelly as red, but equal parts of white and red make a beautiful jelly. Use only the best sugar for all jellies. Put over jelly, when cold, a tissue paper wet in brandy, and cover the jars or moulds, with paper cut to fit and notched, wet with the white of eggs beaten stiff. The jelly bag may be pressed, and a solid but cloudy jelly made from the juice obtained. It is as good for cakes and gravies as the other.

GRAPE JAM.—Heat grapes over water until the juice begins to flow; then put them on the fire and boil gently half an hour; when cool enough to handle put them in a fine colander that will not let the seeds of the grape through. Press the pulp through, weigh it, and allow one pound two ounces of sugar for every pound of grape; put the sugar and pulp together, and cook gently, stirring constantly until it forms a thick jam. The wild grape will do for this preserve, but is not as good as the cultivated varieties, as it will not form a jam solid enough to retain the form when turned out. Green grapes make a very nice preserve prepared in this manner; put the jam in small moulds, and cover as directed in the currant jelly.

GRAPE JELLY.—Take cultivated grapes hardly ripe, or green. If a light-colored jelly is desired, take them quite green. Boil gently until the juice is flowing and the pulp half dissolved. Cool them, and press them through a strong but thin bag, which will allow most of the dissolved pulp to pass through. Weigh the pulp, and allow one pound two ounces of sugar to one pound of fruit, boil the jelly until considerably reduced, and then add the sugar; boil with the sugar fifteen minutes, when it will be ready to put into moulds; cover as already directed in currant jelly. Wild grapes make a jelly; but it will not form so as to retain the shape of the mould when turned out.

BLACK CURRANT JAM.—Weigh the fruit, and allow equal weight of sugar; jam the fruit, and heat it gradually; boil fifteen minutes, then add the sugar; stir it constantly fifteen minutes while steadily boiling, and then put it into moulds; cover with paper wet with egg, as particularly directed in CURRANT JELLY.

BLACK CURRANT JELLY.—It is necessary to add a little water to the fruit, in order to strain it, it is so very thick, unless jam is made at the same time, when a part can be strained for the jelly, and the remainder used for jam. After it is boiled so as to heat the fruit through, press it little by little until all the juice is extracted; measure the juice, and allow one pound of sugar to every pint of juice; mix the juice and sugar, and boil ten minutes gently, stirring constantly, when it will be ready to put in moulds. Cover as directed in CURRANT JELLY.

GOOSEBERRY JELLY.—This is made exactly as black currant jelly; use no water with the fruit, but press it firmly, and make the remains of the pulp into jam; if desired to remove the skins, pass the pulp through a colander, allow one pound of sugar for one of jam.

To PRESERVE HERMETICALLY-SEALED GOOSEBERRIES WHOLE.—Prick nice large gooseberries, free from mildew, several times; put them in a strong syrup (*See* SYRUPS, Part III., Chap. XII.); warm the syrup with the fruit in it to 160°, and let them remain overnight; repeat this until the berries are completely preserved with the syrup, then heat them gently to near boiling heat, say 200°; let them remain to cool until the next day, then put them in bottles with the syrup equally divided; cork and wire them, and put the bottles in the cold bath, and heat the bath to boiling heat. If, before the water boils, the fruit shows any appearance of cracking, remove them immediately and seal the bottles tightly; if not, seal them when the water boils.

WHORTLEBERRY JELLY.—Heat whortleberries over water, press the juice, allow one pound of sugar for every pint of juice. Boil the juice, add the sugar, and put it in jars as soon as it shows signs of setting, which will be very soon if the fruit is in a right state; no fruit will make a jelly if in the least inclining to fermentation. Cover with egg paper as directed in CURRANT JELLY.

BLACKBERRY JELLY.—Prepare the fruit as above, and make the jelly in the same manner.

RASPBERRY JELLY.—Prepare the fruit as directed in CURRANT JELLY, and make the jelly as there directed. If raspberries are scarce, use one pint of currant juice to two of the raspberry, and the flavor will be quite as pleasant.

RASPBERRY OR BLACKBERRY JAM.—Boil the fruit after it is weighed until reduced one-third, then add as many pounds of sugar as there was fruit, stir in the sugar gradually, and as soon as it melts and becomes boiling hot, put it in small bottles with large corks while boiling hot, cork immediately and seal carefully. If the bottles are put in cold water, and heated to boiling heat, and drained over heat, and filled while hot, they will not break with the jam; but if cold when the preserve is put in the bottles, they may crack.

To Preserve Raspberries or Blackberries, Hermetically Sealed.—Weigh the fruit, and allow equal weight of sugar; put alternate layers of sugar and raspberries in wide-mouthed jars until the bottles are full, let them stand until the next day. If the bottles are too full, drain off the juice; if not full enough, add more fruit and sugar; the fruit should be three inches from the cork; cork the bottles tightly and wire the corks down; place the bottles in the cold bath, heat them to boiling heat, let them stand in the bath until ready to seal; be careful to seal tightly, and set them in a cool place. Watch them for one month, and turn them up daily to prevent their moulding. Label the bottles with the date of preserving, before putting them away for the winter. Plain preserves may be made with half the sugar.

Ripe Currants, Hermetically Sealed and Preserved.—Prepare the fruit exactly as for jelly without heating; drain off one quarter of the juice without bruising, weigh the remainder, and allow equal parts of sugar and fruit; mash the fruit and stir the sugar gently into it, put the preserves in bottles, and manage as directed in the preceding receipt.

To Preserve and Hermetically Seal Strawberries.—Select large strawberries hardly ripe, the firmer the berry the better; soft berries, as for instance the Ohio Mammoth, do not make fine preserves. Weigh the fruit, and allow one-fourth of a pound of sugar for one pound of fruit. Put the sugar and fruit in layers, in a flat earthen dish, set the dish in a cool place until the next morning, then drain off the juice that has settled from the fruit without disturbing the berries; weigh the juice, and take it from the weight of the fruit, weigh the same number of pounds of sugar, as the fruit without the juice, deducting one-fourth of a pound for the sugar already in the fruit. Pack the fruit and sugar in layers, in bottles, cork and wire tightly, put them in the water bath, and heat to boiling heat; remove the bottles from the bath as soon as the water reaches 212°, and seal immediately. Be particularly careful to seal so as to make them air-tight, or the fruit will ferment and break the bottles. If perfectly sealed, the fruit will keep years. Examine daily for six weeks, and turn the bottles often to prevent mould, but do not shake them to break the fruit; if turned up each day, so as to disturb the fruit for six weeks, it will seldom mould afterward.

To HERMETICALLY SEAL STRAWBERRIES, RASPBERRIES, WHORTLEBERRIES, BLACKBERRIES, RIPE CURRANTS, IN TIN CANS, No. 1.—Pick the fruit before it is perfectly ripe; all fruit loses flavor as soon as ripe. A species of fermentation takes place in all fruits, whether on the tree or gathered as soon as it is what is usually termed dead ripe. For a quart can of fruit allow half a pint of the best sugar, put the sugar in the bottom of the can, and fill to within one inch of the top of the can with the fruit; solder the cap on the can, have ready a kettle of water boiling hot, or as near to it as possible without boiling, about 209° tested by a thermometer. *To Test Cans.*—Put the cans, after they are soldered up, in the hot water one by one; watch them closely, if any bubbles arise from them, air is escaping from the cans and they are not tight; mark the spots where the bubbles come out and have them soldered; try them again until they appear perfect, when they will be ready for the bath.

To MAKE A BATH FOR FINE FRUITS.—It is important that it is arranged in such a manner that the heat can be equally maintained from twenty minutes to half an hour over a fire. Water either increases in, or loses, heat. If a steam-pipe is carried to a bath, the heat can be regulated by stop-cocks; but as few families have this convenience we must give some other plan. Take the wash boiler, have a pan fitted to the boiler six inches deep, with a pipe through the middle two inches in diameter, and seven inches high. Fill the boiler to within three inches of the pan with cold water; fill the basin with sufficient cold water to come within one inch of the top of the cans. Make a fire under the boiler, test the water in the basin often, and when it is raised to 150°, punch the cans with a small awl, and let them remain in the bath; if the water rises over the cans, dip out some. Test the water often with a thermometer to know when it reaches the proper heat, which is 170° for small fruits; when this is the heat of the water, notice the time and leave the strawberries in for twenty minutes; raspberries, twenty-five; blackberries, the same; currants and whortleberries, half an hour. Solder the holes in the cans before taking them from the water; as soon as they are soldered, take them from the bath, and turn them upside down until morning, and then examine them; if the ends are drawn in, the cans will probably prove perfect; if not, they are not airtight. If the leak can be found, solder it, and repeat the process; if not, use the fruit, or change it to another can, or it will soon ferment, and burst the cans. Mark the cans, and put them away where they can be seen without trouble. If any swell, open them, use the fruit immediately, as they will certainly spoil, and you will lose both fruit and can. No tin cans should be used for acid fruits the second time. If intended to keep long, varnish them to save the tin from rust.

To HERMETICALLY SEAL ALL SMALL FRUITS WITHOUT SUGAR IN CANS, No. 2.—Put the fruit in the cans, filling them to within one inch of the top. To green currants and gooseberries, add half a pint of soft water; to whortleberries and blackberries, one gill; to strawberries, raspberries, and ripe currants none, and then proceed exactly as before directed with sugar. All small fruits may be preserved in bottles, but are in danger of moulding; put the fruit in bottles, and add water as directed in pie fruit plums, Part V., Chap. IV. Directions for making small fruit pies, and using hermetically sealed small fruits, will be found in Part III., Chap. VII.

To HERMETICALLY SEAL SMALL FRUITS WITHOUT PIERCING THE CAN, No. 3.—Sugar the fruit, let it stand overnight in an earthen dish. In the morning fill the cans to about two inches of the top, solder on the cap, test thoroughly with the hot water, solder all imperfect places, put them in the bath with the water to the top of the can, and heat gradually; when the water reaches the heat of 170°, take the basin from the boiler, or fill the boiler with cold water through the tube to reduce the heat ten degrees, and let them remain twenty minutes. The next day put the cans in boiling water, one by one, a few moments to test them; if tight, no bubbles will rise; if not, solder the imperfect places and heat the cans over; fruit put up in this manner retains the flavor better, than if punched and soldered hot.

STRAWBERRY JAM.—Boil the strawberries until reduced to paste; have ready as many pounds of the best sugar as there was fruit before boiling; add the sugar, stirring constantly until the jam is reduced to a stiff paste; pack it in jars while hot, and cover with paper wet with egg. (*See* CURRANT JELLY.)

STRAWBERRY JELLY.—This is made with one ounce of gelatine to one pint and three gills of strawberry syrup. Soak the gelatine overnight in one gill of water, heat it gradually, and when dissolved, add it to the syrup; let it boil up, and pass it through a jelly bag until clear, after which mould it. If made in the summer, set it on ice; in the winter it will keep some time, but will soon melt in the summer.

To Dry Strawberries.—Spread the fruit on plates, scatter over it granulated sugar, and dry in the sun. Before putting it away, scald it by putting the fruit in a bright tin pan or enamelled kettle over hot water; stir it often until hot enough to destroy any insects' eggs that may have been laid in the fruit while drying. Put the berries in small paper bags, and paste them together; the bags should hold about a pint; use the contents of a bag when opened. Keep them out of the reach of rats and mice. The fruit can be dried without sugar, though not as nice.

To Dry Blackberries and Raspberries.—The best raspberries to dry are the wild black; spread them thin, and dry in the sun. Blackberries are not as nice dried as raspberries. Select the best fruit for drying, not overripe; dry in the sun, and heat over hot water before putting away in paper bags. (*See* Dried Strawberries.)

To Dry Whortleberries.—Select the large blueberry, the inferior berries are all seeds when dried, and worthless; scald and pack them in bags after they are fully dried. (*See* Dried Strawberries.) When used they must soak all night, and are improved by adding a few currants or raspberries to them; dried whortleberries are mostly used for pies; add acid, if no acid fruit is mixed with them.

To Dry Currants.—Pick them before dead ripe, stew them without crushing, spread them on plates, scatter over them good coffee sugar, and dry them in the oven. These are pleasant to eat, but worth little to cook. Soak them overnight, if to be stewed; they should be kept in paper bags. (*See* Dried Strawberries.)

Cranberry Jelly and Jam.—Make it exactly like currant jelly; do not press the jelly bag. To make the jam, pass the pulp through a sieve, add as many pounds of sugar as fruit, boil gently until clear, and mould it; cover with paper wet in egg, etc. (*See* Currant Jelly.)

To Preserve Cranberries for Winter Use.—Keep the fruit in a tub of water, change the water occasionally to keep it fresh, and throw out the imperfect fruit.

To Stew Cranberries.—Pick them over carefully, allow half as much sugar as fruit, put the fruit in the stew-pan, cook slowly a few moments, jam the fruit, add the sugar, and stew until quite clear. It can be moulded.

To PRESERVE GRAPES FOR WINTER USE, No. 1.—Notice the stem of the grape, and you will find that it is dried and withered near the branch; cut in dry weather as near the branch as possible; remove all imperfect fruit, and pack them in boxes, with layers of the nicest wadding between, not suffering the fruit to touch; paper should be placed between the grapes and the wadding, as the cotton often sticks to the grapes, and is troublesome to pick off. Keep the grapes in a cool place, to preserve the fruit from the unpleasant flavor of the cotton. Should the season be backward and the stem still green, cut the grapes as close to the branch as possible, and dip the ends of the stem in melted sealing wax immediately. ' Grapes preserve beautifully by pursuing this course, most of the winter.

To PRESERVE GRAPES IN SAWDUST, No. 2.—Procure sawdust of tasteless wood, sift and dry it in the oven; have ready a seasoned white-wood box; scatter a layer of sawdust, one inch thick, in the bottom of the box, pack fresh picked fruit perfectly dry and free from blemishes on the sawdust without allowing the bunches to touch; scatter the sawdust evenly until the fruit is covered two inches deep. Fasten narrow strips of cotton across the box, sides, and ends, forming squares to support the next layer; scatter on sawdust; pack the grapes as the first layer, fill the box with the sawdust, screw (not nail) on the cover, and keep the box in a dry place, and as cool as possible without freezing. (*See* gathering, in No. 1

To PRESERVE GRAPES IN SAND, No. 3.—Use fine lake sand sifted free from gravel and fine dust, and dried perfectly in an oven. Prepare a dry white-wood box with handles. Fasten strong twine firmly to the sides of the box, and hang fine perfect bunches of dry, fresh-gathered grapes on the twine, so that there will be a space of one inch between the top, bottom, and sides of the grapes, and then sift in, slowly and evenly, sufficient sand to cover the fruit two inches deep. Screw on the cover instead of nailing it, as pounding would jar the grapes. Set the box in a room free from dampness, where the temperature is just above freezing point. (*See* gathering, in No. 1.)

PART VI.

WINES, FRUIT BRANDIES, FRUIT VINEGARS, CORDIALS, &c.

CHAPTER I.

WINES AND TABLE BEER.

WHORTLEBERRY WINE.—Pour over whortleberries sufficient boiling water to cover them, let the fruit remain in the water overnight; in the morning press out the juice and measure it; allow to every gallon two pounds of sugar; put it in a barrel, and add spices or not, as desired. When the wine has ceased to ferment, close the bung, and place the barrel where it will remain undisturbed for several months. Bottle when the wine is nine months old. If not clear, filter it before bottling.

GRAPE WINE, No. 1.—Five gallons of ripe grapes crushed and soaked in four and a half gallons of soft water seven days; seventeen and a half pounds of nice sugar. Wash all the juice from the grapes into the water, and remove the seeds, skin, and pulp; put it in a clean cask, leave open the barrel until fermentation ceases, then stop the bung tightly.

SWEET CURRANT WINE.—To every quart of juice allow three pounds No. 1 coffee sugar, and two quarts of clean soft water. Never let the currants stand overnight without scalding. Press out the juice, and mix in it the water and sugar; this is the receipt for one gallon of wine. If a barrel is used, be particular to have it clean and sweet. Pour the mixture in the barrel, and tack over tne bung cotton cloth, to prevent the wine from running over. The barrel should contain thirty gallons, allowing three gallons for fermenting room; as soon as the fermentation ceases, close the bung-hole, and place the barrel where it will remain for six months. The longer wine remains without bottling, the more wine there will be to the gallon, and the greater will be the body of the wine. The currant wine already described is the rule which we have followed for several years, and the wine has been mistaken for raisin wine by persons who are called good judges. The older the better. The following rules for currant wines are from the best authority, but untested by ourselves.

WHITE CURRANT WINE.—Heat forty pounds of white currants, press out the juice, and add four gallons of soft water. Dissolve twenty-five pounds of white sugar in the juice, wash out the pulp with more water, strain and add it to the juice, and fill up with soft water until the whole measures nineteen gallons. In respect to managing the wine, the first rule gives full directions.

RED CURRANT WINE.—Eight gallons of currants, and one quart of raspberries; scald and press out the juice, and to the seeds and skins add eleven gallons of cold water, add two pounds of beet-root sliced thin as possible; let them remain with the pulp and water twelve hours; then press out the mixture, and add the liquor to the juice. Dissolve in the mixture twenty pounds of good coffee sugar, and three ounces of red tartar in powder. When the fermentation ceases, close the bung, and leave the barrel stationary until wanted for bottling.

BLACK CURRANT WINE, No. 1.—Follow either of the above receipts, except the beets and raspberries, and allow for the same quantity of wine, two gallons less of fruit, than in the red currant wine.

BLACK CURRANT WINE, No. 2.—Six gallons of black currants, three of strawberries scalded, four ounces of red tartar, and twenty-five pounds good sugar; add eleven gallons soft water.

SPICED ELDERBERRY WINE.—Ten gallons of elderberries, ten gallons of soft water, boil and strain; eight ounces red tartar, forty-five pounds of white sugar; ferment with yeast. When in the cask add ginger, cloves, nutmeg, mace, in all four ounces of spices, and three ounces of bitter almonds. After fermentation has ceased, close the barrel tight, and rack it off when convenient.

CHERRY WINE.—Select morello cherries not overripe; pick them free from the stems, bruise the pulp without breaking the pits, and add to each gallon three pounds of sugar; let it remain over night, then pass it through a fine colander, put it in a cask, let it ferment, and draw off the wine as soon as clear. Some add a part of the kernels.

DAMSON WINE.—Boil eight gallons of fruit in eleven of water; strain, and add thirty pounds of sugar, six ounces of red tartar; strain and ferment as usual.

FRENCH CHERRY WINE.—Bruise, and extract the juice after heating to boiling heat, fifteen pounds of cherries, and two of red currants; add two-thirds of the kernels to each gallon of juice, with two pounds of sugar; cover the bung with cloth while fermenting. The cask should be as full of the mixture as possible without running over in fermenting. Bottle in two months if convenient; if not, close the bung, and leave the barrel undisturbed.

MULBERRY WINE.—Bruise the mulberries before they are quite ripe; add as many gallons of soft water as there is fruit; let it stand over night, then press out the juice, and to every gallon of liquor allow three pounds of sugar. Ferment in the usual manner.

APRICOT OR PEACH WINE.—Bruise the fruit when nearly ripe, and reduce the pulp to paste; to eight pounds allow one quart of water; bring it to a boil; squeeze out the juice; add to every gallon two pounds loaf-sugar. Ferment in the usual method. Bottle when clear, if convenient; if not, leave the cask undisturbed, and the bung tightly plugged.

STRAWBERRY WINE, No. 1.—Scald the fruit, press out the juice; to every quart add three pounds of loaf-sugar and two quarts of water; pour the water over the pulp of the fruit, wash it well, and strain it in the juice. Ferment as directed for currant wine. Leave the barrel six months undisturbed before bottling.

STRAWBERRY WINE, No. 2.—Prepare as above, allowing to one quart of juice two pounds of sugar and one quart of soft water. Ferment as directed for currant wine.

RASPBERRY WINE, No. 1.—Allow for every gallon of juice eight pounds of sugar and eight quarts of water. Ferment as other wines.

RASPBERRY WINE, No. 2.—To every quart of juice add two quarts of soft water and three pounds of loaf-sugar; boil the fruit, press out the juice, wash the pulp in the water, and strain it in the wine.

GINGER WINE, No. 1.—Boil in nine gallons of soft water twelve ounces of bruised ginger until the water is highly flavored; add eighteen pounds nice sugar, and when nearly cold, a little hop yeast. Rack off as soon as clear, and bottle immediately.

GOOSEBERRY WINE.—Take forty pounds of nice large gooseberries before they commence to turn ripe, but not before fully grown; remove the blossoms and tails; bruise the fruit without crushing the seeds or skins; add to the pulp four gallons of soft water, stir and mash the fruit in the water until the whole pulp is cleared from the skin; let it stand for six hours, strain it through a coarse bag or sieve that will not let through the seeds; bring the water and juice to boiling heat, and dissolve thirty pounds of white sugar, and add it to the liquor; pass a gallon of water through the mass, strain, and add it to the mixture; measure the wine, and add soft water until it measures ten gallons. Let it ferment as currant wine. Leave the barrel tightly bunged after the fermentation has ceased, until it is drawn off to bottle.

RHUBARB WINE, No. 1.—Chop the rhubarb plant, drain off the juice, and add to every quart, one quart of water and two of sugar. Let it ferment, and bottle when clear.

RHUBARB WINE, No. 2.—Chop the stalks to fifty pounds of rhubarb, allow thirty pounds of sugar, press the juice, add the sugar and sufficient water to make nine gallons of wine; put it in a cask, cover with cloth until fermentation ceases, plug the barrel for three months, and then draw off the wine and bottle it. If not convenient to bottle, draw it off in a clean cask that it will fill entirely full. Wine barrels ought always to be filled full after the fermentation is over.

RAISIN WINE, No. 1.—Procure fresh raisins (the Smyrna or Malaga make the best wine), pick the raisins free from stems, dried, and imperfect fruit; soak in three gallons of hot water thirty pounds of chopped raisins, let them steep twenty-four hours, then press the fruit through a strong canvas bag or sieve to obtain all the juice possible from the fruit without crushing the seeds of the raisins; add an ounce of rude tartar, set the barrel in a warm cellar, and add to the liquor three pounds of white sugar dissolved in two gallons more of hot water, shake well to mix the liquors, set it in a moderately warm cellar, and cover the barrel with a blanket as soon as the first fermentation has ceased. Rack off the wine into a clean cask, bung it up, and leave the wine without disturbing the barrel for three months; rack it again in a clean cask and close the bung. It will be fit to bottle in twelve months.

RAISIN WINE, No. 2.—Soak in three gallons of hot water for forty-eight hours, sixty pounds of chopped Smyrna raisins, wash out the pulp, and pass it through a coarse sieve, discarding the skins and seeds; add another gallon of water to the mash, wash the pulp clean, and strain it as before; add an ounce of red tartar in powder, shake well, set the barrel in the cellar, and keep it covered with a blanket through the first fermentation, to preserve equality of temperature in the wine; when the first fermentation ceases, rack off the wine in a clean cask, and be particular to preserve equality of temperature in the cellar; at the end of three months again rack the wine, and bottle in about twelve months.

RAISIN WINE, No. 3.—Three pounds of raisins chopped fine, one pound of sugar, and one gallon of water; to the chopped raisins pour one quart of water heated to 120°, let it stand half an hour to dissolve the sugar of the raisins; stir the fruit and water with the hand until the sugar is entirely dissolved; pour the fruit and water over a coarse sieve, and let it drain, pressing but little; take up the skins and press them in the hand, and then return them to the dish or tub in which they were first soaked; heat a quart of water to 160°, and pour it over the mash; go over the same process as before, and repeat the process the third and fourth time. Dissolve one pound of white sugar in the liquor, warm the cask in which the wine is to be put, and keep up the temperature to from 55° to 60°. Let the wine remain in the cask ten months before bottling.

RAISIN SHERRY.—One pound of chopped raisins, one quart of soft water boiled and cooled; mix and let it stand one month, stirring frequently; take the raisins from the cask and put the liquor in a closely stopped vessel; in four weeks rack it clear, leaving out all sediment; if, at the first racking, it is muddy in the least, repeat the process until the liquor is perfectly clear; measure and add to every five gallons, three pounds of loaf-sugar, the juice of six oranges, and the yellow rind infused in one quart of white French brandy; mix the whole in a cask, keep the temperature even, and bottle in about three months.

GRAPE WINE, No. 2.—One gallon of grapes free from stems and blemishes, one gallon of soft boiled water; bruise the grapes and let them stand with the water seven days without stirring; draw off the liquor, and to every gallon allow three pounds of loaf-sugar; put it in a barrel, cover with a blanket, and close the bung as soon as the wine ceases to hiss. It will be fit for bottling in from six to nine months.

GRAPE WINE, No. 3.—Pick over carefully Catawba grapes, bruise, and add to each gallon of fruit one quart of soft boiled water; let it stand one week, draw off the juice, and to each gallon allow one pound of loaf-sugar; let the bung remain open until the wine ceases to hiss, and then close tightly. Keep a blanket over the barrel until the wine is bottled, unless the cellar maintains a temperature of from 55° to 60°. It will be fit to bottle in from nine to twelve months.

EXCELLENT GINGER WINE, No. 2.—Ten gallons soft water, fifteen pounds loaf-sugar clarified with the whites of six eggs; bruise half a pound of white ginger, boil half an hour; rub off the thin yellow rind of twelve lemons, and pour on the lemon peel the liquor boiling hot; when cool, mix into the liquor a gill of good yeast, and put it in a cask, retaining two quarts of the liquor, in which dissolve two ounces of shred isinglass; mix it with the wine and shake well; let it stand open over night, then close the bung, and bottle in three weeks. It will be fit to use in three months.

PARSNIP WINE.—To eighteen pounds of sweet parsnips add three gallons of water, boil soft, and press the liquor through a sieve; add to each gill three pounds of loaf-sugar; when nearly cold, add yeast; let the wine stand open ten days, stirring from the bottom several times each day; then put it in a cask, and fill up with liquor reserved for the purpose, as it works over.

*TOMATO WINE.—One quart of the juice to one pound of sugar; it will ferment without yeast; this wine is much thought of in some places, and is easy to make.

TO CLEANSE A WINE BARREL.—It is necessary, in preparing a new barrel for wine, to scald it in salt and water, and afterwards soak it in two cold waters; after which heat a little wine or pure spirits and rinse out the barrel; when an old cask is emptied, drain it thoroughly, burn a brimstone match in the barrel, and close the bung immediately. The wine casks should be raised from the cellar floor about six inches. The temperature should be kept between 55° and 60°, the cellar clean, and protected from currents of air.

SPRUCE BEER.—Boil to a jelly half a pound of fine starch, and add to it one and a half pound of strained honey, and one gallon of soft water, allow for three times this receipt two ounces of the essence of spruce, add yeast, and close the cask as soon as fermentation ceases. It will be fit to use in two days, and will not keep a very long time.

MOLASSES BEER.—Mix four quarts of molasses with thirteen gallons of water and three ounces of hops, boil for half an hour, strain and add yeast.

BOTTLED TABLE BEER.—Nine gallons of water, six pounds of molasses, and eight ounces of the essence of spruce, and a half-pint of yeast; skim off the yeast as it rises, and when the fermentation has nearly ceased, bottle the beer in strong bottles, and wire down the corks. Ginger, lemon, or any other flavoring can be substituted for spruce.

BLACKBERRY WINE, No. 1.—Scald the fruit, press out the juice, and allow for every quart two of soft water and three pounds of white coffee sugar; let the bung remain open until all fermentation ceases, after which close the bung and place the barrel where it will not be disturbed for several months. Bottle the wine eight months after it is made.

BLACKBERRY WINE, No. 2.—Cover the fruit with boiling water; when sufficiently cool, bruise the fruit, and let it stand until the berries begin to rise to the top, then drain off the clear liquor; measure, and add to every gallon two pounds of sugar; stir it well, and let it stand open a week or ten days, then draw off the wine, and pass it through a jelly bag. Dissolve in a little of the wine half an ounce of isinglass to every three gallons, and mix it through the wine; if not quite clear, filter before bottling.

CHAPTER II.

FRUIT BRANDIES.

PEACH BRANDY, No. 1.—Take one gallon nice-flavored peaches, remove the skins, mash and put them in two gallons of white French brandy, crack the pits from one peck of peaches, and add the whole nut to the brandy; let it stand two months, then strain the liquor through filtering paper, and bottle it. It is fine for sauces.

ANOTHER PEACH BRANDY, No. 2.—Take four gallons of deodorized pure spirits; peel half a bushel of peaches, crack the pits, and put the whole in a thin cotton bag; put the bag in a clean cask, head it up, and pour in the pure spirits; shake it frequently, and when it is needed it will be found a pleasant flavored liquor for cooking purposes.

PLUM BRANDY, No. 1.—Take two gallons of plums, bruise them and break the pits; put the fruit in a four-gallon keg, and fill it with French brandy.

ANOTHER PLUM BRANDY, No. 2.—Take two gallons of green gages very ripe, boil them in just enough water to cover them; to the fruit add one gallon of white French brandy and two pounds of sugar; cork tightly, and after two months filter the liquor.

STRAWBERRY BRANDY, No. 1.—Take eight quarts of strawberries, mash them, and add to them four pounds loaf-sugar; stir them in one gallon of French brandy, put them in a four-gallon jug, tie over the mouth of the jug a cotton cloth, let it stand three weeks, then cork tightly; bottle when six months old.

STRAWBERRY BRANDY, No. 2.—To every gallon of strawberries, add one of deodorized pure spirits, let it stand three months before drawing off; when ready to bottle, pass the liquor through a filtering paper, until quite clear.

WHITE CURRANT BRANDY.—To one gallon of currant juice, add two quarts of deodorized pure spirits, and four pounds of sugar; let it stand three months before bottling.

RED CURRANT BRANDY.—To one gallon of the juice add five pounds of sugar, and two quarts of deodorized pure spirits; draw off and bottle the brandy after three months.

BLACK CURRANT BRANDY.—Boil a half-bushel of black currants with two gallons of water, half an hour; after the fruit cools, add four gallons of the best deodorized pure spirits, stir it briskly, and strain the liquor, squeezing it until all the juice is out of the fruit; add to the liquor eight pounds of sugar, put it in a clean cask, wash the fruit again in one gallon of water and one of pure spirits mixed; press it well, and add four pounds more sugar, put this in the cask, and shake it thoroughly. It can be used in one month, but will improve by age; is useful in bowel complaints.

ELDERBERRY BRANDY.—To every gallon of brandy, add one of elderberries; let it stand one month before using. It can be spiced if desirable.

BLACKBERRY BRANDY, No. 1.—Take equal parts of brandy and blackberry juice; add to every gallon one pound of loaf-sugar. This is excellent for bowel complaints.

BLACKBERRY BRANDY, No. 2.—To every gallon of the fruit, allow one of deodorized pure spirits; mix them in a barrel, and let the berries dissolve in the spirits. This is made in large quantities, and sold at high prices for bowel complaints, under the name of blackberry brandy.

RASPBERRY BRANDY, No. 1.—Allow for every quart of the juice of the fruit, one pound of sugar and one quart of brandy.

RASPBERRY BRANDY, No. 2.—Put in a barrel eight gallons of raspberries, twelve pounds of sugar, three gallons of water, and twelve gallons of deodorized pure spirits; stir it up every day for two weeks, and then let it stand; when bottled it must be filtered.

CHERRY BRANDY.—Crush cherries, allowing one quart to every gallon of spirits; it can be made of any variety of the cherry, and with either deodorized pure spirits, or brandy. These extracts of fruit in brandy will be found much better for pudding sauces than any brandy that can be bought at the shops.

CHAPTER III.

FRUIT VINEGARS

CURRANT VINEGAR.—To make a barrel, mash two bushels of currants, press out the juice, and wash the pulp free from the acid of the fruit in filtered rain-water; put the juice in a barrel; add to the water in which the pulp was washed two gallons of molasses; dissolve it thoroughly, and pour it in the barrel; add sufficient rain-water to make the barrel three-quarters full. Stir into one gallon of water a teacup of hop yeast, and add it to the other ingredients. If the vinegar is not needed until winter, omit the yeast. Set the barrel in the sun, and place in the bung-hole a junk bottle. The next fall add eight gallons of soft rain-water, which will make the barrel full of vinegar; shake the barrel, while turning, every day.

STRAWBERRY VINEGAR.—Take two gallons of strawberries, small inferior ones are just as good as any, mix in them eight pounds of sugar, and jam them very fine; add four gallons of soft water, and put the whole into a clean cask, where it will keep warm.

RASPBERRY VINEGAR.—Take six quarts of raspberry juice, twelve pounds of sugar, and three gallons of water; put the juice, water, and sugar together, and put them in a clean cask; shake them well; put the pulp of the fruit in one gallon of water, with three table-spoons of yeast, and one pound of sugar; let it stand until it has well worked, then strain it and add the liquid to the cask.

PEACH VINEGAR.—Mash overripe peaches, and mix them in water; there should be enough of the fruit to flavor the water, so as to taste as strong of peaches as cider vinegar, half reduced with water, does of apples; to every gallon of the water add four ounces of brown sugar, and a little yeast until turned, set the cask in the sun with a junk bottle in the bung-hole.

CHERRY VINEGAR.—Beat up three bushels of cherries in a tuo, and fill it with water; let them soak two days, then drain them, and press the fruit in a bag to save all the juice; to this water and juice add half as many gallons of water as there is of the liquid, and add four ounces of sugar to each gallon of the preparation. Keep it warm while fermenting.

PLUM VINEGAR.—Allow for each gallon of water two quarts of any common plum, and soak the fruit until the whole flavor is imparted to the water; to each gallon allow half a pint of sugar; set the barrel in a warm place and shake it daily; there should be kept in the bung a black junk bottle.

GOOSEBERRY VINEGAR.—To two quarts of mashed gooseberries full grown, but green, allow three quarts of water; let the fruit soak two days, then strain; press out the juice, and add a pint of sugar to each gallon; add yeast, and let it ferment.

BLACKBERRY VINEGAR.—To every gallon of mashed blackberries allow two of water and half a pound of sugar; mix them together, and put pulp and all in a clean cask; add a little yeast if it is necessary to hasten fermentation; if not, set the barrel in the sun, and shake three times every day; put in the bung-hole a junk bottle; when it is drawn for use, commence near the top of the barrel, and draw down, boring new holes as needed, or the pulp will be in the way. If convenient, drain it off after a few months.

PEAR VINEGAR.—If you have more pears than you can use, and they are spoiling, make them into vinegar. We have made excellent vinegar from the water in which pears were boiled for preserves. The pears should be ground and pressed like apples for cider, and used the same way; or they may be boiled and pressed, and the juice and water sweetened with molasses.

WHORTLEBERRY VINEGAR.—Press the fruit, and add to each gallon of mashed fruit six quarts of water and one pound of sugar; or it may be made with one quart of the juice of the fruit to two of water, and no sugar. When it is drawn for use, commence near the top of the barrel and draw down, or the pulp will be in the way. If desired, it can be racked off after it is soured.

RHUBARB VINEGAR.—Pick the stalks, chop them fine, and drain off the juice; to every quart of the juice allow three of water and one pound of sugar; add the mother from vinegar, and put the whole in a clean cask; set it in a warm place until soured.

APPLE VINEGAR.—Whenever apples are used in the family, boil the skins and cores in as little water as will cover them; sweeten slightly with the rinsings of sweetmeats, and put it in a cask or jug; when making cider apple sauce, a half-barrel can be made with but little trouble. If apples are decaying, boil them up, strain the liquor, and make vinegar. It will take but little molasses to sweeten it.

CRAB APPLE VINEGAR.—Grind the apples, press the juice, and reduce it one-third, after which treat it like common cider vinegar. (*See* CIDER VINEGAR.)

GRAPE VINEGAR.—Take wild grapes, press out the juice, reduce it one-half, and add to a barrel three gallons of molasses; keep it warm, and let it work well before putting in the bung.

CHAPTER IV.

CORDIALS, EXTRACTS, ETC.

THE FAMOUS CREAM OF NECTAR—*An English Recipe.*—Four pounds of white sugar and three of water; put it over a slow fire in a porcelain kettle; when milk-warm, add the whites of two well-beaten eggs; bring it nearly to boiling heat; skim well and bring it to a boil, and strain immediately; when cool add six ounces tartaric acid. Steep a quarter of a teaspoonful of cloves with the water and sugar, or when cool add some other flavoring. It should stand two days before using. Add a wine-glass to a glass of ice-water, in which is dissolved half a teaspoonful of super-carbonate of soda.

CREAM OF ORANGES.—Two dozen oranges, six pounds of loaf-sugar, orange-flower water one gill, spirits of wine three quarts, tincture of saffron one-fourth of an ounce; chop the oranges fine, and let the ingredients remain together one month, then filter and bottle.

CARAWAY CORDIAL.—Put into one quart of brandy two ounces of caraway seed and half a pound of loaf-sugar; draw it off after it has steeped two weeks.

LEMON CORDIAL.—Take two dozen of fine lemons, and four pounds of loaf-sugar; steep the yellow part only of the skin in one gallon of the best French brandy. Having rolled the lemons, squeeze out all the juice and the pulp in one gallon of water, dissolve the sugar in the water, and pass it through a jelly-bag. The peel of the lemon should have been steeping for twenty-four hours in the brandy;

strain it in the acid water and sugar, and add three pints of boiling hot milk. Let it stand twenty-four hours, and then strain clear and bottle it.

EXTRACT OF ROSE.—Take a gallon bottle, fill it nearly full of rose-leaves packed tight, and fill the bottle with best brandy; as the leaves dissolve, add more.

EXTRACT OF PEACH.—Blanch a pint of peach pits, and add to them one quart of the best brandy or pure deodorized spirits.

EXTRACT OF NECTARINE.—Blanch one pint of nectarine pits and half a pint of peach, pour over them one quart of pure deodorized spirits.

EXTRACT OF LEMON.—Use the yellow only of the peel; if any of the white is used the extract will be bitter. To a dozen lemons, juice and peel, allow one quart of the best brandy and four pounds of sugar.

EXTRACT OF LEMON PEEL.—Grate carefully the thin yellow rind of two dozen lemons, pour over it one quart of deodorized pure spirits, and cork tight. Strain it as needed.

ORANGE PEEL EXTRACT.—Rub one pound of loaf-sugar on two dozen oranges, so as to extract all the oil; wet the sugar with one quart of the best pure deodorized spirits, and cork tight.

EXTRACT OF CELERY SEED.—To an ounce of celery seed put a pint of deodorized spirits, and cork tightly; shake the bottle frequently.

EXTRACT OF SAGE.—Take a gallon bottle, fill it two-thirds full of sage wilted in the sun; press it tight, and fill the bottle with pure deodorized spirits; use the extract in place of the dried sage.

LEMONADE.—Rub some of the sugar on the peel of the lemon to extract the oil; roll the lemons under the hand on the table, and press out all the juice; add to every lemon two heaping table-spoons of loaf-sugar; mix it thoroughly with the lemon; fill the pitcher one-quarter full of broken ice, and add water.

ORANGEADE is made as above with less sugar. Oranges and lemons mixed make a fine ade.

PINEAPPLEADE.—Cut the pineapple fine, and mix the fruit with sugar and ice and water. Orange, lemon, and pineapple mixed are fine.

CURRANTADE.—Take a goblet one-quarter full of currant juice; add sugar and a table-spoonful of pounded ice, and fill with cold water.

STRAWBERRYADE.—Mash strawberries, sweeten to taste; fill the glass half-full of pounded ice, and fill up with the sweetened juice. The two above are very nice for invalids, and can be made of the syrups, though the fresh fruit is better.

RASPBERRY VINEGAR FOR A BEVERAGE.—Pour one quart of wine vinegar over three quarts of raspberries; let it stand one day; press out the liquid, and continue the same operation for three days, and then bottle the liquid. Use it in ice water, with or without sugar.

TO MULL WINE.—Boil any spices in very little water, strain, and to half a pint of spiced water add one pint of wine, with sugar to taste. Serve hot with slices of toasted bread; add lemon or orange if desirable.

EGG NOG.—Beat the yolks and whites of six eggs separately; add to the yolks sugar, a quart of new milk or thin sweet cream, and half a pint of French brandy; add the whites of the eggs beaten stiff, and stir them through the nog.

SANGAREE.—Take half Madeira wine and half water, and the juice of a lemon.

ENGLISH MILK PUNCH.—Add boiling milk to lemonade; strain, and add brandy and spices.

COMMON MILK PUNCH.—Beat an egg light, mix it in milk, and add brandy and nutmeg.

MISSISSIPPI TRAVELLER.—Squeeze half a lemon with two teaspoonfuls of loaf-sugar; add one fresh egg, and wine to double the quantity; then add two table-spoons of water and sufficient ice broken the size of a small hickory nut to fill the tumbler; put over the tumbler a tin lemonade mixer, which is a tin tumbler holding about a pint, shake the mixture briskly until the egg is cut and in a perfect froth. The best wine for this is pure port, though currant and other domestic wines do very well as a substitute.

PART VII.

CATSUPS, SALADS, FLAVORED VINEGARS, PICKLES, AND MANGOES.

CHAPTER I.

CATSUPS.

MUSHROOM CATSUP.—Put layers of mushroom and salt in an earthen dish, or if a large quantity of the catsup is to be made, in a cask; let them lie three hours, by which time the salt will have penetrated the mushrooms; then bruise them in a mortar or in some other efficient manner, and let them remain three days, stirring them from the bottom three times each day; then put them in a jar, and add a few peppercorns, cloves, and allspice. Set the jar in cold water, bring it to boiling heat, and boil gently one hour; after which drain off the juice without pressure, and boil gently until it is reduced one-half, skimming it as it boils. When sufficiently reduced pour it in a crock, let it stand a day to settle, and strain it through a thick cloth, without disturbing the sediment at the bottom; bottle in half-pint bottles; add to each bottle one teaspoon of brandy and cork tight. If it moulds it must be boiled again.

WALNUT CATSUP, No. 1.—Bruise green walnuts, and press out the juice of the nut; boil the juice until half reduced; add a little essence of anchovy, mace, cloves, and pepper, without grinding, in equal parts, a clove of garlic, and a little salt; let the catsup and spices simmer together until the liquor measures one-third of the original amount; strain out all the spices; add half as much of the very best wine vinegar as the liquor measures; let it stand in an earthen jar until it settles, then filter it until clear; bottle and seal tight.

WALNUT CATSUP, No. 2.—Bruise the nuts, press out the juice; add to a gallon an ounce of cinnamon, half an ounce of mace, and a quarter of an ounce of cloves; put the spices in a bag without rolling or grinding; boil until the liquor is half reduced; pour it in a jar; add a little salt; let it settle two days, and filter until clear; bottle in pints or half-pints, and seal the corks. It is better two years old.

OYSTER CATSUP.—Pound fine fresh oysters in a mortar with a few cloves, mace, salt, and Cayenne; pass them through a sieve, and thin with strong vinegar poured over boiling hot; bottle and seal tightly. In this catsup the cloves must be barely perceived; if too strong the other spices will be lost.

CATSUP FOR MUTTON CHOPS.—Three teaspoons of black pepper, three of mustard, one of allspice, three of salt, mix the spices with two quarts of grated horseradish, half an onion or not, as desired; beat the ingredients together quickly; strain the liquor from the radish, add one-quarter as much ten per cent. vinegar as there is liquid; bottle in half-pint bottles, and cork immediately.

CELERY CATSUP.—Mix an ounce of celery seed ground, with a teaspoon of ground white pepper; bruise half a dozen oysters with a teaspoon of salt; mix and pass the whole through a sieve; pour over the mixture one quart of the best white wine vinegar; bottle and seal tight.

PEACH CATSUP.—Boil ripe peaches over steam with the pits; press out all the juice; to every quart allow a pound of loaf-sugar; boil without the sugar until it is reduced one-third; add to each quart of juice before boiling a teaspoon of broken, not ground, mace, two of cinnamon, half a teaspoon of cloves, and one of peppercorns; boil all together; when half reduced remove the spices, add the sugar, boil until quite thick, and reduce to a convenient consistency for bottling with strong vinegar.

PLUM CATSUP.—Boil whole plums over steam; press out the juice; pass the pulp through the sieve; boil in a quart of the juice a teaspoon of broken cinnamon, one of mace, and half as much of cloves and pepper until reduced half; add this to the pulp, with two pounds of loaf-sugar, and heat it, stirring constantly; when the sugar is dissolved, reduce the catsup with one quart of ten per cent. vinegar.

CHERRY CATSUP.—To every pound of fruit allow one pound of coffee sugar; boil the fruit and sugar together, drain off the syrup, and to every quart add a teaspoon of pepper, one of mace, two of cinnamon, one of ginger, and half a teaspoon of cloves; boil until the syrup is highly flavored; pass the fruit through a sieve, strain the syrup, add it to the pulp; boil all together until of the consistency of very thick molasses; thin with ten per cent. vinegar until it is only of the consistency of common catsup. Bottle while hot and seal immediately.

GOOSEBERRY CATSUP.—Pick clean ripe gooseberries, allow a pint of water for two quarts of fruit; boil it until the fruit is quite tender; then add a teaspoon of ground cinnamon, one of mace, half as much pepper, and the same of cloves; stir the spices in the fruit; let it simmer a few moments, and press out all the juice; add to each quart one pound of sugar; reduce until the syrup is near to becoming a jelly, and then thin with the best vinegar until of the consistency of molasses. Bottle and cork tightly.

GRAPE CATSUP.—Boil grapes over water; to each quart allow a teaspoon of broken cinnamon, one of mace, one half-teaspoon of cloves; simmer over water one hour; strain, and add to every quart one pound of sugar; reduce nearly to jelly, and add wine or vinegar to thin it to the proper consistency.

BLACKBERRY CATSUP.—Cover the fruit with boiling water; press out the liquor, add whole pepper, mace, cinnamon, white mustard, each one teaspoonful for every two quarts; reduce by boiling one quarter; strain and boil until very thick, and reduce with vinegar of the best quality. Bottle hot and seal immediately.

RASPBERRY CATSUP.—Boil one gallon of the fruit in one quart of vinegar; strain, and add mace, cinnamon, mustard, and ginger, each half a teaspoonful without grinding; boil half an hour slowly; strain, and measure the liquor; to every quart add one pound of sugar; boil until of proper consistency; if not sufficiently acid, add citric acid dissolved in very little vinegar.

WHORTLEBERRY CATSUP.—Add to every gallon of fruit two quarts of boiling water; let it stand all night; in the morning draw off the juice; pass the pulp through a sieve; add to each gallon of the liquor a teaspoonful of each of the following spices: mace, cinnamon, white mustard, ginger, pepper; boil one hour gently; strain off the liquor; add to every quart half a pound of sugar; stir in the pulp, and boil it in the spiced juice; dissolve a teaspoon of the citric acid in a little of the juice reserved for the purpose; add it to the catsup, and if too thick thin with vinegar or wine.

CUCUMBER CATSUP.—Grate large cucumbers before they begin to turn yellow; drain out the juice and put the pulp through a sieve to remove the large seeds; fill a bottle half-full of the pulp, discarding the juice, and add the same quantity of ten per cent. vinegar; cork tightly; when used, add pepper and salt; salt kills the vinegar if put in when made. This is almost like a fresh-sliced cucumber when opened for use.

TOMATO CATSUP.—Select tomatoes not overripe, skin and strain the tomatoes; to every gallon add three table-spoons of salt, three of ground black pepper, three of mustard, and one teaspoon of ground allspice; mix the spices in a part of the tomato, and strain them through a sieve; put in a small bag four large pods of sweet peppers, and if relished, one onion, and boil them with the catsup while it is being reduced; add the expressed juice of one quart of horseradish, and reduce it until it is of the proper consistency to pour from the bottles without difficulty; let the catsup remain in the bottles, with a piece of cotton cloth tied loosely on the neck, for three months to ripen, when cork and seal tightly.

CHAPTER II.

SALADS.

To DRESS LETTUCE.—Bring in a head or more of lettuce one hour before dinner; lay it in cold water; look it over carefully, and lay the leaves, one by one, around the edge of the dish, leaving the heart in the centre. (*See* Part III., Chap. VII.)

SALAD OF LETTUCE, No. 1.—Select lettuce; examine each leaf carefully; chop very slightly; boil four eggs hard; slice them; lay them around the plate; dust over pepper, salt, and a dust of mustard; and pour over the whole, cold vinegar.

SALAD OF LETTUCE, No. 2.—Look over lettuce very carefully; chop it sufficiently fine to eat at table without cutting with the knife; prepare a dressing with egg, butter, salt, pepper, and mustard worked to a paste; add vinegar, and pour the dressing over the lettuce.

SALAD OF WILTED LETTUCE, No. 3.—Having examined the lettuce leaf by leaf, chop it fine; heat sufficient vinegar boiling hot to cover the salad, beat up two eggs very light, and mix them in the vinegar; when it is nearly boiling hot, add a table-spoonful of butter, pepper, salt, and mixed mustard, and pour it over the lettuce.

LETTUCE WITH FINE EGG SALAD, No. 4.—Beat up the yolks of two eggs very light; mix in a table-spoon of cold butter, a teaspoon of mustard, half as much black pepper, and the same of salt; beat the eggs and other ingredients together. Heat nearly boiling hot a half pint of strong vinegar, remove it from the fire, and thicken it with the egg, butter, and spices; if not hot enough to thicken by the partial cooking of the egg, heat it, beating it constantly while heating; when a little thickened, cool it quickly, or it will be either too thick or curdle; if too thick, thin with vinegar. Having looked over the lettuce, chop it slightly, and pour the sauce over the salad cold.

COMMON SALAD DRESSING, No. 1.—Boil eggs hard, peel them, and while hot add butter, pepper, salt, and mustard, work these ingredients well together, and then add vinegar.

CHICKEN SALAD, No. 2.—Boil tender two good-sized chickens, skin and pick them free from bones, using only the white meat. Boil nine eggs one hour, and work them to a smooth paste with a wooden spoon, add half a pint of melted butter, and work into the egg and butter mustard, salt, and pepper to suit the taste; it should be highly seasoned; mix the ingredients well, and add a small teacup of grated horseradish, and one pint of strong vinegar. Chop fine half a head of cabbage and as much blanched celery; mix the chicken, cabbage, and celery together, and just before serving add the sauce. If celery can be had in abundance use no cabbage; if celery cannot be obtained, use cabbage, with extract of celery. If neither cabbage nor celery is in season, use blanched lettuce. (*See* Part III., Chap. VII.)

CHICKEN SALAD, No. 1, under the head of celery.

A VERY FINE SALAD SAUCE, No. 2.—Pass through a sieve with a wooden spoon, the yolks of two hard-boiled eggs, add two table-spoonfuls of sweet oil, or melted butter, work the butter and egg to a paste, add a teaspoon of made mustard, and half as much salt, and pepper; work these ingredients well together, and add gradually three table-spoons of strong vinegar. Mince lettuce, and just before serving, mix with it lobster, chicken, the white meat of veal, or any cold fowl, and add the sauce.

SALAD DRESSING WITHOUT EGGS, No. 3.—Take one part fresh salad oil and two parts strong vinegar, add pepper, salt, and mustard; send it to the table in a boat, with the leaves of the salad nicely washed, slightly chopped or not, as desired.

SWEET SALAD SAUCE, No. 4.—To one pint of strong vinegar, add one-fourth of a pound of sugar; pour it over the lettuce cold, after it is on the table.

LOBSTER SALAD.—Abstract all the meat from the body and claws of a well-boiled lobster, cut it fine, and mash the coral with a wooden spoon. Wash the blanched part of a head of lettuce, chop it fine, and mix it with the lobster. To make the sauce: take a pinch of salt, half as much Cayenne, a teaspoon of French mustard, four large table-spoons of fresh salad oil, and four table-spoons of the strongest vinegar; have ready the yolks of three boiled eggs, mash them to a paste, and mix them and the coral in the sauce; the sauce should be added to the salad just before serving.

HORSERADISH.—Wash the roots, and scrape them free from the outside skin, grate them finely, and mix it with strong vinegar, and add to one pint of the grated horseradish, a teaspoon of loaf-sugar.

TO MIX MUSTARD.—One table-spoonful of best mustard, a salt-spoon of salt, one teaspoon of sugar, and water enough to make a paste; mix thoroughly, and add sufficient boiling water to cook and stiffen the mustard; work well, and add hot water, until it is of the proper consistency.

CUCUMBERS FOR THE AGED.—Peel nice young cucumbers, chop or grate them as fine as possible, saving all the liquor of the vegetable; chop two small onions fine, and mix them with the cucumbers; add strong vinegar, pepper, and salt; this salad should be served as soon as prepared, as the cucumbers soon wilt. The onions can be omitted.

CABBAGES AND CUCUMBERS.—Chop cabbage very fine, add to one quart of the chopped cabbage, a teacup of chopped cucumber, season with pepper, salt, and vinegar; this, when cucumbers are high, will be found a good substitute. It can be made during the winter with vinegar of cucumbers, or cucumber catsup; onions can be added, if relished; some persons who cannot eat cucumbers, will relish this salad.

RADISHES FOR THE AGED.—Peel tender radishes, grate them, add salt, and vinegar if desired. This manner of preparing radishes is more healthy for all; especially for persons who have poor teeth, and children who do not take time to masticate their food. Winter radishes grate nicely, and will be found a fine relish, when fresh salads cannot be obtained. (*See* Part III., Chap. VII.)

CELERY FOR THE AGED.—Take the blanched celery, cut it as fine as possible, add salt, and send it to the table, where vinegar and egg can be added, if desired. This salad should be served as soon as prepared, as it will be apt to turn brown; ornament the dish with green celery leaves. Onions can be prepared in the same manner, and will make a fine salad, for those who relish them.

TOMATO CHOWDER.—Four quarts of finely chopped green tomatoes, press the juice from the tomatoes, scald them in vinegar, but do not heat boiling hot, drain off all the vinegar, add three pods of large green peppers, and three onions chopped fine, one quart of grated horseradish, one-fourth of a box of mustard, black pepper the same, salt to the taste; cover with the best of vinegar, press it firmly, and set it in a cool place; the vinegar should completely cover the chowder, the onions can be omitted, adding more horseradish. It can be varied by adding chopped cucumbers to the tomatoes.

CHAPTER III.

FLAVORED VINEGARS.

CELERY VINEGAR.—Obtain ten per cent. vinegar; put into a muslin bag four ounces of celery seed, put the bag in a wide-mouthed bottle, holding three or four quarts, fill with the extra strong vinegar, and cork tight; set the bottle in cold water, heat it to boiling heat, take it from the bath, cork tightly, and set it in a cool place; this will be found a good substitute for celery, in all salads where this flavor is required.

VINEGAR OF MUSTARD.—Boil black mustard seed in strong vinegar until it is highly impregnated, then strain clear, and bottle for use; use it in salad sauces, which are to be made without thickening.

VINEGAR OF NASTURTIUMS.—Pick young nasturtium seeds, and put them in vinegar; when all the strength is extracted, throw out the seeds, and add more until the vinegar is very strongly flavored.

VINEGAR OF CUCUMBERS.—Chop cucumbers, pour over them cold vinegar very strong; as fast as the strength of the cucumbers is extracted, add more; the vinegar should be ten per cent. If the vinegar is not strong, it will become too much reduced by the juice of the fruit; when it is sufficiently strong, it should be equal, after it is flavored, to four per cent. vinegar, which is as strong as the common vinegar of the shops.

PEACH VINEGAR.—Blanch, by putting them in boiling water, one pint of peach pits; pour over them cold vinegar, as strong as can be obtained, and cork tightly.

ONION VINEGAR.—Take onions, or cloves of garlic, and put them in strong vinegar; it will take but a few drops to flavor salads.

CHILI VINEGAR.—Infuse fifty small ripe Cayenne peppers, chopped fine, in a quart of ten per cent. vinegar, for two weeks; when it will be ready to strain, and bottle.

BASIL VINEGAR.—Infuse basil leaves in best wine vinegar; when it has steeped two weeks, drain it off, press the basil, and add fresh leaves; continue to do this until the vinegar has the desired flavor, when cork and wire down.

GARLIC VINEGAR.—Take one quart of white wine vinegar, the juice of four lemons, six cloves of garlic, six cloves, half a nutmeg, and a few basil leaves; set the bottle in cold water, and heat it to boiling heat, cork tight, and let it stand for two weeks; then strain and cork tightly. It will take but two or three drops to add the flavor to soups, or sauces if desired. If the flavor of garlic is fairly discerned, it is disagreeable.

Eschalot Vinegar.—Chop eschalots, and to one quart of ten per cent. vinegar, put four ounces of eschalots; shake often for two weeks, then drain off, bottle and cork tight.

Tarragon Vinegar.—Fill a large wide-mouthed bottle with fresh tarragon leaves, picked from the stalk before the plant flowers; steep them in strong vinegar for fourteen days, or longer if convenient; strain clear; fill half-pint bottles with the vinegar, and cork tightly; this is used to flavor mustard and salads.

Vinegar of Marjoram.—Pick sweet marjoram leaves before the plant flowers; wilt them a little, and steep them in strong vinegar for two weeks, then bottle and cork tightly.

Savory Vinegar.—Steep summer savory in strong vinegar; when the vinegar is highly impregnated, strain, bottle, and cork.

Borage Vinegar.—Pick the flowers of borage; put them in a wide-mouthed jar, fill with strong vinegar, let them steep for three weeks, then strain, bottle, and cork. The flavor is somewhat like cucumbers.

Burnet Vinegar.—Pick the leaves before it flowers, pack them in jars, and pour over them strong vinegar, and steep one month; then strain off and cork.

Cinnamon Vinegar.—Bruise cassia buds and steep them in vinegar; let the buds remain, and strain the vinegar when wanted, as the strength of the buds is long in extracting.

Clove Vinegar.—Bruise two ounces of cloves, add one pint of strong vinegar, let it steep six weeks, then filter until clear, bottle in half-pint bottles, and cork tightly.

Cherry Vinegar.—Pick morello cherries free from stems, bruise them, and to one quart of fruit put two quarts of strong vinegar; let them steep one month, then strain and bottle.

Oyster Vinegar.—Boil oysters in strong vinegar, until the vinegar is highly flavored; add clove, mace, and pepper, to suit the taste, then strain and bottle.

Vinegar of Walnuts.—Bruise butternuts when not larger than a small hickory-nut, steep them in strong vinegar for two weeks, after which strain and bottle. It can be flavored with spices, or not, as desired, and is used to flavor fish sauces.

HORSERADISH VINEGAR.—Make this in the spring; to one quart of grated horseradish add one quart of strong vinegar, press the liquor out as soon as possible, bottle, cork, and seal immediately. This must be made as speedily as possible, or the flavor will escape before bottling; use one ounce bottles, as it will become tasteless if open one day.

VINEGAR OF GINGER.—Steep four ounces of crushed white ginger in two quarts of the strongest vinegar for two months; strain until quite clear, bottle, and cork tight.

VINEGAR OF MACE.—To one quart of the best white-wine vinegar put one ounce of rolled mace, cork the bottle, set it in cold water, and heat until it is nearly boiling hot, let it steep for four weeks before straining, or longer if convenient, then bottle and cork tightly.

VINEGAR FOR SOUSE.—Steep black peppercorns and white mustard seed in strong vinegar for four weeks, strain, and pour it over the souse after it is boiled tender.

VINEGAR FOR SOUSED FISH.—Steep in strong vinegar a few cloves, more peppercorns, mustard seed, and young walnuts bruised, until the vinegar is highly spiced; then strain, and cover the fish with the spiced vinegar; the fish must be boiled before it is soused.

WORMWOOD VINEGAR.—Bruise green wormwood; to one pound add one quart of strong vinegar, steep the wormwood and vinegar together, by setting the bottle in cold water, and heating to boiling heat; let the wormwood and vinegar remain together for two weeks, then strain, press out all the juice, and bottle. This is excellent for all sprains, and ought to be ready to use at any time.

HOP VINEGAR.—Steep one quarter of a pound of ripe, but not dry hops in one quart of strong vinegar, let it steep two weeks, and then press out the liquor; keep it for colds, quinsy, and throat troubles.

CHAPTER IV.

PICKLES AND MANGOES.

REMARKS ON PICKLING.—In the first place, be quite sure that the salt of which the brines are made is pure; much of the common barrelled salt is mixed with lime, in which case it will neither preserve meat nor vegetables. The object of using salt on vegetables is to reduce their fluids; if cucumbers are put in common strength vinegar when fresh picked, their natural fluid will reduce the vinegar so much, that there will not be sufficient strength left to preserve the pickles. Vinegar must be of proper strength; if too strong, it will eat the pickles; if not of sufficient strength, mould will form, and the pickles become soft and worthless. It is of no use to scald vinegar that moulds. It is want of strength that produces it; either add ten per cent. vinegar, until the percentage of the vinegar is raised to four per cent., or throw it away, and put fresh vinegar to the pickles. There is no better vinegar to be obtained for pickles than pure distilled high wine vinegar; this can be bought of the maker from ten to four per cent.; four per cent. is the proper strength for preserving cucumber pickles. Onions and mixed pickles require it much stronger. The strength of vinegar can be ascertained by the use of a glass tube called by vinegar makers Acetometer; the proper name for it is Acet-meter. The tincture of litmus is first put into the tube, then vinegar, and afterwards ammonia. It is impossible to give an idea of the instrument, but every housekeeper who makes her own pickles should possess one. They cost from three to twelve dollars; our own cost but three, and is in every respect equal to the high-price tubes. To ascertain the percentage of vinegar, pour into the tube the tincture of litmus, until it reaches the first mark on the scale; add vinegar to reach the third mark, turn the tube up and down, pressing your thumb on the mouth until the liquid turns red; then add ammonia until the vinegar has turned blue, which will give the percentage of the vinegar. When buying the tube, get directions of a chemist in regard to the proper strength of the ammonia. The measuring must be done with great accuracy, as half a drop makes a difference in the percentage. This is the only instrument that can be depended upon, to ascertain to a certainty the amount of acetic acid in vinegar, and without this knowledge of the strength of vinegar, housekeepers are liable to fail in their pickling.

To PICKLE CUCUMBERS.—Cut the cucumbers from the vines without bruising the stems; lay them carefully in a basket; take them to the cellar; sort and pack them in barrels, putting different sizes in separate barrels, spread a layer of salt between each layer of cucumbers; there should be sufficient salt to entirely cover the pickles between the layers. Continue to pack the cucumbers daily as they are picked, never using any but fine cucumbers, discarding all that are crooked or of slow growth. Keep boards over the pickles, and weight to press them under the brine, which will be formed without the addition of water, with the juice extracted from the fruit by the salt. Pickles packed in this manner may be preserved for years, if there are no impurities in the salt; but if the salt is mixed with lime, they will soon soften and spoil. In two months after the barrel is filled, take them from the brine, freshen and green. To green cucumbers, prepare alum-water; put the pickles in a vat or boiler, lined with tinned copper; heat the alum-water, and pour it over the pickles. This is the process which is usually employed by pickle-makers, except that they throw steam into the vats to heat the alum-water, and if managed properly the pickles may be greened with less action of copper than when scalded in the usual method in bright brass kettles. Take the pickles from the vat when a little green, and pour over them water boiling hot. If not greened sufficiently, repeat the hot water until they are the desired color, and when cold, put them in four per cent vinegar, let them remain until quite soured; then change to fresh vinegar, of four and a half per cent., which will keep the pickles hard and sour; add to a barrel six large peppers, without bruising, and keep the pickles under the vinegar with weights.

GHERKINS, OR PRICKLY CUCUMBERS.—Pick the gherkins when from half to two-thirds grown. Put them in strong brine in which a little alum has been dissolved; keep the pickles under the brine with weights; let them remain in the salted water three days; then take them out, and green them by covering with alum-water in a brass kettle half a day; then take them from the kettle, even if they have not greened, pour over them hot water, let them nearly cool, and repeat the process until the color is right. It takes heat to bring out the color. If soaked sufficiently in the brass to green without heat, the pickles would be poisoned; but in pursuing the course recommended in this chapter, the skin is slightly acted upon by the metal, and the after soaking in the hot water removes what little was absorbed of the acetate of copper by the vegetable. When pickles have a clear light green color, they have absorbed so much verdigris as to make them unhealthy; the color should be a dark green, nearly the color of grass. When the gherkins are freshened, and greened, put them in a keg, and pour over them hot vinegar; put a weight on them to keep them under the vinegar, and let them remain until quite sour, then add fresh vinegar. If to be spiced, steep spices in the first vinegar, but put none in the second, which should be four per cent., and put on cold. Unless gherkins are pickled when prime, and with care, they wilt and become flabby; unless they are brittle, they are a miserable pickle. Those who like can sugar the last vinegar.

Spiced Pickled Cucumbers, No. 1.—Cut carefully from the vines small cucumbers which have grown fast, and are neither crooked nor spotted. Put them in a jar, and pour over them weak salt and water. The next morning heat over the brine, and add more salt and a teaspoonful of pounded alum to every gallon. Let the cucumbers remain in the brine one week. Heat in a brass, not copper, kettle, a pail of water in which is dissolved a piece of alum as large as a butternut; heat the alum-water to boiling heat, put the cucumbers in the kettle, let them lie one hour; then pour over them boiling water three successive times, letting them stand each time sufficiently long to cool the water to blood heat, after which heat vinegar with spices and pour it over the cucumbers; let them stand one week. Then cover them with fresh vinegar, with more spices, and pour over them cold. The vinegar for spiced pickles should be full five per cent.

Spiced Cucumber Pickles, No. 2.—Having salted small cucumbers with brine, or by packing in salt, cover the bottom and sides of a brass kettle with leaves from a grape vine; put a layer of leaves and a layer of pickles in the kettle until it is quite full, covering over the top with the leaves; heat to boiling a pail of water, dissolve in the water two table-spoons of alum, pour the water over the pickles, and cover tight, and let them remain until cold; if not sufficiently greened, drain off the water without disturbing the cucumbers, heat the water again, and pour it over the pickles; do not let them stand in the kettle overnight, to become impregnated with the verdigris of the kettle; it is only necessary to set the color of the cucumber skins. Take out the cucumbers, and pour over them three times boiling water; this may be done three successive days, or all in the same day, as convenient; then pour over them hot vinegar, and leave them one week; then change the vinegar, and scatter in the keg ginger root, cloves, cinnamon, mustard, horseradish root, nasturtium seeds, and one pepper.

AN EASY METHOD OF PREPARING SPICED PICKLES, No. 3.—Take them from the brine when sufficiently salted, put them in a brass kettle with a table-spoonful of alum to a pailful of water, heat them, stirring frequently until the water is too hot to allow the cucumbers to be stirred with the hand. Let them cool in the kettle, and while cooling heat in a wash-boiler four pails of water to boiling heat, take the boiler from the fire, and put the cucumbers in a tub; when the water has cooled ten minutes, pour half of it on the cucumbers, stir them round, pour off the water and add the remainder; cover and let them cool gradually. The next day taste the pickles; if the taste of salt is perceived, and they are not sufficiently greened, pour over them again hot water; but if greened to suit, cover with cold water and repeat the operation until they are quite fresh; then scald a few spices in strong vinegar, and pour over the pickles, cover tight, and let them remain two weeks, then add fresh cold vinegar, with more spices. Pickles to spice should be picked quite small. The smaller the cucumbers, the sooner will they green and freshen.

To PREPARE SUMMER PICKLES.—Pick very small cucumbers, pour over them weak hot brine, let them cool, and pour over them hot vinegar and spices to the taste, they will be fit to use in twenty-four hours; but will not keep long.

CUCUMBERS PICKLED IN SUGAR.—Cut very small young cucumbers from the vines without bruising the spines or stem; put them in a colander, and pour water gently through it so as to rinse the cucumbers without bruising the spines; place in the bottom of the keg a thin layer of cheap sugar; that left in the bottom of molasses hogsheads, if dried, is as good as the best; add a layer of cucumbers and a layer of sugar until the keg is full, putting a good covering of sugar on the top; put a board and weight on the top to keep the cucumbers under the liquid, which will form with the juice of the fruit and the sugar. There should be as much sugar used, in preserving pickles in this manner, as there is salt when packing in salt. The juice and sugar ferment and form a vinegar which preserves the cucumbers beautifully, and leaves them a good color, without the trouble of greening. After the vinegar is well formed, and the cucumbers soured sufficiently, spices can be added if desirable.

Sweet Cucumber Pickles.—Freshen and green pickles as already described, then cover them with vinegar in which sugar is dissolved, in the proportion of one pound to the gallon, add spices or not, according to the taste.

Whiskey Pickled Cucumbers.—Select the cucumbers, pack them in barrels, and pour over them whiskey and rain water in equal proportions. The liquor must be the usual strength, and pure from sulphuric acid. Test the whiskey with litmus paper; if, on wetting it, the paper turns red, you may be sure it is diluted with water, sulphuric acid, and probably Cayenne. The whiskey and water should be added as the cucumbers are packed, always keeping them under the liquor by weights; the barrel should stand in a warm cellar, and when full may be placed in the sun. Cucumbers pickled in this manner are very acid, hard, and green, retaining the natural flavor of the fresh fruit, more than when salted. Peppers should be added when the vinegar has quite turned, and the pickles sufficiently soured. If spiced pickles are preferred, a few can be put in a crock with the vinegar spiced and peppered to suit the taste, or a few can be flavored by putting them in the mango tub.

Ripe Cucumbers.—Select cucumbers that show a little yellow; cut them open, remove the seeds, cut them lengthwise, in strips one and a half inch wide, soak them in salted water and alum two days. Then soak them half a day in cold water. Take two quarts of strong vinegar, scald and pour it over the cucumbers hot, let them stand overnight, then pack the cucumbers in a large-mouthed bottle; dissolve in one quart of strong vinegar, one pound of sugar, strew in the bottle spices to suit the taste, cover the fruit with the sweetened vinegar, cork, and let it stand all night; the next morning set the bottle in the water bath, and heat the water to boiling heat; cork and set in a cool place.

Pickled Beans.—Select young crispy beans, and string them; put them in hot, not boiling, brine overnight; the next day green by pouring over them hot alum water heated in a brass kettle, let them stand until cold; then pour hot water over them until greened; when freshened, pour over them hot vinegar strongly spiced, let them lie for three or four days; then put the beans in bottles, cover with four per cent. vinegar, and cork tight; if desired sweet, add sugar.

SOUR MARTENEAS OR MOUSE PICKLES.—Pick the marteneas when the size of a small mouse; leave on the stem, put them in very strong cold brine, let them lie three days; take them from the brine, cover with strong alum, and soak three hours; then cover with cold water to freshen them, changing the water as fast as it becomes salt; when entirely fresh, pour over them hot spiced vinegar; let them lie until seasoned through, then bottle, and pour over them strong vinegar.

SWEET MARTENEAS.—Pour over marteneas hot brine with a little alum; let them lie four days, put them in a brass kettle, pour over them hot water with a little alum, and let them lie. Sugar being an antidote for copper, they may be well greened in the kettle without danger. Heat over the water until the marteneas are very green; make a syrup of vinegar and sugar, allowing two pounds of sugar to the quart; take half a pound of sugar and a pint of vinegar, and melt to a syrup, wipe the marteneas, and put them, a few at a time, in the syrup, and heat over steam until quite hot, without cooking in the least; as fast as they are passed through the syrup, pack them in bottles with spices, and pour over them the vinegar syrup hot, have them quite covered with the syrup, and cork tightly.

MELON MANGOES.—Select small green muskmelons, pack them in a tub, pour over them hot brine in which alum has been dissolved; repeat this process three times, adding salt and alum to keep the brine the same strength; let them remain in the brine six days after the last scald, making in all nine days. Then put them in a brass kettle, pour over them boiling water, and let them stand covered six hours; remove them to a tub, pour over them boiling water, let them remain until nearly cool; pour over them fresh hot water three times, and soak them two days; now remove a strip of the melon, cutting in the natural creases; with the fingers scrape out all the inside, wash them clean, and soak overnight in weak vinegar. Have ready horseradish root scraped, and split in fine strips, nasturtium seeds, small button onions peeled, radish pods, young beans, green grapes, cucumbers no larger than the little finger, minute melon, young gherkins, small tomatoes, young marteneas, ginger root, cinnamon, cloves, white mustard, young peppers, a ball of twine, and a large needle.. Drain the melons, place them on the table with the pieces belonging to each melon lying by them; commence with the cloves, put in each melon six, then cinnamon, ginger root, and a teaspoon of mustard; put in each several bits of horseradish, beans, and every other vegetable prepared for the filling of the melons. . When some of each are in, crowd the melon with what is left, using more cucumbers than any other of the vegetables, and lastly crowding in as much of the mustard seed as possible. If the family do not use onions, these can be omitted; one only should be allowed for each mango; now place the pieces of melon on each mango, as they belong, heat enough vinegar to cover them, in which spices have been steeped; as fast as the pieces are sewed in, lay them in the tub with the openings uppermost; when all are in the tub, pour over them the hot spiced vinegar, cover tightly, and let them remain one week; then drain off the spiced vinegar, and cover with five per cent. vinegar. A weight should be put on the mangoes before the first vinegar was poured on, to prevent their rising, which being left on while this was drained off, will prevent the spiced vinegar, which has filled the mangoes, from escaping; the last vinegar will need no spices if the first was highly flavored. If the vinegar moulds, pour it off, drain the mangoes, and add new spiced vinegar cold; mangoes well made with vinegar of proper strength, will keep until melons are again in season.

PICKLED ONIONS.—Peel small white onions, soak them one week in strong brine, changing the brine every day; scald them in milk and water without cooking, rinse in hot water, and soak for one day in weak alum water, or vinegar in which is dissolved a little alum. Pour over the onions ten per cent. vinegar, and bottle; pour on the top of each bottle two table-spoonfuls of sweet oil to prevent the vinegar from losing strength, add spices if desired; onions will turn dark if spiced. The vinegar can be flavored with extracts, when their color will not change.

TOMATOES, TO PICKLE GREEN.—Select small green tomatoes, put them in very strong brine with a little alum, nine days; green as gherkins, and put them in ten per cent. vinegar.

RIPE TOMATOES.—Select small tomatoes when turning red but not soft. Put them immediately in bottles, and pour over them ten per cent. vinegar; add sugar and spices, if desired.

To PICKLE GREEN WALNUTS.—Gather the walnuts, or, what is better, butternuts, when very small, prick them several times through and through, pack them in alternate layers of salt and nuts; when they have made a brine, drain them and repack with fresh salt; let them remain eight days. Wash them free from salt, and wipe them, lay them to dry three days; steep spices in strong vinegar, heat it boiling hot, and pour it over the nuts, let them stand one week, then pack the nuts in jars with spices; heat ten per cent. vinegar near to boiling heat, fill the jars, let them become entirely cold, and then cork tightly; the vinegar can be used in fish sauces after the pickles are used.

CAULIFLOWER.—Select fine cauliflower heads, break them in pieces as they naturally part, and lay them in salted water overnight. The next morning scald in a water made quite acid by dissolving a tablespoonful of citric acid in three quarts of water; heat nearly, but not quite boiling hot, and after draining well, put the cauliflower in ten per cent. vinegar, and pack in large bottles; this pickle looks very pretty colored pink, with red cabbage; although white when first pickled, it soon turns dark.

PICKLED CABBAGE, RED.—Select firm small heads, quarter them, shake salt in the leaves, and let them lie all night; in the morning shake out the salt, and scald vinegar and pour it over the cabbage hot; let it remain in the first vinegar three days; in the mean time, steep cinnamon, mustard seed, ginger root, peppercorns, and a few cloves in strong vinegar three days; drain off the first vinegar, and strain the spiced vinegar over the cabbage, and keep it well covered.

SHRED CABBAGE, RED OR WHITE.—Slice cabbage very fine, and scatter through very little salt; when it dissolves, drain off the brine, turn over hot spiced vinegar, and let it remain a few days, after which renew the vinegar, and put on a weight to keep the cabbage under the vinegar.

PICALILLY.—Take any vegetables, cabbage, cauliflower, tomato, carrot, cucumbers, onion, pepper, beans, etc.; salt them, pickle in vinegar, and mix with the addition of strong spiced vinegar to suit the taste and fancy; they can be sliced or chopped.

TOMATOES AND ONIONS.—Slice tomatoes and onions, allow four times as many tomatoes as onions; drain well, and cover with strong spiced vinegar poured on boiling hot. If the tomatoes and onions destroy the life of the vinegar, drain the pickles thoroughly, and add fresh cold vinegar to cover them.

PICKLED MUSHROOMS.—Get the button mushrooms; put them in

cold water; dip a flannel in salt and rub them off, and throw them in fresh water; put them in a stew-pan; scatter over a little salt; cover close, and set them in a boiling pot until the salt has drawn the juice from them; then lay them between two towels until quite cold; then pack in jars, and cover with strong distilled vinegar; add very little mace, and put a table-spoon of salad oil on the top; cork tightly, and keep them in a cool place.

PEACH MANGOES.—Take fine large freestone peaches; rub off the down with a small, stiff brush; open them; remove the pit, and fill with spices; and pour over them four per cent. vinegar. If preferred, add sugar to the vinegar. (*See* FRUIT PICKLES, in Part V.)

PEPPER MANGOES, No. 1.—Open large sweet peppers; fill them with the same vegetables and spices as the melon mangoes, omitting the pepper, and cover with boiling vinegar. When removing the seeds, have a basin of milk near, in which to dip the hands, or the peppers will cause intense suffering.

PEPPER MANGOES, No. 2.—Fill tomato-shaped, or any other peppers, with picalilly, or cabbage and celery chopped together and seasoned with mustard seeds; sew them firmly and cover with hot vinegar.

SMALL MELON PICKLES.—Pick muskmelons no larger than a walnut; prick them, and lay them in brine two days; then freshen, and green as directed for other pickles, and put them in hot spiced vinegar; they make an excellent brittle pickle.

PICKLED CAYENNE PEPPERS.—Pick the small peppers; prick them, and put them in ten per cent. vinegar.

PICKLED NASTURTIUMS.—Gather the seeds very young, and put them in the strongest vinegar, and cork tightly; use them in place of capers for sauces.

RIPE MUSKMELON PICKLES.—Take hard muskmelons, after they are sufficiently ripe to be well flavored; slice them lengthwise; scrape out the seeds, and lay the melon in salt overnight; wash and wipe dry, and put them in alum-water one hour; wash and wipe them again, cut them in slices, and pack them in glass jars; pour over a syrup of vinegar with spices, and set them in a boiler of cold water;

heat gradually to boiling; remove the bottles, and cork as soon as cold. They can be peeled if preferred, or cut in rings.

To PICKLE CARROT.—Boil carrot until tender; cut them in fancy shapes, and put them in strong vinegar. This is a pretty garnish and an excellent pickle. It can be spiced or flavored to suit the taste.

To GREEN CUCUMBERS WITH GRAPE-VINE LEAVES.—Many persons have a prejudice against cucumbers greened with alum, in copper; and indeed, without the closest attention to the process described, there is danger of the pickles becoming impregnated more or less with the copper. For those who would like fine-looking pickles, and do not mind trouble, the following directions may be useful; although they must not expect to get their pickles a very beautiful color, they will look much better than if no effort is made to green them. When packing the cucumbers in the salt, line the barrel, bottom and sides, with grape leaves, and pack between the layers of cucumbers a quantity of the fresh leaves, until the barrel is full. When salted through, remove them from the brine, and pour upon the pickles, several times, boiling water. If not the desired color, line a tub in the same manner that the barrel was prepared, and pack the pickles with a large quantity of the leaves. Heat vinegar boiling hot, pour it over the pickles, and cover them tight. If, the next morning, they are not sufficiently greened, drain off the vinegar, reheat it, and pour it again over them; repeat the process until of the color desired. When they are sufficiently greened, pour over them hot vinegar; if they taste of the vine leaves, change the vinegar after a week. Pickles, put down with sugar, or made with whiskey, will be nearly as green without any trouble in greening, as those greened with vine leaves. The sugar-made pickles may be considered as a first-rate family pickle, and not so expensive as would seem, without remembering that there is no vinegar to be bought for them.

PART VIII.

CHAPTER I.

KITCHEN GARDEN, WITH PLAN.

REMARKS.—The writer designs in this chapter to give some general directions to those who are entirely ignorant of agriculture in all its divisions, having been accustomed to live where a patch of green was a luxury only enjoyed by the millionnaire; but who, happily, find themselves snugly settled in a little home of their own, in a quiet country village, where an acre of ground is only too small for the comfort of a family; in such towns no vegetable market for the summer is to be depended upon; every family raise their own, and friends take as much interest in looking at the thrifty vegetables in each other's gardens, as in more fashionable places, in examining the expensive exotics which adorn the parlor or green-house. Many beginners in gardening fail for want of the knowledge of a few of the first principles in the science of horti- and agriculture. The first requisite is to prepare the soil in such a manner as to insure the healthy growth of tree or root. It is absurd to think of any plants thriving in a cold, wet, hard soil, yet many plant valuable trees and vines in just such, losing eventually both tree and time. Roots cannot live in water, or destitute of air. In low, wet soils, with clay subsoil, the roots of vines and trees become mouldy, the fruit drops, and the tree becomes worthless; the reason of this is, the air cannot penetrate stiff, wet clay soils, so as to reach the roots, which is absolutely necessary if a thrifty growth of tree or plant is desired. The most money will be saved in the end by a proper preparation of the soil, before planting either tree or plant. After what has been advanced in respect to water and air, it will be readily seen that a wet soil must be drained, and hard clay broken up. The object now will be to show the most efficient mode of accomplishing these desirable results, so as to produce the most permanent good.

UNDERDRAINING is considered by all to be the only method to be depended upon for the thorough draining of wet land. We will describe fully the particular manner to accomplish this with the least possible expense. First engage a good ditcher to do your work: there is as great difference in ditchers as in mechanics; measure the ground, and decide how the drains shall run; if they are three feet deep, forty feet apart is sufficient; if one and a half, twenty will do, etc.; a fall of from one to two inches to the hundred feet is all that is needed; they must be dug in a straight line, and made very even on the bottom; this will be the most easily accomplished with a hoe; if tile is used, thin sod placed over the joints will prevent the soil from working into the tile; when tile cannot be procured, use white oak boards, entirely free from sap, from five to nine inches wide, according to the amount of water to be carried off, and fully one inch thick; place the edges of two boards together, so that the opening shall be the same width as the boards of which the drains are formed; fasten them in place, with three tenpenny nails, one at each end, and one in the middle; be very careful, in laying them in the drains, to keep them in the right position, as the manner described forms the strongest arch; before putting the tile or boards into the drain, be sure that you have the right descent; if dug in a wet time, the proper declivity will be readily ascertained by the movement of the water, which should be very slow. In a dry time resort should be had to a level; when a level is used, pins should be driven in the bottom of the drain, as a guide for finishing it. When the drains are ready which have before been formed, the two boards of equal length, nailed as before directed, may be carefully laid in the ditch, so as not to move them from the right position; sufficient straw is then put in to fill the crevices, and clay, if it is on hand, thrown in to fill the ditch; sand, if thrown in next the straw, is apt to work in and fill the drains; but clay will form a hard pan, so that when the straw decays, the crevices will be protected from the loose sand which would otherwise fill it up. Board drains will last from fifteen to twenty years, and tile a whole lifetime. Even if land is dry, underdrains are a great benefit to the soil; as experience shows that lands so treated, suffer comparatively little by drought or wet; they also save much of the ammonia of the rain-water, taking it up so suddenly as to prevent evaporation by the influence of the sun. A large drain should be constructed, into which all the small drains can flow; this should be sufficiently deep to allow the water to fall into it slowly. There is generally some natural outlet or public drain into which this can empty.

TRENCHING.—After the draining is accomplished, the next object is to deepen, and if hard, to soften the soil. The very best method of benefiting such land permanently, is to trench, and at the same time, manure it. Proceed as follows: open a trench two feet wide; throw the top soil into a cart, or wheelbarrow, and dump it down on the opposite side of the bed that is to be trenched. This soil is usually about six inches to one foot deep; throw out a foot of soil from the bottom of the trench, and cart that to the other side of the bed, so that it can be shovelled into the last trench, after the top soil; spade up so as to loosen the soil in the trench, one spade deep; throw into the trench one foot of long manure, and then proceed as before. To open another trench, throw the top soil from this into the first trench, and afterwards the clay, and so proceed until each bed in the garden is finished; this should be done late in the summer, or early in the fall, so that the frost can act upon the clay; a great change in it being effected by the freezing. In the spring, the soil will be found soft and crumbling; it should then have a coat of manure, a sprinkling of salt, and a little ashes, spread evenly over it, and be thoroughly spaded; after it has lain an hour, it should be raked, or if pretty dry, immediately; should the trenching be done in the spring, the top soil must be left on the top; the clay can be thrown up the next fall to freeze. Before this process is gone over, the garden should be laid out, and the walks decided upon (*see Plan of Garden*), as it is unnecessary to trench where they are to be; indeed, the harder the walks, the better.

MANURING.—Should the soil be a light sand, deep manuring will be found equally important, though the extra loosening of the trench before manuring is unnecessary. The lighter the soil, the more manure will be needed in the spring top dressing, before spading. Solid manure will be more benefit to light lands than that mixed with straw; and light manures are the best for heavy lands. If this process is thought too expensive, procure a person who understands ploughing, and have the whole trenched with the plough, a person going after, and throwing manure into each furrow, so that the next furrow will cover it, etc.; none but an experienced ploughman can plough land in this fashion. Let the land remain rough until spring, then drag and plough again, running the furrows the opposite way from the first. It should be manured in the spring, before ploughing, and a little ashes and salt thrown over the land, as directed, before spring spading. The land should be dragged and all the lumps broken, before the beds are laid out. Unless very pliable, it will still need for small seeds, both careful spading and raking.

After the ground is ready, if not before done, proceed to lay out the garden; decide how many trees you will plant; prepare the border for currants, strawberry bed, raspberry border, etc. For a family of six, the following is about the proportion of ground wanted for each vegetable: asparagus-bed three feet wide and twenty feet long, or two beds, each three wide and ten long; beans, a bed three by nine is all sufficient; beets will need a bed three by twenty; cabbage will take a large spot, if it is intended to grow for winter use; but as this vegetable is usually very cheap in the fall, only the small summer varieties are grown in gardens; thirty heads of Early York can be grown on a bed three feet wide and twelve long; cauliflowers will take the same room for fifteen plants; for carrots, a bed three by six will be all that is needed; of celery, fifty heads can be grown in a trench fifty feet long; the room taken up in width for a trench is about three feet; six egg plants will occupy a bed three feet by eight; lettuce can be grown on the borders of the cabbage and cauliflower-beds; a small seedling bed, three by three, will furnish plants; water and muskmelon will need a square fifteen by twenty; cucumbers the same; corn, twenty square feet for the first, and the same for the second planting; the first peas will require two borders three feet by nine, the second the same; martenaes and okra, each occupy three feet to a plant; nasturtiums spread very much, a bed three by six, with six plants, would be sufficient; peppers, a bed three by six; parsley the same, or it can be used as borders for other beds; parsnips three by nine, will be sufficient for summer use; they can be bought very low in the fall and spring; onions three by nine; early potatoes, a square of twenty feet; squash, four hills, occupying nine square feet; radishes, the first crop can be grown on the borders of other beds; the second on a bed of three by six feet; salsify will take a bed three by twelve, if the family make much use of it; for spinach, a bed three by nine will be all that is needed; for turnips, a small bed only for summer use, three by twelve; for tomato, each plant will require three or four feet, according to the variety; a bed three by six for sage, the same for summer-savory, half as much room for thyme and sweet marjoram;. a bed three by six containing wormwood, tansy, Old Man, etc. Beds, for vegetables, should never be over four feet wide. The garden should first be laid out in squares with a border round the whole; this border can be occupied with currants, and if so large as to contain more than is needed for the family, raspberries and blackberries can be added; though the latter will do better in a more roomy part of the premises, as they grow very straggling. The squares for melons, cucumbers, and squashes should be as far apart as possible, and separated by high plants, as corn and peas.

SPINACH.—Plant this in the fall, as it is only useful as an early green; a little litter must be scattered over it, if the seed comes up before frost sets in.

PEAS are the first seeds usually planted in the spring; soak the peas in saltpetre water (*see* PURE SALTPETRE), to prevent the ravages of the wire-worm. If the season is favorable, plant the first week in April, or as soon as the ground is free from frost, and sufficiently dry to work; this rule will hold good for all climates. Make two drills one foot apart, and plant each seed separately one inch apart; as soon as they are three inches high, draw a little soil up to them; do this every week, until they commence running, when they must have sticks, placed for them to fasten on; drive each stick firmly in the ground, first on one side and then on the other, so as to meet half-way between the drills; they will stand much firmer thus, than if driven straight in the ground; each row separately staked. The seed should be two years old. Make the drills two inches deep.

PARSNIPS can be sown as soon as the frost is out of the ground; cover the seed lightly, and press the soil firmly, by placing a short board over the drills, and standing on it. Thin as soon as the plants have grown two inches high; so that each plant will be four inches apart; when they are wanted to boil for summer use, thin again, leaving them eight inches apart. Plant the sugar or hallow-crown.

DOUBLE-CURLED PARSLEY can be sown in the fall, or early in the spring; thin the plants as soon as well up, to an inch apart; and again when large enough to use; it should stand one foot apart when sufficiently thinned. It bears its seed the second year, and then dies. Old seed vegetates sooner than fresh.

ONIONS can be planted as soon as the soil can be prepared. The bed should be very richly manured, and the soil finely pulverized. If the black seed is planted, they must be thinned to stand four inches apart. Onions must not be hoed so as to have the bulbs covered. The whole bulb should be exposed, the roots only covered. If they do not incline to bottom, bend the tops gently, this will generally have the desired effect. Gather them as soon as the tops dry; leave them in the sun, and when dry, spread them in a cool dry cellar.

SALSIFY OR VEGETABLE OYSTERS.—Plant in rows about one foot apart, the seeds not nearer than two inches from each other; press the soil firmly, and thin to four inches. Leave some for the next year's seed in the ground all winter. Pull those needed for winter use as directed, before frost, etc. They are the best in the spring.

BEETS.—Extra early varieties should be first planted. Drop the seeds in drills three inches apart, unless wanted for greens; if so, plant two inches. Thin early; what is usually called the beet seed is in reality several seeds enclosed in cells, so that this vegetable will need much thinning. When about four inches high they will do for greens. For winter select long blood, or Whyte's new blood, and plant the 1st of July. Beet seeds should always be soaked in saltpetre water, as this will not only prevent the attack of the wireworm, but also give the young beet a start it would otherwise not have. Cover all seeds the size of beets a half-inch, and press down the soil.

BEANS.—Plant early six weeks. Soak the beans as directed for beets. Plant the hills one foot apart each way. Put into each hill six beans, in this manner: draw a circle four inches across, plant the beans at equal distances, when three inches high thin them, leaving three in each hill. Draw the soil up to the roots as they grow, making slight hills; continue this until they nearly cover the ground. As soon as the stems dry, pull up most of the roots, leaving a few to ripen seed for the next season.

CABBAGE, EARLY YORK.—Set the plants one foot apart in the bed, after first winding them, as far as the leaves, with brown paper, to prevent the cut-worms from destroying them. Draw the soil around the roots of the plant, as fast as they grow. Do not let the stumps remain in the ground after cutting the head, as they only waste the best part of the soil.

CAULIFLOWER.—This vegetable will not bear hot weather; it is necessary, therefore, to get it started early for the first crop to take advantage of the coolest part of the season. In order to do this, plant the seed in autumn, and protect the plants in a cold frame during the cold weather, and put them out as soon as all danger of frost is over, in soil as rich as it can be made; to insure a quick and thrifty growth of the plant, they should stand at least two feet apart. Wrap the stems in brown paper two inches above the surface of the soil, and the cut-worm will not touch them. Stir the soil frequently, and draw it to the plant. As soon as it shows flower, bend the leaves and tie them together, to protect them from sun and rain. When fit to cut, cook immediately; it should not lie an hour without being dressed, as it soon discolors.

BROCCOLI.—Cultivate in the same manner as cauliflower. Some varieties are nearly as good.

CELERY.—Sow the seeds in rich soil in open ground in autumn; or, if this has been neglected, in a gentle hot-bed in April; sometimes, however, it can be raised in open ground in the spring. It is very slow to germinate without heat, and must be soaked in a little water some time. Thin the plants to four inches, and when pretty strong plant them in a rich border, after removing a part of the leaves and a piece of the tap root. Let them remain in the border until the middle of June, when a trench should be dug four feet deep, the bottom two wide, and widening to three across the top. In the bottom of this trench lay a foot of good decomposed manure, and nine inches of the best soil to be had; sprinkle on a little salt and ashes, and mix it all together; let it lie one week before planting. Have ready a pail of mud; lift each plant carefully; if the roots are exposed, dip each in the mud, and plant immediately, one foot distant from each other. Soak them in water after planting, (not sprinkle, as most people water,) and cover from the sun; keep them protected from the sun during the day for a week, and take off the covering at night or if it rains. Give the plants plenty of water; if the season is dry, soak the trench twice a week. It is a marsh plant, and will do nothing if dry. House slops diluted are a good stimulant, but the leaves must not be wet with it; another watering will be necessary, when this is used, to rinse any from the plants that may have been sprinkled on them. Stir the soil often. Before commencing to blanch, let the plants become strong and stocky, and if possible draw the earth to them in bright weather, crumble the soil, take the leaves in the left hand, and carefully pack the fine soil around each separate plant, being careful each time not to cover the crown. If dirt gets into the crown, the celery will rust. The watering must be continued while the plant is growing. Draw the earth frequently up to the plant as it grows, being careful not to break the stalks. Celery is fit to commence blanching when one foot high, and should be continued until the last of autumn. When lifted, be cautious how you use the spade; it is, or should be, very brittle, and of course will break easily. It can be blanched two feet, though it is often seen less than one. When started very early in a hot-bed, it is apt to run to seed. If a few roots are set out and allowed to seed, it will sow itself, which is perhaps as sure a way to obtain good strong plants as there is. Seymour's White Solid is perhaps the best variety; Giant White is much esteemed by some, but no seed, however great its name, will raise good celery with poor cultivation; while any common variety will be found superior with it. Directions for its preservation will be found in another part of this work, under the head of VEGETABLES PRESERVED FOR WINTER USE BY STORING AND BURYING.

CUCUMBERS AND MELONS.—For table use we prefer Early Russian, a small brittle cucumber, more highly flavored than any other kind. It is the earliest cucumber known. It makes a good, but not handsome pickle, if gathered very young. For pickles, the early frame, and long green, are highly esteemed. Gherkins are excellent when quite young, and bear a good crop when the season is too dry and hot for other vines. They are oval and covered with prickles, and are called by some, prickly cucumbers. Prepare hills with plenty of rich manure; they should be the size of a halfbushel in circumference, raised two inches only above the bed, and five feet apart. Soak the seeds overnight in saltpetre water; plant six seeds on the north side, considerably scattered; in three days plant the same quantity on the south; in three days again plant the same on the east; and in three days more on the west. Melons and squashes are to be planted in the same manner. This may seem superfluous, and sometimes it is unnecessary, but the frost and worms often destroy the first crops entirely, and a few days may make a great difference. Leave two, or at the most three, plants in each hill; if they are crowded, so that in removing the superfluous plants the remainder will be injured, thin very early; but if a few inches apart, let them remain quite thick, until the season for bugs has passed. When the vine puts forth its first runner, pinch it off, to make it branch and fruit earlier. In melons, as soon as all the fruit is set which will ripen, stop every runner as fast as they put out. Lime scattered on the vines while the dew is on, is an excellent remedy for the striped bug; it must be repeated when washed off by showers. (*See* INSECTS.) We raise the finest melons and cucumbers by pursuing the following plan: Trench the whole bed, burying a foot of coarse litter from the stable, mostly straw, one foot under the surface, and then proceeding exactly as before. Or we remove the soil from a pit three feet square to the depth of two feet, and fill it with coarse litter and manure fresh from the stable, and then throw back the best of the soil, well enriched; in this we plant seeds in the four corners, leaving one in each to mature. Where it is almost impossible to raise melons, especially the watermelon, this plan will generally succeed. The finest muskmelons are the Persian, but they require a very favorable season at the North to mature. Nutmeg, Turk-cap, and netted citron are good enough, and more sure. White-cored mountain sprout, with seeds entirely white, is a variety but little known East; at the West it is very superior. Long Island is a mongrel, but an excellent melon. Red-cored mountain sprout, Imperial, and for late use, the Black Spanish, are among the best. Carolina, with us, is large but poorly flavored. There is a winter variety which ripens late and keeps well. It is insipid, only valued as a curiosity. Melons deteriorate if planted near other vines. One pumpkin vine will spoil a whole garden of melons, cucumbers, or fine squashes. Seeds of cucumbers and melons should be at least three years old; they will vegetate when six. The theory is, that seeds produce more fruit and less vine when the powers of germination are almost extinct. The last efforts of nature being to reproduce itself, the whole strength of the seed goes to flower and fruit instead of vine and leaf. Florists take advantage of this fact to produce double blooms in great profusion, from seed ripened from single flowers.

HERBS.—Thyme and sage should be planted where they can remain three years; thin the plants to one foot apart. Summer-savory and sweet marjoram are annuals, and can be sown more thickly; tansy, wormwood, and Old Man are perennials, they must seldom be transplanted; sage is tender and needs a little protection. The time for cutting herbs is when in flower; they do not need rich soil; the flavor is stronger in poor soil.

NASTURTIUM.—This needs only planting and thinning, if allowed to cover the bed; they can be trained on a trellis; in which case the soil should be drawn to the stem. The green seeds are what are used;

they flavor vinegar finely for pickles, and are sometimes substituted for capers. The flower is showy, and should be placed in a conspicuous part of the garden.

OKRA.—Plant the seeds, and thin them; they are a large plant, and want room; three feet to each plant is about what they will need.

EGG PLANT.—*(See particulars in* HOT BEDS.) After the plant is large enough to transplant, take it up carefully, having first prepared the hole for them; dip the roots in mud, and set them out as soon as possible. All plants of large size taken from the hot-beds, will need protection in the same manner as the cabbage; they are so tender, that cut-worms will take them in preference to a slow-grown plant. Shade the plants from the sun for a few days. If there is danger of frost, protect them, as they are very tender, even cold winds are injurious, putting them back for weeks.

CARROTS.—Follow the directions for beets, except in covering the seeds; one-fourth of an inch is sufficient for seeds of this size. For family use, Early Short Horn, a French variety, is to be preferred.

LETTUCE.—For the earliest, plant Early Butter or Cabbage, a small bed should be sown as soon as the ground can be worked. When the leaves are two or three inches high, transplant them carefully to the edges of the cabbage or cauliflower beds, and let them head. The seedling bed can be thinned for use as fast as it grows. For a late salad, plant Ice Leaf, or Drumhead; the Cos are fine, but require more managing to blanch them.

PEPPERGRASS needs only sowing in drills; it grows quickly, and can be used very small, if the cook has patience to dress it.

HORSERADISH.—A few roots should be planted for spring use; scrape the small roots, and lay them almost horizontally in the ground. It is well always to keep this in the same place in the garden, as when once rooted, it is difficult to eradicate it.

RADISHES.—The turnip radish is the earliest, but the Early Scarlet Short Top is the best; plant both; these can be sown early in the spring on the edges of other beds, and for late crops by themselves; they delight in light, quick soil; the faster they grow, the more tender. It is said that wheat-bran raked in the bed will prevent the worms eating the root. Thin radishes as soon as possible, or they will grow to stalk instead of root. Let some plants ripen for the sake of the seed pods, which make a fine pickle. Winter radishes must be planted very thinly from the first to the middle of July, and gathered before frost. The Black Spanish is a good variety.

SWEET CORN.—Prepare hills at regular distances, from three to four feet apart; soak the corn overnight in saltpetre water, and plant six kernels in each hill equally distant from each other, the whole occupying a space as large as a peck measure; watch it well, examine some of the corn to see if germination has commenced; if no signs of sprouting appear, the seed is bad; procure other, and plant again. When fairly up, it is often cut off by the cut-worm; should any spears be cut off, examine every morning for worms, and destroy them, and in the mean time, soak more seed, and plant it in the same hills, as they often take every spear, in spite of every precaution. A farmer informed me last season, that he saved his corn by digging small holes near the hills, which acted as traps, and caught multitudes of these ravenous creatures. He went to the field every morning before sunrise, and gathered them in a basin to feed his fowls. When all danger from the worms has passed, thin the corn, leaving three stalks in each hill; hoe frequently, but do not draw the soil to the roots; if suckers appear, slip them carefully off, without wounding the main stalk. Early Darling is the best for the first crop; it ripens within a week of the Tuscarora, the earliest corn. Large Sugar, is the finest variety, much before Stowel or any of the new varieties. Corn will soon run out, if planted on the same ground; for that reason the seed should be often changed.

EARLY POTATOES.—Procure early varieties, such as Ladyfingers, Early June, etc.; plant in rows, running north and south if convenient, that they may all have the early sun alike; the seed end is said to be a week earlier than the other parts of the potato; for that reason the two parts better be planted separately; drop the sets in the rows, six inches apart, and cover; hoe frequently, but do not ridge the rows much. Potatoes can be forwarded by cutting the sets early, partly drying them by the air (not by heat), and then allowing them to sprout either in pots in a hot bed, or boxes by the kitchen stove; they must be planted out carefully, so as not to break the sprouts, and unless the weather is warm, protected by a light litter for a week or so. Potatoes for winter can be bought of farmers cheaper than they can be raised in a garden.

SWEET POTATOES.—These require warm, dry soil, sand is the best; make hills six feet apart, as large in circumference as a half-bushel, and four inches above the level of the ground; procure sets from a hot bed (*see* HOT BEDS), and plant two small or one very strong plant, in the centre of each hill; they must be protected from cut-worms, and the only cultivation required is, to keep the ground free from weeds, and lift the vines once every week from the hill, to prevent their taking root, as they will do, if not disturbed, producing small roots from every joint, which prevents the growth of the tubers. Gather the potatoes before they are touched by the frost.

RHUBARB.—Procure Early Red and Victoria rhubarb plants, two or three years old; prepare a richly manured bed, set the Victoria four and Early Red three feet apart; do not cut them the first season. Two-year-old plants are as large as are profitable to purchase. The Giant, or Mammoth sorts, are not as pleasant flavored as the smaller kinds. The principal thing is, to have them early; cover the crown with coarse litter from the stable, before frost sets in; in the spring remove it from the crown, letting it lie for a month, or until the plant has made several leaves, after which, fork it into the ground; do not allow it to bloom unless wanting the seed; if this is desired, select the most desirable root, and let the first seed stalk grow, discarding all others; select a centre blossom, and pull off the remainder. Gather the seed as soon as ripe, by cutting the whole stalk; as it is very light, it will fall, if allowed to become dry, and be blown away. The second year cut moderately; a barrel without heads, set over the plant, as soon as the weather becomes mild, will make the stalks more tender and less acid; they must be removed when the hot summer weather comes on. If plants are raised from the seed, they must be planted in a shady place, or else shaded from the sun at midday; they require the first season, plenty water; the stalks can be cut the third season; the plants will not always prove the same variety as the seed, they are sometimes better and often not as good as the parent plant.

ASPARAGUS.—To raise from seed, select seed from strong plants, and sow it thinly on a bed of unusually rich soil; let them remain one year, keeping the bed free from weeds, and the soil loose; the plants will be one year behind those purchased from the nursery. Prepare the bed in the following manner, and remember it cannot be made too rich: remove the whole soil four feet deep, put a layer of bone from the slaughter-house, of about six inches, throw in six inches of long manure, and pack it to the bones; sprinkle in a layer of salt, throw in about three inches of soil, then put in one foot of fresh manure from the stable, just as it is with the straw, mixed with it; have ready, if possible, a pile of old manure, well decomposed, that has not been exposed to weather, and two barrels of house slop; put six inches of good soil on the manure, and a layer of salt; throw on it the house water; this is to furnish ready-made ammonia for the young plants. We have now two and a half feet of the bed filled; the bed must now be filled up with the old manure, and the best part of the soil, with a sprinkling of salt and ashes, mixed thoroughly together; when finished, it should be six inches higher than the other parts of the garden, to allow for the settling of the long manure, etc.; if the bed has been made early enough, let it settle a week before planting, though this is not important; draw a line both length and breadthwise of the bed, so as to form squares, and mark it out regularly in diamond form, allowing each plant to be eighteen inches apart, and put a stake where each plant is to be set; open the ground sufficiently deep to allow the roots to spread out as they naturally grow, and at the same time cover the crowns two inches with the soil; leave the stakes for the first year, that the plants can be replaced without trouble, should any fail. The first of April is the most certain time to transplant the plants, as they often winter-kill when removed in the fall; the bed can be prepared in the fall, if more convenient, and planted in April. If plants are procured at the nurseries, choose those one year old of the variety called Purple Top; always cover the bed every fall with coarse litter from the barn. After the first season, sprinkle the beds, so that they look white, with salt, every autumn, and empty all the old brine on them in the spring; the beds will do to cut lightly the third year; use a pointed knife, and be careful in cutting not to wound the young sprouts below the surface of the ground; stop cutting the first of July, or the beds will become exhausted. It would be well never to let the seeds form, but at least they should not be allowed to fall on the bed, as they will grow, and fill it in a few years with young seedlings. Never allow branches to be cut from the bed while in the growing state. When the leaves turn yellow, cut the stalks, and remove them to the manure pile; if they have seeds, throw them to the chickens, or the whole garden will become an asparagus bed; dress the bed, removing all weeds, salt and cover with litter as before directed; in the spring, remove the litter and spade it in the walks between the beds; let it remain until fall, then throw some of the rich soil from the walks on the bed, and carefully fork it in; do this yearly, and an asparagus bed will last prime twenty years. The Giant varieties are only the old varieties highly cultivated.

PLAN OF KITCHEN GARDEN EXPLAINED.—The outside borders are four feet wide, principal walks the same width, the smaller two feet wide, the squares fourteen by sixteen, the whole occupying eighty by eighty-four feet; fruit and vegetable together eighty-four, by one hundred and forty; No. 39, squash; 40, sweet corn; 41, tomatoes; 42, melons; 43, peas; 44, celery and beans; 45, cucumbers; 46, early beets, parsnips, salsify, turnips; 47, late beets, nasturtiums, peppers, onions, egg plant, each a bed; 48, early potatoes; 49, cauliflower and early York cabbage; 50, sweet potatoes; 35, okra, marteneas, and herbs; 36, strawberries; 37, asparagus; 38, rhubarb. Parsley, lettuce, radishes, and peppergrass, can be grown on the edges of the borders or beds. This plan is intended to occupy a half-acre, with the comforts of life, and at the same time, so arrange the garden that it will make a good appearance without devoting most of the land to ornamental shrubbery, etc. The front and side yards can be arranged to suit the taste.

CHAPTER II.

FRUIT GARDEN.

REMARKS.—On a half-acre of ground it would be absurd to plant winter fruit, as this can always be obtained in favorable seasons for comparatively small prices from farmers who raise quantities for market. I shall only notice such trees and fruits as are valuable in the garden, because rarely to be found in a country market, and consequently high-priced. Early apples often bring from twelve shillings to two dollars per bushel, while in the same market good fall and winter fruit can be bought for from two to four shillings. Peaches grow fast, take less room, and consequently are more valuable to the family; a limited supply of cherries; one or two standard, and a few dwarf pears and cherries; two or three plums, raspberries, currants, and strawberries, will be all that can be grown with profit in a small fruit-yard. Many crowd the kitchen-garden, clothes-yard, etc., with every tree they hear of as being superior, which in the end prevents their enjoying any fruit worth mentioning from their own trees. Fruit trees must have room, or the roots soon interlace, the trees become sickly, and disappoint the planter, who has waited in vain for the fruits of his toil. One tree properly grown is worth a dozen such as are usually seen in crowded yards and gardens. Apple trees should never be nearer each other than twenty feet, and even then the roots ought to be pruned. In orchards we place them from thirty to forty feet apart. Pears and cherries the same distance. Peaches and dwarfs will do at ten and twelve, by low-heading and root-pruning. This will be found described in another part of the work. Each tree ought to be staked when planted, for two reasons: the first, that the roots may remain in one position to insure the growth of the tree, and the other, for the sake of symmetry, as a tree will generally bend to the wind, and become crooked, until quite large. Care must be taken when staking trees not to bind or chafe them. If bound, the sap cannot flow with equality, and ridges are often made by the bindings. Examine often, especially if the trees are in a thrifty state, that this danger may be avoided. The tallies are often forgotten until the wire is grown over by the bark, when the tree must be nearly girded to remove it. Leave no tallies on trees, but draw a plan of your fruit garden, or orchard, numbering each tree, and you will find it much safer than to depend on tallies or memory for the names of your fruit.

PLAN OF FRUIT GARDEN.—Sixty feet wide and eighty-eight long. No. 1, early harvest apple; No. 2, early sweet bough; No. 3, summer queen; No. 4, the Bartlett pear; No. 5, Flemish beauty; No. 6, Governor Wood cherry; No. 7, Downer's late; No. 8, black heart; No. 9, green gage plum; No. 10, frost gage, or winter damson; No. 11, Breda apricot; No. 12, nectarine violet; No. 13, red Siberian crab; No. 14, dwarf cherry plumstone morello; No. 15, Downer's early; No. 16, American heart; No. 17, dwarf pears, Maria Louisa; No. 18, white Doyanne; No. 19, Louisa Bonne, of Jersey; No. 20, Orange Quince; No. 21, early York serate peach; No. 22, large early York; No. 23, George IV.; No. 24, Cooledge's favorite; No. 25, Crawford's late; No. 26, old Mixon free; No. 27, Morris white; No. 28, snow. The apples, pears, plums, and cherries, stand twenty feet apart; the rows commencing four feet inside the fence. The borders around the garden are occupied by small fruit; the border next the side fence (No. 24) is intended to extend through the kitchen-garden, and is the best spot for blackberries; it will contain twenty-three plants six feet apart. Plant one root to each stool; procure the New Rochelle. Against the back fence (No. 30) plant raspberries; the

Hudson River Antwerp, three plants to each stool, four feet apart. It will take seventy-five plants, making twenty-five stools. On the opposite side of the kitchen-garden (No. 31) plant one dozen stools of Ohio ever-bearing, and a dozen American white. The border of the fruit-garden (No. 32) is the best place for gooseberries; Houghton's seedling is the only variety entirely free from mould. There are many large varieties, but, unless extra pains are taken with them, they are entirely worthless, by reason of the mildew which gathers upon them. This border will take fourteen bushes, four feet apart. Borders 33 and 34 are designed for currants; each will grow twenty-one plants, four feet apart. Select for these, ten of old red Dutch, four of white grape, seven of Prince Albert, six of Victoria, seven of long bunched red, seven of cherry, four English black, and three of white Dutch. This variety gives currants a longer season than the one old variety. Border 35 in kitchen-garden is intended for grapes; there will be room for ten vines eight feet apart. Procure for the West and North, Isabella, Concord, and Diana. These are the only *tested* varieties that do well at the North and West. I would advise but one Isabella, as they do not always ripen; four Diana, a light-colored sweet grape, resembling the Catawba in flavor, and five of the Concord, which seldom fails to ripen its fruit. Trellises must be constructed for the grapes. Particular directions for their cultivation will be given in another part of this work. The peaches and dwarfs stand ten feet apart. The borders are four feet wide, small walks the same; the walk between the fruit and vegetable garden is eight feet wide. For four or five years peaches or any dwarf trees can be placed between the apples, but after this they should be removed. The ground occupied by all the fruit trees can be planted with vegetables, if desired, for a few years; no high crops, like corn, should be allowed. If seeded down, a ring as large as the branches must be left free from grass, and the soil should be frequently stirred. (*See* PLAN OF KITCHEN GARDEN.)

PLANTING TREES AND SMALL FRUITS.—If possible, plant those fruits troubled by the curculio by themselves. (*See* PREVENTIVES OF CURCULIO, ETC.) Having fixed on a plan, prepared the soil, and chosen the trees, the next thing is to set them properly. Never allow trees or roots of any kind to be exposed to frost, sun, or wind. As soon as received from the nursery bury the roots in a trench, unless the ground is frosty; if so, wrap them in matting, old carpet, or any other convenient article, pour water over, and lay them on the cellar bottom.

14*

Prepare holes for planting before taking out the roots. For apples they ought to be three feet deep; the first foot filled with coarse bones, the next with long manure, and the remaining foot with rich soil, mixed with fine old manure. The ground should be two inches lower in the hole than the surrounding soil. Having the holes ready, proceed to trim the roots; cut off every wounded spot smoothly with a sharp knife, and remove any branches broken or superfluous. Trim always for a low head; the first branch should be not over two feet from the ground, if very low heads are desired. This trimming should be done where the wind will not dry, or the sun scorch the roots. Dip them immediately in a batter of mud, and have a pailful ready, rather thin, to pour on the tree when planted. Drive the stakes firmly in the centre of the holes, taking sight from one to the other, to be sure they are straight from every point. Place the body of the tree firmly against the stake, in the same position in which it stood in the nursery, that the bark may not be obliged to become acclimated the second time. With the hand, work the fine soil into every crevice, pressing it firmly as you proceed; when nearly finished, dash on with force a pail of water, and then a pail of mud and water, not too thick to flow; fill the hole immediately, and press the soil very lightly. The tree when finished planting, should stand four inches higher than the other parts of the garden. If the garden has been trenched, as described before, it will not be necessary to prepare the holes as described. Bone-dust can be added as a top dressing at any other time. Mulch with coarse litter, chip manure, spent tanbark, or sawdust, four inches thick, and let it remain all summer. Wrap the tree with some soft material, and fasten it to the stake with a leather strap. Examine often, for fear the strap may become too tight, and bind the tree. Standard pears and cherries should grow slowly, and therefore do not need as much stimulating manure as apples. Dwarfs can hardly be too highly manured. The holes for standard pears can be filled with bones, ashes, and good soil. Cherries, but little manure, ashes, lime, bones, etc. If the cherry grows too fast, the bark splits; and the standard pear, when too highly stimulated, is in more danger from fire-blight. The reason why dwarf pears require high manuring is, that the roots of the quince being so very small they are incapable of taking up sufficient nourishment to perfect the fruit, unless it is ready prepared for them. The roots of most standards reach after the richest of the earth, and unless drowned or choked, will by their own unaided efforts thrive and flourish; while the poor dwarf, like a Chinese lady, must be cared for by its friends, or become a worthless cumberer of the ground. Peaches require high manuring, but only for the time being. The food furnished for the apples is calculated to last for years; but the peach, being comparatively a short-lived tree, needs its nourishment nearer the surface. Iron is necessary for the peach, it will be well to bury old iron near the root. Brimstone, put near the trunk of the tree, only covered with soil, is said to prevent the ravages of the borer. (*See* BORER.) Manure plums pretty high, with bones, lime, ashes, and salt, not too much of the latter; for small trees, a quart below the manure, and another scattered on the soil, is sufficient. Plums grow wild on the borders of salt marshes, and naturally like salt, though too much would kill them; give the tree a good dressing of ashes, mixed with the other manures. It is best to dig holes for every tree, and, unless the soil has before been trenched, as deep as three feet for every kind of fruit except the peach; two is sufficient for them. Quinces need as rich soil as the dwarf pear to do well; they also like salt, and will bear considerable, like the plum, yearly. Apricots and nectarines are to be treated like the peach. Currants, to be as fine as possible, need high and deep manuring. Raspberries and gooseberries, to do well, must have rich soil with plenty of old manure. Blackberries should, the growers say, be as well cared for as raspberries, to insure a good crop of fine berries.

GRAPES.—Grapes should be manured very much like the apple, only using more ashes, mixing them in well, as the border is filled; when a number is to be planted, the whole border should be prepared; if the border has been trenched, it will be sufficient to spade in ashes before planting, and top dress with bone-dust; all roots should be panted as directed for apples.

STRAWBERRIES.—These need deep tillage ; Downing advises burying two feet of long manure one foot below the surface, and filling up the other foot with rich soil mixed with chip and stable manure well decomposed, but not wasted by rain and evaporation; they also like ashes. Plant the large varieties two and the smaller one and a half feet apart. · April is the most sure month for planting, but on account of obtaining new plants, it is usually put off until August. The pistillate varieties will not bear perfect fruit without a staminate or perfect blossom near ; it requires one perfect plant to three pistillates; but it is unnecessary to mix the plants in the bed; a row near of the perfect blossoms will fertilize three rows of the pistillate. A person, by observing, can readily distinguish the difference in the flowers; the perfect has both stamens and pistils; the pistillate has no perfect stamens, but a pistil; the barren has many stamens but no pistil; the latter is of course worthless, and, while so many good, perfect varieties can be obtained, entirely unnecessary. Dip the plants in mud, after first taking off all but one or two of the youngest leaves; if the season is dry, water thoroughly the hole before putting in the plant, and cover immediately from the sun; remove the covering at night, that the dew may have effect, and keep down the runners; the easiest way to do this is to have a sort of chopping-knife, made with a long handle, with which the cultivator can cut the runners without stooping, by passing the knife along the line of the plants, removing the runners or not, as desired. The soil should be frequently stirred, and a slight covering thrown over them before frost sets in. The next spring clear the beds, and loosen the soil; when the plants are in bloom, scatter between the rows ashes or lime, and rake it in. A mulch of clean straw, or something of the kind, should be spread around the plants to protect the berries from the sand, and the plants from the sun. If the season is dry, plenty of water must be artificially supplied; indeed, the berries are sweeter when watered in this manner, than by rain. If no plants are wanted, do not let them run, but keep the beds in good order the whole season; cover lightly every fall, and the beds will last prime three years, and do pretty well the fourth.

Perfect Flowers: Wilson's Albany, a fine, rather acid berry; Chilian, very fine; Boston Pine, needs moisture and high cultivation; Le Barron, is a good berry and fair bearer; and Longworth's Prolific. There are many others equally good, we presume, which we have not as yet tested.

The best pistillates which we have tested, are the Monroe Scarlet, a good bearer, rather tart; Prolific Orange, good bearer, sweeter than the preceding; Hovey's Seedling, succeeds in some localities, and in others fails entirely; M'Aboy's Superior; and a seedling of our own, which we have named the Peninsular Berry, is a very fine berry, large, prolific, fine-flavored, and continues in bearing a long time.

The Early Scarlet is a small berry, much recommended formerly as a fertilizer, but as there are now so many large berries with perfect blossoms in cultivation, they are going out of use. The Ohio Mammoth is a large, hollow berry, very sour, and, when better can be had for fertilizing, should be discarded.

GOOSEBERRIES.—After the border is well prepared, set the plants three feet distant from each other in the row, placing them in the centre of the bed. Mildew is the most effectually prevented by keeping the whole border cool and damp, by mulching six inches deep, through the whole season; salt hay is the best article to mulch with; where this cannot be obtained, fine soft hay, that will pack readily, will do, sprinkled with salted water. Uncover the roots early in the spring, and work around each plant one or two shovelfuls of good manure; train on a single stem six inches from the ground; trim in February or March, thinning out the shoots quite freely; when a bush needs renewing, cut back to a good bud near the main stem; when the border is prepared for the season, put on the mulch as before directed. Another method of preventing mildew is the renewing system, with high cultivation and mulching. Plant in the spring, two feet apart, well-rooted plants, from twelve to fifteen inches high, one year old, trimmed to one straight stem; stake, and let them grow at random for the first season, keeping the soil well worked; the next February, cut off nearly a third of the last season's growth of the first bush, leaving it a good shape; the second bush, cut back to one or two buds near the main stem; the third bush as the first, and so on, until the whole are trimmed. When the frost is out of the ground, work into the border around each root, two or three shovels of manure, and mulch six inches with salted hay, even though it reaches the first branches; the following winter reverse the process. A northern aspect, is said to be the best for gooseberries; mildew is also said to be prevented by cutting out all shoots of a light green color, and also by pinching out the points of the growing shoots, during the early development of the fruit, and afterwards by rubbing any buds bursting into growth while the crop is maturing. It is a good plan to sprinkle the bushes with suds every washing day; some advise sprinkling with water a little salted; but if this is used, care must be taken that the water is not too salt, as this would kill the leaves. Gooseberries are increased by suckers and cuttings; some of the largest are, Crown Bob, Bunkerhill, Green Ocean, and Walnut; in England, these large varieties do well, but in this country they usually are worthless, though it is said, high cultivation will insure a good crop of perfect fruit.

BLACKBERRIES.—It is useless to attempt cultivating the common blackberry; it will be found labor lost. The New Rochelle, however, well repays the cultivator by its large crops of delicious fruit, for all his care and expense. It will, like the currant, bear fruit without extra labor and expense in the preparation of the soil, and, like it, also will pay for good care and deep culture; they delight in a deep soil, moist and light, with considerable vegetable matter, but not sandy; it should be deeply trenched, as before described, but instead of a foot of manure in the bottom of the trenches, use straw litter from the barn, leaves or any other vegetable matter, with now and then a sprinkling of ashes, and fill up with rich soil, composed of a mixture of decomposed vegetable matter, some barnyard manure, and good soil; set them six feet apart, and if put out in rows, eight feet between the rows. The ground should be kept loose and free from weeds. The next spring cut off one-third of every branch and stem, and mulch six inches deep with straw. In the fall, cut out all the old, and shorten the new canes, to about five feet high; they can be trained to upright stakes, or be confined in place, by means of wire run through posts five feet high; the first, one foot from the ground, the next two, and the third eighteen inches, or two others the same distance as the two first; the canes can be tied with strings to the wires, or bent while young, and fastened by weaving in and out through them; the old canes must be cut out every fall, and in the spring the new canes shortened, the mulching spaded in with a very little ashes, and new applied. Plants trained in this manner will well repay the trouble by their large crops and superior fruit. Our opinion is, that a dozen well cared for, would be worth more than a dozen and a half entirely neglected. The old saying, " A thing well done, is twice done," is never more truly spoken than when applied to agriculture. Blackberries are increased by suckers.

RASPBERRIES.—These require rich, deep soil, with a large proportion of vegetable matter; therefore about the same preparation of soil is needed as for blackberries. The stools should be composed of three plants, six inches from each other, set in a triangular form, and distant the one from the other, four feet; the old canes should be cut out as soon as the plant has fruited. In the spring dig into the border a good dressing of well-prepared compost, or if not at hand, a layer of stable litter, ashes, and chip manure. The raspberry will pay well for extra care; mulching is very beneficial; train to posts, set between the stools, so as to bring them within four feet from each post, and two from each plant; nail firmly, a flat piece of webbing or soft leather on one side of the post, have a slit cut in the other end, and a strong brass or iron knob driven into the post; divide the stools, taking half the canes of one, and half of another, lay the ends together on the posts, and button them down with the webbing nailed to the post. This should be done in the spring, and at the same time, the canes, if too long, can be cut off; in the fall, the young canes should be laid down, and some of the soil thrown over them; or if preferred, they can be covered with straw without bending, but the first method is the least trouble. The Everbearing should have one-third to one-half of the canes cut down to within six inches of the ground to insure a fall crop. Birds can be kept from the fruit by means of nets, but in no other way. Some raspberries are propagated from suckers, and others grow by layers only; the American White is one of the latter class; the Antwerps, and all of that class, should have from one inch to a foot cut from each branch in August. (*See* BORER.)

CURRANTS, if planted from cuttings, should have all the buds cut out below the surface; they should be cut late in the fall, and buried below frost; or very early in the spring, when the bushes are not frozen; plant in a cool border, after cutting them smooth and pointed. When a year old, prepare a border, no matter how rich, and plant them four feet from each other; take good care of them, keeping the soil loose, and you will not be obliged to pick over little half-grown currants, and the neighbors will wonder where you obtained your fine variety. Their only enemy is the borer.

PRUNING.—The *Apple* needs less pruning than some other fruits. If there is too much wood it should be removed, and the head be pruned to give a good shape, all branches that cross each other must be removed before they are of much size. It is an injury to a tree to be obliged to saw off large limbs, though by carelessness it is often necessary.

Apricots need only to be kept in good shape, without too large a head for the body.

The *Cherry* needs but little pruning, only sufficient to keep the tree in shape. The *Bigaroons* need as much as any, if not more; the long shoots that extend beyond the head should be shortened every September.

The *Peach* should have one-third of its last year's growth cut off early every spring.

Nectarines should be treated in every way as a peach.

Pear—trim to form a fine head, and afterwards keep the centre of the tree rather open; do not cut or saw large branches, if it can be avoided.

Plum; trim by the same rule as the pear.

Quinces need but little pruning, merely sufficient to form a good-shaped bush.

Currants; give a good supply of manure every spring; thin the shoots to allow them to stand some distance from each other, and shorten the young wood to about three inches of the preceding year's growth.

Gooseberries; trim closely, keeping the centre of the bush clear for the large varieties; Houghton's seedling needs but little pruning.

Raspberries; cut out the canes as soon as fruited, and shorten those left in the spring six inches; the tender varieties, if not all, should be stopped in August.

GRAPES.—*First Year:* let one branch grow, and cut it to two or three buds late in the fall.

Second Year: Let two branches grow; in November cut them off, leaving them four or five feet long. The trellis must now be built, if not already done, and these two branches fastened, one to the right, and the other to the left, on the lower rail of the trellis.

Third Season: Let each bud on the branches grow, and train the branches which they produce, perpendicular to the top of the trellis.

Fourth Season: The vine is now ready to fruit, and will produce its first crop. After gathering the fruit, cut the lateral branches which have grown through the season, from the upright branches, to two buds each.

Fifth Season: Allow but one bud on each lateral to grow, pinching off all others; the bud left should be the one nearest the parent, unless weak; if so, the next one.

Sixth Season: Cut off that part of the old spur which extends beyond the base of the new branch, and cut the new branch to two buds.

Seventh Season: Allow the bud nearest the main branch to grow, unless weaker than the other; if so, pinch it off, and allow the further bud to grow. Continue this yearly. To procure new wood, allow six branches to grow trained in an upright manner; cut two of these to one bud one year, two others the next, and two the next, which will give new wood every three years. The common method of pruning the native grape, is to cut to from four to six buds of the previous year's growth on each branch. The grape is a great feeder, and must have plenty of rich manure; wash-water is an excellent stimulant for it, applied once every week. The foreign grapes that ripen in out-door air need to be more closely pruned; from two to three buds is all that should be left. The cuttings of last year's growth cut smooth at the end, and set in a cool border, with two eyes below, and one above the ground, will make nice plants in a year, of proper size for a vineyard. The cultivators of the present day vary in their opinions of the best methods of summer pruning, but all advise the removal of the late pushing buds, that would produce blossoms at midsummer, and green fruit in the fall; we succeed well by pinching off each branch as fast as it has made five buds beyond the bunch of fruit highest on the vine. Remove also what the Germans call the wild wood, or, what is better, the buds from which it would grow; these become small side branches, worse than useless to the vine. Look out for the grape worms. (*See* INSECTS.)

A SAFE WASH FOR TREES.—Heat over charcoal in an iron kettle, until red hot, six pounds of the common sal soda of the shops; when perfectly free from moisture, having parted with its carbonic acid and water, it resembles whitish ashes, and is ready for use. Dissolve one pound of this caustic soda in a gallon of soft water, and scrub the trees. It removes decayed bark, is death to all insects, (*see* INSECTS;) and never kills the tree as potash is too apt to do, when applied strong. If diseased pears are treated with this or any other wash, it is safe to use a part of the preparation for them, with a separate brush, for fear of communicating the disease to healthy trees. This is useful to currants or any other small fruits.

CHAPTER III.

FLOWERS.

FLOWER GARDEN.—Nothing is a greater promoter of health than agreeable exercise in the open air, and in no way can the rich and the poor so surely secure health and pleasure united, as in the cultivation of flowers. The taste for floriculture improves rapidly by cultivation, and none truly value flowers, who do not enjoy the care of them. The best benefits to be derived from the flower-garden can not be obtained through a finished gardener, as a good dinner is enjoyed through the cook. Flowers, to impart the highest pleasure, should be cultivated by the same hand that gathers them. Those, who do not know from experience, would hardly believe how much happiness a bed of flowers, well cared for, may be the means of imparting. Exercise in the air, to be beneficial, consists in something more than machine locomotion; the mind needs change as much or more than the body. A walk for the sake of exercise alone, with no present enjoyment, fatigues more than it invigorates; school girls feel this without analyzing the cause, excusing themselves, if possible, from the formal walks of the seminary; but when a nutting, berrying, or botanizing expedition is under consideration, the walk is anticipated as a great treat, and enjoyed as such, to the benefit of mind and body. A motive for the exercise is highly important, if the person is to be benefited by it, and for this reason, in nine cases out of ten, the walks prescribed by the physician injure instead of invigorating the patient. When a lady commences gardening, she gets along very well until she finds herself quite lame; as soon as this occurs, she decides that gardening disagrees with her, and gives it up. Now, if she will reason a little, the cause for the lameness will be found, generally, to be of little consequence, being merely muscular fatigue arising from the new use of the muscles alone, which will gradually cease to trouble her, as they become accustomed to their new exercise and position, and once overcome, the trouble is over entirely for the first season, and will be found of much less moment ever after. The hard, rough work is of course too fatiguing for ladies, but by the use of light tools, after the garden is once spaded and raked, the whole cultivation of flowers will be found a light and pleasant employment, adapted peculiarly to ladies and children; the health of whom will be far better than if they are occupied with needlework or any other indoor employment the whole day, and no doubt the trifling expense attending the garden will be fully met by the decrease of doctors' bills, journeys for health, tonics, etc. This chapter does not contain all that it would be pleasant and useful to know of the art of floriculture, by any means; but sufficient information is imparted on the subject, to enable any one to cultivate, with success, a choice collection of annuals, biennials, perennials, roses, bulbs, etc. Flowers should be arranged to form good contrasts in the garden, as well as in bouquets. (*See* CUTTING AND ARRANGING FLOWERS.)

A FEW HINTS ON THE CULTIVATION OF FLOWERS.—Flowers should not be planted with vegetables. A small spot of ground devoted to flowers alone will give more satisfaction than much more room on borders surrounding the kitchen garden. The soil for flowers should be spaded very deep, and highy manured with a well-prepared compost. Fresh manure is filled with seeds of weeds, and is too stimulating, while fermenting, for delicate seeds and plants; if fresh, or, as it is called, long manure is used, it should be buried three feet deep, and the top soil prepared with old manure or composts. Chicken manure, finely pulverized, and mixed with four parts of fine soil, is an excellent top dressing for a flower-garden. Borders, for small seeds, should be thoroughly pulverized and finely raked; lumps of clay often prevent delicate seeds from throwing up their seed leaves, after germination has taken place. Small seeds should be covered lightly, the soil pressed firmly, and, if dry, watered a little every day, or as often as the surface becomes dry. A weak solution of saltpetre will save the seed from the depredation of insects, but be careful the saltpetre is pure, as much of it is crystallized with rock salt. Large seeds, as peas, Balsams, Convolvulus, etc., should stand overnight in a weak solution of soda or saltpetre; large seeds must be planted deeper than small seeds, peas half, Balsams one-fourth of an inch deep, and other seeds by the same rule according to their size. It is well to put a part of each packet of seeds in the soil early, and the remainder a week later; sometimes the early, and sometimes the late sown, doing the best. A good rule in all localities, is to sow flower seeds when the peach trees first bloom; some seeds, however, should be sown in the fall, as soon as ripe. It is usually considered that nature indicates what seeds should be sown thus, though it is not always safe to follow this rule, our flowers being, in so many cases, exotics which need nursing to insure their growth. Flowers, that cast their seeds as soon as ripe, should, as a general thing, be allowed to sow themselves, or the seeds should be taken just before the seed-vessel bursts, and sown immediately. The following list comprises most of the flowers in general cultivation which do better for fall sowing.

ANNUALS THAT BEAR TRANSPLANTING, TO SOW IN SEPTEMBER.

Asters, also in hot-beds,
Chinese Pinks,
Coreopsis,
Marigold,
Orange Amaranthus,
Ageratum,
Portulaca,
Balsams, also in hot beds,
Petunias,

Mignonette,
Drummond Phlox,
Verbenas,
Forget-me-nots,
Pansies,
Sweet Alyssum,
Hibiscus,
Emeralds,
Zinnias,

THOSE THAT WILL NOT BEAR TRANSPLANTING WITHOUT RETARDING THEIR GROWTH.

Candytuft,
Clarkia,
Collinsia Bicolor,
Larkspurs,
Convolvulus,
Grove Love,
Bartonia Aurea,

Leptosiphon Densiflorus,
Poppies,
Eschscholtzia,
Shell Plant,
And most of the California annuals.

LIST OF SEEDS THAT SHOULD BE SOWN IN A HOT-BED.

Asters,
Coxcombs,
Verbenas,
Vineas,
Clintonias,

Balsams,
Choice Petunias,
Lophospermums,
Everlastings,

And any other plant desired to bloom early that will bear transplanting.

To Sow FLOWER SEEDS.—Usually flower seeds are sown too thickly. Fine seed should be mixed with dry sand, and scattered evenly in the soil, and larger seeds planted at equal distances, so far apart that they can be thinned by transplanting without disturbing those that remain. Sow seeds of low plants on the borders, and higher bloomers back of them, as, for instance, on a border of four feet, sow first pansies, and back of them balsams, etc. The catalogues usually designate the height of each advertised flower. Peas like good soil that was manured the previous year. Balsams require very high fertilizing. Amaranths should have rather a poor light soil. Stocks prefer rich soil, with a little lime or chalk. Coxcombs must be stimulated highly to do well. Larkspurs like rich soil, mixed with pulverized charcoal. Pansies should be highly stimulated, and the soil kept moist around them. California annuals prefer warm soil and but little thinning; if exposed to the sun too much, they will soon wither; they must cover the ground. Asters must have rich soil, and be transplanted when two inches high to do well. Mignonette is most fragrant on sandy soil. Verbenas like good soil, not very light, with no decomposed manure. Soil cannot be too good for pinks; they like a sprinkling of salt over the soil every season. All flowering plants that incline to throw out roots from the stem should have the earth drawn up to them; as the balsam, the four o'clock, etc. The seeds of biennial and perennial plants, if sown as soon as ripe, will bloom the next season. Weeds must be removed from among seedlings when very small, or they will soon destroy the young plants; but, as many flowers resemble our common weeds when quite young, great care must be taken, or the flowers will be mistaken for weeds.

SEED SAVING.—Be sure the seeds are ripe. Dry them well before putting them away. Bottles are very convenient for seed; they should be labelled thus: "Balsams, 1860." If the label reaches round the bottle, it can be used many years, erasing the previous and adding the current year each season. To those who practise giving their neighbors seeds yearly, it will save much trouble, and will also insure the seeds from the depredations of mice. Vines should be furnished with supports as soon as they incline to twine. Asters, and all plants needing support, should be tied to neat stakes, or the first hard rain will ruin them. Pinks need frames to keep the blossoms from the ground. Larkspurs should be thinned to one foot apart when quite young; candy tuft to six inches; if the branching, to one foot, and other plants in proportion. One stalk of coxcomb, if thrifty, looks better than more; it should be trimmed tree-shaped. They grow three and four feet high, if well cared for, with combs measuring six inches. The same rule will apply to all coarse growing plants; only small plants should be clustered. Very low plants should be used as borders, unless the garden has box, grass, or other permanent borders. Large seeds improve by age, some retaining their vegetating properties several years. All seeds as large as the Balsams can be kept two years; peas, longer; while the minute seeds should be sown the season after ripening. Pansies will seldom vegetate the second year, etc. It is impossible to enumerate half the annuals now in cultivation, but catalogues, describing the old and many new flowers, can be had of all seedsmen.

THE CARE OF FLOWERS IN A DROUGHT.—Unless a plant is efficiently and regularly watered, it had better be left to nature alone. If the soil is deep, a frequent stirring of the surface will be much more advantageous to the garden than a mere sprinkling of water. Shading the ground with straw, moss, flat stones, bits of board, or sawdust, will protect the plants materially from the sun and heat. When watering is absolutely necessary, remove the soil around the plant without exposing the root, pour in two quarts at least to each, and after it has well soaked in the ground, cover with the dry displaced earth; after this, a mulch of moss, or something else, will keep the plant moist several days; but if watering is once commenced, and the roots again allowed to dry, the plant will suffer more than if no water had been used. Water to be used in the garden should stand in the sun during the day, and be applied to the plants after the sun has set. Liquid manure is the most beneficial, when applied during, or just before a rain.

TRANSPLANTING ANNUALS.—Select cloudy weather, if possible. Water, if the soil is dry, the plants to be removed, the evening previous, and the place to which the plant is to be removed. Lift it carefully with a garden trowel, having previously removed the soil from the spot intended for the plant; by the same instrument, that it may carry the plant on the trowel, insert it into the hole prepared for it, and press it gently in place. If young, it will need no pruning, but if the roots are disturbed, pinch off the end of the root, and remove one quarter of the leaves. Water and shade until it is well rooted.

GRUBS.—These are very troublesome to some flowering plants, especially balsams, and other watery stems. (*See* INSECTS.)

CUTTING AND ARRANGING FLOWERS.—Never break off blossoms, cut them with shears. Select the first and finest blooms to ripen, so as to secure good seed. In arranging, do not crowd the bouquet or confuse the colors. The following colors form good contrast: Blue and orange; purple and yellow; pink and white; scarlet, white, and dark purple; blue and white; crimson and white; maroon and dark blue; rose and green, etc. All the colors can be combined in the same bouquet, but each combination should be a distinct bouquet of itself, separated by greens or white. White flowers are indispensable in the artistic arrangement of flowers, whether in baskets, vases, or hand bouquets, to give effect to the other colors. Delicate greens, unless geranium leaf can be obtained, are the most appropriate and graceful in floral combinations. If flowers are to be sent to a distance, wrap the stick which forms the handle of the bouquet, and the stem of each flower, with wet cotton or moss before arranging them. Be careful, too, to select blooms that are hardly in their prime, as many flowers fade as soon as perfected.

GENERAL DIRECTIONS FOR CULTIVATING BULBS.—Bulbs require deep, rich, at the same time, light soil. Dig the beds from eighteen inches to two feet deep, placing about four inches of decayed manure on the bottom of the trench, and enrich the top with decomposed manure and soil from the woods, and let it remain, at least, one month before planting the bulbs. The time for planting bulbs is from the middle of October to the middle of November; the bed which was prepared should be dug over, raised a little above the walk, and well raked. Tulips should be planted six inches apart; make holes four inches deep, with a stick rounded at one end, much in the shape of a tulip bulb, but larger than the largest tulip; put in each hole half an inch of sand from the lake shore, or what is usually called mason's sand, used by them in making mortar; put a bulb in each hole, cover with the hand, and press the soil firmly by beating it with the back of the spade, and before the severe season comes on, protect them with tan, straw, or boards. If wanted to increase, let them remain three years; if not, take them up as soon after flowering, as the leaves have disappeared, and replant in other beds prepared as directed at first. They will do very well, however, to leave two years, enriching the soil after the leaves die, with prepared compost, without cutting the bulbs; never disturb them in the spring. Hyacinths; plant much as tulips, though it is well to cover the bulbs with sand before putting on the soil; the holes for hyacinths should be deep enough to allow four inches of soil over the crown of the plant when finished; protect with cow manure. Remove all protection from bulbs the last week in March, and if frost threatens, they must be protected with boxes or any thing that will not break the foliage. The beds should be dressed as soon as frost is out of the ground, and all weeds removed as soon as they appear. Tulips and hyacinths should be supported by stakes, neatly made and painted green, which can be numbered to designate the color of each bulb. Lift hyacinths about five weeks after flowering, dry them slowly in the air without exposure to the sun, after which lay them away in a dry garret. Never allow the seed to ripen on bulbs, but break off the blossom as soon as its beauty has passed away. Crocuses; plant in rows two inches deep; the bulbs can remain four years without lifting. Jonquils; treat as tulips, except, as they do not bloom well the first year, they should not be lifted oftener than every third year, and may remain four. Tuberoses, Tigridas, and Amaryllis will not bear freezing; lift the bulbs after the first frost, dry, and pack them in dry sand until spring. Lilies; most of the lilies are quite hardy; they require rich deep soil. Narcissus requires a richer soil than the lily. Pæonias, are quite hardy; the soil should be rich and deep, plant them in the fall; they are propagated by dividing the roots; it will not do to lift them in the spring. Dahlias; the dahlia, if too highly stimulated, will make more branches and leaves than blossoms; the soil should be a good, sandy loam, which will not retain moisture; the border should be dug deeply, and a strong stake be driven firmly into the ground for each plant. If a gentle hot bed is at hand, hasten the sprouting of the plant by planting them in it; if not, place them near the furnace, or in some other warm situation, to sprout. The eyes of the plant are around the neck, not on the tubers, as in potatoes. The crowns should not be covered while sprouting, as the moisture of the hot bed will be apt to induce decay. When the sprouts are three inches, cut them from the plant near the base, using only a small piece of the old tuber, and plant the cutting in a pot filled with good loam mixed with soil from the woods, and place the pots in a gentle hot bed until time to plant it out in the open air; care must be taken to shade them until they have formed roots; they will do very well, however, if planted in the border as soon as of sufficient size to cut from the old tuber without potting. Shade for a week, and keep the soil moist, not wet, until the roots commence to form. Cut the stalks to within one foot of the ground as soon as touched by frost, and before the soil freezes; lift the whole root, dry it thoroughly, pack them away, and keep them in a dry place free from frost until spring. Some say, pack in dry sand; others, hang them by the stalk in the cellar; and others advise to lay the roots on shelves, and cover to the stem with dry sand. The principal requisites to insure their keeping are freedom from moisture and protection from frost; in a warm cellar where there is a furnace they might become too dry, so as to wrinkle, which is nearly as bad as moisture; the tubers should remain plump and smooth.

ROSES, TO PROPAGATE.—Roses can be increased by layering, budding, and grafting. Many of the hybrid perpetuals are difficult to grow from layers, taking two or more years to form roots, while others form good plants in one season. Roses are no more difficult to bud than peaches, were the thorns not troublesome. There are two methods of layering roses and other plants, which will be described. Select a young branch of the current year's growth, bend it to the ground, and split it an inch or more; some split the upper, and others the lower side of the branch; cover it as deep as convenient in the soil, and keep it in place, by pegging it down with a notched stick; support the end of the branch firmly in an upright position, and lay a flat stone over the part slit to keep the soil moist while the roots are forming. The other method is as follows: take a young growing shoot, run the knife under each eye, and place a splinter in each split, then cover the whole branch, peg it firmly in place, and let it remain all the season. There will be as many plants as slits, each eye making a shoot.

ROSES, TO BUD.—Select a shoot of the current year from the rose desired to propagate, and another of from one to three years, in which the bud is to be inserted. With a sharp pen, or, what is better, a budding knife, carefully remove the bud with a portion of the bark, and the wood attached above and below the footstalks of a leaf, in the axil of which the bud to be inserted is situated. To remove the bud insert the knife about three-fourths of an inch below the bud, and slip it carefully underneath it, making a smooth cut, taking but little wood with the bud, to half an inch above it; that is, the bark below the bud should be three-fourths, and above it, half an inch in length, the whole cut one and a quarter inch in length. Remove part of the leaf, and proceed to prepare the stock; make a slit lengthwise on the back of the stock, and another across the top of the first slit, leaving the incision in the shape of the letter T. Open the slit at the top without wounding the bark, slip the bud under the bark, and push it down as far as possible with the knife handle, being careful to place the bud in its natural position; press the bark firmly, and secure it in its place with strips of bass matting, wrapped evenly around it. As soon as the bud has united with the stock, which will be in about a month or six weeks if it does well, loosen the matting, and in two or three weeks after remove it entirely. Some advise removing the bit of wood adhering to the bud before inserting it, but if cut closely, it will be better to let it remain. If the wood is thick, it may prevent the buds uniting with the stock, but if properly cut, it will stiffen the bud, so that it will bear crowding down better, and also retain moisture longer than without it.

GRAFTING, REMARKS ON.—Although several kinds of grafting are practised, the same condition, to insure success, is essential to each, namely, that the inner bark of the scion should be closely united to the inner bark of the stock. Propagation of roses by grafting is less certain than by budding, on account of the pithy nature of the stem.

CLEFT GRAFTING.—This is the most sure method of grafting roses. Cut the scion before the buds swell, and shade them until needed, which will be as soon as the buds in the stock show signs of swelling.

15

At the proper time cut the stock horizontally the desired height; split the stock downward one or two inches, cut the scion from two and a half to three inches long, and shape the lower end with a sharp knife, in form of a wedge, insert the wedge end in the split made in the stock, holding it firmly, so that the back of the stock and scion will be brought into close contact. Bind it firmly in place with bass matting, and cover the whole top of the stock with grafting wax; in August or September cut the ligatures.

WHIP, OR SPLICE GRAFTING.—Select the scion and stock as near the same size as possible; the former should consist of from three to five buds, the latter may be cut to the ground or left at any height chosen. For standards it should be three, four, or more feet. Cut both scion and stock slanting, so as to fit perfectly. Make a dovetail notch in the stock on which to rest the scion; place the two together, and bind them firmly in place with a strand of bass matting, and cover the whole with grafting-clay, or wax. If the stock is much larger than the scion, the scion may be fitted to the side of the stock, so as to bring the two inner barks in contact. This is a very simple mode of grafting, and applicable to any shrub or fruit. Grafting wax is composed of rosin, beeswax, and tallow; to use it, melt the wax, and while warm dip in strips of cotton cloth, and wind the graft before the wax cools. Layering can be done when convenient, from spring until autumn. Budding can be performed from July until September; grafting is done in April. The buds will generally remain dormant until the next spring, when the stock may be headed down to within three inches of the budding; as the bud grows, tie it to the stock with strips of cotton or matting, without binding, to prevent the circulation of the sap. The graft, if it takes, will grow the same season it is put in. Some roses make layers in three, some six months, and some take years.

HONEYSUCKLES.—These are increased by layers; most of them are hardy, but some of the Chinese varieties need slight protection. Young sprouts should be allowed to grow as very often the old branches are winter-killed. It is well, when the principal branch becomes very woody, to cut it to the ground, and let it start anew.

LILACS.—Never allow the seed to ripen, and remove all suckers. Twinberries, Snowballs, and Flowering Currants, these grow from the slip, and are perfectly hardy; they all sucker badly; give them plenty room.

FLOWERS. 339

PRIVET HEDGES.—This grows from cuttings, and will make a fine hedge in three or four years. Allow room for the hedge to spread four feet from the base. Plant the cuttings in April about six inches apart; there should be three buds below the surface of the soil. Let it grow until fall or the next spring, and then cut it to two buds. The next season it is cut at midsummer, trimming both tops and sides, leaving the hedge six inches high. It is trimmed again in the spring, and so on, until it is as thick as desired, after which, to look well, it should be trimmed as often as is necessary to keep it in fine shape.

Box.—This makes a fine hedge, and the dwarf is beautiful for bordering, but winter kills it badly, where the winters are severe and open.

LIST OF HARDY FLOWERING SHRUBS GENERALLY CULTIVATED, BY THEIR COMMON OR VULGAR NAMES.

Purple Lilac.
White Lilac.
Red Persian Lilac.
White Persian Lilac.
Spiræas, pink and white.
Twinberry, or Shrub Honeysuckle.
Double-flowering Almond.
Bride's, or St. Peter's, Wreath, white.
Flowering Currants, yellow.

Double White Syringo.
Single White, called Mock Orange.
Snowball.
Privets, pink and white.
Waxberry, red and white.
Flowering Quince.
Double Peach.
Fringe. Tree, white and brown.
Rose Acacia.

LIST OF HARDY TWINING PLANTS WITH WOODY STEMS.

Coral Honeysuckle,
White Monthly Honeysuckle,
Fragrant Monthly   "
Chinese Twining   "
Woodbine,
Virginia Creeper,
Wistaria,
Bitter Sweet,
Trumpet Vine,

Hardy Passion Vine,
Irish Ivy, the most hardy of the Ivies,
Common Virgin's Bower Clematis, or sweet-scented; double red, and
Clematis Aurea Grandiflora, a blue variety, are the most beautiful of this family.

LIST OF HERBACEOUS CLIMBERS.

Calystegia pubescens, rose-colored. Plant this in boxes buried beneath the surface, as they soon become a base weed if allowed to grow in the garden.

Adlumia, a half hardy biennial, rose-colored, with graceful foliage.

ANNUAL CLIMBERS.

Cypress Vine, red,
" " white, } delicate and graceful.

Hyacinth Beans, many varieties.
Balsam Apple, " "
Sweet Pea, " "
Morning Glories, " "

Beside many other woody, herbaceous biennals, and annual climbers.

Roses.—No ornament of the garden more fully repays extra care than does the rose. The soil should be well drained, deep, rich, and highly manured; liquid manures, charcoal finely pulverized, and other stimulants, applied just before the flower buds, show their colors, enlarge the blooms, and brighten the colors materially. The time for transplanting in the spring is as soon as the frost is out of the ground, and at autumn, the last of September. June, or hardy roses, require but little pruning. The wood that shows age should be removed regularly, and if the branches crowd each other, they must be entirely removed. The hips of roses should be gathered as fast as the leaves fade, and the bushes often searched for the insects that infest them. We give a list of a few of the roses included in this class.

LIST OF HARDY ROSES.

Red Moss,
White Moss,
Marbled Moss,
Partout, or Moss upon Moss,
Persian Yellow,
Marbled,

Madame Hardy, white,
Cabbage, pink,
African, black,
Baron de Stael, cherry color,
King of Rome, red,
Queen of Violets,

and many others distinct from those named. The dwarf Scotch roses are very pretty, of which there are many varieties.

HARDY CLIMBING ROSES.

Greville, or Seven Sisters,
Queen of the Prairie,

Baltimore Belle,
Queen of the Belgians,

and many other natural climbers, can be made to cover arbors with very little trouble; they look very pretty twined round a pillar. The old branches must be removed every two or three years, to insure perfect blooming; but the ends should never be shortened.

LIST OF HYBRID CHINESE ROSES.

Blanchefleur, white.
Parny, bluish or dove color.
Lady Stewart, blush.
Fulgens, bright scarlet.

Coup de Hebe, pink.
Louis Philippe, dark.
Victor Hugo, rosy violet.
William IV., blush red.

The hybrid Chinese bloom but once in the season; they are perfectly hardy, luxuriant growers, fine bloomers, and many of them delightful for their fragrance. They can be used to cover arbors, pillars, or trellises to advantage, being quite flexible. If the shoots crowd, remove them entirely, but never shorten the ends of those left; leave them to grow naturally, but give them support as fast as they need it.

LIST OF HARDY PERPETUAL ROSES.

Blanch Vibert, pure white.
Duchess de Nemours, pale rose.
Duc d'Aumale, crimson.
La Reine, rosy lilac.

Baron Provost, dark rose.
Edward Jesse, pale red.
Du Roi, red capped.
Lane, bright carmine.

Youlande d'Arragon, pale rose, one of the best.

These, at the north, need a slight protection. They require deep, rich soil, richly manured every year. If they grow with luxuriance, they will need pruning twice yearly. If the rose to be pruned is budded, take care that in trimming you do not cut the inserted rose below the bud, and leave only the worthless stock. This is often done by a careless or ignorant gardener, and the nurseryman blamed for the poor rose that appears in the place of the one expected. The first pruning is usually performed the last of October or the first of November. Cut off two-thirds of each shoot that grew the preceding summer, and if the branches crowd, remove some entirely. The next June they will throw out a great number of shoots; which, to insure autumnal blooming, will need to be severely pruned. Leave about half of the new shoots to flower, and cut off full half the length of the remainder. In July and August the shortened branches will be full of blooms, paying well for the sacrifice of the June blossoms. The third blooming will commence in September, and continue until freezing weather comes on.

BOURBON ROSES.—These are mostly hardy, though a slight protection will prove beneficial at the north. Being constant bloomers, mostly fragrant, and in growth luxuriant, they may be considered one of the greatest ornaments of the garden. They should be pruned much in the same manner as the hybrid roses. Those named can be relied upon as fine roses, true to the description, if cultivated with care.

LIST OF BOURBON ROSES.

Souvenir de la Malmaison, pale, blush and large.
Madame Desprez, dark, perfectly double.
Paul Joseph, crimson.
Henry Clay, carmine.
Doctor Roques, dark crimson.
Acidalie, white.

Hermosa, bright rose.
Duval, bright scarlet and crimson.
Queen of the Bourbons, waxy blush.
Madame Angelina, creamy white.
Duc de Chartres, rosy pink.
Monthly Cabbage, bright rose.

NOISETTE ROSES.—These require a slight protection at the North. Give them a rich soil with plenty manure, prune in the same manner as the Bourbons, and they will give a profusion of blooms from June until November. The following are some of the best old tested varieties:

LIST OF NOISETTE ROSES.

Aimee Vibert, white dwarfish, one of the best.
Champney's Pink Cluster, light pink, profuse bloomer.
Luxembourg, rosy, purple, fragrant.
Fellenberg, bright crimson; a fine rose.
Bologne, dark, crimson, dwarfish.
Joan d'Arc, yellowish white.

There are many others equally fine, which might be described did our limits permit.

LIST OF HARDY BIENNIALS.

Digitalis, or Foxglove, several colors.
Campanula, or Canterbury-bell, in colors.
Antirrhinum, or Snap-dragon, and perennial, many colors.
Althea rosea, or Hollyhock, various colors.
Ipomopsis elegans, scarlet.
Dianthus barbatus, or Sweet-William.
Pansies, of many colors.

PERENNIALS.

Aconitums, or monkshood, various colors.
Bellis perennis, or daisy, many colors.
Delphinums, or larkspurs, blue.
Funkia, or day lily, different colors.
Iris, or fleur-de-lis, many colors.
Lychnis, many varieties.
Agrostemma flos-cuculi, or ragged robin, pink.
Phlox, white, pink, and purple.
Primulas, including cowslips, primroses, and auriculas.
Spiræas, white and pink.
Viola, or the double violets of many sorts.
Dianthus, pinks.
Yuca, or Adam's needle, and many others that cannot be enumerated in this work. Lilies, bulbs, peonies, etc., are included under perennials.

Biennials, if sown one year, bloom the next, ripen their seed, and die; some of the choice biennials, that do not come true to the seed, can be layered and continued from year to year; as, for instance, the finer sorts of snap-dragon, etc. Lilies of all sorts are mostly hardy; they need rich deep soil, and many of them are among the most beautiful of the garden ornaments. They should be lifted and changed to other parts of the garden once in four years. The high growing sorts should be supported by tying the stalks to neat stakes. Some are very fragrant, lading the air with perfume; the Chinese varieties are the most beautiful, but our native sorts are very fine.

CHAPTER IV.

DIRECTIONS FOR MAKING HOT-BEDS.

PROCURE fresh manure from the stables; it will take, for a bed four by six feet, a heap of manure eight feet wide, ten long, and four deep. Fork it over three times; if dry, sprinkle; it must neither be wet nor dry, but damp only. Throw out all that has burned before coming from the stable; cover with straw or boards to keep off the wind and rain; do not turn it in windy weather, unless absolutely necessary; and be careful not to lose too much heat. The object in turning it so often is to insure equality in the temperature of the manure; if this is not done, the bed will be of little use, the manure will be very hot at the first, and become cold very soon. Prepare a place for the bed, if possible where it will be protected from the north and east winds; the ground should slope a little towards the south. Lay down a little brush under the bed, or make a drain of strong plank, to let off the surface water quickly. It usually takes from two to three weeks to prepare the manure fit for the beds. When the manure is in the right state, evenly heated all through, proceed to make the bed; lay the manure evenly, and beat it down with the fork as each layer is put on, making it lie as compactly as possible. The manure should reach one foot beyond the frame all round. If the bed is to be planted in February, it should be four feet deep; if in March, three; if the 1st of April, two; and if only intended for forwarding plants, eighteen inches will do. Let the frames and sash now be put on, and cover the outside with straw, or boards, to keep in the heat. When the manure is all spread, put on the frames and sash, keeping it closed for a day or two to draw up the heat; the sash should then be tilted to let off the steam; this generally takes from three to four days. Be careful not to let the heat become too much reduced before making up the bed, or the plants will turn yellow instead of being a fine green. When the manure is in a right state, lay evenly over it the soil, which should be light and rich; the best soil is the top surface from the woods. When finished, it should be about six inches to one foot deep. Close the sash, and let it remain two or three days. Rake thoroughly to destroy the weeds and remove the lumps. If the bed is too hot, the ground will look whitish and cracked. To remedy this, drive sticks in as far as the manure in several places, and leave open the holes for a day. If the soil is burned take fresh ground, and proceed to plant the seed. Sow more seed than is needed, to allow for losses, and thin out the plants as soon as they have made two or three leaves. A novice cannot depend on feeling to regulate the heat of hot-beds; a thermometer must be used. During the day, with tilted sash, the heat should never be above 80°, or below 75°. At night it should never fall below 50° with the sash closed. Cover the beds at night to keep off the cold winds, as long as there is any danger of chilling the plants. If the heat rises, with the sash closed, above 80, tilt the sash at the back; and in the middle of the day, when there is no wind and the sun bright, push the sash nearly down. Plants need *air* as well as *heat*, and will no more thrive without the one than the other. In cold weather they are apt to damp off for want of air, and for this reason it must be admitted whenever it will do; but, at the same time, cold wind is very injurious. When the sash is tilted, it will be necessary to lay over the crack something to prevent the wind from blowing directly on the plants. Persons who do not understand this, fail in the management of their hot-beds, and the plants damping off, they become quite discouraged. Never allow the surface of the bed to become dry; water in the morning, during the early part of the season of forcing, and in the afternoon when the sun is hot. The water should be the same temperature as the bed, and, once a week, be slightly impregnated with pigeon manure or any other stimulus of the same nature. Rinse off the plants always with fresh water after watering with the liquid manure. Keep on hand a heap of compost, composed of decayed sod, weeds, stable manure, a sprinkling of salt, and some plaster, to mix with the soil in the beds, and furnish every plant, as far as possible, with the soil best adapted to its growth. This bed is proper for raising cucumbers, tomatoes, cauliflowers, cabbage, peppers, and celery. If the heat decreases, line the edges of the beds with fresh manure, and make holes in the sides to let in the heat from the outside. If the heat is too strong, the sun hot, and the wind blows, so that the sash cannot be let down, tilt the sash, and cover the glass with a sprinkling of straw. Cabbage and cauliflowers will do better raised in cold frames in the fall, and protected in them all winter. Celery should have a little salt raked in the soil, as it is a marsh plant; give it also plenty of the manure from the compost heap. Do not let the plants stand too thick, or they will be weak instead of stocky.

DIRECTIONS FOR RAISING CUCUMBERS.—Prepare the beds as directed, raise the soil within one foot of the glass. Prepare hills with compost about three inches high, so as to raise them within nine inches of the glass, plant a dozen seeds in each hill, and let them grow until they have made two or three leaves; then remove all but one in each hill. When the plants have made three leaves, pinch them off, to induce them to branch and fruit early. Draw the soil to the roots as they grow, tilt the frames whenever the weather will allow; the temperature should never fall below 60° or rise above 80° during the day, or fall below 50° at night. When the sun is hot, give plenty of air; but when it is hot, with a cold wind, cover the glass with a little straw, and keep the wind from blowing directly on the plants. As soon as flowers appear, give plenty water, and fertilize the plants, by taking those that are barren and turn the stamens in the centre of those that show fruit; one will impregnate two or three. In two weeks after, they should be fit to cut, if managed rightly. If the plants look yellow, there is not enough heat; line the beds with fresh manure. If bugs appear, sprinkle with lime. The early Russian is small, but very early, and does not run. Seeds should be three years old; old seeds make less vine and more fruit than fresh ones.

To GROW RADISHES.—These require a foot of soil; plant thinly, and as soon as the plants are up give plenty air and water, every day, not allowing the bed to become dry.

HOT-BEDS FOR FORWARDING PLANTS.—For forwarding plants in the spring, prepare a bed as follows: Make a pit and place over it the frame; spread in the pit twenty inches of manure, well prepared; cover it with eight inches of good mould; the surface soil from the woods is the very best to use for this purpose; and cover the beds, to draw up the steam; tilt the sash to let off the steam. In two or three days rake the soil, and plant the seeds. When the seeds are up give plenty air, and do not allow them to stand nearer each other than three or four inches. This is intended to apply principally to cabbages, cauliflowers, lettuce, celery, and tomatoes. Protect the plants during the severe weather, with mats at night, and give air when they will not chill, by raising the sash every night one-fourth of an inch. If this is not done they will decay. If cauliflower is injured by heat, it never recovers.

FORWARDING CUCUMBERS AND MELONS IN POTS.—Plant seeds in small pots one-third full of charcoal, and filled up with rich soil. Place them as near the glass as convenient, say six inches; when they grow, remove all but one plant in each pot. As soon as they have made three leaves, pinch them off. Turn the plants in the ground as soon as all danger of frost is over, without disturbing the roots. Early in April is soon enough to plant them in the pots at the north. If they are too large before planting out, they will not do as well.

To START TOMATOES.—Plant the seed thinly, and when up, give plenty air, and thin to two inches. Transplant them three times before the final planting, and trim off all the laterals as far as the first fruit branch; continue this practice all summer; remove them to the garden when all danger of frost is over and the soil is warm; shade them from the sun for a few days, sprinkle the leaves, and water well when first planted. Tomatoes managed in this manner will not feel the transplanting, and will fruit very early. Tomatoes incline to sucker.

EGG PLANT.—This requires more heat than other vegetables, and cannot well be grown with those requiring more air and less heat. The temperature for egg plant should never be below 80° during the day, and may rise to 100°, without harm. The lowest temperature at night should be 70°. Give air when the weather will allow, but be careful not to chill the plants, as they will not recover from it but always remain stunted. Transplant to another bed as soon as the plants have grown four inches; or add a new lining to the old bed, and transplant them to the other side of the frame. This is done to induce them to throw out roots for future use. If the plants can be transplanted two or three times without chilling, they will be better prepared to endure their change when finally transplanted into the garden. Water them well, and shade until fairly rooted, and afterwards give plenty air; gradually harden them, and when transplanted they will hardly feel the removal into the garden. Stake or put a frame to them when transplanted, and trim off all superfluous branches.

PEPPERS should be managed much like egg plants, but require very rich light soil; water with manured water, without touching the plants, twice a week, being careful that the water is not too highly impregnated. Soapsuds from the wash is beneficial once a week, if not too strong.

LETTUCE.—Plant early, and transplant to vacant spots to head; lettuce that has lived through the winter in the garden will head nicely. Sow peppergrass often, if relished by the family.

SWEET POTATOES.—Procure small sound tubers. The bed should be of gentle heat; mix a little plaster with the soil; lay the tubers three inches apart; cover lightly with the soil, and keep the bed barely damp. When the sprouts are four inches long remove them; and if too soon to plant out, bury the roots in the bed. More sprouts will grow from the same eyes. The 20th of March is early enough at the north to put them in the beds, and the 20th of May early enough to plant them out. They prefer sand enriched with vegetable manure. On heavy soil they are apt to be watery.

CUT-WORM.—The cut-worm prefers plants from hot-beds to others, as they are more tender than slow-grown plants. Wrap the stem of all plants, before transplanting to the garden, with brown paper two inches above the surface of the soil.

REMARKS.—Plants that incline to sucker, like the tomato, should be planted deeper every time they are transplanted, to induce the formation of new roots. Water can be left in the hot-bed, if there is room for the sprinkler, overnight; but if not, should be tested with a thermometer. Cucumber, melon, and other long-keeping seeds, ought not to be too fresh to plant in hot-beds, as they incline more to leaves than fruit. It is a maxim that the last effort of nature is to reproduce itself, and consequently old seeds make the most fruit. Celery, egg plant, pepper, lettuce, should be quite fresh and plump. All seed for the hot-bed should be soaked; a weak solution of saltpetre is, perhaps, the best for soaking them in, but it must be pure; much of the salts of nitre sold in the shops, is mixed with rock salt. Examine often to know if the seeds are germinating or rotted; frequently much time is lost expecting poor seeds to make their appearance, and, before it is known that they are worthless, the best heat of the bed has passed off. Seeds bought from many seedsmen are but little to be depended on. Buist, of Philadelphia, is probably as reliable a seedsman as there is to be found, though the seedsman is not always in fault; the bed may have been too warm, and the young plants have been burned after germination had taken place. If the soil of the bed is filled with weeds, it will be necessary to leave it several days, that all the weed seed may germinate, and be destroyed before putting in the seed. As fast as weeds appear, remove them, or the plants will soon be choked. Remember not to crowd the bed, a dozen good strong plants are worth fifty starved ones. At first thin but slightly, as many plants are lost by damping off; as soon as this danger is past, remove all that are not needed, without delay, and those left will pay for the trouble. Increase the air as the weather becomes mild, and plants strong, and gradually inure them to outdoor exposure. Gentle showers are always useful if warm, but cold, beating rains are decidedly injurious, chilling and breaking the tender plants. Long, cold rains are very deleterious. It will not do to keep the air from the plants long; the manure round the beds becomes soaked, and often the plants are ruined. Lay boards on the manure, to lead off the moisture, and dig drains a little distance from the bed to receive the water and carry it away. Raise the sash all round, and place boards aslant to prevent the rain beating in. Whenever the sun shows itself, air, if only for ten minutes. As plants grow, raise the sash so that the leaves will not touch the glass. The frames should have side pieces to fit them, two or three inches wide, to use as the plants increase in size. A record should be kept of the bed; when seeds were planted, when they germinated, and when transplanted. Tallies should also be put by every patch of seed, and as the moisture often obliterates the names from them, numbers or notches cut in them corresponding to the record in the diary, will be found more certainly to be depended upon. A corresponding number on the seed packet will be convenient to replant from, if need be. When through with the frames and sash, they should be put in order, and carefully stored where the sash cannot be broken or weather-beaten; if the paint is poor, now is the time to add a coat. If done in the spring, it will last but little time, having no time to season. A hot-bed, six feet square, will furnish many comforts to a small family, or forward a large number of plants, and the manure is but little injured as it is usually used. Every family that has a garden will find them a great comfort, fully paying for their trouble, as well as a source of much pleasure.

CHAPTER V.

INSECTS INJURIOUS TO AGRICULTURE, AND TROUBLESOME TO THE HOUSEKEEPER.

REMARKS.—In a work of this character, it is quite impossible to enter into a scientific description of the many insects, troublesome alike to the farmer, fruit cultivator, gardener, and florist. The naturalist would find a scientific description agreeable to the taste, but to the utilitarian, all that is necessary is a knowledge of the habits, modes of propagation, haunts, senses, duration of life, to this class of insects. Those destructive to grain and troublesome to cotton will not be noticed, as this work is not intended for the agriculturist alone, but principally for the use of families, in the cultivation of small gardens of fruits, flowers, and vegetables.

LIST OF INSECTS.—The following are the most destructive to the vegetable garden: wire-worm, larva of the May-beetle, tomato worm, striped-bug, squash-bug, strawberry worm, aphis, radish-maggot, and rose-bug.

Cut Worm.—This worm is an annual, or as it might, in some cases, be called biennial, the late perfected insects laying their eggs late in the fall, which being hatched just before winter, live until the spring, continuing their ravages through May and June. The millers are timid, and seek hiding-places to lay their eggs; they select pink borders, or any broad-leaved plant; thousands of them have been destroyed in the author's garden, under the leaves of the rhubarb plants. The color of the worm or caterpillar is brown of different shades, and they are found from the size of a knitting needle, an eighth of an inch or less long, to the size of a man's little finger, one and a half inch long. They dislike the heat and brightness of the sun, feed at night, or before the sun is high in the morning, hiding under leaves, or just below the surface of the soil near where they have been feeding. If searched for early in the morning, they will be found without difficulty. The greater part of these worms will cease their ravages with the commencement of July, but some will be found until winter sets in. Nothing offends them by the senses, except heat and cold. The only way to get rid of these pests is to gather and destroy them, but as their death often takes place after the mischief has been done, it seems much like shutting the gate after hogs have destroyed the garden. These creatures seem to have but little choice in their food, taking any thing that is tender enough for them to bite, from the sweet young corn to the smarting pepper. They cut the plant just above the soil, seldom reaching half an inch above the stem. Transplanted plants can be protected by wrapping the tender stems in brown paper two inches above their insertion in the soil; those not transplanted can be protected by rings of tin, made to clasp together, one or two inches high, making a ring about four inches in diameter. Search the soil for the worm before putting the ring around the plant, and press it slightly in the soil. Our gardener uses hundreds of these rings; they are gathered when the plants toughen, and taken care of from year to year. In a field of corn, these rings would be too expensive a protection; we have saved our corn by sowing lettuce broadcast in the field with the corn, at the time of planting the corn; the lettuce being more tender than the corn, is preferred by the worm, and by the time it is consumed the corn is too tough to be in much danger. It is well, too, to plant half as much more corn as will crop the field, to allow for losses. Many cut-worms' winter-quarters are disturbed by raking off all the rubbish of the garden. Lifting the borders and raking out the soil, will expose many young grubs to the cold, if done just before freezing weather comes on.

INSECTS INJURIOUS TO AGRICULTURE. 351

Chickens let out in the morning before the sun rises will destroy great numbers, and if shut up by eight, will do but little other mischief; at least, the good will overbalance the evil. As soon in autumn as the crops which chickens would trouble are gathered, let them have a free run of the garden, also keep hens in coops, with chickens, in the garden during the whole season, and these creatures will be very much diminished in numbers.

WIRE-WORM.—This worm lives, from its hatching until it takes a perfect form, seven years; it destroys roots, seeds, grasses, etc. It seems to have but little choice in the selection of food; destroys seeds especially corn and peas. It is usually seen of a yellowish brown, more of the yellow than brown predominating in the color. When found white, it has just cast its skin, which it does frequently. These worms may be destroyed in numbers when the spading is done. If the workman will throw the soil so as to pulverize it, he will see them immediately. They can be entrapped if very troublesome; the barren tubers of dahlias suit them well; where they are very troublesome, in small gardens it pays well to raise dahlias, and use the tubers in this manner; dozens will be found in one tuber; they should be examined once each week, the worms destroyed, and the tubers replanted. Whenever weeding is done by hand, they will be found in the roots of the grass and weeds, particularly young dock. Throwing up the garden in ridges late in autumn will kill numbers. Corn cobs spaded in the ground are said to destroy them; the worm eats into the centre of the cob and perishes, not being able to extricate itself to seek winter-quarters. The cobs should be near the surface, so as to be reached by the frost to kill the worm. To prevent the destruction of seeds by this worm, soak them in a solution of pure saltpetre; taste the solution; if saline, there is rock salt mixed with the saltpetre, and will retard the germination of the seed.

LARVA OF THE COCKCHAFER, DORR BEETLE, OR MAY-BUG.—This worm, called familiarly by farmers the corn-worm, is the larva of the May-bug, or as it is usually called, the horn-bug. It is a large, disgusting maggot, of a dirty white, with reddish head, large mouth, and red legs, usually curls up when touched. It is found of all sizes, the largest being about one and a half inch long, and as thick as a man's little finger. The beetle deposits her eggs in the ground in June and July, they are hatched in from two to three months, and continue in the larva state from three to four years, devouring indiscriminately every root within their reach. They particularly fancy the roots of corn and strawberries, though they will eat any thing, even to bark the roots of young apple trees. We lost, one season, five thousand strawberry plants, that had fruited once. These grubs will be found curled around or near the crowns of the plants on which they are feasting; their manner of proceeding in fibrous-rooted, is to eat the bark from the root near the surface, thus destroying all connection between the fibrous roots and the crown. If they would content themselves with the fibres or tap roots, the injury they occasion would be much less. In potatoes and tubers they eat into the heart; we have seen them nearly covered by the tuber they were eating. To destroy them effectually, so as to rid a garden, the beetles must themselves be caught. Early in May, they will be seen emerging from their winter-quarters, where they have taken the form of the perfect insect. They come out, principally, at evening; now, if the chickens are at hand, they can have a feast; if not, children should gather them, and feed the chickens. If fires are made every evening during May, June, and July, numbers will be decoyed into the blaze, as they always fly towards a light, and at the same time, the moths of the different parts of the garden will share the same fate. If fires are made, shake the cherry and other trees, to dislodge the lazy ones, and set them flying to their grave. This is to boys a great source of amusement, and can always be accomplished if there is a spot to build the fire, without scorching trees and plants. In spading, many of the torpid bugs will be turned up as well as worms, pass none by, destroy all, without mercy. If they are among the strawberries, examine each plant, and remove them; one grub will eat a whole row, passing from one to the other, as though they worked by a line. Allow no birds to be shot on the premises; they had better take their share of fruit with the grubs, than to take no grubs. In the garden, when the green corn is used for the table, pull up the roots and destroy the grubs. There is no use liming, sooting, sulphuring, or in any way frightening them; they can not be driven. Extermination by prevention and death is the only remedy worth trying.

TOMATO WORM.—This great worm is known to all who grow tomatoes; they strip a plant of the leaves, and then attack the green fruit; there is no remedy but fowls, birds, and hand-picking. These are annual, and many of the chrysalis will be found in the spring, where tomatoes were grown. They are nearly or quite as large as the worm, and a reddish color; destroy all you find.

STRAWBERRY WORM.—A small green maggot appears on the vines of the thinnest-leaved strawberry, which eats the whole of the leaf except the veins; I have not been able to discover what the green maggot was. The only remedy is to coop young chickens near, which will soon remedy the evil. If not checked, they will destroy the vines, root and branch.

RADISH MAGGOT.—In new soils, this maggot is seldom troublesome. Grow the radishes fast, scatter and rake in the soil wheat bran for the maggots to eat, instead of the root. Light sand is less infested with this plague to lovers of good radishes, than dark rich soil.

STRIPED BUG, OR JUNE BUG.—This is a small yellow bug, usually most plenty in June, though often lasting the whole season. We have found that they may be kept in check by the use of quicklime, sifted over the plants. On a patch of two or more acres, we seldom lose a vine; our plan is, to sift lime over each vine when the first bug is seen, not wait until the vines are overrun with them, and we never fail to save them, even when our neighbors are unable to raise a melon or cucumber. The lime must be applied at sundown, when the dew is on the leaves, or after a slight shower, and this must be repeated as often as the lime is washed off by rains. Air-slacked lime of full strength is what we use, old lime would not be as effective. Many advise sulphur, soot, ashes, snuff, manure, water, etc., each of which we tried before lime, but for several years have used lime alone, with the best success; it is also a benefit to the plants, furnishing them with a useful stimulant.

SQUASH-BUG.—This miserable bug is a dirty brown, so near the color of the ground as to be imperceptible to an inattentive observer, and so timid, that without the utmost caution in approaching them they hide so as not to be found. They are very injurious to the plant, seeking the juices, or poisoning every stalk they pierce, so that it will wither, making its removal necessary. They emit, in crushing, a very disagreeable odor, resembling the bed-bug. Their eggs will be found on the underside of the leaf, where, if undisturbed, they will soon hatch, and destroy the whole plant; crush the eggs; sprinkle with flour of sulphur, look over the plants daily, and destroy the bugs.

APHIS, OR PLANT-LOUSE.—The common aphis, or plant-louse, found more or less on the stems, leaves, buds, and often the roots of most plants, is a small, soft, usually green-colored insect with a short, oval body, small head, round eyes, long tubular beak, long tapering antennæ, long slender legs, two jointed feet, and a tube at the hinder extremity, from which it ejects at pleasure drops of sweet fluid. The females are wingless. In the autumn, the winged insects or males may be seen, immediately after which the female lays her eggs, and both die. Early in the spring the eggs hatch, producing females only, which are immediately in a state to continue their kind. In the course of forty-eight hours these produce alive nearly or quite twenty young lice, in the same state as their parent. These again bring forth their young as did their parent; and thus brood after brood is produced for seven generations, without the appearance of a male. The last brood, consisting of males and females, pair, lay their eggs, and become extinct until the next season. These little creatures do much mischief, sucking the sap from the tender branches of the plants they infest, and would be far more injurious had they not some natural enemies, to thin their ranks. Their enemies are birds, the larva of the lady-bird, the young of the golden-eyed, laced-winged fly, and the maggots of the flies, belonging to the genus Syrphus. The aphis has, however, one friend which protects and watches it with anxious care. Wherever the plant-lice are to be found, there may be seen ants, running up and down the trunk or stem of the tree or plant, gathering the sweet drops which exude from the lice, often hastening the periods of its discharge, by caressing the insects with their antennæ. They protect the lice which infest the roots of plants, with the same care they do their own young; and look after the eggs, often moistening them with their tongue. Plants infested with lice should be protected from the ants; chalk the tree, or place a ring of chalk close to the body, and below the surface, around the plant or tree. Water with an infusion of quassia chips, or tobacco, and rinse the plants after a short time. When the plants infested are delicate, they had better be brushed off, than wet with either of the above infusions. If the first lice are destroyed, there will be no future trouble; cabbages and other vegetables may be dusted with lime or ashes. To destroy lice on the roots of plants; water with soapsuds, or a weak solution of saltpetre, and mix chalk with the soil. There are also other colored plant-lice beside the common green, or the aphis rosea; those on the cabbage have a mealy appearance; those found on the willow are of a black color, which, when crushed, leave a reddish stain; those found on roots are white. Some inhabit tumors, growing upon leaves, and are usually without honey tubes, and clothed with a white down. There is also a species of this insect, called by some the woolly aphis; it is found on the tender branches and suckers of apple trees; when crushed, they leave a stain, resembling blood. Cut off the suckers and infested branches, and burn them; remove the soil from the trunk, and scrub the whole tree to the root, with the wash recommended for apple trees.

BARK LICE, OR SCALY APHIS.—These are of different shapes; some are oval, others convex, kidney shaped, globular, like a muscle or bottom of a boat. They subsist principally on the juices of the stem and trunk of tree or plant; some, however, inhabit the leaves, and a few the roots of plants. The best way to rid a tree of these insects, is to scrub the whole tree early in the spring with the prepared soda wash. Remove the soil, and wash the trunk to the roots, and water with strong soapsuds, soaking the soil as far as the roots extend. If the tree is very bad, repeat the washing the first of June.

ROSE-BUG OR SAW-FLY.—The larva of this bug infests the bud of the rose, and many other plants, but from its being so very troublesome to the rose cultivator, it has of late been called the rose-bug almost entirely. The perfect insect, which is a beautiful creature, lays its eggs in the flower-bud, in which the grub is hatched, eating its way out, destroying the petals in its way. The rose has an insect called a leaf roller, and another which is called a leaf miner, which cuts the pulp of the leaf, marking its course by yellowish zigzag lines; the only method that effectually rids the rose of these pests is hand picking. Dust with sulphur, and water with quassia, if very numerous.

APPLE-BORER.—The apple borer is a deceitful foe, doing its mischief unseen; when only a few small holes can be seen, the whole wood inside the bark may be reduced to powder. The perfect insect is a brown and white striped beetle, half an inch long, seldom seen by day, as it flies by night. It deposits eggs in the bark near the surface of the ground, late in the spring, or the first of summer. Its presence is first indicated by small holes, as large as buck-shot, from which ere long a fine dust will be ejected; this is the borings of the insect. Unless the tree is taken in time it will be impossible to save it. If the insect has only perforated the bark, it can be cut out; if deeper in the wood, follow it with a wire and crush it in its den; if it cannot be reached, plug the holes, that the insect may not emerge and lay its eggs. To prevent the insect from laying its eggs, remove the soil from the roots, and wash the tree around its base with a mixture of the soda wash, tobacco, and flour of sulphur; or with a receipt of Mr. Thomas, which is: "To one pint of sulphur a gallon of soft soap, and sufficient strong tobacco water to reduce the whole to the consistency of paint." It is also recommended to inject this preparation in the holes of the insects. The quince is also troubled by this borer.

THE CATERPILLAR.—The common orchard caterpillar is hatched at the same time the leaf buds begin to open. At first it is very minute, but rapidly increases in size until it measures two inches in length, when it spins a cocoon and passes to the pupa state. In the latter part of summer it comes out in the form of a yellowish brown miller, deposits its eggs in rings, encircling the smaller branches, near the extremities, containing from three to five hundred. These are protected by a sort of varnish, where they remain until spring, and are hatched as has already been described. These caterpillars very materially injure the fruit, as the leaves are entirely destroyed, looking much like a branch burned by fire. Search the trees late in autumn, and cut off all the nests of eggs. If one is neglected until it is hatched, remove it as speedily as possible.

THE CANKER WORM.—This worm attacks both fruit and flower. They cover the tree with small webs, and destroy the foliage, which gives to the tree the appearance of having been scorched by fire. The only remedy recommended by Thomas is to encircle the tree with a canvas belt coated with tar and train oil.

THE APPLE-WORM.—This attacks the fruit at the blossom end, eating its way to the core. Destroy all imperfect fruit, and keep up fires at night to attract the millers.

PEACH-BORER.—The perfect insect somewhat resembles the wasp, though destitute of the sting, and in other respects entirely distinct. It deposits its eggs at the foot of the tree, from June until the latter part of autumn, which hatch and enter the bark of the tree; the peach-borer does not perforate the wood, like the apple-borer, but does its mischief by girdling the tree. Its presence is indicated by exudations of gum, when the insect should be searched for and probed to death, or cut out. Ashes piled round the tree, allowing a peck to a tree, will prevent their entering the root, though they sometimes will enter above the ashes; wrapping the tree in canvas, with the ashes below, is also a good plan. Scalding the trees will prevent the eggs hatching, though if this is carried to too great an extent it will kill the trees. Sulphur is also efficacious as a preventive, and the paint of sulphur, tobacco, and soap, advised for the apple-borer, will be found useful.

CURCULIO.—The curculio, to a common observer, is well described by saying it as much resembles a ripe hemp-seed as any thing. This pest of the plum and its varieties commences, almost as soon as the blossoms fall, to puncture the fruit, making a crescent shaped incision. The egg soon hatches, and the young larva makes its way to the centre of the plum, feeding in its way on the pulp of the fruit, causing it to fall to the ground before maturing. Many remedies have been tried, some with partial, and others with entire success. Jarring the trees, salting the soil, allowing half a peck to a good sized tree, throwing lime, sulphur, and ashes on the trees dry, and also injecting them with a syringe mixed to the consistency of paint. Tying tansy in the tree has been also found useful, and smoking with sulphur and tobacco. All the imperfect fruit should be destroyed as it falls, and one of the above remedies resorted to until something better is known. It is to be hoped, if there is a better remedy, it will soon be made public. I would advise trying chalk around the tree, so as to touch the trunk, and extend one or two feet around it; also to wash in the soda water wash, scrubbing the bark with a stiff brush. If a tree is planted where the family pass it constantly, or so near water that the branches reach over the stream, or so near a barn that the fermenting manure will trouble the insect, it is probable it would perfect its fruit without further trouble. A bed of herbs, such as tansy, camomile, and wormwood, might perhaps offend them. Camomile is particularly offensive to all insects.

CURRANT-BORER.—Remove all the wood infested by the borer, following it up until the insect is found; wash the bushes in the paint of sulphur, tobacco, and soap, recommended for the apple-borer. Remove the soil from around them early in autumn, and replace with fresh, to destroy the cocoons, if there are any.

RASPBERRY-BORER.—Remove all infested canes, and renew the soil around the stools.

CATERPILLAR ON GOOSEBERRY.—Dust with sulphur, sprinkle with soapsuds, and with water slightly impregnated with salt.

GRAPE-WORM.—To rid a vine of small insects, syringe with a solution of whale-oil soap. Gather the beetles and destroy them, and pick off the caterpillars.

ANT-HILLS, ETC.—Scald the hills, when it can be done without destroying plants, with hot soda water. Use lime or chalk to starve them out, making circles around their hills, which they will never cross. Chalk is to them probably poisonous, as an ant never crosses a chalk line under any circumstances. Make rings of chalk around the shrubs and plants they trouble, three inches from the plant or stem, and they will not ascend it.

BED-BUGS.—Young housekeepers should have every bedstead oiled before setting up, with the following receipt, and continue to use it once every year, in the month of March. If there are bugs in the house and bedsteads, oil the cracks of the rooms where they are, and the bedsteads, every month, until they disappear, and afterwards yearly. To one pint of spirits of turpentine, add one ounce of corrosive sublimate, put it in a bottle and shake well. Apply with a feather. Label the bottle, "Bed-bug POISON."

MOTHS.—Procure an old whiskey barrel, perfectly tight, and free from worm holes; place it in a dry garret; dust it out, but do not wet it; shake all the furs and woollens free from dust, and if they have lain until May, lay them in the sun. Then pack the goods and furs smoothly in the barrel and close tightly. If you please, put a half-ounce of Bergamot in the barrel with the goods, to prevent them from having an unpleasant odor from the whiskey. Camphor, shavings of red cedar, cloves, and tobacco, are all preventives. Furs and shawls wrapped in newspaper are seldom troubled with them; this will be well to remember in putting down carpets where moths have been found in the cracks of the floor. Carpets are sometimes ruined while in use, before their presence is observed.

CRICKETS.—Arsenic on apple or cabbage leaves will destroy crickets. Cayenne pepper will drive them from their haunts if it can be ejected into the cracks where they are.

To Entrap Red Ants.—Set a plate of sugar on the shelf where they congregate, and burn the insects as fast as the plate fills. Hickory and maple-bark also attract ants. The bark can be burned and renewed frequently, which will soon thin them.

To Protect from Ants.—Chalk the sides of jars containing sweetmeats, sugar barrels, or any thing which these insects infest, and they will not trouble them. If the shelves of the buttery are chalked for half an inch all around the wall, both upper and lower sides, the ants will not cross the chalk, and thus the shelves will be entirely protected. If any dishes are allowed to touch the wall, the ants will soon cross over on them, and the chalking be of no avail.

Rats.—Chloride of lime, scattered in the cellar, is said to drive off rats.

Fleas.—Camomile and pennyroyal is said to be repulsive to fleas, and to effectually prevent their attacks on children who have a bag of these herbs about their person. In some localities children suffer greatly by the sting of these insects. Wash the bites in a solution of ammonia.

To Destroy Flies.—If mosquito bars are used in the windows, and doors are kept closed, flies will trouble the parlors but little. Cobalt wet on plates will destroy them, but is very poisonous, and must be kept where children cannot reach it. Black pepper, with sugar and water, or cream, is also a good thing to use for the same purpose, and much less dangerous than cobalt where there are young children.

Spiders.—Sweep down and destroy all nests, out of doors and in, until through the month of August, and there will be but few left to trouble the housekeeper during autumn.

Mosquitoes.—Where they abound in numbers, bars should be used around the beds. If a few light on the wall, touch them lightly with the blaze of a candle, without burning or smoking the paper. Ammonia is useful to remove the poison of the bites.

Cockroaches.—Cats will destroy numbers if they can get at them. Strychnine, spread on bread, butter, and sugar, will destroy numbers. It is a deadly poison, and must be used with great caution. Remove all eatables before using it, and wash the shelves thoroughly, to remove all the poison.

PART IX.

CHAPTER I.

CURING MEATS, AND DAIRY.

REMARKS.—It is usually thought that the parts of the animal which contain the fewest large blood-vessels are the best for salting. Salt has the property of dissolving fibre, thus reducing the amount of fluid in the meat. If too much is used, too much of the fibre will be dissolved, and the meat, if very lean, will be hard and unhealthy. The only salt safe to use in curing meats is the evaporated salt; the common barrel salt is so often adulterated with lime as to render it unsafe to use. Saltpetre too is now often adulterated with salt, rendering it almost worthless. Pork must never be packed in a beef barrel, no matter how well cleansed; there is something about the two that will not allow them to come in contact. If a small piece of beef should be laid in the pork barrel the whole would soon be ruined. All animal heat should be removed from meats as soon as possible after being killed. The animal should not be cut until it is cold, or if cut, not salted. Meat preserves much better without bone; remove all that is possible before salting. If you do not understand cutting up a creature properly, employ a butcher, and notice his movements, that you may be prepared for the next season. If dried beef is wanted, the hind quarter should be selected. It is the best for family use, whether the ham is dried or not, as it makes fine pieces for slicing cold.

TO CURE HAMS FINELY.—Allow for every hundred pounds of ham two pounds of brown sugar, four pounds of rock salt pulverized, or evaporated salt ground fine, one-fourth of a pound of saltpetre pulverized; mix these together, and add sufficient molasses to make a thick batter. Rub the hams thoroughly with the batter, pack them close in a keg, skin side down; let them lie five days; then take them out, rub each ham again, and repack, putting the top one down, thus reversing the order of the hams, laying the skin side down. Let them lie five days longer. Take lye, made of clean house ashes, strong enough to bear an egg; reduce it half; there should be sufficient lye to form a pickle that will cover the hams; add to the lye all the rock salt it will dissolve cold; let it settle, and skim well; then pour it over the hams, and let them lie in the pickle until cured through. Medium hams, in a temperature above freezing, will cure in about twenty days. If difficult to make lye, use a pound of saleratus dissolved in soft water. When the hams are cured, hang them in a cool place to drain; when a little dried, smoke them. The best smoke is from corncobs. If you put under the hams a piece of brimstone as large as a small hickory nut three times, they will smoke in two or three days; or, if the smoke continues all night, in sixty hours; the brimstone leaves no smell or taste whatever. If no brimstone is used, they will need to smoke from six to ten days. When the hams are smoked, sew them up in cotton, covering every part, and whitewash them; then put each ham in a large paper bag, paste it together, and hang them in a cool place, away from rats. They preserve all summer, if they are wrapped in paper and buried in wood-ashes. A ham, unless protected, in fly time will soon become filled with vermin.

To CURE DRIED BEEF.—For one hundred pounds of beef, allow ten pounds rock salt, four ounces of saltpetre, and two pounds of brown sugar. Dissolve the ingredients mentioned in clean soft water, boil the pickle, remove the scum, and pour it on the beef when cool; when cured through, drain and smoke very little. If brimstone, the size of a hickory nut, is used with the smoke, it will be sufficiently smoked in twenty-four hours; it may be preserved in the same way as ham in ashes. To keep it from becoming hard, pack it closely in a strong box or keg, and compress with great weights. Large quantities can be kept soft for shipping by packing it in strong casks, and pressing by steam to almost a solid body; this has been practised to some extent by packers, to good advantage.

CORNED BEEF.—For one hundred pounds of beef, take five quarts of solar salt, five ounces of pure saltpetre, dissolve in two pails of soft water, boil and skim. Pack the beef closely in the barrel, and pour over the brine while boiling hot, sink the beef with a weight, and cover tight. It will be fit to boil in twenty-four hours. This mode of curing beef is very fine, but will not keep longer than the first of April. If the brine does not cover the beef, make more, as after it is once scalded with this brine it will take no more salt. Test the saltpetre; if adulterated with salt, the beef will not be a bright color. Dried beef and venison may be cured in this manner. If desired to corn beef for summer, use double the amount of salt when the brine is first made; salt added after the brine is first put on, will not add to its saltness.

To SALT PORK.—Lay in the bottom of the barrel a layer of solar salt, one and a half inch thick; pack the pork edgewise as compact as possible, cover it with a layer of salt as thick as the bottom layer, then pack another layer of pork and the same quantity of salt, etc., until the whole is packed, finishing with a layer of salt. Make a brine as strong as possible of solar salt, put a weight on the pork, and pour on the brine, until it is covered several inches. A hog weighing two hundred and fifty pounds is the best weight to buy; be sure the hog is cornfed, not fatted on still-slops, as the pork to be hard must be fatted on corn. When pork is taken from the barrel, be careful that no part of the meat is left above the brine; if this happens, it will become wormy. All bone and lean meat should be removed when the hog is cut up. Lean salt pork is worthless; use it in the family, or make sausages.

To CURE BACON.—Bacon is side pork; it may be cured and managed like ham.

To CURE TONGUE.—For fifty pounds, take five quarts salt, five ounces saltpetre, dissolved in a pail and a half of soft water; boil and skim, and pour on the brine hot; sink the tongues and cover tight; they may be boiled as soon as the brine is cold.

CHAPTER II.

THE DAIRY.

CARE OF A COW AND HER MILK.—If pastured, be sure that the cowboy does not hurry her to and from the pasture; if she becomes heated, her milk will be unhealthy; the nearer the pasture, the more milk will she give with the same amount of feed. If not pastured, she should be slopped night and morning at regular hours, to induce her to come home in season; a cow that will not come home regularly, and cannot be pastured, is not worth the trouble of keeping. Milking should be done at regular hours night and morning; a slow milker will soon dry a cow, the faster she is milked, the better; cows should be stripped until no milk can be obtained, or they will gradually fail in milk, let the feed be what it may. Some cows discharge their milk; it is said that faithfully rubbing the whole bag while giving no milk, and a month after, with tallow, will cure this entirely. Milk is affected by the food of the cow; if she eats turnips or cabbage, it injures her milk materially. Most persons use new cow's milk the fourth milking, but it is well to test it; if it boils without curdling, it is fit for use; if not, throw it out. If milk becomes stringy or curdles, there is something the matter with the cow, and she should have the advice of a person experienced in the diseases of cattle. Bran for cows is much better if scalded, but they must not eat it hot; scald a pailful at night for the morning meal, and in the morning for the evening; they ought to be fed very early in the morning, and about five at evening; they require a large supply of water, and if there is none in the pasture, should be allowed to drink all they will, morning and evening. Milk should be strained into shallow pans as soon as the froth goes down; the greater surface the milk has, the more cream will rise. Set milk in a cool, dark cellar, free from impurities; milk will absorb and retain unpleasant and strong odors. In hot weather, it will remain sweet longer if scalded, but the cream is not as good as when allowed to rise naturally.

To MAKE BUTTER,—Skim the milk before it becomes very sour, merely turned, or what is called blue; pass a silver spoon handle around the edge of the pan, and lift the cream with a perforated skimmer, and put it immediately into the cream crock; the cream should not be in summer over two days gathering, and if there were sufficient cream to churn daily, it would be better still; stir the cream two or three times each day briskly until it is ready to churn, when usually it will come quickly. Churning should be done, during warm weather, early in the morning in a cool place; the dasher ought to be moved regularly, not sometimes fast and then slow, but with a regular motion, until the butter separates from the milk; the dasher may then be moved more gently, turning round the handle at each plunge of the dasher; when the butter is gathered, wet the bowl and ladle in ice water, pour out the water and take up the butter, drain off as much of the buttermilk as possible, pressing the butter a moment gently with the ladle. Make indentations in the butter with the ladle, fill them with nice solar salt, and set the bowl in a cool place, (or if wanted soon, in ice water;) at evening, when the butter is hard, work it gently without breaking the grain, and squeeze out all the milk that can be removed without too much pressure; salt as before, and let it stand until morning; then finish it, making it in rolls or cakes with as little pressure as possible. If butter is worked with a heavy hand, it becomes smooth like a salve. If to be used immediately, it is now finished, but if to be put down for winter, add, before the last working, to every two pounds of butter, a teaspoonful of pure loaf-sugar and a saltspoon of pulverized saltpetre; work it gently through the butter with the salt, cool it on ice, put it in a press in a cool cellar, surrounded with a thin cloth, and press it gently until all the milk is entirely discharged, then pack it in small jars for the winter. If the jar is not full with one churning, (which is a much better plan than to fill it with several successive days' churnings,) scatter salt between each new layer, and finish by a layer of salt on the top; lastly, paste strong paper over the mouth of the jar with the beaten white of egg, varnish it with the same, add another paper before it is dry, cover it with the egg, and keep it in a cool place until needed for winter use, when it will turn out as sweet as fresh-made butter. May and June are the best months to lay down butter for winter use; if the grass starts early in April, May is much to be preferred.

CHEESE-MAKING.—The utensils needed for cheese-making are a *Cheese tub*, in which the milk is mixed with the rennet water to form the curd; *Cheese knife*, sometimes formed of wood, for cutting or breaking the curd; *Cheese ladder*, a wooden frame used to rest the vat upon, while the whey is draining from the curd; *Vat*, or hoop turned from solid wood, usually elm, with a loose bottom, which, with the sides, is perforated with holes to let off the whey, while the cheese is in the press; *Cheese press, Cheese boards*, and *Cheese cloth*, which is made of strong linen, woven very open. Cheese is made from May until October, if the season is favorable, although October is often too cold for the operation to be well performed. The curd is produced with rennet water made by soaking the rennet in clear water until of the proper strength. It requires experience to know how much rennet is needed for a certain amount of milk; if too little is used, the curd will not form; if too much, the cheese will heave, and have a strong, rank taste. A little salt assists the formation of the curd. After the rennet is put into the milk, mix it thoroughly with a wooden spoon, cover the tub tightly with a wooden cover, and spread over it a thick blanket, to prevent the passing off of the heat during the coagulation of the milk. The milk ought not to lose over from five to seven degrees of its natural heat, while the curd is forming. The temperature of the milk should be from 85° to 90°, which is about the natural heat of milk when drawn from the cows. If the cows have been racing, and the milk heated above the usual animal heat, it should be cooled as soon as possible to the desired heat. If milk is too warm when the rennet is added, the cheese will heave, become spongy, hard, and possess but little flavor; if not warm enough, the curd will be tender, never forming a firm cheese, and will bulge out at the sides. If the cheese is to be made from two milkings, set the milk in shallow pans in a cool place; when used, remove all the cream, bring the skimmed milk to little more than the desired heat, mix it with the new milk, and stir in the cream. Test the milk; if too warm, cool it; if too cool, add very little hot milk until it has the desired heat. If there is the right proportion of rennet, and the milk is the proper temperature, the curd will set in one, or at most two hours; when the curd is firm, cut it gently and slowly across the curd, reaching the knife to the bottom, making the incisions about an inch apart, after which cut across in the opposite direction and around the tub, to allow the whey to rise above the curd, which will sink to the bottom of the tub. Remove the whey as it rises, without disturbing the curd; after a little time, slowly cut the curd into finer, until reduced to small pieces. The tub is then again covered, and allowed to stand from fifteen to twenty minutes; it is then tilted, and the curd gathered to the upper side. A semicircle board, fitting loosely one half of the tub's bottom, is now introduced into the tub; the board, with from forty to sixty pounds weight, according to the size of the cheese, is placed over the curd, until the whey has passed off. The curd is now cut into still finer pieces, and pressed by the hand and the weight as long as any whey is discharged. When the whey assumes a slightly greenish color, it is a proof that the curd was properly formed, but if white, it shows that the coagulation was imperfectly produced, and it may well be understood that the cheese will not be prime. The cheese is now ready to be transferred to the vat. The curd is now divided into convenient quantities, broken very fine, and salted; after the salt is well incorporated with the curd, it is ready to transfer to the vat; when all is prepared, the cheese-cloth is placed over the vat, and the curd is placed in it. The curd should be heaped in the centre of the vat, the corners of the cloth turned over the cheese, and pressed gently with the hand until it adheres sufficiently to allow a board to be put over it with a part of the cheese-cloth separating it from the curd. The whole is then put into the press, with the pressure of from forty to sixty pounds, according to the size of the cheese, and remains in the press from two to three hours. *The cheese is then taken from the vat,* and put for one hour into hot whey, for the purpose of hardening the skin, after which it is wiped dry, and again put into the vat. The upper part of the cheese being still above the vat, it is bound round with a strong binding, called a *cheese-fillet;* or a hoop is put around it, over the cloth which covers the cheese, to preserve its shape, and is again put into the press, where it remains from twelve to fourteen hours; after half an hour the cheese, is turned in the vat, bottom side up, and another cheese-cloth put in the vat; it should press forty-eight hours, being turned several times during the time. The cheese being completed is placed on a cheese-board, and carried to the cheese-room, which should be dry, airy, and well ventilated, of moderate and even temperature, not exposed to currents of air or sunbeams, as the wind and sun dries the cheeses too fast to allow them to ripen well. Cheeses are turned daily and rubbed with butter for some time, and three times every week until perfectly cured or ripened. Rich cheeses need no coloring matter; it is the poor ones that require this, to give them a fair appearance in market. Sage cheese is made by incorporating the juice of green sage with the curd, before it is put into the vat. To preserve cheeses from flies, after being cut, a cheese-box is almost indispensable; one with a wire cover is to be preferred.

PART X.

CHAPTER I.

SPRING WORK.

MARCH.—The nits or eggs of all vermin which have lain dormant through the cold months, will now begin to hatch, and unless preventives are promptly applied, the increase of *bedbugs* and *cockroaches* will be without number. Search for the bugs, kill all that can be found, and oil all bedsteads with *corrosive sublimate*, mixed with turpentine (*see* BEDBUGS); lift boards and barrels in the cellar; scald all the bugs under them with boiling water; spread bread and butter with *arsenic*, to lay in their haunts; wet crevices with the preparation of *mercury*, mentioned above, and prepare the same in whiskey for the edges of shelves where food is stored; but be careful that none is dropped on the shelves to come in contact with food, as it is a deadly poison.

APRIL.—By the first of April, the cellar should be carefully looked over, and all impurities removed; if the soap-grease has not been thrown into lye (as it accumulated during the winter), it should now be sent to the factory, or be mixed with strong lye, preparatory to soap-making. All refuse vegetables ought to be thrown out; the potatoes selected; the small ones given to the cow, if there is one, and the best reserved for spring use. The meat barrels will now need looking after; if there is much corned beef on hand, unless very salt, it should be used as fast as possible. See that the pork is well covered with brine, and the sides of the barrel free from vermin; have the barrels cleansed on the outside from all soil; examine the lard; if it appears soft, as though mixed with water, heat it boiling hot; strain it into jars, and paste a paper over each while hot. If the hams have not been protected before, bag and bury them in a barrel of strong, hard-wood ashes, and do the same with dried beef; examine the cheese; if inclined to mould, or infested with vermin, make it into pot or brandy cheese. To do this properly, proceed as follows: first remove all mould or vermin; cut or crumble the cheese fine; for pot cheese, pound it hard, with a little sweet butter between each layer, thoroughly incorporating the butter with the cheese. Brandy cheese is prepared in the same manner; using the best brandy in the place of butter; when finished, cover the cheese with paper wet in brandy, and paste strong, brown paper over the mouth of the jar. It will be fit to use in a month. Examine the pickles and sweetmeats; if pickles are moulding, renew the vinegar (see PICKLES); if preserves are fermenting, boil them up for tarts; if entirely spoiled, put the syrup in the vinegar-barrel; wash and scald the jars and bottles that have been emptied during the winter; turn them up to drain; when dry, send them to the store-room and throw the corks away; it is unsafe to use them twice for sweetmeats; if jars or bottles with ground stoppers are used, tie each stopper to the jar it is fitted for, before washing; if misplaced, it will be almost impossible to remove them when the fruit is needed, and the jars will very likely be broken in the effort. If there is butter on hand, in danger of becoming rancid, melt it over water slowly; when melted, let it boil up once with slices of raw potatoes cut very thin, boiled in it; strain it in very small jars while boiling hot, stirring the salt through the butter while it is straining; cover each jar, while hot, with paper, pasted firmly to the edge of the jar, and afterwards varnish the paper with the beaten whites of eggs; use the butter for sauces, gravies, etc. If butter is well prepared in autumn, it will remain sweet until the next May. After all impurities are removed from the cellar, sweep down the walls, destroy all vermin, and whitewash thoroughly; cleanse the windows, shelves, etc.; and if the floor is damp, scatter lime over it; arrange the contents of the cellar most convenient to yourselves; place all barrels on a low staging, to prevent their moulding; scatter lime under each; when the cellar will be ready for the summer, and a good beginning made toward house-cleaning. Now proceed to the attic; look over the patches, and send off all useless rags; examine the summer clothing; distribute to the poor every article which cannot be used in the family; especially woollen goods, which form good hiding-places for moths. Many persons fill their houses with moths, by allowing useless woollen garments to accumulate, year after year, in the garret. Air well all furs and woollen goods laid aside for the next season, and pack them away (*see chapter on* INSECTS); destroy all spider-webs, and thoroughly cleanse the garret; bring down all the spring clothing; if not repaired in the fall, now is the time to do it: never allow your work to drive you, but keep it ahead of your necessities. The storeroom is next in order. Take out all movable articles; if not done in March, touch with a feather, dipped in a preparation of *corrosive sublimate* and whiskey, all the cracks in the wall, floor, back of the shelves, and around the casing; let it remain several hours before cleaning, if convenient overnight; this, if carefully done every spring, will preserve the storeroom from cockroaches and other vermin, which are apt to infest such places. When the poison has lain sufficiently long, cleanse the shelves, whitewash the wall, and wipe off the floor. While the room is drying, look over the contents of the room; cleanse the boxes containing spices, etc.; examine, and scald the dried fruit (if it was not put into paper bags after being scalded in the fall); to do this without injury to the fruit, great care must be taken, or it will not stew soft. The safest method to accomplish this object, is to spread it thin in a pan, and set the vessel containing it, over boiling water until heated through. When the room is perfectly dry, and well aired, return the different articles to their places; turn the cans and jars of fruit label-side out, so that any article needed, can be reached without disarranging others, and another part of the house is ready for the summer. Examine china closets; if crockery is tea-stained, boil it up in white lye; mend dishes that have been broken, or replace them by new ware, matching the old as nearly as possible; if plated ware is worn, it can be replated at but little cost; if knives have rusted, send them to the emery-mill, to be polished; send any articles of furniture that are broken to the shop for repairs; if windows are cracked or broken, send for the glazier; if locks are out of order, for the locksmith, etc.; look over drawers and closets; pack away all furs and woollen goods (*see* MOTHS), fill the spaces with spring clothing, nicely repaired, and ready for use; engage whitewashers, painters, and extra help, before the rush for house-cleaners comes on. Have the yards raked, and the last of the month, the tender shrubs uncovered, etc., and you are ready to commence the hard part of general house-cleaning.

MAY.—As soon as the weather settles, take down most of the stoves; oil or varnish them, and place them in the attic, or some other dry place. Fires in grates will sometimes be needed morning and evening, or in the nursery stove, until the first of June. When cleaning is fairly commenced, it is best to begin in the upper story; examine beds; if the ticks are soiled, they should be cleansed, and laid in the sun. Cover all furniture, pictures, and books, before taking up carpets; throw the carpets from the windows; have them shaken until free from dust, and laid where the sun will heat them; turn them once, that both sides may be heated, to destroy moths; sweep the floors, dust the wall-paper, wood-work, windows, and furniture, wipe the dust from the floor, and whitewash the walls; if the paint contains or is covered with varnish, rub no soap on the cleaning cloth, and as little as possible if not varnished; rub the paint with a soft cloth wrung from warm suds, or very weak white lye; rinse in clear water as soon as cleansed, washing but a small space before rinsing, and wipe dry without leaving the marks of the cloth; be careful that the corners and mouldings are clean, and wiped quite dry. Wash the floor around the sides of the room perfectly clean before washing the base boards; rub the blinds with a soft cloth, wrung dry from *clear water*, until free from dust; lastly, wash the windows in hot suds, cleansing the corners, and rinse thoroughly; wipe dry and rub them with paper until bright. When the rooms are perfectly dry, put down the carpets; if troubled with moths, lay camphor gum, red cedar shavings, or some other preventives under the carpet; especially where it will be covered by furniture, and in the corners; bring in the beds, and arrange the rooms before tearing up below. Proceed in the same manner with the remaining stories, until the whole is finished, being particular to take down curtains; cover books, pictures, furniture, etc., before removing the carpets; as soon as the blankets are not needed on the beds, wash them (*see* WASHING BLANKETS), and lay them away where they will be safe from moths; wash other bedding requiring it, do up the curtains (*see* WASHING CURTAINS), put them in place, and house-cleaning, the dread of the family, old and young, will be through with for the next half-year; when, with the exception of a few things, which will be reversed, the same routine of work will be again necessary for the comfort of the family.

PART XI.

SICK ROOM, REMEDIES, INFANTS, COOKERY FOR THE SICK.

CHAPTER I.

SICK ROOM.

SELECT, if possible, a large, airy room, with a cheerful prospect from the window. Let the furniture of the room be neat and comfortable, but no more of it than is necessary. It fatigues and disturbs an invalid to see furniture dusted and the room arranged; therefore, every superfluity should be dispensed with. The curtains of the windows should be of plain, dark-colored material; it is impossible for an invalid to avoid tracing the figures in the drapery of the room, and none but those who have experienced it know how fatigued a nervous person will become by this effort of the eye and mind. For the same reason the paper or wall should be plain, free from cracks and defects. If the sick room is over the family rooms, it will be noisy; therefore remove it as far as possible from that part of the house. There should be a closet for medicines; nothing gives a more forlorn appearance to a sick room, or makes more confusion, than a great array of bottles to be lifted and dusted two or three times each day; and then, too, the patient is often worried by the breaking and spilling of contents on the table and floor. None but the medicines in constant use should be in the room, and if a nurse is in attendance, these ought to be out of the patient's sight. A room, communicating with the sick room, to which all offensive clothing, etc., can be removed, is highly important. In this room the close stool, slop-pails, and other conveniences, should be kept, that the nurse need not be obliged often to call a servant, or leave her patient. If the weather is warm, matting is much better than carpeting on the floor. A thermometer should hang in the room, by which to regulate the temperature. The room should be kept neat and tidy, and the bed often aired. The sheets used by day should be spread at evening to air for the next day; and those used at night be aired for the next night. The practice of putting on sheets and using them night and day for two or three successive days and nights, is very deleterious to the sick. A mattress, on elliptic springs, with an under bed of husks, is probably the most comfortable bed for an invalid. There are many easy chairs, of different make, more or less comfortable. The reclining chair will be found a great luxury to a consumptive patient, or one suffering with diseased spine. For a person with spinal abscess, a bedstead manufactured by the "Elliptic Spring Bed Company," in New York, is not only a comfort, but almost indispensable; it is arranged with hinges and springs, by which the mattress and patient are lifted together to any desired height, allowing the invalid to sit or recline at pleasure, much after the plan of the reclining chair. Bedsteads can be made after the same idea without infringing on the patent. One seen by the author was made of black walnut, three feet wide, with a joint, and notches in the frame, to which were fitted pieces of hickory about three inches wide, and long enough to raise the patient to a sitting posture; these pieces, when not in use, folded under the slats or sacking of the bed, and rested on the frame, entirely out of sight; such a bedstead could be made for five or six dollars, and would be found extremely convenient to all invalids. Never crowd a sick room with company, or allow either loud talking or whispering; of the two, loud talking is to be preferred; but all conversation is better carried on in an ordinary tone of voice. If whispering is allowed while the patient sleeps, it will waken much sooner than talking. If the talking is in an undertone, sad and mournful, it gives the idea to the patient that his case is worse than it really is. If the patient is weak, very little, if any, company should be allowed during the day, and none during the latter part of the afternoon, when the patient needs rest. All visits to the sick should be made during the forenoon, while the invalid is fresh. Do not put off until late in the evening the preparations for the night. If the patient is to take a sponge bath, let it be commenced early, so that the operation need not be hurried; a hasty bath accomplishes but a small part of the object for which it is used;

it is not only to invigorate, or cleanse the skin, that this important part of the nurse's duty is performed, but to allay extreme nervousness, and induce sleep; a gentle nurse often soothes her patient into a quiet sleep while taking the spirit bath, when without it she would toss all night with nervous restlessness. Be careful to follow to the letter the directions of the attending physician; if he does not suit, dismiss him, and engage another; but while he is employed, he should be implicitly obeyed. In the preparations of medicines, be particular to disguise powders and prepare liquids in such a manner as to make them as little disgusting as possible. There is more art in covering powders than is usually supposed; any medicine is less nauseous taken in fluid than in a half-covered powder. Make yourself acquainted with the good and bad effects of the medicines which are being taken by the patient, that you may use discretion in the administration of them. Wear in the sick room light easy slippers, so that in walking, the floor will neither be jarred by heavy uncertain steps, nor the patient annoyed by creaking; heels on leather shoes are annoying, particularly so if high and narrow. Avoid taking hold of the bedposts; patients who are suffering with spinal trouble often suffer acutely from a person merely supporting themselves by holding the posts with the hand, or leaning over the footboard, and to any one suffering with extreme debility it is very fatiguing. Rocking back and forth in a rocker is often very distressing to an invalid, particularly one suffering with a nervous affection of the head and brain; they cannot avoid watching the motion of the chair, without shutting their eyes, and often become almost crazed before allowing themselves to speak of it. Motions of the body, trotting the foot, scraping the throat, blowing the nose, picking the teeth, and coughing, should all be avoided as much as possible. The more quiet the nurse the better. Often sewing, knitting, or any other employment which would assist the nurse in passing the time, proves a source of real suffering to her patient. Reading in a quiet voice, combing the hair, gently rubbing the palms of the hand, will often induce sleep, when anodynes fail. Another important matter not to be lost sight of in a nurse is a cheerful obliging temper. Be always ready to humor a sick person in every thing that will do them no harm; never think of your own trouble, when you can, in the smallest particular, add to the comfort of the sick; what to you is so small a trifle as to be hardly worth mentioning, seems to an invalid a weighty matter. It is not well to cross a sick person, if it can be avoided. A person with a gloomy disposition is unfit to take charge of the sick. A nurse soured by trouble, carrying on her face the sorrows of a life-time, is wholly unfit for her office, and should be banished at once; such a disposition will affect a nervous person most unfavorably. Sympathy is a quality to be appreciated in a nurse; at the same time she should use her judgment in expressing it. If the patient is inclined to make the most of the illness, the nurse should endeavor to present them in a more favorable light. If her nervous restlessness shows itself in too much talking, the nurse should be quiet, avoiding subjects of conversation. If inclined to despondency, she may tell cheerful anecdotes; or if the patient is sufficiently strong, introduce subjects of conversation which will lead the invalid to forget self and personal sufferings. If the patient is confined to the bed, turn and shake up the pillows as often as they become heated; bathe the face and hands with a damp towel frequently; smooth the hair; keep the bedclothes in order, and in numberless trifles make the sufferer comfortable. It is only those who have lain on beds of suffering month after month that will understand the full value of these minute directions to the nurse; but all who have thus suffered know that it is not in great matters that the sick chamber can be made comfortable. The little nothings, hardly worth a name, hinted at in this chapter, do not embrace all the means of comfort which a judicious nurse can employ to lighten the invalids burden. To purify the air of a sick room, burn coffee on a hot shovel; or if the patient cannot endure the smoke, scatter a little sulphuric ether over the carpet; or burn vinegar on a hot shovel. In preparations of food for the sick, select such as suit the case, and vary the selection of dishes as much as possible. (*See* COOKERY FOR THE SICK.)

CHAPTER II.

REMEDIES.

BURN SALVE.—Grate finely Peruvian Nut Gall, and mix it with cold lard, until it forms a paste; this is an excellent salve for burns after the fire is out.

BURN LINIMENT.—Take strong clear lime-water, and mix with it as much linseed oil as it will cut; apply, as soon as possible, after the accident. It is the best cure for burns that can be had, and no housekeeper should be without a bottle in the house, ready prepared. Shake the bottle before applying, wrap the burn in cotton wadding, saturated with it, wet it as often as it appears dry, without removing the cotton from the burn for nine days, when the new skin will probably be found ready formed.

QUICK REMEDY FOR BURNS.—If there is none of the liniment in the house, cover the scald or burn with flour and cotton immediately, and leave it on until it heals. The liniment can be applied over the flour, by wetting the cotton with it, without exposing the scald to the air.

CUTS.—Press a cut together, and bind it firmly without cording; if it bleeds, use ashes, salt, or what is better, spiders' webs.

To CLEANSE SORES.—Prepare a solution of nitrate of silver, and wash the sore until the foul matter is destroyed.

PUTRID SORES.—Work together from one to two parts of coal tar with one hundred parts of commercial plaster of paris, very finely powdered. When well incorporated, it forms a grayish plaster. To apply it, make it into a paste with linseed or olive oil; it removes all odor, and produces no pain.

CHAPPED HANDS.—If persons would always dry their hands by friction, rubbing them together until a little of the oil of the skin moistens them, they would never chap. Bran water, mutton tallow, camphor, ice, white wax, and sweet oil, simmered together, are each useful. If salve or oil is used, apply it at night, and wear soft leather gloves. Rubber gloves are very unhealthy, and although they soften the hand, should never be used; they cause the hand to perspire too freely, for health. Boil and skim honey, keep it free from dust on the washstand, and rub a drop on the hands after washing.

WAHLER'S FROST SALVE.—24 ounces mutton tallow; 24 do. hog's lard; 4 do. peroxide of iron (red iron rust); 4 do. Venice turpentine; 2 do. oil of Bergamot; 2 do. of Armenian bole, rubbed to a paste with olive oil. Heat together the tallow, lard, and iron rust in an iron vessel, stirring constantly with an iron spoon, until the mass assumes a perfectly black color. Add gradually the other ingredients, stirring until perfectly mixed. Apply on linen daily.

CAMPHOR ICE FOR CHAPPED HANDS.—3 drachms gum camphor;

3 do. white wax; 3 do. spermacetti;. 2 ounces of olive oil. Melt slowly in an earthen bowl, and stir together; continue to stir briskly, until entirely cold. It will form a white salve; anoint at night, and put on gloves.

CHILBLAINS.—Soak in a pail of water in which turnips have been boiled. Mash the turnips, leave them in the water, and set the feet into them. A poultice of mashed turnips is also useful. The writer has seen bad cases of chilblains entirely removed, by merely soaking the feet several times.

RECEIPT FOR CHILBLAINS.—One part of muriatic acid, six parts of water; bathe the parts affected, nightly.

CURE FOR DYSENTERY.—Procure a lump of mutton suet fresh from the sheep, as large as a coffee-cup, and a lump of loaf-sugar one-third as large; put the suet in an earthen bowl, and lay the sugar on it; set it before the fire, where the heat will gradually melt the sugar and suet together; when rightly prepared, the tallow and sugar is browned together in one mass. There must be no heat under the dish, or the suet will melt faster than it should. For an adult, a dose is one teaspoonful every hour, of the browned sediment in the bowl. If feverish, the patient should drink freely of nitre in water, in the usual proportion, and take no other nourishment. This rule has cured cases of this disease given over by the physicians.

DYSENTERY RECEIPT.—Boil two quarts of oats in a gallon of water, until reduced to two quarts; sweeten with double-refined loaf-sugar, and give two gills every half-hour, until the disease is checked.

DIARRHŒA.—One teaspoon of grated Turkey rhubarb root; do not depend on the pulverized rhubarb of the shops; half a teaspoon of sub carbonate of soda, one teaspoon of pure essence of peppermint. Steep, without heating, to boiling heat, a teacup of soft water, in which steep the rhubarb. When steeped, strain; add the other ingredients, two table-spoons of loaf-sugar, and lastly, the peppermint; shake together. Dose for an adult, a table-spoonful once an hour; for an infant, a tea-spoonful.

DYSENTERY OR DIARRHŒA.—One table-spoon of pulverized maple charcoal; mix with one table-spoon of boiled molasses, add two table-spoons of fourth-proof West India rum, and half a glass of sweet oil.

PULMONIC WAFERS.—Seven pounds loaf-sugar; syrup of ipecac four ounces, antimonial wine two ounces, morphine ten grains, dissolved in a table-spoonful of water, with ten drops of sulphuric acid, tincture of bloodroot one ounce, syrup of Tolu two ounces, add to the sugar, and make the mixture into lozenges. Use from six to twelve in the course of twenty-four hours.

SCALD HEAD.—Examine the roots of the hair by pulling out a few with the tweezers. If minute bags of water are found at the roots of the hair, the disease is the scald head, or some other form of diseased hair. The only cure is to remove the hairs one by one with tweezers, until every diseased hair is removed from the head. We have known a number of individuals afflicted with this disease, perfectly cured by this simple remedy, who had been under the care of doctors for years, being injured rather than benefited by their treatment. Use a wash of copperas water, very weak, to loosen the hair. Wash in Castile soap, and remove daily as many hairs as the patient can bear; it will take but a short time to perfect a cure.

MALIGNANT SORE THROAT.—Wrap the whole throat in tow, wet in common tar; if tow cannot be obtained, use flexible linen cloth, or cotton batting.

QUINSY.—Make a poultice of hops and strong vinegar, apply to the throat, changing often. Inhale through a tube, Cayenne and vinegar as strong and hot as the patient can bear.

SPRAINS.—Wormwood pounded with vinegar and warmed, is an excellent remedy for sprains. Pouring cold water on the joint as long as the patient can bear it, holding the pitcher four feet above the limb, is a sure remedy for a sprained ankle.

HICCOUGH.—A single drop of oil of cinnamon dropped on sugar, dissolved in the mouth.

OINTMENT FOR THE ITCH.—Heat lard, and melt in it a quantity of brimstone; apply over the whole body three times at night, rubbing in well before a hot fire.

FOR NERVOUS AFFECTIONS.—Compound spirits of lavender and sulphuric ether, equal parts. Take a teaspoonful once an hour until relieved.

TO BREAK UP AN OBSTINATE COUGH.—Take a dessert-spoonful of ipecac, mix it with a little vinegar to remove the lumps, add the juice of two lemons, and as much loaf-sugar as can be stirred into the mixture; take just sufficient, once every hour, to keep the stomach nauseated; continue to use the mixture until the cough is broken up. The patient should guard from cold, and remain housed while using the mixture. Lemon and sugar, alone, will often break up a cough, that is tight, without the ipecac.

LINIMENT OF SALTPETRE FOR RHEUMATISM.—One ounce of saltpetre dissolved in one ounce of sweet oil; rub the parts affected.

NEURALGIA.—One teacup of melted, not boiling, lard; mix in it one ounce of the oil of organum, and stir until thick; then add one ounce strong laudanum, stir well together, and cork tightly. Rub the parts affected as often as necessary. Good for rheumatism also.

EARACHE.—Equal parts of sulphuric ether, and strong laudanum; drop the mixture on cotton, and put it in the ear.

TINCTURE FOR TEETH.—Infuse, in half a pint of brandy, one ounce of Peruvian bark, coarsely powdered, and gargle the mouth with the infusion every morning.

ALUM FOR TEETH.—One of the finest sets of teeth ever seen by the author, were preserved, by dissolving a small bit of alum in the mouth every morning before breakfast.

To CLEAN THE TEETH.—Powder one ounce of myrrh, a tablespoon of green sage, and mix them in white honey; wet the teeth and gums night and morning.

CHARCOAL POWDER FOR THE TEETH.—Pulverize charcoal; burn it on a red-hot shovel; when cold, sift it through muslin, and put it in water, or not, as most convenient.

TOOTHACHE.—Chloroform half an ounce, alum five grains, sulphate of morphine three grains; mix, and apply with cotton.

ANTIDOTES FOR POISONS, ETC.

FOR AN OVERDOSE OF LAUDANUM.—Strong coffee is the best, though strong tea is also efficacious.

FOR MERCURY.—Sulphur is an antidote; mixed with molasses, it is useful as a wash for calomel sore mouth.

For Oil of Vitriol.—Mix an ounce of calcined magnesia in a pint of water; give a glassful every two minutes.

For Soda, Ammonia, Etc.—Use strong vinegar, lemon or lime juice.

For Corrosive Sublimate.—Mix the whites of fifteen eggs with one quart of cold water; take a half-pint of the mixture in half a pint of milk every two minutes.

For Arsenic.—Give strong sugar syrup, as fast as possible, until the patient vomits.

For Verdigris.—Give large quantities of syrup, and a preparation of eggs and milk.

For Antimony.—Give sugar and water; if after the sugar the patient has vomited several times, and still continues to do so, give a grain of opium in a glass of sweetened water.

For Nitrate of Silver.—Give strong salt and water until the patient vomits.

For Sugar of Lead.—Give immediately a large dose of Glauber salts, at least three table-spoonfuls, in a pint of water.

To Remove a Bone, Pin, or any other Obstruction, from the Throat.—Fasten a piece of fine dry sponge firmly, as large as a filbert, on a fine wire, sufficiently stiff to push the sponge past the obstruction without bending; then swell the sponge by pouring water down the patient's throat, and pull up the sponge; the obstruction will come with it.

Simple Cathartic.—Take a bit of sal soda, as large as a kidney bean, dissolve it in one gill of water; add two table-spoons of best pulverized rhubarb; work it free from lumps, and add sufficient water to make the whole measure two gills. Take a table-spoonful every hour until it has the desired effect.

To Prepare Medicines.—Castor oil for adults is taken in boiling coffee clear; in hot milk; or hot whiskey, or brandy sling. To give a child a pill, tell it to open its mouth while you give it, and pass it down the throat; a child cannot be made to understand how to swallow a pill. Cover powders in roasted apples. Salts are taken dissolved in water; sweet milk will remove the taste of them from the mouth. Cayenne pepper must be taken in milk sweetened with plenty sugar. Magnesia is best taken in milk.

FOR FROSTBITTEN HANDS AND FEET.—Wash the parts often in sugar of lead. If badly frosted, wet linen cloths, and keep them on the frozen parts.

RINGWORMS.—Verdigris and mercurial ointments are both efficacious.

TO SCATTER RUN-ROUNDS.—Make a strong lye, and soak the finger until the nail is so soft it can be scraped. Wet the nail in acid to destroy the alkali.

TO CURE FELON.—Soft soap and quick-lime, made into a paste; make a bag; fill it full, and put the finger in it, and renew frequently until the pain subsides.

INFLAMMATION OF BREASTS.—Two table-spoons of linseed oil, one of fresh lard, one of honey; warm, and stir these ingredients together. When cool, add ten grains of sugar of lead. Apply by spreading the mixture on a cloth, and lay on frequently. If it is desirable to partially dry the milk, bathe with camphor, and rub with lard.

ABSCESS, OR GATHERED BREAST.—Equal parts of linseed oil and strained honey, and sufficient Burgundy pitch to make a soft plaster; melt together; warm, and spread on a cloth, and apply frequently. If suppuration has taken place, apply a warm flaxseed poultice, rubbed over with lard, to prevent its sticking. Tender nipples should be washed in a solution of borax. One of the best remedies for this trouble to mothers is, the skin and pulp of a large raisin, freed from seed, drawn over, and tied on the nipple. It should be changed often until the soreness is removed.

EYE WATER.—Ten grains of sulphate of zinc, twenty grains of sugar of lead dissolved in three ounces of filtered rain water. When the eyes are highly inflamed, make compresses of linen, and lay on, keeping them constantly wet until the inflammation is reduced. If too strong, dilute with filtered rain-water. Laudanum and water, and salt and water, are both useful in weak eyes.

HAIR.—Brandy and salt will prevent the hair from falling out

DYSPEPTIC LYE.—One quart hickory ashes, six ounces of soot, one gallon of boiling water; mix and stir frequently. At the end of twenty-four hours pour off the clear liquor. Take one teacupful three times a day.

TO STOP A BLEEDING OF THE NOSE.—Tie a string tightly around the little finger, so as to cord it. Elevate the arm, or pour cold water on the back of the neck.

CURE FOR WARTS.—Pare the hard skin, and touch them with strong acetic acid twice a day. If it touches the hand it will take off the skin. Milkweed will cure warts, if applied frequently.

CORNS.—Wet the corns every morning with saliva, and paste on them young peach leaves.

CHAPTER III.

INFANTS.

NEW-BORN infants should be wrapped in soft flannel as soon as born, for half an hour, or longer, if the mother needs the attention of the nurse. Before washing, place the child's clothing, pins, a bottle of sweet oil, etc., on a chair or frame convenient to the fire; wash the infant in water as warm as it would be standing in the sun during a warm summer day. Use sweet oil, and the finest soap, to assist in the cleansing; let the operation of washing be performed in a warm room, and as expeditiously as possible. The navel should be dressed with mutton tallow warmed, and spread on soft fine linen, with a dust of nutmeg grated finely over the tallow. The first article put on, after a napkin, should be a flannel band, from four to four and a half inches wide; pin it snugly, but not tight enough to bind, and make the babe uncomfortable; the little shirt is the next article of dress to be put on the child; this should be open at the front, and folded smoothly, so as to leave no wrinkles; the pinner comes next; lay the infant on its stomach, fold the shirt smoothly on its back, fasten the shirt and pinner together with a small pin, leaving the point covered, so as to prick neither child nor nurse; wrap its feet in the pinner, and pin it as close as possible without cramping its limbs; then take the flannel skirt in the right hand, putting the arm entirely through it, leaving the band towards the wrist; lift the feet of the babe with the right hand, and with the left draw the shirt in place; fold the shirt over, and fasten shirt, band, pinner, and skirt, together with two pins, near the arms, being particular to have the head of each towards the arms, and the points hid in the clothing. After drawing and preparing the fastenings of the slip, which should be of soft material, entirely free from starch, take it on the right arm, in the same manner as the skirt, and draw it in place with the left, lifting the child's body with the right hand; turn the babe once more, fasten the dress, and the little one is ready for presentation; wrap it in warm flannel, and put it immediately to its mother's breast. When the child has drawn a little while, remove it to its own bed in the crib, which should be of soft materials; a new-born infant should not be put on a cold, hard bed; the covering of the crib should be light and warm. Soft blankets are probably the best covering for young infants. If the little one obtained no nourishment from its mother, give it again to her, and do this frequently until the natural aliment is furnished, after which give it its food at regular intervals.

Food.—Infants are often overloaded, to relieve their mothers; this is very improper: the mother's milk should be drawn by some other means, than the overfeeding of the child. If the mother is in health, the child usually needs, during the early period of its existence, no medicines whatever; should any be necessary, only the simplest remedies ought to be resorted to: as sweet oil, manna, magnesia, etc.; for wind colic, anise-seed steeped, is an almost universal remedy. If the child is much distressed by griping, let the mother take daily, a teaspoonful of the essence, which will usually prevent the suffering of the child. If a nurse must be employed, select one with a sound constitution, free from diseases of the skin, with habits and temper good; and a particularly cheerful disposition. An infant can be as regularly fed as an adult, but much oftener; a young child needs a full supply of food once in an hour; as it increases in age, the time between its meals can be lengthened: an infant of nine months will do well, fed once in three hours; a child of a year, once in four. If a child must be fed, there is nothing better for it than barley-water, milk warm, slightly sweetened with a few drops of sweet cream; if the bowels are out of order by teething, or any derangement from cold, scorch the barley, and make it into a coffee, until the bowels are corrected. In preparing the barley, be careful to look it over thoroughly; wash it well, and boil long and slowly in soft water; it must be made morning and evening, or it will become sour. When on a journey, use pearl barley, as it takes but a short time to cook it, while the common barley would require from two to three hours' boiling. Goat's milk is perhaps the best food for children that are fed; but a child will thrive much better on barley than cow's milk. Never waken a child from its sleep, neither allow it rocked, to continue a dozing sleep, after its nap is over; either is injurious. Put the child to bed at regular hours, and teach it to sleep without rocking or nursing; to many this sounds absurd, but if a healthy child is managed rightly from its birth, there will be no trouble in forming regular habits in all things; but if dressed, nursed, and put to sleep when most convenient to the nurse or mother, it will naturally have no fixed habits; the want of which may, and often does, trouble them through life. A child should have, after the first month of its life, in mild weather, regular daily exercise in the open air; a wagon is much better than the nurse's arms, but an airing in a carriage is better than either. Be careful that a young child does not strain nor injure its eyes by being kept in too light a room, or by gazing at the sun, fire, or lamp; if by any chance its eyes become weak, a little breast-milk is as good as any thing to remove the irritation. If the navel becomes inflamed, spread on it the pulp and skin of a large raisin. A child should be well rubbed in every part of its body except under the arms, which needs only to be thoroughly dried. See that infants are kept warm; this part of a child's comfort is often too much neglected: keep socks on after the child is two months old; before this, its pinners will be sufficient protection. The first month a child nurses very often, and sleeps most of the time; but even thus early, infants' habits can be commenced; when possible, do not allow it quite to lose itself in sleep, before taking it from the mother; this will teach it to go to sleep without rocking; an infant will sleep less and less until it is about six months old, when it should have two periods of slumber daily. The first slumber of an infant is usually immediately after being dressed, and the other about two in the afternoon; these naps, to be of service to the child, should be one and a half to two hours long; when it wakens, amuse it a short time without exercising, before it takes its food; when fairly awake and lively, and before it cries, give it all it requires. It is a bad plan to allow a child to cry for what it needs; all its wants should be attended to without this trial of its temper; children have enough real grief to cry for, to expand and strengthen their lungs, without crying from

17

hunger or want of attention. When a child is three months old, commence to give its body strength by exercise; the nurse can toss it in her arms, and in many ways give the exercise it needs. It will now begin to notice, and whenever it is observed intently looking at an object, be particular not to disturb its meditations; it is no doubt, that by thus disturbing children, many parents prevent their forming habits of concentration, thus making fickle characters for life. If you desire your child to possess a cheerful, happy temper, meets its eye with a smile, and never allow it to hear harsh tones of voice. Sometimes a child may inherit a very nervous temperament, needing constant soothing: such a child more particularly feels the changes in the mother's temper; with such children, the nursery should be guarded as faithfully from ill humor as from the influence of noxious air. It is in the cradle, children's characters are formed; many a mother unconsciously prepares a darling child for a life of infamy and shame, when she would willingly give her right arm to shield it from all harm. Never give up to a child's will, no matter how young it is; if proper care is taken, the temper of an infant need not be roused; but if once it gets the master of the mother, it will soon know how to gain its ends. If taken in time, a decided tone of voice will usually quiet a child crying for will alone; if not, a little pat will make it understand that it must obey its mother. A mother writing, once made a remark like this: "The three first years of my child's life, I expect to obey it, but after that, it must obey me." Our opinion is, that a child can, and many are made, to obey from their birth the wishes of its mother.

At five months, the child usually is sufficiently strong to sit alone; it should be gradually taught to balance while sitting, as soon as it can support itself without danger of falling over; let it sit half an hour, or less; if left sitting too long, it will injure its spine, or fatigue it too much for health. If the child gains strength, it will generally begin to creep between six and seven months; this exercise should be encouraged: some mothers so dislike to see their children's clothes soiled, that they prevent their creeping, if possible. Creeping not only furnishes the child much pleasure, but expands the chest, strengthens the muscles, and straightens the limbs. When a child shows a disposition to creep, shorten its clothes that it may have free use of its limbs, and protect its feet with stockings and shoes. When its limbs are sufficiently strong to bear its own weight, it will pull up by chairs, and with little assistance, will soon learn the art of balancing, and walk alone; and unless it gets hurt by falls, so as to lose confidence, will soon give up creeping entirely. Few children walk before they are one year old; it is best to let nature take her own time; if children walk before they have strength, their limbs will most surely be bent by the weight of their body. The teeth of infants usually commence to trouble them between the fifth and seventh month; the child drools, and shows inclination to press its gums; on examination, they will appear rounded, and often hot; after a time, the shape and color of the teeth can be discerned. Sometimes it becomes necessary to lance the gums, but unless the child is suffering severely, it is better to let nature do its own work; sometimes a rash is occasioned by dentition; nurses and mothers usually think, when this is the case, that it is on the whole better for the irritability of the stomach to show itself on the skin than in a bowel complaint. If the bowels are slightly affected, rhubarb, syrups, and other gentle alteratives better be used; if these fail of the desired effect, a physician should be consulted. Many children suffer much in teething, especially in warm weather; and more deaths occur from dentition than any other of the diseases of infancy. Give children, while teething, gentle exercise in the open air; guard carefully against colds, and be as systematic in their diet as possible. If possible, a child should nurse until it has cut at least eight teeth; if the mother's health permits, it is well to nurse a child through the second summer, as this is probably the most trying period of an infant's existence; more children dying at the age of one year, than at any period of childhood. Weaning should be performed gradually; commencing first by feeding light food, a little daily, and nursing but seldom; then cease giving any nurse to the child during the day, and finally wean entirely. The food of a weaned child ought to be light and nutritious; rice, sago pearl barley, rusked bread, barley groats, arrow root, wheat flour pap, or, if it agrees with the child, cow's milk. Its food should not be warmer than its mother's milk; neither ought it to be entirely cold; be careful not to overload its stomach, and if the bowels show derangement, give simple alteratives, avoiding what does not well agree with its stomach.

SIMPLE DISEASES OF INFANTS.—Thrush is often produced by the lactic acid of milk formed in the mouth from the milk of the mother; to prevent this, wipe the infant's mouth and lips with a soft linen, every time it nurses; wash the mouth with a weak decoction of golden seal, if already sore.

RED GUM.—This disease is of little moment; use gentle herb teas, if any thing; usually nothing is necessary, but to let nature take its course.

VOMITING.—If the milk thrown off by the child is merely white curd, it is of very little account; but if the matter vomited is yellowish, the child's bowels are probably constipated; use gentle laxatives.

COLIC.—If occasioned by wind alone, use anise-seed cordial; if from acidity, use magnesia; if from an overloaded stomach, give less food.

DIARRHŒA.—If simple, use barley coffee, made of scorched barley; if the bowels need correcting, use gentle alteratives; but if severe, consult a physician; rhubarb, syrups, and remedies for bowel complaints, all good, may be found in the chapter of Remedies. The mutton suet and sugar remedy is peculiarly adapted to infants, and young children.

WORMS.—If a child is troubled with worms, its cheeks will be bright red, while the color around its mouth will be pale, breath fetid, appetite irregular, and the nose troubled with itching; it often starts in its sleep, and is sometimes thrown into convulsions. Sage tea is a simple remedy, it should be sweetened and drank warm; salt and water, or turpentine, will turn them down, if rising in the throat. It will do children who have worms, no harm to eat a little pure sugar every day. To expel worms, use worm lozenges, or other preparations for the purpose. If mercury is used, stupefy the worms with pink tea made very sweet, the day before the calomel is taken. To expel pin worms, use sulphur and honey; but these are better brought away by clysters of lard and turpentine.

CROUP.—The symptoms are a peculiar hoarse cough, which is well known when heard, though difficult to describe. For simple croup symptoms, use wine of ipecac; for a child of six months, use one-third of a teaspoon of the ipecac to a table-spoon of sweetened water, repeat often enough to keep the stomach nauseated; apply to the throat and chest, lard spread on thin paper; if there is no ipecac at hand, give goose, sweet, or castor oil, mixed in molasses; garlic syrup is useful in a hoarse cold, but it should not be used after the membrane has formed. The wine of ipecac should always be kept in the house when there are young children in the family. If the simple remedies do not, within a few hours, afford relief, consult a physician immediately. It is the colds that are the longest developing the croups, that are the most fatal; in such cases, the membrane is often formed before the mother suspects danger. The author knew of one instance of a child being saved, who was almost gone with this disease, by excessive bleeding; he was bled until he fainted from loss of blood, and when recovered from the faint, breathed perfectly free. It was, however, in this case, the last resort of the physician to save his life, and when he fainted, was himself uncertain about his breathing again. Watch the symptoms of this disease with the utmost care, if you would learn to control it.

WHOOPING-COUGH.—If possible, keep all young children from the contagion. A child should reach its sixth year before taking the disease. If the child has not been vaccinated before taking the cough, have it done immediately, and it will generally break up the cough. If a child commences to cough in the spring, it will usually recover during the hot weather of summer; but if the disease commences in the fall, they will cough until the next spring returns, with fine clear weather. Sweet oil and molasses, cochineal and water sweetened with loaf-sugar, or a tea of sweet alder (not the poison), made into tea, and sweetened with honey or sugar, are all useful, but the cough will take its course, unless vaccination is performed, no matter what medicine is used.

MEASLES.—The first symptoms resemble a slight cold; the eyes are weak, and discharge a watery fluid; the patient coughs, and appears languid; if this disease is preceded or followed by the whooping-cough, it is often fatal; both diseases very much affecting the lungs. The chief danger from measles is in the inflammation of the lungs; some seasons it is so very light as to require no medical advice; when this is the case, use light diet, keep the body open by gentle laxatives, avoid currents of cold air, keep the temperature neither warm nor cold; if the measles come out well, and the cough is not severe, there will be but little trouble. Nursing infants usually feel the effects of this disease less than older children.

INJURIES FROM FALLS PREVENTED.—If a child in falling, hurts the head, on no account allow it to sleep for several hours; bathe its head with cold water, and give a gentle cathartic; if this plan of treatment is pursued, but few falls would produce the sad results which too often follow in their wake. If in falling, the bruise appears like a bag of water, wet paper in camphor, and change it often, until the water is absorbed. If bruised to discolor, bind on brown paper wet in vinegar; if a limb is injured, swathe it in a cloth wet in wormwood and vinegar; for a sudden cold, induce perspiration, and give gentle cathartics. For scarlet fever, consult a physician. (*See* REMEDY FOR SCARLET FEVERS, in the chapter of Remedies.)

FOR CANKER SORE MOUTH.—Use immediately, a corrective for the stomach; and in the spots, sage, honey, and alum, simmered together and strained.

FOR ERUPTIONS, use cream of tartar and sulphur, equal parts, mixed in molasses; give what would lie on a five-cent piece, three times daily.

FOR EARACHE in an infant, use roast onion or almond oil. For an overdose of paregoric, use strong coffee; for clysters to move the bowels only, molasses and water warmed blood-heat.

IN CONVULSIONS, put the child in a warm bath, and send immediately for the physician; if the convulsions are from worms, force open the mouth, and get down spirits of turpentine and sugar; if there is none in the house, use salt and water.

RHUBARB SYRUP FOR INFANTS.—One table-spoonful of best pulverized rhubarb, one teaspoon of pearlash, two gills of soft water, two gills of best French brandy, and loaf-sugar sufficient to make a rich syrup; shake it together briskly, and let it stand twenty-four hours. For a cure of severe bowel complaint, give a teaspoonful every two hours until it operates, and afterwards three times each day. For slight diarrhœa, give three times daily, until the disease is removed.

CRANESBILL FOR BOWEL COMPLAINTS.—Pound the root, and steep it until the strength is extracted; a dose for a grown person is a teacup of the infusion, three times each day. Root and herb teas should be covered tight while steeping. This is an astringent tonic for obstinate diarrhœas, after the stomach has been corrected, and will often cure, when other means fail.

CHAPTER IV.

COOKING FOR THE INVALID.

INDIAN MEAL GRUEL.—Put into a spider one quart of cold water; stir in a teacup of cold water, a large tablespoon of sweet Indian meal; stir this in the water, add a little salt, and boil it gently fifteen minutes, stirring constantly for five; it can be enriched with a spoonful of sweet cream, sweetened or spiced to suit. For a convalescent, boil raisins in the gruel; add sugar, nutmeg, and little butter; break into the gruel a nice fresh cracker, or toasted bread.

OATMEAL GRUEL.—Mix three ounces of oatmeal in a paste, and add water until it is about as thick as rich cream; put it in a sauce-pan, add one quart of water; stir the gruel until it boils constantly, and afterward frequently; let it boil half an hour, and add salt to suit the taste; eat it with milk, or alone, as desired.

BARLEY GRUEL.—Boil pearl barley until tender, reduce it to pulp, pass it through a sieve, add water until of the right consistency, boil fifteen minutes, and season to suit the taste.

RICE FLOUR GRUEL.—Make this exactly like Indian meal gruel, using less of the rice flour than of the Indian meal for the same quantity.

FLOUR GRUEL.—Tie a teacup of flour in a strong cloth, and boil it six hours; when it is done, it will be a hard cake, of flour; dry it, and grate a large teaspoonful, mix it in paste with cold water, and stir it in boiled milk; let the gruel boil gently ten minutes, and add salt. This is excellent for patients suffering with bowel complaints.

MILK PORRIDGE.—Take equal parts of milk and water, boil it, and thicken the porridge with flour, made into a smooth paste, with cold water; boil five minutes, add salt, and pepper if not too stimulating. It can be thickened with rice flour, groats, barley, oatmeal, arrow-root, or corn starch.

ARROW-ROOT GRUEL.—Boil a pint of morning's milk; make a spoonful of arrow-root into a paste, with cold milk; stir it in the gruel, and boil five minutes, stirring constantly; season with salt. There is danger of being cheated in arrow-root; for an invalid it should be pure.

GROUND RICE MILK.—Take a dessert-spoon of rice flour, mix it in a smooth paste with cold milk, boil one quart, stir in the paste; boil five minutes, and season to suit the taste.

SAGO MILK.—Wash a table-spoonful of sago, put it into a quart of new milk, stir until it has boiled, then let it simmer until reduced one-half, and season to suit the taste.

TO COOK SAGO OR TAPIOCA.—Cleanse it in several waters, and soak it in water an hour; then boil it in water until clear; season to suit the taste; cook tapioca in the same way.

BARLEY MILK.—Boil pearl barley in milk until it becomes as thick as thin cream; flavor to suit.

JELLY OF RICE OR TAPIOCA.—Boil either until they form a mass; pass through a sieve; season to taste, and mould.

WINE JELLY.—Dissolve one ounce of isinglass in half a pint of water, add nutmeg, cinnamon, very little mace, three cloves, simmer gently half an hour without scorching; strain it, and set it away to cool; take a pint of wine, cut into it the jelly, simmer in an earthen jar until the jelly dissolves, add sugar, another pint of wine, warm all together, strain, and put in moulds. Many of the jellies mentioned in this work are useful to the sick.

CAUDLE.—Make a smooth thick gruel with groats, or Indian meal; stir it while cooling, and add nutmeg, sugar, and wine, to suit the taste.

MULLED EGG, IN TEA OR COFFEE.—Beat the yolk of one egg very light; have ready a hot cup of tea or coffee, seasoned with sugar and cream, or boiled milk, to suit the taste; pour it gradually in the egg, beating the egg briskly, while mixing. This is both nourishing and palatable for an invalid breakfast.

EGG MULLED IN WINE OR WATER.—Beat the yolk very light, have the wine or water hot but not boiling; flavor to suit, with sugar, nutmeg, or mace, and stir it into the egg, beating constantly while mixing; if the egg is stirred into the wine or water, it will curdle instead of thickening.

MILK AND WINE FOR AN INVALID.—Put a gill of wine in a pint tumbler; add sugar and nutmeg to suit the taste; hold the tumbler containing the wine, some distance from the cow, and strip the milk into it as fast as possible, until the foam reaches the top of the glass, and drink it immediately; this is very strengthening for a feeble person; it should be drunk morning and evening.

EGG MULLED WITH MILK.—Beat a yolk, and add to it boiled milk, sugar, and spice to the taste.

RAW EGG AND MILK.—Beat a yolk very light, add it to a tumbler three-fourths full of milk; beat until it foams; add sugar, and flavor with orange syrup.

RAW EGG AND WINE.—Drop an egg in wine, and drink it without breaking the egg; or beat the yolk, add it to the wine; beat them together; flavor to suit; beat the whites as light as possible, and then beat them through the yolk, wine, sugar, and spices; drink immediately after mixing.

MEAT AND BREAD PANADA.—Mince so small that it will pass through a coarse sieve, the white meat of a cold chicken, beef, or mutton; boil broth or water, season with salt, and thicken with the minced meat; stir it constantly while boiling, and serve with nice toasted bread broken in bits. Bread may be used in the same manner with mutton or chicken soup.

BREAD PANADA WITH WINE.—Boil equal parts of wine and water; grate bread crumbs and thicken the wine with them; beat constantly while boiling, and season to suit the taste. A bread panada may be made with the juices of fruit and water in place of the wine and water.

DRINKS FOR AN INVALID.

TOAST WATER.—Toast bread slowly without burning: the bread should be browned through and through; put it in a bowl, pour over the toast boiling water, and cover while it steeps; or more bread may be used, and cold water poured over the toast. The usual method of burning bread for toast water, is as absurd as burning coffee to a coal, instead of browning it chestnut color; and there is as much difference in the toast coffee, well prepared or not, as in a good or indifferent cup of coffee. All dishes cooked for the sick, should be prepared as nicely as possible, and served with taste.

LEMON WATER.—Cut into a small covered earthen jar, half a

lemon, sugar to taste, a little syrup of oranges, and pour over the whole a pint of boiling water; cover closely for two hours, and let it steep, when it will be fit to drink; if ice is allowed, add a little to each glass. Apple water, tamarind water, or any fruit water, may be made in the same manner.

MILK WHEY.—Steep a piece of rennet, an inch and a half square, in a teacup of hot water, for four or five hours; then strain the water into two quarts of new milk; when the curd has well formed, press it gently in a sieve until the whey and curd are separated. It may be drank warm or cold, as preferred.

WINE WHEY.—Take equal parts of milk and water, both together measuring about one pint; boil both together, and while boiling, add two gills of white wine; boil a few moments, until the curd settles to the bottom, leaving the whey clear; strain, and season to suit the taste. When taken warm, it promotes perspiration, but if used cold, is a gentle stimulant.

LEMON OR VINEGAR WHEY.—Instead of the wine, use sufficient juice of lemon or vinegar to form a curd; boil and strain clear. This is less stimulating than a wine whey.

NITRE WHEY.—Pour into a pint of boiling milk, a table-spoonful of the sweet spirits of nitre; strain and sweeten; let it be drunk warm. It is used to promote perspiration.

FRUIT ADES.—Take one part of the juice of any fruit to one of water, and one of ice, and sweeten to suit the taste.

FRUIT COBBLERS.—Take half a glass of the juice of any fruit; sweeten to the taste, and fill up the glass with ice, broken very fine.

SHERRY COBBLERS.—Take a glass one-half full of sherry wine; sweeten, and fill with fine ice.

BARLEY WATER.—Wash pearl barley; allow half an ounce to a quart of boiling water; let the barley and water simmer gently one hour in a covered sauce-pan, then strain the liquor; if time is allowed, merely soak the barley in the boiling water from eight to twelve hours. If allowed, add lemon-juice and sugar.

BARLEY NEGUS.—One pint of barley water, half a pint of wine, a table-spoon of lemon-juice, nutmeg and sugar, to suit the taste.

BARLEY PUNCH.—Take the juice of one orange, and half a lemon; add loaf-sugar, and half a pint of good brandy; after the sugar is dissolved, add one pint of rich barley water, or more, if the drink is too stimulating for the patient.

BARLEY OR CORN COFFEE.—Get common barley, wash it in several waters, dry and brown it without burning. Grind the barley, mix it with egg, and pour over it boiling water; let it boil a few moments, and strain it clear; season as the patient likes. This is excellent drink for persons troubled with bowel complaint. Corn coffee is made in the same manner, and is used to settle the stomach.

RASPBERRY, STRAWBERRY, OR OTHER FRUIT VINEGARS.—Put into a tumbler one gill of fruit vinegar; add sugar, one gill of pounded ice, and water, to make the goblet full.

PUNCH.—Heat to 109° a quart of water; measure half a pint of powdered loaf-sugar, take a lump of loaf-sugar, and extract all the oil from one fresh lemon, by rubbing the rind with the sugar; press the juice of the lemon on the sugar; mix well, add half a pint of rum, and one gill of brandy; stir until the sugar is dissolved; beat well and long; now add the water heated to the degree described. strain the whole immediately, and let it settle a little before drinking. Whiskey may be substituted in place of the other liquors. Punches are taken for sudden colds; it may be made with green tea in place of water, if better for the patient.

TO MAKE A CREAM TOAST FOR A SICK PERSON.—Toast the bread nicely; boil milk, add very little flour and salt, and strain it through a sieve on the toast. If butter is allowed, add very little. (*See* MILK AND BUTTER TOASTS.)

EGG AND TOAST FOR THE SICK.—Let the whites only of the egg congeal; toast one-third of a slice of bread; dip it in hot water, a little salted, and lay on it the egg. Season with salt only.

MOLASSES TOAST FOR THE SICK.—Toast the bread; add to molasses a little hot water and salt; boil it together; remove the scum from the molasses, and dip in the toast.

RUSK OF BARLEY OR CORN.—Brown barley or corn; grind in the coffee-mill, and eat it in milk. It is excellent.

NEUDLE SOUP.—Six eggs well beaten, a teaspoon of salt, and flour to make a paste to roll. Roll it as thin as paper, fold it, and shred it fine. Boil it in a gallon of any meat broth, and season with salt and pepper. For an invalid, boil it in milk and water, slightly thickened if desired.

NEUDLE PUDDING.—Three eggs beat light, add a little salt and flour, to make a paste that will roll. Roll the paste an eighth of an inch thick; fold the paste and shred fine; boil in clear water, with little salt; put them in the water while it is boiling, and do not allow them to stick together, or uncover the pot for ten minutes. Take them out and drain well; bake them one hour; beat two eggs light, mix them in a quart of milk, and stir in the neudles; add salt, sugar, and spices to suit the taste, and bake as custard.

PUDDINGS FOR AN INVALID.—Grate boiled flour, (*see* FLOUR GRUEL,) make it into a stiff paste; add salt and one egg; stir into a teacupful one pint of hot milk, little by little, boil it over steam half an hour, and serve with maple syrup, or sugar and cream. Cottage pudding is also light for an invalid; also mush, plain rice, or milk stiffened with rice flour salted, and sugared, either boiled or baked.

GRIDDLE CAKES FOR THE SICK.—Boil pearl barley to a jelly; grate boiled flour; take a table-spoonful of the flour, two of the barley jelly, and one egg; beat them well together; then thin to a batter; add salt.

CAKES FOR THE SICK.—Sponge cake and simple cookies, are the best cakes for an invalid. Rich plum cakes should be avoided.

GERMAN SPONGE.—Boil one teacup of milk, with a spoon of butter; add flour to make it stiff. Boil it over water until it cleaves from the pan; let it cool, and add gradually the yolks of four eggs well beaten, a spoon of sugar, salt and spice to the taste. Beat the whites of the eggs stiff, mix them with the sponge, and beat the whole thoroughly; have ready veal, chicken, or mutton soup; cut the sponges with a teaspoon, and boil them in the soup; when they are in, do not uncover the pot for ten minutes; when, unless there are too many in the pot, they will be well done. For a change, boil them in milk and water, a little salted.

TO DRESS A CHICKEN QUICKLY.—Cut the legs off at the second joint; pull out the tail and wing feathers; cut off the head; split the skin down the breast, and remove the skin and feathers together; then draw the chicken and wash out the blood.

To MAKE CHICKEN TEA.—Cut the meat from the bones, put it in a bottle with a little water, cork and wire the bottle, put it into cold water, and boil one hour; season with salt.

CHICKEN AND MEAT BROTHS.—Put the chicken, after the fat is removed and the parts jointed, in cold water; let it boil gently, and remove all the scum and superfluous fat. It will be ready to use in half an hour, and may boil an hour longer; season with salt and pepper, if allowed. All meat broths are made in the same manner.

BEEF TEA.—Cut up a pint of juicy sirloin beef in small bits; put it in a quart bottle, with half a pint of cold water; cork and wire firmly, and boil fifteen minutes; then press the meat, salt the tea, and use it as directed by the physician.

EXTRACT OF MEAT, No. 1.—Cut lean juicy beef or mutton in small bits; fill a quart bottle three-fourths full; cork and wire tightly, and put the bottle in a kettle of cold water; let it boil gently one hour; when it is removed, press the meat, to obtain the juice which may yet remain in the meat.

EXTRACT OF BEEF, No. 2.—Have ready a bright bed of coal; rub a thick juicy steak with very little salt; broil quickly, and press out all the juice as fast as it gathers. It may be made boiling hot, or used as it leaves the beef. If used without cooking over, it will be more stimulating than if changed by heat.

HERB AND ROOT TEAS.—All herb and root teas should be made with the same care as green tea. Steep them in earthen, tightly closed, and use the drinks while fresh. Most nurses imagine that herb teas are boiled herbs. The infusions lose life as readily as green tea, by long steeping and exposure to air. Strain the teas before taking them to the patient, and do not let it become insipidly flat before it reaches them.

PART XII.

CHAPTER I.

MISCELLANEOUS RECEIPTS.

To CLEAN DUST FROM WALL PAPER.—Make a mop of single cotton yarn, and wipe the paper; this should be done yearly.

To REMOVE FRUIT STAINS FROM THE HANDS.—Rub your hands with rhubarb stalks or sorrel.

To REMOVE ODOR FROM WARE.—Boil the ware in soap-suds, putting the articles in the wash boiler when the suds is cold.

To MAKE A GOOD WHITEWASH.—Six quarts clean, white, well-burnt lime in lumps; slack with hot water covered tightly; pass it in fluid state through a fine sieve; add one-fourth of a pound of burnt alum pulverized, one of pound loaf-sugar, three pints rice flour, made into a thin well-boiled paste, one pound clean glue dissolved, and add five gallons hot water. If used outside, put it on warm. It takes one pint to the square yard. It may be colored if desired.

COMMON WHITEWASH.—Slack good lime with hot water; thin it with skimmed milk; add alum, and stir it often while putting it on. If desired buff, add a bit of copperas as large as a filbert to one pailful. Rinse the brush in cold water when not in use, or to put away. The lime eats the bristles.

GELATINE.—This is prepared for jellies by soaking overnight in very little water; allow one ounce for each quart of jelly. If the isinglass is not pure, it must be clarified. Mix in a half-pint of water a teaspoon of the white of egg, and a little lemon juice; beat well, and stir it into two ounces of isinglass, which is dissolved in half a pint of water; heat these together gradually, constantly stirring; remove all the scum, and pass it through a flannel jelly bag.

To KEEP BRITANNIA BRIGHT.—Wash the ware every time it is used, in hot suds of fine soap; rinse with boiling water inside; when hot, pour over it boiling water, and dry while hot with a soft towel. Once each week rub the metal with wash leather and very little whiting. Take care of silver in the same manner.

To REMOVE A BROKEN CORK FROM A BOTTLE.—If you have no cork extractor, which is merely four wires twisted together, bent slightly, to take up the cork, use a cord tied in a loop, drop it into the bottle, loop it around the cork, and draw it out.

CEMENT FOR JARS AND BOTTLES.—Use one-fourth beeswax, and three-fourths rosin, melted together.

CAMPHOR SPIRITS.—Cut in a pint of spirits of wine an ounce of camphor gum.

To KEEP A MUFF SMOOTH.—Before returning the muff to the box, twirl it, to straighten every hair.

To REMOVE SPOTS FROM FURNITURE.—Rub hard in a mixture of equal parts of sweet oil and turpentine; when the spots are removed, wash the furniture in fine soap-suds, and polish by rubbing briskly.

To CLEANSE FURNITURE.—Wash furniture in fine soap-suds, and rub until polished. This is much better than oiling furniture.

To REMOVE OIL FROM A FLOOR.—Cover the spot with hot ashes, and continue the process until the grease is extracted; or, wet the spot with concentrated lye, as strong as it can be dissolved.

To CLEAN VIALS.—Put them in cold water with ashes, and boil them.

To REMOVE OIL FROM LAMP SHADES.—Fill a kettle with strong suds; place a towel in the bottom of the kettle, and put in the shades; let them boil one hour, being careful that the shades are entirely covered with the suds while boiling; if not covered, the glass will be marked where they rise above the suds. Rinse in boiling water immediately, and wipe dry. If shades are rubbed to remove grease, spots resembling oil will be left on the glass.

To REMOVE INK-SPOTS.—If ink is spilled on carpets that will not spot with acids, wipe up the ink, and wash in white vinegar. If acids will spot the carpet, wash in clear water immediately. For linen or cotton, use lemon juice, or a weak solution of oxalic acid. If ink is spilled on prints which will not bear acids, soak the goods immediately in sweet milk.

To PREPARE RENNET.—Take a calf's stomach, take out the curd; wash it clean; salt it thoroughly, inside and out, leaving a white coat of salt in every part; now lay it in a jar for three or four days, where it will form a pickle; then drain it for two days; resalt, and put it again in the jar; cover it with paper pasted over the jar, and let it lie for twelve months; it may, however, be used within a few days, but is not as strong as when left in the brine for a long time. When used for curds, the rennet is soaked in cold water, and the water is used for forming the curd.

To REMOVE SPERMACETI.—Scrape off the spots; place a brown paper, the size of the iron, on the garment or floor, covering the spots, and put a warm iron on the paper until the oil shows through; continue the process until no oil is drawn to the paper.

THREAD LACE TO LOOK NEW.—Wrap bottles with cotton cloth; wrap the lace on the bottles; leaving the edge exposed at every turn; soak for two days; then boil half an hour; rinse in two clear waters, and lastly in clean, fine soap suds; hang it to dry; when nearly bone-dry, remove it; pick out the edge; pass a stiletto through the eyelets, and wrap the lace smoothly on a ribbon-block; wrap it in cloth, a little damp, one hour; then press with the hand on the block, and dry in the sun, or by the fire; when perfectly dry, lay it away on the block until needed. Sew thread lace to collars very slightly, and rip it off before washing. It looks badly stiffened, and the starch makes it tender.

To WASH BLACK LACE VEIL.—Prepare two suds with fine soap and beef's gall; strain the suds; dissolve a bit of glue as large as a ten-cent piece in a gallon of water; boil and strain it. To the second suds and the glue water, add a quart of water, very darkly colored with indigo, and strained; put a pint in each. Now soak the lace in the first suds five minutes; then squeeze it, without rubbing, several minutes, and pass it through the suds; squeeze it, and shake it gently; pass it through the second suds in the same manner; then rinse in blued water; squeeze dry, and open out, and dip it up and down in the glue water; squeeze it in a towel, and open it out; shake it gently in the wind until partially dried; then pick out the edge; open the eyelets with a stiletto; spread on the carpet, or a large table, a folded blanket; cover it with black silk or cambric; pin the veil out smooth; cover it with black silk or cambric, and lay on it a marble slab, or some other flat, even weight; when it has lain one hour, fold the vail evenly, in the same manner it was originally folded; lay it on the table, and press until bone-dry. Black edging may be washed as above.

To RENEW BLACK TISSUE VEILS.—Dip them in thin glue water; shake them gently until nearly dry; spread black silk or cambric on the ironing blanket, and press with a moderate iron.

To REMOVE WATER SPOTS FROM BLACK CRAPE.—Clap crape, that has been wet, until dry. The best way to do this is to spread the spot on the hand, and slap it with the other until the spot disappears. If dried before the spot was noticed, it will need dampening.

To STIFFEN CRAPE.—Hold crape over patatoes or rice while boiling, and let it dry by the fire.

To REMOVE BROKEN SPOTS FROM VELVET.—Hold the wrong side of the velvet over steam, and while damp draw the wrong side across a clean stove-pipe, or warm iron, several times. This is the only proper method to press velvets.

To IRON RIBBONS.—Heat an iron, turn it on the side, and draw the wrong side of the ribbons over it, holding them firmly to the iron. Ribbons ironed in the usual way look badly.

To WASH RIBBONS.—Make a suds with fine hand soap, lay them flat on a plate, take a brush, dip it in the soap, and first brush the soiled spots; rinse it up and down in clear water, dip it in the suds, take a soft cloth and draw the ribbon through it until it looks clear, dipping the ribbon each time in the suds, but not letting it lie; rinse in the same manner, and draw it through a towel until dry, and press as above. If left to soak, the colors run and fade; if rubbed, the silk wrinkles and will not press smooth ; if dried without rubbing through the towel, the colors will run and the ribbon will be stiff.

To CLEANSE KID GLOVES.—Put the gloves on a person's hand; have ready some old skim milk perfectly sweet, and some fine white soap; dampen a soft white cloth, wrap it around the forefinger, rub it once on soap, and rub the spots from the gloves, change the place in the cloth when it looks soiled; go over the whole gloves without wetting through; when it is quite clean, take it off, pull and stretch the leather so as to stretch every grain several ways ; now shape the glove, and polish it with French chalk if light, or by friction of the hand if dark. White gloves may be cleansed several times in this manner; they may be cleansed without putting on the gloves, but not as perfectly; if allowed to dry damp, they will be ruined.

To SAVE WET GLOVES.—If gloves are wet through by rain or perspiration, wring them in a towel, and stretch the leather until quite dry; if dried before this can be done, wet them again, and stretch until dry.

To WASH DOESKIN GLOVES.—Wash them in water of blood-heat, wring as dry as possible, and let them hang in the house, away from heat, until two-thirds dry ; then stretch until soft. Wash leather, used for cleaning glass or silver, may be washed as above ; also buckskin mittens, shirts, etc.

To REMOVE IRON MOULDS.—Dissolve oxalic acid in water, wet the spot, rub it a little, and hang it by the window in the sun; be careful that the liquid is not so strong as to eat the fabric; it is rank poison : keep it from children.

To REMOVE FRUIT STAINS.—Pour through linen, stained by fruit, boiling water (*see* WASHING) before it is wet.

TEA AND COFFEE STAINS.—Tea and coffee are set by alkali or copperas ; rinse out stains of tea or coffee in warm water.

To SCOUR A CARPET.—If there is a fulling-mill near, the best plan would be to rip the carpet, shake the dust well out, and have it passed through the mill; if not, after it is shook and ripped, lay it on a clean floor; have ready plenty suds and ox-gall, mix a part of the gall with the suds, and scour the carpet with a common scrubbing-brush, until quite clean ; rinse it, until the water is clear, without wringing ; if a river is near, tie to each breadth a rope, and float it in the water until clear; then rinse in water, a little stiffened with bran, to make it sweep clean; dry it in the wind, and press with a tailor's goose when nearly dry, until bone dry.

BLEACHING FLUID.—Put into a quart jar four ounces of chloride of lime : add a little water, and stir it until the lumps are all broken and the chloride unites with the water, forming a mortar; then fill the bottle nearly full of water, and let it stand corked two weeks; open the bottle twice daily to let off the gas; or the bottle may break; be careful not to inhale the gas when opening the bottle; do not let the bottle remain open over a moment each time; dilute with water, and soak linen that is yellow, in it, or add very little to the boiling suds.

To REMOVE SPOTS OF PAINT.—Rub the paint with spirits of turpentine; if dry, drop it on the paint and let it lie; rub the spot, and if not removed, repeat the process. Pitch or tar may be removed in the same manner.

RECEIPT FOR CLEANING HEARTH RUGS.—Dissolve in a quart of warm water, one and a half ounce of alum; the same weight of fuller's earth, in another quart; put a gill of each in a gallon of water, and add a table-spoon of beef-gall; wash the spot in this mixture with a white flannel, brush it over with soap, wash it off, and rub dry; then make a suds; add a gill of the two preparations to one gallon of suds; wash it over and rub it as dry as possible. A whole carpet may be washed as above.

To REMOVE SOIL FROM CARPETS.—Sprinkle the carpet all over with dry Indian meal or wheat bran, and sweep it hard.

To BLEACH WHITE SILKS OR FLANNEL.—Wash the articles clean, rinse in suds, and smoke with brimstone while wet; the silk must be brushed or washed with a sponge; if rubbed, it will never press smoothly; expose the goods to the air, and the odor will soon pass off.

To CLEANSE WHITE OR FAWN-COLORED FEATHERS.—Dissolve fine soap in boiling water; add a lump of soda, strain the suds and cool a little; when you can bear the heat of the water, pass the feathers through it, squeezing them gently, and passing them through the hand; repeat the process with weak suds, without soda; rinse them in cold water, and strike them on the left hand until nearly dry; then take a small silver or some other blunt-edged knife, and draw each fibre over the edge, curling it as you please; if desired flat, it may then be pressed between the leaves of a large book. Black feathers are cleansed with gall water, and dried as above.

To Prevent White Silks, Merinoes, or Feathers turning Yellow.—Pack them in boxes lined with brown paper, and lay white beeswax in the box.

To Prevent a Hat from being Dusted in a Bandbox.—When travelling with a bandbox, paste paper over the edge of the cover, to keep dust from sifting in.

To Renew Feathers.—Put the feathers in a barrel of suds; pound them well through three suds, rinse in two waters, wring in a cloth, and put them in a small room with no carpet; spread them on a clean floor, and whip them daily with a small, long stick; tie up your head, and cover your face with a veil when beating them. Old feathers will be as light as new treated in this manner.

To Wash Feather Beds.—Lay the beds on a clean floor, and scrub them with a clean stiff brush or broom; first one side, and then the other; rinse in the same manner, and dry in the sun; shake them up four or five times daily. This renews the feathers, and cleanses the ticks at the same time. It is a good plan to lay old feather-beds in the rain after scouring.

To Protect Carpets from Moths.—Scatter camphor under the carpet before laying down.

To Save Stair Carpets.—Nail several thicknesses of old carpet or canvas over the edge of each stair. It is a good plan to buy more carpet than is needed to cover the stairs, and move it several times each season, so that the whole will wear evenly; if stair carpets cannot be changed in this way, they will not last long.

To Cleanse Hair Brushes.—Rub them in dry Indian meal, until the oil and dust are extracted.

To Cleanse Baking Plates.—Boil them in strong soap suds.

To Cleanse Inside of Teapots.—Pour into them strong lye, but do not spill any on the outside, as it will discolor them; tea steepers, and coffee pots also, may be cleansed with a weaker lye, or be filled with ashes and water, and boiled out.

To CLEANSE WINDOWS.—After the windows are cleansed, and the corners freed from dust, rub them bright with newspapers.

To CLEAN HOUSE.—Commence with the cellar; when that is in order, go to the garret; then regulate the closets; after which, take up the carpets from the upper story, clean the paint, etc., put down the carpets, and then take the next story, until the house is cleansed.

To WASH WHITE PAINT.—Make a solution of soda-water; wipe off the paint without soap, and rinse with clear water; soap injures paint. If not so strong as to eat the hands, it will not injure paint. (This rule was obtained from a painter.)

To SHAKE CARPETS.—Carpets should be shook in the sun, to destroy any moths which may have lain in them during the winter; shake them until no dust escapes. It is useless to clean house and put down dusty carpets.

To PACK A TRUNK.—Fold each article flat without wrinkles: more can be pressed into a trunk flat, than in bundles.

To PRESERVE TRUNKS.—Have rollers put on all heavy trunks, and cover them with strong canvas.

To PRESERVE GILT FRAMES.—Varnish them with a thin white varnish, made for the purpose, touching them lightly with the brush.

To WASH OIL CLOTHS.—Take equal parts of skimmed milk and water, wash off the dust, and wipe dry.

To PRESERVE OIL CLOTHS.—Varnish oil cloths every spring, that are used in winter, and let them lie until wanted, spread out. Varnish those covering rooms in the summer and in the fall, and let them lie until spring; if used while the varnish is green, it will turn if washed with nothing but water; and the varnish will come off if washed with suds. English oil cloths are the best, because the oldest; Americans send theirs to market while green.

To WASH DOWN.—If sewed on cloth, wash in suds until clean; rinse in blue water, shake and whip until perfectly light.

To CUT AND SEW FUR.—Turn fur on the skin side, draw across it a sharp knife, not quite separating the skin, then pull it apart; if cut with scissors, the fur will be cut with the skin; sew it over hand on the wrong side.

To REMOVE GREASE FROM A LEATHER-COVERED BOOK.—Rub the leather with white flannel, briskly, and repeat the operation until it disappears. Grease may be removed from any goods that will bear rubbing in the same manner.

To POLISH STOVES.—Use British lustre; black them cold and polish with a stiff broom. If polished hot, they soon burn off.

To CLEAN MARBLE.—Pulverize a little stone blue with four ounces of whiting; mix them with an ounce of soda dissolved in very little water, and four ounces of soft soap; boil the mixture fifteen minutes over a slow fire, stirring constantly; lay it on the marble with a brush while hot, and let it lie half an hour; wash it in warm water, with flannel and scrubbing-brush, and wipe it dry.

To REMOVE PAINT AND PUTTY FROM GLASS.—Make a strong solution of soda, and wet the glass several times.

CREAKING HINGES.—Rub hinges with very little soft soap if they creak.

To REMOVE A GLASS STOPPER.—Dip in boiling water the neck of the bottle.

RED INK.—Best carmine four grains; pure filtered rain-water one ounce; spirits of ammonia, forty drops; a piece of gum-arabic as large as a kidney bean.

BLUE INK.—Half an ounce Prussian blue, and half an ounce oxalic acid; powder them finely; add pure soft water to make a paste, and work them until fine; leave it four days, then add water, and a small piece of gum-arabic, until of the proper consistency.

INDELIBLE INK.—Nitrate of silver, three-fourths of an ounce, dissolved in liquor ammoniac fortissime, two ounces and seven-eighths of an ounce; gum-mucilage, six ounces; orchel three-eighths of an ounce: use it without any preparation. Always try indelible ink on cotton cloth before marking, as it sometimes eats.

ELDERBERRY SYRUP.—One quart of juice, half a pound of loaf-sugar, one table-spoon heaping full of cinnamon, just pulverized, the same of cloves and nutmeg; boil the juice and spices together half an hour, strain and add the sugar, boil and skim well; when cold, put it in a bottle, and add half a pint of fourth brandy.

BLACKBERRY SYRUP.—One quart of juice, one table-spoon of cinnamon, one of nutmeg, half as much cloves, one pound loaf-sugar; mix all together, add one pint brandy, bottle, and in two weeks strain. These two receipts are used for children's bowel complaints.

IRON WARE.

GRIDIRON.—The gridiron should be neither light nor heavy, with the bars bevelling; keep the bars bright by scouring.

IRON BASIN.—The bottom should be rounding, and of light ware.

ENAMELLED KETTLES.—Never cook solids in these kettles; if the glazing cleaves off, it will poison the food. Cleanse with ashes and water if discolored by fruit; never set them empty on the stove, or partly filled, on the hearth. If the glazing cracks, they are unsafe to use.

WAFFLE IRONS.—Select those that bake four cakes, and are deep enough; some are very shallow, and let the butter run over. To grease waffle well and economically, a swab is necessary; melt butter, dip in the swab, and grease when hot; when the cakes are baked, wipe the irons on the outside, but leave the inside greased, or they will rust before again used.

SPIDERS.—Buy one with an iron cover, if possible.

OMELETTE PAN.—These are very small frying pans; a large pan spreads the omelette too much.

IRON BAKE OVENS.—A moderate iron bake oven is very convenient in any family; they may be used on a stove, instead of putting them on coals.

To CLEAN A GRIDDLE.—Scour a griddle with salt and rusked bread, and always wipe it clean around the edge before putting it away.

To CLEAN A BRASS KETTLE.—Wash it in vinegar, and salt and rinse it well before using. To clean one to set away, use no acids; it will corrode if cleaned with vinegar; scour it with Bath brick until bright.

To PRESERVE BUTTER.—Press out the liquid, and work into every two pounds two teaspoons of salt and one of loaf-sugar, a salt-spoon of saltpetre, and pack it tight.

To MEND IRON POTS.—Make a paste of white of egg and lime, work it fine, and stir in iron filings; stop the cracks and let the pots stand one week. They may be mended by the tinner with a preparation of muriatic acid and zinc, used in place of rosin and hard solder.

FLAT IRONS.—Never set them on their faces, or allow nuts to be cracked on them.

To CLEAN IVORY.—Rub ivory knife-handles with fine sand-paper, and polish with pumice stone, powdered fine.

To SCOUR STEEL, AND KEEP BRIGHT.—Rub steel with fine emery sand; wrap shovel and tongs in doeskin or oil silk during the summer; wrap knives in doeskin to keep them from rusting.

To REMOVE MILDEW.—Moisten the linen with soft soap, fill the soap with whiting, and lay it on the grass; continue the process until it disappears. Sour milk often removes fresh mildew.

LABOR-SAVING SOAP.—Dissolve two pounds of soda in five gallons of water; melt in this five pounds of hard soap, add one pint of turpentine; mix all together, and stir until cold; make a suds of this for boiling clothes, as strong as is usually used; rinse in three waters; do not rub the clothes except where very badly soiled, and then but little; soak the clothes overnight in suds; from this soap, in the morning, rub the wristbands and neck bindings, and boil one hour; rinse in three waters.

To REMOVE RUST.—Scour with emery, sand, and sweet oil; leave the oil on a day, and then polish with finest sand-paper.

To PREPARE LIME WATER.—Pour over quicklime as much water as it will take up; let the bottle stand undisturbed until it settles clear, and then pour it off. Liebig advises using it in bread made with hop-yeast. Use one gill for four large loaves, or a pint half reduced. Mix with linseed oil for burns. (*See* REMEDIES.)

To DYE DRAB OR TEA-COLOR.—Save all the tea-grounds in an old iron kettle; when full, boil them; if not very rusty, add a piece of copperas as large as a filbert; boil all together, dip the goods in strong suds, and boil in the tea; if woollen, only allow them to scald, if cotton, they may boil some time.

To Dye Buff.—Dissolve a teaspoon of copperas in a kettle of the strongest suds, or weak lye, and boil the cotton.

To Dye Black.—Put four pounds of logwood in a rusty kettle, throw in all the rusty iron you can find, and cover the logwood with strong vinegar; let it soak, stir up the dye several times daily with a stick with a swab on the end; wipe the rust from the kettle into the dye; let it soak one month, and when you find rusty iron, throw it in; add vinegar as it dries away; then wet the goods in strong soap suds, and lay them in the kettle, airing several times the first day (this will color four pounds of woollen); let the goods lie several days, take them out and expose them ten minutes to the air three times each day; then dry and wash until the dye does not wash out; steep them in hot urine, or a decoction of hickory bark, two days, then wash and dry. The coloring may be performed sooner with the aid of copperas, but there is danger of its eating the goods.

Green or Blue Dye.—Reduce half an ounce Spanish indigo to powder, add a pound of sulphuric acid, stir them together; add soda the size of a pea; when the fermentation ceases, bottle it; it will be ready to use in forty-eight hours. This dye is for silks; scald, not boil, the silks in suds until white, then rinse out all the suds, and dip them in cold alum-water; air the goods often, and do not let them boil; they must not crowd the kettle. This dye is a deadly poison, and will corrode cotton even if reduced, and woollen at full strength. To color green, dip the silks in yellow dye, after they are colored blue.

To Color Silk Yellow.—For twelve pounds silks, take two pounds of weld or quercitron bark; tie the bark in a bag, put it in cold water, soak it for some time, and heat it to 100°; dip the silk in cold alum-water, and then immerse it in the dye, until the desired shade is produced; air often, and rinse in clear water. Chalk or pearlash, will deepen the color.

To Dye Brown.—Steep walnut peel, and scald the goods in them; let them lie until the desired tint is produced.

18

To Dye with Peach-Leaves.—Boil peach-leaves in a brass kettle in alum-water, cool to 100°; having dipped the silks in cold alum-water, soak them in the dye, and air often; rinse in warm water, and add in the last water a teaspoon of the oil of vitriol.

To Dye with Saffron.—Steep saffron in alum-water, and scald, not boil, the silks.

To Dye Scarlet.—For every pound of goods, allow two ounces pure cream of tartar, one ounce best powdered cochineal, and two ounces of solution of tin; mix the tartar in pure warm water, in a brass kettle; when a little warm, add the cochineal; mix well, and add the tin; stir, and when it boils, wet the goods, put it in the dye, move it around, and boil twenty minutes; rinse in cold water. For silks, heat the dye to 180°, wet the silk in cold alum-water, move it constantly, and do not allow the dye to boil; rinse in cold water, without wringing.

To Preserve Bird Cages from Mites.—When the cage is new, anoint it with red precipitate; if made of wood, let it remain a day or two, and wash it in boiling water *without soap*, before putting in the bird; if of wire, unscrew the top, anoint the screw and between the wires, leaving none of the ointment where the bird can reach it; if the cages are old, scald them in boiling water, and anoint them as directed above; do this four times a year, and mites will not trouble the birds.

To Raise Chickens.—When the hen has hatched all the eggs which are not addled, prepare an airy coop, and put her in it; anoint the chickens with red precipitate ointment, and put them with the hen; feed the brood with sour milk, bread soaked in milk or water, or Indian meal wet with milk or water. It is well to give, at times, different food; keep food and clean water by them constantly; the hen will need corn and lime.

To Make Hens Lay in Winter.—Keep them warm, and give them daily fresh meat; do not feed them corn in the usual manner, but keep it by them constantly.

To Keep Cream from Rising.—Take the milk fresh from the cow, and stir it until all the animal is gone; milk prepared thus, is much better for family use than when the cream rises.

LIST OF CONVENIENT KITCHEN FURNITURE.

Ash pail.
Apple parer.
Apple corer.
Acid-ometer.
Bake pan.
Bird spit.
Bread pan.
Bread grater.
Bread board.
Bread box.
Bread knife.
Bread blanket.
Bread toaster.
Basting ladle.
Basting pan.
Butter bowl.
Butter ladle.
Butter print.
Butter cooler.
Butcher's knife.
Bags for twine, etc.
Bottle cleaner.
Bone saw.
Biscuit cutter.
Brooms.
Brushes.
Bell.
Bellows.
Cheese box.
Cheese tub.
Cheese press.
Cheese ladder.
Cheese knife.
Cheese hoop.
Cheese packer.
Cheese grater.
Cheese toaster.
Churn.
Cream crock.
Cream whipper.
Cream beater.
Carving knife.
Cake pans.
Cork screw.
Cork removers.
Coffee mill.
Coffee roaster.

Coffee boiler.
Colander.
Custard baker.
Chocolate mill.
Chocolate boiler.
Chocolate grater.
Candlestick.
Candle box.
Cinder shovel.
Coal sifter.
Chafing dishes.
Crumb brushes.
Carpet brush.
Carpet claw.
Carpet hammer.
Carpet stretcher.
Carpet sweeper.
Clothes basket.
Clothes pins.
Clothes line.
Clothes boiler.
Chopping knife.
Chopping board.
Chopping bowl.
Cleaver.
Covers.
Cracker breaker.
Dippers.
Dishes.
Dish pan.
Dish brushes.
Dutch oven.
Dust pans.
Dust brushes.
Dripping pans.
Egg beaters.
Egg coolers.
Egg basket.
Egg scalder, of wire.
Egg lifter, of wire.
Frying pan.
Flour chest.
Flour sieve.
Flour shaker, or dredge.
Funnels of different sizes.
Furnaces for charcoal.
Furniture brushes.

Freezers for ices.
Faucets.
Fish kettle for boiling fish.
Fish boards.
Fish knives for cleaning fish.
Fish bakers for baking fish.
Fire box.
Forks, large and small.
Fluid can, with caps.
Flat irons.
Forms for cake baking.
Gridirons.
Griddle.
Graters.
Grindstone for knives.
Hammers.
Hatchet.
Hand basin.
Horseradish grater.
Herb steeper.
Herb strainer and sifter.
Iron stands for flats.
Iron lifters.
Iron hooks.
Iron basins, with
Iron spoons of different sizes.
Iron forks, large.
Iron ladle.
Jacks for roasting.
Jelly moulders.
Jelly bags of flannel.
Japanned pails.
Japanned canisters for spices, etc.
Knife boxes.
Knife cleaners.
Knife sharpeners.
Kettles of different sizes.
Lobster crackers.
Larding pins.
Lamps.
Lantern.
Lemon squeezers.
Lard knife of wood.

Milk pans.
Milk pails.
Milk strainer.
Milk skimmer.
Milking stool.
Meat board.
Meat saw.
Meat screen.
Meat chopper.
Meat tongues.
Mats for tables.
Mats for feet.
Market basket.
Match safe.
Mousetrap.
Marble slab for rolling pastry.
Marble rolling pin.
Marble mortar.
Mortar of iron.
Meal tubs or boxes.
Mills for spices and coffee.
Mallet.
Measures, bushel, peck, gallon, quart, and pint.
Nutmeg grater.
Nut cracker.
Oyster knife.
Oyster shells.
Oil can.
Omelet pans.
Pie plates.
Pudding bakers.
Pudding boilers.
Patty pans.
Paste cutter.
Paste roller.
Paste jagger.
Paste moulds.
Plate rack.
Plate warmer.
Pickling tubs.

Pork and beef barrel.
Preserving kettles.
Press boards for ironing pants.
Pepper shaker.
Poker.
Potato masher.
Potato knife.
Plane for shaving dried beef.
Porcelain kettles and stew pans.
Paper bags.
Roller for towels.
Rings for griddles.
Rolling pins.
Skimmers.
Strainers.
Sieves of different sorts.
Sugar sifter.
Sugar sieve.
Sugar bowl.
Sugar box.
Spits.
Skewers.
Stew pans.
Stays.
Saucepans.
Stockpans.
Soup ladles.
Soup pot.
Soup strainer.
Steak beaters.
Steak tongs.
Shears.
Scissors.
Stairs or steps for cleaning.
Sponges for cleaning.
Silver plate brushes.
Salt boxes.
Spice boxes.
Scales.

Shovel.
Salad forks.
Salad spoons of wood.
Salad bowls of wood.
Soap tub.
Soap bowl.
Soap dish.
Scrub brushes.
Stove brushes.
Starch basin.
Starch strainer.
Starch box.
Steamers.
Steers, or oven shovels.
Tubs.
Tables.
Towels.
Towel racks.
Tongs for the fire.
Tongs for meat.
Thermometer.
Toaster.
Toast rack.
Toasting fork.
Twine.
Vegetable drainer.
Vegetable steamer.
Vegetable boiler.
Vegetable lifter.
Vegetable stewpan.
Weights.
Waffle irons.
Wash tubs.
Wash boiler.
Wash board.
Wash bowl.
Water pails.
Water filterer.
Water cooler.
Wood box.
Wedge for breaking ice.
Wine cooler.
Window brushes.

MEAT TONGS.—Small tongs, used to turn steaks, instead of forks, which pierce the meat, causing the juices of the steak to waste.

KITCHEN FURNITURE. 413

OMELET PAN.—A small iron pan, with a short handle, resembling a very small, shallow, frying-pan. Used for frying omelets.

BROILING SPIDER.—This is a spider with a movable frame of iron fitting it, on which the steak is laid. To use it, heat the spider with the frame hot, lay on the steak, and broil it quickly.

FISH KETTLE.—This is an oval pan with handles, a closely fitting cover, and false bottom, perforated with small holes, to which wire handles are affixed to lift the fish by. To use, place the fish on the strainer, put it in the pan, and cover it with the water; when cooked lift the fish on the strainer, drain it free from water, or evaporate all the moisture in the oven, before turning it from the strainer.

SCALLOP SHELL.—This is the shell of the scallop, an earthen dish made to represent it, or a scalloped dish.

CHOCOLATE MILL.—This is a tin vessel, with a handle of wood passing through the cover, to the bottom of which is fastened a wheel of wood or metal, resembling a churn-dasher. To prepare chocolate well, it needs to be milled or beat until perfectly smooth, without settlings of grated chocolate. To use the mill, take the pot from the fire; turn the handle briskly, rolling it in the hand for several minutes; put the pot on the fire again, let it simmer a few moments, and repeat the milling as many times as is necessary to insure a smooth pot of chocolate; usually two millings is sufficient. (*See* CHOCOLATE.)

CREAM SQUIRT.—This is a small syringe of tin or other metal; to use, place the tube in the cream, draw the handle, and push it up quickly, forcing the cream out of the tube.

SUGAR SIFTER.—A small silver box with a finely punctured cover, used to dust powdered sugar over cakes and pastry.

GRAVY POT.—This is of iron, lined with porcelain, and shaped much like the old-fashioned iron tea-kettles, with a little longer spout. Used to keep gravies hot until needed for the table, and also for making broths.

THERMOMETER.—This, for the kitchen, should be cased in japanned tin, the figures on the scale ought to be large and distinct. To use it, dip the ball into the water or syrup; or, for testing the oven, hold in the oven and notice how high the mercury runs. No kitchen should be without one. They may be used to test the wetting for the bread, which should be about 84°; for testing the water bath for fruits; temperature of the room where dough is rising, which should be from 70°, to 84°, and to test ovens, which should be about 270°. This is a much safer guide than feeling. If a cook uses a thermometer, she will know, after one or two experiments, the proper heat of the oven for each kind of bread, pastry, cake, and pudding, which will save much anxiety.

(The following receipts should have been in other parts of the book, but are too valuable to be omitted.)

Howe's Cookies.—This is a receipt from one of the best of the New York bakers, and is superior :—Mix together five pounds of flour, one pound of butter, two and a half pounds of sugar; after the ingredients are well mixed, add caraway seed, and mix the cakes to a paste that will roll out, with a pint of water in which is dissolved one ounce of soda; roll the dough thin, and bake thoroughly, without burning. If they become stale, freshen them by heating them through in a rather cool oven.

Mrs. Hunt's Pork Pudding.—Chop one teacup of salt pork as fine as mince meat; pour over it hot water to freshen it; after which add a teacup of sweet milk, a teaspoon of soda, a teacup of chopped raisins, and flour to make the whole the consistency of cupcake.

Mrs. Hunt's Omelet.—This is a very superior omelet as well as a beautiful dish for the table. Beat the yolks of six eggs light, and mix them in a little sweet milk, say about a cupful, and add a trifle of salt; beat together a table-spoon of sweet butter, and the same of flour, until smooth; add the mixture to the custard, and beat the whole together; pour it into a well-buttered omelet pan, and when it begins to thicken pour over it the whites of the eggs beaten as stiff as possible; sift a trifle of the purest and finest salt over the whites, and when the whole is stiff remove the omelet to a plate, without breaking or bending.

A New Method of Cooking Rice.—Take three pints and one gill of the juice of red currant, or of any other acid fruit; add three pints of water, sugar to suit the taste, and flavor with almond or any spices relished; boil this mixture, and stir into it, gradually, one and a quarter pound of ground rice, or a pound of sago; let it boil very gently, stirring often, fifteen minutes; when well cooked, mould it in fancy moulds, or small cups; serve with cream and sugar, or a boiled custard.

Mrs. L.'s Wine Whey.—To a pint of milk, when boiling, add a wine-glass of wine; let it boil for a moment, and when the curd sets, turn off the whey, and sweeten with loaf-sugar.

Mrs. Dicson's Crackers.—One cup of lard, one cup of warm water, in which is dissolved two and a half teaspoons of cream of tartar, and another cup with a teaspoon of soda, dissolved in it, and salt to suit the taste; sift into the bread bowl a large quart of flour, rub the lard through the flour, mix the dough with the soda and cream of tartar, adding enough flour to make the dough quite stiff. They are better if rolled in separate crackers, but are very good rolled thin and cut with a cracker cutter; bake thoroughly without burning, and after they are all baked, set the pan containing them in a cool oven until they are dry and crisp; or they may be baked over as wanted, each day.

Mrs. L.'s Quick Beer.—Four table-spoons of ginger, one quart of home hop yeast, one quart of molasses, and fourteen quarts of cold water; mix well, and strain through a fine sieve, and bottle it immediately; it will be ready for use in twenty-four hours.

Elder Flower Wine.—Strip the blossoms from the stalks; to every quart of flowers allow a gallon of water, and three pounds of sugar; boil and skim the sugar and water, and pour it while hot over the flowers; add the juice of one lemon to every gallon of the liquor, and a small table-spoon of home brewed hop yeast, stir thoroughly through the whole; let it ferment three days in an open vessel of wood or earthen, covered entirely with a thick woollen blanket, then strain the wine through a sieve; add the white of one egg beaten to a froth; whisk the eggs through the wine, chop three or four pounds of raisins to every six gallons of wine, and put them in the bottom of the cask; then pour in the wine, and immediately close the bung; it will be fit to bottle in six months, and will be found delicious wine.

SCALLOPED CLAMS.—Chop your clams raw; boil five eggs hard, and chop them; butter the sides and bottoms of a pudding dish, and spread crumbs of bread around it, mix the eggs and clams; season to suit the taste, and place layers of clams and bread alternately, adding small bits of sweet butter until the dish is full, and bake in a slow oven one hour.

MRS. L.'s FROSTING.—Two pounds of double refined loaf-sugar, powdered, and sifted through gauze, and the whites of six eggs beaten stiff; after the sugar is all stirred into the egg, beat it for some time, and add the juice of half a lemon.

CRACKER PIES.—One Boston cracker, one cup of sugar, one lemon, one cup of water; roll the crackers, mix all together, and bake it in an open pie.

MRS. WEBSTER'S CORN CAKES.—Six ears of corn grated from the cob, the yolks of six eggs, six table-spoons of flour and salt.

COCOANUT CUSTARD.—The white part of one grated cocoanut, five well-beaten eggs, one quart of milk, sugar, and a little salt; bake twenty minutes, and when done, cover the top with macaroons.

SARATOGA PUDDING.—One quart of boiled milk, two table-spoons of flour, three of sugar, three beaten eggs, and a little salt; beat the flour, sugar, and eggs together, and then pour the boiling milk in the mixture; beat all together, and bake fifteen minutes.

BOILED FLOUR PUDDING.—One quart of milk, eight beaten eggs, eight table-spoonfuls of flour, and a little salt; boil one hour.

COCOANUT CAKE.—One pound of grated cocoanut, one pound of sugar, half a pound of butter, six well-beaten eggs, and half a pound of flour; add the cocoanut to the cake just before it goes into the oven.

RAISED MUFFINS.—One pint of milk, four eggs, a piece of butter the size of a butternut, flour to make a batter, and yeast.

SOFT JUMBLES.—One pound and a quarter of flour, one pound of butter, one pound of pulverized loaf-sugar, six eggs, and nutmeg.

MRS. L.'S RUSK.—One quart of milk, home hop yeast in much greater proportion than for bread (there should be as much yeast used as possible, without making the rusks bitter); add sufficient flour to make a thin batter, and let it stand until light, then add one pound of sugar with one pound of butter, stirred together, eight eggs, and flour to make up the rusk; let them stand until very light before baking; when done, cover the tops with sugar and egg.

MRS. L.'S BLANC-MANGE.—Dissolve one ounce of isinglass in half a pint of sweet milk, by gently heating it over water; when dissolved, strain it through a jelly bag, and add it to one quart of thin, sweet cream; sweeten and flavor the cream to suit the taste, and let it stand until the sediment settles to the bottom; then wet the moulds in ice-water, pour in the mixture, and set it on ice to cool.

AMBROSIA.— Grate cocoanut, and mix it with powdered loaf-sugar to suit the taste; slice sweet oranges and sift over them powdered loaf-sugar, fill a fancy glass, dish with layers of the oranges and cocoa, heaping the dish with the cocoa.

MISS F.'S MEAD.—To three pounds of sugar, pour three pints of boiling water, one pint of molasses, one-fourth of a pound of tartaric acid, and one ounce essence of sassafras, bottle and cork tight: it is not necessary to seal it; put three table-spoons of the mead in three-fourths of a glass of ice-water, and stir in a quarter of a teaspoon of soda dissolved in a little water, to make it effervesce.

SUNDERLAND PUDDING.—Six eggs, three table-spoons of flour, one pint of milk, and a little salt; beat the yolks as light as possible, mix them smoothly with the flour, and then add the milk, beat the whites stiff, and add them just before baking; serve with a wine sauce.

ST. CHARLES' INDIAN BREAD.—Beat two eggs very light, and mix them with one pint of sour milk; add a teaspoon of soda or saleratus, and stir in one pint of Indian meal, and one table-spoon of melted butter, beat a long time, and bake in common bake pans in a quick oven; they are to be eaten hot or cold.

SWEET BREADS; FRENCH STYLE.—Put three large sweet breads in hot water, and let them boil ten minutes; when cool, skim, but do not break them; season with salt and pepper, and dredge them with a little flour; then fry them slowly in butter, a light brown on both sides; when done, place them on a dish, and remove all the brown particles from the pan, retaining the oiled butter; pour into the frying-pan while off the fire one gill of boiling water, and dredge in one dessert spoonful of browned flour, stirring it all the time; season with salt and pepper to the taste; let it come to a boil, and stir into the gravy two table-spoons of Madeira wine, pour it over the sweet breads, which should have been kept warm, and send them to the table hot, in a covered dish.

Mrs. B.'s Lemon Pudding.—Beat together two coffee-cups of powdered loaf-sugar, and half a coffee-cup of sweet butter, add the juice and oil of one large lemon, six beaten eggs, and one coffee-cup of milk; bake in a puff paste; the oil is best extracted by rubbing the rind of the lemon with lump sugar, which may be dissolved in the milk.

Orange Salad.—Slice oranges thin, put a layer of orange in the bottom of the dish, sift over sugar, add a little lemon-juice, and a teaspoon of wine, and continue the layers until the dish is full.

Cream Cakes.—One quart of flour, one pint and a half of milk, a half pint of sweet cream, four beaten eggs, and one small teaspoon of salt; mix all together, and bake in small buttered tins. To be eaten warm.

Mrs. W.'s Orange Custard.—Rub the rind of four large oranges with loaf-sugar to extract the oil; squeeze out the juice from the oranges, and mix it with a teacup of cold water; beat nine eggs very light, and add them to the juice and water, beat well, sweeten with flavored sugar to suit the taste; pour the mixture in custard cups, and let them stand in boiling water ten minutes; when done, set them in a cold place. Any other fruit can be used in the same manner.

Miss Dey's Kisses.—Six ounces of powdered loaf-sugar, and three ounces of butter; beat to a cream, add the whites of three beaten eggs, soda the size of a pea, dissolved in a table-spoonful of hot water (and strained), and flour to make it sufficiently stiff to roll out in very thin sheets; cut them in small cakes.

Boiled Indian Puddings.—Our grandmothers made simple boiled Indian puddings, after the two following rules, which were very good:

heat milk boiling hot, stir into the hot milk Indian meal, making the butter as stiff as it will pour, and let it swell one hour, add salt; have a pot of water boiling; allow one-fourth of the pudding bag for the swelling of the pudding, and boil steadily two or three hours; serve with cream and sugar, or syrup of maple sugar. Another mode; mix in a quart of Indian meal, a small teacup of chopped suet, add a half teacup of molasses, and a teaspoon of salt, stir into the pudding boiling water until the batter will pour, then fill the pudding bag two-thirds full, and boil as above; turn the pudding several times while boiling; dried fruit may be added. Usually boiled with salt meats.

MACARONI.—Boil until tender, four ounces of macaroni in veal or chicken broth; when done, drain it, add two table-spoons of sweet cream, an ounce of butter, and flavoring to suit; put it in a dish, cover the top with beaten eggs, and brown it in the oven; or mix the above with two table-spoons of dry grated cheese; season with pepper and salt; scatter over the top grated cheese, and brown it nicely; it should be Parmesan cheese.

MACARONI TOAST.—Macaroni may be prepared in either the above methods, and spread on nicely toasted bread, dipped in melted butter, or cream, and be browned in the oven, or not, as desired.

LABOR-SAVING SOAP.—For those who cannot obtain the patent soaps labor-saving, the following rule will be found useful: Dissolve two pounds of sal soda in ten quarts of boiling rain-water, add two pounds of common hard soap cut fine, and boil two hours. To use, put the clothes in soak the night before they are to be washed; rub the wristbands, collars, and articles stained, with the skin in one suds; boil in a strong suds of the prepared soap, one hour; suds and rinse well. The clothes look well, and are not injured by the soap.

To CLEANSE GREASE.—Boil drippings, or any other grease left from meats, in water, and let it cool until the next day; scrape off all the impurities settled to the bottom (which is only fit for soap), and boil the pure grease until the water is entirely evaporated; strain it and pour it in a crock for future use.

(The following rules were forgotten, and not inserted in their proper place. *See* SOUPS, SAUCES, AND GRAVIES.)

ROLLED BUTTER.—Lay flour on the moulding board, roll small bits of butter in flour, until it is thickly coated with it, lay it on the moulding board and roll it thin. It should be prepared in a cool room.

CREAMED OR DRAWN BUTTER.—Stir together sweet butter and fine flour, until it forms a smooth paste; stir in at first a table-spoon only of hot water, beat it up, and add another spoonful, and so continue until as much water is added as is needed; when all the water is in, hold the saucepan over the fire, moving it one way until it boils, after which set it where it will gently boil a moment or two. It is sometimes made with sweet milk.

BROWNED BUTTER.—Put a lump of butter in the frying-pan, move it over the fire until it becomes brown; sift in some brown flour, or add flour without browning, and stir it until it is a little scorched.

CAPER SAUCE.—Add to drawn or creamed butter, capers with a little of their vinegar; stir constantly until the sauce boils, and dish immediately. Nasturtiums may be used in the same manner.

INDEX.

	PAGE
Abscess in breast	382
Accidental company, how to treat	26
Advice to young housekeepers	1
chambermaids	34
cooks	32
housekeepers	31
husbands	27
maids of all work	35
nurse maids	35
Additional receipts	414
Ade, currant	285
lemon	284
orange	284
pineapple	285
strawberry	285
À-la-mode beef	87
dressing for	71
pork	92
Almond cake	188
macaroons	199
Alum for the teeth	380
Ambrosia	417
Ant hills	358
Ants, to protect from	359
red, to entrap	359
Antidotes for poisons	380
arsenic	381
antimony	381
Anchovy butter	81
Annuals for fall sowing	331
that will not bear transplanting	332
sowed in hot beds	332
Aphis, or green fly	354
April, work for	367
Apricots, to candy	192
to preserve	253
Apples	229
autumn	229
butter	231
boiled or steamed	234
baked	234
baked, sweet	234
borer	355
cider	230
cider, boiled	231
cider, apple-sauce	231
cook, dried apples	231
crab-apple jelly	233
crab-apple preserves	233
drying	231

	PAGE
Apples	
dumplings, No. 1	233
dumplings, No. 2	149
fritters	234
gathering	229
green	235
hermetically sealed in cans	235
hermetically sealed in bottles	235
jelly	232
late winter and spring use	229
marmalade	232
pie	234
pudding	234
pudding, Boston improved	136
pudding, Berkshire	144
pruning, trees	327
preserving for spring shipments	235
planting, trees	321
remarks on	329
rice dumpling	234
summer use	229
sweetmeats	232
tarts	234
winter late, and spring	229
winter, early use	229
worm	356
wash for trees	329
varieties	229
vinegar	282
Arranging bouquets	334
Arrow-root gruel	391
Artichokes, to cook	116
to preserve through winter	131
Asparagus, to cook	116
to cultivate	317
greens	116
hermetically sealed	117
omelet	216
soup	116
select at market	54
Bacon, to cure	862
to boil	92
Bags more convenient than boxes	7
Baked Indian pudding	148
Baking plates, to cleanse	404
Bark lice	355
Barberries, to preserve	263
Barley coffee	395
gruel	391
griddle cakes	188

	PAGE
Barley	
for infants	384
negus	394
punch	395
pearl	385
water	394
Basil vinegar	294
Batter pudding, plain raised	140
pudding, boiled	149
pudding, baked	149
Bath for fruits	268
Beans, to cook	117
to cultivate	311
lima	118
pickled	300
string, to preserve for winter	118
Windsor	118
Beer	278
bottled	278
molasses	278
mead	417
spruce	278
quick	415
Beef, a-la-mode	87
corned	361
corned, to use cold	88
corned, dried, to prepare	361
corned, dried to preserve soft	361
dried, to cook	90
French	87
general directions for boiling and roasting	84
mock venison of corned beef	90
roast, remarks on	86
sirloin, to roast	86
steak, stewed, No. 1	87
steak, stewed brown	88
fried	88
gravy	88
to broil rare	89
to suit all	89
fried, to resemble broiling	91
and oysters and clams	90
pie	90
Beets, to cook	117
to preserve for winter	132
select at market	55
Berry puddings	146
Berkshire puddings	144
Bird's-nest pudding	145
Bird-cages, to free from mites	410
Biscuit of brewer's yeast	164
of hops	163
of sour milk	165
of sour cream	165
soda and cream of tartar, No. 1	164
soda and cream of tartar, No. 2	165
Black cake	178
lace veil to wash	400
tissue veil to renew	401
crape, to remove spots	401
to color	409
tea	207
berry catsup	288
berry jelly	266
berry, hermetically sealed	267
berry syrup	407
berry wine	278
berry brandy	280
currant jam	265
currant jelly	266

	PAGE
Black	
currant brandy	280
currant wine	273
raspberries dried	270
birds, dressing for	71
Blankets, to wash	24
Bleeding nose	377
Blanc-mange, corn starch,	148
calves' foot	138
Mrs. L's	417
isinglass	152
fruit	136
Bleaching Fluid	403
Board for shirt-bosoms	15
for skirts	14
Bone, to remove from the throat	381
Borage vinegar	294
Box hedges	239
Boston cake	178
cream cake, genuine	187
pudding, improved	136
Bombazines, to wash	23
Boiled bacon	92
bass	76
batter puddings	149
beef, corned	85
beef, fresh	84
beef, remarks on	84
beets	117
beans	117
cabbage	118
cauliflower	119
crab cider	283
cod's head and shoulders	75
cod, salt	77
eggs	74
fish	74
flour pudding	416
fancy pudding, rice	147
fowls	108, 109
geese	109
ham, salt	91
ham, fresh	96
ham, cold to serve	97
indian pudding	416
leg of lamb	101
mutton chops	102
leg of mutton	102
neck of mutton	102
milk for coffee	210
parsnips	125
pike	76
peas	127
pork, salt	91
potatoes	128
prairie chicken	114
rice puddings	141, 147
rabbit	113
salmon, fresh	76
salmon, salt	77
sturgeon	77
sea-fish	75
shad	76
turbot	77
white-fish	76
Brandy cherries	260
cream	197
from fruits	279
green gages	251
peaches	236
plums	258

INDEX.

Brandy	PAGE
sauces	72
Brass kettle, to clean	407
Bread	159
balls	226
bran yeast	163
brewers' yeast	162
carroway	167
dry to use	125
fried	226
fried cakes	185
French	165
Graham	162
griddle cakes	125
hop yeast	160
Indian, St. John	417
milk, rising	169
panada, with wine	393
potato	168
pumpkin	167
pudding, Mrs. F.'s	148
remarks on	159
rice	168
rye	168
rye and Indian	167
sauce for poultry and game	69
wheat and Indian	166
Breakfast tea, to prepare	207
dishes	212
Breast, inflammation of	382
gathering	382
of veal, to carve	40
of veal to roast	103
Bride's cake	172
Britannia, to keep bright	399
Broiled beef	89
beef, with oysters and clams	90
fish	79
ham	95
lamb steaks	101
mutton chops	102
oysters	82
pork, fresh	93
pork, salt	95
Broiling spider, described	413
Browning coffee	208
Brown, to color	409
Broccoli, to cook	118
to cultivate	312
Broken cake pudding	224
Buckwheat flour, to select	56
cakes	189
Buff, to color	409
Bugs, to destroy	367
Bulbs, to cultivate	334
Buns	167
Burn Salve	374
liniment	374
quick remedy	375
salve, whalers'	375
Burnet vinegar	274
Butchers' divisions of meats	37
Butter, browned	68, 420
creamed	420
clarified	67
churned	363
drawn	67
preserved for winter	408
oiled	68
rancid, to restore	368
rolled	420

Butter	PAGE
peach	238
prepared	363
prepared for winter use	364
Cabbage, early York	118
to cultivate	311
boiled	118
boiled with meat	118
hot slaw	119
cold	119
to pickle	303
Cakes	169
Cake baking, to prepare for	172
almond	183
barley, griddle	188
Boston	173
brides	172
bread fried	185
Boston cream, genuine	187
black	178
buckwheat, mock	188
buckwheat, quick	188
buckwheat, raised No. 1	189
buckwheat, raised No. 2	183
chestnut	184
cup cake, Mrs. F.'s	174
cookies, Mrs. Case, No. 1	181
soft	181
Howe's	414
winter, No. 2	182
winter, No. 3	182
rich, No. 4	182
pound, No. 5	182
New Year's, No. 6	182
German New Years	181
cream cake, Boston	187
cream drop	187
cream cakes	172
griddles, No. 4	188
chocolate, soft	183
hard	183
corn starch cup	172
corn cakes, Mrs. Webster's	416
clay	177
crullers, Mrs. F	184
crumpets	168
Carolina cake	178
cocoanut cakes	416
coffee	185
cream cakes	418
children's loaf	179
composition	190
delicate, No. 1	174
No. 2	174
soda, No. 3	174
cup, No. 4	174
cup, Mrs. F.'s	173
eggs, to beat	171
fried, plain	184
fried, Mrs. W.'s superior	190
rich	184
without eggs and milk	185
fritters	185
fruit cup cake, Mrs. F	177
fruit, rich	178
federal	180
German pepper nuts	177
cornucopia	177
ladies' fingers	177

Cake, German	PAGE
steamed neudles	166
raised waffles	186
waffles, rich	186
soft chocolate	183
ginger bread, No. 1	170
cake, No. 2	170
cake, No. 3	170
bread, superior, No. 4	170
Mrs. L., No. 5	170
hard, No. 6	170
Mrs. W., No. 7	171
hard, No. 8	171
soft, Mrs. F. No. 9	171
soft, No. 10	171
snaps	171
griddle cakes, Indian, without milk	189
raised buckwheat, No. 1	189
raised buckwheat, No. 2	189
quick buckwheat	189
mock buckwheat	188
indian meal, without milk	189
Graham	189
rice	188
barley	188
sweet milk, No. 1	187
sour milk, No. 2	188
very nice, No. 3	188
cream, No. 4	188
hard German chocolate	183
Harrison, Mrs. F.	180
hoe cake	168
indian muffins	168
jelly	181
jumbles, pound, No. 2	183
johnny, No. 1	189
johnny, No. 2	189
kisses, Mrs. Dey's	418
soft jumbles	417
ladies' fingers	176
loaf, Mrs. S	179
molasses cakes, remarks	169
marmalade	180
muffins, Mrs. W	187
muffins, Mrs. L.	416
Madison	180
pound, Mrs. F., No. 1	178
No. 2	178
quick, loaf	179
rusk, Mrs. L.'s	417
soda, rich, No. 1	174
yellow, No. 2	175
No. 3	175
No. 4	175
strawberry	181
sponge, No. 1	175
Mrs. F., No. 2	176
excellent, No. 3	176
arrow root, No. 4	176
convenient, No. 5	175
drop	183
Sally Lunn	187
tea, very plain	173
thanksgiving	180
vanities	185
white	173
white, cup	174
white mountain	177
wedding, 1818	179
Washington	180
waffle, pound	186

Cake, German	PAGE
plain	186
good	186
American raised	186
Cake, French method of icing	198
to prepare for icing	198
Candy apricots	192
greengages	192
ice cream	194
maple sugar	193
molasses	193
nectarines	192
plums	192
Calves' brains	106
head to boil	105
light and liver	106
feet and ears	106
kidney	106
foot jelly dessert	137
blanc mange	138
Canvas-back Ducks to truss	107
to roast	112
Candying syrups	191
Carving	37
butchers' divisions of meats	37
breast of veal	40
cod's head	42
divisions of meats	37
eels	42
fillet of veal	40
forequarter lamb	40
fowl	41
fish	42
fish, baked	42
fish pan	42
haddock	42
ham	40
haunch of venison	39
hare or rabbit	41
leg of mutton	39
leg of lamb	40
loin of veal	39
mackerel	42
mutton, leg of	39
saddle of	39
shoulder of	39
partridge	41
pidgeon and quail	41
roast beef	88
roast pig	40
saddle of mutton	39
shoulder of mutton	39
salmon	42
soup to serve	42
turkey or goose	41
tongue	40
turbot	42
veal fillet	40
veal loin	39
Camphor, spirits	399
Canker sore mouth	390
Carpet, to protect from moths	404
to shake	405
to scour	402
remove soil from	403
Caterpillars	356
on gooseberries	358
Catsup	286
blackberry	288
celery	287
cherry	288

INDEX.

Catsup	PAGE
cucumber	289
gooseberry	288
grape	288
mutton chop,	287
mushroom	286
oyster	287
plum	287
peach	287
raspberry	288
tomato	289
walnut, No. 1	286
No. 2	287
whortleberry	289
Cauliflower, to cook	119
to pickle	305
to cultivate	315
Carrots, to cook	119
to pickle	308
to cultivate	313
Cassarole of fish	381
Cement for jars	399
Cellar, to cleanse	367
Celery, to use	119
preserved for winter	132
to grow	312
for the aged	292
Chintz, with red grounds to wash	20
with brown	20
with green	19
Chops, mutton, broiled	102
Chambermaid, advice to	34
Charlotte Russe, No. 1	135
No. 2	136
No. 3	136
fruit	136
Chocolate mill	413
Chocolate	210–211
Chilblains, to cure	376
Cheese	364
Cherries	257
Cherry brandy	280
Cherries—	
Black Hawk, to preserve	258
dried, No. 1	262
No. 2	263
dried, to cook	263
duke and Morella, to preserve	259
fancy preserves	258
history of	257
hermetically seal, natural preservers, in bottles, No. 1	259
No. 2	250
hermetically seal for pies, in glass	261
in cans	262
for table	262
pickled, No. 1	260
No. 2	261
No. 3	261
No. 4.	261
pie	263
pie from can fruit	263
pudding, No. 1	145
No. 2	146
trees to plant, remarks	321
vinegar	281
varieties	257
Chickens, to fricassee	115
pie and pot-pie	115
tea	397
quickly to dress	396

Chicken	PAGE
salads	119, 390
Cocoa kisses	194
Cocoanut cake	416
Cocoa snow	135
whips	152
flummery	152
cream	137
cakes	190
custard	416
pudding	143
Comfits	194
candying	192
Coffee cream	211
Coffee cream ice	197
Coffee	207
aroma preserved	208
cream, mock, for	211
browned	208
boiling	209
boilers, care of	211
description of plant	207
egg in milk for	210
mixing	209
proportion for an extra cup	210
preparation for market	207
remarks	210
storing	209
sugar for	210
serve	210
varieties	208
Cork broken to remove	399
Cow, to milk, etc.	362
Confectionery, chapter on	190
Counterpane, to wash	24
Cotton sheets, to iron	24
Corned beef hash	217
Codfish hash	218
balls	219
toast	214
picked up	80
salt to boil	77
tongues and sounds	78
head and shoulders	75
Cordials and extracts	283
of lemon	283
of carroway	283
Corn, to cook	120
cakes, green	121
muffins	121
oysters	121
and beans, succotash	121
dried, to prepare to cook	121
dried, to cook	122
hermetically sealed	122
to dry for winter use	122
sweet, to cultivate	316
worm	351
Cockchafer	351
Cockroaches	359
Cook, advice to	32
Cranberry jelly and jam	270
pies and tarts	158
stewed	270
preserved for winter	
Cream ice, to freeze	195
brandy, a dessert of 1818	197
whipped	151
of nectar	288
custard	151
orange	283

	PAGE		PAGE
Cream ice		Cultivation of	
cake	172	herbs	314
drop	187	horseradish	315
Boston, genuine	187	lettuces	315
griddle cakes	188	manuring	308
dinner creams	136	melons	313
snow	153	nasturtiums	314
toast	213	onions	310
to prevent rising	410	okra	315
Crackers, Mrs. Dicson's	415	peas	310
Mrs. P.'s	169	parsley	310
Crabs	75	parsnips	310
Crayfish	83	peppergrass or cress	315
Curing meats	360	potatoes, early	316
beef, corned	361	sweet	317
bacon	362	remarks on	306
ham	360	radishes	315
pork	362	rhubarb	317
Curtains, lace, etc., to wash	23	salsify	311
Custard, boiled	150	sweet corn	316
thickened	150	spinach	310
baked	150	tomatoes	346
frozen	197		
and whey	150	Dairy work	360
and cream	151	Damask, to iron	248
Cucumbers, to buy	54	Damsons, to preserve	248
to cultivate	313	Delaines, printed, to wash	18
catsup	289	plain, to wash	19
to green, with grape leaves	305	scarlet, to wash	20
to fry, etc	123	Delicate-colored merino	19
to grow in hot beds	345	Dicson's, Mrs., crackers	415
pickled	297	Diarrhœa	376
spiced, No. 1	298	of infants	387
spiced, No. 2	298	Description of coffee tree	207
spiced, No. 3	299	of tea-plant	204
summer	299	of chocolate mill	413
sugar, sour	299	Dinner-parties	24
sugar, sweet	300	desserts	150
in whiskey	300	of quinces	247
ripe	300	creams	136
salad for the aged	291	cold, arranged	226
and cabbage	292	Dishes, washed	6
to select	54	Discoloration by bruises removed	378
vinegar	293	Dipped butter toast	214
Cutlets of lamb	102	Directions for carving	87
of veal	104	cooking generally	58
of fish	81	cakes	169
Cutworm	350	catsups	286
Curculio	357	chocolate	209
Currant-borer	357	coffee	207
Currants, dried	270	cordials	283
Currant jam	264	creams and confectioneries	190
jelly	264	cold dinners	226
hermetically sealed	267	infants	388
pies	157	cooking for invalids	391
Curled cress, to dress	120	cultivating fruit	319
to grow	315	" flowers	329
Cultivation of fruit garden	319	" vegetables	306
of flower garden	329	cooking vegetables	116
asparagus	317	curing meats	360
beets	311	cooking beef	84
beans	311	biscuit and bread	159
broccoli	312	breakfasts	212
cabbages	311	brandies from fruits	279
cauliflowers	311	dairy work	360
celery	312	dinner desserts	133
cucumbers	313	" parties	24
carrots	315	economy dishes	223
corn, sweet	316	eggs	219
double curled parsley	310	entertaining visitors	24
egg-plant	315	extracts	283

INDEX.

Directions for	PAGE
fruit garden	319
flowers	329
fish	74
furnishing a house	1
gravies	67
game	106
hashes	217
hot-beds	348
to husbands	27
kitchen furniture	1
" garden	306
lamb	100
management of servants	4
marketing	51
mutton	100
pastry and pies	153
pickling	296
pork	91
poultry	106
puddings	133
preservation of vegetables through winter	116
preserving apples	229
" cherries	257
" peaches	286
" pears	244
" plums	248
" quinces	247
salads	289
sauces	71
servants	81
sick-room	371
soups	58
small fruits, preserving	268
spring work	367
tea	207
venison	100
vinegars	281
" flavored	292
washing, ironing, etc.	12
wines and beer	272
Down, to wash	405
Doeskin, to wash	402
Duck, canvas-back, to truss	107
wild, to truss	107
canvas-back, to roast	112
wild, to roast	112
Draining land for gardens	307
Drab, to color	409
Drawn butter	67
Dress chickens quickly	396
of servants	36
Dressing for a-la-mode beef	71
beef, a-la-mode	71
blackbirds	71
boiled pigeons	71
" turkey	70
duck	70
fish	70
fowls	70
fowls for market	106
for partridges	71
pigeons	71
pigs	70
quails	71
turkeys	70
salad, common No. 1	290
" very fine No. 2	291
" without eggs, No. 3	291
" sweet, No. 4	291

Dressing	PAGE
infants	383
Dried beef, to cure	861
apples	231
cherries	262
corn, to cook	122
to prepare for succotash	121
to prepare for winter	122
currants	122
blackberries	267
fruits, care of	367
berries	56
peaches	289
plums	256
quinces	248
raspberries	270
strawberries	270
whortleberries	270
Dye brown	409
black	409
blue	409
buff	409
drab	408
green	409
peach leaves, with	410
scarlet	410
yellow	409
Dysentery, cure for	376
receipt for	376
or diarrhœa	376
Dyspeptic lye	383
Ear-ache of infants	390
Economy	7
dishes	228
in cooking well	7
cheerfulness	8
small matters	9
Edging or thread lace, to wash	22
Eggs	219
boil	221
breakfast dish	215
closing the pores of shells with hot water	220
considered as food	221
cooked whole	228
English rule for preserving	220
fried hard	222
soft	221
grease removed by yolks of	13
of insects, to destroy	367
Italian method	228
mass, cooked in	223
mulled in wine and water	392
nog	285
mulled in tea and coffee	392
raw in milk	893
and milk	393
omelet, hard	222
soft	222
puff, Mrs. Hunt's	414
souffle	222
pack	221
poached	222
preserved for winter use	220
plant, cultivated	315
cooked	128
cold, to use	225
selection at market	54
shells useful	228
selected fresh	219

Eggs	PAGE
scambled	232
sauce for fish	69
puddings	73
toast	212
for invalids	395
used to remove grease	18
whole, cooked in a mass	223
Eels broil	80
fry	79
general directions	78
to select	54
soup	61
to select	54
Elderberry syrup	406
wine, spiced	273
flowers, wine	415
Elegantly preserved peaches	241
Elements of food necessary for the family	47
Embroideries, to wash, starch, and iron	21
Embroidered curtains, to wash	23
Enamelled kettles	407
Entertainment of company	24
English plum puddings	143, 144
Eruptions of infants	390
Evening parties	26
Excuses for the housekeeper	31
Extracts and cordials	283
of celery	284
lemon	284
" peel	284
nectarines	284
orange peel	284
peaches	284
roses	284
sage	284
Family bed-room	3
Fancy dinner desserts	150
jellies	195
rice boiler	147
Fault-finding	30
Feathers colored, to cleanse	403
to renew	404
Felon, to cure	382
Figs, to select	57
Fillet of veal, to boil	103
to roast	103
Fish	74
anchovy butter	81
bake a large fish whole	78
boil, general directions	74
broil, general directions	79
clean	74
cod fish, picked up	80
cod fish, salt, to boil	77
cod, tongues and sounds, to boil	78
cod, head and shoulders, to boil	75
cod, to select	53
crabs, to boil	75
crabs, to select	53
casserole of fish	81
croquette of fish	81
cutlets	81
clams, to fry with eggs and crackers	85
clams, stewed	85
clams, scalloped	416
clams, hashed	83
clams, hard-shelled, to boil	82
cray fish, to cook	83

Fish	PAGE
cray fish, to select	54
eels, to fry	79
eels, to select	54
eels, to broil	80
fresh-water fish, to select	53
fry, general directions	78
halibut, to select	54
kedgeree of fish	81
kettle described	413
lobsters, to roast	78
" to boil	75
" to dress	63
" balls	84
" patties	84
mackerel, fresh, to fry	79
fresh, to broil	80
to boil	75
salt, to soak	80
to broil	80
to boil	77
muscles, stewed	83
oysters, to fry	82
to broil	82
to stew	82
scalloped	82
patties	82
pies	82
scalloped, Mrs. W	81
prawns and shrimps, to select	53
perch, to select	54
pike, boiled	76
to select	54
rock bass and small fish, to fry	79
rock fish and bass, to boil	76
shad, fresh, to bake	78
to fry	79
to boil	76
salt, to boil	77
salmon, fresh, to boil	76
salt, to boil	77
to select	53
sturgeon, fresh, to boil	77
seal fish, fresh, to boil	75
soak, salt fish	80
scalloped fish	81
soused fish	81
sandwiches	81
scallops, to cook	83
sprawns, to cook	83
shrimps, to cook	83
turtle, stewed	83
to select	54
patties	83
trout, to fry	79
to select	53
turbot, to boil	77
to select	53
white fish, to boil	76
to broil	80
Flat irons	403
Fourth of July pudding	139
Flannel, to wash	17
Flavored vinegars	286
Flax-seed jelly, for coughs	378
Fleas	359
Flies	359
Flour, buckwheat, to select	56
gruel	391
puddings, baked	134
pudding boiled	416

	PAGE		PAGE
Flour		Fruit	
wheat, to select	56	frozen	198
Flowers of elderberry wine	415	garden	319
garden	329	gathering apples	229
Floating islands	150	stains to remove from hands	398
Floor, to remove oil from	399	hermetically sealed apples	235
Flummery of cocoa-nuts	152	sealed berries	267
Fowls	106	cherries	259–262
to bake	110	currants	267
to boil	108	peaches	241–243
to boil	109	pears	246
dressed for market	196	plums	250–256
dressing for	70	pineapple	200–201
cold, to use	223	raspberries	267
to fry	115	quinces	247
to roast	110	small	263
to truss	106	stains removed from hands	398
to select	52	strawberries	270
Fresh-water fish, to select	58	tomatoes	181
French bread	165	whortleberries	263
French method of candying fruit	192	trees	321
icing cake	198	insects injurious to	349
preserving apricots	253	manure for	322
Fried apples	94	planting	321
beef	88	pruning	327
bread	226	pudding bread	140
chops	101	vinegars	291
chickens	115	stains to remove from hands	398
cucumbers	123	" from linen	402
eggs, hard	222	Furniture, to cleanse	399
soft	221	to remove spots from	399
with oysters	215	Fur, to cut and sew	405
fish	74	to protect from moths	358
ham	95		
lamb chops	101		
mutton chops	102	Game, to truss	106
oysters	82	black-birds to roast	112
with egg	215	to truss	107
onions	125	duck to roast	112
parsnips	126	to truss	107
potatoes	128	hare and rabbit to roast	111
pork, fresh	98	to truss	107
salt, plain	94	moor fowl to roast	111
superior	95	to truss	107
salsify	130	partridges to boil	114
vegetable oyster	130	to roast	114
Fritters	185	to truss	107
apple	284	pheasant to broil	114
egg plant	123	to roast	111
turnip	126	pigeon to roast	110
Fricassee of chicken, brown	115	pie	114
" white	116	to truss	107
veal	104	prairie chicken to broil	114
parsnips	126	to roast	112
potatoes	129	quail to broil	114
Frost-bitten hands and feet	382	pie	114
salve	375	to roast	113
Wahler's	375	reed birds to truss	108
Frozen creams	195	small birds to roast	112
fruits	198	snipe to roast	112
jellies	195	widgeons and teals to roast	118
Fruit ades	284	woodcocks to roast	111
bath for preserving	268	Garden fruit	319
brandies	277	flowers	329
blanc-manges	136	vegetables	306
catsups	286	Garlic vinegar	293
candied	192	Geese to boil	109
coblers	394	to roast	111
cultivated	319	to truss	108
dried to protect from vermin	270	Gelatine, to prepare	398
eggs of insects in, dried to destroy	367	General directions for cookery	3

430   INDEX.

	PAGE
General directions	
house work	6
German cherry sauce for puddings	70
cookies, New Year's	181
chocolate	211
cakes hard	183
soft	183
pepper nuts	177
cornucopia cakes	177
ladies' fingers	177
steamed neudles	166
waffles	186
sponge for invalids	396
Giblet sauce	70
Gilt frames, to preserve	405
Gingham, to wash	21
Gingerbread	170, 171
Gingerbread pudding	146
Ginger green	201
wine	275
wine, excellent	277
vinegar	295
Glass stopper to remove	406
Gloves, wet to save	402
Gooseberries	324
caterpillar	356
catsup	288
jelly	266
sauce for lamb	69
tarts	158
mildew	325
wine	275
Graham rice flour pudding	142
flour to select	56
pudding raised	141
Gravies and sauces	67
for beef roasts	68
steaks etc	68
lamb	68
mutton	68
veal	68
venison	68
Gravy pot described	413
Grease, to remove from book covers	406
to cleanse	419
Green corn, to select	54
Greens, asparagus	116
mustard	124
Green to color	409
Green fly or aphis	354
gages to candy	192
ginger to preserve	201
gages to preserve in brandy	251
tomatoes preserved	202
tea, to choose	205
Greening pickles without alum	305
Gherkins pickled	297
Gridiron	407
Griddle to clean	407
Gruel arrow root	391
barley	391
flour	391
Indian meal	391
rice	391
Grubs	334
Hair brushes, to cleanse	404
to prevent falling out	382
Hall furniture	2
Halibut	
to select	54

	PAGE
Ham	
boiled, salt	91
fresh	96
carved	40
cold served	47
cured	360
baked	92
broiled	95
fried	95
protector from vermin	361
Hands, chapped	375
to remove fruit stains	398
Hardy biennials	342
climbing roses	340
perpetual roses	341
twining plants	339
Hares and rabbits, to cook	111
to truss	108
Hashes	217
beef, fresh	218
browned	217
balls of corned beef	217
calf's head	105
corned beef	217
cod fish	218
balls	219
fish hash	218
fresh beef	218
meats with toast	218
pork	218
pork and parsnips	218
" and potatoes	218
Hat, to protect from dust	404
Heavy plum pudding, to use	224
Hearth rugs, to cleanse	403
Hens, to make lay in winter	410
Herbaceous climbers	339
Herb or root teas	397
Hermetically sealed and cooked apples	229
" cherries	257
" peaches	236
" pears	244
" plums	248
" quinces	247
" small fruit	268
Hints on cultivating flowers	330
Hiccough	379
Honey-suckles	338
Hop	
Horse radish	291
vinegar	295
Hop "	295
Hot bed	343
House cleaning	405
general	370
House, to select and furnish	2
Hyacinth	335
Hybrid Chinese roses	341
Ice cream, directions for	195
candy	194
flavored with coffee	197
" chocolate	197
oranges	198
strawberries	198
thickened with arrow-root	196
superior	196
without cream	196
quick	197
Mrs. A.'s	197
puddings	142
Iced jellies	195

INDEX.

	PAGE
Iced fruits	198
Ices, water, of fruits	198
Icing, cake to prepare for	199
common	198
confectioneries	199
French method	198
Mrs. L.'s frosting	416
India muslins, washed	14
Indian meal gruel	391
griddle cakes	189
bread, St. Charles	417
and rye bread	167
wheat "	166
pumpkin bread	167
hoe cakes	168
pudding, boiled	418
baked	148
Johnny cakes	189
muffins	168
Indelible ink	406
Infants, care of from birth to weaning	383
Injuries from falls prevented	389
Infantile diseases	387
canker, sore mouth	390
convulsions	390
diarrhœa	388
eruptions	390
measles	389
red gum	387
worms	388
whooping cough	389
vomiting	388
Ink, blue	406
red	406
indelible	406
spots, to remove	400
Ironing generally	14
Iron mould, to remove	402
ware	407
Iron pots, to mend	408
ware not in general use	407
described	412
Insects, injurious to gardens	349
troublesome to housekeepers	349
ant-hills	358
ants, to protect from	359
red, to entrap	359
apple-borer	355
worm	356
aphis, or green fly	354
bark-lice	355
bed-bugs	358
cut-worm	350
caterpillar	356
canker-worm	356
curculio	357
currant-borer	357
caterpillar on gooseberries	358
crickets	358
cockchafer	351
cockroach	359
egg of, in dried fruit, to kill	367
fleas	359
flies, to destroy	359
grape-worm	358
list of	349
May-bug, larva of	351
mosquitoes	359
moths	358
peach-borer	356

	PAGE
Insects, radish-maggot	353
rose-bug	355
remarks	349
raspberry borer	358
red ants	359
rats	359
strawberry-worm	353
striped bug	353
squash	353
scaly aphis	355
spiders	359
tomato-worm	352
wire-worm	351
Invalid's cookery	391
arrow-root gruel	391
barley-gruel	391
milk	392
water	394
negus	394
punch	395
or corn coffee	395
bread panada, with wine	393
beef-tea	397
caudle	392
cream-toast	395
cakes	396
chicken, to dress quickly	396
tea, to make	397
and meat broths	397
drinks for an invalid	393
egg mulled in wine or water	392
raw, and wine	393
raw, and milk	393
mulled with milk	393
and toast	395
extract of meat, No. 1	397
No. 2	397
flour gruel	391
fruit ades	394
vinegars	395
cobblers	394
ground rice milk	392
griddle cakes	396
German sponge	396
herb or root teas	397
Indian meal gruel	391
jelly wine	392
of rice or tapioca	396
lemon-water	393
whey	394
milk porridge	391
and wine	392
meat and bread panada	393
milk whey	394
molasses toast	395
mulled egg in tea or coffee	392
nitre whey	394
needle pudding, German	396
soup	395
oatmeal gruel	391
punch	395
pudding	396
rice-flour gruel	391
jelly	396
raspberry and strawberry vinegar	395
rusk of barley or corn	395
sago-milk	392
sago or tapioca, to cook	392
sherry cobbler	394
toast-water	393

432   INDEX.

Invalid's	PAGE
wine jelly	392
whey	394
whey, Mrs. L.	415
Italian method of cooking eggs	223
Ivory, to clean	408
Jams, currant, black	265
red	264
grape	265
cranberry	270
plum	256
peach	238
hermetically sealed	242
" No. 2	242
raspberry	266
strawberry	269
Jellies, apple	232
cake	181
crab	238
pine	201
blackberry	266
currant, black	266
cranberry	270
currant red	264
calves' foot	137
crab apple	233
flummery	151
frozen	195
fancy	175
and whips	152
grape	265
gooseberry	266
peach	238
quince	248
raspberry	266
rice	392
small fruits	263, 271
tapioca	392
whortleberry	266
wine	392
Johnny cakes	189
Jumbles	183
pound	183
soft	417
Kettle, enameled	407
Kid gloves, to cleanse	402
Kitchen furniture	2
Kisses, very nice by long beating	194
to make quickly	194
cocoa	194
jelly	195
orange	194
pineapple	194
pyramid of	195
Miss Dey's	418
Knives, to take care of	7
Lace veil, black, to wash	400
to wash	400
Lard	97
Lamb chops, fried	101
cutlets	102
quarter, roasted	101
selected	51
steaks, broiled	101
Late winter and spring apples	229
Leason, to make	67
Leather peach, to prepare	239
plum, to prepare	256

Leg of	PAGE
lamb, boiled	101
carved	40
mutton, boiled	102
carved	39
Lettuce, dressed	124
grown	315
hot beds	347
salads	289, 290
selected	55
Lemonade	284
Lemon cordial	283
cakes	195
extract	284
drops	193
macaroons	199
puffs	190
pears	246
water	393
whey	394
Lights, calves	106
Liver, "	106
Lip salve	378
List of annual flowers that bear transplanting	331
of annual flowers that will not bear transplanting	332
of annual flowers for hot beds	332
hardy flowering shrubs	339
twining plants	339
annual climbers	340
roses	340
climbing roses	340
hybrid Chinese roses	341
hardy perpetual "	341
Bourbon	342
noisettes	342
hardy biennials, plant	342
perennials	343
kitchen furniture	411
Lobster balls	64
dressed	63
patties	84
selection	58
soup	61
sauce	60
salad	291
Lunches, prepared	228
Macaroni	419
toast	419
soup	67
Macaroons, common	191
almond	199
lemon	197
orange	199
vanilla	199
Mackerel, boiled	75
broiled fresh	80
carved	42
salted	77
soaked	80
broiled	80
and herring selected at market	58
Madison bake	180
Maids, chamber	84
all work	35
laundry	84
nurse	35
Malignant sore throat	308
Mangoes, peach	304

INDEX.

Mangoes,	PAGE
pepper	314
melon	301
and pickles	296
Manuring gardens	308
Maple sugar candy	193
syrup for puddings	72
March, work for	367
Marjoram vinegar	294
Marketing	51
asparagus, to select	54
beans, to select	54
buckwheat flour, to select	56
bulls head	54
beets	55
beef	51
blackbirds	53
black tea	56
cabbage	54
cauliflower	54
corn, green	54
carrots	54
cucumbers	54
crab and cray fish	53
coffee, to choose	56
ducks	52
dried fruit	56
apples	57
egg plant, to select	54
eels	54
figs	57
flour	56
fresh water fish	53
green corn	54
tea	56
geese	52
grapes	57
Graham flour	56
hares and rabbits	53
hallibut	54
Indian meal	56
lamb	51
lettuce	55
lobster	53
melons	55
mackerel and herrings	53
mutton	51
oysters	53
okra	55
onions	55
oranges	57
pigeons	52
partridges	52
prairie chickens	52
pineapple	57
prawns and shrimps	53
pike	54
perch	54
parsley	55
parsnips	55
peas	55
pork	51
potatoes	55
sweet	55
poultry	52
quail	52
rabbits	53
rice	57
raisins	56
radishes	55
rhubarb	55

Marketing,	PAGE
quails	52
sugar	56
salsify	55
string beans	54
spinach	55
salmon	53
squash	55
tea, to choose	56
trout	53
turbot	53
turtle	54
tomatoes	56
turnips	56
turkeys	52
veal	51
vegetables	54
venison	52
woodcocks	52
Marteneas, sweet, pickled	301
sour, pickled	301
Marmalade, apple	233
cake	180
orange	201
peach	238
pineapple	201
quince	243
Mashed potatoes	123
May-bug or beetle	351
May, work for	369
Medicines, to prepare	83
Mead	417
Meal, Indian, gruel	391
Measles	389
Meats, cured	360
hashed with toast	218
and gristle of soups used	223
and bread panada for invalids	393
tongs	412
Melons, to grow	313
mangoes	301
musk, to pickle ripe	304
small	304
to preserve ripe	204
nutmeg, to preserve	203
Meringues, strawberry	194
Mercury, antidote for	380
Milk, barley for invalids	392
boiled for coffee	210
cure of	362
ground rice for invalids	392
mulled with eggs	393
punch, common	285
English	285
porridge for invalids	391
sago	392
toast No. 1	213
No. 2	213
whey	394
and wine for invalids	392
Mince pies	153
Minute pudding, nice	147
Mississippi traveller	285
Mixing and boiling coffee	209
Mock cream for coffee	211
toast	213
turtle soup	66
venison of corned beef	99
Molasses beer	278
candy	193
toast for invalids	213, 395

19

INDEX.

	PAGE
Morello cherries, preserved	259
Mosquitoes	359
Moths	358
Muff, to preserve the fur smooth	399
Muffins, Mrs. W.'s	187
corn	121
Indian	168
raised	416
Mull wine	285
Mulled egg in wine	392
in tea and coffee	392
Mushroom catsup	286
Mushrooms, pickled	303
sauce	69
Musk melons, pickled ripe	304
mangoes	301
small pickled	304
Muslins, India, with fast colors, to wash and iron	15
India, doubtful, with fast colors, to wash and iron	16
India, to wash and iron	17
Swiss	17
Mustard, Greens	124
mixed	291
vinegar	293
Mush, to make of Indian meal	147
Mutton chops, broiled	102
fried	103
Mutton—	
haunch of, roasted	102
leg of, boiled	102
carved	89
loin of, stewed, to resemble venison	102
neck of	102
saddle of, carved	89
shoulder of, carved	89
selection at market	51
soup	63
Nasturtium, grown	314
pickled	304
vinegar	293
Natural roast goose	111
Necessary furniture for the house	2
Necessity of system, order, etc	4
Nectarines and apricots, candied	192
extract of	284
preserved, French method	253
pickled	257
trimmed, etc	327
Negus of Barley	394
Nervous affections	379
head-aches	378
Needle pudding for invalids, German	396
soup " " "	395
New Year's cookies	182
German	181
Nice cold dinners prepared	266, 268
lunches	268
Nitrate of silver, antidote for	381
Nitre whey	394
Nurse maid	35
Nutrition	43
Nutmeg melon, preserved	203
Okra, or gumbo grown	315
stewed	124
soup	124

	PAGE
Okra, selected	55
Obstinate cough, to break up	379
Orangeade	284
Orange cream, iced	198
a beverage	283
cream	158
and cream ambrosia	417
custard, Mrs. W.'s	418
extract	284
kisses	194
macaroons	199
marmalade	201
salad	418
sauce	78
Oranges, selected	57
Order and system at table, etc	4
Oysters fried with eggs	215
omelet	215
pie	82
patties	82
toast	215
soup for the city	63
country	63
Mrs. W.'s superior scalloped	81
scalloped	82
selected	53
Omelets, hard	222
mushroom	216
oyster	215
soft	222
souffle	222
Mrs. Hunt's	414
Omelet pan	413
Onions boiled	125
fried	125
pickled	302
with tomatoes	303
preserved for winter	133
vinegar	293
Ointment for itch	379
Oil, to remove from book covers	406
floors	399
lamp shades	399
Ovens, heated	161
iron bake ovens	407
Parsnip	125
plain	125
broiled	125
cutlet	126
fried	126
fritters	126
fricassee	126
preserved for winter	132
Partridges, dressing for	71
trussed	107
selected	52
Parsley, preserved for winter	125
Pastry	153
Pies, custard	154
Paste, for dumplings	156
French pastry	156
plain	154
puff, to prepare for	153
nice	154
for pumpkin pies	154
Patties, oyster	82
lobster	84
Peaches	266
brandy, No. 1	279

INDEX.

	PAGE
Peaches, brandy, No. 2	279
brandy peaches	236
borer	356
butter	238
dried, with sugar, No. 1	239
No. 2	239
common, No. 3	239
extract	284
fresh, hermetically sealed, No. 1	243
without sugar, No. 2	244
No. 3	241
in cans, No. 4	243
elegantly preserved in bottles, etc.	241
water ice	238
jam	238
jelly	288
jam, hermetically sealed, No. 1	242
No. 2	242
leather	239
mangoes	304
marmalade	238
preserved in sour syrup	237
plain sauce	237
preserved, rich	240
hermetically sealed	240
natural	241
very plain	242
elegantly	241
pie	244
pudding, No. 1	244
rich, No. 2	244
remarks	236
sour, spiced	237
sweet, spiced	237
syrup, brandy	239
stewed, dried	239
trees, to plant	321
pruned	327
varieties of	320
vinegar	281
water, ice	238
Peas	244
boiled	244
brandy	245
baked, hermetically sealed	247
ginger	245
hermetically sealed, fresh	246
lemon	246
plain, boiled	244
preserved	244
pickled	246
plain preserves, hermetically sealed	246
trees, to plant	321
pruned	327
varieties of	320
vinegar	282
Pickles and mangoes	296
Pickles—	
apricots	255
beans	300
with grape leaves	305
cabbage, red	303
shred, red or white	303
cucumbers, to green, with grape leaves	305
gherkins, or prickly cucumbers	297
greening, without alum or brass	305
cherries, part 5, No. 1	260
No. 2	261
No. 3	261

	PAGE
Pickles—cherries, part 5, No. 4	261
cauliflower	303
cayenne pepper	304
carrots	305
greening cucumbers with grape leaves	305
cucumbers	297
ripe	300
spiced, No. 1	298
No. 2	288
No. 3	299
summer pickles	299
in sugar, sour	299
sweet	300
in whiskey	300
peach pickles, part 5	237
pear	246
plum	254
plum	255
remarks	296
mushroom	303
marteneas, or mouse, sour	301
sweet	301
melon, small melon pickles	304
mangoes	301
muskmelon, ripe	304
nasturtium	304
nectarines	255
onions	302
picalilly	303
remarks on pickling	296
red cabbage	303
pepper mangoes	304
peach mangoes	304
shred cabbage	303
tomato, green	302
ripe	302
and onions	303
walnuts	302
Pig, roaster	97
force meat for	70
feet, pickled	97
Pie, beefsteak	90
oyster	82
pork	93
pot, chicken	115
chicken	115
quails	114
Pigeons, boiled	71
dressing for	71
roasted	71
dressing for	71
broiled	114
curried	41
roasted	114
pie	114
trussed	107
Pike, selected	54
Perch, selected	54
Pineapple, best method of preserving	
without cooking	200
fresh, hermetically sealed, No. 1	200
No. 2	201
jelly	201
marmalade	201
Pies	153
apple	233
blackberry	157
cherry	263
boiled, salt	91

Pies

	PAGE
cream	157
crackers	416
cranberry	158
custard	156
currant	157
gooseberry	157
lemon	158
mince	158
peach	244
pumpkins	156
rhubarb	158
raspberry	157
strawberry	158
whortleberry	157
Pig, roasted	97
sausages	97
souse	97
Pigs' feet, pickled	97
headcheese	99
Plums	248
brandy	279
brandied	251
brandied, French	251
family preserve	251
blue, preserved	253
candied	192
catsup	287
compote	250
dry, without sugar	256
with sugar	256
egg plum, hermetically sealed and preserved	252
greengage, hermetically sealed No. 1	250
No. 2	251
No. 3	251
hermetically sealed natural preserves in glass	255
hermetically sealed pie fruit, glass	255
cans	256
table fruit, cans	256
natural preserves in cans	256
ice for syrup	254
jam	244
plain jam	256
leather	256
leaves to die with	410
preserve, winter damson	248
paste	250
syrup and jelly	253
pickled No. 1	254
sour No. 2	254
No. 3	255
remarks	248
tarts	257
trees to plant	321
vinegar	282
Pork, a-la-mode	92
boiled, salt	91
baked "	93
with beans, superior	96
broiled, fresh	93
boiled, plain salt	95
superior	95
cutlets	99
fritters, salt, with apples	94
fried, salt, plain	94
cream gravy	94
steak	93
with parsnips	95

Pork

	PAGE
pancakes, salt	93
pie, fresh	93
pot-pie, fresh	99
roast, cold, to serve	97
steak, to serve	93
stewed, "	92
stew, "	92
scrambled "	93
selected	51
tenderloins, to boil	99
nice method of frying fresh	99
bacon, bacon cured	360
boiled bacon	92
ham, salt	91
fresh	96
cold, to serve	97
baked ham	92
broiled ham	93
fried bacon	96
fried ham	95
ham cured	360
lard	97
Potatoes, baked	129
boiled	127
broiled	128
crisped	128
early potatoes, boiled	127
fried	128
fried	214
fricassee	129
hashed	129
steamed	129
preserved for the winter	132
selected	55
Poultry and game	106
black and small birds, to truss	103
chickens to dress quickly	396
to fry	115
fricassee brown	115
white	116
pie	115
pot-pie	115
salad	290, 291
duck, wild, to truss	107
to roast	112
canvas-back, to truss	107
to roast	112
fowls to dress for market	106
and game to truss	106
to truss for boiling	107
in French style	107
to roast	110
to bake	110
steamed	109
cold	115
to boil No. 1	108
No. 2	108
No. 3	108
No. 4	109
broil	113
goose, to truss	108
boil	109
roast	110
natural	111
green, roasted	111
hare, to roast	113
hare and rabbit, to prepare	103
moor fowl, to truss	107
to roast	111
pigeon, to roast	114

INDEX.

Poultry and game,	PAGE
pigeon and quail pie	114
to truss	107
partridges, to truss	107
to roast	114
to boil	114
pheasant, to boil	114
to roast	111
prairie chicken, to broil	114
to roast	112
quail, to broil	114
black and small birds, to roast	112
rabbit, to boil	113
to roast	113
reed birds, to truss	108
snipe, to roast	112
turkey, boiled	109
bake	110
roast	110
widgeons and teal, to roast	113
woodcock, to roast	111
Preserved apples	232
drying	231
for spring shipments	235
for winter	229
hermetically, in cans	235
in bottles	235
jelly	232
marmalade	233
crab	233
jelly	233
pine, No. 1	200
without cooking	200
hermetically sealed, No. 1	200
No. 2	201
jelly	201
marmalade	201
apricots, candied	192
biscuit	257
French	253
pickle	255
bath for	268
barberries	263
blackberries, dried	270
hermetically sealed	267
jelly	266
black currant jam	265
jelly	266
currant, red, jelly	264
jam, No. 1	264
No. 2	264
cherries, brandy, No. 1	260
No. 2	260
Black Hawk	258
dried, No. 1	262
No. 2	263
duke	259
fancy	258
hermetically, for pies, in glass	261
in cans	262
hermetically sealed, natural preserves, in bottles	259
No. 2	259
table fruit	262
pickled, No. 1	260
No. 2	261
No. 3	261
No. 4	261
citron, American	202
currant, black, in jam	265
in jelly	266

Preserved	PAGE
cranberries, jelly and jam	270
fresh ice-water, for winter	270
currants, hermetically sealed	267
cucumbers, very sour, syrup	300
damsons, winter	248
egg-plums, hermetically seal and preserve	252
grapes, in cotton, for winter, No. 1	271
saw-dust, for winter, No. 2	271
sand, for winter, No. 3	271
jelly	265
jam	265
gooseberry, jelly	266
hermetically sealed and preserved	266
ginger, green, No. 1	201
No. 2	201
gages, green, to candy	192
brandy	251
French	251
No. 3	251
muskmelon, No. 1	203
No. 2	204
orange, marmalade	201
peaches	236
brandy	236
butter	238
dried, with sugar, No. 1	239
No. 2	239
common, No. 3	239
fresh, hermetically sealed, No. 1	243
No. 2	244
No. 3	241
No. 4	243
elegantly, in bottles	241
jam	238
jelly	238
jam, hermetically sealed, No. 1	242
No. 2	242
leather	239
marmalade	238
plain sauce	237
rich, hermetically sealed	240
hermetically, natural	241
very plain, hermetically sealed	242
elegantly, hermetically sealed	241
sour, spiced	237
sweet, spiced	237
syrup, brandy	239
pears, brandy	245
baked, hermetically sealed	247
ginger	245
fresh, hermetically sealed	246
lemon	246
pickled	246
plain, hermetically sealed	246
sweetmeats	244
pineapple, No. 1	200
No. 2	200
hermetically sealed, No. 1	200
No. 2	201
jelly	201
marmalade	201
plums	248
brandy gages	251
family use	251
French	251
No. 3	251
blue	253
compote	250

438 INDEX.

Preserved — PAGE
  plums, dry, without sugar........ 256
    dry, with sugar.............. 256
    egg, hermetically sealed....... 252
    greengages, hermetically sealed and preserved, No. 1..... 250
                    No. 2..... 251
                    No. 3..... 251
    hermetically sealed, natural preserves, in glass.......... 255
    pie-fruit, in glass............ 255
          in cans.............. 256
    natural preserves, in cans..... 256
    jam......................... 256
    jelly........................ 253
    leather...................... 256
    nectarines, French............. 253
    paste........................ 250
    pickled, No. 1................ 254
        sour, No. 2................. 254
            No. 3................. 255
  pumpkin chips................. 204
    hermetically sealed........... 130
  quinces....................... 247
    dry......................... 248
    hermetically sealed........... 247
    jelly........................ 248
    marmalade................... 248
    sweetmeats.................. 247
  raspberries.................... 266
    jelly........................ 266
    hermetically sealed and preserved................... 267
    jam......................... 266
  rhubarb, hermetically sealed...... 129
  small fruits, hermetically sealed and preserved.................. 268
  squash, hermetically sealed...... 130
  strawberries, dried.............. 270
    jam......................... 269
    jelly........................ 269
    hermetically sealed and preserved................... 267
  tomatoes, hermetically sealed..... 131
    green, preserved.............. 202
  whortleberries, hermetically sealed 268
    jelly........................ 266
    to dry...................... 270
Pudding, apple................. 144, 234
  dumpling................... 149, 234
  Boston, improved.............. 136
  butter, plain, raised 140
  boiled, rice, baked.............. 141
    No. 1....................... 146
    No. 2....................... 147
    in fruit syrups................ 415
    fancy....................... 147
  baked rice, flour, No. 1......... 141
              No. 2 .... 141, 147
  Berkshire..................... 144
  bird's-nest.................... 145
  berry......................... 146
  barley........................ 146
  bread, Mrs. F.'s............... 148
  batter, boiled.................. 149
    baked...................... 149
  baked, Indian................. 148
  cottage....................... 134
  cocoa-nut..................... 143
  corn starch................... 148
  custard....................... 145

Pudding, — PAGE
  cream, No. 1.................. 149
    No. 2...................... 149
    No. 3...................... 150
    No. 4...................... 150
  cherry, No. 1.................. 145
    No. 2...................... 146
  custard....................... 145
  English bread,................. 143
  plum, No. 1................... 142
    No. 2...................... 143
    rich........................ 144
  fruit, raised................... 140
  Fourth of July................. 139
  flour, boiled................... 416
  German rice................... 138
    raised...................... 138
    rye bread................... 139
  ginger bread.................. 146
  Indian, boiled................. 416
    baked...................... 148
  ice cream..................... 142
  lemon................... 134, 418
  minute....................... 147
  mush......................... 147
    neudles, German............ 396
  pork, Mrs. Hunt's.............. 414
  for invalids................... 396
  pineapple..................... 135
  plum, rich.................... 144
  peach, plain, No. 1............ 244
    No. 2...................... 244
    No. 3...................... 145
    rich, No. 4................. 145
  quick......................... 139
  Pennsylvania.................. 141
  quince........................ 145
  raised fruit................... 140
    Coventry.................... 140
    Graham..................... 141
  rice flour, baked, No. 1......... 141
              No. 2.................... 141
    Graham, No. 3............. 142
    rich,   No. 4............. 142
  boiled, fancy.................. 147
  new, with fruit syrup..... 415
  German....................... 138
  sago...................... 144, 392
  Sunderland.................... 417
  sponge, Mrs. W.'s............. 148
  strawberry.................... 135
  Saratoga...................... 416
  tapioca No. 1.................. 142
    No. 2...................... 142
  whortleberry.................. 146
  wine.......................... 140
Pudding sauces.................. 71
  brandy sauce.................. 72
  cherry " 71
  cream " 72
  dyspepsia sauce............... 73
  egg " 73
  German cherry sauce........... 71
  hard " 71
  maple syrup " 72
  orange " 73
  peach " 72
  plain sweet " 73
  plain sour " 73
  rose hip " 71
  sour " 71

	PAGE
Pudding	
sweet sauce	72
wine " No. 1	73
" No. 2	73
" No. 3	73
West India molasses sauce	72
punch "	395
punch barley "	395
milk "	285
Quails, broiled	114
pie	114
to roast	112
select	52
Quick ice cream	197
beer	415
remedy for burns	378
Quinces	247
dinner dessert	247
dried	248
hermetically sealed	247
jelly	248
marmalade	248
pudding	145
sweetmeats	247
Quinsy	379
Rabbit, boiled	113
Rabbits, to prepare	108
roasted	113
Radishes, grown	317
in hot bed	346
maggot	353
salad	129
for aged	282
selected	55
Raisins	56
sherry	276
wine	276
Raise chickens	410
Raspberry borer	358
brandy	280
catsup	288
cultivation	326
hermetically sealed	267
jam	266
jelly	266
pie	157
pudding	135
pruned	328
vinegar, a drink for invalids	395
vinegar	281
wine	274
Rats	359
Raw eggs and milk	393
wine	393
Red ants	359
Relishes for breakfast	216
Remarks on apples	229
bread making	159
coffee	210
cold dinners	226, 228
hot beds	346
insects	349
fruit culture	319
flowers	329
kitchen garden	306
peaches	236
pickling	296
plums	248
roast beef	86

	PAGE
Remarks on venison	100
Remedies—	
antidote for poison	380
mercury	380
oil vitriol	381
laudanum	380
soda	381
arsenic	381
verdigris	381
corrosive sublimate	381
nitrate of silver	381
antimony	381
sugar of lead	381
alum for teeth	380
abscess, or gathering of breast	382
bone to remove from the throat	381
burn, salve	374
liniment	374
quick remedy	375
blackberry syrup	407
blood, to stop	377
bleeding nose, to stop	377
breast, inflammation of	382
cuts	375
camphor ice	375
cleanse sores	378
chilblains	376
chapped hands	375
chilblains, receipt	376
cough syrup	378
cough, cure for	378
cough, obstinate, to break	379
charcoal powder, for teeth	380
cathartic, simple	381
cure for warts	383
cure for corns	383
dysentery, cure for	376
receipt	376
diarrhœa	376
dysentery or diarrhœa	376
discoloration by bruising, to remove	378
dyspeptic lye	383
earache	380
eye water	382
elderberry syrup	406
frost-bitten hands and feet	382
flax-seed jelly	378
felon, to cure	382
frost salve	375
hands, chapped	375
hiccough	379
hair, to prevent falling out	382
liniment of saltpetre	380
lip salve	378
lobelia cough mixture	378
liniment, rheumatism and neuralgia	380
liquorice syrup	378
malignant sore throat	379
mouth, sore, wash for	377
medicine, to prepare	381
nervous headache	378
affection	379
nose, bleeding, to stop	377
putrid sores	375
pulmonic wafers	379
quinsy	379
rheumatism	377
rhubarb syrup	390
rheumatism, receipt	377

INDEX.

Remedies—
  remove a bone or pin from the throat 381
  ringworm 382
  run-round, to scatter 382
  sores, to cleanse 375
    putrid sores 375
  sore mouth, wash 377
  scarlet fever 377
  stings of insects 378
  scald head 379
  sprains 379
  tincture for teeth 386
  teeth to clean 380
  toothache 380
  whalers' burn salve 375
Rheumatism 377
  receipt for 377
Rhubarb 129
  hermetically sealed 129
  grown 317
  pie 158
  selected 55
  syrup 390
  vinegar 282
  wine 275
Rice, new method 415
  milk 392
  flour gruel 391
  griddle cakes 188
  bread 168
  boiled 147
  flour pudding 141
Roast beef 86
  duck, canvas-back 112
    wild 112
  fowl 110
  goose 110
    green 111
    natural 111
  hare 118
  lamb, quarter of 101
  lobster 78
  moor fowl 110
  mutton, haunch 102
    shoulder or neck 100
  partridge 111
  pheasant 111
  pigeon 114
  sauce for 71
  pig 97
    dressing 71
  prairie chicken 112
  snipe 112
  turkey 110
  veal, breast of 103
    shoulder of 103
  widgeon and teal 113
Rolled butter 419
Rose-bugs 355
Roses, budded 337
Roses, grafted 337
  cleft 337
  whip 338
  propagated 336
  Bourbon 342
  Chinese 341
  climbers 340
  hardy 340
  noisette 342
  perpetual 341

Rose flip sauce for puddings 71
Rusked bread 225
Rusks, Mrs. L.'s 417
  corn or barley 395
Rust, to remove 408

Saffron dye 110
Sage, extract of 284
Sago, cooked 392
  milk 392
  pudding 144
Salads 289
  chicken, No. 1 119
    No 2 290
  see celery 119
  cucumber, for the aged 291
  cabbage and cucumbers 292
  celery, for the aged 292
  dressing, common, No. 1 290
  very fine, No. 2 291
  sauce, without eggs, No. 3 291
    sweet 291
  horseradish 291
  lettuce, to dress 289
    salad, No. 1 289
    No. 2 290
    No. 3 290
    No. 4 290
  lobster 291
  mustard, mixed 291
  orange 418
  radishes, for the aged 292
  tomato, chowder 292
Sally Lunn 187
Salmon, carved 42
  cutlets 78
  fresh 76
  selected 53
Salted beef, boiled 85
  cured 361
  and dried 361
  cooked 90
  cod 77
  balls 219
  toast, hash 214, 218
  picked up 80
  fish soaked 80
  mackerel 77
  shad 78
  ham, boiled 91
  baked 92
  served cold 97
  cured 360
  pork 362
Salsify cakes 130
  grown 311
  selected 55
Sandwiches of fish 81
Sangaree 285
Saratoga pudding 416
Sauce, brandy, for pudding 72
  bread, for poultry and game .. 69
  butter 67
  caper 420
  cherry, for puddings 71
    German, for puddings .. 71
  cream, for puddings 73
  catsup, for fish 69
  dyspepsia, for puddings 73
  egg, " " 73

	PAGE		PAGE
Sauce,		Soups—	
egg, for salt fish	68	asparagus	116
giblet	70	beef soup, No. 1	59
gooseberry, for lamb	69	No. 2	59
hard, for puddings	71	No. 3	60
leason, to make for	67	No. 4	60
liver	70	No. 5	60
lobster	69	chicken, brown	64
maple syrup, for puddings	72	white	64
mint	68	clam, No. 1	62
molasses, improved	73	No. 2	62
mushroom	69	eel	61
oyster	68	gumbo	124
orange, for puddings	73	lobster	61
peach, " "	72	leason, to make for	67
poultry and game	69	macaroni	67
rose hip, for puddings	71	mutton	63
salad	291	neudle, for invalids	395
sour, rich, for puddings	73	oyster, for the city	63
plum, " "	73	country	63
sour, for venison	69	pea	127
sweet, rich, for puddings	72	remarks on	58
plain, " "	73	salsify	130
venison, for	69	turtle	66
wine, for venison	69	mock	65
for puddings, No. 1	73	vermicelli	66
No. 2	73	veal, No. 1	60
No. 3	73	No. 2	60
Sausages	98	No. 3	61
Savory vinegar	294	economical, No. 4	61
Scarlet, dye	410	veal stock for	66
fever	377	vegetable, French	64
Scald head, cured	379	Soused fish	87
Scalloped, clams	416	pigs' feet, etc	98
fish	81	Sowing, seed	332
oysters	82	Spermaceti, spots of, to remove	400
Mrs. W.'s	81	Spinach	180
shells	413	grown	310
Scambled, eggs	222	Spirits of camphor	399
pork	98	Sponge cakes	175, 176
Scour carpets	402	drop cakes	183
Sea-fish	75	German	396
Seed, saving	333	Spots, to remove from furniture	399
sowing	332	Spring work	367
Serving a good dinner for gentlemen	24	Squash bugs	353
soup	82	cooked	130
Servants, advice to	31	hermetically sealed	130
dress	36	selected	55
rooms	3	Stair carpets protected	404
Sewing furs	405	Starching shirts and collars	13
Shad, baked	78	Starch for embroideries	22
fresh	76	shirts	22
fried	79	Steel, scoured	408
salted	77	rust removed from	408
Shades of lamps cleansed from oil	399	Stew of calves' head	105
Shaking carpets	405	Stewed clams	83
Sherry cobblers	394	muscles	83
Sheets, cotton, to iron	24	oysters	82
Sick room	371	turtle	83
Simple diseases of infants	367	Strawberry ade	285
cathartics	361	cake	181
Skirts, to iron	14	dried	270
Slaw, cold	119	Strawberries, cultivated	323
hot	119	brandy	279
Small fruits, preserved, etc	263	hermetically sealed	269, 276
fish	74	jam	269
Snow cream	153	jelly	269
Soda cake	175	pudding	135
Soil removed from carpets	403	vinegar	294
Sores cleansed	375	wine	281
Soups—		whips	151

INDEX.

	PAGE
Strawberries,	
worm	353
String beans for winter	118
Striped bugs	353
Sturgeon, boiled	77
Sweetbreads, French	417
Sweetbreads	106
Sweet corn, grown	316
Sweetmeats, apple	232
apricots	253
barberries	263
blackberries	267
cherries	258
currants	267
damsons	248
egg plums	252
ginger, green	201
greengages	250
nectarines, French	253
peaches, elegant	241
pears	244
pineapple	200
pumpkin chips	204
quinces	247
raspberries	267
strawberries	267
Sweet potatoes	317
grown in hot beds	347
Swiss muslin, to wash, etc	17
Succotash	121
Sugar hearts	194
sifter	413
selected	56
of lead, antidote for	381
Sillabubs and whips	151
Syrups for candying	191
of proper strength	191
plum	258
System and management of servants, etc	3
Tapioca, to cook for invalids	382
puddings	142
Tarts, apple	234
cranberry	158
gooseberry	158
plum	257
lemon or pie	148
Tea, black, prepared	207
breakfast prepared	207
chosen	205
description of plant	207
green, steeped	205
prepared for market	207
served	206
varieties of	205
selected	56
with egg mulled in it	392
Tenderloin of pork, broiled	99
Thanksgiving cake, a recipe of 1818	180
Thermometer for testing ovens, fruit baths, etc	413
Thrush	387
Tincture for teeth	380
Toast, asparagus	116
cream	213
cracker	214
codfish	214
dip	214
dry	214
dry butter	214

	PAGE
Toast,	
Graham or Indian bread	214
egg and toast for invalids	395
egg, No. 1	212
No. 2	212
milk	213
without butter	213
mock cream	213
molasses, for invalids	395
molasses	213
tomato, superior	214
tomato	181
soft butter	212
water for invalids	393
Tomato catsup	289
Tomatoes, chowder	292
hermetically sealed	181
green, preserved	202
forwarded in hot-beds	346
pickled	302
with onions	303
toast	181
superior	214
wine	277
worm	352
Tongs for turning steaks	412
Tongues, cured	360
carved	40
Transplanting annuals	334
trees and small fruits	331
Trees transplanted	331
Trout, fried	79
selected	53
Trussing poultry and game	106
Turbot	77
selected	53
Turkey, boiled	104
baked	110
selected	52
roasted	110
Turtle balls	83
stew	83
patties	83
selected	34
Twist bread, French	165
Underdraining	307
Used, economically—	
beefsteaks left over	223
bread that is dry	225, 226
broken cake for puddings	224
cake that is heavy	224
cold cabbage	224
corn	225
eggs	223
egg-plant	225
fish	224
fowl	224
ham	224
meats	223
mush	224
potatoes	225
peas	225
rice	224
soup-meat and gristle	223
veal	224
pie crust left over	224
remains of preserves	225
Vanilla flummery	151
macaroons	199

INDEX. 443

	PAGE
Varieties	185
Veal, breast of, roasted	103
with oysters or clams	104
cutlets	104
fillet, boiled	103
roasted	103
fricassee	104
gravy for roast	68
loin of roasted	103
pot-pie	104
pie	104
soup	60, 61
stock for soups, French	66
stewed	104
Verdigris, antidote for	381
Vegetables, to cook	116
artichokes	116
to preserve through the winter	131
asparagus	116
toast	116
soup	116
greens	116
hermetically sealed	117
beets, to boil	117
preserve through winter	132
beet greens	117
beans, to boil	117
stewed	117
baked	117
Lima, dried	118
Windsor	118
string to preserve for winter	118
broccoli	118
cabbage, early York	118
boiled	118
with meat	118
hot slaw	118
cold slaw	119
chicken salad with cabbage	119
cauliflower, to cook	119
carrots	119
celery	119
to preserve for winter	132
chicken salad, No. 1	119
curled cress	120
corn	120
an excellent method	120
No. 2	120
No. 3	120
corn cakes, green	121
muffins	121
oysters	121
succotash	121
to prepare for succotash	121
to cook	122
dried for winter	122
hermetically sealed	122
cucumbers	123
to fry	123
egg-plant, to cook, No. 1	123
No. 2	123
No. 3	123
No. 4	123
to bake	123
lettuce, Dutch method	124
No. 2	124
to serve in heads	124
mustard greens	124

Vegetables,	PAGE
okra	124
or gumbo soups	124
stewed	124
onions	125
to preserve for winter	133
boiled	125
fried	125
parsley	125
to preserve for winter	132
parsnips, plain	125
boiled	125
fried	126
fritters	126
cutlet	126
fricassee	126
to preserve for winter	132
peas	126
steamed	127
soup	127
dried	127
hermetically sealed	127
potatoes, early, to cook	127
to preserve for winter	132
ripe, to boil	127
mashed	128
fried crisp	128
fried	128
boiled	128
fricasseed	129
hashed	129
baked	129
steamed	129
warmed	129
pumpkin	129
radishes	129
to preserve for winter use	132
rhubarb	129
hermetically sealed	129
salsify patties	130
to preserve through winter	133
soup	130
cakes	129
spinach	130
squash	130
winter	133
baked	130
hermetically sealed	130
tomatoes, to stew	131
toast	131
hermetically sealed	131
turnips	131
to preserve through winter	133
plain boiled	131
mashed	131
cellar	133
Venison, remarks on	100
roasted	100
mock, of corned beef	90
selected	52
steak	111
stewed	100
Vermicelli soup	66
Vials, to cleanse	399
Vines, flowering, list of	339, 340
Vinegar, remarks on	296
tester, or acet-meter	296
Vinegars flavored with—	
basil	293
borage	294
burnet	294

INDEX.

	PAGE
Vinegars, flavored with—	
celery	292
cucumbers	293
Chili	293
cinnamon	294
cloves	294
cherry	294
eschalot	294
flavored	292
garlick	293
ginger	295
horseradish	295
hop	295
mustard	293
marjoram	294
mace	295
nasturtium	293
oyster	294
onion	293
peach	293
savory	294
Vinegar for souse	295
soused fish	295
tarragon	294
walnuts	294
wormwood	295
Vinegar from fruits	281
apple	282
blackberry	282
currant	281
cherry	281
crabapple	283
cider, see part 5, chapter 1	230
gooseberry	282
grape	283
peach	281
plum	282
pear	282
raspberry	281
rhubarb	282
strawberry	281
whortleberry	282
Waffles, American raised	186
German "	186
" rich	186
good	186
pound	186
Warmed over, potatoes	129
Warts, cure for	383
Water of barley	394
for eyes	382
of lemons	394
of toast	394
Washing blankets	24
bombazines	23
black merinoes	20
lace veils	400
brown merinoes	20
blue "	20
chintz with blue grounds	20
brown "	19
green "	19
red "	20
counterpanes	24
curtains	23
delaines with delicate colors	19
plain	18
colored	18
down	405
doubtful colored muslins	16

	PAGE
Washing	
doubtful colored prints	16
embroideries	21
or lace curtains	23
feather beds	404
flannels	17
ginghams	21
generally	12
India muslins	17
printed	15
merinoes, colored	18
delicate colored	18
blue	20
brown	20
printed	18
scarlet	20
mourning prints	17
muslins, doubtful colors	16
India	17
Swiss	17
oil cloths	405
prints with doubtful colors	16
fast "	16
printed India muslins	15
delaines	18
merinoes	19
ribbons	401
scarlet merinoes	20
silks	22
sore mouth, for	377
thread lace to look like new	400
Wash, trees, fruit	329
Washington cake	177
Wash veils	400
Walnut catsup	296, 297
pickles	302
vinegar	294
Wet gloves, to save	402
Whalers' frost salve	375
Whey, nitre	394
milk	394
lemon	393
wine	394
Wheat and Indian bread	166
White chicken soup	64
White counterpane washed	24
currant brandy	279
wine	373
White feathers cleansed	403
fish boiled	76
silks or feathers preserved white	404
Whitewash, superior	399
common	399
White mountain cake	177
cup "	174
Whips of cream	151
cocoa	152
and jelly	152
strawberries	151
sillabubs	151
Whip grafting	333
Whooping cough	399
Whortleberries, dried	270
catsup	289
hermetically sealed	268
jelly	366
pie	157
vinegar	282
wine	272
Wedding cake of 1818	179
Widgeons and teals	118

INDEX.

	PAGE		PAGE
Wild duck trussed	107	Wine, raspberry, No. 2	274
roasted	112	rhubarb, No. 1	275
Windsor beans	118	No. 2	275
Winter cookies	182	raisins, No. 1	275
radishes	132	No. 2	276
vegetables preserved for	131	No. 3	276
squash	183	sherry	276
Wine	272	sweet currant	272
apricot	274	strawberry, No. 1	274
barrel, to cleanse	277	No. 2	274
blackberry, No. 1	278	tomato	277
No. 2	278	whortleberry	272
black currant, No. 1	273	white currant	273
No. 2	273	and milk	392
cherry	274	with egg mulled in it	392
French	274	mulled	285
currant, sweet	272	with raw eggs for invalids	393
white	273	panada for invalids	393
red	273	pudding	140
black, No. 1	273	sauces for pudding	73
No. 2	273	sauce for venison	69
damson	274	whey	394
elderberry, spiced	273	Mrs. L.'s	415
flowers	415	Woodcocks, roasted	111
grape, No. 1	272	trussed	107
No. 2	277	Worms, infants troubled with	388
No. 3	277	corn	851
ginger, No. 1	275	cut	847
excellent, No. 2	277	strawberry	353
gooseberry	275	tomato	352
mulberry	274	wire	351
peach	274		
parsnip	277	Yellow dye for silks	409
red currant	273	soda cake	175
raspberry, No. 1	274		

Any of these Books sent free by mail to any address on receipt of Price.

RECENT PUBLICATIONS

OF

D. APPLETON & CO.,

443 & 445 BROADWAY, NEW YORK

The Life and Correspondence of

THEODORE PARKER, Minister of the Twenty-eighth Congregational Society, Boston. By JOHN WEISS. With two Portraits on Steel, fac-simile of Handwriting, and nineteen Wood Engravings. 2 vols., 8vo. 1,008 pages. Price, $6.

"These volumes contain an account of Mr. Parker's childhood and self-education ; of the development of his theological ideas ; of his scholarly and philosophical pursuits ; and of his relation to the Anti-Slavery cause, and to the epoch in America which preceded the civil war. His two visits to Europe are described in letters and extracts from his journal. An autobiographical fragment is introduced in relation to Mr. Parker's early life, and his letters of friendship on literary, speculative, and political topics are freely interspersed. The illustrations represent scenes connected with various periods of Mr. Parker's life, the houses he dwelt in, his country haunts, the meeting house, his library, and the Music Hall in which he preached."

Catechism of the Steam Engine,

In its various Applications to Mines, Mills, Steam Navigation, Railways, and Agriculture. With Practical Instructions for the Manufacture and Management of Engines of every Class. By JOHN BOURNE, C. E. New and Revised Edition. 1 vol., 12mo. Illustrated. Cloth. $2.

"In offering to the American public a reprint of a work on the Steam Engine so deservedly successful, and so long considered standard, the Publishers have not thought it necessary that it should be an exact copy of the English edition. There were some details in which they thought it could be improved and better adapted to the use of American Engineers. On this account the size of the page has been increased to a full 12mo. to admit of larger illustrations, which, in the English edition, are often on too small a scale, and some of the illustrations themselves have been supplied by others equally applicable, more recent, and to us more familiar examples. The first part of Chapter XI., devoted in the English edition to English portable and fixed agricultural engines, in this edition gives place entirely to illustrations from American practice, of steam engines as applied to different purposes, and of appliances and machines necessary to them. But with the exception of some of the illustrations and the description of them, and the correction of a few typographical errors, this edition is a faithful transcript of the latest English edition."

D. APPLETON & CO.'S PUBLICATIONS.

History of the Romans under the

Empire. By CHARLES MERIVALE, B. D., late Fellow of St. John's College. 7 vols., small 8vo. Handsomely printed on tinted paper. Price, in cloth, $2 per vol. Half Morocco extra, $3 50.

CONTENTS:

Vols. I. and II.—Comprising the History to the Fall of Julius Cæsar.
Vol. III.—To the Establishment of the Monarchy by Augustus.
Vols. IV. and V.—From Augustus to Claudius, B. C. 27 to A. D. 54.
Vol. VI.—From the Reign of Nero, A. D. 54, to the Fall of Jerusalem, A. D. 70.
Vol. VII.—From the Destruction of Jerusalem, A. D. 70, to the Death of M. Aurelius.

This valuable work terminates at the point where the narrative of Gibbon commences.

. . . " When we enter on a more searching criticism of the two writers, it must be admitted that Merivale has as firm a grasp of his subject as Gibbon, and that his work is characterized by a greater freedom from prejudice, and a sounder philosophy.

. . . " This history must always stand as a splendid monument of his learning, his candor, and his vigorous grasp of intellect. Though he is in some respects inferior to Macaulay and Grote, he must still be classed with them, as one of the second great triumvirate of English historians."—*North American Review, April,* 1863.

Practice in the Executive De-

partment of the Government, under the Pension, Bounty, and Prize Laws of the United States, with Forms and Instructions for Collecting Arrears of Pay, Bounty, and Prize Money, and for Obtaining Pensions. By ROBERT SEWELL, Counsellor at Law. 1 vol., 8vo. Sheep. Price, $3 50.

" I offer this little book with confidence to the profession, as certain to save lawyers, in one case, if they never have any more, more time and trouble than its cost. To the public generally, the book is offered as containing a large amount of useful information on a subject now, unfortunately, brought home to half the families in the land. To the officers and soldiers of the Army it will also be found a useful companion ; and it is hoped that by it an amount of information of great value to the soldiers, and to their families at home, will be disseminated, and the prevailing ignorance respecting the subject treated of in a great degree removed."—*Extract from Preface.*

Hints to Riflemen.

By H. W. S. CLEVELAND. 1 vol., 12mo. Illustrated, with numerous Designs of Rifles and Rifle Practice. Cloth. Price, $1 50.

" I offer these hints as the contribution of an old sportsman, and if I succeed in any degree in exciting an interest in the subject, my end will be accomplished, even if the future investigations of those who are thus attracted should prove any of my opinions to be erroneous."—*Extract from Preface.*

D. APPLETON & CO.'S PUBLICATIONS.

Laws and Principles of Whist,

Stated and Explained, and its Practice Illustrated on an Original System, by means of hands played completely through. By CAVENDISH. From the fifth London edition. 1 vol., square 16mo. Gilt edge. $1 25.

"An excellent and very clearly written treatise; the rules of the game thoroughly explained; its practice illustrated by means of hands played completely through, and much of the minutiæ and finesse of the game given that we have never seen in any other volume of the kind. Whist players will recognize it as an authority; and that it is a success is proved by its having already gone through five editions. It is got out very neatly, in blue and gold, by the publishers."—*Com. Bulletin.*

Roba di Roma.

By W. W. STORY. 2 vols., 12mo. Cloth, $3.

"Till Rome shall fall, the City of the Seven Hills will be inexhaustible as a subject of interest. 'Roba di Roma' contains the gatherings of an honest observer and a real artist. . . . It has permanent value to entitle it to a place of honor on the shelf which contains every lover of Italy's Rome-books."
—*Athenæum.*

Heat considered as a Mode of

Motion. Being a Course of Twelve Lectures delivered at the Royal Institution of Great Britain. By JOHN TYNDALL, F.R.S. Author of "The Glaciers of the Alps." 1 vol., 12mo. With 101 illustrations. Cloth. $2.

"No one can read Dr. Tyndall's book without being impressed with the intensity of the author's conviction of the truth of the theory which it is his object to illustrate, or with the boldness with which he confronts the difficulties which he encounters. * * * * * * * Dr. Tyndall's is the first work in which the undulatory or mechanical theory of heat has been placed in a popular light; but we are sure that no one, however profound his knowledge upon the subject of which it treats, will rise from its perusal without a feeling that he has been both gratified and instructed in a high degree while reading its pages."—*London Reader.*

Life of Edward Livingston,

Mayor of the City of New York; Member of Congress; Senator of the United States; Secretary of State; Minister to France; Author of a System of Penal Law for Louisiana; Member of the Institute of France, etc. By CHARLES H. HUNT, with an Introduction by GEORGE BANCROFT. 1 vol., 8vo. Cloth, $3.50.

"One of the purest of statesmen and the most genial of men, was Edward Livingston, whose career is presented in this volume. * * *
"The author of this volume has done the country a service. He has given us in a becoming form an appropriate memorial of one whom succeeding generations will be proud to name as an American jurist and statesman."—*Evangelist.*

D APPLETON & CO.'S PUBLICATIONS.

Round the Block.

An American Novel. With Illustrations. 1 vol., 12mo. Cloth. Price, $1 50.

"The story is remarkably clever. It presents the most vivid and various pictures of men and manners in the great Metropolis. Unlike most novels that now appear, it has no 'mission,' the author being neither a politician nor a reformer, but a story teller, according to the old pattern, and a capital story he has produced, written in the happiest style, and full of wit and action. He evidently knows his ground, and moves over it with the foot of a master. It is a work that will be read and admired, unless all love for good novels has departed from us; and we know that such is not the case."—*Boston Traveler.*

The History of Civilization in

England. By HENRY THOMAS BUCKLE. 2 vols., 8vo. Cloth. $6.

"Whoever misses reading this book, will miss reading what is, in various respects, to the best of our judgment and experience, the most remarkable book of the day—one, indeed, that no thoughtful, inquiring mind would miss reading for a good deal. Let the reader be as averse as he may to the writer's philosophy, let him be as devoted to the obstructive as Mr. Buckle is to the progress party, let him be as orthodox in church creed as the other is heterodox, as dogmatic as his author is sceptical—let him, in short, find his prejudices shocked at every turn of the argument, and all his prepossessions whistled down the wind—still there is so much in this extraordinary volume to stimulate reflection, and excite to inquiry, and provoke to earnest investigation, perhaps (to this or that reader) on a track hitherto untrodden, and across the virgin soil of untilled fields, fresh woods, and pastures new—that we may fairly defy the most hostile spirit, the most mistrustful and least sympathetic, to read it through without being glad of having done so, or having begun it, or even glanced at almost any one of its pages, to pass it away unread."—*New Monthly (London) Magazine.*

Illustrations of Universal Prog-

ress. A Series of Essays. By HERBERT SPENCER, Author of "The Principles of Psychology;" "Social Statics;" "Education." 1 vol., 12mo. Cloth, $1 75.

"The readers who have made the acquaintance of Mr. Herbert Spencer through his work on Education, and are interested in his views upon a larger range of subjects, will welcome this new volume of 'Essays.' Passing by the more scientific and philosophical speculations, we may call attention to a group of articles upon moral and political subjects, which are very pertinent to the present condition of affairs."—*Tribune.*

Thirty Poems.

By WM. CULLEN BRYANT. 1 vol., 12mo. Cloth, $1.25; cloth gilt, $1.75; mor., $3.50.

"No English poet surpasses him in knowledge of nature, and but few are his equals. He is better than Cowper and Thomson in their special walks of poetry, and the equal of Wordsworth, that great high priest of nature."—*The World.*

D. APPLETON & CO.'S PUBLICATIONS.

An Introduction to Municipal

Law, designed for General Readers, and for Students in Colleges and High Schools. By JOHN NORTON POMEROY. 1 vol., 8vo. 544 pages. Cloth, $3.

"I have spent nearly four days in reading your book, and am willing to say, in reference to it, that, when considered in reference to its scope and the design had in view in entering upon is, it is a work of great merit. The topics are presented clearly, discussed with ability, and in the main satisfactory results arrived at. Parts I. and II., I think, may prove very useful to students at law and young lawyers, as there is a great deal in the history of the law, and especially in its sources, both common and civil, that is very clearly, briefly, and logically stated, and more available in the manner presented in your work than in any other that I am acquainted with."—*From* AMOS DEAN, *Esq., Albany Law School.*

Thackeray;

The Humorist and Man of Letters, the Story of his Life, with particulars of his early career never before made public. By THEODORE TAYLOR, Esq. Illustrated with a Portrait, one of the latest taken from life; View of Thackeray's House; Fac-simile of his Handwriting; Humorous Illustrations by George Cruikshank; and other Pictures and Sketches. One vol., 12mo. Cloth. Price, $1 25.

"The author, Mr. T. Taylor, long resident in Paris, has been collecting in-formation for many years, and has much to say of Mr. Thackeray's artist life in that city. The book is illustrated with a portrait and some curious original sketches."—*From the Guardian.*

The Iron Manufacture of Great

Britain. Theoretically and Practically considered: Including Descriptive Details of the Ores, Fuels, and Fluxes employed; the Preliminary Operation of Calcination; the Blast, Refining, and Puddling Furnaces; Engines and Machinery; and the Various Processes in Union, etc., etc. By W. TRURAN, C. E., formerly Engineer at the Dowlais Iron Works, under the late Sir John Guest, Bart. Second Edition, revised from the manuscripts of the late Mr. Truran, by J. ARTHUR PHILLIPS, Author of "A Manual of Metallurgy," "Records of Mining," etc., and WM. H. DORMAN. One vol., imperial 8vo. Con-taining 84 Plates. Price, $10.

D. APPLETON & CO.'S PUBLICATIONS

Principles of Political Economy.

With some of their Applications of Social Philosophy. By JOHN STUART MILL. 2 vols., 8vo. Printed on tinted paper. Cloth, $6.

"In the whole range of extant authorship on political economy, there is no writer except Adam Smith with whom John Stuart Mill can, without injustice, be compared. In originality, Adam Smith, as being the acknowledged father of the science, takes the precedence, as he does also in exuberance of apt illustration. But in rectitude of understanding, clearness and sagacity, Mill is fully his peer; in precision of method, range of topics, and adaptation to the present state of society, he is altogether his superior. The 'Wealth of Nations' now belongs, indeed, rather to the history of the science than to its exposition. But the 'Principles of Political Economy' is an orderly, symmetrical, and lucid exposition of the science in its present advanced state. In extent of information, breadth of treatment, pertinence of fresh illustration, and accommodation to the present wants of the statesman, the merchant, and the social philosopher, this work is unrivalled. It is written in a luminous and smooth, yet clear-cut style; and there is diffused over it a soft atmosphere of feeling, derived from the author's unaffected humanity and enlightened interest in the welfare of the masses."

The New American Cyclopædia.

Edited by GEORGE RIPLEY and CHARLES A. DANA. Now complete, in 16 vols., 8vo., double columns, 750 pages each. Cloth, $4; Sheep, $4 75; Half Mor., $5; Half Russia, $5 50 per volume.

The leading claims to public consideration which the *New American Cyclopædia* possesses may be thus briefly stated :

"1. It surpasses all other works in the fullness and ability of the articles relating to the United States.

"2. No other work contains so many reliable biographies of the leading men of this and other nations. In this respect it is far superior even to the more bulky Encyclopædia Britannica.

"3. The best minds in this country have been employed in enriching its pages with the latest data, and the most recent discoveries in every branch of manufactures, mechanics, and general science.

"4. It is a library in itself, where every topic is treated, and where information can be gleaned which will enable a student, if he is so disposed, to consult other authorities, thus affording him an invaluable key to knowledge.

"5. It is neatly printed, with readable type, on good paper, and contains a most copious index.

"6. It is the only work which gives anything approaching correct descriptions of cities and towns of America, or embraces reliable statistics showing the wonderful growth of all sections."

Queen Mab.

A New Novel. By JULIA KAVANAGH. 1 vol., 12mo. Cloth, $1 50.

"No English novelist of the present day ought to hold, we think, a higher rank in her own peculiar walk of literature than Miss Kavanagh. There is a freshness of originality about all her works, and an individual character stamped on each,—there is, moreover, a unity of thought and feeling, a harmony, so to speak, pervading each separate work, that plainly speaks original genius, while the womanly grace of her etchings of character, is a marvel of artistic excellence."—*Tablet.*

D. APPLETON & CO.'S PUBLICATIONS.

THE
NEW AMERICAN CYCLOPÆDIA.

EDITED BY

GEORGE RIPLEY AND CHARLES A. DANA.

PUBLISHED BY

D. APPLETON & COMPANY, New York

In 16 Vols. 8vo, Double Columns, 750 Pages each.

Price, Cloth, $4. ; *Sheep,* 4.75 ; *Half Mor.,* $5.00 ; *Half Russ.,* $5.5C
per *Volume.*

———•◦•———

EVERY one that reads, every one that mingles in society, is constantly meeting with allusions to subjects on which he needs and desires further information. In conversation, in trade, in professional life, on the farm, in the family, practical questions are continually arising, which no man, well read or not, can always satisfactorily answer. If facilities for reference are at hand, they are consulted, and not only is the curiosity gratified, and the stock of knowledge increased, but perhaps information is gained and ideas are suggested that will directly contribute to the business success of the party concerned.

With a Cyclopædia, embracing every conceivable subject, and having its topics alphabetically arranged, not a moment is lost. The matter in question is found at once, digested, condensed, stripped of all that is irrelevant and unnecessary, and verified by a comparison of the best authorities. Moreover, while only men of fortune can collect a library complete in all the departments of knowledge, a Cyclopædia, worth in itself, for purposes of reference, at least a thousand volumes, is within the reach of all—the clerk, the merchant, the professional man, the farmer, the mechanic. In a country like ours, where the humblest may be called to responsible positions requiring intelligence and general information, the value of such a work can not be over-estimated.

PLAN OF THE CYCLOPÆDIA.

The New American Cyclopædia presents a panoramic view of all human knowledge, as it exists at the present moment. It embraces and popularizes every subject that can be thought of. In its successive volumes is contained an inexhaustible fund of accurate and practical information on Art and Science in all their branches, including Mechanics, Mathematics, Astronomy, Philosophy, Chemistry, and Physiology; on Agriculture, Commerce, and Manufactures; on Law, Medicine, and Theology; on Biography and History, Geography and Ethnology; on Political Economy, the Trades, Inventions, Politics, the Things of Common Life, and General Literature.

The Industrial Arts and those branches of Practical Science which have a direct bearing on our every-day life, such as Domestic Economy, Ventilation, the Heating of Houses, Diet, &c., are treated with the thoroughness which their great importance demands.

The department of Biography is full and complete, embracing the lives of all eminent persons, ancient and modern. In American biography, particularly, great pains have been taken to present the most comprehensive and accurate record that has yet been attempted.

In History, the New American Cyclopædia gives no mere catalogue of barren dates, but a copious and spirited narrative, under their appropriate heads, of the principal events in the annals of the world. So in Geography, it not only serves as a general Gazetteer, but it gives interesting descriptions of the principal localities mentioned, derived from books of travel and other fresh and authentic sources.

As far as is consistent with thoroughness of research and exactness of statement, the popular method has been pursued. The wants of the people in a work of this kind have been carefully kept in view throughout.

It is hardly necessary to add that, throughout the whole, perfect fairness to all sections of country, local institutions, public men, political creeds, and religious denominations, has been a sacred principle and leading aim. Nothing that can be construed into an invidious or offensive allusion has been admitted.

DISTINGUISHING EXCELLENCES.

While we prefer that the work should speak for itself, and that others should herald its excellences, we cannot refrain from calling attention to the following points, in which we take an honest pride in believing that the New American Cyclopædia surpasses all others:—

I. IN ACCURACY AND FRESHNESS OF INFORMATION.—The value of a work of this kind is exactly proportioned to its correctness. It must preclude the necessity of having other books. Its decision must be final. It must be an ultimatum of reference, or it is good for nothing.

II. IN IMPARTIALITY.—Our work has undergone the examination of Argus eyes. It has stood the ordeal. It is pronounced by distinguished men and leading reviews in all parts of the Union, strictly fair and national. Eschewing all expressions of opinion on controverted points of science, philosophy, religion, and politics, it aims at an accurate representation of facts and institutions, of the results of physical research, of the prominent events in the history of the world, of the most significant productions of literature and art, and of the celebrated individuals whose names have become associated with the conspicuous phenomena of their age—doing justice to all men, all creeds, all sections.

III. IN COMPLETENESS.—It treats of every subject, in a terse and condensed style, but fully and exhaustively. It is believed that but few omissions will be found; but whatever topics may, through any oversight, be wanting, are supplied in an Appendix.

IV. IN AMERICAN CHARACTER.—The New Cyclopædia is intended to meet the intellectual wants of the American people. It is not, therefore, modelled after European works of a similar design; but, while it embraces all their excellences, has added to them a peculiar and unmistakable American character. It is the production mainly of American mind.

V. IN PRACTICAL BEARING.—The day of philosophical abstraction and speculation has passed away. This is an age of action. *Cui bono* is the universal touchstone. Feeling this, we have made our Cyclopædia thoroughly practical. No man of action, be his sphere humble or exalted, can afford to do without it.

VI. IN INTEREST OF STYLE.—The cold, formal, and repulsive style usual in works of this kind, has been replaced with a style sparkling and emphatically readable. It has been the aim to interest and please, as well as instruct. Many of our writers are men who hold the foremost rank in general literature, and their articles have been characterized by our best critics as models of elegance, force, and beauty.

VII. IN CONVENIENCE OF FORM.—No ponderous quartos, crowded with fine type that strains the eyes and wearies the brain, are here presented. The volumes are just the right size to handle conveniently; the paper is thick and white, the type large, the binding elegant and durable.

VIII. IN CHEAPNESS.—Our Cyclopædia has been universally pronounced a miracle of cheapness. We determined, at the outset, to enlarge its sphere of usefulness, and make it emphatically a book for the people, by putting it at the lowest possible price.

Such being the character of the New American Cyclopædia, an accurate, fresh, impartial, complete, practical, interesting, convenient, cheap Dictionary of General Knowledge, we ask, who can afford to do without it? Can the merchant, the statesman, the lawyer, the physician, the clergyman, to whom it gives thorough and complete information on every point connected with their several callings? Can the teacher, who is enabled, by the outside information it affords, to make his instructions doubly interesting and profitable? Can the farmer, to whom it offers the latest results of agricultural research and experiment? Can the young man, to whom it affords the means of storing his mind with useful knowledge bearing no any vocation he may have selected? Can the intelligent mechanic, who wishes to understand what he reads in his daily paper? Can the mother of a family, whom it initiates into the mysteries of domestic economy, and teaches a thousand things which more than saves its cost in a single year? In a word, can any intelligent American, who desires to understand the institutions of his country, its past history and present condition, and his own duties as a citizen, deny himself this great American digest of all human knowledge, universally pronounced the est Cyclopædia and the most valuable work ever published?

www.ingramcontent.com/pod-product-compliance
Lightning Source LLC
Chambersburg PA
CBHW030322020526
44117CB00030B/625